THE HISPANIC POPULATION
OF THE UNITED STATES

THE POPULATION OF THE UNITED STATES IN THE 1980s

A Census Monograph Series

THE HISPANIC POPULATION OF THE UNITED STATES

Frank D. Bean
and
Marta Tienda

for the
National Committee for Research
on the 1980 Census

RUSSELL SAGE FOUNDATION / NEW YORK

The Russell Sage Foundation

The Russell Sage Foundation, one of the oldest of America's general purpose foundations, was established in 1907 by Mrs. Margaret Olivia Sage for "the improvement of social and living conditions in the United States." The Foundation seeks to fulfill this mandate by fostering the development and dissemination of knowledge about the political, social, and economic problems of America. It conducts research in the social sciences and public policy, and publishes books and pamphlets that derive from this research.

The Board of Trustees is responsible for oversight and the general policies of the Foundation, while administrative direction of the program and staff is vested in the President, assisted by the officers and staff. The President bears final responsibility for the decision to publish a manuscript as a Russell Sage Foundation book. In reaching a judgment on the competence, accuracy, and objectivity of each study, the President is advised by the staff and selected expert readers. The conclusions and interpretations in Russell Sage Foundation publications are those of the authors and not of the Foundation, its Trustees, or its staff. Publication by the Foundation, therefore, does not imply endorsement of the contents of the study.

Library of Congress Cataloging-in-Publication Data

Bean, Frank D.
    The Hispanic population of the United States.
    (The Population of the United States in the 1980s)
    Bibliography: p.
    Includes index.
    1. Hispanic Americans—Social conditions. 2. Hispanic Americans—Economic conditions.
I. Tienda, Marta. II. National Committee for Research on the 1980 Census.
III. Title. IV. Series.
E184.S75B4   1987   305.8′68073   87-9748
ISBN 0-87154-104-1
ISBN 0-87154-105-x (pbk)

First Paperback Edition 1990

Cover and text design: HUGUETTE FRANCO

10 9 8 7 6 5 4 3

The National Committee for Research on the 1980 Census

The committee is sponsored by the Social Science Research Council, the Russell Sage Foundation, and the Alfred P. Sloan Foundation, in collaboration with the U.S. Bureau of the Census. The opinions, findings, and conclusions or recommendations expressed in the monographs supported by the committee are those of the author(s) and do not necessarily reflect the views of the committee or its sponsors.

Foreword

The Hispanic Population of the United States is one of an ambitious series of volumes aimed at converting the vast statistical yield of the 1980 census into authoritative analyses of major changes and trends in American life. This series, "The Population of the United States in the 1980s," represents an important episode in social science research and revives a long tradition of independent census analysis. First in 1930, and then again in 1950 and 1960, teams of social scientists worked with the U.S. Bureau of the Census to investigate significant social, economic, and demographic developments revealed by the decennial censuses. These census projects produced three landmark series of studies, providing a firm foundation and setting a high standard for our present undertaking.

There is, in fact, more than a theoretical continuity between those earlier census projects and the present one. Like those previous efforts, this new census project has benefited from close cooperation between the Census Bureau and a distinguished, interdisciplinary group of scholars. Like the 1950 and 1960 research projects, research on the 1980 census was initiated by the Social Science Research Council and the Russell Sage Foundation. In deciding once again to promote a coordinated program of census analysis, Russell Sage and the Council were mindful not only of the severe budgetary restrictions imposed on the Census Bureau's own publishing and dissemination activities in the 1980s, but also of the extraordinary changes that have occurred in so many dimensions of American life over the past two decades.

The studies constituting "The Population of the United States in the 1980s" were planned, commissioned, and monitored by the National Committee for Research on the 1980 Census, a special committee appointed by the Social Science Research Council and sponsored by the Council, the Russell Sage Foundation, and the Alfred P. Sloan Foundation, with the collaboration of the U.S. Bureau of the Census. This committee includes leading social scientists from a broad range of fields—demography, economics, education, geography, history, political science, sociology, and statistics. It has been the committee's task to select the main topics for research, obtain highly qualified specialists to carry out that research, and provide the structure necessary to facilitate coordination among researchers and with the Census Bureau.

The topics treated in this series span virtually all the major features of American society—ethnic groups (blacks, Hispanics, foreign-born); spatial dimensions (migration, neighborhoods, housing, regional and metropolitan growth and decline); and status groups (income levels, families and households, women). Authors were encouraged to draw not only on the 1980 census but also on previous censuses and on subsequent national data. Each individual research project was assigned a special advisory panel made up of one committee member, one member nominated by the Census Bureau, one nominated by the National Science Foundation, and one or two other experts. These advisory panels were responsible for project liaison and review and for recommendations to the National Committee regarding the readiness of each manuscript for publication. With the final approval of the chairman of the National Committee, each report was released to the Russell Sage Foundation for publication and distribution.

The debts of gratitude incurred by a project of such scope and organizational complexity are necessarily large and numerous. The committee must thank, first, its sponsors—the Social Science Research Council; the Russell Sage Foundation; and the Alfred P. Sloan Foundation. The long-range vision and day-to-day persistence of these organizations and individuals sustained this research program over many years. The active and willing cooperation of the Bureau of the Census was clearly invaluable at all stages of this project, and the extra commitment of time and effort made by Bureau economist James R. Wetzel must be singled out for special recognition. A special tribute is also due to David L. Sills of the Social Science Research Council, staff member of the committee, whose organizational, administrative, and diplomatic skills kept this complicated project running smoothly.

The committee also wishes to thank those organizations that contributed additional funding to the 1980 census project—the Ford Foundation and its deputy vice president, Louis Winnick, the National Science Foundation, the National Institute on Aging, and the National Institute of Child Health and Human Development. Their support of the research program in general and of several particular studies is gratefully acknowledged.

The ultimate goal of the National Committee and its sponsors has been to produce a definitive, accurate, and comprehensive picture of the

U.S. population in the 1980s, a picture that would be primarily descriptive but also enriched by a historical perspective and a sense of the challenges for the future inherent in the trends of today. We hope our readers will agree that the present volume takes a significant step toward achieving that goal.

CHARLES F. WESTOFF

Chairman and Executive Director
National Committee for Research
on the 1980 Census

To our fathers, Frank and Toribio

Acknowledgments

Completion of this book was made possible by financial assistance from the Russell Sage Foundation through the National Committee for Research on the 1980 Census, from our respective institutions, and from other granting agencies. Funding for the research conducted at the University of Texas was provided by grants from the University of Texas' University Research and Policy Research Institutes, as well as by grants from the Center for Population Research at the National Institute for Child Health and Human Development (grants HD-18834, HD-18084, and HD-12812) and the Hewlett Foundation. Also, computer programming assistance at the University of Texas was supported by a grant to the Population Research Center (HD-06160). At the University of Wisconsin (Marta Tienda's institutional affiliation during the preparation of this volume), the major share of funding was provided by grants from the Graduate School Research Committee, the Department of Health and Human Services to the Institute for Research on Poverty, and a Hatch grant to the Department of Rural Sociology. In addition, all computational work at the University of Wisconsin was supported by a grant to the Center for Demography and Ecology from the Center for Population Research at the National Institute of Child Health and Human Development (HD-05876). Both the Population Research Center at Texas and the Center for Demography and Ecology at Wisconsin provided collegial and supportive research environments for the research.

The manuscript has been greatly improved by the critical readings of our review committee. Charles F. Westoff, chairman and executive director of the National Committee for Research on the 1980 Census, and Douglas S. Massey, of the University of Chicago, provided especially thorough and constructive criticisms as the manuscript was being written. At the University of Texas, we profited from W. Parker Frisbie's reading and suggestions for improvement of the manuscript once it was completed. Finally, George J. Borjas (of the University of California at

Santa Barbara, a member of our advisory panel) provided helpful comments on the first few chapters. Our readers certainly improved the final product, but we assume responsibility for any shortcomings that remain.

Many other individuals participated in the production of this work, either by assisting with the research for individual chapters or by providing technical, computational, or typing assistance. At Texas, Wolfgang Opitz and Elizabeth H. Stephen were extremely valuable research associates. B. Lindsay Lowell also provided research assistance, and Fran Milfeld and Sherry Young helped with typing and word processing. At Wisconsin, Wayne Bigelow and Cheryl Knobeloch prepared the master extracts used for Chapters 2, 8, 9, and 10 and for some of the material in Chapter 3. Vilma Ortiz and Candace Nelson collaborated in the analyses which resulted in Appendix A and Chapter 8, respectively. At Wisconsin, numerous students made invaluable substantive and technical contributions to the research, including Ding Tzann Lii, Leif Jensen, John Marcotte, Alberto Martini, Rebecca Hilliker, Susan Robinson, Susan Walsh, Diane Duesterhoeft, and Gary Heiserer.

Chapters 1, 3, and 4 were authored collaboratively. Primary responsibility for Chapter 2 and Chapters 8 through 10 belonged to Marta Tienda, and primary responsibility for Chapters 5 through 7 and the Epilogue to Frank D. Bean. Douglas S. Massey contributed a section to Chapter 5. The material in the technical appendixes was prepared by Marta Tienda.

FRANK D. BEAN
University of Texas at Austin

MARTA TIENDA
University of Chicago

Contents

List of Tables   *xv*

List of Figures   *xxiii*

INTRODUCTION   *1*

1 THE STRUCTURING OF HISPANIC ETHNICITY:
   THEORETICAL AND HISTORICAL CONSIDERATIONS   *7*

2 THE HISPANIC POPULATION IN NUMBERS:
   CENSUS DEFINITIONS IN HISTORICAL PERSPECTIVE   *36*

3 A DEMOGRAPHIC AND SOCIOECONOMIC PROFILE
   OF THE HISPANIC POPULATION: PERSISTENCE,
   DIVERSITY, AND CHANGE OVER TWO DECADES   *56*

4 IMMIGRATION   *104*

5 GEOGRAPHICAL DISTRIBUTION, INTERNAL MIGRATION,
   AND RESIDENTIAL SEGREGATION *(written in collaboration
   with Douglas S. Massey)*   *137*

6 MARRIAGE, FAMILY, AND HOUSEHOLD   *178*

7 FERTILITY PATTERNS WITHIN THE SPANISH
   ORIGIN POPULATIONS   *205*

8 THE EDUCATIONAL STANDING OF HISPANICS:
   SIGNS OF HOPE AND STRESS   *233*

9   HISPANICS IN THE U.S. LABOR FORCE   *280*

10   EARNINGS AND ECONOMIC WELL-BEING   *338*

11   EPILOGUE   *397*

     APPENDIX A   *401*

     APPENDIX B   *409*

     APPENDIX C   *412*

     Bibliography   *419*
     Name Index   *435*
     Subject Index   *440*

List of Tables

2.1   Identifiers Used to Enumerate the Hispanic Population, U.S. Censuses of Population and Housing: 1950–1980   *41*

2.2   Hispanic Origin Population, 1970–1980: Census Enumerations and CPS Estimates   *53*

3.1   Growth of the U.S. Hispanic Population: 1960–1980   *59*

3.2   Estimated Components of Change in Mexican Origin Population (1970–1980) and Change Due to Immigration   *64*

3.3   Median Age of the Hispanic Population by Type of Origin and Nativity: 1960–1980   *68*

3.4   Metro and Nonmetro Residential Distribution of the Hispanic Population by National Origin: 1960–1980   *85*

3.5   Selected Demographic Characteristics of the Hispanic Population by Type of Origin: 1980   *90*

3.6   Selected Social and Economic Characteristics of the Hispanic Population Aged 16 and Over by National Origin: 1980   *92*

3.7   Language Characteristics of the Hispanic Population Aged 25 and Over by National Origin: 1980   *93*

3.8   Country of Origin and Nativity Composition of the Central/South American Origin Population: 1960–1980   *96*

3.9   Changing Age Structure of the Central/South American Origin Population by Country of Origin: 1960–1980   *99*

3.10   State of Residence Distribution of the Central/South American Origin Population by Country of Origin: 1980   *100*

4.1   Hispanic Immigration to the United States by Origin Group: 1950–1980   *105*

4.2   Mexican Legal Immigration to the United States: 1821–
        1984   106
4.3   Naturalizations by Country of Former Allegiance and
        Period of Entry Expressed as a Percentage of Immi-
        grants Entering Five Years Previously   108
4.4   Percentage Distribution of the Hispanic Origin Popula-
        tions by Nativity: 1960–1980   110
4.5   Distribution of the Hispanic Origin Populations by Na-
        tivity and Year of Arrival: 1980   111
4.6   Distribution of the Central/South American Origin
        Population by Timing of Arrival and Country of Ori-
        gin: 1980   112
4.7   Selected Alternative Estimates of the Number of Illegal
        Migrants of Mexican Origin Living in the United
        States in 1980   119
4.8   Estimates of the Size of the Illegal Mexican Population
        Living in the United States in 1980 Under Alternative
        Assumptions About Undercount Rates for Illegal
        Mexicans   121
4.9   Immigrants Admitted by Type of Admission, Country
        or Region of Birth, and Period of Entry   124
4.10   Age Distribution by Immigrant Status and Sex, as Well
        as Sex Ratios by Immigrant Status and Age: Mexican
        Origin Population, 1980   128
4.11   Education Level Completed by Persons Aged 18 and
        Over and English Proficiency Distributions by Immi-
        grant Status and Sex: Mexican Origin Population,
        1980   130
4.12   Industry Classification by Immigrant Status and Sex:
        Mexican Origin Population, 1980   132
5.1   Percentage Distributions of the Spanish Origin Popula-
        tions by Census Region: 1960–1980   139
5.2   Percentage Distributions of the Spanish Origin Popula-
        tions by Region and Nativity: 1980   140
5.3   Percentage State Distribution of the Spanish Origin
        Populations: 1960–1980   142
5.4   Indexes of Dissimilarity Between the State Distribu-
        tions of the Spanish Origin Populations and the Total
        United States Population: 1960–1980   144
5.5   Percentage of the Spanish Origin Populations Living in
        Metropolitan Areas by Nativity: 1960–1980   146
5.6   Percentage of the Spanish Origin Metropolitan Popula-

	tions Living Within Central Cities by Nativity: 1960– 1980	*147*
5.7	Standard Metropolitan Statistical Areas with 100,000 or More Spanish Origin Persons: 1980	*148*
5.8	Standard Metropolitan Statistical Areas with 100,000 or More Spanish Origin Persons by Origin Type: 1980	*150*
5.9	Percentage Change Between 1970 and 1980 in the Sizes of the Total and Hispanic Populations of SMSAs with 100,000 or More Hispanics in 1980	*151*
5.10	Total Net Migration and Rates for Census Regions by Type of Spanish Origin, Indexed to Non-Hispanic Whites: 1980	*154*
5.11	Regional Destinations of Migrants by Regions of Origin and Type of Spanish Origin: 1980	*158*
5.12	Ratio of the Number of Inmigrants to Outmigrants by Region and Type of Spanish Origin: 1980	*160*
5.13	Classification of Hispanic Tracts by Type of Residential Change: 60 SMSAs by Census Region	*165*
5.14	Classification of Hispanic Tracts by Type of Residential Change, 1970–1980: 10 Hispanic SMSAs	*166*
5.15	Dissimilarity between Hispanics and Anglos in 60 SMSAs by Region and the 10 Largest Hispanic SMSAs	*169*
5.16	Probabilities of Residential Contact Between Hispanics and Anglos by Region and for 10 Largest Hispanic SMSAs	*172*
5.17	Dissimilarities and Contact Probabilities Between Selected Hispanic Groups and Anglos in 60 SMSAs by Region and 10 Largest Hispanic SMSAs: 1980	*174*
6.1	Marital Status by Sex and Spanish Origin Group, Persons Aged 14 and Over: 1980	*183*
6.2	Percentage of Ever-Married 25-Year-Olds by Sex and Spanish Origin Group: 1960–1980	*184*
6.3	Median Age at First Marriage by Sex and Type of Spanish Origin: 1960–1980	*185*
6.4	Age-Standardized Percentages Experiencing Marital Instability Among Females Aged 15–64 by Type of Spanish Origin: 1960–1980	*186*
6.5	Mean Household Size and Mean Number of Adults per Household: 1960–1980	*187*
6.6	Change in Mean Household Size and Decomposition into Change in Mean Number of Adults and Mean Number of Children: 1960–1970 and 1970–1980	*188*

6.7   Mean Household Size and Percentage Distribution by
        Family Type and Ethnic Group: 1960–1980   190
6.8   Female Headship Rates and Percentage of Children in
        Two-Parent Families, Standardized for Age: 1980   192
6.9   Percentage Distribution of Marital Status of Female
        Household Heads, Standardized for Age: 1980   193
6.10   Mean Number of Adults per Household and Percentage
        of Households with Three or More Adults, Standard-
        ized for Age: 1980   195
6.11   Presence of Adult Relatives in Husband-Wife Families,
        Standardized for Age: 1980   196
6.12   Percentage of Never-Married Persons Aged 18–24 Who
        Are Living in Parental Households   197
6.13   Per Capita and Mean Household Income for All House-
        holds by Ethnic Group: 1960–1980   198
6.14   Per Capita and Mean Household Income by Family
        Type and Ethnic Group: 1960–1980   200
6.15   Decomposition of Differentials in Average per Capita
        Income of Mexicans and Puerto Ricans from Non-
        Hispanic Whites into Income and Family Type Distri-
        bution Components: 1960–1980   202
7.1   Number of Children Ever Born per 1,000 Women Aged
        15–44 by Race and Type of Spanish Origin: 1960–
        1980   207
7.2   Number of Children Ever Born per 1,000 Women Aged
        15–44 by Type of Spanish Origin and Age: 1960–1980   209
7.3   Mean Numbers of Children Ever Born and Under Age 3
        by Ethnicity and Age Groups, Ever-Married Spanish
        Origin and Non-Spanish Origin White Women Aged
        15–44: 1980   217
7.4   Mean Numbers of Children Ever Born and Under Age 3
        by Generational Status and Ethnicity, Ever-Married
        Spanish Origin and Non-Hispanic White Women
        Aged 15–44: 1980   218
7.5   Gross and Net Mean Fertility Deviations for Spanish
        Origin from Non-Hispanic White Women by Genera-
        tional Status, Ever-Married Women Aged 15–44: 1980   219
7.6   Mean Numbers of Children Ever Born by Education,
        Generational Status, and Ethnicity, Ever-Married
        Spanish Origin and Non-Hispanic White Women
        Aged 15–44: 1980   222
7.7   Mean Numbers of Children Under Age 3 by Education,
        Generational Status, and Ethnicity, Ever-Married

	Spanish Origin and Non-Hispanic White Women Aged 15–44: 1980	223
7.8	Number and Percentage Distributions by Education and Generational Status, Ever-Married Spanish Origin and Non-Hispanic White Women Aged 15–44: 1980	224
7.9	Net Mean Fertility Differences Between Spanish Origin Groups and Non-Hispanic Whites by Education and Generational Status, Ever-Married Women Aged 15–44: 1980	226
7.10	Net Mean Fertility Differences Between Mexican Origin and Non-Hispanic White Women, Controlling for Age at Marriage, Ever-Married Mexican Origin Women Aged 15–44: 1980	228
7.11	Net Mean Fertility Differences Between Mexican Origin and Non-Hispanic White Women, Ever-Married Women Aged 15–44: 1970	228
7.12	Net Mean Fertility Deviations Between Mexican Origin and Non-Hispanic White Women by Generational Status and English Proficiency, Ever-Married Women Aged 15–44: 1980	229
8.1	Median Years of Schooling of the Adult Population Aged 25 and Over by Race, Hispanic Origin, and Nativity: 1960–1980	234
8.2	Percentage Distribution of Adults Aged 25 and Over by Levels of School Completed, Race, Hispanic Origin, and Nativity: 1960–1980	238
8.3	Selected Characteristics of Adults Aged 25 Completing Less Than High School and Four or More Years of College by Race and Hispanic Origin: 1970–1980	244
8.4	School Enrollment Status of the Hispanic Population Aged 14–34 by National Origin, Education Level, and Age Group: 1980	250
8.5	School Enrollment Status of Hispanic Youth Aged 5–25 by National Origin, Living Arrangements, and Age Group: 1980	252
8.6	Selected Characteristics of Hispanic Youth Aged 5–25 by National Origin, School Enrollment Status, and Living Arrangements: 1980	255
8.7	Rates of Grade Delay Among Enrolled Hispanic Youth by National Origin, Nativity, and Selected Student and Household Correlates of Educational Achievement: 1980	262
8.8	Adjusted Effects of Individual and Household Charac-	

	teristics on the Probability of School Grade Delay Among Enrolled Hispanic Youth Aged 5–25	266
8.9	School Noncompletion Rates Among Hispanic Origin Youth Aged 18–25 by National Origin, Nativity, and Selected Student and Household Correlates of Educational Achievement: 1980	272
8.10	Adjusted Effects of Individual and Household Characteristics on the Probability of School Noncompletion Among Hispanic Youth Aged 18 and Over Living with Parents	275
9.1	Labor Force Participation Rates of Persons Aged 16–64 by Race, National Origin, Nativity, and Gender: 1960–1980	290
9.2	Labor Force Participation Rates of Central/South Americans Aged 16–64 by Gender and Country of Origin: 1980	293
9.3	Adjusted 1980 Labor Force Participation Differentials by National Origin: Hispanic Men Aged 16–64	296
9.4	Adjusted 1980 Labor Force Participation Differentials by National Origin: Hispanic Women Aged 16–64	298
9.5	Unemployment Rates by Hispanic National Origin, Race, Gender, Nativity, and Age: 1960–1980	306
9.6	Sectoral Allocation of Men Aged 16–64 by Nativity: 1960–1980	312
9.7	Allocation Scheme for Sectors and Industries	314
9.8	Sectoral Allocation of Women Aged 16–64 by Nativity: 1960–1980	316
9.9	Occupational Distribution of Men Aged 16–64 by Nativity: 1960–1980	328
9.10	Occupational Distribution of Women Aged 16–64 by Nativity: 1960–1980	334
10.1	Income Distribution and Median Income of Families by Hispanic National Origin and Race: 1970–1980	341
10.2	Differentials in Median Family Income According to Selected Head and Family Characteristics, Hispanic National Origin, and Race: 1970–1980	346
10.3	Components of Mean Family Income by Hispanic National Origin and Race: 1970–1980	350
10.4	Differential Poverty Rates for Families by Hispanic National Origin and Race: 1970–1980	356
10.5	Differentials in Receipt of Public Assistance Income by Families According to Hispanic National Origin and Race: 1970–1980	359

10.6	Components of Mean Personal Income of Men and Women Aged 16 and Over by Hispanic National Origin and Race: 1960–1980	*368*
10.7	Differential Poverty Rates of Persons by Hispanic National Origin and Race: 1970–1980	*371*
10.8	Median Earnings Differentials of Individual Workers Aged 16–64 by Hispanic National Origin, Race, and Gender: 1970–1980	*376*
10.9	Median Earnings for Full-Time, Year-Round Central and South American Workers Aged 16–64 by Gender and Country of Origin: 1980	*379*
10.10	Earnings Determination of Hispanic Men by National Origin: 1980	*380*
10.11	Earnings Determination of Hispanic Women by National Origin: 1980	*384*
10.12	Description of Variables Used in Earnings Regression Analyses	*387*
A.1	Percentage Distribution of Hispanic Subgroups: 1960–1980	*406*
B.1	Total Hispanic Distribution by State: 1960–1980	*409*
B.2	Residential Redistribution of the Hispanic Population Aged 5 and Over by National Origin: 1960–1980	*411*
C.1	Operational and Conceptual Definition of Dependent and Independent Variables for Analysis of Delay and Dropping Out	*414*

List of Figures

1.1 Structuring of Hispanic Ethnicity: A Conceptual Framework   *15*

2.1 The Spanish Origin Question in the 1970 and 1980 Censuses   *50*

3.1 Persons of Hispanic Origin in the United States: 1980   *60*

3.2 Growth of the Hispanic Population: 1970–1980   *61*

3.3 Age-Sex Composition of the Hispanic Population: 1980   *65*

3.4 Age-Sex Composition of the Total U.S. Population: 1980   *66*

3.5 Age-Sex Composition of Persons of Mexican Origin by Nativity: 1980   *67*

3.6 Age-Sex Composition of Persons of Puerto Rican Origin by Birthplace: 1980   *69*

3.7 Age-Sex Composition of Persons of Cuban Origin by Nativity: 1980

3.8 Age-Sex Composition of Persons of Central/South American Origin by Nativity: 1980   *74*

3.9 Age-Sex Composition of Persons of Other Hispanic Origin by Nativity: 1980   *75*

3.10 Residential Distribution of the Total Hispanic Population by State: 1980   *77*

3.11 Distribution of the Hispanic Population by Type of Origin by State: 1980   *78*

3.12 Percentage Hispanic of Total Population by State: 1970–1980   *81*

3.13 Residential Configuration of the White Spanish Surname Population by Urban-Rural Residence for the Southwest: 1950–1980   *87*

4.1 Emigrants from the Spanish-Speaking Latin American Countries to the United States: 1980   *113*

5.1   Interregional Net Migration Flows: 1975–1980   *155*
5.2   Interregional Net Migration Flows: 1975–1980   *156*
5.3   Interregional Net Migration Flows: 1975–1980   *157*
5.4   New York and Florida Migration Flows by Spanish Origin Type: 1975–1980   *161*
5.5   Migration Flows of the Mexican Origin Population for Selected States: 1975–1980   *162*
8.1   Median Education of the Hispanic Population Aged 25 and Over by Type of Origin and Broad Age Groups: 1960–1980   *236*
8.2   Proportion of the Hispanic Population Aged 25 and Over Not Completing High School by Type of Origin and Broad Age Groups: 1960–1980   *242*
9.1   Labor Force Participation Rates of Men and Women Aged 16–64 by Race and Hispanic National Origin: 1980   *288*
9.2   Unemployment Rates of Men and Women Aged 16–64 by Race and Hispanic National Origin: 1980   *304*
9.3   Occupational Distribution for Mexicans Aged 16–64 by Year and Gender: 1960–1980   *323*
9.4   Occupational Distribution for Puerto Ricans Aged 16–64 by Year and Gender: 1960–1980   *324*
9.5   Occupational Distribution for Cubans Aged 16–64 by Year and Gender: 1960–1980   *325*
9.6   Occupational Distribution for Central/South Americans Aged 16–64 by Year and Gender: 1960–1980   *326*
9.7   Occupational Distribution for Other Hispanics Aged 16–64 by Year and Gender: 1960–1980   *327*
10.1 Median Family Income by Hispanic National Origin: 1968–1980   *342*
10.2 Percentage of Families in Poverty by National Origin and Race: 1970–1980   *354*
10.3 Mean Personal Income of Men and Women Aged 16 and Over by Hispanic National Origin and Race: 1960–1980   *362*
10.4 Age Earnings Profiles for Hispanic Men: 1980   *386*
10.5 Age Earnings Profiles for Hispanic Women: 1980   *389*

INTRODUCTION

O VER THE past two decades peoples of Hispanic descent have had an increasing impact on the ethnic, socioeconomic, and demographic features of the United States population. Persons whose national origin is Mexico, Puerto Rico, Cuba, or any of the Central or South American or other Hispanic countries—any of some 23 different nations altogether—have captured the national attention as the public policy issues of immigration, population growth, bilingual education, discrimination, and unemployment have assumed a more prominent place on political agendas. Although the Hispanic presence in the United States predates the formation of the American nation, the impact of the first settlers—direct descendants from the Spanish Conquistadores—was overshadowed by the political and military events leading to the geographic expansion and consolidation of the United States. Furthermore, the regional concentration of the Mexican origin population in the five southwestern states—which continues to the present day—made it relatively easy for the rest of the country to overlook even this largest and oldest of the Spanish-speaking populations. However, as the social consciousness of the 1960s increasingly called attention both to the cultural diversity and to the disadvantaged economic position of most Hispanic groups, and as Latino immigration to already growing Sunbelt states increased during the 1970s, the national visibility of the Hispanic population grew substantially.

Interest in the Spanish origin population increased on the part of both federal and local leaders during the post–civil rights period. This stemmed not only from social movements that gave political legitimacy to claims for social and economic justice, but also occurred as a result of other sociodemographic changes that strengthened the position of Spanish origin peoples outside the Southwest. Puerto Ricans from the tiny island Commonwealth began their influx shortly after World War II. Their numbers gained momentum during the 1950s, when the average annual flow averaged about 40,000 individuals. That most Puerto Rican migrants were destined for New York City may have limited their national visibility for a decade or two, but this situation began to change during the late 1960s and continued throughout the 1970s as the second generation of Puerto Ricans, as well as new migrants, began to settle outside the Northeast. Between 1970 and 1980 Puerto Ricans residing on the mainland became more residentially dispersed both within the Northeast and outside this region. The early concentration of Puerto Ricans in New York City, however, while limiting national visibility, did serve to foster the development of an endogenous community leadership that has become increasingly more proficient in articulating Puerto Rican interests in the national arena.

A third major event that contributed to the increased presence and diversification of Hispanics in the United States was the large-scale admission of refugees from Cuba following the Communist revolution on this island nation located 90 miles from the southernmost tip of Florida. Although the program designed to help Cuban refugees resettle in this country has tried to prevent their geographic concentration in Miami, the major port of entry during the early stages of the program, the Cuban presence in the United States remains highly concentrated in the Southeast, with Florida containing the vast majority of refugees and their descendants. Thus, while the three major Hispanic origin groups continue to be regionally concentrated and relatively geographically isolated from one another, their collective national presence differs dramatically from that of the pre–World War II period. In a relatively short period—two or three decades at most—peoples of Hispanic origin have become national rather than regional in distribution.

Taken together, persons of Mexican, Puerto Rican, Cuban, and Central or South American origin constitute roughly 86 percent of what is commonly termed the Hispanic population. Our empirical analyses illustrate extensive diversity among these three groups and thus challenge the idea that a single Hispanic population exists (as well as suggest that it is misleading to use "Hispanic" as an ethnic label). We also acknowledge the importance and diversity of a rather substantial residual group frequently denoted "Other Hispanics" for reasons of terminological convenience. This is the most heterogeneous Spanish-speaking group, both in terms of the number of national origins encompassed and in terms of sociodemographic characteristics. For this reason it is important not to attach undue significance to comparisons of "Other Hispanics" with groups whose members are of Mexican, Puerto Rican, or Cuban origin. The same might be said for Central or South Americans, although the members of this latter group may have more in common by virtue of identification with Latin America.

Recent and previous immigrants from Caribbean countries and Spain, including their native-born offspring, make up a considerable share of the "Other Hispanic" population. Also included are the *Hispanos,* the direct descendants of the Spaniards who participated in the conquest and settlement of selected areas of the present-day Southwest. In contrast to the individuals who trace their ancestry to Caribbean countries and are largely foreign-born, *Hispanos* are native-born citizens whose ancestors have been in the United States for several generations. That *Hispanos* maintain a separate ethnic identity reflects their common historical experience and relatively secluded residence patterns in the United States. Historically, *Hispanos* resided in present-day New Mexico and southern Colorado, but available data make it virtually impossible to trace changes in the residential dispersion and cultural integration of this group. What is certain is that while the *Hispano* population absorbed Indian influence through miscegenation and cultural commingling that took place during the colonization phase of United States history, most *Hispanos* emphasize their European origins, tracing their ancestry to the original Spanish settlers.

With the exception of information on Mexicans, data on the various Hispanic origin populations are almost nonexistent prior to 1960. And even for Mexicans nationally representative data were not available until 1970. However, as the Hispanic presence in the United States has become more pronounced both demographically and politically, the availability of data suitable for national level studies has also increased. More and better data about peoples of Hispanic origin have permitted many researchers working independently to document the changes in the social and economic position of the various national origin groups. Collectively, these individual efforts have enhanced our understanding of the changing position of Spanish-speaking people in a complex and multiethnic society. In this book we aim to advance this understanding by drawing together the findings of past studies with new evidence from the 1980 Census of Population and Housing. Where appropriate and feasible, we introduce more recent data, as well as data from earlier censuses in order to document changes that have occurred since 1960.

Given the extensive social, demographic, and ethnic diversity among the Hispanic groups, we begin our study of the underlying commonalities and differences with a theoretical discussion in Chapter 1 of the meaning of Hispanic ethnicity. Since we think it is fruitful to conceive of ethnicity as a process rather than as an ascribed trait, we develop our theoretical arguments with brief historical vignettes on the incorporation of each of the three major groups into United States society. Our purpose is to set a historical backdrop for interpreting the contemporary expression of socioeconomic and ethnic differentiation among Mexican, Puerto Rican, and Cuban origin peoples.

Chapter 2 is devoted to defining the population and to providing a critical discussion of the data used to portray changes in the characteristics of Hispanic origin peoples. While this discussion is based largely on data from the 1980 census, attention is also given to 1960 and 1970 census data in order to identify the strengths and limitations of the items used to enumerate the Spanish origin population over time. We also consider how changes in enumeration practices and in definitions of specific items limit the accuracy of measurement, and especially the representation of temporal change.

The remainder of the book is dedicated to compiling a comprehensive profile of the demographic and socioeconomic characteristics of the Hispanic origin populations, emphasizing the vast diversity among them through comparisons of Mexicans, Puerto Ricans, and Cubans; Central/South Americans; and, where appropriate, blacks and non-Hispanic whites. The book is organized by subject matter rather than by nationality of the groups. This approach enables us to focus the results and analyses around the themes of persistence and change, and when comparing the groups, around patterns of diversity and uniformity. This strategy also allows us to identify the ways in which the Hispanic origin groups and the non-Hispanic white majority are becoming more similar and dissimilar and to note which groups are involved in patterns of convergence (or divergence).

Our analyses begin with a general demographic profile in Chapter 3, which considers the size of the population, as well as its changing age and sex composition, rates of growth, and residential distribution. Data limitations require us to restrict this discussion to the 1960–1980 period since data prior to 1950 are less comparable. Since the rapid growth of the population has resulted from both high fertility and high rates of immigration during the 1960s and 1970s, we devote separate chapters to each of these topics. We also devote a chapter to patterns of spatial distribution and internal migration. Another full chapter is devoted to the marriage patterns and living arrangements of Hispanic origin groups and, where data permit, changes over time. The latter is a topic of great social and political importance, and one that has received very spotty attention by past researchers. Our discussion of the social and economic positioning of the Hispanic population will be presented in three chapters about the educational, labor market, and economic well-being of the population.

Other topics of special importance to Hispanic origin groups, such as linguistic practices, are not covered in extensive detail as separate chapters, but rather are discussed in conjunction with the topics in the chapters enumerated above. For example, the importance of proficiency in English and Spanish-English bilingualism is explored in great detail in the chapter about the educational attainment of the Hispanic populations. Linguistic traits are also considered in conjunction with labor market activity and indicators of economic wellbeing. Because many of the topics and results presented are policy-relevant, we explore their implications in several of the chapters. A final, brief chapter reiterates in synopsis form the major conclusions of the study.

1

THE STRUCTURING
OF HISPANIC ETHNICITY:
THEORETICAL AND HISTORICAL
CONSIDERATIONS

ALTHOUGH common ancestral ties to Spain and/or Latin America, as well as frequent usage of the Spanish language, might seem to imply an underlying cultural similarity among peoples of Hispanic origin, the diverse settlement and immigration experiences of Mexicans, Puerto Ricans, Cubans, and other Hispanic groups have created distinct subpopulations with discernible demographic and economic characteristics. Persisting socioeconomic differences among these groups not only challenge the idea that the term "Hispanic" is appropriate as an ethnic label, they also suggest that a careful scrutiny of the historical commonalities and divergencies among these groups as they have settled in the United States is relevant to understanding their contemporary sociodemographic situations. This chapter attempts such a scrutiny.[1]

Our purpose is to lay the theoretical and historical groundwork for interpreting the extensive variation in demographic and socioeconomic characteristics of peoples of Spanish origin in 1980, as well as for understanding changes in these characteristics since 1960. A portion of this effort involves examining the concept of ethnicity, which Yinger defines as "a segment of a larger society whose members are thought, by them-

---

[1]Parts of this chapter originally appeared in Candace Nelson and Marta Tienda, "The Structuring of Hispanic Ethnicity: Historical and Contemporary Perspectives," *Ethnic and Racial Studies* 8 (1985):49–74.

selves and/or others, to have a common origin and to share important segments of a common culture and who, in addition, participate in shared activities in which the common origin and culture are significant ingredients."[2] In an attempt to clarify the meaning of Hispanic ethnicity in contemporary United States society, we explore how each of the major Hispanic national origin groups has entered the country and how this has shaped their definitions of ethnicity. This task initially requires separating conceptually the structural elements of ethnicity from its cultural manifestations. To assist us in accomplishing this objective we draw upon historical comparisons among Mexicans, Puerto Ricans, and Cubans—the three largest Hispanic groups each of which has come from a single national origin—calling attention to the social and political factors affecting their migration to this country, their incorporation into the labor market, and their settlement patterns. Although our primary goal is to describe the demographic and social history of these Spanish origin groups, we also comment on the usefulness of the idea of Hispanic ethnicity and on the extent to which it constitutes a sociopolitical force shaping the contemporary pattern of ethnic stratification in the United States.

On the Social Construction of Ethnicity: Theoretical Considerations

In the context of the United States as a nation of immigrants, it is impossible to define ethnicity simply as a collection of ascriptive traits. While the importance of such traits as rallying points for people of similar cultural backgrounds cannot be denied, primordial ties—defined by Geertz as "the longing not to belong to any other group"[3]—are not sufficient to explain ethnic group solidarity. Ethnicity is also a social phenomenon. This is demonstrated by the fact that ethnic group boundaries are defined not only by socially produced rules of descent, but also can be changed by group members themselves. One becomes an ethnic by virtue of leaving the homeland and by virtue of one's social status vis-à-vis the dominant majority in the receiving society. Frequently a common sense of nationality emerges only after immigration. This was the case with many European immigrants and can be seen today in the emergence to a certain degree of a common sense of identification among Hispanics and Asian Americans who have come from previously

---

[2]Milton Yinger, "Ethnicity," *Annual Review of Sociology* 11 (1985):151–80.
[3]C. Geertz, *Old Societies and New States* (New York: Free Press, 1963), p. 109.

distinct and often hostile national groups.[4] But the very fact that recent ethnic labels for Hispanics have been ever-changing—from Latins to Hispanics to Latinos—itself reflects the social tensions that render the concept of Hispanic ethnicity problematic and the political cohesion of the diverse groups questionable.

The complexities involved in interpreting ethnicity are aptly demonstrated in the case of the United States Hispanic population. Although their presence in the United States predates the emergence of the American nation, their political strength and national visibility, resulting in part from high fertility and the continued influx of new immigrants, presents a challenge for students of ethnic stratification. "Hispanic" as a label combines second-generation natives and their offspring, foreigners, and political refugees under one ethnic umbrella, but the adequacy of this and other singular labels is questionable on theoretical and historical grounds.

As the flow of immigrants from Latin America and the Spanish-speaking Caribbean into the United States continues to increase the size of the Hispanic population, a partially unified sense of nationality seems to be emerging among Hispanic origin groups. However, this sense of identification is fragile for political and demographic reasons. Not only do the short-term social goals of the various national origin groups differ, but the varying geographical distributions of the groups undermine the possibility of an overarching cohesion. Moreover, unlike the European immigrants of the nineteenth and early twentieth centuries, many Hispanics, perhaps because they are more recent immigrants, have not yet become fully integrated into the broader society. And, in contrast to the case of other white immigrants, use of the mother tongue has not disappeared among third- or later-generation Mexicans and Puerto Ricans reared in the United States. Today Hispanic enclaves and the Spanish language thrive in different regions of the country, although considerable linguistic acculturation can be observed among all Spanish-speaking national origin groups who have lived in the United States for longer than a generation. That these processes have not occurred at uniform rates among various national origin and cultural groups lends support to the view that ethnicity is socially produced.

A frequent depiction of the social and economic experiences of U.S. immigrants is that most groups have confronted similar opportunities in the host society. Without taking into account differences in the historical contexts of the migrations, differences in the ways the various

[4]Edna Bonacich, "Class Approaches to Ethnicity and Race," *Insurgent Sociologist* 10 (1980):9–23; William Yancey, Eugene Erikson, and Richard Juliani, "Emergent Ethnicity: A Review and Reformulation," *American Sociological Review* 41 (1976):391–403.

groups have been received in the new society, and differences in the nature of the migration process itself, many observers often evaluate ethnic groups in terms of how they fare in "becoming American." "Americanization," however, is a multifaceted process which encompasses cultural, social, and psychological dimensions as well as those which are purely economic, yet the latter seem to weigh most heavily in assessments of which groups have and which have not become well integrated into the American mainstream. Those who do not succeed socially or economically—the unmeltable ethnics—undermine the idea that the "melting pot" is the dominant metaphor guiding our understanding of ethnic relations. Despite alternative interpretations that have surfaced to explain the social significance of ethnicity and the persistence of racial and ethnic stratification in contemporary U.S. society, the melting pot metaphor has yet to be replaced.

One perspective on the persistence of racial and ethnic stratification maintains that ethnic cohesion persists as the natural extension of primordial ties. This view gives rise to the notion that the disadvantaged, marginal position of certain ethnic and racial groups results from their cultural deficiencies, and that these disappear as individuals assimilate into the dominant culture. A contrasting theoretical perspective views ethnic divisions as mere reflections of class divisions. Several variants of the class interpretation of persisting ethnic differentiation exist, but the unifying theme is their focus on economic rather than cultural factors as determinants of ethnic inequality and their emphasis on structural instead of individual factors in the explanation of rates of assimilation. The great diversity in the ethnic experience in the United States challenges both of these perspectives and most that fall between them. Reducing ethnic stratification to a class phenomenon is reasonable only under the assumption that all members of an ethnic group are in the same class. Similarly, because ethnic identity and solidarity shift across groups and historical eras, it is equally inappropriate to deny the importance of social factors in molding ethnicity over time and place. Members of ethnic groups who combine high levels of economic success with strong ethnic identifications present a troublesome inconsistency for theories that would see ethnicity and class as nearly perfectly overlapping categories.[5]

In acknowledging that ascriptive traits are far less salient determinants of ethnic group boundaries than socially constructed membership rules, we believe that ethnicity is predominantly a social phenomenon organized around outwardly visible physical and cultural differences be-

---

[5]Charles Hirschman, "America's Melting Pot Reconsidered," *Annual Review of Sociology* 9 (1982):397–423.

tween two or more groups. Moreover, the fact that ethnic boundaries can be changed by group members to make the collectivity more or less inclusive requires a dynamic conception of ethnicity and a view that is sensitive to the historical setting in which it occurs. Finally, whether an individual is a member of an ethnic group depends not only on outwardly visible ascriptive traits, but also on the person's identification with a particular ethnic group.

That ethnic boundaries are defined by a constellation of social forces, including the degree of ethnic and racial antagonism in the host society, calls attention to a third aspect of the social construction of ethnicity—that is, its interactive character. While the common sense of nationality which constitutes the minimum criterion for ethnic identification emerges only after immigration and the ensuing process of social comparison between the newcomers and the members of the majority group, the extent to which ethnic boundaries become clearly defined varies directly with the reception the group experiences in the host society at the time of immigration and for some time following. For many groups the elaboration of ethnicity is a direct reaction to manifestations of ethnic antagonism and hostility against newcomers who are perceived to be in direct competition for a limited pool of social and economic resources.[6] Whether immigrant groups are eventually successful in overcoming such hostility is a critical distinction between those who become disadvantaged and those who do not.

Ideas about the social construction of ethnicity are illustrated in the work of William Yancey and his associates which focuses on European immigrants and their experiences in becoming part of American society.[7] Although quite different in many ways, the comparison of the European and Latin American immigration experiences can fruitfully illustrate the importance of social and historical factors in structuring the dimensions and manifestations of ethnicity. Although the amalgamation experiences of the predominantly white European immigrants gave birth to the melting pot metaphor, it remains to be seen whether the relatively more recent experiences of Latin American and Asian immigrants will lead to a similar result. That many Hispanic immigrants and their descendants have yet to assimilate culturally or socially and occupy lower socioeconomic positions raises the possibility that a greater congruence of ethnic distinctiveness and socioeconomic position may characterize their experience. This issue needs to be further explored in

---

[6]Susan Olzak, "Contemporary Ethnic Mobilization," *Annual Review of Sociology* 9 (1980):355–74; Stanley Lieberson, "A Societal Theory of Race and Ethnic Relations," *American Sociological Review* 26 (1961):902–10.

[7]Yancey, Erikson, and Juliani, "Emergent Ethnicity."

both theoretical and empirical terms if we are to understand the experiences of Hispanic immigrant groups in the United States.

Starting with the idea that ethnicity is a variable, William Yancey and his associates identify several factors that contribute to the emergence of ethnicity among immigrant groups, including (1) the legal and political guidelines determining who can immigrate, (2) the need for and availability of wage labor, (3) the changing structure of industry, and (4) the ecological configuration of urban areas. Yancey and his collaborators argue that these structural variables played an important role in shaping the integration experiences of European immigrants. They claim—and we agree—that these supra-individual variables better explain the residential and occupational concentration of foreign-born groups than the traditional notion of cultural disposition or preference for certain types of work. Accordingly, we argue below that similar factors have operated for Hispanic groups.

Two factors—residential and occupational concentration—are especially crucial to the formation of ethnic group solidarity in that they produce common interests, lifestyles, and friendships. When the ethnic experience includes rejection, discrimination, and oppression, ethnic ties provide a ready system of support for groups that are readily distinguishable by race, national origin, and/or language. As we will see below, the migration and settlement patterns, and the ensuing labor market experiences of Hispanic origin groups, have had much more to do with contemporary expressions of socioeconomic differentiation among peoples of Spanish origin than have any tendencies to embrace aspects of a common Latin American or Spanish culture.

In order to distinguish between and compare the waves of immigration from Europe, about which Yancey and his colleagues wrote, and the historically later Hispanic flow, one must also draw attention to the timing of immigration and to the various modes of entry and integration of specific national origin groups. Time of immigration is crucial because of temporal changes in employment opportunities and changing demand for various skills as the economy has shifted from goods to service production. Europeans settled in large eastern and western cities during a period of industrial expansion.[8] In contrast, the early Hispanic influx, involving mostly Mexicans, began as a rural phenomenon.[9] As a predominantly urban population after the 1950s, Hispanics have faced

[8]Pastora San Juan Cafferty, Barry R. Chiswick, Andrew M. Greeley, and Teresa A. Sullivan, *The Dilemma of American Immigration* (New Brunswick, NJ: Transaction Books, 1985).
[9]Marta Tienda, "The Mexican American Population," in Amos Hawley and Sara Mills Mazie, eds., *Nonmetropolitan America in Transition* (Chapel Hill: University of North Carolina Press, 1981).

an economic system characterized by periods of restricted growth coupled with dramatic changes in the structure of production.[10] Race and racial discrimination must also be considered as a force shaping the integration experiences of Hispanics, especially those of Puerto Rican origin, even though a racial classification of Hispanics is complicated by the fact that they are brown, black, and white. The changes in the political and legal rights of people of color in the United States should enhance opportunities in the world of work and schooling, but evidence of such outcomes is limited.

A critical question is why certain ethnic groups are singled out for segregation in the least desirable low-skill, low-paying jobs, while others are not. A related and perhaps more central question for understanding the persistence and nature of ethnic stratification is why some groups manage to experience mobility from low- to high-status jobs while others do not. Racism is an important element in this explanation, but it is a mistake to view the situation of white European immigrants as completely distinct from that of racial minorities. At the time of initial entry European immigrants served many of the same functions that racial and ethnic minority workers currently do and also were segregated residentially and occupationally by national origin.[11] The key issue is why Europeans made the transition from low-status occupational positions to the higher-status, better-paying jobs while blacks and Hispanics have not yet done so.

More than any other single comparison, these contrasting outcomes make a critical distinction between ethnic groups and minority groups. Minority groups and ethnic groups are not isomorphic, yet virtually all minorities are distinguishable by ethnic (and/or racial) traits. However, many ethnic groups are not minorities in the sense of being ethnically identifiable and economically disadvantaged. For example, Cubans and other Latin American immigrants are seldom identified as a minority group, but Mexicans and Puerto Ricans usually are. The reason, we maintain, has to do with their very different modes of incorporation and socioeconomic integration experiences.

Vincent has elaborated at some length the distinction between minorities and ethnics, and her interpretation is helpful for understanding the diverse experiences of Hispanics in the United States. A

---

[10]Joachim Singelmann and Marta Tienda, "The Process of Occupational Change in a Service Society: The Case of the United States, 1960–1980," in Bryan Roberts, Ruth Finnegan, and Duncan Gallie, eds., *New Approaches to Economic Life: Economic Restructuring, Unemployment and the Social Division of Labor* (Manchester, England: University of Manchester Press, 1985).

[11]Stanley Lieberson, *A Piece of the Pie: Black and White Immigrants Since 1980* (Berkeley: University of California Press, 1980).

minority, according to Vincent, is a group whose members are treated unequally by a dominant group, usually through prejudice and discrimination. Ethnic groups, on the other hand, are collectivities sharing common cultural norms, values, identities, and behaviors, and who both recognize themselves and are recognized by others as being ethnic.[12]

The extent to which ethnicity is a matter of individual choice depends on the group's access (or lack thereof) to the reward system of the dominant society. For members of lower socioeconomic strata opportunities to elaborate or conceal national origin are considerably more limited, if they exist at all. In this light the convergence of ethnic origin and economic disadvantage requires an investigation of the circumstances that translate ethnicity into a disadvantaged economic position for some and a symbolic identity with few if any socioeconomic consequences for others.[13] Such a pursuit might fruitfully uncover the areas of convergence and divergence among Hispanic origin groups and help to clarify the origins of the differential access to resources and social rewards that impart a different socioeconomic connotation to the phrase "Hispanic ethnicity" for Mexicans, Puerto Ricans, Cubans, and other Latin Americans.

The Emergence and Consolidation of "Hispanicity"

To guide our interpretation of the historical circumstances that have shaped the integration of the diverse Hispanic origin groups into the U.S. society and economy, we first set forth the theoretical framework which outlines the processes underlying the emergence, consolidation, and reformulation of Hispanic ethnicity. For this outline we draw heavily on the work of Yancey and his associates,[14] adapting the particulars of their analysis of European ethnics to the experience of Hispanics. Subsequently we compile brief historical vignettes of the integration experiences of Mexican, Puerto Rican, and Cuban origin populations in an attempt to illustrate the diversity of experiences which help explain the extensive socioeconomic and demographic heterogeneity of the peoples of Spanish origin.

[12]Joan Vincent, "The Structuring of Ethnicity," *Human Organization* 33 (1974):375–79.

[13]Herbert J. Gans, "Symbolic Ethnicity: The Future of Ethnic Groups and Cultures in America," *Ethnic and Racial Studies* 2 (1979):1–19.

[14]Yancey, Erikson, and Juliani, "Emergent Ethnicity."

FIGURE 1.1
Structuring of Hispanic Ethnicity: A Conceptual Framework

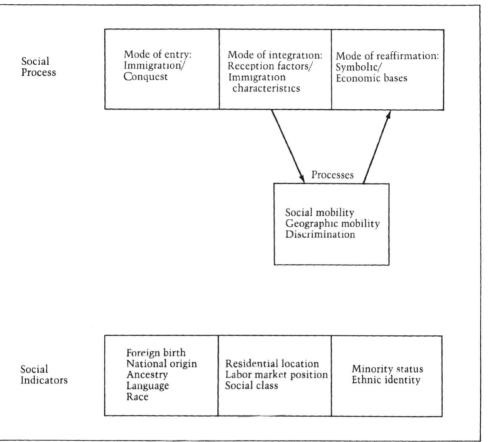

Figure 1.1 maps the major historical and social processes describing the emergence, transformation, and reformulation of ethnicity which help in interpreting the diverse integration experiences and socioeconomic standing of Hispanics. These processes are by nature interactive, and the ways in which the social and historical dimensions intersect are central to understanding the relegation of Hispanics to a minority group status, or their eventual adoption of a more symbolic ethnicity, one less intertwined with economic and social standing.

The Hispanic population emerged as an ethnic group historically through international migration and, to a lesser extent in the Mexican case, through conquest. The reasons for their entry into the United States, combined with the historical moment of that entry, affected both the composition of the Spanish-speaking groups according to national origin and their eventual geographical configuration and socioeconomic standing. Patterns of interethnic contact, once established, were determined by occupational and residential segregation and the changing climate of prejudice and xenophobic sentiment. Integration processes also changed in accordance with shifting economic conditions, the passing of generations, and legal prescriptions governing both immigration flows and labor practices.

Once consolidated, ethnic groups can reformulate their position vis-à-vis the dominant society in response to any number of circumstances. Hispanics having more "successful" integration experiences are more likely to have maintained a symbolic connection to their ethnic heritage, as manifested by the continued observance of holidays, the revival of ethnic foods, the practice of cultural rituals, and so on, while in the areas of occupation, education, language, and residence they have increasingly modeled Anglos. The elaboration of these ethnic traits acquires a symbolic character which reinforces the validity of cultural pluralism as a perspective on ethnic stratification. In a stratified society it is possible for some members of a group to be socioeconomically successful while the group as a whole occupies a disadvantaged position vis-à-vis the dominant majority.

Alternatively, for Hispanics who have not gained access to new opportunities, and for whom isolation within minority occupational and residential enclaves and systematic discrimination have remained the rule, ethnicity becomes synonymous with minority status. For ethnic minorities the significance of ethnicity not only extends beyond the symbolic manifestations of cultural heritage, but it also is more than a simple reflection of economic relationships. The survival of distinct ethnic cultures, while structurally determined, attests to the reflexive nature of ethnicity as it offers refuge to its adherents against the very system that produces stratification and oppression.

Theoretical constructs such as those abstractly presented thus far need to be translated into concrete social experiences through the stories of real people. It is to these that our focus now shifts. In discussing the very different integration experiences of Mexicans, Puerto Ricans, and Cubans in the United States, the elements that translated Hispanic origin to a symbolic ethnicity for some and a minority status for others will become apparent. So, too, will the fluid character of Hispanic ethnicity as a social construct.

Mexicans

In comparison with other national and immigrant minorities, including Puerto Ricans, Cubans, and other Latin Americans, Chicanos[15] are distinguished because for some of the members of this group entry into the United States came about through conquest and subordination.[16] Historically and today residentially concentrated in the Southwest, the Mexican ancestry population is not only the largest of the Spanish-speaking nationalities, constituting roughly 60 percent of the total Hispanic population in 1980 (see Chapter 3), but also the most heterogeneous in socioeconomic characteristics and generational composition.[17] The social antecedents of this heterogeneity are rooted in the history of U.S. westward expansion, the geographic proximity and poverty of Mexico that has facilitated continued immigration, and the historical labor functions of Mexican workers in the U.S. economy. These factors, along with changes in immigration policies and the resurgence of Mexican ethnicity that accompanied the Chicano movement of the 1960s, were decisive in molding the contemporary socioeconomic position of people of Mexican origin.

By annexing the states of California, Arizona, New Mexico, Colorado, and Texas at the conclusion of the Mexican-American War, the Treaty of Guadalupe Hidalgo which ended the war also created the Mexican American population as a people. Beyond its political and military implications, the territorial annexation of the Southwest was socially significant in establishing the social destiny of the Mexican American population. Unlike other immigrant groups who voluntarily migrated to the United States and whose sense of peoplehood and ethnicity was shaped by the immigration process and subsequent reception in the new society, Mexicans residing on U.S. territory at that time had neither cause nor power to challenge the new Anglo rulers. Not only did a rapid

---

[15]We use the terms "Mexican American" and "Chicano" interchangeably to refer to populations of Mexican origin and descent, irrespective of generational status. However, the terms differ in their sociopolitical connotation. The term "Chicano" rather than "Mexican American" appears to be more closely associated with the rising level of ethnic consciousness and the movement for equitable treatment. The term "Chicano" eulogizes the Mestizo (Spanish and Indian) heritages and a legacy of exploitation.

[16]Tomas Almaguer, "Historical Notes on Chicano Oppression: The Dialectics of Race and Class Domination in North America," *Aztlan* 5 (1974):1; Edward Murguia, *Assimilation, Colonialism and the Mexican American People*, Mexican American Monograph Series no. 1 (Austin: Center for Mexican American Studies, University of Texas, 1975).

[17]Tienda, "Mexican American Population"; Frank D. Bean, E. Stephen, and W. Opitz, "The Mexican Origin Population in the United States: A Demographic Overview," in R. de la Garza, F. Bean, C. Bonjean, R. Romo, and R. Alvarez, eds., *The Mexican American Experience: An Interdisciplinary Anthology* (Austin: University of Texas Press, 1985).

and clear break with the parent country occur, together with ensuing socioeconomic and cultural subjugation, but the land itself that the indigenous population considered its own was often lost.[18]

Once conquered, the Southwest was opened for Anglo "settlement." This invitation resulted in an influx of thousands of non-Hispanic whites who took control of the land and brought about the eventual destruction or transformation of the indigenous social systems governing the lives of the original Mexican residents. The subsequent development of the area by Anglos depended on the abundant and cheap labor of foreigners in the three major economic sectors—agriculture, mining, and the railroad industry. As Cardoso has described, the construction of the railroads in the Southwest was very important in providing employment and determining settlement patterns.[19] Also, the expansion of commercial agriculture in the West contributed significantly to capital accumulation that made the economic transformation of the area possible. However, this economic growth came at the social expense of the Mexican people who were paid "Mexican wages" for Mexican work. While mechanization began to affect grain crops prior to World War II, fruits, vegetables, and cotton remained labor intensive into the 1960s and early 1970s. Their importance as a commercial crop for agricultural corporations rose steadily and required a large seasonal labor force. Because of the historical role of Chicanos in the development of U.S. agriculture, Chicano workers constituted up to 85 percent of common labor employed in the fields well into the twentieth century.[20]

As Chicanos lost their land, their social mobility became blocked, and this eventually led to a deterioration of their social position vis-à-vis Anglos. Racism was employed to pursue economic interests (all racial minorities in the area were subjected to similar treatment); although Mexicans are white, their brown skin and indigenous features encouraged racism and discrimination by the Anglo majority. That Mexicans were viewed as "non-white" is attested to by the fact that they were classified as a racial group in the 1930 census. The results of racial discrimination and subordination led to a set of conditions that both structured the lives of Chicanos and gave racial and ethnic prejudice a life of its own in the Southwest, but particularly in Texas.

Equally important to an understanding of Chicano ethnicity is the phenomenon of immigration which gained momentum after the Mexican Revolution of 1910 and propelled thousands north of the Rio Grande

[18]Rodolfo Alvarez, "The Psycho-Historical and Socioeconomic Development of the Chicano Community in the United States," *Social Science Quarterly* 53 (1973):4.

[19]L. Cardoso, *Mexican Emigration to the United States: 1897–1931* (Tucson: University of Arizona Press, 1980).

[20]Almaguer, "Historical Notes on Chicano Oppression."

in search of refuge and employment. Initially the flow of workers over the United States–Mexico border was relatively slow. For the 30-year period following the annexation of the Southwest territory there was relatively little migratory movement over the newly established boundary between Mexico and the United States. In many ways the American Southwest operated as an isolated area that was culturally and economically removed from the rest of the country.[21] However, this situation changed dramatically after 1880. At that point immigration became the main vehicle by which the Mexican population grew and consolidated its regional and residential segregation in the Southwest; its social and demographic significance cannot be overstated.

The increased flow of Mexican workers into the United States after 1880 coincided with the rapid economic development of the Southwest largely owing to the expansion of employment opportunities in commercial agriculture, mining, and railroad construction. Massive political upheavals in Mexico which culminated in a bloody revolution (1910–1917) further drove thousands of Mexicans to "El Norte" in search of employment opportunities and political refuge. Employers in the United States gladly hired Mexicans as cheap laborers, especially as labor shortages resulting from World War I diminished output and profit margins.

The history of Mexican immigration in the twentieth century is cyclical, with the doors open in times of labor shortages, followed by restrictive policies and even massive deportations during periods of economic recession.[22] Between 1880 and 1929, when Mexican workers began to enter the United States in significant numbers and the U.S. economy expanded, Mexican immigration policy was relatively unrestricted. Consequently, by the time of the Great Depression, the U.S. Census enumerated over 1 million persons of Mexican ancestry in the United States.[23] However, the flow of immigrants from Mexico ebbed considerably during the 1930s when widespread domestic unemployment contributed to a wave of anti-Mexican sentiment which culminated in a massive repatriation campaign that, unfortunately, affected native-born residents as well as the foreign-born. Although the Mexican origin population declined during the 1930s as a consequence of forced and voluntary emigration,[24] by that time the Mexican origin population was

[21]Douglas Massey, *The Demographic and Economic Position of Hispanics in the United States: The Decade of the 1970s* (Washington, DC: National Commission for Employment Policy, 1983).
[22]Rudolfo Acuña, *Occupied America: The Chicano Struggle Toward Liberation* (San Francisco: Canfield Press, 1971); Julian Samora, *Los Mojados: The Wetback Story* (Notre Dame, IN: University of Notre Dame Press, 1971).
[23]Massey, *Demographic and Economic Position of Hispanics*.
[24]A. J. Jaffe, R. M. Cullen, and T. D. Boswell, *The Changing Demography of Spanish Americans* (New York: Academic Press, 1980).

firmly established in the Southwest and selected communities of the industrial Midwest.

World War II triggered another period of labor shortages, particularly in the agricultural industry which had not yet mechanized, and led to the establishment of the contract labor system between Mexico and the United States. Conceived as a temporary solution to the labor shortages in agriculture, the bracero program, which lasted from 1942 to 1964, revived the tradition of regular migration to the United States and reversed the emigration of Mexicans witnessed during the 1930s. Since the mid-1950s the volume of immigration from Mexico has continued to increase, and during the latter 1970s legal immigration reached levels not experienced since the 1920s. However, as the restrictions on who could enter limited the number of legal immigrants from Mexico, the volume of illegal entrants has also increased.[25]

The significance of the pre-1930 immigrant flow for the structuring of Chicano ethnicity was far-reaching. First, it increased the size of the Mexican origin population of the United States while consolidating its regional and residential segregation in the Southwest. Second, it reinforced the relegation of the Mexican origin people to a virtually unnegotiable—at least until the 1960s—low-status position in the social hierarchy. This legacy of social and economic disadvantage persists until the present day. Third, it channeled a significant share of the Mexican origin work force into the rural economy as a largely mobile, seasonal, and docile agricultural work force.[26] Like the rest of the U.S. population during the 1930s, 1940s, and 1950s, the Chicano population became an increasingly urban population during this period, especially as the mechanization of cotton production and that of several fruits and vegetables reduced the demand for agricultural labor.

The dimensions of immigration from Mexico to the United States in the twentieth century are so staggering that some have argued that the process has become self-sustaining via kinship ties and ethnic barrios which provide contacts and resources for incoming workers.[27] This helps explain its apparently "irrational" continuation despite the stricter immigration policies and the shrinking job market of the 1970s and 1980s. The relationship between family networks and ongoing migra-

[25]Samora, Los Mojados; D. S. Massey, "Dimensions of the New Immigration to the United States and the Prospects for Assimilation," Annual Review of Sociology 7 (1981):57–85; C. B. Keely, U. S. Immigration: A Policy Analysis (New York: Population Council, 1979).

[26]Alvarez, "Psycho-Historical and Socioeconomic Development"; Tienda, "Mexican American Population."

[27]Mario Barrera, Race and Class in the Southwest (Notre Dame, IN: University of Notre Dame Press, 1979); Marta Tienda, "Familism and Structural Assimilation of Mexican Immigrants in the United States," International Migration Review 14 (1980):383–408.

tion has several implications for Chicano ethnicity. Reliance of low-wage Chicano workers on assistance from their families is a form of subsidy to employers in that their wages do not have to cover all of their maintenance costs.[28] Also, the influx of recent arrivals from the Mexican community juxtaposes the values of Mexican culture and those of Anglo culture as transmitted through the schools, mass media, industrial discipline, and so on, thus serving as a constant reminder of differences between the two.[29] If the numbers of immigrants created excess labor supply during much of the first half of the twentieth century, exerting downward pressure on wages and undermining efforts at union organization, it also resulted in resentment on the part of Anglo workers. This hostility, which combined with opposition from small farmers who were unable to compete with large enterprises employing cheap labor, isolated Chicanos from the Anglo working class and further cut them off from potential avenues of integration into the social and economic mainstream. The racism practiced by employers resulted in a set of conditions that both structured the lives of Chicanos and augmented racial and ethnic prejudice in the Southwest. The continuing entry of new immigrants maintains and renews this process.

The longer history of Mexicans in the United States makes them more generationally diverse than other Hispanic origin groups. After the hysteria of the repatriation of the 1930s subsided, a segment of the Mexican origin population—largely urban, upwardly mobile natives—developed a sense of cultural loyalty to the United States. Their receptivity to cultural assimilation was advanced by several factors, including the transition from an agricultural, nonmetropolitan, and foreign-born population to a blue-collar, metropolitan, and native-born group. Noticeable advances in education, income, and political efficacy engendered in this segment a false sense of social acceptance and security, one fueled by the belief of brighter prospects for their offspring.[30] However, the Chicano movement of the late 1960s rekindled the pain of social rejection and accumulated disadvantages. Moreover, the critical absence of older role models with certified middle-class status bolstered the development of a new consciousness among the supporters of the Chicano movement. The more militant advocated separation and decolonization, whereas the resurgence of Mexican ethnicity among the less militant

[28]Michael Burawoy, "The Functions and Reproduction of Migrant Labor: Comparative Material from Southern Africa and the U.S.," *American Journal of Sociology* 81 (1976):1050–87; Tienda, "Familism and Structural Assimilation."
[29]Alex Saragoza, "The Conceptualization of the History of the Chicano Family," in Armando Valdez, Albert Camarillo, and Tomas Almaguer, eds., *The State of Chicano Research in Family, Labor and Migration: Proceedings of the Symposium on Work, Family, and Migration* (Palo Alto: Stanford Center for Chicano Research, 1983).
[30]Tienda, "Mexican American Population."

activists was articulated in demands for self-determination, equality, and a cultural self-redefinition as Chicanos rather than as Mexican Americans.[31]

Despite the success of the Chicano movement of the mid-1960s in calling attention to the social injustices endured by earlier generations of Mexican and Mexican American workers, a decade later the imprint of social inequality persists. Today, although the historical legacy remains, dramatic changes have occurred in the residence patterns and the structure of opportunity open to Chicanos. Although Mexicans as a group are principally now an urban-based population, one clear vestige of the rural origins characteristic of part of the population is their current disproportionate representation in agriculture—not as farmers, but as seasonal and permanent laborers. That these vestiges should persist, despite gains from unionization efforts and legal sanctions against discriminatory practices, is a reminder of the strength of their influence in the past. However, urban residence has provided access to a wider range of employment opportunities and has gradually eroded the viability of the colonial labor system. Cultural manifestations of changes associated with the urbanization experience include the trend toward a language shift away from Spanish,[32] the declining isolation of the barrio,[33] and indicators pointing to a greater degree of assimilation into Anglo society.[34] Mario Barrera concedes that the segmentation line separating Chicanos from the majority culture across all classes has been weakening since World War II.[35] This indicates that class divisions could become more salient than ethnic ones as Chicanos become more integrated into the nonsubordinate part of the labor force, but the prospects of this occurring also depend on the process of immigration and the vitality of the U.S. economy. The historical record to date is mixed, providing signs of hope as well as signs of distress.

Puerto Ricans

Compared with Mexicans, Puerto Ricans have a much shorter history in the United States, and they make up a smaller share of all Hispanics than do Mexicans. In 1980 Puerto Ricans constituted approxi-

[31]Charles P. Loomis, "A Backward Glance at Self-identification of Blacks and Chicanos," *Rural Sociology* 39 (1974):96.

[32]Bruce Gardner, *Bilingual Schooling and the Survival of Spanish in the United States* (Rowley, MA: Newbury House, 1977); Carlos H. Arce, "A Reconsideration of Chicano Culture and Identity," *Daedalus* 110 (1981):177–91.

[33]Joan Moore, "Colonialism: The Case of the Mexican Americans," *Social Problems* 17 (1970):463–72.

[34]Massey, "Dimensions of the New Immigration."

[35]Barrera, *Race and Class in the Southwest.*

mately 14 percent of the Hispanic population living on the mainland (see Chapter 3). Designated a U.S. territory at the culmination of the Spanish-American war in 1898, Puerto Rico became a semi-autonomous Commonwealth in 1952. This status has obliterated economic boundaries and protective mechanisms that many Third World nations employ to defend local interests and has fostered the economic dependency of the island on the United States. The processes set in motion by the United States' domination of the island's economy have been intense since the island acquired Commonwealth status, bringing on rapid economic changes, restructuring class relations, and introducing new value conflicts largely owing to an extensive migration process that continues to the present day.[36] As time passes, the nature of the relationship between the island Commonwealth and the United States makes it even more difficult to define the island culturally or ethnically, for that which is Puerto Rican is partly North American as well.

While the island is self-governing in all domestic matters, the governance structure is bounded by the provisions of the federal constitution.[37] Commonwealth status confers on the Puerto Rican population several privileges and obligations. Among the former are "common citizenship, common defense, common currency, and a common loyalty to the value of democracy."[38] That Puerto Rican island residents may not vote in U.S. presidential elections, are not represented in the U.S. Senate, and have a nonvoting Resident Commission in the House of Representatives attests to their second-class citizenship. Moreover, the privilege of citizenship which gives Puerto Ricans unrestricted entry to the United States mainland is a mixed blessing. With the benefit of national defense comes the requirement of military service. In exchange for unequal representation and voting privileges, the U.S. Congress has exempted Puerto Rican residents from federal income taxes and federal excise taxes.

Puerto Ricans have lived in the continental United States for more than a century, but the emergence of a visible Puerto Rican community is essentially a post–World War II phenomenon. Like most ethnic communities in the United States (with the notable exceptions of the Mexican and Native American populations), the Puerto Rican population on the mainland emerged through migration. Although there existed a small Puerto Rican community in New York before World War II, the major exodus from the island to the continental United States began in

---

[36]Sidney Mintz, "Puerto Rico: An Essay in the Definition of National Culture," in Francesco Cordasco and Eugene Bucchioni, eds., *The Puerto Rican Experience* (Totowa, NJ: Rowan and Littlefield, 1973).

[37]Jaffe et al., *Changing Demography of Spanish Americans.*

[38]National Puerto Rican Coalition, *Puerto Ricans in the Mid '80s: An American Challenge* (Washington, DC: National Puerto Rican Coalition, 1985).

the 1940s and accelerated after 1950. Average migration rates from Puerto Rico to New York more than doubled during the 1950s, rising from an average annual flow of 18,700 persons between 1940 and 1950 to 41,200 between 1950 and 1960. The sharp decline in the average annual Puerto Rican conflux between 1960 and 1970 is even more impressive, falling to less than 15,000 per year.[39] Presumably a circular migration flow, which is characteristic of Puerto Ricans, underlies these dramatic changes in the number of Puerto Rican migrants arriving on the mainland.

As a result of this massive migration process, the Puerto Rican population residing in the continental United States increased from roughly 70,000 in 1940 to over 300,000 in 1950 and 893,000 in 1960. With the drop in migration during the 1960s, the growth rate of the stateside Puerto Rican population also slowed. Even with moderate migrant inflows, the Puerto Rican population continued to increase, reaching 1.4 million in 1970 and 1.8 million in 1980.[40] While the 56 and 29 percent increases in the size of the Puerto Rican population during the 1960s and 1970s, respectively, are impressive by most standards, they are strikingly low compared with the three- to four-fold increases experienced during the two prior decades.

These sharp demographic changes are largely the result of a decision to transform and develop Puerto Rico's plantation economy through a program of rapid industrialization. The apparent success of the infamous Operation Bootstrap (in effect from 1948 to 1965) hinged on several key factors, including unrestricted migration between the mainland and the island. Even with the help of the burgeoning Commonwealth bureaucracy (employing three workers in ten by 1976), the new industrial order could not absorb the available workers, whose numbers rose steadily, owing to population growth and to a severe employment decline in the plantation sector. Agricultural employment dropped from 50 to 10 percent of all jobs between 1940 and 1970.[41] Migration to the mainland provided a temporary solution to the acute unemployment problem. So intense was the outflow of wage laborers that during the 1950s Puerto Rico provided the unusual spectacle of a booming economy with a shrinking labor force.[42]

Other influences on the migration flows from Puerto Rico to the U.S. mainland included easy, inexpensive air travel;[43] the impact of

---

[39]Centro de Estudios Puertorriqueños, "The History Task Force," in *Labor Migration Under Capitalism* (New York: Monthly Review Press, 1979).

[40]Massey, *Demographic and Economic Position.*

[41]Centro de Estudios Puertorriqueños, "History Task Force."

[42]Centro de Estudios Puertorriqueños, "History Task Force."

[43]Jaffe notes that following the end of World War II the conversion of surplus military aircraft to commercial use considerably lowered the cost of travel between the island and the mainland.

mass communication on potential job-seekers; obligatory military service; and the absence of immigration restrictions—all of which were rooted in the special relationship between Puerto Rico and the United States.[44] One might expect, then, that the relatively easy access of Puerto Ricans to the United States and their legal status as U.S. citizens would facilitate their integration into U.S. society by giving them a comparative advantage in securing employment and living quarters. Oftentimes the opposite occurred. As we will see in subsequent chapters, Puerto Ricans were often relegated to the lowest levels of the labor market. They frequently experienced social deprivation and discrimination in both the housing and job markets, and they often fared as badly or worse economically than blacks who migrated to the North.

It is both striking and significant for an understanding of the contemporary socioeconomic position of Puerto Ricans that of the 400,000 foreign contract workers brought to the United States during World War II, few were Puerto Rican, despite a 100 percent increase in unemployment on the island and despite the fact that Puerto Ricans were legal U.S. citizens who were serving in the military. This unfortunate fact concurs with the view that Puerto Ricans were incorporated into the mainland society as a second-class citizenry, one whose social and economic welfare was never represented in the national immigration policies (via relocation assistance such as that received by Cubans or recent Southeast Asian refugees) or in the economic policies allegedly designed to improve the vitality of the island economy.

The persistent inability of many island migrants to secure steady employment on the mainland, coupled with the displacement of Puerto Rican workers from declining textile and garment industries in the Northeast during the decade of the 1970s, set in motion a return migration process whose scale and duration cannot be predicted. The worsening labor market position of Puerto Rican men and women during the 1970s makes more glaring their position vis-à-vis other Hispanics, and their marginal labor market position carries over to other indicators of social well-being. Of all Hispanic origin groups they have the lowest labor force participation rates, the highest unemployment levels, the highest incidence of poverty, and the lowest levels of education.[45]

Despite the very different circumstances leading to the establishment of the Puerto Rican and Mexican communities in the United States, there are several parallels between them which are pertinent to an understanding of the contemporary socioeconomic positioning of the

[44]Clara Rodriguez, "Economic Factors Affecting Puerto Ricans in New York," in *Labor Migration Under Capitalism* (New York: Monthly Review Press, 1979).

[45]Marta Tienda, "The Puerto Rican Worker:Current Labor Market Status and Future Prospects," in National Puerto Rican Coalition, *Puerto Ricans in the Mid '80s: An American Challenge* (Washington, DC: National Puerto Rican Coalition, 1984).

two groups.[46] First, both migratory movements were fundamentally wage labor flows destined for unskilled blue collar jobs. Second, both groups were destined for regional labor markets, the industrial Northeast in the case of Puerto Ricans and the agricultural Southwest in the case of Mexicans. Third, like Mexicans in the Southwest, Puerto Ricans in the Northeast have been the victims of intense discrimination and prejudice, perhaps even greater than that experienced by Mexicans in Texas.[47]

Similarities between the Mexican and Puerto Rican experiences should not be overstated.[48] Unlike Mexicans, whose labor market integration began as a largely agricultural experience, Puerto Ricans have been almost exclusively urban-based and concentrated in the manufacturing and service sectors of New York City.[49] Thus, more than most groups—immigrants and natives alike—Puerto Ricans have disproportionately entered industries whose operations are seasonal in nature and in the declining manufacturing sector of the city; the suburbanization of industry, coupled with inadequate mass transit, has further restricted opportunities for those tied to their central city neighborhoods. This situation seemed to worsen during the 1970s as the flight of industry from the Frostbelt to the lower-wage Sunbelt progressed. Finally, the fact that Puerto Ricans are citizens by birth differentiates their entry to the mainland society from that of Mexicans, particularly those who enter in an undocumented status. Theoretically, their citizenship could give them greater political leverage in lobbying for their interests in the future, but this has not happened. Such a prospect depends much on the effectiveness of the community leaders in setting and pursuing a social agenda to rectify past injustices.[50]

In brief, circular migration and relegation to the lowest levels of the socioeconomic ladder are two important defining features of the ethnic structuring process for Puerto Ricans.[51] These two dimensions are interrelated in complex and fluid ways. The circular migration means that the island population and mainland community are two parts of a

[46]Massey, Demographic and Economic Position.

[47]U.S. Commission on Civil Rights, Puerto Ricans in the United States: An Uncertain Future (Washington, DC: U.S. Government Printing Office, 1976); Douglas Massey and Brooks Bitterman, "Explaining the Paradox of Puerto Rican Segregation," Social Forces 64 (1985):306–31.

[48]Massey, Demographic and Economic Position.

[49]Tienda, "Puerto Rican Worker."

[50]National Puerto Rican Coalition, Puerto Ricans in the Mid '80s.

[51]The U.S. Commission on Civil Rights' Puerto Ricans in the United States reported that in 1969–70 alone 129,000 persons returned to Puerto Rico. By 1972 14 percent of the island's population consisted of return migrants, according to Alberto Lopez, "The Puerto Rican Diaspora," in Alberto Lopez and James Petras, eds., Puerto Rico and Puerto Ricans (Cambridge, MA: Schenkman, 1974).

whole. It means that elements of both cultures thrive in both places, which requires a dual functional ability: Children must be able to switch school systems and must cope with competing value systems. It has resulted, as Frank Bonilla states, in "an unprecedented job of psychological and cultural reconstitution and construction that must rest on a very special political and economic infrastructure."[52]

Despite the strong cultural and economic ties between Puerto Rico and the United States, the image of a single monolithic Puerto Rican community spanning the two locations is not entirely accurate. Members of the second generation raised in New York City have been dubbed "Nuyoricans," indicating their simultaneous separateness from Puerto Rico and their connection to it. Being caught between two value systems, especially with respect to race and ethnicity, is not only a feature of life on the mainland but also, given the U.S. domination over the island, plays an important role there as well, producing ideological divisions that transcend those of class hierarchy.

Thus, Puerto Rican ethnicity can be interpreted as structurally determined by their dependent status, a pattern of migration that places Puerto Ricans between two worlds, and extreme occupational segregation. All of these contribute to their marginality vis-à-vis the rest of society. Their reaction is found in the maintenance of strong ethnic communities, low intermarriage rates,[53] and the rejection of a quick transfer of cultural identity. Although in part a response to and protection against oppression, the persistence of ethnic distinctiveness, despite massive pressure toward a homogeneous consumer culture, can also be interpreted as a form of protest. The settings for most Puerto Ricans—the schools, the streets, the military, the prisons, and the sweatshops—are radicalizing contexts. That Puerto Rican ethnicity is reaffirmed here is "a sign of remarkable survival in the face of radical ambiguity."[54]

Cubans

The experience of Cubans, who by 1980 constituted roughly 6 percent of all Hispanic origin persons in the United States, presents a case of quite different features and outcomes that both challenges and supports the theoretical assumptions made with respect to the Mexican and

[52]Frank Bonilla, "Por que seguiremos siendo puertorriqueños," in Alberto Lopez and James Petras, eds., *Puerto Rico and Puerto Ricans* (Cambridge, MA: Schenkman, 1974).

[53]Joseph P. Fitzpatrick, and Douglas M. Gurak, *Hispanic Intermarriage in New York City,* Hispanic Research Center Monograph (New York: Fordham University, 1979).

[54]Bonilla, "Por que seguiremos siendo puertorriquenos."

Puerto Rican experiences. That Cubans have been relatively successful socioeconomically relative to Puerto Ricans and Mexicans is of critical comparative value in distinguishing their incorporation experience from that of the other groups. Three factors stand out. First, the early immigrants were primarily political rather than economic refugees. Second, during the early phase of the exodus from Cuba, individuals from professional, urban, and more highly educated sectors were greatly overrepresented. Third, their reception in this country, especially their early reception, was not the tacit acceptance by employers hungry for cheap labor but rather a public welcome by the federal government eager to harbor those seeking refuge from a Communist dictatorship.

Although the 1950 census enumerated roughly 34,000 persons of Cuban birth, the Cuban presence in the United States increased during the late 1950s and throughout the 1960s because of the exit of thousands seeking asylum from the Castro regime.[55] So intense was the initial exodus from the tiny island located just 90 miles from Key West that the 1960 census enumerated over 79,000 Cuban-born persons, representing more than a two-fold increase in less than two years following the 1959 Cuban Revolution. The flow of refugees intensified throughout the 1960s so that by 1970 more than half a million Cuban origin persons resided in the United States, with nearly 80 percent born in Cuba.[56] By the time the Cuban government imposed restrictions on the exodus of Cubans seeking asylum in the United States during the early 1970s, Cuban communities were firmly established and highly visible in southern Florida and large northeastern cities.

Owing largely to the volume of the refugee flow, the Cuban stock population had increased 25-fold in a 30-year period, rising to approximately 831,000 by 1980.[57] Following the Mariel incident of 1980, when over 125,000 Cuban refugees were admitted to the United States,[58] the Cuban population exceeded 1 million, but these individuals were not included in the 1980 enumeration because they entered several weeks after the census was taken. Given their relatively recent immigration history, Cubans also show relatively little generational diversity, with the clear majority being first-generation immigrants or offspring of foreign-born (see Chapters 3 and 4).

---

[55]Jaffe et al., *Changing Demography of Spanish Americans.*

[56]Massey, *Demographic and Economic Position.*

[57]U.S. Bureau of the Census, "Population Profile of the United States: 1980," *Current Population Reports,* series P-20, no. 363 (Washington, DC: U.S. Government Printing Office, 1981).

[58]Robert L. Bach, "The New Cuban Immigrants: Their Background and Prospects," *Monthly Labor Review* 103 (1980):39–46; Robert L. Bach, Jennifer B. Bach, and Timothy Triplett, "The Flotilla 'Entrants': Latest and Most Controversial," *Cuban Studies* 11 (1981):29–49.

Until the Cuban refugees arrived, no other immigrant group in this hemisphere has been so advantaged in terms of socioeconomic background and host country reception. That individuals from the upper and middle classes were dominant among the early exiles[59] led some to characterize the Cuban exodus as "the greatest brain drain ever to occur, leaving the Cuban middle class virtually gutted."[60] However, this popular portrayal overlooks the fact that Cuban émigrés arrived in several successive waves, with the latter ones greatly diversifying the exile population. That is, while the earliest waves consisted of elite wealthy Batistianos, upper-class landholders, and businessmen who were able to leave with their wealth and possessions, those who arrived after the Bay of Pigs invasion had their assets confiscated and were left only the barest necessities.[61]

Successive waves were younger and less well educated, neither rich nor part of the pre-Castro establishment. Roughly 40 percent of the refugees who came during the airlift years between 1965 and 1973 were students, women, and children joining relatives already in the United States.[62] Thus, while the label of self-imposed political exiles is largely an accurate description of Cubans who left during the early 1960s, studies of later waves have found significant numbers resembling traditional immigrants whose decisions to leave were governed by economic factors.[63]

In marked contrast to the reception of Mexican and Puerto Rican immigrants, the arrival of the Cubans involved the United States in the largest refugee aid operation in its history to that point. Any portrayal of the reception extended to Cubans must take this as its point of departure. Like the Puerto Rican migrants, Cuban exiles were offered cheap air transportation and permission to enter the United States without visas, not as immigrants but as special entrants, pending the possibility that the Communist government would not last. Unlike Puerto Ricans, Cuban refugees were provided with some resettlement assistance. Included in the Cuban refugee resettlement program were provisions for job training, professional recertification, assistance in securing employment, reimbursement to public schools for costs incurred by the entrance of Spanish-speaking Cuban children, and funds for special research and teaching opportunities for Cuban scholars.[64]

---

[59]A. Portes, J. M. Clark, and R. L. Bach, "The New Wave: A Statistical Profile of Recent Cuban Exiles to the United States," *Cuban Studies* 7 (1977):1–32.

[60]Lourdes Casal and Andres Hernandez, "Cubans in the U.S.: A Survey of the Literature," *Cuban Studies* 5 (1975):25–51.

[61]Eleanor Rogg, *The Assimilation of Cuban Exiles: The Role of Community and Class* (New York: Aberdeen Press, 1974).

[62]Casal and Hernandez, "Cubans in the U.S."

[63]Bach, "New Cuban Immigrants."

[64]Rogg, *Assimilation of Cuban Exiles.*

The Cuban influx into Miami, combined with restrictive state aid laws, caused Florida authorities to appeal to the federal government for help with their resettlement. President Eisenhower's emergency relief measures were followed by Kennedy's Cuban Refugee Program in providing extensive aid for relocation away from Miami. Of the 251,000 Cubans initially registered with the government's refugee program in 1967, 153,000 (or 60 percent) had been relocated away from Miami.[65] However, this policy of dispersal proved largely futile, as by 1970 two Cubans in three were living in either the Miami or the New York urbanized areas,[66] and recent census data indicate that the gravitation toward Miami has continued. Massey estimated that about 56 percent of all Cubans lived in Miami in 1980, up from 40 percent in 1970.[67]

Given that the early waves of Cubans were from advantaged socioeconomic backgrounds and received modest help from the federal government in relocating themselves in the United States, their socioeconomic success would not be surprising were it not for the serious obstacles they initially faced. Not the least of these was their widespread downward occupational mobility vis-à-vis positions held in Cuba. A comparison of early occupational positions in the United States with last occupations held in Cuba showed that in Miami the percentage of unskilled laborers had doubled. Cubans who had been employed as professionals, managers, and technicians dropped from 48 percent in Cuba to 13 percent in the United States.[68]

In many ways Cubans found themselves in a situation similar to that of many other immigrants during the 1960s. They were residentially segregated, they were concentrated in blue collar "ethnic" jobs, they were lacking English language skills, and they were tied to their ethnic communities. In New York and Miami they formed strong ethnically enclosed communities of extended families and friends who relied on each other for support and financial assistance. Whether this implied an affirmation of cultural identity is unclear, but their common national origin and political orientations provided a ready basis for the elaboration and cementing of intragroup social relations. Initially, their "commitments to old values and to a 'return' goal, together with a strong identification with Cuba and their past lives, [were] the most

[65]Kenneth L. Wilson and Alejandro Portes, "Immigrant Enclaves: An Analysis of the Labor Market Experiences of Cubans in Miami," *American Journal of Sociology* 86 (1980):295-319.

[66]D. S. Massey, *"Residential Segregation of Spanish Americans in United States Urbanized Areas,"* unpublished doctoral dissertation, Department of Sociology, Princeton University, 1978.

[67]Massey, *Demographic and Economic Position.*

[68]Casal and Hernandez, "Cubans in the U.S."

potent forces working against the Cubans' integration into the United States."[69]

Despite the initial handicaps they encountered, and the belief by many that their stay in the United States would be temporary, Cubans were never restricted to a position of second-class workers in an ethnically split labor market, nor was their success patterned after the gradual integration patterns of earlier European immigrants. In addition to the warm welcome and massive aid received under the auspices of the Cuban Refugee Program, two factors help explain their very different integration experience. These are class background and the formation of an ethnic enclave economy in Miami.[70]

Unlike Puerto Ricans and Mexicans, Cubans did not enter the United States as predominantly subordinate workers. They were fleeing the real and perceived persecution and harassment of a new regime. The same individualism that led upper- and middle-class Cubans to reject Castro provided both the cultural link to the socioeconomic values of the United States and the basis for effective competition. Their strong individualism and an orientation toward the future often compensated the initial loss of occupational position. Moreover, the opportunities for economic and social integration that the Cuban Refugee Program offered were perhaps more valuable for their symbolic political message than for the cash and in-kind resettlement assistance provided the Spanish-speaking newcomers.

Once it became clear that an eventual return to Cuba would not be possible, middle-class Cubans aggressively sought to learn English and new skills necessary for the economic rewards that would eventually signal their social integration. In this undertaking, class background proved indispensable. Because of the downward mobility initially experienced by the Cuban exiles, and particularly the early arrivals, occupational position in Cuba was unrelated to first job acquired in the United States. However, last job in Cuba was found to be a principal factor affecting subsequent upward mobility, along with education and age on arrival.[71] Clearly, then, the current advantaged position of Cubans relative to other Hispanics is partly the result of the differential attitudes and resources derived from their class background.[72]

---

[69]Alejandro Portes, "Dilemmas of a Golden Exile: Integration of Refugee Families in Milwaukee," *American Sociological Review* 34 (1969):505–19.

[70]Wilson and Portes, "Immigrant Enclaves"; Alejandro Portes and Robert Bach, "Immigrant Earnings: Cuban and Mexican Immigrants in the United States," *International Migration Review* 14 (1980):315–41.

[71]Eleanor Rogg and Rosemary Cooney, *Adaptation and Adjustment of Cubans: West New York, N.J.*, Hispanic Research Center Monograph (New York: Fordham University, 1980).

[72]Portes, "Dilemmas of a Golden Exile."

The emergence of the Cuban enclave economy (also class-related) is the second key factor in understanding the Cuban experience in the United States. Close to one third of all businesses in Miami are Cuban-owned, while 75 percent of the work force in construction is Cuban and 40 percent of the industry is Cuban-owned.[73] Twenty percent of the Miami banks are controlled by Cubans, who account for 16 out of 62 bank presidents and 250 vice presidents.[74] Other ethnic strongholds in the enclave economy include textiles, food, cigars, and trade with Latin America.

In Miami one can proceed from birth to death "Cuban style."[75] For the refugee with fewer marketable skills, the enclave not only provides a home, but also can shelter workers from the harsh realities of the open competitive market. Its success depends on low wages paid to Cuban workers, ethnic preference in hiring, *and* the reciprocal obligation to help fellow ethnic members in their own financial ventures. The other crucial components are, of course, sufficient operating capital and entrepreneurial skills to initiate a successful enterprise, as well as an economic climate conducive to the flourishing of small-scale, private enterprises. The early Cuban exodus, with its upper-class bias and access to financial credit, was able to provide both elements. Later arrivals, however, became the working class for the "golden exiles" of the 1960s. As Bach concludes, "Thus there has been a total transplantation of the pre-revolutionary Cuban social structure to Miami, with all the implications of unequal wealth, power and prestige."[76]

The importance of the Cuban enclave economy together with similar structures in other ethnic groups (that is, the Japanese and the Koreans) requires that it be added to any theoretical explanations of the immigrant experience. Enclave workers, while ethnically segregated and often paid lower wages, cannot be considered a mere extension of the secondary sector in an ethnically split labor market. Wilson and Portes report that ethnic workers integrated in an enclave experience a pay-off to human capital investments similar to those workers in the primary sector, thus providing them with advantages usually unavailable to minorities employed in the peripheral industries of the economy.[77] The nagging question is whether subsequent generations will follow suit in expanding or protecting the forms and functions of the enclave econ-

---

[73]Bach, "New Cuban Immigrants."
[74]Wilson and Portes, "Immigrant Enclaves."
[75]Bach, "New Cuban Immigrants."
[76]Bach, "New Cuban Immigrants."
[77]Wilson and Portes, "Immigrant Enclaves."

omy. Not enough time has passed to make this assessment, but recent survey data provide a unique opportunity to begin this evaluation.[78]

Summary and Conclusion

This chapter has outlined features of the Mexican, Puerto Rican, and Cuban immigration experiences. Although other Hispanic national origin groups are much smaller and thus are not discussed here, the Central and South American and other Hispanic cases are similarly diverse. Our purpose has been to demonstrate that each of the major Hispanic groups has been subjected to a distinctive set of experiences that have shaped their economic and cultural integration into American society and that have affected the development of Hispanic ethnicity. The Puerto Rican case provides the strongest support for an isomorphic link between ethnicity and lower socioeconomic status. That Cubans have not remained segregated in a secondary labor market, have been the most successful of all groups, and are demonstrating strong tendencies toward integration into the larger society provides evidence in the other direction. Their distinct status at entry and their more favorable economic resources are the most significant factors distinguishing Cuban refugees from Mexican and Puerto Rican and other Latin American immigrants. The greater diversity of the Mexican American experience, which results in part from this group's greater numerical size and longer history in the United States, makes an analysis of the development of ethnicity in the case of this group more ambiguous.

Indicators pointing to increasing assimilation of Chicanos must be weighed against the isolation, extreme poverty, and lack of control over life as it exists in the barrios. In contrast to Barrera's claim to class integration, can the small rising Chicano middle class play the role of native elite within a group whose initial entry into the United States came about by conquest?[79] How is one to interpret ongoing intraethnic contact as it exists between social class groups (as Chicano businesses, for example, increasingly rely on a Chicano clientele) or as it is affected by continued immigration of lower-status Mexicans? For Chicanos it is difficult to envision a future when ethnic distinctions within social class divisions will fade away. The cloudiness of what Barrera has la-

---

[78]Alejandro Portes and Robert L. Bach, *Latin Journey* (Berkeley: University of California Press, 1985).

[79]Almaguer, "Historical Notes on Chicano Oppression."

beled "the current period of confusion and redefinition" is maintained by the continuing influx of new immigrants.

For Mexicans and Puerto Ricans isolation in ethnic communities and other manifestations of ethnicity are structurally produced by their concentrations in minority labor markets and by the continued influx of immigrants who help to renew cultural traditions and subsequently elaborate them as a basis for social solidarity. In turn, ethnically based solidarity serves as a protection and source of resistance against oppression. For Cubans the cohesiveness of their ethnic community has been a key factor facilitating initial adjustment and success. Whether that success will ensure the survival of the ethnically enclosed community or lead to its decline remains to be seen. Initial evidence based on the most recent census suggests a decline as the first generation of native-born Cubans demonstrates an unusual ability to assimilate.[80]

In summary, although we have introduced many aspects of the immigration experiences of Hispanics, we wish to close our discussion by emphasizing four factors in particular as important in shaping the ethnicity of Hispanic groups in the United States, especially when viewed in comparison with the experience of European immigrants. First, a crucial difference between Europeans and Hispanics is that European immigration was concentrated in a 40-year period from 1880 to 1920, after which it virtually ceased, leaving the United States 60 years to "assimilate" these massive immigrant cohorts. By contrast, Hispanic immigration has been relatively strong since 1942 and will probably not abate in the near future, so the United States may not have a comparably long period within which to assimilate the recent cohorts. This may render assimilation more difficult and affect tendencies toward ethnic identification on the part of the Hispanic groups, depending on differences among them in their immigration histories, which we have discussed at length above. Second, the economic order which the immigrant groups encounter shapes and determines ethnicity. The industrial regime prevailing between 1880 and 1920 tended to concentrate immigrants spatially and occupationally, while the post-industrial economy of the 1970s and 1980s acts to disperse immigrants both socially and spatially. Third, European immigrants were all white, while Hispanics are a mixture of blacks, Amerindians, and whites. This factor is especially important for groups with a large black admixture, like Puerto Ricans and, increasingly, Cubans. Fourth, an ethnic group is *created* by the entry of an immigrant group into American society, and its initial configuration depends on the characteristics of both the group and the society at the

---

[80]Nelson and Tienda, "Structure of Hispanic Ethnicity."

point of contact. Ethnicity is subsequently shaped by the social and economic experiences of the group in a changing society. Key elements in creating ethnicity include the ensuing immigration history of the group itself, changes in the economic organization of society, and prevailing patterns of racial and ethnic prejudice.

2

THE HISPANIC POPULATION
IN NUMBERS: CENSUS DEFINITIONS
IN HISTORICAL PERSPECTIVE

INCREASED interest in Hispanics heightened the need for current, reliable and detailed statistics about the people of Spanish origin residing in the United States.[1] Unfortunately, owing to changes over time in the definitions, labels, and procedures used to enumerate Hispanics, seemingly straightforward questions about the size, characteristics, and growth both of the population as a whole and of its constituent national origin subgroups pose challenging technical and operational problems for researchers. Thus, before addressing such questions, we discuss in this chapter the Census Bureau's solutions to the challenge of enumerating Hispanics over time and our operational criteria for delineating groups whose members are Mexican, Puerto Rican, Cuban, Central/South American, or Other Hispanic origin.

There are several reasons why the Census Bureau since 1960 has modified extensively its procedures for identifying and enumerating Hispanics and has increased the quantity of detailed tabulations produced about each of the major national origin groups. One reason is the increased numerical visibility of Hispanics. A second reason is the grow-

---

[1]Marta Tienda and Elizabeth Evanson, *Statistical Policy and Data Needs for Hispanic Studies,* Final Report to the Ford Foundation (Madison: Institute for Research on Poverty, University of Wisconsin, 1983).

ing diversity of the Hispanic subpopulations. In many ways the changed labels and concepts used to identify peoples of Spanish origin[2] are an important expression of the cultural and ethnic evolution of this population and must be recognized accordingly. Increased political leverage to produce more and better data about Hispanics constitutes a third reason why the Census Bureau has changed its enumeration procedures with respect to Hispanics. That Congress in 1976 enacted legislation requiring the reporting of Hispanic origin on government censuses and surveys starkly illustrates the political and social nature of what could be construed as a largely technical problem.[3] Finally, deliberate attempts to improve upon previous censuses and surveys also fostered changes in identification and enumeration procedures.

Changes in the questions used to identify Hispanics, and in the procedures for tabulating and publishing information about their social and economic characteristics, limit the accuracy of intercensal comparisons to varying degrees. Because our central purpose in this monograph is to document—based on 1980 data—the demographic, social, and economic characteristics of the Hispanic origin population and, where feasible, changes in these characteristics over time, this chapter discusses the strengths and limitations of census data for this purpose. Another concrete objective of this chapter is to define operationally the Hispanic population with data from the 1960, 1970, and 1980 censuses. We place greatest emphasis on the 1980 data, as, in our judgment, these provide the most complete national coverage of the Hispanic population to date. A third purpose is to discuss in historical perspectives changes in the criteria used to identify Hispanics and to highlight the direct implications of these modifications for our period comparisons. We do not dwell on the data prior to 1950 because the analyses presented in the following chapters largely draw upon only the 1960, 1970, and 1980 censuses. However, a brief overview of the evolution of enumeration practices and identifiers used prior to 1960 brings into focus the Census Bureau's rationale for having introduced new identifiers during the past two decades. This discussion provides a sociological as well as technical

---

[2]We use the terms "Spanish origin" and "Hispanic" interchangeably. These are the two most recent labels used by the Census Bureau, but at this writing the term "Latino" is becoming acceptable among some groups.

[3]In response to pressure from various interest groups, in 1976 Congress passed the Roybal Resolution (Public Law 94-311), which requires that a self-identification question on Spanish origin or descent be included on government censuses and surveys. This question now is the primary means of identifying people of Hispanic/Spanish origin, although not all units of the statistical reporting system have responded promptly to the federal mandate. See Tienda and Evanson, *Statistical Policy*, for further discussion of the limitations of data presently available to study Hispanics.

understanding of the difficulties of using census data to demarcate ethnic boundaries in a population.[4]

We organize our discussion both chronologically and comparatively. That is, first we summarize the items used to identify the Hispanic population prior to 1980. Until 1950 it mainly involved peoples of Mexican and Puerto Rican origin or descent. We trace in greater detail the changes in the procedures and items used to identify Hispanics from 1950 to 1980, placing particular emphasis on the comparison between the 1970 and 1980 censuses. The comparative aspect of our analysis highlights the continuities and discontinuities among the items used to identify Hispanics in the 1960, 1970, and 1980 censuses and draws out the implications of these discontinuities for the period comparisons presented in the chapters which follow.

Toward an Operational Definition of Hispanics: Hispanic Identifiers and Concepts

Ethnicity denotes a social identity deriving from group membership based on common race, religion, language, national origin, or some combination of these factors.[5] Most Hispanics are white, most are Catholic, and most trace their ancestry to a Spanish-speaking country. But beyond these broad generalizations, no clear agreement exists about how to demarcate the boundaries between Hispanics and non-Hispanics.[6] Less debated is that Hispanic ethnicity is a multidimensional construct based on both subjective and objective criteria, as well as individual and communal perceptions of these criteria.[7]

The notion that it is possible to demarcate ethnic boundaries for the Hispanic population as a whole derives from a communal perception that substantial cultural commonalities exist among Spanish-speaking nationalities, which, in spite of variation among national origin groups, are greater than those between Hispanics and non-Hispanics. Individual

[4]To limit the amount of technical detail presented in the text of this chapter, we have prepared an appendix (see Appendix A) which summarizes the selection criteria and operational procedures used to define Hispanics in the 1960, 1970, and 1980 censuses.

[5]Ira S. Lowry, "The Science and Politics of Ethnic Enumeration," Rand Paper Series no. P-6435 (Santa Monica, CA: Rand Corporation, 1980).

[6]Douglas Massey, *The Demographic and Economic Position of Hispanics in the United States: The Decade of the 1970s* (Washington, DC: National Commission for Employment Policy, 1983).

[7]Marta Tienda and Vilma Ortiz, "Hispanicity and the 1980 Census," Working Paper no. 84-23 (Madison: Center for Demography and Ecology, University of Wisconsin, 1984).

attribution of ethnicity derives from an acknowledgment of the ethnic content of such objective attributes as language, surname, birthplace, and race and such subjective attributes as perceived and self-reported ethnic identity or ancestry.

Historically, the Census Bureau has relied more on objective indicators than on subjective indicators to establish Hispanic origin or descent. However, this practice changed with the introduction of the self-identification Spanish origin item which was first used on an experimental basis in the 1969 Current Population Survey and the following year included in the 5 percent sample schedule of the 1970 census. The self-identification Spanish origin item, discussed in greater detail below, represents the closest approximation to the sociological concept of ethnic identity.[8] Ultimately, this identifier permitted the Census Bureau to enumerate the Hispanic population for the entire nation.

Efforts to enumerate the Hispanic population on a national, as opposed to a regional, basis are relatively recent, dating back to the late 1960s and early 1970s (see Appendix A).[9] In fact, prior to the 1970 census not only was the notion of a national Hispanic population an emergent phenomenon,[10] but no single indicator rendered a suitable nationwide operational definition which could be used with reasonable consistency over time. Instead, users of census data, including Census Bureau and private researchers, had to manipulate several Hispanic identifiers (some of which are available only on a regional basis) to establish the ethnic boundaries for Hispanics.

Among the various items used to identify people of Spanish origin prior to 1970 were respondent's place of birth; parent's place of birth; mother tongue; Spanish surname; and, on one occasion, race.[11] Which tabulations were actually produced and published for use by the general public largely reflected the size and visibility of a particular group, as well as user demands for specific information.[12] However, beginning in the 1950s the Census Bureau published information on persons of

---

[8]Jose Hernandez, Leo Estrada, and David Alvirez, "Census Data and the Problem of Conceptually Defining the Mexican American Population," *Social Science Quarterly* 53 (1973):671–87.

[9]Morris J. Newman, "A Profile of Hispanics in the U.S. Work Force," *Monthly Labor Review* 101 (1978):3–14.

[10]Cary Davis, Carl Haub, and JoAnne Willette, "U.S. Hispanics: Changing the Face of America," *Population Bulletin*, vol. 38, no. 3 (Washington, DC: Population Reference Bureau, 1983).

[11]In 1930 Mexicans were identified as a separate race, but this practice was discontinued in the 1940 census and all those since. Subsequently, the racial tabulations for 1930 were adjusted to reclassify Mexicans in the white racial category in several 1940 published tabulations, thereby increasing interdecade comparability.

[12]Hernandez et al., "Census Data."

Puerto Rican stock, that is, persons whose parents or who themselves were born in Puerto Rico. For the first time in 1970 the Census Bureau published tabulations on people of Cuban birth or parentage. Both divisions for special publications were motivated by a large interdecade influx of Puerto Ricans and Cubans which generated a demand for more detailed statistics about these populations. The level of detail provided in published tabulations also increased over time, as information requirements rose, and the Hispanic population became larger and more diverse.[13]

In what follows we summarize the conceptual and methodological problems encountered when attempting to identify Hispanics prior to 1980. For ease of presentation, we organize this discussion according to identifiers and present them roughly in the sequence they appeared. This format allows us to trace the evolution of identifiers in historical time, while helping to indicate how more recent items were designed to improve upon those that preceded.

Foreign Stock

With some limitations, segments of the Hispanic population can be traced as far back as 1850, when the Census Bureau first asked respondents their place of birth. Although the usefulness of this item for identifying people of Hispanic origin was restricted to the foreign-born population, most people of Spanish origin or descent residing in the United States in 1850 were Mexican, and virtually all were foreign-born at that time. Recall that the Southwest Territory had been annexed to the United States in 1848, at the culmination of the Mexican American War. Two decades later, in 1870, the Census Bureau added a question about parents' birthplace, generally referred to as the parentage identifier. This item, which was included in all schedules through and including the 1970 census, made it possible to distinguish the native-born descendants of immigrants, or mixed-native and foreign-born parents, from individuals who were native-born of native parents. Combined, the parentage and foreign birth items define the foreign stock population.

One advantage of the foreign stock concept is its utility for time trend analyses. Parentage and birthplace data are available for a period

[13]For a list of publications available through the mid-1970s, see Leo F. Estrada, Jose Hernandez, and David Alvirez, "Using Census Data to Study the Spanish Heritage Population of the United States," in *Cuantos Somos: A Demographic Study of the Mexican-American Population.* Monograph no. 2 (Austin: Center for Mexican American Studies, University of Texas, 1977).

TABLE 2.1

Identifiers Used to Enumerate the Hispanic Population,
U.S. Censuses of Population and Housing: 1950–1980
(percentages of U.S. population sampled)

Identifier	1950	1960	1970	1980
Birthplace[a]	100%	25%	20%	20%
Foreign Parentage	20	25	15	*
Mother Tongue[b]	*	25	15	*
Home Language Other Than English	*	*	*	20
Spanish Surname[c]	5 Southwest states	5 Southwest states	5 Southwest states	5 Southwest states
Spanish Origin or Descent[d]	*	*	5	100
Ancestry[e]	*	*	*	20

[a]The 1970 20 percent sample results from two independent samples of 15 percent and 5 percent.
[b]In 1960 this item was obtained for the foreign-born population only, but in 1970 applied to both the native- and the foreign-born population.
[c]Post-enumeration coding of questionnaires for 5 Southwest states. Lists used in 1950 and 1960 were identical, but an expanded list of more than 8,000 entries was used in 1970, and yet another list consisting of more than 12,000 names was used in 1980. Prior to 1970 the coding was restricted to white persons.
[d]The questions used in 1970 and 1980 are not strictly comparable. See text discussion.
[e]For most respondents, two ancestry responses were coded.
*Not applicable.

spanning 100 years (130 years for the birthplace data—from 1850 to 1980), but unfortunately the parentage item was dropped in 1980. The birthplace item, however, was retained, and in both 1970 and 1980 year of immigration was ascertained for the foreign-born. Other differences in the availability of the parentage and birthplace items derive from the percentage of the population queried about these items. As Table 2.1 shows, in 1950 all persons were asked the birthplace question, but in successive censuses only one questionnaire in four, or one in five, required respondents to provide this information. In 1950 a 20 percent sample of the population provided information about the birthplace of their parents, while in 1960 and 1970, 25 and 15 percent samples, respectively, produced this information.

In common usage, academic researchers and the popular media have referred to immigrants as a first generation, while the natives of foreign or mixed (native and foreign) parentage and the natives of native parentage have been called, respectively, second and third generations. Alma and Karl Taeuber[14] have discussed at some length the inferential problems associated with using the three foreign stock groups—the foreign-born, the natives of foreign or mixed parentage, and the natives of native parentage—as proxies for generations in the conventional sense of the term. Beyond the technical non-equivalence of these three categories with real generations, a major limitation of the foreign stock criterion for enumerating Hispanics is its inadequacy for identifying third or higher-order generations.

The main problem is essentially one of coverage. To be identified with the parentage item, Hispanics must have been born, or have at least one parent who was born, in a Spanish-speaking country, as this is the only basis for determining their ancestry or descent. This coverage problem is most acute for the Mexican origin population whose presence in the United States dates back to the mid-1800s and who, consequently, are much more generationally diverse. The coverage limitations of this item for Mexicans are especially severe in censuses after 1930. However, this problem is less serious for Puerto Ricans, Cubans, and other Central or South Americans, among whom the first and second generations (that is, immigrants and natives of foreign parents) constituted over 90 percent of these groups as recently as 1980.

The 1980 census was the first to include the self-identification question on ancestry which replaced the parentage indicator used during the previous 100 years. In contrast to the approximate generational referent of the parentage items, the ancestry question—"What is this person's ancestry?"— is ambiguous about how many prior generations

---

[14]See Alma Taeuber and Karl Taeuber, "Recent Immigration and the Foreign Born," *Demography* 4 (1967):798–808. Despite the population references to the native-born off-spring of foreign parents as a second generation, this interpretation, which assumes a closed population, is technically incorrect. Taeuber and Taeuber's succinct cautionary note is worth quoting at length:

Meaningful intergenerational occupational comparisons are made most easily if the data pertain to father-son comparisons at corresponding life-cycle stages. But, in [many] studies the so-called "fathers" include many individuals who (by virtue of fertility patterns or death or emigration of children) either have no sons or have two or more sons among the enumerated second-generation labor force, and in a similar fashion the so-called "sons" include many whose fathers are not among the enumerated first-generation labor force. With census-based data there is no one-to-one match of each first-generation father with a second-generation "son." [p. 799]

Their reservations about the use of parentage data to roughly outline "generations" is most serious for analyses of social mobility. Although we do not use the parentage data for that purpose, we nonetheless caution readers about the limitations of the parentage and foreign birth items for the study of socioeconomic and ethnic assimilation, as similar criticisms generally apply.

should be used to establish one's descent,[15] about what the term means,[16] and about how many responses to include in the likely event of multiple ancestries.[17] This change from the parentage item to the ancestry item is unfortunate in that it breaks the 100-year time series about the foreign stock population.[18] Fortunately, with some statistically inconsequential exceptions, Hispanics were highly consistent in reporting Hispanic ancestry codes and other identifiers of Hispanic origin.[19] The major exceptions were individuals of mixed origins, including those involving mixed Hispanic or Hispanic and non-Hispanic ancestors, and Cubans, who were more apt to report Spanish or European origin rather than Latin American ancestry.[20]

Spanish Language

Census data about the use of Spanish is important for enumerating the Hispanic population for several reasons. First, despite the numerous socioeconomic and demographic differences among the Hispanic national origin groups, affinities to Spanish language cultures are a common denominator. The strength and nature of linguistic practices, however, vary considerably among the groups according to length of time in the United States, patterns of residential concentration, and other demographic and social indicators. Furthermore, variation in linguistic

[15]Conceivably, some national origin groups would be more inclined than others to go back further in time in determining their ancestry. For example, Cubans were much more likely to report *Spanish* ancestry (meaning descendants from Spain) than either Mexicans or Puerto Ricans. This practice distorts to some extent the value of this item for Hispanics. See Candace Nelson and Marta Tienda, "The Structuring of Hispanic Ethnicity: Historical and Contemporary Perspectives," *Ethnic and Racial Studies* 8 (1985):49–74.

[16]The ancestry question assumes that most individuals understood the meaning or intention of the word "ancestry." Examples provided below the space for a written response cued for a nationality of one form or another, but included constructed terms, such as Afro-American.

[17]Individuals were allowed to report multiple ancestries, and the Census Bureau coded all single and double ancestry responses. In addition, the bureau coded 17 triple-origin categories, but none of these involved Hispanics.

[18]Subjected to much pressure and protest from various segments of the user community, the Census Bureau is considering reinstating this item in the 1990 census, but it is unclear whether the ancestry item, which was intended to replace the parentage item, will be eliminated.

[19]See Tienda and Ortiz, "Hispanicity."

[20]See Nelson and Tienda, "Structuring of Hispanic Ethnicity," for a discussion of consistency of responses based on a comparison of the ancestry and Spanish origin items and patterns of linguistic assimilation.

attributes and practices is a key indicator of cultural assimilation.[21] Presumably, people of Hispanic origin who are more structurally assimilated—that is, integrated into the social and economic institutions of the mainstream English-speaking society, should use Spanish less (if at all) than those who are less well integrated. Finally, Spanish language background and current linguistic practices are important contemporary cultural expressions of Hispanic ethnicity.

Consistent with its historical preference for objective over subjective criteria to define ethnic boundaries, the Census Bureau has obtained information about Spanish mother tongue in all censuses from 1910 to 1970, with the exception of 1950. However, the comparability of the mother tongue item is somewhat restricted because of period variation in the wording of the question, differences in the population from which the information was sought, and differences in the criteria used to tabulate information for peoples of Spanish mother tongue. Lack of comparability for the Spanish language items is most severe for the 1950–1980 period.[22]

As Table 2.1 shows, the Census Bureau in 1960 solicited information about mother tongue—that is, the language spoken at home when the respondent was a child—for only 25 percent of the foreign-born population. Although this question was intended to solicit information on ethnic ancestry, in the absence of more direct information it has been used, with mixed success, as an indicator of language practices.

In 1970 the criteria for soliciting information about mother tongue were changed substantially. That the Census Bureau decided to ask mother tongue of a smaller sample of the population in 1970 was of lesser consequence for comparability purposes than the decisions to query both native- and foreign-born respondents and to expand the Spanish language concept based on mother tongue from an individual to a household basis in tabulations. Specifically, the Spanish language population in 1970 refers to *all* persons in households where either the head or spouse reported having been raised in a Spanish-speaking environment, irrespective of whether the language was then used by any members of the household. This conceptual expansion of the Spanish language population in 1970 represents a significant departure from

---

[21]Milton Gordon, *Assimilation in American Life: The Role of Race, Religion and National Origins* (New York: Oxford University Press, 1964).

[22]For most years information about mother tongue is available only for persons of foreign birth or foreign parentage, but specifications as to the groups included range widely, depending on whether the first generation, or the first and the second generations were used as the base population(s), and whether these were further restricted by race. See Hernandez et al., "Census Data," p. 673.

previous years when mother tongue was based on individual responses and seriously hampers the utility of this item for delineating ethnic boundaries over time. Interdecade noncomparability for the mother tongue items is particularly severe in published tabulations because users are unable to manipulate the data to achieve greater comparability. Not surprisingly, as a direct consequence of the conceptual expansion of the mother tongue concept, the Spanish language population in 1970 was considerably larger than in all prior years—an obvious artifact of changed enumeration procedures.

Because information about Spanish mother tongue was at one time solicited only of the foreign-born population, this identifier of the Hispanic population shares many of the limitations of the parentage and foreign stock item. Furthermore, the concept of mother tongue is ambiguous with respect to linguistic ability of individuals residing in Spanish language households. To remedy this problem, in 1980 the Census Bureau modified the foreign language question to focus on actual current usage and, in addition, included a question about proficiency in English. A set of three questions were used in 1980 to determine Spanish language home use: (13a) "Does this person speak a language other than English at home?" If the response was yes, it was followed by two questions: (13b) "What is this language?" and (13c) "How well does this person speak English?" Combined, these three questions provide information about the extent of bilingualism and the pace of linguistic assimilation among ethnic populations for the first time in the history of the U.S. census.[23]

Spanish Surname

Information about Spanish surnames involves a costly manual coding procedure which is done on a post-enumeration basis. This process was begun in 1950 as a means of identifying the native or native parentage population of Mexican origin which, with passing time, was less adequately captured by the foreign birth or parentage items used to designate the foreign stock population. This item has been coded mechanically on a post-enumeration basis through a matching procedure for the

---

[23]Several intercensal surveys, such as the 1976 Survey of Income and Education, and special supplements of the Current Population Survey, contain extensive language data. However, 1980 was the first census which solicited information on English proficiency *and* current home languages other than English.

five southwestern states for successive censuses through and including 1980, thus making possible longitudinal comparisons of this population over a 30-year period.

The principal advantages of the surname identifier of the Hispanic population stem from its high degree of comparability over time, but especially between 1950 and 1970. Next to the foreign stock identifiers Spanish surname ranks second in terms of consistency and continuity over time, although it is available for a much shorter period. Considerable expansion of the list of Spanish surnames after 1960 hampers the comparability of this identifier, however. This noncomparability problem is most serious for 1970–1980, when the list was expanded from over 8,000 names to over 12,000 names, but the 1970 list is also more inclusive than that used in 1960. An additional noncomparability problem stems from restricting in 1960 the list of eligible names to white persons, although this limitation is not likely to be great since there were relatively few non-white Hispanics residing in the southwestern United States prior to 1970.[24]

More serious disadvantages of this identifier are its regional focus on the five southwestern states that at most captured 85 percent of the Mexican origin population which the item was designed to enumerate, and its ambiguities with respect to non-Hispanic names in related romance languages, especially those of Italians, Portuguese, and Filipinos. As a criterion to identify Hispanics (Mexicans), the Spanish surname item is unable to differentiate between those who acquire or who lose their Spanish surnames through intermarriage with non-Hispanics and those who acquire their names through birth. It is unclear whether the misclassification of non-Hispanic origin persons with Spanish surnames acquired through marriage and Hispanics who lost their Spanish surnames through marriage are mutually offsetting. What is clear, however, is that as the extent of interethnic marriages continues, and the Mexican origin population becomes more residentially dispersed, the usefulness of this identifier will continue to diminish. Finally, as we show in the following chapter, the presence of many persons from Central and South America in the southwestern states increased notably during the 1970s. For this reason, as well as the two noted above, the Spanish surname indicator may become an increasingly less useful way to identify the Mexican origin population.

---

[24]For further detail about the surname list used in 1980, see Jeffrey S. Passel and David L. Word, "Constructing the List of Spanish Surnames for the 1980 Census: An Application of Bayes' Theorem," paper presented at the annual meeting of the Population Association of America, Denver, April 1980. In 1980 approximately 19 percent of all Spanish surnames were sampled and coded from the southwestern states.

Spanish Heritage

Growing dissatisfaction with the inability of any single item to designate the Hispanic population in 1970 prompted the Census Bureau to devise a composite concept—Spanish Heritage—based on the parentage, surname, and language items. This post-enumeration designation of Hispanics included persons of Puerto Rican stock residing in three Middle Atlantic states (New York, New Jersey, and Pennsylvania), persons of Spanish surname residing in the five southwestern states, and persons of Spanish language (Spanish mother tongue) in all remaining states. While the Spanish heritage concept represented an important stride toward establishing ethnic boundaries for the Hispanic population on a national basis, the use of several different identifiers confused many data users who tried to interpret varying population counts for peoples of Spanish origin.[25] Moreover, federal laws and increased data requirements by governmental agencies made starkly evident the need for a single and unequivocal identifier to enumerate Hispanics.[26]

After the 1970 census and the criticism of the data on Hispanics, the major task confronting the Census Bureau in attempting to delineate the ethnic boundaries of the Hispanic population was to obtain clarity and objectivity without regional limitations and to develop a sufficiently broad concept that could accommodate all national origin groups.[27] Fortunately, considerable progress has been made in devising alternative indicators to identify the Hispanic origin population on a national basis which allow for more precise differentiation according to country or region of origin and which are not regionally restricted. The shift toward the use of a self-identification Spanish origin item can best be understood in this light.

Spanish Origin

For both political and statistical reasons, efforts to improve the coverage of the Hispanic origin population at a national level resulted in several items designating Hispanic national origin or descent in the 1980 census. The single most significant was the self-identification item which required all persons to indicate whether they were of Spanish/

[25]See tabulations in Estrada et al., "Using Census Data"; and Hernandez et al., "Census Data."

[26]See Edward Ferdandez and Nampeo R. McKinney, "Identification of the Hispanic Population: A Review of Census Bureau Practices," paper presented at the annual meeting of the American Statistical Association, Houston, Texas, August 11–14, 1980.

[27]Estrada et al., "Using Census Data"; Hernandez et al., "Census Data."

Hispanic origin or descent. The Spanish/Hispanic origin item is subjective in that individuals indicate whether they perceive themselves to be Hispanic. This identifier is the closest approximation to the sociological concept of ethnic group identity.[28] Its inclusion in the 1970 census schedule not only marks a departure in Census Bureau practices favoring objective over subjective indicators of Hispanic ethnicity, but also represents an attempt to enumerate more precisely the various Hispanic national origin groups than was previously possible using combinations of the birthplace, parentage, language, surname, and region criteria. The need for an alternative identifier was becoming particularly salient for the Mexican origin population owing to the inability of existing items, particularly the parentage, surname, and language criteria, to classify adequately the growing third and higher-order generations.

Although included in the 1970 census questionnaire, the Spanish origin item was not the major identifier used to enumerate the Hispanic population until 1980.[29] The decision to include the Spanish/Hispanic origin item on the full enumeration questionnaire— that is, it was asked on the complete count questionnaire given to all respondents—testifies to the growing concern with the limitations of previous procedures to enumerate Hispanics. Part of the motivation for soliciting information about Hispanic origin on the full enumeration questionnaire was to produce data for Hispanics in small geographic areas, something that had not been previously possible.[30] However, this decision also reflected the increased political clout of advocates and users of Hispanic data who desired to collect the most detailed information possible. The pressure on the Census Bureau to develop an alternative item for identifying Hispanics was further aggravated by allegations that the Hispanic origin population, but particularly the population of Mexican origin, had been seriously undercounted in 1970.[31] These allegations find some support in various official estimates of the Hispanic origin population, which we discuss later in this chapter (see Table 2.2).

Despite the apparent similarity of the Spanish/Hispanic origin

[28]See Hernandez et al., "Census Data."

[29]U.S. Bureau of the Census, *Census of Population and Housing: 1980*, Public Use Microdata Samples, Technical Documentation (Washington, DC: U.S. Government Printing Office, 1983). See more extensive discussion of this point in Estrada et al., "Using Census Data."

[30]Davis et al., "U.S. Hispanics," p. 6.

[31]Marta Tienda, "The Mexican American Population," in Amos Hawley and Sara Mills Mazie, eds., *Nonmetropolitan America in Transition* (Chapel Hill: University of North Carolina Press, 1981). The author identified three potentially significant sources of undercount of Mexican Americans in 1970, including (1) failure to include mobile illegal aliens, (2) exclusion of young mobile families, and (3) exclusion of families of agricultural laborers.

items used in the 1980 and 1970 censuses, substantial differences in the wording and sampling bases in each year distort to some extent the comparability of this item over time. A facsimile of Spanish origin questions which appeared in the 1970 and 1980 census questionnaires illustrates substantial differences between them. Besides the sharp difference in the proportion of the population required to respond to these questions, the two items are dissimilar in the wording of the question, in the number of response categories used, and in the placement of the non-Spanish origin response. Thus, all of the changes in 1980 were designed to improve upon the item used in 1970 which met with mixed, but promising success.[32]

Although seemingly trivial, the differences between the 1970 and 1980 Spanish origin items were of major consequence for the enumeration itself (compare columns 1 and 6 on Table 2.2) and for the quality of the data produced.[33] First, the placement of the non-Spanish response category first, rather than last, was intended to facilitate responses of non-Hispanics—clearly the majority at 93 percent of the total population. Second, the elimination of the Central or South American response category was intended to reduce misreporting by individuals residing in central and southern parts of the country.[34] Finally, the changed wording of the question was designed to accommodate various constituencies of the Mexican origin population who objected to the 1970 label and preferred an alternative label, such as Chicano or Mexican American.[35]

Another important difference between the 1970 and 1980 Spanish origin items—the percentage of the populations sampled—has direct implications for the success of the most recent identifier in reducing undercount. It appears that the 1980 enumeration of the Hispanic origin population at 14.6 million on April 1, 1980, is the most complete in the recent history of the U.S. Census. However, the success of the self-identification Spanish origin item for eliciting accurate responses from Hispanics varied by national origin. This variability stems partly from the lack of a rigorous definition of "Spanish/Hispanic origin or descent" in the accompanying instructions (see Figure 2.1), partly from the vague-

---

[32]Jacob Siegel and Jeffrey S. Passel, "Coverage of the Hispanic Population of the United States in the 1970 Census: A Methodological Analysis," *Current Population Reports*, special studies, P-23, no. 82 (Washington, DC: U.S. Government Printing Office, 1979).

[33]Tienda and Ortiz, "Hispanicity"; Davis et al., "U.S. Hispanics."

[34]Siegel and Passel, "Coverage of the Hispanic Population."

[35]In addition, the Census Bureau coded as Mexican those who wrote in entries such as "La Raza" and as Puerto Rican those who wrote in entries such as "Boricua."

FIGURE 2.1

The Spanish Origin Question in the 1970 and 1980 Censuses

1970	b. Is this person's origin or descent—(fill one circle)	
	○ Mexican	○ Central or South American
	○ Puerto Rican	○ Other Spanish
	○ Cuban	○ No, none of these

1980	7. Is this person of Spanish/Hispanic origin or descent? (fill one circle)	○ No (Not Spanish/Hispanic) ○ Yes, Mexican, Mexican-American, Chicano ○ Yes, Puerto Rican ○ Yes, Cuban ○ Yes, other Spanish/Hispanic

INSTRUCTIONS TO THE RESPONDENT FOR 1980 SPANISH-ORIGIN QUESTION.

7. A person is of Spanish/Hispanic origin or descent if the person identifies his or her ancestry with one of the listed groups, that is, Mexican, Puerto Rican, etc. Origin or descent (ancestry) may be viewed as the nationality group, the lineage, or country in which the person or the person's parents or ancestors were born.

SOURCE: Cary Davis, Carl Haub, and JoAnne Willette, "U.S. Hispanics: Changing the Face of America,' *Population Bulletin*, vol. 38, no. 3 (Washington, DC: Population Reference Bureau, 1983).

ness of the race item which preceded the Spanish origin item in the census questionnaire,[36] and partly from other sources of response error.

Recognizing that the performance of this subjective item also depended on the willingness of individuals to identify themselves as Hispanics, we conducted several tests of internal consistency to check the extent of discrepancies in reporting Spanish/Hispanic origin or descent

[36]Question 4, designed to tap color or race, defies typological classification and does not even mention the word "race." Given the format of this question, it was not surprising that 40 percent of all persons who identified themselves to be of Spanish/Hispanic origin or descent responded to Question 4 by writing in a Spanish national origin. This resulted partly because the question cued for national origin in several of the response choices. For further discussion, see William Petersen, "Politics and the Measurement of Ethnicity," in William Alonso and Paul Starr, eds., *The Politics of Numbers* (New York: Russell Sage Foundation, 1987).

using alternative indicators of Hispanic ethnicity.[37] The long schedule, which was administered to 20 percent of all households, includes several items that can be used to identify Hispanic ethnics and to assess the extent of agreement with the full enumeration Hispanic identifier. These include country of birth, home language, ancestry, Spanish surnames, and a Spanish write-in response to the open-ended race item (see footnote 36). Our analyses revealed that, overall, Hispanics were quite consistent in reporting their ethnicity by responding affirmatively to the Spanish origin item *and* subsequently reporting two or more additional Hispanic ethnic identifiers.[38] Moreover, even when we adjusted the Spanish origin population by making it more *restrictive;* that is, by selecting only those individuals whose responses to the various Hispanic identifiers were internally consistent, or more *inclusive;* that is, by including as Hispanics all individuals who reported any Hispanic trait, whether or not they responded affirmatively to the Spanish origin item, there were no significant differences in the socioeconomic characteristics of the population.

Given the above evidence we concluded that inferences based on an analysis of the full-enumeration Spanish/Hispanic origin item should be virtually identical to those based on an adjusted population definition which takes into account additional ethnic indicators. In the interest of simplicity and comparability with published tabulations, and because we determined that an adjusted definition of the Hispanic population was statistically inconsequential for portraying the social and economic characteristics of the population, we chose to use the Spanish origin item to set the ethnic boundaries of the Hispanic population in 1980. The only exception to this was the exclusion of the persons of Mexican origin who also reported their race as black and who reside outside the five southwestern states. Evidence indicates the vast bulk of these were

[37]Tienda and Ortiz, "Hispanicity." A similar analysis was not possible for the 1970 census because most of the ethnic items of interest were from the 15 percent sample questionnaire, while the Spanish origin item appeared in the 5 percent sample questionnaire. As these were independent samples, it was not possible to cross-tabulate the identifiers of interest.

[38]This supports earlier evidence by Charles E. Johnson, Jr., "Consistency of Reporting of Ethnic Origin in the Census Population Survey," *Current Population Survey*, Technical Paper no. 31 (Washington, DC: U.S. Government Printing Office, 1974). A more recent Census Bureau publication showed that Hispanics were among the most consistent ethnics in reporting their origin across multiple items designed to elicit ancestry or descent. See U.S. Bureau of the Census, "Ancestry and Language in the United States: November, 1979," *Current Population Reports*, series P-23, no. 116 (Washington, DC: U.S. Government Printing Office, 1982).

poorly educated blacks who mistakenly identified themselves in the Mexican origin category.[39]

That the 1980 enumeration of the Hispanic population based on the Spanish origin item represented an improved coverage over the prior decade is indicated by the success of the Census Bureau in counting more Hispanics than had been expected. The data in Table 2.2, which summarize the Hispanic enumerations for the 1970 and 1980 censuses, as well as several intercensal population estimates based on Current Population Surveys, provide an empirical basis for assessing the performance of the Spanish origin item. Not only do these data suggest an improvement of coverage in 1980, but they also support allegations that the Mexican origin population was underenumerated in 1980. The total Hispanic population increased by 60 percent during the decade, if the official enumerations and estimates are taken at face value. Moreover, the Hispanic population increased by 16 percent during the three years immediately following the census. That the Hispanic population estimate based on the March 1980 Current Population Survey, taken just one month *before* the census, resulted in a population estimate 1.4 million *below* the census count of 14.6 million provides further support for the allegation that the Hispanic population was underestimated throughout the 1970s, probably as a result of the underenumeration of Mexicans in the 1970 census. However, since the underenumeration issue is clouded by the inclusion of an unknown number of undocumented immigrants from Mexico and Central and South America in 1980, it is difficult to determine with much precision the size of the 1970 undercount, although results from CPS surveys just before and after the 1970 census suggest that as many as 10 percent of persons of Mexican origin may have failed to so identify themselves.[40]

The data in Table 2.2 also help to illustrate intertemporal comparability of definitions and concepts for measuring change over time. For example, the national origin composition of the Hispanic population differs appreciably between 1970 and 1980. The most obvious difference is the share of Mexicans, which ranged from a low of 50 percent in 1970 to approximately 60 percent in 1980. Although some might hastily conclude that this compositional change resulted largely from the increased

---

[39]Available evidence indicates that the misreporting may have occurred in only selected areas where the Hispanic population is relatively sparse. Further discussion of this point is provided in U.S. Bureau of the Census, "Persons of Spanish Origin by State: 1980," Supplementary Report, PC80-S1-7 (Washington, DC: U.S. Government Printing Office, 1982) and in Tienda and Ortiz, "Hispanicity"; see also Frank D. Bean, H. L. Browning, and W. P. Frisbie, "The Sociodemographic Characteristics of Mexican Immigrant Status Groups: Implications for Studying Undocumented Mexicans," *International Migration Review* 18 (1984):672–91.

[40]Jeffrey S. Passel, personal communication, 1986.

TABLE 2.2

Hispanic Origin Population, 1970–1980:
Census Enumerations and CPS Estimates

	1970 Census (April)	1973 CPS (March)	1976 CPS (March)	1979 CPS (March)	1980[a] CPS (March)	1980 Census (April)
Mexican	50.0%	59.5%	59.3%	60.6%	59.9%	59.6%
Puerto Rican	15.8	14.6	15.8	14.5	13.8	13.8
Cuban	6.0	6.9	6.2	6.6	6.3	5.5
Central or South American		5.6	6.8	7.0	7.7	
	28.3 }					{ 20.9
Other Hispanic		13.3	12.0	11.4	12.3	
Population Size (in millions)	9.1	10.6	11.1	12.1	13.2	14.6

SOURCES: U.S. Bureau of the Census, *Census of Population: 1980* "Persons of Spanish Origin by State: 1980," Supplementary Report PC80-S1-7 (Washington, DC: U.S. Government Printing Office, August 1982); "Persons of Spanish Origin in the United States: March, 1973," *Current Population Reports,* series P-20, no. 264 (Washington, DC: U.S. Government Printing Office, May 1974), table A; "Persons of Spanish Origin in the United States: March, 1976 (Advance Report)," *Current Population Reports,* series P-20, no. 302 (Washington, DC: U.S. Government Printing Office, November 1976), table 1; "Persons of Spanish Origin in the United States: March, 1979 (Advance Report)," *Current Population Reports,* series P-20, no. 347 (Washington, DC: U.S. Government Printing Office, October 1979), table 1; "Population Profile of the United States: 1980," *Current Population Reports,* series P-20, no. 363 (Washington, DC: U.S. Government Printing Office, June 1981).

March 1980 estimate includes 300,000 Spanish origin persons who were not included in the March 1979 CPS estimates.

illegal immigration from Mexico during the period, as well as from the increased number of these aliens actually included in the census, these explanations are insufficient. It is likely that an underenumeration of the Mexican origin population in 1970 was also responsible for the changed national origin composition of the Hispanic populations between 1970 and 1980.

We base this conclusion on two facts. First, in 1970 the estimate of the Mexican origin population residing in the Southwest, as identified with the Spanish surname criterion, was similar to that based on the Mexican origin item—roughly 4.5 million—despite the fact that roughly 15 percent of the Chicano population was estimated to have resided outside of the Southwest during that period.[41] Second, the 1973 estimate of the Mexican origin population at 6.3 million, based on the Current Population Survey, implied an unlikely increase of 1.8 million Mexicans, or

[41]Tienda, "Mexican American Population."

a 40 percent increase, in just three years! Part of this increase resulted when the Census Bureau changed its algorithm for assigning children under age 14 to the Spanish origin category. This changed practice added some 400,000 children to the Hispanic population between 1972 and 1973, but this new procedure does not account for the huge increase in the size of the Hispanic origin population between 1970 and 1973.[42]

Thus, while variation in the national origin composition was less extensive for other groups than for Mexicans, the data in Table 2.2 clearly indicate that problems of temporal comparability in identifying the Hispanic population exist, even if one relies on the seemingly identical Spanish origin identifiers.

Summary and Conclusions

There are three principal means by which the Census Bureau has identified ethnic populations in the past. These involve classifying individuals using an objective criterion, such as foreign birthplace, parental birthplace, Spanish surname, language, or some combination of these; allowing individuals to select an ethnic label, as in the self-identification Spanish origin and ancestry items; or some combination of these. Over the past three decades the Census Bureau has used subjective and objective indicators to enumerate the Hispanic population, but the extent of reliance on subjective criteria has increased during the past two decades compared with all prior censuses. Both subjective and objective indicators have their advantages and disadvantages, and the usefulness of these for deriving meaningful group designations also changes as the populations become more generationally diverse and as the social and political climate of the nation and its constituent ethnic population changes.

Thus, the continuing challenge to the Census Bureau is to arrive at a broad concept of the Hispanic population which not only includes all ethnic groups of Hispanic ancestry, but also accommodates the subjective and objective diversity among the national origin groups. The greatest strides toward this goal were made in 1980 with the introduction of the full-enumeration origin item, which provided a solid basis for assessing the size and composition of the Hispanic population. However, for the analyses reported in the remainder of this monograph, there remain several problems which impair the temporal comparability of the Hispanic population as a whole and its constituent subgroups.

[42] Massey, *Demographic and Economic Position.*

One major difficulty that hampers comparability over time stems from the suspected underenumerations of Hispanics, particularly persons of Mexican origin or descent, between the 1970 and 1980 censuses. This problem, highlighted by the summary statistics in Table 2.2, was also reflected in the various intercensal estimates of the Hispanic population based on the Current Population Surveys of the 1970s. Problems of comparability were further exacerbated when, in 1973, the Census Bureau changed its algorithm for assigning children under age 14 to the Spanish origin category. An additional factor confounding the comparability of the 1970 and 1980 enumerations of the Hispanic population is the inclusion of an unknown number of undocumented aliens in the most recent census. Not only does this source of noncomparability contaminate estimates of the growth of the population over the decade, but it systematically biases the assessments of changes in the characteristics of Hispanics over time. To the extent that large numbers of undocumented aliens are included in the Hispanic population count, the socioeconomic position of Hispanics will be downwardly biased and the assessment of intercensal changes in the socioeconomic position of Hispanics will be similarly understated.[43]

One main conclusion to be drawn from the preceding discussion is that the evolution of Census Bureau practices in collecting data about the Hispanic population imposes certain limitations on the temporal dimensions of this study. Specifically, the lack of comparability over time among various identifiers, the changes in the wording and implementation of the Spanish origin item and the Spanish surname criteria, the regional focus of Spanish surname and Puerto Rican stock, and the lack of continuity of most identifiers (including parentage, Spanish/Hispanic origin, Spanish home language, and ancestry) make it difficult to assess in a completely reliable fashion the trends of change, even during the most recent period. Although we attempt to delineate Hispanic ethnic boundaries in the most consistent fashion possible using the Public Use Microdata Sample tapes, as we elaborate in Appendix A, our success in achieving comparability cannot entirely overcome the inconsistencies stemming from the discontinuation or introduction of items or from variance in the population segments to which these indicators were applied.

---

[43]Bean, Browning, and Frisbie, "The Sociodemographic Characteristics of Mexican Immigrant Status Groups."

3

A DEMOGRAPHIC AND SOCIOECONOMIC PROFILE OF THE HISPANIC POPULATION: PERSISTENCE, DIVERSITY, AND CHANGE OVER TWO DECADES

THE GROWING awareness of the Hispanic presence in the United States during the 1960s and the 1970s can be traced largely to two demographic phenomena: the rapid growth of the population and a pronounced regional concentration which heightened the national visibility of Hispanics as an ethnic group. At the same time increased study of this population has revealed great diversity among the peoples of Spanish origin. One purpose of this chapter is thus to provide a summary overview of the size, growth, and residential distribution of the Hispanic populations over the past two decades. We also examine the extensive social, economic, and demographic differences among the populations through a comparison of the marital and household characteristics, education and employment status, and language practices of the five major groups. Finally, we devote special attention to the Central/South American population because it is comparatively new and uniquely diverse in terms of national origin composition.

Our main objectives are to provide answers to basic questions about the size and national origin composition of the Hispanic population and to set an empirical foundation for the theme of diversity which runs through the remaining topical chapters. Rapid growth, regional concentration, and socioeconomic differentiation according to national origin are three features which distinguish Hispanics from other ethnic groups in the United States. This chapter thus lays the groundwork for a more detailed treatment of these topics in the remainder of the monograph. Examining the size, growth, and national origin composition of the total Hispanic population, using 1980 as a point of reference and viewing change retrospectively, allows us to focus on the contemporary demographic situation of the Hispanic origin population and to make general inferences about its prospects for change. We discuss only briefly the growth rate of the population which, because of data limitations, is quite imprecise. Instead we dwell on the components of growth and attempt to document the role of immigration in contributing to the intercensal growth of the Hispanic populations and in shaping the age-sex structure of each major group.

Patterns of residential concentration of the population at the regional and state levels are discussed, as is the increasing metropolitan character of the Hispanic population since 1960. The third section of the chapter compares selected demographic and social characteristics of the population, highlighting the themes of diversity and change in the demography of the Hispanic population. The need to distinguish among national origin groups when discussing the implications of rapid growth and geographic concentration for the socioeconomic positioning of the population is also emphasized. Finally, in the last section we underscore further the theme of diversity by focusing on the Central and South American origin populations. Although there are places in the remainder of the monograph where we distinguish the national origin groups that constitute this population, for the most part we treat this group as a single population, even though we are fully aware that this masks considerable diversity.

Size, Growth, and National Origin Composition

The two most basic questions that can be asked about any population are: How many persons are in the population and who are they? In 1980 the Census Bureau enumerated 14.6 million persons of Hispanic origin residing in the continental United States. An additional 3.2 million people—most of them Hispanics—resided on the island of Puerto Rico in 1980. Of 226 million people enumerated in 1980, Hispanics represented 6.4 percent of the U.S. population, up from 4.5 percent in 1970.[1] The 1980 enumeration represents an increase of 61 percent over

---

[1] U.S. Bureau of the Census, "Persons of Spanish Origin by State: 1980," Supplementary Report, PC80-S1-7 (Washington, DC: U.S. Government Printing Office, 1982).

the 1970 count of 9.1 million, a rise almost seven times greater than the 9 percent growth registered for non-Hispanics during the period.[2]

However, part of this growth is an artifact of improvements in the coverage of the Hispanic population resulting from changes in the design of census questionnaires and from the initiation of an effective public relations campaign aimed at reducing undercount among ethnic populations.[3] The better coverage of the Hispanic population in 1980 than in 1970 is also one factor contributing to the inclusion of a substantial number of illegal immigrants in 1980 census counts.[4] Because of these and other changes, a strict comparison of the 1970 and 1980 Hispanic population totals overstates the true amount of intercensal growth. Similar problems of noncomparability affect the 1960 enumeration.

These reservations notwithstanding, the data in Table 3.1 provide a rough indication about the size and relative growth of the Hispanic population since 1960.[5] The first entry for 1970, 9.1 million, is the official count produced by the Census Bureau; the second, 10.5 million, is an estimate produced by the Population Reference Bureau in an effort to account for some of the data deficiencies prior to 1980, particularly the underenumeration of Mexicans in 1970. That Census Bureau analysts and researchers who have written about this problem do not agree about how to arrive at a "best" estimate of the Hispanic population in 1970 greatly complicates the task of computing reasonably accurate growth rates. Part of the difficulty in settling this problem arises from the increased number of undocumented immigrants counted in the 1980 census.[6]

---

[2]U.S. Bureau of the Census, *The Condition of Hispanics in America Today* (Washington, DC: U.S. Government Printing Office, 1984), p. 4.

[3]U.S. Bureau of the Census, *Condition of Hispanics*, p. 6. The analysts at Development Associates and the Population Reference Bureau who prepared the intercensal growth estimates of the Hispanic population believe that despite the improvements in the enumeration of Hispanics in 1980, the 14.6 million figure represents an undercount, although of much lesser magnitude than that which occurred in 1970. They estimated that the Hispanic undercount fell between the white rate of 1.9 percent and the black rate of 7.7 percent; see Cary Davis, Carl Haub, and JoAnne Willette, "U.S. Hispanics: Changing the Face of America," *Population Bulletin*, vol. 38, no. 3 (Washington, DC: Population Reference Bureau, 1983).

[4]Robert Warren and Jeffrey S. Passel, "A Count of the Uncountable: Estimates of Undocumented Aliens Counted in the 1980 United States Census," *Demography* (forthcoming). These authors estimate that the 1980 census included about 2.1 million illegal aliens. Latin America, including Mexico, Cuba, Dominican Republic, and other Central or South American or Caribbean countries, contributed an estimated 1.6 million, or 76 percent of the total illegal population counted in the 1980 census. Mexico alone was estimated to have contributed 1,131,000, or about 55 percent of the illegal alien population.

[5]Davis et al., "U.S. Hispanics."

[6]Warren and Passel, "Count of the Uncountable"; Jeffrey S. Passel and Karen A. Woodrow, "Geographic Distribution of Undocumented Immigrants: Estimates of Undocumented Aliens Counted in the 1980 Census by State," *International Migration Review* 18 (1984):642–71.

TABLE 3.1

Growth of the U.S. Hispanic Population: 1960–1980
(in millions)

Year	Total U.S. Population	Hispanic Population	Hispanic Intercensal Increase	Hispanic As Percentage of U.S. Population
1960	179.3	6.9	2.9	3.9%
1970[a]	203.2	9.1	2.2	4.5
1970[b]	203.2	10.5	3.6	5.2
1980	226.5	14.6	4.1	6.4

SOURCE: Adapted from Cary Davis, Carl Haub, and JoAnne Willette, "U.S. Hispanics: Changing the Face of America," *Population Bulletin,* vol. 38, no. 3 (Washington, DC: Population Reference Bureau, 1983): 8, table 2.

[a]Official Census Bureau estimate.
[b]Adjusted estimate prepared by the Population Reference Bureau staff.

Reservations of comparability and undercount notwithstanding, the data in Table 3.1 reveal an extraordinary growth of the Hispanic population between 1960 and 1980. Even discounting the underenumeration problems encountered in 1970 and earlier, there is no doubt that the growth rate of the Hispanic population, which averaged 6.1 percent on an annual basis during the 1970s, far exceeded that of blacks (1.8 percent) and other whites (0.6 percent).[7] Whether one uses the official or the adjusted counts of Hispanics in 1970, the percentage increases in the population are unusually large. These range from 39 to 61 percent during the 1970s and from 32 to 52 percent during the 1960s based on the adjusted and official estimates, respectively. These intercensal increases are particularly striking compared with those of other racial and ethnic groups, with the exception of Asians.[8]

Two factors stand out in accounting for the phenomenal growth of the Hispanic population since 1960. These are an increased immigration from Latin America and migration from Puerto Rico, on the one hand, and relatively higher fertility among Hispanic origin women, on the other. [9] Both of these topics—immigration and fertility—are treated in

[7]Hispanic Policy Development Project, *The Hispanic Almanac* (Lebanon, PA: Sowers, 1984).

[8]The loosening of admission restrictions on immigration from Asian countries after 1965, and the admission of thousands of refugees from Southeast Asia after the fall of U.S.-backed governments in Indochina, has resulted in higher intercensal increases for Asians during the 1970–80 decade. See Robert W. Gardner, Peter C. Smith, and Herbert R. Barringer, "The Demography of Asian Americans: Growth, Change and Heterogeneity," paper presented at the annual meeting of the Population Association of America, Boston, March 28–30, 1985.

[9]U.S. Bureau of the Census, *Condition of Hispanics.*

some detail in chapters 4 and 7. Our concern of the moment is with the relative importance of these factors in contributing to changes in the size and composition of the Hispanic population during the 1970s, and what they portend for future increases in the population.

Differing rates of immigration and fertility among Hispanics have diversified the national origin composition of the population and will probably continue to do so for some time in the future. Of the 14.6 million Hispanics enumerated in 1980, approximately 60 percent were Mexican in origin, 14 percent were Puerto Rican, 6 percent were Cuban, 7 percent were Central or South American, and 14 percent were Other Hispanic (Figure 3.1). The latter group includes not only part-Hispanics,

FIGURE 3.1

Persons of Hispanic Origin in the United States: 1980

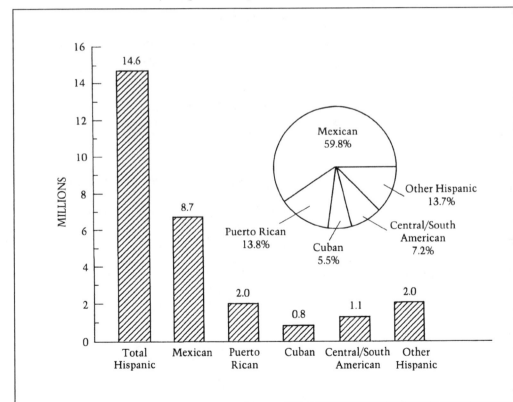

SOURCES: U.S. Bureau of the Census, "Persons of Spanish Origin by State: 1980," Supplementary Report PC80-S1-7 (Washington, DC: U.S. Government Printing Office, 1982); and special tabulations of the Public Use Microdata Sample A (5%) file.

FIGURE 3.2

Growth of the Hispanic Population: 1970–1980 (percentage change)

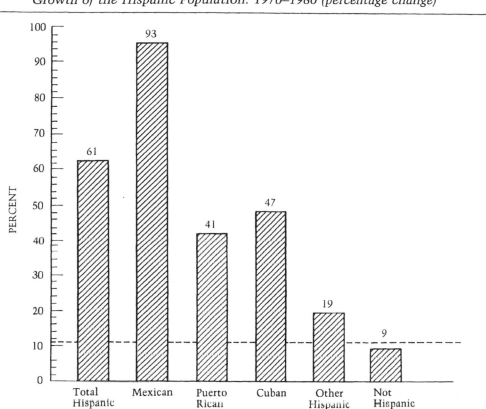

OURCE: U.S. Bureau of the Census, *The Condition of Hispanics in America Today* (Washington, DC: .S. Government Printing Office, 1984).

that is, offspring from Hispanic and non-Hispanic parents, but also persons of mixed Hispanic origin, that is, offspring of marriages between two members of different Hispanic subgroups, and Hispanos, the long-term residents of the Southwest whose origins are traced to Spanish and Mexican/Indian stock.[10]

Figure 3.2 shows that the major national origin groups did not contribute uniformly to the impressive intercensal growth of the total Hispanic population. While all of the groups grew rapidly between 1970 and 1980, the Mexican origin population, which is the largest of the major

[10]Hispanic Policy Development Project, *Hispanic Almanac*.

subgroups, increased by almost 93 percent during the decade. This is almost twice as much as the increase experienced by the Puerto Rican and Cuban populations, whose percentage increases were 41 and 47 percent, respectively, and considerably greater than the 19 percent increase of the Other Hispanic origin population. For the latter, which in the case of published data includes Central and South Americans, most of the intercensal growth resulted from the immigration and fertility of the population from Central or South American countries.[11]

Although few would deny that the Hispanic population increased rapidly during the 1970s, it is highly unlikely that a 61 percent change for the total population, or a 93 percent increase for the Mexican origin population, represents *real growth* over the 10-year period. Even with high levels of legal and illegal immigration, and with fertility levels 35 to 40 percent above those of Anglos (see Chapter 7), a near doubling of the Mexican origin population between 1970 and 1980 seems highly implausible. Therefore, in the following section we discuss in very general terms the relative importance of measurement error, immigration, and natural increase in producing the large intercensal Hispanic increase.

Components of Growth: An Approximation

Besides natural increase and net migration, which are the only true sources of growth of a population, the measured change in the size of the Hispanic population reflects coverage and classification errors in both periods. That the existence of such errors differed among the national origin groups further complicates the task of sorting out the natural increase and net immigration components of growth for the Hispanic population.[12] Thus, while there is no way to know precisely the "true" intercensal population growth rate,[13] information about the de-

---

[11]Published statistics do not distinguish between Central/South Americans and Other Hispanics. Thus, we were forced to combine this group in some figures and tables, such as Figure 3.2. Where possible, we estimated population characteristics separately for Central or South Americans versus Other Hispanics.

[12]The problems of studying the coverage of the Hispanic population in 1970 are discussed in detail by Jacob S. Siegel and Jeffrey S. Passel, "Coverage of the Hispanic Population of the United States in the 1970 Census: A Methodological Analysis," *Current Population Reports*, series P-23, no. 82 (Washington, DC: U.S. Government Printing Office, 1979).

[13]JoAnne Willette, Robert Haupt, Carl Haub, Leon Bouvier, and Cary Davis, "The Demographic and Socioeconomic Characteristics of the Hispanic Population in the United States: 1950–80," report prepared by Development Associates and the Population Reference Bureau for the U.S. Department of Health and Human Services (Washington, DC: Development Associates, 1982). In their comprehensive report on the social and demographic characteristics of the Hispanic population, Willette and her associates similarly cautioned against attempting to compute growth rates for the Hispanic population and its constituent segments.

mographic structure of the Hispanic subpopulations, together with official statistics about the volume of immigration from Mexico, Cuba, and other Spanish-speaking countries during the 1970s, provides a general idea about the relative importance of immigration and natural increase in producing the observed growth of the Hispanic population. Since rapid growth is one of the three distinguishing features of the Hispanic population, it is essential to develop a knowledgeable interpretation of the published statistics that imply very high growth rates.

First, a cautionary note. We must emphasize that the business of estimating a rate of growth for the total Hispanic population, or for its constituent subgroups, is a highly technical enterprise. It is nonetheless one that is necessarily inaccurate because of the coverage problems in the 1970 census and the enumeration of a nontrivial number of undocumented aliens in 1980. Our goal in discussing the components of growth is not to produce adjusted growth rates for the total population or for the major national origin groups based on alternative assumptions about fertility, mortality, net migration, and net coverage error. Rather, our more modest objective is simply to render more intelligible the widely disparate rates of growth observed among the major national origin groups, as well as to provide a general idea about the relative importance of natural increase versus immigration in producing the observed differential growth rates.

A second reason for elaborating on the components of growth, even if in a highly approximate way, stems from popular and often unfounded conceptions about how much immigration has contributed to the rapid growth of the Hispanic population. As we briefly document here and in greater detail in Chapter 4, immigration from Mexico, the Spanish-speaking Caribbean, and Latin America increased substantially during the 1970s. Its impact is differentially manifested in the age structure and national origin composition of the Hispanic population. Based on the data we present here, we find little evidence to support the claim that immigration accounts for more than half of the growth of the total Hispanic population. However, we acknowledge that the importance of immigration differed among the national origin groups.

Mexicans. For Mexicans the issue of immigration has become increasingly controversial because of the attention devoted to the problem of illegal immigration. As the data and computations in Table 3.2 show, the question of assessing the growth of the Mexican origin population during the decade is a complicated one. First of all, the enumeration in 1980 compared with 1970 includes a large number of persons who misclassified themselves as being of Mexican origin, a large number of illegals, and some "extra" number of persons who were enumerated because of coverage improvements in 1980 (rows B, C, and D of Table

TABLE 3.2

*Estimated Components of Change
in Mexican Origin Population (1970–1980)
and Change Due to Immigration (in thousands)*

Row Label	Description	Formula	Count or Percentage
A	Mexican Origin Population: 1980 Census	*	8,740
B	Misreporting of Mexican Origin: 1980 Census[a]	*	200
C	Estimated Number of Undocumented Mexicans Included in 1980 Census[b]	*	1,130
D	Coverage Improvement: 1980 Census Over 1970 Census[b]	*	100
E	Adjusted 1980 Legal Mexican Origin Population	A-B-C-D	7,310
F	Mexican Origin Population: 1970 Census	*	4,530
G	Estimate of 1970 Classification Error[c]	*	500
H	Adjusted 1970 Mexican Origin Population	F + G	5,030
I	1970 to 1980 Legal Increase	E-H	2,280
J	Number of Legal Immigrants from Mexico as of April 1, 1980[b]	*	575
K	Number of Mexican Illegal Immigrants in 1980 who entered 1970–1980[b]	*	902
L	1970 to 1980 Total Increase	I + K	3,182
M	Total Immigration as a Percentage of Total Increase	K + J/L	46.4%
N	Legal Immigration as a Percentage of Legal Increase	J/I	25.2%

[a]U.S. Bureau of the Census, "Persons of Spanish Origin by State: 1980," Supplementary Report, PC80-S1-7 (Washington, DC: U.S. Government Printing Office, 1982).
[b]Robert Warren and Jeffrey S. Passel, "A Count of the Uncountable: Estimates of Undocumented Aliens Counted in the 1980 United States Census," *Demography* (forthcoming).
[c]Jeffrey S. Passel, personal communication, 1986.

*Not applicable.

3.2).[14] Also, the 1970 enumeration gave low results compared with totals from CPS surveys taken just before and after the census (row G).[15] Taking all of these factors into account, we find that a more "accurate" amount of increase over the decade would be about 2.3 million rather than 4.2 million persons (row I), assuming that we base our calculations on legal persons only. The figure would be about 3.2 million persons (row L) if we based them on both legal and illegal persons. The former represents an increase of 45.3 percent over the decade, and the latter an

[14]Warren and Passel, "Count of the Uncountable."
[15]Jeffrey S. Passel, personal communication, 1986.

increase of 63.3 percent. Certainly the former is more consistent with "plausibility" than is the 93 percent increase that is obtained if none of these complicating factors is taken into consideration. Finally, when we calculate immigration as a percentage of increase, we obtain figures of 46.4 percent and 25.2 percent (rows M and N), depending on whether or not we include estimates of the number of illegal immigrants coming to the United States during the decade in our calculations.[16] In either case,

FIGURE 3.3

Age-Sex Composition of the Hispanic Population: 1980

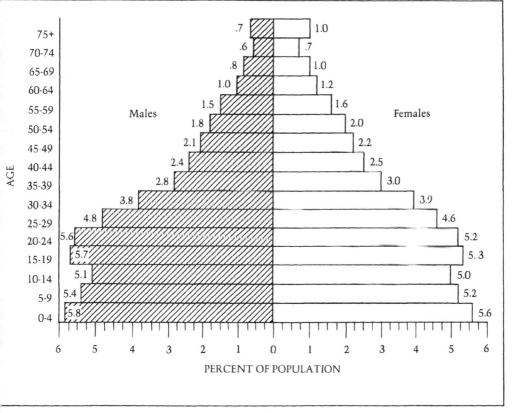

SOURCE: U.S. Bureau of the Census, *Census of Population: 1980* "Age, Sex, Race and Spanish Origin of the Population by Regions, Divisions, and States: 1980," Supplementary Report, PC80-S1-1 (Washington, DC: U.S. Government Printing Office, 1981).

[16]Warren and Passel, "Count of the Uncountable."

however, measured immigration represents less than half of the measured population increase from 1970 to 1980.

Our contention that immigration was responsible for less than half (and substantially less than half in the case of legal immigration) of the growth of the Mexican origin population finds further support in Figures 3.3–3.5, which show how recent immigration (1970–1980) and that prior to 1970 altered the age-sex pyramid of the Mexican origin population. The wide base shows the influence of high fertility during the 1960s and before. Compared with the base of the total U.S. population pyramid,

FIGURE 3.4

Age-Sex Composition of the Total U.S. Population: 1980

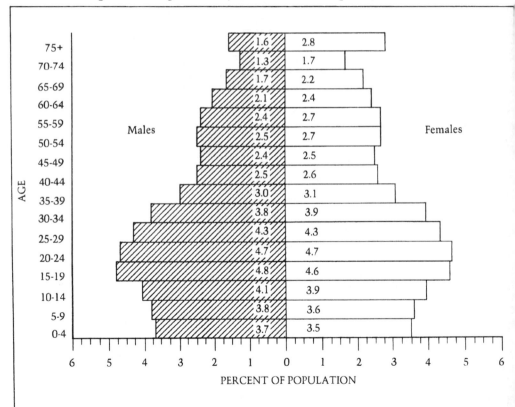

SOURCE: U.S. Bureau of the Census, *Census of Population: 1980* "Age, Sex, Race and Spanish Origin of the Population by Regions, Divisions, and States: 1980, " Supplementary Report, PC80-S1-1 (Washington DC: U.S. Government Printing Office, 1981).

FIGURE 3.5

Age-Sex Composition of Persons of Mexican Origin by Nativity: 1980

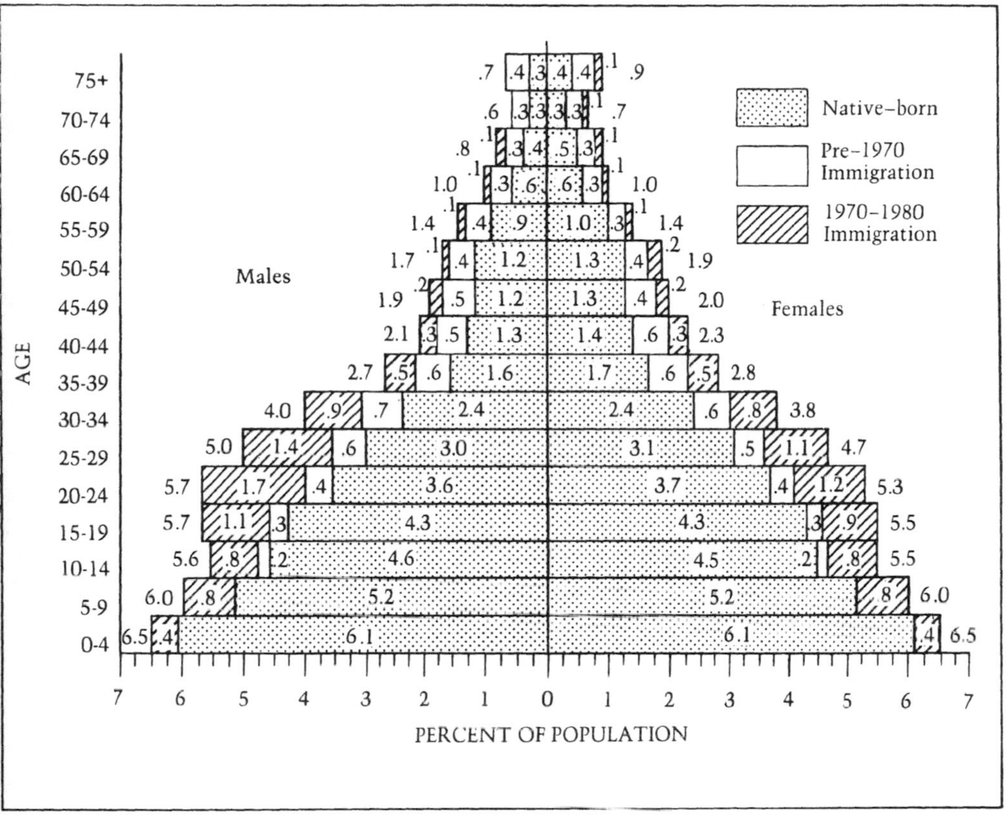

AGE	Males				Females			
					Native–born			
					Pre–1970 Immigration			
					1970–1980 Immigration			
75+		.7	.4 .3 .4 .4	.1	.9			
70-74		.6	.3 .3 .3	.1	.7			
65-69		.8	.1 .3 .4 .5 .3	.1				
60-64	1.0	.1	.3 .6 .6 .3	1.0				
55-59	1.4	.1	.4 .9 1.0 .3	.1 1.4				
50-54	1.7	.1	.4 1.2 1.3 .4	1.9				
45-49	1.9	.2	.5 1.2 1.3 .4	.2 2.0				
40-44	2.1	.3	.5 1.3 1.4 .6	.3 2.3				
35-39	2.7	.5	.6 1.6 1.7 .6	.5 2.8				
30-34	4.0	.9	.7 2.4 2.4 .6	.8 3.8				
25-29	5.0	1.4	.6 3.0 3.1 .5	1.1 4.7				
20-24	5.7	1.7	.4 3.6 3.7 .4	1.2 5.3				
15-19	5.7	1.1	.3 4.3 4.3 .3	.9 5.5				
10-14	5.6	.8	.2 4.6 4.5 .2	.8 5.5				
5-9	6.0	.8	5.2 5.2	.8 6.0				
0-4	6.5	.4	6.1 6.1	.4 6.5				

PERCENT OF POPULATION
7 6 5 4 3 2 1 0 1 2 3 4 5 6 7

SOURCE: 1980 Public Use Microdata Sample A file.

that of Mexicans is much wider. Moreover, at ages 14 and under, the foreign-born never reach one fifth of the age-sex population segment; for ages 15 to 44 the foreign-born constitute anywhere from 22 to 41 percent of the respective age-sex segment. As a result of the changing age structure of recent immigrants and the aging of earlier immigrants, the foreign-born Mexican origin population became more youthful between 1960 and 1980, with the median age declining from 42 in 1960 to 29 in 1980 (Table 3.3). Recent Mexican immigration largely involved young adults, but women participated more in recent streams than they did in the past.

TABLE 3.3

Median Age of the Hispanic Population by Type of Origin and Nativity: 1960–1980

	1960			1970			1980		
	Native	Foreign	Total	Native	Foreign	Total	Native	Foreign	Total
Mexican	15.1	42.0	18.4	16.7	34.7	19.3	17.0	28.9	20.5
Puerto Rican	4.6	26.7	20.4	8.4	28.6	18.4	11.8	32.7	20.9
Cuban	16.0	32.6	29.3	9.6	35.2	29.5	11.4	43.1	36.5
Central/South American	10.7	30.7	24.8	8.2	29.1	24.4	7.9	30.3	27.8
Other Hispanic	35.2	56.0	46.3	29.2	44.2	34.8	19.6	34.3	22.3
Total	13.9	32.9	18.8	14.9	31.8	20.2	16.7	31.0	19.5

SOURCE: 1980 Public Use Microdata Sample A file.

Puerto Ricans. In a strict sense it is not possible to discuss the role of immigration in contributing to the growth of the Puerto Rican population during the 1970s. However, net migration between the mainland and island can contribute to increase in the mainland population. And, indeed, the movement of Puerto Ricans between the island and the mainland is not trivial, as evidenced by the fact that fully half of the Puerto Rican origin population residing in the continental United States in 1980 was born in Puerto Rico (see Chapter 4).

Unfortunately, the Census Bureau did not collect information about the timing of first arrival on the mainland for Puerto Ricans, but the data on residence five years ago allow us to approximate the recency of arrival of island-born residents. These tabulations showed that nearly 8 percent of island-born Puerto Ricans residing on the mainland at the time of the census had arrived between 1975 and 1980 (see Chapter 4). It is quite likely that many of these "recent migrants" are repeat rather than first-time migrants, but the empirical evidence for the phenomenon of circular migration is scanty, and census data are inadequate to address this question.

If we assumed, simply for the sake of argument, that the movement of Puerto Ricans from the island to the mainland was uniform during both five-year intervals, and that return migration was also constant throughout the period (an unlikely assumption), the net migration could have accounted for anywhere between 12 and 15 percent of the intercensal change in Puerto Rican population, or 70,000 to 88,000 persons. This leaves over 80 percent of the total net increase of 585,000 to be explained by natural increase and by improvements in the coverage of the Puerto Rican population in 1980.

By and large, this description of the components of population change among Puerto Ricans is consistent with that put forth by others. For example, Willette and her associates estimated that net migration between Puerto Rico and the U.S. mainland had slowed considerably from its peak during the 1950–1960 decade, when net migration from the island to the mainland was estimated at roughly 470,000 to 209,000 during the 1960s and 47,000 during the 1970s.[17]

The Puerto Rican age-sex pyramid, which has a large base, points to the importance of fertility in the growth of the population. Figure 3.6 shows that the impact of migration on the age-sex structure dominates

FIGURE 3.6
Age-Sex Composition of Persons of Puerto Rican Origin by Birthplace: 1980

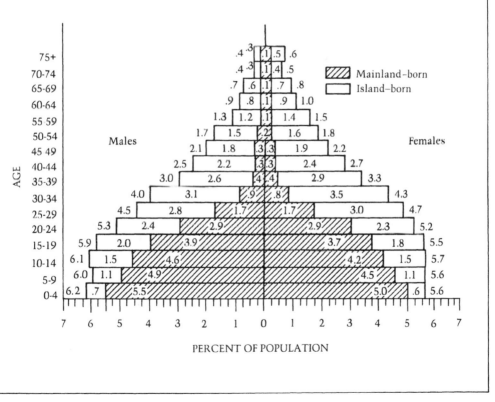

SOURCE: 1980 Public Use Microdata Sample A file.

[17]Willette et al., "Demographic and Socioeconomic Characteristics," table 2-7, p. 50.

the population segment over age 29, thus indicating that migration between the island and the mainland largely involved adults. From this information and from that in Table 3.3 showing changes in the median ages by nativity, we can see that the Puerto Rican population is less generationally diverse than the Mexican origin population. The median age of Puerto Ricans born on the U.S. mainland rose from 4.6 in 1960 to 11.8 in 1980, but the 20-year age differential between the island- and mainland-born segments of this population remained relatively stable over the 1960–1980 period.

Cubans. In some ways, estimating the growth rate for the Cuban population during the 1970s is less problematic than it is for Mexicans because the role of immigration is straightforward. Also, the coverage problems for this group in 1970 appear to have been less serious. The Immigration and Naturalization Service (INS) reported that approximately 277,000 Cubans were legally admitted to the United States between 1971 and 1980—and prior to the Mariel boatlift.[18] That the more than 120,000 Cubans who entered during the sealift in the spring of 1980 were not counted in the 1980 census further simplifies the task of sorting out the components of growth of the Cuban population during the most recent intercensal decade. Census data on the timing of arrival (see Chapter 4) show that approximately 20 percent, or roughly 167,000 Cubans, entered during the 1970s.[19]

Two striking features of the Cuban population are its largely foreign character and its relatively older age composition (Figure 3.7). The dramatic increase of the Cuban population over a two-decade period— roughly a 220 percent increase—was possible because at the time of Castro's revolutionary victory in 1959 the size of the Cuban population in the United States was quite small, just over 200,000. A large volume of adult migration during the 1960s and 1970s and a relatively low fertility level explain the high median age of this population. The influence of low Cuban fertility levels on the base of the population pyramid stands in sharp contrast to those of Mexican, Puerto Rican, and Other Hispanic origin groups.

[18]U.S. Department of Justice, *Statistical Yearbook of the Immigration and Naturalization Service: 1980* (Washington, DC: U.S. Government Printing Office, 1981), table 13.

[19]This figure is approximately 110,000 less than the number of official admissions reported by the Immigration and Naturalization Service. At first blush, this discrepancy appears to be substantial and highly discrepant with the census enumeration which indicates a net change of 258,626 over the 10-year period. To interpret these discrepancies requires some understanding of the refugee character of Cuban immigration which largely has been governed by a series of legislative mandates specifying the conditions under which refugees are entitled to apply for legal resident status. Not only does admission as a refugee not automatically confer an applicant legal alien status, but the waiting period required to initiate adjustment of status proceedings has itself varied over time. These circumstances complicate the estimation of net immigration for Cubans and other refugees.

FIGURE 3.7

Age-Sex Composition of Persons of Cuban Origin by Nativity: 1980

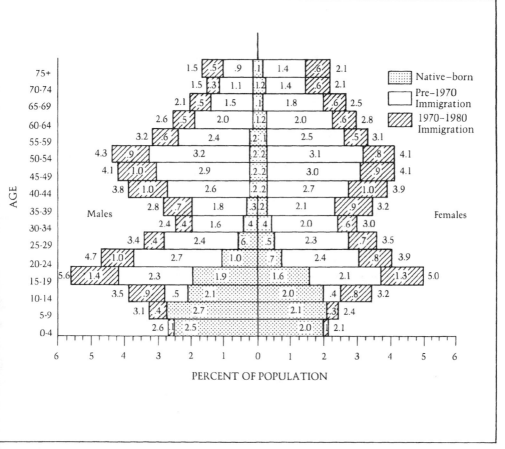

The age-sex pyramids and the nativity composition of the Cuban population suggest two conclusions about the components of growth. First, natural increase through fertility, although a smaller component than that observed among other Hispanic origin groups, has contributed to the growth of the Cuban population during the 1970s. By 1980 almost 25 percent of all Cubans were U.S.-born compared with nearly 40 percent in 1960,[20] when the population base was much smaller. That the proportion of foreign-born Cubans did not change much during the

[20]Special tabulations of the 1960 and 1970 Public Use Samples.

71

1970s suggests that natural increase and immigration were of nearly equal importance in contributing to population growth between 1970 and 1980.

Second, and largely because of the refugee character of Cuban immigration, the role of immigration in increasing the size of the Cuban population diminished gradually, after having reached a peak during the 1965–1969 period. This diminishing flow is consistent with the political and institutional barriers imposed on the emigration of Cubans from their homeland, but it does not preclude sudden and unexpected refugee flows, such as that which occurred during the spring of 1980. The Mariel refugee population, estimated to number over 125,000,[21] surely will manifest itself as an important component of population growth in the 1990 census, not only because these individuals raised the size of the post-census Cuban population to over 1 million, but because many will themselves contribute to the growing native-born Cuban population through their fertility.

Central and South Americans. Although the coverage error of Hispanics in 1970 seems to have been most severe for Mexicans, for Central and South Americans the error apparently resulted in an overcount of this group. This overcount stemmed from a misunderstanding of the response category "Central and South American" by many persons residing in central and southern regions of the United States. This source of coverage error, essentially a classification error, partly explains the apparently slower growth of what the Census Bureau terms the Other Hispanic population between 1970 and 1980 and led to a decision not to include a separate response category for Central and South Americans in 1980.[22]

The Central and South American population is the only group for which immigration clearly was the dominant component of population growth between 1970 and 1980. In 1980 recent immigrants constituted well over half (60 percent) of the Central and South American population born abroad (see Chapter 4). Inasmuch as this group constituted less than 8 percent of the total Hispanic population in both 1970 and 1980, immigration from Central and South American countries represented less than 25 percent of the growth of the total foreign-born Hispanic population during the 1970s,[23] even though it was the most prominent source of growth for this segment of the population during the 1970s.

---

[21]Robert L. Bach, "The New Cuban Immigrants: Their Background and Prospects," *Monthly Labor Review* 103 (1980):30–46.

[22]Some perspective on the magnitude of the error is afforded by comparing the estimates of the Central and South Americans based on the Current Population Surveys taken just prior to and following the 1970 census. This problem explains why Census Bureau tabulations do not differentiate between Central/South Americans and Other Hispanics after 1976.

[23]See Davis et al., "U.S. Hispanics," table 11.

Immigration and Naturalization Service statistics show that about 900,000 persons were legally admitted from Central and South America between 1970 and 1980.[24] Compared with the estimated size of the 1980 Central/South American population of 1.1 million and under the assumption of no emigration, the 900,000 immigration figure suggests a Central/South American population of approximately 200,000 in 1970. This population estimate is roughly 350,000 less than the estimate of 550,000 based on the 1969 Current Population Survey.[25] Although the coverage errors for the Central and South American origin population in 1970 render it difficult, if not impossible, to estimate the intercensal growth of this segment of the Hispanic population, the preliminary evidence indicates that emigration may be important in offsetting demographic increase of this group due to immigration.

The supplementary information in Figure 3.8 and in Table 3.3 shows the impact on the age-sex structure of a rising level of adult migration throughout the 1970s. Clearly, immigration was the major component of growth during the most recent intercensal period, and for the 25–29 age segment, three persons in every four were recent immigrants. At the same time, the darkened interior of the age-sex pyramid shows a growing base of native-born persons whose ancestors were from Central or South America. By 1980 the native-born segment of this population constituted one fifth of the total. Should the levels of immigration from Central and South America witnessed during the 1970s continue throughout the 1980s, this group could become one of the fastest growing in the country. The youthfulness of its population will be maintained by a relatively small, but growing segment of native-born offspring (see Table 3.3), whose median age declined from 10.7 years in 1960 to just under 8 years in 1980.

Other Hispanics. In the case of the population of Other Hispanic origin, which in 1980 was as large as the Cuban and Central/South American population combined, immigration played a small part in the measured intercensal growth. Presumably, a large proportion of the foreign-born in this group are from Spain, but this residual group also includes mixed and part Hispanics who were born in other countries. Our tabulations show that 8.5 percent of the enumerated Other Hispanics population consisted of recent immigrants—the lowest share of the five major groups—which amounts to approximately 170,000 new arrivals. Of these, nearly 40,000, or 24 percent, were immigrants from Spain, and the remainder were Hispanics of other nationalities who were born in countries other than those of their ancestors.

[24]U.S. Department of Justice, *Statistical Yearbook*, table 13.
[25]U.S. Bureau of the Census, "Persons of Spanish Origin in the United States: November, 1969," *Current Population Reports*, series P-20, no. 213 (Washington, DC: U.S. Government Printing Office, 1971).

FIGURE 3.8

Age-Sex Composition of Persons of Central/South American Origin by Nativity: 19

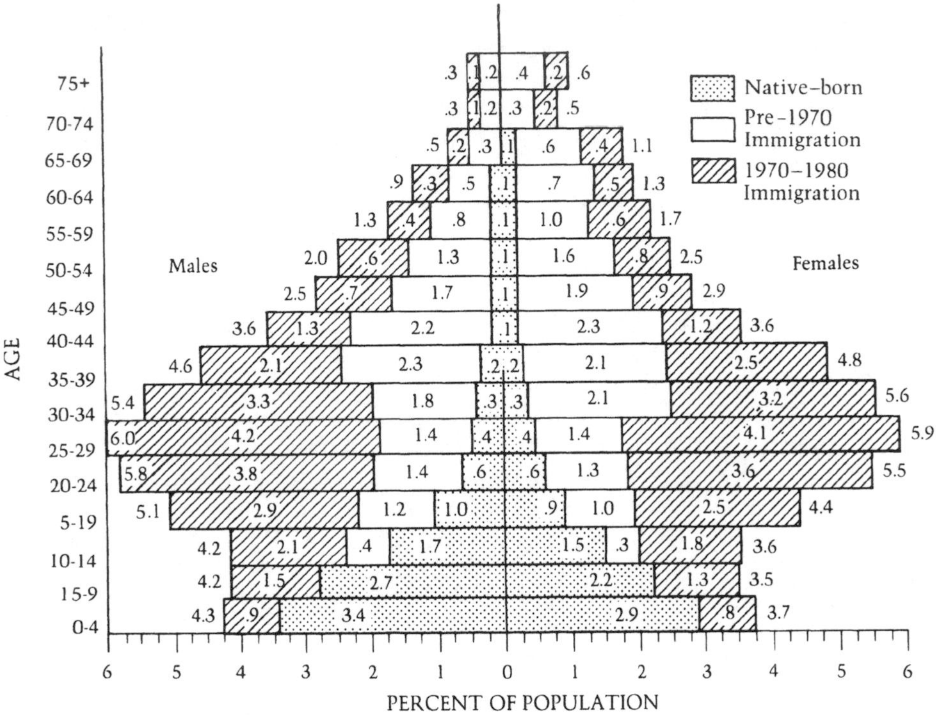

AGE / PERCENT OF POPULATION

Males — Females

Legend:
Native–born
Pre-1970 Immigration
1970–1980 Immigration

Age	Males				Females		
75+		.3	1.2	.4	1.2	.6	
70-74		.3	1.2	.3	1.2	.5	
65-69		.5	.2 .3	.1	.6	.4	1.1
60-64		.9	.3 .5	.1	.7	.5	1.3
55-59		1.3	.4 .8	.1	1.0	.6	1.7
50-54	2.0	.6	1.3	.1	1.6	.8	2.5
45-49	2.5	.7	1.7	.1	1.9	.9	2.9
40-44	3.6	1.3	2.2	.1	2.3	1.2	3.6
35-39	4.6	2.1	2.3	.2 .2	2.1	2.5	4.8
30-34	5.4	3.3	1.8	.3 .3	2.1	3.2	5.6
25-29	6.0	4.2	1.4	.4 .4	1.4	4.1	5.9
20-24	5.8	3.8	1.4	.6 .6	1.3	3.6	5.5
5-19	5.1	2.9	1.2	1.0 .9	1.0	2.5	4.4
10-14	4.2	2.1	.4 1.7	1.5 .3	1.8	3.6	
15-9	4.2	1.5	2.7	2.2	1.3	3.5	
0-4	4.3	.9	3.4	2.9	.8	3.7	

PERCENT OF POPULATION 6 5 4 3 2 1 0 1 2 3 4 5 6

SOURCE: 1980 Public Use Microdata Sample A file.

Evaluating the role of natural increase and immigration for this segment of the Hispanic population has some of the complexities (resulting from classification error) described for the Mexicans and the Central and South Americans. The most serious problems stem from the difficulty of differentiating third- and later-generation Mexican Americans from Other Hispanics who trace their ancestry to the original Spanish settlers (called Hispanos) and the difficulty of sorting mixed from part Hispanics. These problems notwithstanding, if we use the 1969 CPS estimate of 1.6 million Other Hispanics as a point of reference, the gross intercensal increase in this segment of the population was relatively small, or approximately 418,000. Despite the problems encountered in trying to define consistently this population over time, even a very simple scenario about the components of population change shows that immigration probably accounted for less than one third of the total increase during the period. That is, of the approximately 420,000 net increase in the number of Other Hispanics between 1970 and 1980, continued immigration of Spanish-speaking people from Spain and other countries could have at most produced one third of the total increase, while the remainder was due either to natural increase or to improved coverage of the population in the latter census.

The Other Hispanic group had the largest share of native-born persons in 1980, when four respondents in five reported a U.S. birthplace.

FIGURE 3.9

Age-Sex Composition of Persons of Other Hispanic Origin by Nativity: 1980

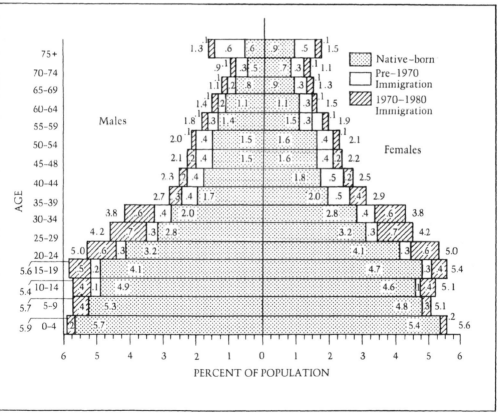

SOURCE: Public Use Microdata Sample A file.

In 1960 almost half of this population was foreign-born, while by 1970 only one Other Hispanic in three was an immigrant. The impact of recent adult migration on the age-sex structure of this group was most pronounced for the group aged 25 to 34 (Figure 3.9), but in no instance did immigrants' share of these age segments ever exceed 20 percent. In 1960 the Other Hispanic group was the oldest of the major nationalities—largely reflecting the impact of adult migration—but with the slowdown of adult migration from Europe, and relatively high fertility during the 1960s, the median age of this group dropped to third place by 1980, exceeded by that of Cubans and that of Central and South Americans.

Summary of Components of Growth

On balance, these numerical exercises are useful in illustrating that, while the Hispanic population grew rapidly during the 1970s, a nontrivial amount of the net change reflects improved coverage of the population in the 1980 census. While this is no longer a disputed point,[26] our general discussion of the components of growth has attempted to put into perspective interpretations of the measured increase in the Hispanic population for the Mexican, Puerto Rican, Cuban, Central/South American, and Other Hispanic populations. Many users of census data, while acknowledging the 1970 undercount problem, present growth rates based on net change as though the reported increase represented "true" growth. Even more serious misunderstandings concerning the future size of the Hispanic population result from basing population projections on the changes in the size of the Hispanic population measured between 1970 and 1980, as some organizations have done.[27] The impact of immigration on intercensal growth has also been misunderstood. What seems clear from the evidence presented above, however, is that immigration probably was not the major source of growth for the Hispanic population during the 1970s, although its impact was quite significant, particularly for the Mexican, Cuban, and Central/South American groups. That other sources of growth were often more important even when the volume of immigration from Mexico and Central and South America was increasing during the 1970s only underscores the need to exercise caution in attributing the major causes of growth rates for the Hispanic populations during the 1970–1980 intercensal period to immigration.

[26]Siegel and Passel, "Coverage of the Hispanic Population."
[27]See, for example, the Hispanic Policy Development Project, *Hispanic Almanac.*

Residential Distribution of the Total Hispanic Population
by State: 1980 (absolute numbers)

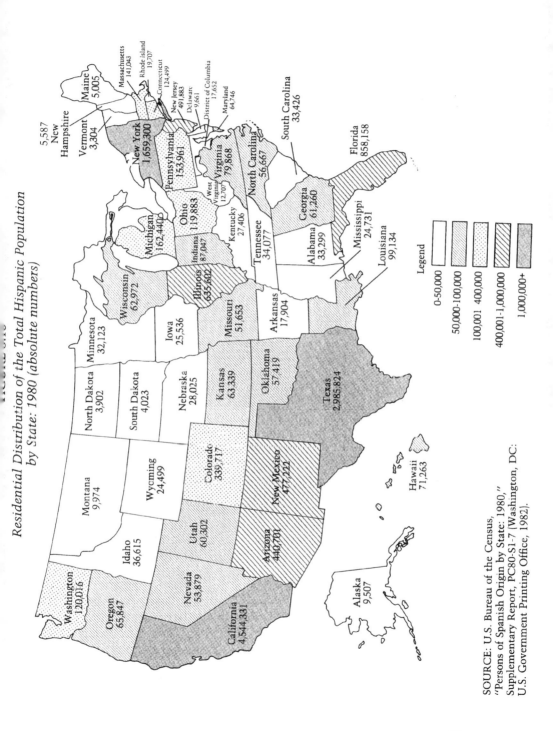

Legend

0-50,000

50,000-100,000

100,001-400,000

400,001-1,000,000

1,000,000+

Maine 5,005
New Hampshire 5,587
Vermont 3,304
Massachusetts 141,043
Rhode Island 19,707
Connecticut 124,499
New Jersey 491,883
Delaware 9,661
District of Columbia 17,652
Maryland 64,746
New York 1,659,300
Pennsylvania 153,961
West Virginia 12,707
Virginia 79,868
North Carolina 56,667
South Carolina 33,426
Florida 858,158
Michigan 162,440
Ohio 119,883
Indiana 87,047
Kentucky 27,406
Tennessee 34,077
Georgia 61,260
Alabama 33,299
Mississippi 24,731
Louisiana 99,134
Wisconsin 62,972
Minnesota 32,123
Illinois 635,602
Iowa 25,536
Missouri 51,653
Arkansas 17,904
North Dakota 3,902
South Dakota 4,023
Nebraska 28,025
Kansas 63,339
Oklahoma 57,419
Texas 2,985,824
Montana 9,974
Wyoming 24,499
Colorado 339,717
New Mexico 477,222
Idaho 36,615
Utah 60,302
Arizona 440,701
Washington 120,016
Oregon 65,847
Nevada 53,879
California 4,544,331
Hawaii 71,263
Alaska 9,507

SOURCE: U.S. Bureau of the Census,
"Persons of Spanish Origin by State: 1980,"
Supplementary Report, PC80-S1-7 (Washington, DC:
U.S. Government Printing Office, 1982).

FIGURE 3.11

Distribution of the Hispanic Population by Type of Origin by State: 1980

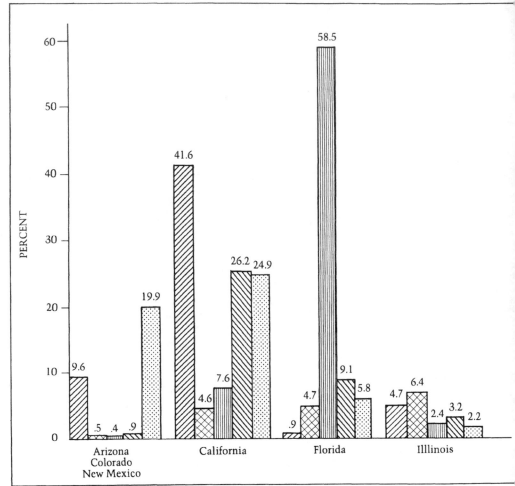

Geographic Distribution of the Hispanic Population: 1960–1980

Regional concentration in the Southwest, the Northeast, Florida, and Illinois is a second distinguishing feature of the Hispanic population (see Figure 3.10). In 1980 over half of the nation's Hispanics lived in two states alone—California and Texas—and an additional 17 percent resided in New York and Florida. Stated differently, in 1980 over two

FIGURE 3.11 *(continued)*

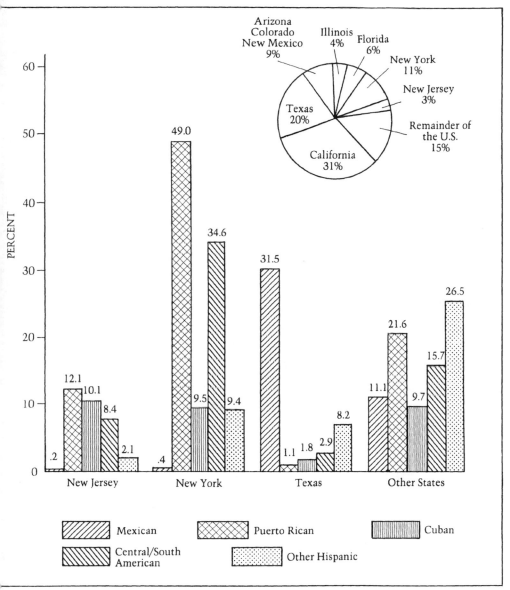

OURCES: U.S. Bureau of the Census, "Persons of Spanish Origin by State: 1980," Supplementary Report,
C80-S1-7 (Washington, DC: U.S. Government Printing Office, 1982); *The Condition of Hispanics in
America Today* (Washington, DC: U.S. Government Printing Office, 1984); and special tabulations of 1980
ublic Use Microdata Sample files.

thirds (69 percent) of the Hispanic population resided in just four states compared with 66 percent in 1970. This general tendency toward increasing concentration among the four states with the largest Hispanic population was offset by a tendency toward dispersion among states that previously contained fewer Hispanics, such as Illinois, New Jersey, Colorado, and several others.[28] On balance, however, these geographic movements had not yet gained momentum during the 1970s, and thus did not alter in any appreciable way the historical concentration of Mexicans and Other Hispanics in the Southwest and of Puerto Ricans in the Northeast. Because the aggregate tendency toward concentration or dispersion can easily mask movements in opposite directions among the national origin groups, we delineate in broad terms below, and in greater detail in Chapter 5, differences in the residential distributions of Mexicans, Puerto Ricans, Cubans, Central/South Americans, and Other Hispanics. Appendix Table B.1 summarizes the relative changes in the state distribution of the total Hispanic population between 1960 and 1980.

Regional Configuration

As Figure 3.11 shows, 85 percent of all Hispanics resided in just 9 states in 1980, while 15 percent were distributed among the remaining 41 states. Compared with 1970, when 82 percent of the Hispanic population lived in these 9 states, the aggregate net residential shift shows greater geographic concentration. However, because of coverage and classification errors in 1970, it is unclear whether this increased concentration represents a real net change or whether it is an artifact of the 1970 underenumeration of Mexicans—most of whom resided in the Southwest.[29]

A somewhat different dimension of the geographic concentration of Hispanics emerges from a comparison of their national origin distribution among states (bar graphs of Figure 3.11) and from an examination of the interdecade change in the Hispanic density of states (Figure 3.12). Among the nine states of highest Hispanic concentration, Mexicans predominated in California and Texas in 1980, as they have since the mid-1800s. Roughly four fifths (83 percent) of all persons of Mexican origin resided in one of the five southwestern states, a proportion slightly below the 1970 figure of 87 percent.[30] Illinois was the preferred state of residence by Mexicans living outside the Southwest in both 1970 and

[28]Hispanic Policy Development Project, *Hispanic Almanac*, p. 23.
[29]If the increased geographic concentration of Hispanics during the 1970s is real change, it would arise from differential growth rates of the various national origin groups, immigrants' residential preferences for areas with large Hispanic populations, and the growing attractiveness of Florida as the preferred state of residence for Cubans.
[30]U.S. Bureau of the Census, "Persons of Spanish Origin," table 7.

FIGURE 3.12

Percentage Hispanic of Total Population by State: 1970–1980

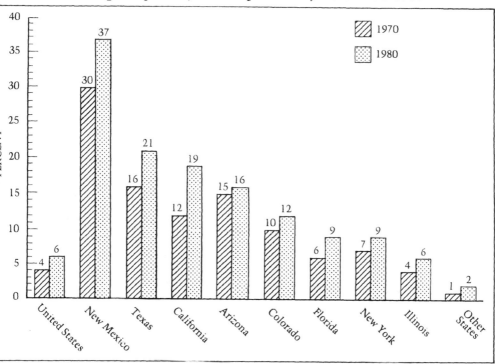

SOURCE: U.S. Bureau of the Census, *The Condition of Hispanics in America Today* (Washington, DC: U.S. Government Printing Office, 1984), chart 6, p. 5.

1980, but because of the seasonal migrant farmworker streams which flourished throughout the 1960s, the presence of Mexican origin people is clearly discernible as well in other midwestern states—Michigan, Ohio, Indiana, Illinois, and Iowa.

As in all previous decades since they were granted U.S. citizenship, Puerto Ricans in 1980 were disproportionately concentrated in the Northeast, with New York and New Jersey accounting for 60 percent and Illinois another 6 percent of the total mainland population. A decade before, in 1970, these three states housed nearly 80 percent of all Puerto Ricans, providing evidence of considerable residential dispersion during the 1970s. While the share of Puerto Ricans residing in Illinois remained stable over the decade, the proportion residing in New York and New Jersey declined considerably. For New Jersey this implied an absolute as well as a relative loss, but the number of Puerto Ricans residing in New York increased (from 916,000 to 986,000) between 1970 and 1980, despite the decline in the relative share of the total who lived there.[31]

Unlike Puerto Ricans and, to a lesser extent Mexicans, who participated in a process of residential dispersion away from states of traditional concentration, Cubans became more concentrated in a single state—Florida—whose climate and geographic proximity to Cuba enable the population to approximate the milieu of the home country more so than is the case for New York or any of the midwestern states. Whereas in 1970 just under half (46 percent) of all Cubans resided in Florida, by 1980 this proportion climbed to nearly 60 percent. During this period the percentage of Cubans living in New Jersey and New York declined from 12.5 to 10.1 percent and from 16.5 to 9.6 percent, respectively. In the latter instance an absolute decline (from 90,000 to 77,000) produced the observed decrease, while in the case of New Jersey the slight relative decline occurred despite a modest absolute increase in the size of the Cuban population.[32]

Because of the coverage problems of Central/South Americans in 1970, and because published tabulations based on the 1980 census do not differentiate this segment of the Spanish origin population from Other Hispanics, it is difficult to comment on the interdecade changes in the residential configuration of these groups. However, Figure 3.11, based on special tabulations from the 1980 Public Use Microdata Sample files, illustrates clear differences in the 1980 residential configurations of Central and South Americans versus Other Hispanics. The former were disproportionately concentrated in New York, while the latter were disproportionately located in the Southwest, where over half (53 percent) of the total resided in 1980. California, which housed roughly half of each group in 1980, was the only state where these two segments of the 1980 Hispanic population intersected to any considerable degree.

The disproportionate presence of Other Hispanics in Colorado, New Mexico, and Arizona, coupled with the virtual absence of Central and South Americans from these states, serves to differentiate these two groups. Also, the Other Hispanic group, which is very diverse in its generational and national origin composition, was more highly represented among states other than the nine which house the majority of the population. From these data, however, it is unclear whether this resulted from increasing dispersion of this group over time or whether this has been the case historically.

The social significance of residential concentration is that it allows for the maintenance of group cohesion and identity through the rein-

[31]U.S. Bureau of the Census, "Persons of Spanish Origin," table 8.
[32]U.S. Bureau of the Census, "Persons of Spanish Origin," table 9.

forcement of ethnic norms and that it renders the Hispanic population more visible than if it were uniformly distributed throughout the United States. Hispanic residential concentration occurs in several regions of the country, although different national origin groups are dominant in each, and makes them appear as a national rather than a regional minority, as was so long the case for the Mexican and, to some extent, the Puerto Rican origin groups. However, it is not only the share of the total Hispanic population residing in a given state which determines the nature and extent of Hispanic cultural influence, but also the Hispanic concentration within states.

Figure 3.12 provides a temporal perspective on this dimension of the Hispanic residential concentration phenomenon. During the 1970s, when the Hispanic share of the total population increased from 4 to 6 percent, the increase in proportion Hispanic ranged from 1 to 2 percent in Arizona, Colorado, New York, and Illinois, and from 5 to 7 percent in Texas, New Mexico, and California. Because Texas and California share boundaries with Mexico and serve as major ports of entry for immigrants from Mexico and Central and South America, the increased Hispanic concentration is less surprising than that observed for New Mexico.[33]

What is striking about Figure 3.12 are the compositional differences among the nine states where 85 percent of all Hispanics live. New Mexico, which by itself housed only 3.3 percent of the total Spanish origin population in 1980, had a Hispanic/non-Hispanic ratio of 1 to 3. This is much higher than the Hispanic/non-Hispanic ratio of 1 to 5 in California and Texas. Although the impact of the Hispanic presence within states also is determined by patterns of residential segregation at the level of cities, districts, and census tracts, higher aggregate Hispanic concentrations provide the ecological basis for the maintenance of a Hispanic ethnic culture. In that sense, "Hispanic ethnicity" will likely continue to flourish in the Southwest, where the absolute and relative size of the Spanish origin population has increased rapidly and where the historical antecedents for the Hispanic presence are more deeply rooted.

That the Hispanic concentration in Florida and New York was less than 10 percent in 1980 does not constitute evidence of a less significant Hispanic impact in these states. Here it is precisely the intrastate concentration of Hispanics—Cubans in Miami, and Puerto Ricans and Central/South Americans in New York City—that distinguishes the Spanish

---

[33]Part of this observed increase could also be an artifact of the underenumeration of people of Mexican origin in 1970 and the inclusion of undocumented migrants from Latin America in 1980, many of whom were of Mexican origin.

origin people from other ethnic groups and makes these nationalities visible within a multiethnic context.

In assessing the intercensal change in the Hispanic concentration among states, one should bear in mind that the meaning of a 2 or 3 percent change in Hispanic concentration depends on the proportion of the population that is Hispanic at the beginning of the decade. In states like Florida and Illinois, where the 1970 Hispanic concentration was relatively low, a 2 to 3 percent change could signify a more substantial ethnic imprint than a comparable change in a state like New Mexico or Texas. This is so for two reasons. First, a small change in the Spanish origin composition of low concentration states, if sustained for a period of time, could significantly alter the ethnic configuration of these states. Second, a compositional change of this order of magnitude marks the entry of Hispanics into traditionally non-Hispanic states and thus contributes to the acceptance and acknowledgment of Hispanics as a (numerical) minority.

Metro-Nonmetro Residence

Another noteworthy dimension of the geographic distribution of the Hispanic population is their allocation between metropolitan and nonmetropolitan areas and, within the former, their relative concentration in central cities. The social significance of this aspect of residential distribution derives from the nature of economic opportunities associated with different labor markets, as well as from the range of possibilities for elaborating ethnic concerns in different ecological niches. The social and economic characteristics of the top 20 Hispanic labor markets are discussed in some length in the *Hispanic Almanac*,[34] and thus we do not elaborate them here. Rather, our modest purpose is to lay the foundation for our more detailed treatment of the recent internal migration patterns of Hispanics by summarizing the changes in the distribution of the major national origin groups between metropolitan and nonmetropolitan areas and briefly commenting on their social and economic significance.

Although Hispanics are largely a metropolitan population—more so than the non-Hispanic white population[35]—this generalization particularly applies to the Puerto Rican, Cuban, and Central/South American segments of the population, as shown in Table 3.4. Because the wage

[34]Hispanic Policy Development Project, *Hispanic Almanac*.
[35]Marta Tienda, "The Mexican American Population," in Amos Hawley and Sara Mills Mazie, eds., *Nonmetropolitan America in Transition* (Chapel Hill: University of North Carolina Press, 1981).

TABLE 3.4
Metro and Nonmetro Residential Distribution
of the Hispanic Population by National Origin: 1960–1980

	1960		1970		1980	
	Metro	Nonmetro	Metro	Nonmetro	Metro	Nonmetro
Mexican	73.6%	26.4%	83.1%	16.9%	80.9%	18.1%
Puerto Rican	96.1	3.9	96.4	3.6	95.8	4.2
Cuban	93.6	6.4	94.0	6.0	93.8	6.2
Central/South American	91.0	9.0	94.7	5.3	96.2	3.8
Other Hispanic	79.8	20.2	73.4	26.6	77.5	22.5

SOURCE: 1960, 1970, and 1980 Public Use Microdata Sample files.

labor streams between Puerto Rico and the U.S. mainland historically have been destined for New York City, Puerto Ricans have been metropolitan residents since the postwar migration flows began. As early as 1960, 96 percent of all Puerto Ricans resided in metropolitan areas—the New York SMSA in particular—and by 1980 this share remained about the same. Cubans are similar to Puerto Ricans with regard to their metropolitan residence pattern. As early as 1960, 94 Cubans in every 100 resided in metropolitan areas, the same figure as in 1980.

Central/South Americans were slightly more likely than Puerto Ricans and Cubans to reside in metropolitan areas in 1980. The main difference between this group, on the one hand, and the Puerto Ricans and Cubans, on the other, is that in the case of the latter groups the high level of metropolitan residence evident in 1980 involved relatively little net change over the previous two decades. This does not mean that Cubans and Puerto Ricans have been geographically immobile during the past two decades. Rather, the internal migration streams of the Cuban and Puerto Rican population involved mainly move between metropolitan areas than between nonmetropolitan and metropolitan areas.

Central and South Americans, on the other hand, experienced a somewhat higher rate of metropolitanization during the 1960s and 1970s. Whereas in 1960, 91 percent of this group resided in metro areas, by 1980, 96 percent did. The large volume of immigration from Central and South America during the 1970s probably explains the increasing metropolitan character of this segment of the Hispanic population. Recency of immigration probably also plays a role. As Appendix Table B-2 shows, in each of the three census years nearly 25 percent of this group arrived within the previous five years. For no other group except Cubans during the 1950s and early 1960s has recency of immigration been such a characteristic feature of the group.

The Mexican and Other Hispanic populations are distinguished from the other three groups in their relatively lower proportions of metro dwellers by 1980, in the substantially higher proportions of non-metro residents at the beginning of the period (1960), and in the more rapid pace of metropolitanization experienced by Mexicans over the past two decades. The higher shares of Mexican and Other Hispanic nonmetropolitan residents throughout the period reflect the historical role of these segments of the Spanish origin population in U.S. agriculture,[36] as well as their incorporation into a rural economy.[37]

It is noteworthy that the metropolitanization of the Mexican origin population has continued to increase during the past two decades. Whereas in 1960 over 75 percent of all persons of Mexican origin resided in metro areas, by 1980 the share of metropolitan dwellers had increased by about 10 percent. Thus, by 1980 more than four persons of Mexican origin in every five resided in metropolitan areas. The participation of the Mexican origin population in this metropolitanization and urbanization process resulted from declining opportunities in agriculture as the mechanization of the industry that began after World War II gained momentum and as the urban service and manufacturing sectors expanded. That a higher share of the Mexican origin population had not become metropolitan residents by 1980 reflects their continued disproportionate representation in agricultural laborer occupations and industries, a theme we elaborate further in Chapter 9.

The Other Hispanic population, which includes a relatively large but unspecifiable segment of descendants from the original Spanish settlers, historically has been isolated in rural enclaves of the Southwest, particularly in northern New Mexico and southern Colorado.[38] Table 3.4 portrays a picture of relative stability, although it masks the very real possibility that many of the nonmetropolitan dwellers lived in urban rather than rural areas or on farms. Figure 3.13, which graphically depicts the changing residential configuration of the white Spanish surname population between 1950 and 1980, provides some support for this

---

[36]Marta Tienda, "Residential Distribution and Internal Migration Patterns of Chicanos: A Critical Assessment," in Armando Valdez, Albert Camarillo, and Tomas Almaguer, eds., *The State of Chicano Research on Family, Labor and Migration: Proceedings of the Symposium on Work, Family, and Migration* (Palo Alto: Stanford Center for Chicano Research, 1983).

[37]See discussion of this topic in Chapter 1. See also Candace Nelson and Marta Tienda, "The Structuring of Hispanic Ethnicity: Historical and Contemporary Perspectives," *Ethnic and Racial Studies* 8 (1985):49–74.

[38]Tienda, "Mexican American Population."

FIGURE 3.13

Residential Configuration of the White Spanish Surname Population
by Urban-Rural Residence for the Southwest: 1950–1980

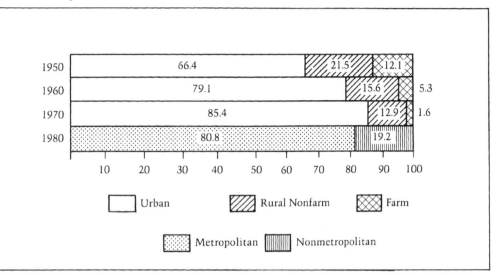

ϽURCE: U.S. Bureau of the Census, *Census of Population: 1950*, table 2; *Census of Population: 1960*,
C (2)-1B, table 2; *Census of Population: 1970*, PC(2)-1D, table 1; and 1980 Public Use Microdata Sample
▌e.

argument.[39] Appendix Table B-2 also documents a nontrivial share of
geographic movement between states, especially during the late 1960s,
but apparently these changes in residence did not dramatically alter the
metro-nonmetro configuration of the population.

Figure 3.13 shows that, as recently as 1970, less than 2 percent of
the white Spanish surname population of the Southwest resided on
farms and a gradually diminishing segment resided in rural nonfarm
areas. In fact, by 1970 less than 15 percent of the Spanish surname population of the Southwest lived in rural areas, including both farm and
nonfarm areas. Given the rural origins of both the Other Hispanic and
Mexican origin population, for whom the Spanish surname identifier
served as a proxy as late as 1970, this aspect of their residential charac-

[39]It is not possible to differentiate the 1980 population into the same residential
categories used between 1950 and 1970. Our inability to differentiate the nonmetropolitan
population into rural and urban components is unfortunate because of the rapid urbanization of this population in a short time period. However, the available evidence for the
1950–1970 period serves to make our basic point.

ter remains as a clear vestige of their ancestors' previous involvement in agriculture. Whether and how much it will change in the future depends on the ways industrial restructuring processes open new employment alternatives for the offspring of agricultural workers, as well as the character of the Hispanic metropolitanization process itself.

Summary of Residential Configuration

Our portrayal of the geographic distribution of the Hispanic population is intended simply to document the diverse patterns of residential concentration and dispersion during the 1960s and 1970s and to consider in very general terms the underlying forces of change. Despite evidence that all groups except Cubans participated in a process of residential dispersion away from their original locations, in 1980 the pronounced regional concentration of Hispanics according to national origin persisted. That is, Mexicans continued as the dominant Spanish-speaking population of the Southwest, Puerto Ricans were predominantly located in the Northeast, and Cubans increasingly resided in the state of Florida. The Other Hispanic population was bifurcated between the Southwest and other states where Hispanics are numerous, while New York and California were the preferred residential locations of the Central and South American populations.

Since 1950 the U.S. Hispanic population has become increasingly an urban population, and this process of urbanization, at least as indicated by metropolitan residence, has proceeded at a faster rate than that observed for the population as a whole.[40] Puerto Ricans, Central/South Americans, and Cubans are almost exclusively metropolitan residents, but the Mexican and Other Hispanic origin populations are less so. Given the direction of change over the past two decades, it is likely that 1990 will witness higher levels of metropolitan dwellers of Mexican and Other Hispanic origin.

Often, a shift from nonmetropolitan to metropolitan status is associated with improvements in socioeconomic status. While this has occurred for the Mexican origin population,[41] there is no general correspondence between the metropolitan character of the subgroups and their socioeconomic standing. As the following segment of this profile chapter documents, Puerto Ricans and Mexicans, one of the most and one of the least metropolitan of the Hispanic nationalities, respectively, occupy the lowest socioeconomic position of all groups, while on most social and economic indicators Cubans placed highest.

[40]Willette et al., "Demographic and Socioeconomic Characteristics," p. 102.
[41]Tienda, "Residential Distribution"; Tienda, "Mexican American Population."

Demographic and Socioeconomic Differentiation: A Contemporary Overview

Diversity with respect to social, demographic, and economic characteristics is the third defining feature of the Hispanic population. So pronounced are some of these differentials that they challenge the very notion of a single Hispanic population. We devote Chapters 8 through 10 to a detailed consideration of social and economic differentiation among the national origin groups. However, as part of our task of introducing the major organizing themes of this book, in this section we briefly survey and highlight the key dimensions of socioeconomic and demographic diversity which differentiate the five major national origin groups.

Demographic Characteristics

Hispanics are a relatively young population, with a mean age of 26 in 1980. But because of their different immigration histories and recent fertility levels, the average age of the groups varies appreciably. Mexicans and Puerto Ricans are the youngest of the five national origin groups, with an average age of roughly 25 in 1980, while Cubans, with a mean age of 37, are a considerably older population. Central/South Americans and Other Hispanics, while, on average, three to four years older than either Mexicans or Puerto Ricans, averaged eight or nine years less than Cubans in 1980 (Table 3.5).

As a result of the changing composition of immigration from Latin America and the Spanish-speaking Caribbean, the average share of each group that is foreign-born differs greatly. The proportion foreign-born in 1980 ranged from a low of about 18 percent for Other Hispanics to a high of about 80 percent for Central/South Americans. Since Puerto Ricans cannot be classified as foreign-born, the statistic reported refers to the share of the population born on the island. In other words, by 1980 roughly half of all Puerto Ricans residing on the mainland were of the second or higher generation. Mexicans, the most generationally diverse of all the groups, are predominantly U.S.-born. Despite the large influx of immigrants from Mexico during the past two decades, and especially during the 1970s, in 1980 about one person in four of Mexican origin was foreign-born. Since this is the largest of the Hispanic subgroups, however, the size of the foreign-born Mexican population is substantial—approximately 2.3 million in 1980, which is comparable to the foreign-born populations of Cubans and Central/South Americans combined.

TABLE 3.5

Selected Demographic Characteristics of the Hispanic Population
by Type of Origin: 1980

	Mexican	Puerto Rican	Cuban	Central/South American	Other Hispanic
Mean Age	24.5	24.6	37.0	28.5	27.5
Percentage Foreign-Born	26.0%	50.6%[a]	77.4%	80.4%	17.4%
Marital Composition (age 15 and over)					
Males					
Single	35.6	39.8	28.3	33.6	35.5
Married	56.1	48.8	62.2	58.2	54.4
Separated	2.3	4.9	2.3	3.2	2.1
Widowed	1.6	1.4	2.0	.7	2.0
Divorced	4.4	5.1	5.3	4.3	5.9
	100.0	100.0	100.1	100.0	99.9
Females					
Single	27.3	31.1	22.3	27.3	27.3
Married	55.6	43.0	54.5	52.4	51.7
Separated	3.8	11.0	3.0	6.8	3.3
Widowed	6.8	5.9	10.9	5.5	9.0
Divorced	6.5	9.0	9.2	7.9	8.6
	100.0	100.0	99.9	99.9	99.9
Mean Persons per Family	4.1	3.7	3.4	3.7	3.6
Percentage of Households Headed by Women	15.3%	33.7%	13.2%	20.1%	17.4%

SOURCE: 1980 Public Use Microdata Sample file.

[a]Refers to individuals born on the island of Puerto Rico.

Since 1960 the share of the total Hispanic population which is foreign-born has increased gradually, rising from 29.6 to 36.0 percent in 1980. This evolution of the nativity composition of the population—a major dimension of socioeconomic differentiation in itself—has not been uniform among the national origin groups. Although among Mexicans the foreign-born segment of the population was stable during the 1960s, it rose sharply between 1970 and 1980. Part of this increase, however, is an artifact of the coverage problems encountered in 1970 (see the first section of this chapter). Among Central/South Americans, on the other hand, the proportion foreign-born dropped from 38 percent in 1960 to 18 percent in 1980.

Hispanics also differ greatly with respect to family and household characteristics. Differences in the proportion single among the groups partly reflect variation in age composition, but they also reflect differences in age at marriage. That Puerto Ricans were considerably less likely than any of the other Hispanic groups to be married in 1980 corresponds to an unusually high level of households headed by women. In this respect, not only do Puerto Ricans stand apart from the other national origin groups, but their female headship rate is more similar to that of blacks.[42] Among Puerto Rican women the lower proportion married results from higher proportions separated, divorced, and widowed, as these transitions usually involve the breakup of families.

Owing partly to differential fertility, and partly to variation in living arrangements, average family size varied from a low of 3.4 persons among Cubans to a high of 4.1 persons among Mexicans. These are, respectively, the lowest and highest fertility groups. However, were these averages based on household rather than family members, we would observe even greater size variation because of clearly different preferences for alternative living arrangements among the national origin groups (see Chapter 6). As shown elsewhere, Cubans are most likely and Puerto Ricans least likely to reside in extended family households.[43] Explanations for observed differences in living arrangements, including the differential prevalence of extended family structure, have focused on socioeconomic factors,[44] demographic factors,[45] and cultural factors.[46] In the following section we highlight the ways in which national origin and nativity—two ascribed demographic characteristics—arrays the extensive socioeconomic variation observed among Hispanics.

Socioeconomic Diversity: A Sketch

As a group U.S. Hispanics are much less educated, much poorer, more likely to be unemployed, and, if employed, more likely to occupy

[42]Marta Tienda and Ronald Angel, "Headship and Household Composition Among Blacks, Hispanics, and Other Whites," Social Forces 61 (1982):508–31.

[43]Marta Tienda and Jennifer Glass, "Household Structure and Labor Force Participation of Black, Hispanic and White Mothers," Demography 22 (1985):38–94; Ronald Angel and Marta Tienda, "Determinants of Extended Household Structure: Cultural Pattern or Economic Need?" American Journal of Sociology 87 (1982):1360–83; Marta Tienda and Jennifer Glass, "Extended Household Composition and Female Labor Force Participation," in Jacques Boulet et al., Understanding the Economic Crisis: The Impact of Poverty and Unemployment on Children and Families. Proceeding of a National Conference by the Bush Program in Child Development and Social Policy (Ann Arbor: University of Michigan, 1985a).

[44]Tienda and Glass, "Household Structure"; Angel and Tienda, "Determinants."

[45]Rosemary S. Cooney, "Demographic Components of Growth in White, Black and Puerto Rican Female-Headed Families: A Comparison of the Cutright and Ross/Sawhill Methodologies," Social Science Research 8 (1979):144–58; Heather Ross and Isabel V. Sawhill, Time of Transition: The Growth of Families Headed by Women (Washington, DC: Urban Institute, 1975).

[46]Angel and Tienda, "Determinants."

TABLE 3.6

Selected Social and Economic Characteristics
of the Hispanic Population Aged 16 and Over
by National Origin: 1980

	Mexican	Puerto Rican	Cuban	Central/South American	Other Hispanic
Median Number of Years of Education[a]	9.1	10.0	11.7	11.7	11.8
Labor Force Participation Rate					
Male	83%	74%	85%	83%	81%
Female	52	42	64	58	57
Percentage of Professional and Managerial Workers	12.4	13.6	21.4	16.8	20.5
Median Family Income, 1984	$15,200	$9,900	$17,500		$15,000[b]
Percentage of Families Below Poverty	20.6%	34.9%	11.7%		16.7[b]
Percentage of Families Below 125% Poverty	28.3	42.4	16.2		22.6[b]

SOURCES: 1980 Public Use Microdata Sample file; U.S. Bureau of the Census, "Persons of Spanish Origin in the United States: March 1980 (Advance Report)," Current Population Reports, series P-20, no. 361 (Washington, DC: U.S. Government Printing Office, May 1981); Census of Population and Housing: 1980 Vol. 1, Characteristics of the Population, U.S. Summary, PC80-1-C1, Ch. C, "General Social and Economic Characteristics," Table 171. "Poverty Status in 1979 of Families and Persons by Spanish Origin, Type of Spanish Origin and Race: 1980" (Washington, DC: U.S. Government Printing Office, December 1983).

[a]Persons aged 25 and over.
[b]Includes Central/South Americans.

low-status, low-paying jobs than the non-Hispanic white population.[47] Table 3.6, which provides a comparative socioeconomic snapshot of the national origin groups, sharply illustrates the extent of diversity in educational attainment, employment status, and poverty among Hispanics. One clear message is that on most socioeconomic indicators Mexicans and Puerto Ricans fare least well, while Cubans and Central/South Americans are typically better educated, have higher rates of labor force participation, and have notably higher family income levels. Likewise, Cubans experience rates of poverty which are considerably lower than those of Mexicans and Puerto Ricans. Specifically, in 1980 Puerto Ri-

[47]George Borjas and Marta Tienda, eds., Hispanics in the U.S. Economy (Orlando, FL: Academic Press, 1985); Davis et al., "U.S. Hispanics."

cans were almost three times more likely, and Mexicans almost twice as likely, to be poor than Cubans. Of course, these averages conceal extensive within-group variation in these socioeconomic indicators according to nativity, geographic location, and degree of acculturation. For example, among men, immigrants participated in the labor force at a higher rate than natives in 1980. These differentials ranged from 10 to 18 percent for Central/South Americans and Cubans and from 5 to 7 percent for Other Hispanics and Mexicans, respectively. We elaborate on the sources of such differentials, as well as their consequences for the economic well-being of Hispanics, in Chapters 9 and 10.

The only indicator of acculturation available in the 1980 census is a measure of English proficiency. Although not a particularly precise measure of acculturation, when evaluated against indicators of socioeconomic status this characteristic is quite revealing. As Table 3.7 shows, among Cubans and Central/South Americans, the economically most prosperous of the Hispanic origin groups, about 94 percent reported Spanish as their home language compared with 86 percent of all Mexicans and only 61 percent of Other Hispanics. As an indicator of acculturation (or nonacculturation) the high proportions of Cubans and Central/South Americans who use Spanish as their main household language are consistent with the high immigrant composition of these groups, as well as with the relative recency of their arrival in the United States. Presumably, with longer periods of U.S. residence, and as the relative size of the native-born population grows, English will become the dominant language both within and outside the household. How-

TABLE 3.7

Language Characteristics of the Hispanic Population Aged 25 and Over by National Origin: 1980

	Mexican	Puerto Rican	Cuban	Central/South American	Other Hispanic
Home Language					
Spanish	86.1%	90.7%	94.4%	94.5%	61.2%
English	13.9	9.3	5.6	5.5	38.3
English Proficiency					
Speaks Only English[a]	13.9	9.3	5.6	5.5	38.8
Speaks Very Well	36.9	37.0	24.4	26.1	34.3
Speaks Well	22.4	26.6	23.4	29.4	15.5
Speaks Not Well	16.2	19.1	25.0	25.2	7.7
Speaks Not at All	10.7	8.0	21.5	13.7	3.8

SOURCE: 1980 Public Use Microdata Sample file.

[a]Not applicable.

ever, this assumption remains to be verified and is challenged by the experience of Mexicans and Puerto Ricans.

Mexicans and Puerto Ricans, who are more generationally diverse than either Cubans or Central/South Americans, exhibit understandably higher levels of linguistic assimilation, as revealed by the extent of English as the home language. Yet, despite their higher levels of linguistic assimilation and greater proficiency in English, these two groups are the most disadvantaged in terms of social and economic status. Cuban immigrants, in contrast, are the least linguistically proficient, yet they are, on average, more successful in the labor market than Mexicans, Puerto Ricans, or Other Hispanics.[48] This suggests that while mastery of English may be a necessary condition for socioeconomic success, it is insufficient by itself. We scrutinize this inference in greater depth in Chapters 8, 9, and 10.

In attempting to explain this apparent anomaly—anomalous from an assimilation perspective which predicts higher levels of socioeconomic success with higher levels of cultural and social assimilation—Nelson and Tienda argued that the privileged class position of Cubans in relation to Mexicans and Puerto Ricans, which has remained intact until the present time, apparently conferred advantages to this population which have not been enjoyed by others, except, perhaps, selected segments of the Central/South American population.[49] Despite the fact that Cubans have a shorter residence in the United States, as a group they have experienced faster cultural assimilation than Mexicans or Puerto Ricans, as shown by patterns of exogamous marriages, persisting middle-class orientations, and high socioeconomic status.[50] This is an issue we pursue in greater detail throughout the following chapters as we attempt to explain the Cuban socioeconomic "success" story against the lesser prosperity of the Mexican, Puerto Rican, and Other Hispanic groups, and the increasing diversity of the Central/South American population.

[48]Candace Nelson and Marta Tienda, "The Structuring of Hispanic Ethnicity: Historical and Contemporary Perspectives," *Ethnic and Racial Studies* 8 (1985):49–74. In their overview essay on the structuring of Hispanic ethnicity, Nelson and Tienda disaggregated variation in English proficiency between Mexicans and Cubans according to nativity, and for the foreign-born, according to year of arrival. Their results suggested that the Cuban linguistic assimilation process may be more rapid, but it also may be tied to the educational background of the groups entering at different periods, as well as to their locational and associational patterns upon arriving in the United States.

[49]Nelson and Tienda, "Structuring of Hispanic Ethnicity."

[50]Eleanor Rogg, *The Assimilation of Cuban Exiles: The Role of Community and Class* (New York: Aberdeen Press, 1974); Eleanor Rogg and Rosemary Cooney, *Adaptation and Adjustment of Cubans: West New York, N.J.*, Hispanic Research Center Monograph (New York: Fordham University, 1980).

Central and South Americans: A Further Look

Because of their relatively recent arrival in the United States and their diversity of national origins, Central/South Americans deserve more detailed scrutiny. The most basic questions one can ask about the Central and South American population of the United States are: What countries do they represent? How has the demographic and socioeconomic significance of this population changed over time? Table 3.8 addresses the first question by showing how the relative shares of Central Americans and Caribbeans[51] compared with South Americans shifted between 1960 and 1980 and what countries were most responsible for these changes. In 1960 South Americans represented just over half of the population (56 percent), while Central Americans and Dominicans accounted for 44 percent. During the 1960s the share of South Americans increased slightly to 58 percent, but declined to 48 percent by 1980. Concomitantly, the share of persons from Central America and the Caribbean increased to just over half, or 52 percent, of this Hispanic group.

The indices of dissimilarity shown in the table indicate that there was a moderate amount of temporal variation in the country of origin distribution within the Central and South American country groupings. For temporal comparisons the index of dissimilarity reveals the degree to which the national origin distribution for one time period would have to shift to give the distribution for the other time period. For example, among Central Americans, approximately 15 to 16 percent of the 1970 and 1980 distributions would have to be shifted in order to achieve the national origin distributions of 1960 and 1970, respectively. The interdecade differences in the national origin distributions can be traced largely to the increasing presence of Dominicans and Salvadorans. While Dominicans constituted roughly 16 percent of the Central American and Caribbean subgroup in 1960, by 1980 they more than doubled their shares to 35 percent. Persons from El Salvador increased their numbers from 9 to 18 percent of all Central Americans during the 20-year period. Guatemalans also constituted a slightly larger share of all Central Americans in 1980 compared with 1960. Owing to the growing presence of Dominicans, Salvadorans, and Guatemalans, the share of persons from other Central American countries decreased in varying amounts. The most substantial decline was in the share of Panamanians which

---

[51]Our decision to group the Dominican Republic with the Central American nations was largely arbitrary, but reflected other considerations such as the relative sizes of the sending countries and the salience of political factors in propelling the 1970s exodus from several Central American countries, especially Guatemala and El Salvador.

TABLE 3.8

Country of Origin and Nativity Composition
of the Central/South American Origin Population: 1960–1980

Country of Origin	1960		1970		1980	
	Distribution by Country of Origin	Percentage[a] Foreign-Born	Distribution by Country of Origin	Percentage[a] Foreign-Born	Distribution by Country of Origin	Percentage[a] Foreign-Born
CENTRAL AMERICA AND THE CARIBBEAN[b]						
Dominican Republic	16.5%	73.8%	30.1%	78.7%	35.4%	80.8%
El Salvador	9.2	66.3	10.7	64.8	18.4	85.9
Guatemala	9.7	44.3	10.1	66.3	12.5	82.6
Nicaragua	15.7	70.5	12.9	54.4	9.1	79.6
Panama	25.1	62.0	13.2	61.9	8.5	75.0
Honduras	14.9	63.5	13.8	63.2	7.7	74.1
Costa Rica	8.8	58.0	9.2	60.6	5.5	81.5
Other Central American	—	—	—	—	2.9	79.6
Total	99.9	63.8	100.0	66.8	100.0	79.6

Dissimilarity Index
1960–1970 = 15.8
1970–1980 = 16.8

Country of Origin						
SOUTH AMERICA						
Colombia	14.8	65.0	23.3	74.6	33.1	80.6
Ecuador	8.2	72.8	13.8	76.1	20.1	81.9
Peru	8.1	60.4	10.0	67.8	12.9	77.2
Argentina	22.6	59.2	21.2	68.7	11.3	86.0
Chile	9.9	50.8	5.8	68.3	7.6	82.7
Venezuela	11.6	69.2	6.1	75.8	6.3	82.2
Bolivia	1.9	75.0	3.5	72.4	3.1	77.4
Uruguay	2.2	50.0	2.2	80.3	2.6	88.4
Paraguay	0.4	80.0	0.9	83.3	0.5	89.3
Other South American	20.2[c]	49.0[c]	13.2[c]	49.8[c]	2.5	80.1
Total	99.9	59.7	100.0	69.4	100.0	81.3

Dissimilarity Index
1960–1970 = 14.6
1970–1980 = 16.0

Central American as Percentage of Pooled	44.2		42.5		52.2	
South American as Percentage of Pooled	55.7		57.6		47.7	

SOURCE: 1960, 1970, and 1980 Public Use Microdata Sample files.
[a]Percentage foreign within each country.
[b]This refers to the Spanish-speaking Caribbean, excluding Cuba and Puerto Rico, countries considered separately.
[c]Includes Other Central Americans.

dropped from 25 percent of all Central Americans in 1960 to less than 10 percent by 1980.

In the aggregate, the country of origin composition of the South American population changed by roughly the same amount as that of the Central American population, approximately 15 to 16 percent for each decade. Another parallel between the two subregion country groupings is that three countries dominated most of the compositional change witnessed during this period. In 1960 the three dominant groups were Argentinian, constituting almost 25 percent of the South American origin population; Colombians, constituting an additional 15 percent; and Venezuelans, who represented just under 12 percent of the subregional total.[52] The growth of the South American population since 1960 can be traced largely to the substantial influx of Colombians and Ecuadorans. In 1980 one South American in three living in the United States was Colombian and one in five was Ecuadoran, while the share of Argentinians had declined to approximately one in ten. Declines in the shares of Chileans, Venezuelans, Bolivians, Uruguayans, and Paraguayans were relatively small as a result of the increased presence of Colombians and Ecuadorans, however. Peruvians increased their share of the subregional total from 8 to 13 percent between 1960 and 1980.

That immigration was largely responsible for the growth of the Central and South American population is reflected in a rising share of foreign-born over time. Among Central Americans and Caribbeans the share of foreign-born increased from 64 to 80 percent for the entire group between 1960 and 1980. Only Panamanians and Hondurans reported shares of foreign-born below the 1980 subregion average, while the share of immigrants among Salvadorans and Guatemalans was slightly above the subregion average. Among South Americans the share of foreign-born rose from 60 to 80 percent between 1960 and 1980, reflecting the dominance of Colombians and Ecuadorans in the most recent immigrant flows. The next chapter, which introduces more detail about country of origin variations in timing of arrival, provides further insight about how changes in the timing and volume of immigrant flows were responsible for the changes in the composition of Central and South American origin population.

Compared with Mexicans, Puerto Ricans, or Cubans, the immigration of Central and South Americans primarily involves adults. Because

[52]Our figures necessarily are approximate because the residual category "Other South American" includes Central Americans whose country was unspecified in 1960 and 1970. This is not the case in 1980, when the unspecified categories were reported separately for Central and South America. Also, the size of the residual category was much greater prior to 1980, when greater effort was devoted to classifying the Hispanic origin population. Unfortunately, there is no easy way to correct for these changes in classification.

adult immigration was responsible for most of the growth of the Central/South American population over the past two decades, the mean age of this Hispanic group has risen. Among Central Americans the average age rose from 24 to 28 between 1960 and 1980, whereas among the South Americans the average age increased one year, on average, from 28 to 29. Thus, during the 1970s and 1980s the average age of the Central and South American subgroups has converged. As the share of persons under age 16 declined (from 39 to 25 percent for Central Americans and from 31 to 24 percent for South Americans), the share of working-age individuals increased. Thus, by 1980 nearly three fourths of the Central/South American population were persons of working age (Table 3.9).

Not surprisingly, and owing to the changed national origin composition and variation in the timing of immigration from Central and South America, the age structure of the population varies by country of origin. In 1960 Guatemalans were the youngest group, with an average age of 20, but because of the continued influx of young and middle-aged adults during the 1960s and 1970s, the average age rose to 27. Hondurans also were younger than the Central American average in 1960, and their mean age also rose during the 1960s and 1970s as higher shares of working-age adults came to the United States. Thus, the age diversity of the Central American population evident in 1960 was diminished by 1980.

The decline in the average age of South Americans between 1960 and 1970 reflects the lessened importance of adult immigration and increased importance of immigrant fertility for this regional subgroup. However, owing to the increased volume of adult immigrants during the 1970s, the mean age of South Americans rose sharply, even surpassing its 1960 average. Again, there was considerable diversity in the age composition of the South American origin population by country of origin. For example, in 1960 Colombians, Ecuadorans, and Venezuelans exhibited average ages slightly below the subregion average, but this situation changed by 1980 owing to the continued immigration of working-age adults during the 1960s and 1970s. The average age of Peruvians fell from 29 to 22 during the 1960s, but increased thereafter in 1980 to 29, roughly comparable to the mean age of the region total. The shares of working-age persons rose substantially between 1960 and 1980, increasing from 60 to 71 percent among Central Americans and Caribbeans and from 64 to 73 percent among South Americans. We examine the labor market implications of these changes in later chapters.

Like most immigrants, the majority from Central and South America settle in three states—California, New York, and Florida. However, as shown in Table 3.10, the concentration of Central and South Ameri-

TABLE 3.9

Changing Age Structure of the Central/South American Origin Population by Country of Origin: 1960–1980

Country of Origin	1960 Mean Age	Percentage under 16 years	Percentage 16–64 years	1970 Mean Age	Percentage under 16 years	Percentage 16–64 years	1980 Mean Age	Percentage under 16 years	Percentage 16–64 years
CENTRAL AMERICA AND THE CARIBBEAN	24.4	39.1%	59.1%	25.3	38.1%	58.7%	28.0	25.4%	71.2%
Dominican Republic	28.0	26.2	70.7	25.8	34.5	62.0	28.2	25.7	70.8
El Salvador	27.7	30.4	66.3	23.7	41.4	56.4	27.3	21.7	76.2
Guatemala	19.8	52.6	46.4	26.6	33.0	63.2	26.9	26.5	71.3
Nicaragua	27.2	29.5	68.6	24.5	42.0	55.0	29.7	24.9	69.3
Panama	22.8	44.0	54.8	26.8	34.2	62.8	29.4	24.0	71.8
Honduras	20.8	50.0	49.3	24.5	43.1	54.1	27.3	28.1	68.8
Costa Rica	24.9	42.0	55.7	24.4	44.5	51.7	30.0	23.1	72.4
Other Central American[a]	—	—	—	—	—	—	21.8	43.8	53.4
SOUTH AMERICA	28.0	31.4	64.5	26.1	35.2	61.0	29.2	23.8	73.2
Colombia	25.1	40.3	56.4	24.7	37.0	60.3	28.7	24.8	72.5
Ecuador	25.0	30.1	68.0	25.0	36.9	61.2	28.8	24.8	72.3
Peru	29.4	23.8	70.3	22.3	44.0	53.7	28.8	26.2	70.9
Argentina	28.6	29.9	68.0	27.8	31.8	64.8	32.0	20.0	76.9
Chile	28.7	27.4	71.0	31.7	23.3	69.3	30.3	23.1	73.1
Venezuela	23.9	34.2	63.7	24.3	41.2	53.1	26.1	21.7	74.7
Bolivia[b]	—	—	—	22.7	38.2	56.9	28.3	24.9	72.1
Uruguay[b]	27.2	42.9	53.6	29.9	29.0	60.5	31.0	20.2	78.1
Paraguay	—	—	—	28.3	43.3	53.3	31.1	17.2	80.3
Other South American	32.5	28.8	61.7	28.7	31.1	63.0	31.2	17.8	78.2
Overall Total	26.1	35.5	62.6	25.8	36.4	60.0	28.5	24.6	72.2

SOURCES: 1960, 1970, and 1980 Public Use Microdata Sample files.

[a]Other Central American and Other South American are combined in 1960 and 1970.

[b]Number is less than 25 (1960).

TABLE 3.10

State of Residence Distribution
of the Central/South American Origin Population
by Country of Origin: 1980

Country of Origin	California	New York	Florida	Other	Total
CENTRAL AMERICA AND THE CARIBBEAN	31.1%	38.3%	6.3%	24.3%	100.0%
Dominican Republic	1.1	77.6	4.6	16.6	99.9
El Salvador	71.4	10.7	2.4	15.6	100.1
Guatemala	57.0	11.1	3.8	28.1	100.0
Nicaragua	51.3	8.8	17.0	22.8	99.9
Panama	15.8	36.5	7.9	39.8	100.0
Honduras	18.8	28.5	11.2	41.5	100.0
Costa Rica	34.3	20.7	9.7	35.3	100.0
Other Central American	38.3	7.7	4.2	49.8	100.0
SOUTH AMERICA	18.8	30.6	12.1	38.5	100.0
Colombia	11.9	33.8	17.2	37.2	100.1
Ecuador	16.0	48.1	5.2	30.7	100.0
Peru	28.5	24.4	8.5	38.5	99.9
Argentina	32.6	22.8	8.7	35.9	100.0
Chile	25.9	18.3	12.4	43.4	100.0
Venezuela	11.0	15.2	24.2	49.6	100.0
Bolivia	25.2	12.5	7.5	54.9	100.1
Uruguay	15.2	24.7	6.9	53.2	100.0
Paraguay	15.6	13.1	3.3	68.0	100.0
Other South American	13.7	23.7	15.4	47.2	100.0
Total	25.2	34.6	9.1	31.1	100.0

SOURCE: 1980 Public Use Microdata Sample file.

cans varies considerably by country of origin. For example, Central
Americans and Dominicans as a group were largely concentrated in
New York State, where almost 40 percent resided in 1980. An additional
one third of Central Americans and Dominicans resided in California,
with the remainder distributed between Florida and other states, including the District of Columbia.

The marked presence of Central Americans in New York State reflects the fact that nearly 80 percent of all Dominicans resided there in
1980, and this group represents roughly one third of the total Central
American and Caribbean population in 1980 (see Table 3.8). That Dominicans are so heavily concentrated in New York State can be traced

to the existence and perpetuation of Dominican communities that have been established and revitalized over the last 20 years,[53] a period that witnessed an increasing flow of immigrants from the Dominican Republic. Also, since Puerto Rico has served as a gateway to New York for the illegal segment of the Dominican population, New York City, the city of greatest Puerto Rican concentration, has become a natural haven for incorporating new Dominican arrivals.[54] By contrast the Salvadorans, Guatemalans, and Nicaraguans were more highly concentrated in California, a circumstance related to the geographic proximity of these countries to the California border.

With the exception of New York, no single state houses up to a quarter of the South American population. Nearly one third of all South Americans resided in the state of New York in 1980, with Colombians, Ecuadorans, Peruvians, and Argentinians dominating. The disproportionate presence of these nationalities in New York resulted from the initial immigrant flows established in the late 1950s and early to mid-1960s. Over time, these flows have perpetuated themselves as established kinship ties continue to recruit new arrivals to this area. The internationalization of the U.S. economy and the bifurcated demand for highly skilled workers in New York City also explain the persistence of a large Latin American immigrant work force in New York City.[55]

Almost 20 percent of all South Americans resided in California in 1980, with Peruvians, Argentinians, Bolivians, and Chileans representing the largest country groups. Venezuelans tend to concentrate in Florida, reflecting the proximity of Miami, the major port of entry, to Caracas, the main origin source for this population. The Venezuelan presence in Miami resulted from the bi-national commerce and residence pattern established by the wealthy classes of Venezuelan society during the 1970s when the oil economy was booming. However, the sharp fall in petroleum prices during the early 1980s slowed the bi-national flows of

[53]Mary M. Kritz and Douglas T. Gurak, "Kinship Networks and the Settlement Process: Dominican and Colombian Immigrants in New York City," paper presented at the meeting of the Population Association of America, Minneapolis, May, 1984; Roger Waldinger, "Immigration and Industrial Change in the New York City Apparel Industry," in George J. Borjas and Marta Tienda, eds., *Hispanics in the U.S. Economy* (Orlando, FL: Academic Press, 1985).

[54]Sherri Grasmuck and Patricia Pessar, "Undocumented Dominican Migration to the United States," Research Project Center for International Studies, Duke University, 1982.

[55]Saskia Sassen-Koob, "Changing Composition and Labor Market Location of Hispanic Immigrants in New York City, 1960–1980," in George J. Borjas and Marta Tienda, eds., *Hispanics in the U.S. Economy* (Orlando, FL: Academic Press, 1985).

people and goods between Caracas and Miami.[56] Moreover, between 1979 and 1983 the number of Venezuelans seeking to immigrate to the United States has nearly doubled and may continue to do so in the future as the economic consequences of the oil crisis intensify.[57] Thus, it is likely that the share of permanent Venezuelan residents will continue to increase during the 1980s, and possibly beyond, but this outcome depends on what happens in the international oil market.

Perhaps the most salient residential characteristic of Central and South Americans is their relative dispersion compared with Mexicans, Puerto Ricans, and Cubans. Anywhere from one third to two thirds of any national origin group does not reside in the three states of largest concentration, but rather are dispersed throughout the United States. A disproportionate share of both Central and South Americans reside in Washington, D.C. This partly reflects the availability of government jobs and international exchange programs in this area, but also the concentrated demand for low-skilled workers to provide services for a large professional work force. Given the importance of kinship and friendship ties as recruitment mechanism for new immigrants, the Spanish-speaking population of Washington, D.C., is likely to increase during the 1980s.

Summary and Conclusions

Our main purpose in this chapter has been to highlight certain aspects of three defining features of the Hispanic population: [1]rapid growth, [2]regional concentration, and [3]extensive demographic and socioeconomic variation according to national origin. We evaluate these topics in greater depth in the chapters that follow. Our introduction to them here, while necessarily sketchy, nonetheless illustrates the themes of diversity and differentiation according to national origin that provide the comparative frame of reference for our monograph. In discussing the rapid growth of the Hispanic population during the past two

[56]Although statistical data are not readily available to document the extent to which wealthy Venezuelans own property in southern Florida or their impact on the commercial establishments in the Miami area, some unobtrusive indicators have become evident as a result of the economic crisis of the 1980s. Not only has the number of dual flights between Caracas and Miami been drastically reduced, but also the number of passengers has declined.

[57]U.S. Department of Justice, *Statistical Yearbook of the Immigration and Naturalization Service: 1983* (Washington, DC: U.S. Government Printing Office, 1983), table 1.3, p. 9. The number of legal Venezuelan immigrants rose from 841 in 1978 to 1,508 in 1983.

decades, we showed that the components of this growth, especially in the case of the Mexican origin population, must be interpreted in light of recent knowledge about the census coverage of the legal and illegal segments of the populations. The importance of rapid growth in making the Hispanic population more visible in the future cannot be understated, particularly in light of the persisting patterns of regional concentration of the major national origin groups.

One of the great challenges faced by scholars interested in the socioeconomic progress of Hispanics is explaining the persistence of wide disparities in socioeconomic status among Mexicans, Puerto Ricans, Cubans, Central/South Americans, and Other Hispanics. In our introductory chapter we suggested mode of entry as a dominant force in structuring the socioeconomic position of Hispanics along national origins. Our distinction between symbolic ethnicity and minority status seems appropriate to distinguish the Cuban from the Mexican and Puerto Rican socioeconomic positions. From the preliminary evidence provided in this thumbnail sketch of socioeconomic differentiation according to national origin, it is difficult to interpret the socioeconomic placement of the Central/South Americans and Other Hispanics. This is a task we address through the more in-depth analyses provided in later chapters of this monograph. What is clear, however, is that in light of the extensive socioeconomic diversity characterizing the national origin groups, it is largely inappropriate to treat Hispanics as a single population.

4

IMMIGRATION

T HE CONTEMPORARY demographic, social, and economic situations of Hispanics in the United States, as we noted in Chapter 2, are molded to a considerable degree by the historical and current patterns of migration of Spanish-speaking groups to this country. The historical features of this immigration are important for understanding the origin and persistence of important demographic and socioeconomic differences both among the Hispanic groups and between these groups and non-Hispanic whites. The contemporary features of immigration—both its real and perceived volume and economic impact—have shaped recent debates about how to change the nation's laws concerning immigration.[1] Other differences are important as well. People emigrate for various reasons, and these can have a bearing on what happens to them in their countries of destination. Moreover, some come legally and others come illegally, which affects not only the immigrants themselves but often the reaction to them on the part of the receiving society. In this chapter we are thus interested in exploring the volume, characteristics, determinants, and impacts of both legal and illegal immigration of Spanish origin persons to the United States.

[1]Frank D. Bean and Teresa Sullivan, "Immigration and its Consequences: Confronting the Problem," *Society* 22 (May-June 1985):67–73.

Historical and Contemporary Features of Hispanic Immigration

No single pattern characterizes the historical circumstances under which the various Hispanic groups have come to the United States. As Table 4.1 shows, Puerto Ricans came to the United States in most concentrated numbers during the 1950s, a time when the United States needed entry-level workers as a result of postwar economic expansion. By virtue of their U.S. citizenship, Puerto Ricans are accorded freedom of entry to this country, and thus, strictly speaking, do not immigrate, but rather migrate to the United States, often returning to the island after a period of time on the mainland.[2] This pattern of circular movement is a feature of Puerto Rican migration that is shared by both legal and (especially) illegal labor migrants from Mexico and which shapes the social and demographic lives of the people involved in it.

In contrast to Puerto Ricans, Cubans have come to the United States largely to escape a political situation in Cuba they find distasteful.[3] Many have come as legal immigrants, and many others have ar-

TABLE 4.1

Hispanic Immigration to the United States by Origin Group:
1950–1980 (in thousands)

Origin Group	1950–1959		1960–1969		1970–1979	
	Number of Migrants	Percentage of Total	Number of Migrants	Percentage of Total	Number of Migrants	Percentage of Total
Mexican	293	30.6%	431	33.2%	567	40.8%
Puerto Rican	480	50.2	222	17.1	41	3.0
Cuban	71	7.4	249	19.2	278	20.0
Central/South American	94	9.8	294	22.7	344	24.8
Other Hispanic	18	1.9	103	7.9	159	11.4
Total	956	99.9	1,299	100.1	1,389	100.0

SOURCES: Cary Davis, Carl Haub, and JoAnne Willette, "U.S. Hispanics: Changing the Face of America," Population Bulletin, vol. 33, no. 3 (Washington, DC: Population Reference Bureau, 1983); U.S. Department of Justice, Immigration and Naturalization Service, *Annual Report* (Washington, DC: U.S. Government Printing Office, 1959, 1961, 1970, 1980, and 1982).

[2]Cary Davis, Carl Haub, and JoAnne Willette, "U.S. Hispanics: Changing the Face of America," *Population Bulletin*, vol. 38, no. 3 (Washington, DC: Population Reference Bureau, 1983).
[3]Davis, Haub, and Willette, "U.S. Hispanics."

rived under the categories "political refugee" and "parolee," especially during the past two decades. Central/South Americans constitute a relatively new group. As Table 4.1 indicates, their numbers have increased rapidly in recent years, in part as a result of the political turmoil in Nicaragua and El Salvador. Other Hispanics come from a variety of places (for example, Spain) and show a slight increase in number over the past three decades.

Unlike Puerto Ricans, Cubans, and Central/South Americans—most of whom have come to the United States since 1950—Mexicans have a long history of legal immigration to this country. This is evident from the data in Table 4.2, which shows the number of legal Mexican immigrants who have arrived since 1821. Some observers have argued that Mexicans differ from the other groups of Hispanic origin in the extent to which they have been voluntary immigrants to the United States. In this view Mexican Americans are a "colonized people," a

TABLE 4.2

Mexican Legal Immigration to the United States: 1821–1984

Period	Number of Immigrants	Percentage of Total Immigrants
1821–1830	4,817	3.40%
1831–1840	6,599	1.10
1841–1850	3,271	0.20
1851–1860	3,078	0.10
1861–1870	2,191	0.10
1871–1880	5,162	0.20
1881–1890[a]	1,913	0.04
1891–1900[a]	971	0.02
1901–1910	49,642	0.60
1911–1920	219,004	3.80
1921–1930	459,287	11.20
1931–1940	22,319	4.20
1941–1950	60,589	5.80
1951–1960	299,811	11.90
1961–1970	453,934	13.70
1971–1980	640,294	14.20
1981	101,268	17.00
1982	56,106	9.40
1983	59,079	10.60
1984	57,557	10.60

SOURCE: U.S. Department of Justice, *Statistical Yearbook of the Immigration and Naturalization Service: 1983* (Washington, DC: U.S. Government Printing Office, 1983), table 2.

[a]No record of immigration from Mexico from 1886 to 1893.

group whose ancestors lived within the present geographical boundaries of the country at the time of the Mexican War.[4] It is thought that this explains why the experience of Mexicans has been very different from that of other immigrant groups. Mexicans, it is argued, have not only been treated more harshly, but the involuntary nature of their "immigration" has impeded their assimilation as a consequence of their continuing identification with Mexico and its culture and customs.[5]

The figures in Table 4.2, however, clearly suggest that the Mexican origin population in the United States in the nineteenth century was not very large.[6] In 1848, when the Treaty of Guadalupe Hidalgo was signed ending the war between the United States and Mexico over territorial rights to Texas, the entire Mexican population of the Southwest was probably no more than about 80,000 persons (or about 4 percent of the population).[7] In short, the size of the Mexican origin population in the United States at the time of the cessation of the war and for some time thereafter was not very large. This would not seem to lend a great deal of support to the view that the contemporary social and economic situations of Mexican Americans can be best understood by considering them a "conquered people."

More impressive is the number of Mexicans who have voluntarily immigrated to the United States since the middle of the nineteenth century. Although not exceeding 1,000 legal immigrants in a single year until 1904,[8] the number began to increase substantially in the first decade of the twentieth century. At the same time, large numbers of "nonstatistical" (that is, nondocumented) Mexicans, perhaps as many as 50,000 in some years, were arriving annually.[9] And with the exception of the decade of the 1930s during the Great Depression, the flow of immigrants from Mexico has remained substantial during the rest of the twentieth century. The idea, then, that Mexican Americans must be viewed as different from other national origin groups who have immi-

[4]R. Acuña, *Occupied America: The Chicano Struggle Toward Liberation* (San Francisco: Canfield, 1971); and R. Blauner, *Racial Oppression in America* (New York: Harper & Row, 1977).

[5]Blauner, *Racial Oppression.*

[6]U.S. Department of Justice, *Statistical Yearbook of the Immigration and Naturalization Service: 1983* (Washington, DC: U.S. Government Printing Office, 1983).

[7]Terry G. Jordan, "The 1887 Census of Texas' Hispanic Population," *Aztlan* 12 (1982):271–77.

[8]U.S. Bureau of the Census, *Historical Statistics of the United States: Colonial Times to 1957* (Washington, DC: U.S. Government Printing Office, 1960), pp. 58–59.

[9]S. Bryan, "Mexican Immigrants in the Labor Market," in W. Moquin and C. Van Doren, eds., *A Documentary History of the Mexican Americans* (New York: Bantam, 1971); and J. Gomez-Quinones, "The First Steps and Chicano Labor, Conflict and Organizing, 1900–20," in M. P. Servin, ed., *An Awakening Minority: The Mexican-Americans* (New York: Free Press, 1974).

TABLE 4.3

Naturalizations by Country of Former Allegiance and Period of Entry Expressed as a Percentage of Immigrants Entering Five Years Previously

Period	Mexico		Cuba		Central/South America		Total	
	Naturalization	Percentage	Naturalization	Percentage	Naturalization	Percentage	Naturalization	Percentage
1975–1979	34,392	11.5%	80,560	79.7%	71,084	33.8%	781,599	40.6%
1980–1984	57,478	18.6	59,718	35.1	103,048	33.8	873,914	37.8

grated to the United States because they are a conquered people instead of voluntary immigrants seems hard to justify in light of these statistics. This is not to say that Mexico's relinquishment of territorial rights to Texas may not have an effect on interethnic relationships in the Southwest, but simply that it is misleading to argue that the members of the Mexican American population are in the United States against their will.

In contrast to the seemingly overwhelming nature of the evidence indicating that the vast majority of Mexican Americans are either immigrants or the descendants of immigrants, however, stands the fact that Mexican immigrants have been much less likely to become naturalized citizens of the United States after fulfilling the five-year residency requirement than have the members of other groups. For example, the Immigration and Naturalization Service (INS) reported for 1975–1979 and 1980–1984 relatively fewer naturalizations for Mexicans (less than one for every five entrants who came five years previously) than for Cubans and Central/South Americans (more than one in three) (see Table 4.3). What interpretation should be attached to this is not at all clear. At a minimum, however, it is highly arguable that this pattern results from some historically derived sense going back to the Mexican War among the members of the Mexican origin population of lesser attachment to the customs and institutions of the United States.

Nativity Composition and Timing of Arrival

Despite the recent increases in the volume of legal Mexican immigration, the foreign-born segment of the Mexican origin population constitutes only a little more than one-fourth of all persons who so identified themselves in 1980 (see Table 4.4). Even though foreign-born persons increased their relative share of the Mexican origin population from 1960 to 1980, this group remains a decided minority, a circumstance that sharply distinguishes the Mexican origin population from all of the other Hispanic populations except Other Hispanics. That most of the non-Mexican groups in the United States are more characteristically comprised of immigrants than is the Mexican population can be seen not only in their much higher percentages of foreign-born persons, but also in the fact that their percentages of foreign-born increased by larger amounts than did Mexicans' since 1960. For example, Central/South Americans moved from about 60 percent foreign-born in 1960 to about 80 percent in 1980 (Table 4.4).

An increasing share of immigrants is characteristic of both the Mexican and Central/South American populations, despite their very differ-

TABLE 4.4

Percentage Distribution of the Hispanic Origin Populations
by Nativity: 1960–1980

Hispanic Population	Census Year		
	1960	1970	1980
Mexican	16.7%	17.9%	26.0%
Foreign-Born			
Native-Born	83.3	82.1	74.0
Puerto Rican			
Foreign-Born	68.2	54.2	50.6
Native-Born	31.8	45.8	49.4
Cuban			
Foreign-Born	64.4	73.4	77.4
Native-Born	35.6	26.6	22.6
Central/South American			
Foreign-Born	61.6	69.4	80.4
Native-Born	38.4	30.6	19.6
Other Hispanic			
Foreign-Born	17.8	12.0	17.4
Native-Born	82.2	88.0	82.6

ent shares of foreign-born persons (Table 4.5). Among Mexicans, for example, fully one-third of the foreign-born arrived in the five-year period just before the 1980 census, and more than one-third did among Central/South Americans. Of course, to a certain (but unknown) extent, the smaller shares among the members of earlier arriving cohorts reflect the effects of attrition owing to mortality and emigration. Nonetheless, when viewed in conjunction with the figures in Table 4.1, it seems evident that the Hispanic population in general, and the Mexican and Central/South American populations in particular, have been increasing their shares of immigrants at an increasing rate.

This phenomenon is especially significant and worth examining in more detail in the case of the Central/South American population because of the relative recency of arrival of this population. That immigration from Central/South American countries is still in its formative stages is evident in the very high proportion of the population that is foreign-born (over 80 percent). Although the share of foreign-born in 1980 was roughly similar for both Central and South Americans, there was considerable variation in immigrant composition by country owing to differences in timing of the flows. Almost half of the Central American origin population residing in the United States in 1980 arrived during the 1970s, whereas less than a third arrived prior to 1970. For South

TABLE 4.5

*Distribution of the Hispanic Origin Populations
by Nativity and Year of Arrival: 1980*

Nativity and Year	Mexican	Puerto Rican[a]	Cuban	Central/South American	Other Hispanic	Total Hispanic Population
Native	74.0	49.4%	22.6%	19.6%	82.6%	71.5%
Foreign	26.0	50.6	77.4	80.4	17.4	28.5
(1975–1980)	(8.7)	(7.9)[b]	(5.0)	(27.9)	(4.7)	(8.3)
(1970–1974)	(6.4)		(15.8)	(19.9)	(3.8)	(6.7)
(1965–1969)	(3.4)		(25.3)	(16.3)	(3.2)	(5.1)
(1960–1964)	(2.3)		(21.9)	(9.5)	(1.8)	(3.6)
(1950–1959)	(2.6)		(7.0)	(4.6)	(1.5)	(2.6)
(Pre-1950)	(2.6)		(2.3)	(2.1)	(2.4)	(2.2)
Total	100.0	100.0	100.0	100.0	100.0	100.0

SOURCE: 1980 Public Use Microdata Sample A file.

For Puerto Ricans, the native-foreign distribution corresponds to mainland-island birthplace.
Percentage of all island-born who moved to the mainland during the five years preceding the census.

Americans the proportions were roughly similar, except that they were lower for the recent immigrants and marginally higher for the share of immigrants who arrived before 1970. Table 4.6 indicates that among the Central Americans, Salvadorans and Guatemalans were most highly represented among recent arrivals, with 67 and 58 percent, respectively, having arrived after 1970. This large share of recent immigration corresponds to the rise of political unrest in these two countries. The share of Dominicans who arrived before and after 1970 was roughly similar to the Central American average; apparently the flow of Dominicans to the United States has been sustained during the 1970s.

Figure 4.1 serves a dual purpose in documenting the large area from which the Central and South American population originated and in summarizing the size of the immigrant population admitted to the United States in 1980. The numbers reported in Figure 4.1 correspond to persons admitted in the year 1980, not during the 1970–1980 period. However, these entries roughly correspond to the discussion above about the role of immigration by country of origin. For example, the number of Colombians, Ecuadorans, and Peruvians immigrating to the United States in 1980 far exceeded the number of persons immigrating from Argentina and other South American nations. Fewer than 1,000 persons immigrated from Bolivia, Paraguay, and Uruguay in 1980, and the number of Venezuelans hovered just over 1,000. INS data for 1971–1983 report the influx of Colombians, Ecuadorans, and Peruvians at

TABLE 4.6

Distribution of the Central/South American Origin Population by Timing of Arrival and Country of Origin: 1980

Country of Origin	Native-Born	Foreign, Arrived Before 1970	Foreign, Arrived 1970–1980	Total
CENTRAL AMERICA AND THE CARIBBEAN	20.5%	30.7%	48.8%	100.0%
Dominican Republic	19.2	35.8	45.0	100.0
El Salvador	14.1	19.2	66.8	100.1
Guatemala	17.4	24.5	58.1	100.0
Nicaragua	20.4	30.5	49.1	100.0
Panama	25.0	40.2	34.8	100.0
Honduras	25.9	32.8	41.3	100.0
Costa Rica	18.5	41.9	39.6	100.0
Other Central American	67.3	14.5	18.2	100.0
SOUTH AMERICA	18.5	34.6	46.8	99.9
Colombia	19.4	35.4	45.3	100.1
Ecuador	18.1	38.0	43.9	100.0
Peru	22.8	29.8	47.4	100.0
Argentina	14.0	44.5	41.6	100.1
Chile	17.3	30.5	52.2	100.0
Venezuela	17.8	18.1	64.1	100.0
Bolivia	22.6	32.5	44.9	100.0
Uruguay	11.6	29.7	58.7	100.0
Paraguay	10.7	36.9	52.5	100.1
Other South American	19.9	40.3	39.7	99.9
Total	19.6	32.6	47.8	100.0

SOURCE: 1980 Public Use Microdata Sample file.

106,000, 64,000, and 42,000, respectively, while the pooled total from all other countries was less than 180,000 for the period.[10]

The number of Dominicans, Salvadorans, and Guatemalans immigrating to the United States in 1980, as well as throughout the 1970s, far exceeded the number of Hondurans and Costa Ricans. The growing presence of Salvadoran immigrants among Central Americans reflects the exodus of refugees seeking political asylum owing to the civil war. INS reports show a steady increase in the number of immigrants from

[10]U.S. Bureau of the Census, *Statistical Abstract of the United States* (Washington, DC: U.S. Government Printing Office, 1986), table 129, p. 86.

FIGURE 4.1

*Emigrants from the Spanish-Speaking Latin American Countries
to the United States: 1980*

SOURCE: U.S. Department of Justice, *Statistical Yearbook of the Immigration and Naturalization Service: 1980* (Washington, DC: U.S. Government Printing Office, 1981), table 6.

El Salvador, rising from 15,000 during the 1960s to 34,000 between 1970 and 1980.[11] Furthermore, as the military operations have escalated within this war-torn country, so has the volume of emigration. Whereas the number of legal Salvadoran immigrants between 1974 and 1976 averaged approximately 2,350 individuals of all ages, by the latter part of the decade (1978–1980), this figure had climbed to roughly 5,500 persons per year.[12] Similarly, the political unrest in Guatemala appears to be largely responsible for the growing number of migrants from this country during the late 1970s. For example, the number of Guatemalans entering the United States legally increased notably during the 1970s, from an average of 1,700 annually during the early- to mid-1970s to roughly over 3,400 per year after 1978.[13]

INS data for the early 1980s show that the number of Guatemalans and Salvadorans seeking refuge in the United States has continued to rise (in fact, there were 13,500 asylum cases from El Salvador pending at the beginning of FY1984).[14] Thus, should the political unrest and economic instability in Central America continue, we might expect the influx of persons from these countries to continue into the more distant future. Unless immigration restrictions limit the number of entrants from the Western Hemisphere—and this does not seem likely in the near future—the size of the Central American origin population will continue to increase rapidly throughout the 1980s and possibly into the 1990s.

Among the South Americans the increasing presence of Venezuelans in the recent flows can be seen in the fact that 64 percent of this group entered the United States after 1970. If the economic crisis resulting from falling petroleum prices in the 1980s continues to intensify, the demand for immigrant visas from Venezuelans may increase over the next few years. However, overall, the net impact on the growth of the South American origin population is likely to be small since in 1980 Venezuelans made up less than 3 percent of the total from South America. Argentinians differed from Venezuelans in the timing of their arrival. Although the share of the total who immigrated during the 1970s was only slightly below the regional average (42 versus 47 percent), the peak of the Argentine influx occurred prior to 1970. Argentina is the only South American country for which the demand for U.S. visas seems to be declining rather than increasing. A changed economic and

[11]U.S. Bureau of the Census, *Statistical Abstract of the United States* (Washington, DC: U.S. Government Printing Office, 1986), table 129, p. 86.

[12]U.S. Department of Justice, *Statistical Yearbook of the Immigration and Naturalization Service: 1983* (Washington, DC: U.S. Government Printing Office, 1983), table 1.3, p. 9.

[13]U.S. Department of Justice, *Statistical Yearbook*, table 1.3, p. 9.

[14]U.S. Department of Justice, *Statistical Yearbook*, table 1.3, p. 9.

political climate largely accounts for the slowdown in immigration from Argentina, but political and economic factors could change this situation in the future. Colombians made up roughly 16 percent of all South Americans living in the United States in 1980 and represented the largest group from any single country from this region. Of these, nearly half arrived since 1970. Recent INS data[15] show that the volume of Colombian immigration has been maintained through the 1980s, accounting for roughly one-fourth of all entrants from South America.

The Context and Consequences of Hispanic Immigration

What are some of the consequences of these patterns and trends in Hispanic immigration? Within what sociohistorical context have they occurred? In interpreting statistics on Hispanic immigration, it is important to realize that since 1960 both the volume and kind of immigration to the United States has changed considerably, largely as the result of three developments.[16] The first was the passage of the 1965 Amendments to the Immigration and Nationality Act, which at once abolished the restrictive provisions of the national origins quota system, raised the annual ceiling on the number of immigrants from 158,000 to 290,000, and increased the number of categories of persons who could enter exempt from the numerical limitations. The second was the passage of legislation that made it much easier for political refugees to enter the country, particularly those from Cuba and Indochina. The third was an apparent increase in undocumented immigration to the United States, a phenomenon that was part of the worldwide emergence during the 1960s of labor migration from less developed to more developed countries.

In the years since 1970 (two years after the 1965 amendments took effect), annual immigration to the United States averaged over 462,000 persons per year compared with 252,000 per year during the 1950s.[17] Moreover, the ethnic composition of legal immigrants changed substantially as well, shifting away from a preponderance of Europeans to a preponderance of Asians and Latin Americans. For example, during the 1950s Europeans still constituted over half (52.7 percent) of all immigrants, whereas in the years since 1970 they have made up only 17 per-

---

[15]U.S. Bureau of the Census, *Statistical Abstract*, table 129, p. 86. These data show that between 1971 and 1980 Colombians made up 27 percent of all immigrants from South America and a roughly similar share of those who entered between 1981 and 1983.

[16]Douglas S. Massey, "Dimensions of the New Immigration to the United States and the Prospects for Assimilation," *Annual Review of Sociology* 7 (1981):57–85.

[17]U.S. Department of Justice, *Statistical Yearbook*.

cent of legal entrants. By contrast, persons of Latin American origin have increased their share of total immigration during this same time span from 24.6 to 40.2 percent.[18] The other group, of course, showing a sizable increase in its proportion of immigrants has been Asians.

What is important about these changing immigration patterns is that they may have heightened awareness of the Hispanic population in the United States. They may also have given impetus to the desire to modify immigration policy, a movement which culminated in the passage of new immigration legislation in 1986 designed to curb illegal immigration.[19] This is suggested by the fact that recent immigration trends parallel rather closely those that occurred in the late nineteenth and early twentieth centuries, trends that played an important role in bringing about the restrictive National Origins Quota System passed during the early 1920s.[20] For example, during the greater part of the nineteenth century most immigrants to the United States came from northwestern Europe. In the later nineteenth century, however, the pattern changed dramatically, and the number of southern and eastern Europeans overtook northwestern Europeans as a proportion of all immigrants. This changing ethnic composition of immigrant streams fueled a growing antiforeign sentiment among native-born Americans in the early twentieth century. It was also a factor contributing to the passage in 1924 of the legislation that restricted immigration by setting quotas on the numbers of new immigrants that could come based on the national origins of the U. S. population in 1920.[21]

If increases in the volume and origin of immigration in the late nineteenth and early twentieth centuries generated restrictive legislation, recent trends might be argued to have had a similar effect. The changes in law adopted since 1965 (but not including the recently passed Simpson-Rodino bill) have resulted in larger numbers of immigrants and have changed their composition. For example, the 601,442 entrants (including 132,781 refugees) granted lawful permanent resident status in the United States in 1978 amounts to a number of new lawful entrants greater than at any time since 1924, when most of the immigrants coming to this country were from eastern and southern Europe.[22] Hence, not only has the volume of immigration been increasing, but relatively more immigrants have been coming from Third World countries, over one-third of whom are Hispanic in origin. Moreover, the His-

[18]U.S. Department of Justice, *Statistical Yearbook.*

[19]*New York Times*, October 25, 1986.

[20]Bean and Sullivan, "Immigration and its Consequences."

[21]John Higham, *Strangers in the Land: Patterns of American Nativism, 1860–1925*, 2nd ed. (New York: Atheneum, 1971), pp. 319–24.

[22]David M. Reimers, "Post–World War II Immigration to the United States: America's Latest Newcomers," *Annals* 454 (1981):1–12.

panic element in the immigration flows has been and continues to be supplemented by sizable numbers of refugees from Cuba and by an uncertain but not trivial number of undocumented migrants from Mexico. That legal immigrants are not only greater in number than at any time since the early 1920s, but perhaps also more visible than at any time in the United States' history, may have reinforced the recent drive to modify immigration policy, a drive that ironically has resulted more in efforts to halt illegal migration than in attempts to change legal immigration.[23] Given this policy emphasis on illegal immigration, it is appropriate that we turn our attention to this phenomenon.

Undocumented Immigration

The term "illegal immigrant" is frequently used to describe persons who enter the United States without appropriate visas.[24] This terminology raises several interesting issues of nomenclature. In the first place, it is important to realize that the different terms that have been used to describe illegal immigrants—"undocumenteds," "irregular immigrants," "wetbacks," and so on—carry different connotations. The term "immigrant," for example, implies someone who comes to the United States with the intention of staying. This is in contrast to the term "migrant" which is more likely to imply someone who is in a given place only temporarily, as would be the case with "migrant workers." Many of the persons who enter the United States illegally come to work for relatively short periods of time, typically less than one year, and have no intention of becoming permanent settlers. For this reason some experts have suggested that the term "illegal migrant" provides a more accurate description of the group that enters the United States outside the channels of legal immigration.[25]

Similarly, the term "illegal" carries strong connotations that may obscure, if not invalidate, its usage to describe the population of nonregular entrants. It is not that the term is inaccurate. Clearly, persons who enter without appropriate visas do so illegally. Rather it is that the term oversimplifies, and in so doing places the onus of "illegality" entirely on the shoulders of the individual migrants rather than in part on the society that in many respects has encouraged their entry. For example, until the recent change in immigration law it was illegal to harbor (for

---

[23]Bean and Sullivan, "Immigration and its Consequences."

[24]See, for example, C. B. Keely, "Illegal Migration," *Scientific America* 246 (1982): 41–47.

[25]Keely, "Illegal Migration."

example, to admit to your home) someone who was in the country without an appropriate visa, but it was *not* illegal to employ this person to clean your home. In recognition of the contradictions this situation entailed, many observers preferred to use adjectives like "undocumented" or "irregular" to describe non-visa entrants, especially those who come to the United States temporarily in order to work.

We mention this issue not because we wish to embrace a particular terminology, but because we wish to emphasize that the language used to describe this group seems to have considerable potential for affecting the way people think about this population. For example, the use of the term "illegal immigrant" immediately places persons who have reservations about some of the procedures proposed to restrict illegal entry into the country on the defensive. No one wishes publicly to condone illegality. Moreover, the desire to build political support for curtailing illegality also may have fostered exaggerations about the extent of the "illegal migrant problem." The number of border apprehensions reported by the Immigration and Naturalization Service, for example, is an exaggerated representation of the number of apprehended migrants, because it includes multiple apprehensions of the same individual. When this figure is further inflated by a factor of two or three on the assumption that an unknown additional number of border crossers "got away" and then is spoken of as if it represented "illegal entrants," at least as much confusion as light is shed on the question of the extent of undocumented immigration to the United States.[26]

This confusion is not without consequence. For example, speculations concerning the numbers residing in the country at any given point in time have ranged from 8 million to 15 million persons.[27] While "educated guesses" as high as these numbers have been generally discredited by the demographers who have systematically analyzed the question,[28] some examples from the heated rhetoric during the congressional debate of 1984 on proposed immigration legislation reveal that the exaggerated figures have often been taken seriously. For example, in debating immigration legislation Representative Peter Rodino exclaimed: "Since the last time we considered this legislation . . . over one million persons were apprehended attempting to cross into our country illegally . . . . It is readily accepted that several million others succeeded in gaining illegal entry."[29] In a similar vein, Representative Hamilton Fish queried, "How many more years of millions of undocumenteds entering

[26]Bean and Sullivan, "Immigration and its Consequences."
[27]See J. Passel, "Undocumented Immigration," *Annals* 487(1986):181–200.
[28]Passel, "Undocumented Immigration."
[29]*New York Times*, June 17, 1984.

at will will our people accept?"[30] Others referred to immigration as a "ticking time bomb" and warned that the United States was "losing control of its borders."[31]

The most systematic and careful empirical analyses, however, have concluded that it is improbable that more than 3 million to 6 million illegals resided in the United States in 1980.[32] Moreover, analysis of the one data source that permits an assessment of the number who have come since 1980 indicates that by April 1983 the size of the illegal population probably had not grown appreciably.[33] Because a majority of illegals are Mexican in origin, and because no other single group constitutes more than a small percentage of this population, questions about the number of illegals residing in the United States must be viewed in large part as queries concerning the size of the illegal Mexican population. Even in this case, however, almost every new piece of evidence that has emerged in recent years points to a smaller number residing in the country than many observers have thought were here. As shown in Table 4.7, for example, demographic analyses of 1980 Mexican census data led to the conclusion that no more than about 1.5 million to 3.8

TABLE 4.7

Selected Alternative Estimates of the Number of Illegal Migrants of Mexican Origin Living in the United States in 1980 (in thousands)

Source for Estimates	Males	Females	Total
Mexican Census Data[a]			
High	2,289	1,511	3,800
Low	913	608	1,521
U.S. Census Data[b]	620	511	1,131

[a]Frank D. Bean, Allan G. King, and Jeffrey S. Passel, "The Number of Illegal Migrants of Mexican Origin in the United States: Sex Ratio Based Estimates for 1980," *Demography* 20 (1983):99–109.
[b]Robert Warren and Jeffrey S. Passel, "A Count of the Uncountable: Estimates of Undocumented Aliens Counted in the 1980 United States Census," *Demography* (forthcoming).

[30]*New York Times*, June 17, 1984.
[31]Bean and Sullivan, "Immigration and its Consequences."
[32]Frank D. Bean, Allan G. King, and Jeffrey S. Passel, "Estimates of the Size of the Illegal Migrant Population of Mexican Origin in the United States: An Assessment, Review and Proposal," in Harley L. Browning and Rodolfo O. de la Garza, eds., *Mexican Immigrants and Mexican Americans: An Evolving Relation* (Austin: Center for Mexican American Studies, University of Texas, 1986).
[33]Jeffrey S. Passel and Karen A. Woodrow, "Growth of the Undocumented Alien Population in the United States, 1979–1983, as Measured by the Current Population Survey and the Decennial Census," (paper presented at the annual meeting of the Population Association of America, Boston, April 1985).

million Mexican nationals could have been living in the United States in 1980,[34] with the figure probably closer to the lower end of that range.[35] Other research has estimated that about 1.1 million undocumented Mexicans were included in the 1980 U.S. Census.[36]

These two sets of analyses (of both Mexican and U.S. census data) taken together provide a basis for narrowing the range of possibilities concerning the number in the United States in 1980. They may be viewed as providing estimates of an upper and lower boundary to the number in the country. For example, the analyses of the Mexican census data suggest that it is very unlikely that more than 3.8 million were here in 1980. The analyses of the U.S. census data tell us that at least the 1.1 million included in the 1980 census were here. In addition, an unknown percentage not included in the census were also here. Although there is no way to know this latter proportion with certainty, the burden of expert opinion and other evidence suggests that no more than half of the undocumented Mexicans in the United States in 1980 were *not* included in the census. For example, Keely has offered the opinion that the 1980 census had an undercount of one-third to one-half of the undocumented aliens in this country,[37] and others have said there is reason to think it is even lower.[38] Moreover, based on an examination of other data, analysts have concluded that the 1980 U.S. Census probably counted most illegals living in Los Angeles County, a large proportion of whom are Mexican.[39] In fact, it seems reasonable to think that a minimum undercount rate for illegal Mexicans in 1980 would not be less than the highest rate measured in the United States for any given group, which was about 20 percent for black males aged 20 to 29 in 1980.[40] Moreover, if it is unlikely that fewer than 1.5 million Mexican

[34]Frank D. Bean, Allan G. King, and Jeffrey S. Passel, "The Number of Illegal Migrants of Mexican Origin in the United States: Sex Ratio Based Estimates for 1980," *Demography* 20 (1983):99–109.

[35]Bean, King, and Passel, "Number of Illegal Migrants."

[36]Robert Warren and Jeffrey S. Passel, "A Count of the Uncountable: Estimates of Undocumented Aliens Counted in the 1980 United States Census," *Demography* (forthcoming).

[37]Charles B. Keely. Affidavit submitted for Plaintiffs in *Cumo et al.* v. *Baldridge et al.*, United States District Court, Southern District of New York, 80 Div. 4550 (JES), 1984.

[38]Jeffrey S. Passel, "Undocumented Immigrants: How Many?" (paper presented at the annual meeting of the American Statistical Association, Social Statistics Section, Las Vegas, August 1985).

[39]David M. Heer and Jeffrey S. Passel, "Comparison of Two Different Methods for Computing the Number of Undocumented Mexican Adults in the Los Angeles SMSA" (paper presented at the annual meeting of the Population Association of America, Boston, April 1985).

[40]J. S. Passel, J. S. Siegel, and J. G. Robinson, "Coverage of the National Population by Age, Sex, and Race in the 1980 Census: Preliminary Estimates by Demographic Analysis," *Current Population Reports*, series P-23, no. 115 (Washington, DC: U.S. Government Printing Office, 1982).

TABLE 4.8

Estimates of the Size of the Illegal Mexican Population
Living in the United States in 1980
Under Alternative Assumptions About Undercount Rates
for Illegal Mexicans (in thousands)

Undercount Rate	Males	Females	Total
50% [a]	1,240	1,022	2,262
33% [b]	1,013	675	1,688
25% [c]	905	603	1,508

[a]C. Keely, "Illegal Immigration," *Scientific American* 246 (1982):41–47.
[b]Keely, "Illegal Immigration."
[c]See text.

undocumenteds were living in the United States, as the results of the analyses of Mexican census data suggest, then a minimum undercount rate of about 25 to 30 percent is implied (for example, the 1.1 million included in the 1980 U.S. Census would be about 73 percent of the 1.5 million figure).

In light of these considerations, Table 4.8 presents an indication of the number of undocumented Mexicans in the United States in 1980 under a range of assumptions about the undercount rate for undocumented Mexicans. The range is based on the expert opinions noted above, but makes no allowance for differential undercount by sex. An undercount rate of about 25 percent would imply that about 1.5 million undocumented Mexicans were living in the United States in 1980, an undercount rate of 33 percent that about 1.7 million were here and an undercount rate of 50 percent that about 2.3 million were here.[41] If the latter figure were correct, and if Mexicans make up about 60 percent of all illegals as the evidence seems to suggest, then one would expect an additional 1.5 million non-Mexicans to have been here in 1980, for a total of about 3.8 million illegals. If one of the smaller figures were correct, the total number of undocumenteds here in 1980 would, of course, have been even less. Hence, careful and systematic consideration of the evidence on the matter points to numbers of illegal aliens living in the United States that are in the lower part of the ranges of the best estimates that have been put forth. These are hardly consistent with the larger speculative guesses that have often been taken as indicative of the size of this population.

[41]That is, if 1.13 million were included, but 25 percent were missed, there would be an additional 37 million in the country.

Future Immigration Flows

Even though evidence about the size of the illegal population suggests figures that do not measure up to the larger numbers often claimed for it, it is not unreasonable to ask whether increased numbers of both legal and illegal immigrants might be expected in the future. Some concerns in this regard have occasionally bordered on the alarmist. In its lead editorial on July 21, 1985, for example, the *New York Times* argued that a "flood" of Hispanic immigrants, the product of Latin American baby booms, is about to inundate the country.[42] This idea was brought forth in support of passage of the immigration reform legislation introduced in the 99th Congress. Ironically again, this legislation is aimed only at illegal migration, although it is recent increases in legal migration from Latin America that the *Times* cites as evidence in support of the "coming flood" of Latin migrants.

Apart from its hazardous reliance on extrapolations from past trends, this argument rests on an overly simplistic and possibly fallacious model of what determines international migration streams. This is a simple "push-pull" model, which assumes that the high urbanization rates and economic conditions in Latin America are synonymous with enormous population and economic pressures in those countries, pressures which will inevitably "push" migrants north to the United States. A number of other factors, however, have generally been found more important in affecting emigration. Orthodox push-pull approaches, which at different times and for different authors have emphasized a variety of factors affecting population migration,[43] have served more as *ex post facto* descriptions of movements that have already taken place rather than as satisfactory bases for predicting movements in the future. Nonetheless, it seems self-evident that, other things being equal, to the extent that economic opportunities are perceived to be better in one area than another, migration to the area thought to be superior is likely to occur.[44]

Other factors are rarely equal, however. Historically, specific labor recruitment efforts undertaken by entrepreneurs in order to attract sources of relatively inexpensive labor for their business enterprises have preceded the emergence and consolidation of migrant flows. This

---

[42]*New York Times*, July 21, 1985.

[43]See the discussion of Alejandro Portes and Robert L. Bach, "Theoretical Overview," in *Latin Journey: Cuban and Mexican Immigrants in the United States* (Berkeley: University of California Press, 1985).

[44]Michael J. Greenwood, "Regional Economic Aspects of Immigrant Location Patterns in the United States," in Mary M. Kritz, ed., *U.S. Immigration and Refugee Policy: Global and Domestic Issues* (Lexington, MA: Lexington Books, 1983).

was true in the case of Italian and eastern European immigration to the United States at the turn of the century and of Mexican labor immigration to the American Southwest.[45] Social relationships and networks are also important in explaining international migration flows.[46] Individuals are often motivated to emigrate because they have family and friends who are emigrating or because they know persons at the place of destination who can assist them in adapting socially and economically to life in a new country. Such mechanisms sustain immigration flows and help to explain why they often persist beyond the point at which economic incentives justify emigration.

Other factors inducing emigration to more developed countries, including the United States, include the nature of the political and economic systems in the countries of origin.[47] Portes, for example, sees international labor migrations as the result of a world economic system involving interdependencies between the United States and other economies. It is important to consider economic interrelationships between countries as a factor influencing migration flows because orthodox push-pull theories imply that immigrants should come from the poorest countries and, within those countries, from the most disadvantaged regions and social groups. Available evidence, however, suggests that this is not what usually occurs. Many Mexican migrants to the United States, for example, come from urban rather than the poorer rural areas;[48] have more education than the general population;[49] and, among those from rural areas, originate in a lower-middle rural stratum rather than among the poorest agricultural laborers.[50] Massey, however, finds that a majority of recent rural migrants are landless day laborers. He argues that, while rural Mexican migration may have begun among those in the middle socioeconomic ranges, in most rural communities it has long since become a mass movement involving persons from almost all strata.[51]

[45]M. J. Piore, *Birds of Passage: Migrant Labor and Industrial Societies* (New York: Cambridge University Press, 1979).

[46]G. M. Anderson, *Networks of Contact: The Portuguese and Toronto* (Waterloo, Ontario: Wilfrid Laurier University Press, 1974).

[47]Portes and Bach, "Theoretical Overview."

[48]Alejandro Portes, "Illegal Immigration and the International System: Lessons from Recent Legal Mexican Immigrants to the United States," *Social Problems* 26 (1979):425–38.

[49]J. A. Bustamante and G. Martinez, "La Emigracion a la Frontera Norte del Pais y a los Estados Unidos," in M. M. Kritz, ed., *Migraciones Internacionales en las Americas* (Caracas: CEPAM, 1980).

[50]I. R. Dinerman, "Patterns of Adaption among Households of U.S.-bound Migrants from Michoacan, Mexico," *International Migration Review* 12 (1978):485–501.

[51]D. Massey, R. Alarion, J. Durand, and H. Gonzalez, *Return to Atzlan* (Berkeley: University of California Press, 1987); and D. Massey, personal communication, 1986.

TABLE 4.9

Immigrants Admitted by Type of Admission,
Country or Region of Birth, and Period of Entry

	Mexico			Cuba		
Period	Numerical Limitation	Exempt	Total	Numerical Limitation	Exempt	Total
1970–1974	189,309	111,030	300,339	96,307	4,759	101,066
	63.0%	37.0%	100.0%	95.3%	4.7%	100.0%
1975–1979	196,446	112,164	308,610	60,050	110,185	170,235
	63.7%	36.3%	100.0%	35.3%	64.7%	100.0%
1980–1984	86,911	142,511	229,422	23,084	30,614	53,698
	37.9%	62.1%	100.0%	43.0%	57.0%	100.0%

NOTE: Omitted from this table are the entrants from Mexico in 1981 and from Cuba in 1977. These are atypical years because both involved special dispensation for the admission of legal entrants.

All of this suggests that the factors impinging on the magnitude of immigration flows are complex and varied. Push-pull approaches to the study of migration, in particular, may be more useful for understanding the "pull" side of the picture than the "push" side. Stated differently, the relative scarcity of unskilled workers projected by some analysts in the United States for the rest of this century might be expected to increase the attractiveness of the United States as a destination for workers in other countries seeking a place where employment and relatively high wages might be more easily obtained.[52] Another factor of importance is the extent to which potential immigrants can be integrated into social networks involving family and friends.[53] If the idea is adopted that migration is a social process in which networks develop to support mass migration, then it is significant that the tradition of Mexican immigration to this country is now over 60 years old, whereas that of Central/South American immigration is still in its formative stages. This can be seen in the figures in Table 4.9, which shows the types of admission by period of entry for Mexicans, Cubans, and Central/South Americans. It is noteworthy that the percentages of immigrants coming to the United States outside the numerical limitations (most of whom qualify on the basis of family reunification criteria) have been increasing for all groups. However, the percentages in this category for Mexicans and Cubans are much higher than they are for Central/South Americans, suggesting a greater potential for future Mexican and Cuban immigration.

[52]Bean and Sullivan, "Immigration and its Consequences."
[53]Massey et al., *Return to Atzlan.*

TABLE 4.9 *(continued)*

Central/South America			All Groups		
Numerical Limitation	Exempt	Total	Numerical Limitation	Exempt	Total
156,946	54,091	211,037	1,408,617	514,796	1,923,413
74.4%	25.6%	100.0%	73.2%	26.8%	100.0%
221,542	79,160	300,702	1,463,416	845.496	2,308,912
73.7%	26.3%	100.0%	63.4%	36.6	100.0%
275,554	124,984	400,538	1,410,866	1,414,170	2,825,036
68.8%	31.2%	100.0%	49.9%	50.1%	100.0%

The Characteristics of Mexican Immigrant Groups

Another issue that is important to consider is the extent to which recent immigrants experience assimilation in the United States. In this section we examine selected socioeconomic and demographic characteristics of Mexican immigrant status groups that vary in the amount of time their members have spent in the United States, as well as in the extent to which their members might be thought to identify with the United States instead of Mexico. We restrict our attention in this exercise to persons of Mexican origin because they are the only group large enough to allow this kind of detailed examination.

It has been estimated that 852,000 persons who were born in Mexico, who reported they were not citizens in 1980, and who entered the United States from 1975 to 1980 were included in the 1980 census.[54] Of this number, 559,000, or 65.6 percent, have been estimated to be undocumented migrants. We thus define our first immigrant status group as consisting of Mexican-born noncitizens who entered the United States between 1975 and 1980. For terminological convenience we call this group post-1975 Mexican-born noncitizens, or Category I for short. Warren and Passel also estimate that 1,474,000 Mexican-born noncitizens entered the United States before 1975.[55] Of this number, 902,000, or 61.2 percent, are estimated to be legal aliens. Again for the sake of terminological convenience, we refer to this subpopulation as pre-1975 Mexican-born noncitizens, or Category II. It should be emphasized that this group is estimated to contain over one-third undocumented migrants and nearly two-thirds legal aliens, whereas the post-1975 group is

[54]Warren and Passel, "Count of the Uncountable."
[55]Warren and Passel, "Count of the Uncountable."

estimated to be made up of two-thirds undocumented migrants.[56] The third group that we examine consists of Mexican-born persons who self-reported that they were naturalized citizens (Category III). There are two reasons for examining these persons separately. The first is that those Mexican-born persons who had actually achieved citizenship (Warren and Passel estimate this number to be 205,000 out of 580,000)[57] are clearly different in their immigrant status from noncitizens and from the native-born. The second is that those who reported they were naturalized citizens but in fact were not (an estimated 375,000 out of 580,000) may be systematically different from those who did not misreport naturalization status.[58] The final group that we define consists of native-born persons who identify themselves as of Mexican origin in the 1980 census. This category we call native-born Mexican Americans, or Category IV.[59]

We contrast these groups here only with respect to their age and sex structure, their levels of educational attainment and English proficiency, and their location in various industry categories. A more complete description is available elsewhere.[60] Our results should not be

---

[56]These compositional differences must be kept in mind in drawing comparisons between the two groups. It must also be remembered that dissimilarities between the two groups may result in part from differences in date of entry into the United States. Not only will those who entered earlier have had longer to assimilate to life in the United States, but also their numbers will be more depleted by return migration than will be the case among those who have been in this country a shorter time. To the extent that it is the less successful and less assimilated who tend to return to Mexico, then differences between the two groups might be accentuated.

[57]Warren and Passel, "Count of the Uncountable."

[58]A comparison of the group of persons who self-report as naturalized citizens with the other groups may provide a clue as to whether undocumenteds or legal aliens are more likely to misreport citizenship. Undocumenteds may misreport citizenship because such a response seems "safe"; legal aliens may misreport it because they are in the process of acquiring citizenship. If undocumenteds are disproportionately represented among misreporters, we would expect the characteristics of the group who self-report as naturalized citizens to resemble more closely the characteristics of Category I than the characteristics of Category II or of native-born persons. If legal aliens are disproportionately represented among misreporters, we would expect the reverse. In either event, the fact that over 65 percent of the persons in the group of self-reported naturalized citizens misreport their status constitutes an important reason in its own right for examining separately the characteristics of persons who report themselves as naturalized citizens.

[59]While this group is more homogeneous than the others, it contains an estimated more than 200,000 Mexican origin persons who reported themselves in the 1980 census as native-born but who in fact were born in Mexico (Warren and Passel, "Count of the Uncountable"). Hence, even this category includes some persons whom we would classify in one of the other categories were it possible to do so at the microlevel, although they represent only a very small percentage of the total.

[60]Frank D. Bean, Harley L. Browning, and W. Parker Frisbie, "The Sociodemographic Characteristics of Mexican Immigrant Status Groups: Implications for Studying Undocumented Mexican Migrants," *International Migration Review* 18 (1984):672-91. Although Bean, Browning, and Frisbie were unable to ascertain the legal status of individuals, they were able to define groups that consisted largely of undocumented aliens, legal aliens, naturalized citizens, and native-born persons of Mexican origin.

construed as providing a sociodemographic profile of undocumented Mexicans included in the 1980 census, for it is impossible to obtain such results. They do, however, provide profiles of certain groups likely to contain substantial proportions of undocumented Mexican immigrants.

The sizes of the various subsamples are shown in Table 4.10, together with the age and sex structure of the various immigrant status groups and sex ratios (the number of males per 100 females) by age. Evidence consistent with the idea that Category I contains substantial numbers of undocumented migrants is evident in the sex ratios for that subpopulation. They increase dramatically from the youngest age group (0–14) to those aged 15 to 19, reaching a peak among persons aged 20 to 29 and dropping off thereafter. In general, the sex ratios for Category I among persons aged 15 to 39, the ages at which undocumented migration is most likely to occur, range from 25 to 40 percent higher than they do for native-born Mexican Americans at comparable ages.[61]

The sex ratios within the primary migrating ages for Categories II and III also reveal the influence of gender selectivity of immigration to the United States from Mexico. In general, the sex ratios for five-year age groups within the 15–39 range average about 5 to 15 percent higher than they do for native-born Mexican Americans at comparable ages. Another interesting feature in this regard is the emergence of somewhat higher than expected sex ratios for Categories II and III at ages 50 to 59. This perhaps reflects the demographic legacy of the bracero program of the 1940s and 1950s, a time when many males came to the United States as temporary workers and then stayed after the program ended in 1962, often with employer assistance in obtaining permanent resident alien visas.

The differences in age patterns that emerge among the subpopulations are thus consistent with the idea that the first category contains a majority of undocumented migrants from Mexico. A much higher percentage of both males and females are aged 20 to 29 in Category I than is the case among the other three groups (also see the median ages in Table 4.10). The subpopulations in Categories II and III are considerably older than is the case for both Categories I and IV, primarily because of the relative absence of children in the latter two groups[62] and because the latter two groups contain significantly large numbers of persons at older ages, perhaps again as a legacy of the bracero program of the 1940s and 1950s.

[61]See Bean, King, and Passel, "Number of Illegal Migrants."
[62]Frank D. Bean and Gray Swicegood, "Generation, Female Education and Fertility Among Mexican Americans," *Social Science Quarterly* 63 (1982):131–44; and Frank D. Bean, Ruth M. Cullen, Elizabeth H. Stephen, and Gray Swicegood, "Generational Differences in Fertility among Mexican Americans: Implications for Assessing Immigration Effects," *Social Science Quarterly* 65 (1984):573–82.

TABLE 4.10

Age Distribution by Immigrant Status and Sex, as Well as Sex Ratios by Immigrant Status and Age: Mexican Origin Population, 1980

Age Group	Males				Females				Sex Ratios			
	I	II	III	IV	I	II	III	IV	I	II	III	IV
0–14 Years	26.3%	9.8%	9.7%	44.4%	30.2%	10.0%	10.4%	42.2%	106.3%	101.9%	99.6%	103.6%
15–19 Years	15.8	7.9	6.4	11.4	14.7	7.7	6.6	11.4	131.1	105.7	103.5	98.5
20–24 Years	23.3	11.2	10.8	9.3	19.9	10.2	9.9	9.7	143.0	113.1	116.5	94.4
25–29 Years	14.5	15.6	12.1	8.0	13.1	13.7	11.4	8.2	135.1	117.2	113.4	96.1
30–34 Years	7.7	13.7	11.6	6.4	7.7	12.8	10.8	6.5	122.1	110.2	114.7	97.0
35–39 Years	4.6	10.2	8.6	4.3	4.7	10.1	9.3	4.6	120.0	104.6	98.8	92.1
40–49 Years	4.7	13.8	12.9	6.8	4.9	14.6	13.6	7.2	117.1	97.4	101.3	93.0
50–59 Years	2.0	8.6	9.8	5.6	2.8	9.1	8.6	5.9	88.0	97.3	121.7	93.5
60 Years and Over	1.1	9.1	18.2	3.8	2.2	11.8	19.5	4.4	61.0	79.5	99.7	85.0
Total	100.0	99.9	100.1	100.0	100.2	100.0	100.1	100.1	122.1	103.0	106.8	98.5
N	17,470	24,469	12,344	155,368	14,313	23,756	11,560	157,767				
Median Age	21.7	32.2	34.7	17.5	21.3	33.3	35.5	18.4				
Median Age for Those Aged 15 and Over	24.5	33.8	37.5	29.4	25.1	35.3	38.3	29.8				

NOTE: I. Mexican-born noncitizens who immigrated to the U.S. in 1975 or later. II. Mexican-born noncitizens who immigrated to the U.S. prior to 1975. III. Mexican-born persons who self-report that they are naturalized citizens. IV. Persons born in the United States who self-identify as being of Mexican origin.

We also examine differences in English proficiency and education. The 1980 U.S. Census for the first time included an item assessing the ability of respondents over age 2 to speak English. The most meaningful cut-point in the English proficiency classification is between the category "Speaks English Well," which denotes proficiency with the language, and the category "Speaks English Not Well," which identifies persons who are limited in their ability to converse in English. In the case of education, we collapse categories to provide a measure that corresponds to certification points. Specifically, we distinguish those with 0–7, 8, 9–11, 12, and more than 12 years of formal education for the adult population (persons aged 18 and over).

The male and female distributions on education and English proficiency are quite similar across the immigrant status typology (Table 4.11). Nearly a third of both males and females who report themselves as naturalized citizens and about half of the native-born population have completed high school. There is a rather remarkable monotonic increase in educational achievement as we move across the immigrant status categories, with the percentage completing at least 8 years of formal education rising from about one-third among post-1975 immigrants to over one-half among those who are or claim to be naturalized citizens.

Similar in direction to the education patterns, but even more striking, are the English proficiency distributions (Table 4.11). Among the most recently arrived Mexican immigrants, whether male or female, approximately 30 percent either speak only English or speak it well or very well compared with more than 90 percent among the native-born. Except for Category I, almost all of the other immigrant groups contain a majority who speak English well. (The one exception is females in Category II, where the figure is 46.1 percent.) A distinguishing feature of all three first-generation groups compared with the native-born, however, is that 29 to 30 percent of the latter speak only English, whereas this proportion never exceeds 5 percent in other groups.

While there are many features of the labor process that it might be useful to examine—for example, the channels through which jobs are obtained, variations in pay and skill levels by work assignments, fluctuations in hours per week worked, and so on[63]—here (Table 4.12) we focus only on the distribution of the subsamples by industry, immigrant classification, and sex. (The occupational distributions, although utilizing different categories, demonstrate much the same pattern as industry, so they are not presented here in tabular form, although we discuss selected results.)

[63]Harley L. Browning and Nestor Rodriguez, "The Migration of Mexican Indocumentados as a Settlement Process: Implications for Work," in George Borjas and Marta Tienda, eds., *Hispanics in the U.S. Economy* (Orlando, FL: Academic Press, 1985); and Portes and Bach, "Theoretical Overview."

TABLE 4.11

Education Level Completed by Persons Aged 18 and Over and English Proficiency Distributions by Immigrant Status and Sex: Mexican Origin Population, 1980

	Males			
	I	II	III	IV
YEARS OF SCHOOLING				
0–7 Years	62.6%	57.5%	48.4%	19.3%
8 Years	6.2	7.0	7.1	6.4
9–11 Years	13.8	13.8	13.8	21.9
12 Years	9.1	11.8	14.9	26.2
More Than 12 Years	8.3	9.9	15.7	26.2
Total	100.0	100.0	99.9	100.0
N	11,638	20,935	10,735	75,002
ENGLISH PROFICIENCY				
Speaks English Only	1.4 ⎤	1.6 ⎤	4.2 ⎤	31.2 ⎤
Speaks English Very Well	10.2 ⎟ 30.6%	22.4 ⎟ 54.1%	34.2 ⎟ 69.1%	39.4 ⎟ 91.0%
Speaks English Well	19.0 ⎦	30.1 ⎦	30.7 ⎦	20.4 ⎦
Speaks English Not Well	35.9 ⎤	31.9 ⎤	21.6 ⎤	7.1 ⎤
Speaks English Not at All	33.5 ⎦ 69.4	14.0 ⎦ 45.9	9.3 ⎦ 30.9	1.9 ⎦ 9.0
Total	100.0	100.0	100.0	100.0
N	16,905	24,469	12,263	138,947

NOTES: For definitions of immigrant status categories, see Table 4.10.
English proficiency is not reported for children under age 3.

The first pattern to note is that agriculture (and mining) is not the dominant source of employment within any of three first-generation immigrant categories. Proportionally, manufacturing is at least twice as important in all of the male immigrant groups, and even more so in the female groups. Indeed, it is of particular interest that among females in Categories I and II more than 40 percent are in manufacturing. Occupationally, both sexes are concentrated in the lower-status "operative" and "laborer" categories, although a consistent decline occurs running from post-1975 aliens to native-born Mexican Americans.

Given that construction always has been considered an entry job for Mexican immigrants, it is interesting to observe that only about a tenth of the most recent male immigrants (Category I) fall into this industry group. Also, there is very little variation in this pattern across the four immigrant status types, although the broadness of the categories may be disguising heterogeneity within them. Among Category I males food retailing evidently is also an entry industry, although this is not true for

TABLE 4.11 (*continued*)

	Females			
	I	II	III	IV
EARS OF SCHOOLING				
0–7 Years	63.9%	59.7%	49.7%	20.7%
8 Years	6.4	7.2	7.3	7.4
9–11 Years	12.5	12.4	13.3	22.3
12 Years	9.5	12.0	16.8	29.3
More Than 12 Years	7.7	·8.7	12.9	20.2
Total	100.0	100.0	100.0	99.9
	8,888	20,306	9,941	79,985
NGLISH PROFICIENCY				
Speaks English Only	1.3⎤	1.5⎤	3.5⎤	29.3⎤
Speaks English Very Well	9.9⎟ 27.9%	21.7⎟ 46.1%	32.2⎟ 61.4%	41.1⎟ 90.4%
Speaks English Well	16.7⎦	22.9⎦	25.7⎦	20.0⎦
Speaks English Not Well	31.7⎤	29.7⎤	22.5⎤	7.1⎤
Speaks English Not at All	40.4⎦ 72.1	24.2⎦ 53.9	16.1⎦ 38.6	2.6⎦ 9.7
Total	100.0	100.0	100.0	100.1
	13,781	23,756	11,462	141,892

females. In contrast, and as would be expected, females are proportionally more represented in the business, repair, and personal services category, as well as in professional services, finance, and public administration. As is generally characteristic of female labor force distributions,
there is a greater concentration of employment in fewer categories than
is the case for males. In this instance two categories account for most
of the variation across female immigrant status groups: the decline in
the percentage in manufacturing and the rise in the percentage in professional, finance, and public administration that occurs as one moves
from Category I to Category IV. Given the fact that educational attainment among females is no greater than among males, it is noteworthy
that females are proportionally much more concentrated in the higher
ranking industry category. But again, as with males in construction, it
may be likely that the Mexican immigrant women occupy low-status
and low-paying positions within this category. In general, however, the
evidence that emerges from this examination is consistent with the idea
that immigrants improve their industry position the longer their families have been in the United States.

TABLE 4.12

Industry Classification by Immigrant Status and Sex: Mexican Origin Population, 1980

Industry Category	Males				Females			
	I	II	III	IV	I	II	III	IV
Agriculture, Mining	17.3%	16.4%	14.9%	9.0%	10.4%	10.8%	8.0%	4.0%
Construction	11.1	11.3	13.0	13.0	.6	.6	.7	.9
Manufacturing	35.3	36.5	28.9	23.7	44.5	41.0	30.9	19.2
Transportation, Communication, Utilities	2.4	4.3	6.7	9.3	1.0	1.5	2.0	3.7
Wholesaling, Nonfood Retailing	8.7	10.3	10.4	12.9	8.4	9.9	11.1	13.5
Food Retailing	12.2	7.1	6.6	7.1	8.0	7.4	7.7	11.0
Business, Repair, Personal Services	8.7	8.1	7.7	7.7	15.3	11.9	11.7	10.8
Professional Services, Finance, Public Administration	4.3	6.0	11.9	17.4	11.8	16.8	27.9	37.0
Total	100.0	100.0	100.1	100.1	100.0	99.9	100.0	100.1
N	11,388	19,566	9,323	71,777	5,127	12,141	5,719	59,340

NOTE: For definitions of immigrant status categories, see Table 4.10.

Labor Market Impacts

It is often thought that undocumented migrants, the majority of whom are Mexicans as we have seen, take jobs and wages away from native-born citizens. For example, Representative Charles Schumer, writing for the *New York Times*, recently said, "It is generally agreed that illegal immigration depresses wages and working conditions for many Americans."[64] More broadly, two-thirds of southern Californians recently queried on the matter expressed the opinion that "undocumented workers tend to bring down the overall level of wages in some occupations."[65] The research evidence on this issue, however, gives a different picture than does public opinion. In thinking about the question, it is important first to remember that many fewer illegal immigrants appear to be in the country than much of the political rhetoric on the subject would lead us to believe. Whatever else we might think about the question, this suggests that the impact of undocumented immigration on employment and earnings is probably not as great as many observers might presume.

Apart from the question of the number of immigrants involved, it has been difficult to study the relationship between illegal immigration and unemployment or wages owing to the lack of data (until recently) on illegal migrants. Studies of the effects of legal immigration on unemployment, however, find little basis to think that a very large impact occurs. For example, an examination of nation-wide and regional data over time in Great Britain found no observable effect of New Commonwealth immigration on unemployment.[66] A study of changes in the unemployment rate in U.S. cities in response to fluctuations in city-rates of immigration revealed no increase in unemployment due to immigration.[67] Further relevant evidence comes from studies of effects on wages based on analyses of various ethnic groups and of legal immigrant and native groups.[68] The results are inconclusive, providing no consistent

---

[64]*New York Times*, May 21, 1985.
[65]T. Muller and T. Espenshade, *The Fourth Wave* (Washington, DC: Urban Institute Press, 1985), p. 201.
[66]K. Jones and A. D. Smith, *The Economic Impact of Commonwealth Immigration* (Cambridge: Cambridge University Press, 1970).
[67]Julian Simon and S. Moore, "The Effect of Immigration Upon Unemployment: An Across-City Estimation," unpublished paper, 1984.
[68]George J. Borjas, "The Earnings of Male Hispanic Immigrants in the United States," *Industrial and Labor Relations Review* 35 (1982)343–53; George J. Borjas, "The Substitutability of Black, Hispanic and White Labor," *Economic Inquiry* 21 (1983):93–106; George J. Borjas, "The Impact of Immigrants on the Earnings of the Native-Born," in V. M. Briggs, Jr., and M. Tienda, eds:, *Immigration: Issues and Policies* (Salt Lake City: Olympus, 1984); Jean B. Grossman, "The Substitutability of Natives and Immigrants in Production," *Review of Economics and Statistics* 54 (1982):596–603; Allan G. King, B. L. Lowell, and Frank D. Bean, "The Effects of Hispanic Immigrants on the Earnings of Native Hispanic Americans," *Social Science Quarterly* 67 (1986):672–89.

evidence that the employment of one group of legal residents depresses the wages of other groups.[69]

These latter results suggest that the impact of illegal immigrants on wages may also be negligible. It seems reasonable to think that if *legal* immigration has little impact, *illegal* immigration is also not likely to make much of a difference, especially if undocumented migrants fill jobs no one else wants to take. As noted above, this question has been hard to address because data on illegals has not been available until recently. A couple of recent studies, however, employ data on undocumented Mexicans to examine the issue. One, conducted by Massey, shows that illegality per se does not cause undocumented immigrants to earn lower wages than legal immigrants.[70] The other, conducted by Bean and his associates, finds that undocumenteds, if anything, exert a small positive effect on the wages of other groups in local labor markets.[71]

In short, when evidence has been systematically brought to bear on the question of labor market impacts, it has not shown adverse effects of undocumented immigration. One reason may be that illegal aliens create some new jobs. Not only is there reason to think that some businesses employing both legal and illegal workers might not exist if some of their jobs could not be filled by undocumented workers,[72] but also other jobs are created to service the illegal aliens working in this country.[73] Also, as noted above, illegal migrants may in fact be filling jobs that American workers are reluctant to take. Whatever the reason, given the relatively low levels of fertility in the United States among non-Spanish whites over the past 20 years, it is possible that the recent legislation passed to restrict undocumented immigration could have the effect of exacerbating shortages of entry-level workers. To the extent that undocumented immigration *increases* the wages of other groups, as the work of Bean and his associates suggests,[74] the absence of undocumented labor might have deleterious rather than beneficial consequences.

---

[69]For further discussion of the issue, see George J. Borjas and Marta Tienda, "The Economic Impact of Immigration," *Science*, February 6, 1987.

[70]D. Massey, "Do Undocumented Migrants Earn Lower Wages?" unpublished paper, 1986.

[71]Frank D. Bean, B. L. Lowell, and L. Taylor, "Undocumented Mexican Immigrants and the Earnings of Other Workers in the United States," *Demography* 25(1988) (forthcoming).

[72]Muller and Espenshade, *The Fourth Wave*.

[73]Browning and Rodriguez, "Migration of Mexican Indocumentados."

[74]Bean, Lowell, and Taylor, "Undocumented Mexican Immigrants."

Summary and Conclusions

This chapter has reviewed the basic aspects of both legal and illegal Hispanic immigration to the United States. Since 1965 immigration has increasingly involved peoples of Hispanic and Asian origin. Most of the Cubans and Central/South Americans came to the United States during this period, and the presence of substantial numbers of Puerto Ricans on the mainland is also a recent phenomenon, occurring almost in its entirety since World War II. Although of longer duration, Mexican immigration, both legal and illegal, has also been of considerable magnitude during the 1960s and 1970s. Hence, immigration has contributed prominently to the growing size and visibility of the various Hispanic groups in recent years.

We have devoted special attention to Mexican immigration, both because Mexicans constitute a majority of all persons of Hispanic origin and because by all accounts they appear to be the largest single group by far among undocumented entrants to this country. In considering the question of the degree to which Mexican Americans might usefully be viewed as a "colonized" rather than an "immigrant" people, as a group involuntarily rather than voluntarily in the United States, we observed that the vast majority of Mexican Americans are either immigrants or the descendants of immigrants rather than the descendants of the small Mexican population residing in the Southwest in 1848 when the Treaty of Guadalupe Hidalgo was signed. We do not take this to mean that the colonial analogy of Mexican Americans as akin to a conquered people is totally devoid of significance for understanding the nature and degree of Mexican American motivation to embrace the cultural and behavioral patterns of the majority society. Rather, we think the voluntary quality that characterizes Mexican immigration to the United States means that the kinds of frameworks and ideas that have proved useful in studying immigrant groups of other national origins are also relevant to the experience of Mexican Americans.

At a policy level, it is interesting to note that the legislation passed by the 99th Congress is designed to have a major impact on illegal immigration although it leaves the law with respect to legal immigration virtually unchanged. Substantial changes in the magnitude and pattern of legal immigration, however, have occurred over the past 20 years. While we know with certainty that the percentage and number of legal immigrants of Hispanic origin have increased substantially, the volume and impact of illegal immigration—most of which involves Mexicans— are known with much less certainty, and perhaps for that reason have been easier to exaggerate. Ironically, it may be the greater visibility of legal immigrants from Third World countries in recent years that has contributed to the seemingly widespread public perception that illegal immigration has been sizable and has had adverse effects. Whatever the case, the data presented in this chapter illustrate many of the ways in which the degree and kind of immigration involving Spanish-speaking persons affect both the immigrants themselves and the society that has received them.

5

GEOGRAPHICAL DISTRIBUTION, INTERNAL MIGRATION, AND RESIDENTIAL SEGREGATION

D ATA PRESENTED in previous chapters have documented recent increases in levels of Hispanic immigration to the United States. Together with high fertility, these increases have resulted in substantial growth in the size of the Hispanic population during the 1970s, thus contributing to a growing awareness in this country that Hispanics constitute an important and increasingly discernible ethnic group. Historically concentrated in the Southwest, the New York metropolitan area, and Florida, the Hispanic population is likely to become an even more visible part of American society as its members disperse more widely throughout the country. The purpose of this chapter is thus to examine the character of and changes in the geographic distribution of the populations of Spanish origin in the United States over the past two decades. Our examination has three foci. The first deals simply with population distribution. Where do the various Spanish origin populations live and how has this changed over the past two decades? The second concerns internal migration. What were the major changes in geographic distribution involving the Spanish origin groups during the 1970s? The third involves residential segregation. To what extent do the members of the Spanish origin populations live in areas that are residentially separate from those of non-Hispanic whites?

NOTE: This chapter was prepared in collaboration with Douglas S. Massey.

Geographic Distribution

The regional concentration of the populations of Spanish origin can be readily seen from the figures presented in Table 5.1, which show the percentage distribution of the various Hispanic populations by major census regions in the United States in 1960, 1970, and 1980. At all three periods about three-fourths of the total Spanish origin population resided in the South (which according to the criteria of the Bureau of the Census includes the state of Texas) or in the West (which includes the southwestern states of Arizona, California, Colorado, and New Mexico).[1] The North Central census region, which contained only 5 percent of all persons of Spanish origin in 1960, showed the greatest relative increase in its share of the Spanish origin population by 1980, jumping to 8.7 percent of all Hispanics, or a gain of 74 percent during the 20-year period. The relative sizes of the total Hispanic population in the remaining three regions did not shift on such a dramatic scale, each retaining over the 20-year period a share roughly comparable to the one it had in 1960.

Such aggregate figures, however, mask important variations among the Spanish origin groups. The most pronounced example occurs in the case of Cubans, who between 1960 and 1980 became increasingly concentrated in the census South, reflecting the growth and increasing dominance of Florida, and especially Miami, as a major center of Cuban American residential and business activity. Whereas Cuban Americans show a pattern of increasingly regional concentration, Mexican Americans and Puerto Ricans exhibit less regional concentration between 1960 and 1980. In the case of Mexicans substantial growth occurred in the population living in the North Central states, although by 1980 this population still represented only 9.3 percent of all persons of Mexican origin in the country. In the case of Puerto Ricans there is evidence of considerable dispersal outside the Northeast, especially between 1970 and 1980. Substantial increases in the size of the Puerto Rican population living in the southern and western states occurred during this decade, as well as a smaller increase in the North Central states. Alto-

[1]The Bureau of the Census defines four major census regions as follows: Northeast— Connecticut, Maine, Massachusetts, New Hampshire, New Jersey, New York, Pennsylvania, Rhode Island, Vermont; North Central—Illinois, Indiana, Iowa, Kansas, Michigan, Minnesota, Missouri, Nebraska, North Dakota, Ohio, South Dakota, Wisconsin; South— Alabama, Arkansas, Delaware, District of Columbia, Florida, Georgia, Kentucky, Louisiana, Maryland, Mississippi, North Carolina, Oklahoma, South Carolina, Tennessee, Texas, Virginia, West Virginia; West—Alaska, Arizona, California, Colorado, Hawaii, Idaho, Montana, Nevada, New Mexico, Oregon, Utah, Washington, Wyoming.

TABLE 5.1

*Percentage Distributions of the Spanish Origin Populations
by Census Region: 1960–1980*

	Northeast	North Central	South	West
Total Spanish Origin				
1960	18.8%	5.0%	32.2%	44.1%
1970	20.7	7.4	29.1	42.7
1980	17.8	8.7	30.6	42.8
Mexican				
1960	0.3	3.9	39.2	56.6
1970	0.2	4.1	34.6	61.1
1980	1.0	9.3	35.5	54.1
Puerto Rican				
1960	82.9	7.6	5.3	4.3
1970	86.3	7.7	2.4	3.5
1980	73.8	10.4	9.1	6.8
Cuban				
1960	43.4	4.2	48.2	4.2
1970	28.4	4.1	59.5	8.0
1980	22.8	4.1	63.9	9.2
Central/South American				
1960	40.6	10.3	21.1	28.1
1970	42.9	9.8	18.2	29.1
1980	37.7	5.9	21.6	34.8
Other Hispanic				
1960	41.6	14.0	0.5	24.0
1970	6.8	48.1	23.5	21.7
1980	19.8	7.5	21.9	50.8

SOURCES: U.S. Bureau of the Census, *Census of Population: 1980*, "General Social and Economic Characteristics," PC80-1-C2–C52 (Washington, DC: U.S. Government Printing Office, 1983), table 100; and 1960 and 1970 Public Use Sample Files.

gether, the proportion of the Puerto Rican population living outside the northeastern states increased between 1960 and 1980 from about 17 percent to about 26 percent.

Central/South Americans reveal less pronounced patterns of population shift, although evidence of some increasing concentration in the West emerges. For example, between 1960 and 1980 the percentage of Central/South Americans living in the West rose from 28.1 to 34.8 percent, a gain of almost 24 percent. In the case of persons of Other Hispanic origin it is almost impossible to try to interpret the figures, because they are largely the product of the changes across census periods in the identifiers that are available to delineate this subgroup.

Nativity Differences

As we observed in the last chapter, one of the factors affecting the volume and character of immigration, as well as settlement patterns among immigrants after they arrive in the United States, is the existence of social networks consisting of family and friends that facilitate the settlement process and the location of employment.[2] This being the case, we would expect to find an even greater geographic concentration of the foreign-born members of the Spanish origin groups than of the native-born. Evidence in support of this idea emerges from the data pre-

TABLE 5.2

Percentage Distributions of the Spanish Origin Populations by Region and Nativity: 1980

	Northeast	North Central	South	West
Total Spanish Origin				
Foreign-Born	17.3%	7.9%	29.3%	45.5%
Native-Born	18.1	9.0	31.1	41.8
Mexican				
Foreign-Born	0.9	9.9	24.1	65.0
Native-Born	1.1	9.1	39.5	50.3
Puerto Rican				
Foreign-Born[a]	71.2	10.5	12.6	5.6
Native-Born[b]	73.9	10.4	8.9	6.8
Cuban				
Foreign-Born	22.3	3.5	65.7	8.5
Native-Born	24.5	6.0	57.7	11.8
Central/South American				
Foreign-Born	42.3	5.5	20.1	32.1
Native-Born	27.1	6.7	25.3	40.9
Other Hispanic				
Foreign-Born	42.4	8.2	20.6	28.8
Native-Born	14.5	7.3	22.2	56.0

SOURCES: U.S. Bureau of the Census, *Census of Population: 1980,* "General Social and Economic Characteristics," PC80-1-C2–C52 (Washington, DC: U.S. Government Printing Office, 1983), table 100; and 1980 Public Use Microdata Sample A File.

[a]Born in Puerto Rico.
[b]Born on the mainland.

[2]See Douglas S. Massey, "The Settlement Process Among Mexican Migrants to the United States: New Methods and Findings," in Daniel Levine, Kenneth Hill, and Robert Warren, eds., *Immigrant Statistics: A Story of Neglect* (Washington, DC: National Academy Press, 1985); and Alejandro Portes and Robert L. Bach, "Theoretical Overview," in *Latin Journey: Cuban and Mexican Immigrants in the United States* (Berkeley: University of California Press, 1985).

sented in Table 5.2, which shows the regional distributions of the Spanish origin subgroups by nativity in 1980. In the case of Mexicans and Cubans, higher proportions of the foreign-born population are found in the regions of the greatest concentration of these populations. For example, 65 percent of foreign-born Mexicans as opposed to only about 50 percent of the native-born live in the West, the region of greatest concentration among Mexican Americans. Similarly, about 66 percent of the foreign-born Cuban Americans live in the South as opposed to only about 58 percent of the native-born. This tendency also emerges in the case of Central/South Americans who are most concentrated in the Northeast. In the case of Puerto Ricans and Other Hispanics, however, the pattern of the foreign-born being more likely to live in regions of greater Hispanic concentration does not appear.

Measures of Concentration

As interesting as such patterns of regional concentration are, they suffer at least two limitations that hamper inferences about whether the populations of Spanish origin are becoming more dispersed throughout the United States over time. The first is that the regional groupings of states are so large that they do not enable the detection of dispersal within regions. The second is that they do not reveal whether the shifts in the distribution of the Spanish origin population over time are distinct from regional shifts occurring in the population at large. In order to obtain a clearer picture about the tendency for the populations of Spanish origin to have distributed themselves more widely throughout the United States, we turn to the state distributions of the populations in 1960, 1970, and 1980 (presented in Table 5.3). Because population shifts in general—such as the tendency for movement to have occurred out of Northeast and North Central states into Sunbelt states during the 1970s[3]—affect the distribution by state of both the total population and the population of Spanish origin, it is desirable to compute a measure of distributional concentration for the populations of Spanish origin in each of the three census years that is free of such general population shifts. A measure of distributional difference that serves this purpose— the index of dissimilarity—was computed between the state distribution of each of the Spanish origin groups and the distribution of the

[3]Jeanne Biggar, "The Sunning of America: Migration to the Sunbelt," *Population Bulletin*, vol. 34, no. 1 (Washington, DC: Population Reference Bureau, 1979); and Brian J. Berry and Lester P. Silverman, eds., *Population Redistribution and Public Policy* (Washington, DC: National Academy of Sciences, 1980).

TABLE 5.3

Percentage State Distributions of the Spanish Origin Populations: 1960–1980

	Mexican			Puerto Rican		
State	1960	1970	1980	1960	1970	1980
Arizona	5.7%	5.1%	4.7%	.2%	.1	.2%
California	38.7	44.0	42.1	3.1	2.9	4.4
Colorado	4.2	4.5	2.4	.1	.1	.2
Connecticut	.0	.0	.0	1.6	2.5	4.5
District of Columbia	.0	.0	.0	.1	.1	.1
Florida	.1	.0	.7	2.1	.2	4.8
Hawaii	.0	.0	.1	.4	.2	1.0
Illinois	1.7	2.1	4.7	3.9	5.3	6.7
Indiana	.3	.3	.7	.9	.5	.6
Kansas	.3	.2	.6	.2	.1	.1
Louisiana	.1	.1	.2	.4	.2	.2
Maryland	.0	.1	.1	.4	.3	.5
Massachusetts	.0	.0	.1	.3	1.7	3.8
Michigan	.6	.7	1.2	.3	.4	.5
Missouri	.2	.1	.3	.1	.1	.1
New Jersey	.1	.0	.1	6.5	11.4	12.2
New Mexico	7.1	6.6	2.7	.0	.0	.1
New York	.1	.1	.4	72.2	66.2	49.2
Ohio	.2	.2	.5	1.3	1.2	1.7
Oklahoma	.1	.1	.4	.1	.1	.1
Oregon	.1	.2	.5	.0	.0	.1
Pennsylvania	.1	.0	.2	2.1	4.5	4.4
Texas	38.7	34.0	32.4	.7	.5	1.0
Utah	.1	.2	.4	.2	.0	.1
Virginia	.0	.1	.2	.3	.2	.5
Washington	.4	.2	.9	.1	.1	.2
Wisconsin	.1	.2	.5	.8	.1	.5
Wyoming	.0	.1	.2	.0	.0	.0
All other states	.5	.5	2.6	1.6	1.2	1.8
Total	99.5	99.7	99.9	100.0	100.2	99.6

SOURCES: 1960 and 1970 Public Use Sample files; and 1980 Public Use Microdata Sample file.

general population in each of the census years.[4] This index varies from a minimum of 0 to a maximum of 100 and can be interpreted as the percentage of the given Spanish origin population that would have to change its state residence in order to result in the same population distribution occurring in the total population.

[4]For a discussion of the strengths and weaknesses of the index, as well as the formula for its computation, see Douglas S. Massey, "On the Measurement of Segregation as a Random Variable," *American Sociological Review* 43 (1979):587–90.

TABLE 5.3 *(continued)*

Cuban			Central/ South American			Other Hispanic		
1960	1970	1980	1960	1970	1980	1960	1970	1980
.0%	.0%	.1%	.6%	.5%	.3%	.3%	.0%	1.8%
3.2	7.1	8.0	24.9	25.9	25.4	12.5	.1	25.0
.1	.3	.2	.7	.5	.4	.3	.0	6.2
2.1	.9	.7	1.9	1.3	1.1	2.8	2.7	.7
.7	.1	.1	1.2	1.0	.6	.6	1.0	.2
43.0	54.0	58.4	5.2	5.7	9.1	9.4	.2	5.9
.0	.0	.1	.0	.1	.1	.6	1.7	2.1
1.9	2.0	2.3	3.7	4.0	3.2	4.1	13.5	2.2
.3	.0	.2	.8	.5	.2	.9	4.9	.5
.1	.1	.1	.2	.2	.2	.8	3.0	.4
1.0	1.5	.9	4.9	3.1	1.6	3.4	3.7	2.2
.2	.6	.5	1.7	1.8	1.7	.4	2.5	1.0
.7	1.3	.8	1.6	1.6	1.8	2.8	2.6	1.5
.2	.7	.4	1.7	1.3	.6	2.4	9.6	1.5
.0	.1	.2	.3	.5	.3	.4	2.9	.6
6.9	11.6	10.7	5.1	6.0	8.4	9.7	.2	3.1
.1	.1	.1	.1	.1	.2	.0	.0	12.1
31.9	13.7	10.1	29.5	32.0	34.9	20.7	.6	9.3
.8	.6	.4	1.7	1.6	.5	4.7	6.1	1.2
.1	.1	.1	.8	.4	.3	.8	2.7	.6
.0	.1	.1	.5	.6	.2	.8	2.4	.8
1.5	.6	.6	1.9	1.7	.8	4.9	.0	1.4
1.1	1.0	1.7	3.3	2.9	2.8	1.3	.0	8.3
.0	.0	.0	.3	.3	.2	.1	5.6	1.0
.4	.9	.5	1.2	1.3	1.7	.6	3.9	1.2
.7	.1	.2	.8	.6	.4	1.1	5.5	1.4
.2	.2	.2	.7	.4	.3	.0	3.4	.4
.0	.0	.0	.0	.1	.0	.1	2.1	.4
3.0	2.1	2.3	4.4	3.6	2.9	14.5	18.9	6.9
100.2	99.8	100.0	99.7	99.6	99.5	100.0	99.8	99.9

The picture that emerges from examining the values for this index (shown in Table 5.4) depends very much on which Spanish origin group is being examined. In the case of Mexican Americans a clear pattern of deconcentration emerges, with the value of the dissimilarity index decreasing from a high of about 80 in 1960 to about 65 in 1980. Although Mexican Americans in 1980 remain highly concentrated in certain states, this concentration is considerably less pronounced than it was in 1960. A similar pattern emerges in the case of Puerto Ricans, although the reduction in the degree of concentration for this subgroup is not

TABLE 5.4

Indexes of Dissimilarity Between the State Distributions
of the Spanish Origin Populations
and the Total United States Population: 1960–1980

	1960	1970	1980
Mexican	79.6%	76.8%	64.6%
Puerto Rican	65.9	66.2	57.8
Cuban	67.0	63.8	64.0
Central/South American	45.6	46.3	52.3
Other Hispanic	39.6	45.2	39.7

SOURCES: 1960 and 1970 Public Use Sample files; and 1980 Public Use Microdata Sample file.

nearly as pronounced as it is in the case of Mexican Americans. Among Cuban Americans the reduction in the index over the 20-year period is slight and does not support the conclusion that much overall dispersal in the population has occurred. While some dispersal throughout the country has occurred, it is offset to a considerable degree by increasing concentration in Florida. Standing in contrast to these trends are Central/South Americans, who exhibit some tendency toward greater concentration during this period, especially since 1970. Given that Central/South Americans are the most recent arrivals to the United States among the Spanish origin groups, this is perhaps not surprising, reflecting the likelihood that immigrant groups will locate in places where others of the same national origin live.

Further insight into this tendency of immigrant groups to settle among persons of their own kind can be obtained by comparing indexes of dissimilarity computed between the state distributions of native-born Mexican Americans and the state distributions of Mexican immigrants classified according to when they entered the United States. In the case of Mexican immigrants who entered the United States before 1970, for example, the index yields a value of 20.4, indicating that slightly more than 20 percent would have to change their state of residence in order to yield the same state distribution that is characteristic of the native-born Mexican American population in 1980. By contrast, those immigrants who entered after 1970 show an index value of 29.4, indicating that a substantially higher percentage would have to change their state of residence to achieve the same population distribution characterizing native-born Mexican Americans. In short, the more recent Mexican immigrants are more concentrated in a few states of residence, whereas those who have been in this country for a longer period of time reveal a state distribution more similar to that of native-born Mexican Americans.

Metropolitanization and Urbanization

Historically, European immigrants to the United States settled in the large cities of the Northeast, thus concentrating in urban areas to a greater degree than was the case with the native-born population.[5] To a considerable extent this pattern has been repeated in the case of Puerto Ricans, Cubans, and Central/South Americans, whose places of settlement have tended to be in the metropolitan areas in and around New York and/or Miami. Early Mexican immigrants, however, were much more likely to be employed in mining, railroads, and agriculture, all nonurban industries. For this reason, as well as because the Southwest was to a considerable degree a rural region before World War II, Mexican Americans during the first half of the twentieth century were a rural population to a much greater degree than other immigrant populations. For example, in 1920 only about 45 percent of the Mexican foreign stock population lived in urban areas in the United States, whereas this proportion for most of the populations of European stock was about 75 percent.[6]

After World War II, however, the Mexican population urbanized more rapidly than the rest of the population.[7] This occurred to such a degree that by 1960 the total Spanish origin population in the United States, including persons of Mexican origin, was more metropolitan in character than the non-Hispanic white population (Table 5.5).[8] Moreover, the tendency toward metropolitanization persisted during the 1960s when large areas of the United States were experiencing a decrease in the percentage of the population living in metropolitan areas (SMSAs).[9] In 1980 all of the Spanish origin groups show a higher concentration of persons living in metropolitan areas than is the case for the

---

[5]Wilbur Zelinsky, *Immigration Settlement Patterns: The Cultural Geography of the U.S.* (Englewood Cliffs, NJ: Prentice-Hall, 1973).

[6]E. P. Hutchinson, *Immigrants and Their Children, 1850–1950* (New York: Wiley, 1956).

[7]Leo Grebler, Joan W. Moore, and Ralph C. Guzman, *The Mexican American People: The Nation's Second Largest Minority* (Glencoe, IL: Free Press, 1970), pp. 112–13. According to census definitions in use since 1960, the urban population consists of persons living in urbanized areas and in places of 2,500 or more inhabitants outside urban areas. An urbanized area consists of at least one city of 50,000 inhabitants and the surrounding closely settled areas.

[8]The metropolitan population consists of persons living in Standard Metropolitan Statistical Areas (SMSAs), whose census definition is complex (see U.S. Bureau of the Census, *Census of Population and Housing: 1980*, Public Use Microdata Samples, Technical Documentation (Washington, DC: U.S. Government Printing Office, 1983), Appendix K.

[9]David L. Brown and Calvin Beale, "Diversity in Post-1970 Population Trends," in Amos Hawley and Sara Mills Mazie, eds., *Nonmetropolitan America in Transition* (Chapel Hill: University of North Carolina Press, 1981); and Dudley Poston and W. Parker Frisbie, "Ecological Models of Migration," *Texas Population Research Center Papers*, no. 6.004 (Austin: University of Texas, 1984).

TABLE 5.5

Percentage of the Spanish Origin Populations
Living in Metropolitan Areas by Nativity: 1960–1980

	1960	1970	1980
Total Non-Hispanic White	62.8%	67.8%	73.3%
Total Spanish Origin	79.7	86.8	84.4
Foreign-Born	87.5	93.2	91.6
Native-Born	76.0	83.7	80.3
Mexican	73.6	83.1	80.9
Foreign-Born	75.5	88.1	87.1
Native-Born	73.2	81.9	78.6
Puerto Rican	96.1	96.4	95.8
Foreign-Born[a]	96.2	96.8	96.4
Native-Born[b]	96.0	95.9	95.1
Cuban	93.6	94.0	93.8
Foreign-Born	96.6	96.4	94.7
Native-Born	88.1	87.7	90.8
Central/South American	91.0	94.7	96.2
Foreign-Born	92.7	94.8	96.3
Native-Born	88.1	94.3	95.7
Other Hispanic	79.8	73.4	77.5
Foreign-Born	75.4	82.3	89.8
Native-Born	80.6	72.2	74.6

SOURCES: 1960 and 1970 Public Use Sample files; 1980 Public Use Microdata Sample file; U.S. Bureau of the Census, Census of Population: 1960, "Standard Metropolitan Statistical Areas," PC(3)-1D; Census of Population: 1970, "General Population Characteristics," PC(1)-B1; Census of Population: 1980, "General Population Characteristics," PC80-1-B1 (Washington, DC: U.S. Government Printing Office, 1963, 1973, and 1983).

[a]Born in Puerto Rico.
[b]Born on the mainland.

non-Hispanic white population, differences that are all the more impressive because the percentages shown in Table 5.5 for 1980 underestimate the true degree of metropolitanization within the Spanish origin groups. This is because the census, in order to protect the confidentiality of respondents, does not provide information on the metropolitan status of persons living in SMSAs of less than 250,000 population in certain states whose total population is small. In the case of Mexicans especially, many of whom live in such small SMSAs, the percentage shown in the third column of Table 5.5 understates the true degree of metropolitanization within this population.

The tendency of immigrants to settle in places where there exists the highest concentration of persons of similar national origin is also revealed in the figures in Table 5.5. The percentage of the foreign-born within each of the Spanish origin groups residing in metropolitan areas in each of the three census years is greater than it is in the case of the native-born. Hence, consistent with the earlier immigration patterns involving Europeans, the foreign-born Spanish origin populations tend to be even more highly concentrated in metropolitan areas than is the case with the native-born population.

In addition to being highly metropolitanized, the various Spanish origin populations also tend to be concentrated within the central cities of metropolitan areas (Table 5.6), although not to as great a degree as is the case among blacks.[10] In 1980 Puerto Ricans exhibited the highest degree of concentration within central cities, and Cubans showed the least. All of the Spanish origin groups, with the possible exception of

TABLE 5.6

*Percentage of the Spanish Origin Metropolitan Populations
Living Within Central Cities by Nativity: 1960–1980*

	1960	1970	1980
Total Non-Hispanic White	30.1%	41.0%	34.7%
Total Spanish Origin	72.6	64.8	65.4
Foreign-Born	80.1	69.0	65.9
Native-Born	62.5	62.5	65.1
Mexican	66.8	59.4	64.6
Foreign-Born	67.2	58.2	64.2
Native-Born	66.6	59.6	64.7
Puerto Rican	89.1	85.4	81.4
Foreign-Born[a]	89.7	87.4	83.0
Native-Born[b]	87.8	82.9	79.8
Cuban	77.3	56.4	45.0
Foreign-Born	80.0	57.8	45.4
Native-Born	71.9	52.1	43.2
Central/South American	74.8	66.2	66.7
Foreign-Born	79.7	69.5	67.0
Native-Born	66.3	58.8	65.3
Other Hispanic	63.7	60.4	58.8
Foreign-Born	76.4	62.7	61.5
Native-Born	61.1	60.1	58.0

SOURCES: 1960 and 1970 Public Use Sample files; 1980 Public Use Microdata Sample file; U.S. Bureau of the Census, *Census of Population: 1960*, "Standard Metropolitan Statistical Areas," PC(3)-1D; *Census of Population: 1970*, "General Population Characteristics," PC(1)-B1; *Census of Population: 1980*, "General Population Characteristics," PC80-1-B1 (Washington, DC: U.S. Government Printing Office, 1963, 1973, and 1983).

[a]Born in Puerto Rico.
[b]Born on the mainland.

[10]See Douglas S. Massey, "Residential Segregation of Spanish Americans in the United States Urbanized Areas," *Demography* 16 (1979):553–64. A central city is the largest city, or one of the largest cities, in an SMSA or urbanized area.

TABLE 5.7

Standard Metropolitan Statistical Areas
with 100,000 or More Spanish Origin Persons: 1980

SMSA	Total Persons	Spanish Origin Number	Spanish Origin Percentage of Total
Los Angeles–Long Beach, CA	7,477,503	2,066,103	27.6%
New York, NY–NJ	9,120,346	1,493,148	16.4
Miami, FL	1,625,781	580,994	35.7
Chicago, IL	7,103,624	580,609	8.2
San Antonio, TX	1,071,954	481,511	44.9
Houston, TX	2,905,353	424,903	14.6
San Francisco–Oakland, CA	3,250,630	351,698	10.8
El Paso, TX	479,899	297,001	61.9
Riverside–San Bernardino–Ontario, CA	1,558,182	290,280	18.6
Anaheim–Santa Ana–Garden Grove, CA	1,932,709	286,339	14.8
San Diego, CA	1,861,846	275,177	14.8
Dallas–Fort Worth, TX	2,974,805	249,614	8.4
McAllen–Pharr–Edinburgh, TX	283,229	230,212	81.3
San Jose, CA	1,295,071	226,611	17.5
Phoenix, AZ	1,509,052	199,003	13.2
Denver–Boulder, CO	1,620,902	173,773	10.7
Albuquerque, NM	454,499	164,200	36.2
Brownsville–Harlingen–San Benito, TX	209,727	161,654	77.1
Corpus Christi, TX	326,228	158,119	48.5
Fresno, CA	514,621	150,790	29.3
Jersey City, NJ	556,972	145,163	26.1
Newark, NJ	1,965,969	132,372	6.7
Philadelphia, PA–NJ	4,716,818	116,280	2.5
Oxnard–Simi Valley–Ventura, CA	529,174	113,192	21.4
Tucson, AZ	531,443	111,418	21.0
Nassau–Suffolk, NY	2,605,813	101,975	3.9
Sacramento, CA	1,014,002	101,694	10.0

SOURCE: U.S. Bureau of the Census, *Census of Population and Housing: 1980*, "General Population Characteristics," PC80-1-B1 (Washington, DC: U.S. Government Printing Office, 1983), table 70.

Mexican Americans, reveal the national trend toward suburbanization (the tendency to live in the non–central city portions of metropolitan areas) typical of the national population over the past two decades.[11] For

[11]William H. Frey, "Population Movement and City-Suburb Redistribution: An Analytic Framework," *Demography* 15 (1978):571–88; Norval Glenn, "Suburbanization in the United States since World War II," in L. H. Massoti and J. K. Hadden, eds., *The Urbanization of the Suburbs* (Beverly Hills, CA: Sage, 1973).

example, the percentage of Cubans living within the central city of metropolitan areas decreased from 77 percent in 1960 to 45 percent in 1980. Smaller decreases over time in the percentage of a group's population living in the central cities of SMSAs also occurred in the cases of the other Spanish origin groups. Interestingly, this tendency obtained among both the foreign-born and native-born, indicating a tendency toward suburbanization on the part of most Spanish origin groups. The one exception occurs among Mexicans, who exhibit a very slight decrease since 1960, but an increase in the percentage of the population residing in central cities since 1970. The fact that this pattern occurs among both foreign-born and native-born Mexican Americans suggests that the result is not due simply to an influx of immigrants, both legal and illegal, who might have been thought more likely than natives to concentrate in the inner parts of major metropolitan areas.

Which of the country's SMSAs contain the largest concentrations of Hispanics? Table 5.7 presents a listing of the SMSAs in the United States that contained 100,000 or more Spanish-origin persons in 1980, ranked in order of the number of such persons in the SMSA. If considered only in and of themselves, the Hispanic populations in at least two of these—Los Angeles–Long Beach and New York—would rank among the largest Spanish-speaking cities in the world.[12] For example, Los Angeles contained over 2 million persons of Spanish origin, who constituted about 28 percent of the total population of the SMSA in 1980. New York contained nearly 1.5 million persons of Spanish origin, who constituted about 16 percent of that city's total population. Even Philadelphia, one of the nation's largest SMSAs, contained more than 100,000 persons of Spanish origin, though they made up only 2.5 percent of the metropolitan area's total population.

In Table 5.8 these same metropolitan areas are shown with their total Spanish origin populations broken down by type. It is evident that most SMSAs with large numbers of Spanish origin persons are predominantly "Mexican" SMSAs. For example, about 80 percent of the Spanish origin population of Los Angeles is of Mexican origin. Not surprisingly, anywhere from 80 percent to well over 90 percent of the Spanish origin populations of most of the California SMSAs and all of the Texas SMSAs listed are of Mexican origin. Even in the case of Chicago, which is outside the Southwest, nearly two-thirds of the Spanish origin population is Mexican in origin. Only two SMSAs—New York and Philadelphia—contain a majority of Puerto Ricans in their Spanish origin populations, although Nassau–Suffolk and Newark come close to 50 percent. Finally, Miami represents the only SMSA whose Spanish origin popula-

---

[12]For example, in 1980 the Hispanic populations of the New York and Los Angeles SMSAs would rank in the top 15 Spanish-speaking cities in the world.

TABLE 5.8

Standard Metropolitan Statistical Areas with 100,000 or More Spanish Origin Persons by Origin Type: 1980

SMSA	Spanish Origin Persons	Mexican		Puerto Rican		Cuban		Other Hispanic	
		Number	Percentage	Number	Percentage	Number	Percentage	Number	Percentage
Los Angeles–Long Beach, Ca	2,066,103	1,650,934	79.9%	36,662	1.8%	44,289	2.1%	334,218	16.2%
New York, NY–NJ	1,493,148	26,332	1.8	892,375	59.8	71,203	4.8	503,238	33.7
Miami, FL	580,994	13,238	2.3	44,656	7.7	407,253	70.1	115,847	19.9
Chicago, IL	580,609	368,981	63.6	126,713	21.8	17,780	3.1	67,135	11.6
San Antonio, TX	481,511	447,416	92.9	3,639	0.8	1,044	0.2	29,412	6.1
Houston, TX	424,903	374,510	88.1	4,397	1.0	6,376	1.5	39,620	9.3
San Francisco–Oakland, CA	351,698	189,742	54.0	19,700	5.6	3,988	1.1	138,268	39.3
El Paso, TX	297,001	282,001	94.9	2,846	1.0	420	0.1	11,734	4.0
Riverside–San Bernardino–Ontario, CA	290,280	252,513	87.0	4,886	1.7	1,750	0.6	31,131	10.7
Anaheim–Santa Ana–Garden Grove, CA	286,339	232,472	81.2	5,734	2.0	4,820	1.7	43,313	15.1
San Diego, CA	275,177	227,943	82.8	6,007	2.2	1,531	0.6	39,696	14.4
Dallas–Fort Worth, TX	249,614	223,105	89.4	2,882	1.2	3,060	1.2	20,567	8.2
McAllen–Pharr–Edinburgh, TX	230,212	221,971	96.4	267	0.1	204	0.1	7,770	3.4
San Jose, CA	226,611	176,838	78.0	6,266	2.8	1,610	0.7	41,897	18.5
Phoenix, AZ	199,003	177,546	89.2	2,152	1.1	545	0.3	18,760	9.4
Denver–Boulder, CO	173,773	108,697	62.6	2,067	1.2	1,169	0.7	61,840	35.6
Albuquerque, NM	164,200	71,617	43.6	748	0.4	396	0.2	91,439	55.7
Brownsville–Harlingen–San Benito, TX	161,654	138,509	85.7	271	0.2	180	0.1	22,694	14.0
Corpus Christi, TX	158,119	151,126	95.6	379	0.2	230	0.1	6,384	4.0
Fresno, CA	150,790	140,976	93.5	705	0.5	128	0.1	8,981	6.0
Jersey City, NJ	145,163	1,385	1.0	55,828	38.4	45,719	31.5	42,231	29.1
Newark, NJ	132,372	3,677	3.8	62,236	47.0	21,073	15.9	45,386	34.3
Philadelphia, PA–NJ	116,280	8,535	7.3	79,564	68.4	4,648	4.0	23,533	20.2
Oxnard–Simi Valley–Ventura, CA	113,192	100,629	88.9	1,239	1.1	486	0.4	10,838	9.6
Tucson, AZ	111,418	100,085	89.8	955	0.8	351	0.3	10,027	9.0
Nassau–Suffolk, NY	101,975	3,354	3.3	49,919	49.0	6,692	6.6	42,010	41.2
Sacramento, CA	101,694	78,597	77.3	2,232	2.2	410	0.4	20,455	20.1

SOURCE: U.S. Bureau of the Census, *Census of Population and Housing: 1980*, "General Population Characteristics," PC80-1-B1 (Washington, DC: U.S. Government Printing Office, 1983), table 70.

TABLE 5.9

Percentage Change Between 1970 and 1980
in the Sizes of the Total and Hispanic Populations
of SMSAs with 100,000 or More Hispanics in 1980

	(1) Total Population	(2) Hispanic Population	Ratio of (2) to (1)
Los Angeles–Long Beach, CA	6.3%	96.5%	15.3
New York, NY–NJ[a]	−21.2	15.8	*
Miami, FL	28.2	107.4	3.8
Chicago, IL	1.8	79.1	43.9
San Antonio, TX	24.1	48.7	2.0
Houston, TX	46.4	133.3	2.9
San Francisco–Oakland, CA	4.5	52.0	11.6
El Paso, TX	33.6	63.4	1.9
Riverside–San Bernardino–Ontario, CA[b]	36.3	89.4	2.5
Anaheim–Santa Ana–Garden Grove, CA	36.1	143.9	4.0
San Diego, CA	37.1	126.5	3.4
Dallas–Fort Worth, TX[c]	91.2	156.8	1.7
McAllen–Pharr–Edinburgh, TX	56.0	74.8	1.3
San Jose, CA	21.6	75.7	3.5
Phoenix, AZ	56.0	77.3	1.4
Denver–Boulder, CO[d]	32.0	68.7	2.1
Albuquerque, NM	43.9	70.2	1.6
Brownsville–Harlingen–San Benito, TX	49.4	62.2	1.2
Corpus Christi, TX	14.5	42.8	3.0
Fresno, CA	24.6	61.3	2.5
Jersey City, NJ	−8.6	60.0	*
Newark, NJ	5.9	66.5	11.3
Philadelphia, PA–NJ	−2.1	47.0	*
Oxnard–Simi Valley–Ventura, CA[e]	40.6	88.2	2.2
Tucson, AZ	51.1	73.7	1.4
Nassau–Suffolk, NY[f]	—	—	—
Sacramento, CA	26.7	76.4	2.9

SOURCES: U.S. Bureau of the Census, *Census of Population and Housing: 1980,* "General Population Characteristics," PC80-1-B1, table 70; "Persons of Spanish Origin," PC(2)-1C, table 13; "Mobility for Metropolitan Areas," PC(2)-2C, List B (Washington, DC: U.S. Government Printing Office, 1973 and 1983).

[a]NJ counties not in NY SMSA in 1970.
[b]1970 SMSA was San Bernardino–Riverside–Ontario, CA.
[c]1970 SMSA did not include Fort Worth, TX.
[d]1970 SMSA did not include Boulder, CO.
[e]1970 SMSA did not include Simi Valley, CA.
[f]Not an SMSA in 1970.

*Indicates that the ratio was not computed due to negative percentage change in the total population.

tion is predominantly Cuban, and Albuquerque the only SMSA whose Spanish origin population contains a majority of persons of Other Hispanic origin.

Persons of Spanish origin not only constitute a notable proportion of the populations of these cities' metropolitan areas, they have also contributed substantially to their growth between 1970 and 1980. Table 5.9 presents the percentage by which the populations of these SMSAs grew (or declined) and the percentage by which the Spanish origin populations increased over the same period. The third column of this table shows the growth rate ratio of the Spanish population to the total population. As is clear from these figures, the growth rates in the Hispanic populations in these SMSAs exceeded the growth rates in their total populations by substantial amounts. For example, in Los Angeles–Long Beach the Hispanic population nearly doubled between 1970 and 1980. The net gain, however, in the size of the Spanish origin population was 1,051,000 persons, meaning that more than 600,000 persons of non-Spanish origin moved out of the SMSA during the decade. Substantial growth rates also occurred in the other SMSAs, with those showing the smallest rates of increase tending to be those containing the highest percentages of Spanish origin population in 1970. Except for SMSAs subject to this "ceiling" effect, those already containing the largest percentage of persons of Spanish origin in 1970 became even more Hispanic in character between 1970 and 1980.[13]

Internal Migration

Historically, the United States has been characterized by three major population movements from one place to another.[14] The first of these was the movement of people from east to west, a pattern of migration that was still evident in the country during the 1970s. The second was a movement of persons from rural to urban areas, a trend, as we saw above, that has been even more characteristic of Mexican Americans than non-Hispanic whites since World War II. The third involved the movement of people out of the South to other regions of the country, a trend that reversed itself during the 1970s as regional economic development increased the attractiveness of Sunbelt states as destinations for migrants.[15]

[13]John D. Kasarda, "Hispanics and City Change," *American Demographics* 6 (1984):25–30.
[14]For example, see Biggar, "Sunning of America."
[15]Berry and Silverman, *Population Redistribution*.

Between 1975 and 1980 the dominant pattern of regional migration in the United States involved the net movement of people out of the Northeast and North Central census regions into the South and West. This can readily be seen in Table 5.10, which presents net migration totals for the major census regions both for non-Hispanic whites and for the total Spanish origin population, as well as for the subpopulations of Spanish origin. For purposes of the present analysis a migrant is defined as someone who changed residence from one state to another between 1975 and 1980.[16] Among non-Hispanic whites, for example, 1.47 more persons aged 5 and over in 1980 left the Northeast for other regions than left these regions for the Northeast. Net movement out of the North Central region occurred on a nearly comparable scale. By contrast, the South gained 1.75 million movers and the West over 1 million.

Among the various Spanish origin groups a similar pattern of geographic mobility occurred. Because the Spanish origin groups are so much smaller than the non-Hispanic white group, it is difficult to compare them using raw numbers of migrants. It is thus of interest to calculate migration rates and compare them with those of non-Hispanic whites in order to ascertain whether the magnitude as well as the direction of movement was similar among these groups. These rates, together with the rates for non-Hispanic whites, which are indexed to a value of 100, are presented in the second and third columns of Table 5.10 under each of the regional headings. It is evident that the Spanish origin groups left the Northeast and North Central regions for the South and West, as was also true of non-Hispanic whites. In some cases this tendency was especially pronounced, as in the case of Cubans who left the Northeast and North Central regions for the South at rates that were respectively, 4 and 7 times as fast as those among non-Hispanic whites.

While these figures indicate the patterns of net gain or loss for the major census regions, they reveal neither the origins of persons going to regions that gained movers nor the destinations of persons going to regions that lost movers. Insight into the former is provided by Figures 5.1–5.3, which show the directions and relative magnitudes of all net positive cross-regional flows for both non-Hispanic whites and the Spanish origin groups. In general, the overall directional pattern is similar for the Spanish origin groups compared with non-Hispanic whites, with the one exception of Other Hispanics, who show a minor deviation from the dominant pattern. This pattern involves the South gaining movers from each of the other three regions, the West gaining from the North Central and the Northeast regions, and the North Central gaining from

---

[16]The Census Bureau sometimes defines a migrant as someone changing counties, but for our purposes a criterion of changing states is preferable.

TABLE 5.10
Total Net Migration and Rates for Census Regions
by Type of Spanish Origin, Indexed to Non-Hispanic Whites: 1980

Group	Northeast			North Central		
	Net Migration[a]	Migration Rate[b]	Index[c]	Net Migration	Migration Rate	Index
Non-Hispanic Whites	-1,478	-38	100	-1,279	-27	100
Total Spanish Origin	-106	-45	118	-31	-28	104
Mexicans	-6	-77	203	-14	-20	74
Puerto Ricans	-33	-25	66	-2	-12	44
Cubans	-28	-158	416	-6	-196	726
Central/South Americans	-22	-48	126	-7	-94	348
Other Hispanics	-17	-55	145	-2	-16	59

Group	South			West		
	Net Migration	Migration Rate	Index	Net Migration	Migration Rate	Index
Non-Hispanic Whites	1,754	33	100	1,003	34	100
Total Spanish Origin	106	27	82	30	5	15
Mexicans	18	7	21	2	1	3
Puerto Ricans	25	152	461	10	87	256
Cubans	32	64	194	3	38	112
Central/South Americans	22	81	245	6	14	41
Other Hispanics	10	28	85	9	11	32

SOURCE: U.S. Bureau of the Census, *Census of Population and Housing: 1980*, "General Social and Economic Characteristics," PC80-1-C2–C52 (Washington, DC: U.S. Government Printing Office, 1983), table 100.

[a]In thousands, for persons aged 5 and over in 1980.
[b]Net migration per 1,000 population aged 5 and over in 1980.
[c]Indexed to the non-Hispanic white net migration rate, which was set equal to 100.

FIGURE 5.1
Interregional Net Migration Flows: 1975–1980

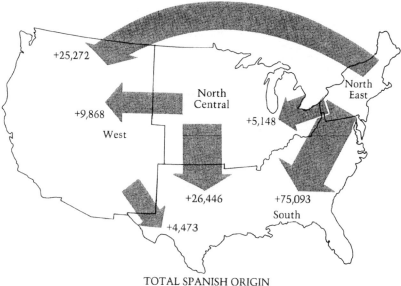

+25,272

North
Central

+9,868

West

+5,148

North
East

+26,446

+75,093
South

+4,473

TOTAL SPANISH ORIGIN

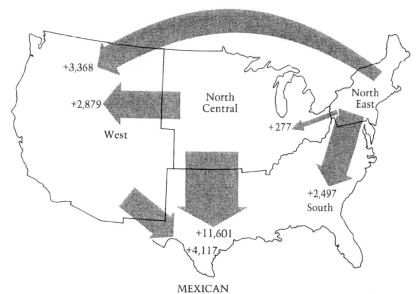

+3,368

North
Central

+2,879

West

+277

North
East

+2,497
South

+11,601

+4,117

MEXICAN

NOTE: Arrows are proportional within figures, but not across figures.

FIGURE 5.2
Interregional Net Migration Flows: 1975–1980

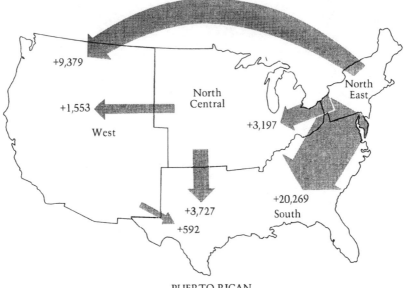

PUERTO RICAN

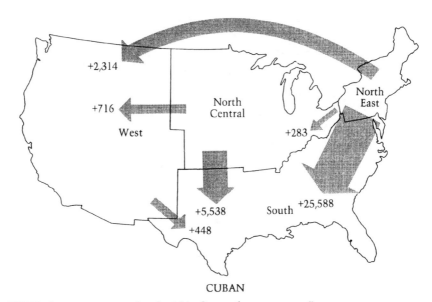

CUBAN

NOTE: Arrows are proportional within figures, but not across figures.

FIGURE 5.3

Interregional Net Migration Flows: 1975–1980

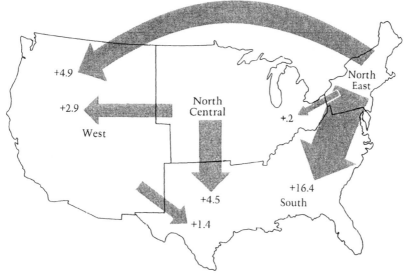

CENTRAL AND SOUTH AMERICAN

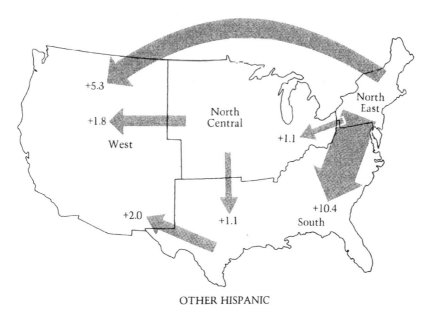

OTHER HISPANIC

NOTE: Arrows are proportional within figures, but not across figures.

TABLE 5.11

Regional Destinations of Migrants by Region of Origin and Type of Spanish Origin: 1980

Region of Origin: 1975	Total Number of Migrants (in thousands)	Percentage Who Stayed in Region
Non-Hispanic White		
Northeast	3,909.0	34.3%
North Central	4,652.6	33.3
South	5,246.1	57.6
West	3,562.6	54.4
Total Spanish Origin		
Northeast	219.9	34.4
North Central	122.6	18.9
South	225.0	40.0
West	281.5	56.1
Mexican		
Northeast	15.9	11.5
North Central	69.0	20.3
South	125.4	33.4
West	167.6	62.8
Puerto Rican		
Northeast	88.9	48.9
North Central	14.7	22.1
South	18.8	42.8
West	11.2	34.3
Cuban		
Northeast	39.4	15.6
North Central	9.2	8.8
South	20.9	52.5
West	6.0	15.2
Central/South American		
Northeast	42.8	32.3
North Central	15.9	13.5
South	33.1	53.0
West	40.0	60.7
Other Hispanic		
Northeast	32.9	31.7
North Central	13.9	21.6
South	26.8	42.8
West	36.0	65.4

SOURCES: U.S. Bureau of the Census, *Census of Population and Housing: 1980*, "General Social and Economic Characteristics," PC80-1-C2–C52 (Washington, DC: U.S. Government Printing Office, 1983), table 100; and 1980 PUMS.

the Northeast region. In the case of Other Hispanics, the West rather than the South region gains movers from all three other regions.

The data presented to this point reveal the overall patterns of net regional gain or loss of movers, as well as the magnitudes of origin-

TABLE 5.11 *(continued)*

	Destination of Those Who Left Their Region		
Northeast	North Central	South	West
—	16.0%	58.0%	26.0%
10.4%	—	53.2	36.4
24.2	38.3	—	37.4
14.1	34.4	51.5	—
—	8.5	66.3	25.2
7.2	—	58.0	34.8
15.2	23.1	—	61.7
8.9	20.0	71.0	—
—	10.1	41.4	48.4
2.1	—	61.4	36.8
4.0	26.3	—	69.7
4.1	20.8	75.0	—
—	14.7	58.5	26.8
30.3	—	46.6	23.1
58.6	15.0	—	26.4
38.2	14.9	46.9	—
—	1.9	89.8	8.3
4.0	—	85.4	10.5
43.4	16.4	—	40.2
8.7	3.6	87.7	—
—	5.1	69.4	25.5
9.0	—	50.9	40.1
24.1	16.0	—	59.8
15.9	16.3	67.8	—
—	9.2	58.7	32.0
8.6	—	42.1	49.2
18.4	22.7	—	58.8
15.1	28.8	56.1	—

specific patterns of net gain. Thus, for example, it is clear that the South incurred a substantial net gain of both Hispanics and non-Hispanic whites and that this net gain involved a component from each of the other regions. Because the sizes of the Spanish origin groups vary so much across regions, however, it is difficult to discern from the relative sizes of the net regional flows shown in Figures 5.1–5.3 whether the South varied in its attractiveness to Hispanic movers depending upon their region of origin. Stated differently, such numbers cannot tell us whether persons from the Northeast, for example, were equally likely to move to the South or West or whether persons from the North Central regions were equally likely to move to the South or West. Information on the regional destination of migrants by origin, however, is provided in Table 5.11. Among non-Hispanic whites, for instance, 58 percent of all migrants leaving the Northeast region were destined for the South. Of those leaving the North Central region 53 percent ended up in the South, and of those leaving the West nearly 52 percent moved to the South. In short, a majority of all migrants from any region moved to the South. Among the Spanish origin populations similar patterns of movement prevailed. There was a decided tendency for each of the Spanish origin groups to migrate to the South. Among Cubans this pattern was especially pronounced. Also similar to the pattern exhibited by non-Hispanic whites was a tendency for the Spanish origin groups (except for Cubans) to move to the West, whatever their region of origin. In short, Spanish origin movers, like their non-Hispanic white counterparts, tended to prefer the South and West as regions of destination irrespective of their regions of origin.

The preponderance of moves out of the Northeast and North Central regions and into the South and West is further revealed in Table 5.12, which presents the ratio of the number of inmigrants to outmigrants by region for the Spanish origin groups and for non-Hispanic whites. In a sense these numbers provide similar information to those presented in Table 5.10, which show the net difference between in and out flows by region. The present numbers, however, show the ratio of in flows to out flows, and thus the net *percentage* difference between in

TABLE 5.12

*Ratio of the Number of Inmigrants to Outmigrants
by Region and Type of Spanish Origin: 1980*

	Northeast	North Central	South	West
Non-Hispanic White	.36	.59	1.79	1.62
Total Spanish Origin	.27	.69	1.79	1.25
Mexican	.59	.74	1.22	1.03
Puerto Rican	.28	.82	3.30	2.43
Cuban	.15	.29	4.19	1.52
Central and South American	.26	.48	2.43	1.40
Other Hispanic	.25	.84	1.62	1.73

SOURCE: Calculated from U.S. Bureau of the Census, *Census of Population and Housing: 1980*, "General Social and Economic Characteristics," PC80-1-C2–C52 (Washington, DC: U.S. Government Printing Office, 1983), table 100.

and out flows. Thus, for example, the flow of Mexicans *into* the Northeast is only 59 percent of the flow of Mexicans *out of* the Northeast. Or the flow of Cubans into the South is 419 percent of the flow of Cubans out of the South. In general the overarching result apparent in these data is that fewer Spanish origin movers migrated to the Northeast and North Central regions than migrated out of these regions, whereas the reverse was true of Spanish origin movers migrating to and from the South and West regions.

In addition to patterns of regional movement, it is also of interest to examine briefly certain aspects of the migration of Spanish origin persons between states and between SMSAs. In particular, the movement of persons out of New York to the South and West has been especially significant. For example, New York was one of only two states (the other was Rhode Island) to incur an overall population decline during the 1970s, largely as the result of a net migration loss of 1.54 million persons over the decade, a change almost equal to the combined total of

FIGURE 5.4

New York and Florida Migration Flows
by Spanish Origin Type: 1975–1980

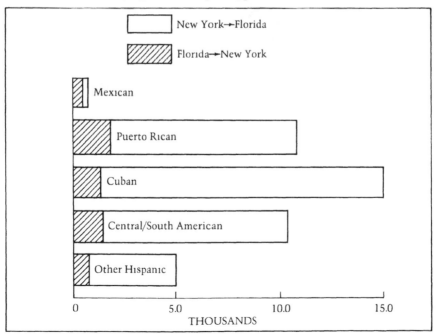

all of the other states in the Northeast and North Central regions.[17] Almost 50 percent (765,000) of this loss derived from movement to the South. Figure 5.4 presents the dimensions of the most significant part of this migration involving Hispanics—migration to and from Florida. As is evident for all Hispanic groups except Mexicans, substantially greater numbers of people left New York for Florida than vice versa. The movement of the Spanish origin groups from New York to Florida, which for the non-Mexican groups represented over half of the net movement from the Northeast to the South, thus paralleled significantly the tendency in the entire population for persons to leave New York State for the South.

In the case of Mexican Americans the major interchanges of persons between states resulting in net gain or loss involved states with substantial populations of Mexican origin persons. Figure 5.5 shows the largest

FIGURE 5.5

*Migration Flows of the Mexican Origin Population
for Selected States: 1975–1980*

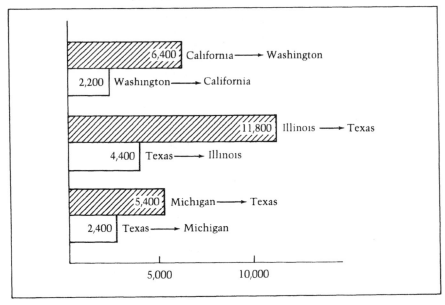

[17]U.S. Bureau of the Census, *Statistical Abstract of the United States: 1982–83* (Washington, DC: U.S. Government Printing Office, 1982); Richard D. Alba and Katherine Trent, "Population Loss and Change in the North: An Exploratory Analysis of New York's Migration to the Sunbelt," unpublished paper, Center for Social and Demographic Analysis, State University of New York at Albany, 1985.

of these, those involving flows of at least 2,000 persons each between 1975 and 1980 with one flow exceeding the other by at least 3,000 persons. Especially interesting is the imbalance in the flows between Illinois and Texas, the former losing more than two-and-one-half as many Mexicans to Texas for every one it gained. Hence, despite a substantial gain in the size of the Mexican origin population in Illinois between 1970 and 1980 due to natural increase and immigration, Illinois still lost migrants of Mexican origin to the state of Texas.

Residential Segregation

Residential segregation is an important facet of a group's position in society. Social and economic resources are distributed unevenly in space, and where one lives strongly affects one's life chances, determining access to such important variables as education, employment, housing, health, and safety. To the extent that residential segregation is imposed on a group, limits are placed on its access to these important resources. But segregation may also be voluntary. People may choose to live in ethnic neighborhoods in order to maintain linguistic or cultural ties or to gain privileged access to jobs within an enclave economy. Research conducted for 1970 showed that Hispanic segregation was mostly voluntary, determined largely by the operation of two basic ecological processes: residential succession and spatial assimilation.[18]

Residential succession refers to the process of neighborhood turnover that occurs as Hispanics enter an area and displace its original Anglo inhabitants. The driving force behind succession is immigration, and an important enabling condition is social distance. The greater the economic, social, and cultural dissimilarity between Anglos and Hispanics, the more likely Anglos are to avoid an area after Hispanics have entered it. In the normal course of residential change, then, Anglos are replaced predominantly by Hispanics, who are guided to the neighborhood by social networks of friends and relatives. If migration continues after an area has become predominantly Hispanic, succession spills over into adjacent areas, expanding the ethnic enclave.

[18]For a review of the 1970 literature on Hispanic segregation and a theoretical review of the ecological foundations of segregation, see Douglas S. Massey, "Ethnic Residential Segregation: A Theoretical Synthesis and Empirical Review," *Sociology and Social Research* 69 (1985):315–50. Research suggesting the voluntary nature of Hispanic segregation includes Stanley Lieberson and Donna K. Carter, "A Model for Inferring the Voluntary and Involuntary Causes of Residential Segregation," *Demography* 19 (1982):511–26; Douglas S. Massey and Brendan P. Mullan, "Processes of Hispanic and Black Spatial Assimilation," *American Journal of Sociology* 89 (1984):836–73; and Douglas S. Massey and Nancy A. Denton, "Spatial Assimilation as a Socioeconomic Outcome," *American Sociological Review* 50 (1985):94–105.

Over time, this process of succession and consolidation produces a segregated residential distribution. However, counteracting residential succession is a process of spatial assimilation. In the United States urban space is highly fragmented by social class and family type, producing an uneven distribution of opportunities, resources, and neighborhood characteristics. In order to improve their position in society, to gain access to richer amenities, or to find a location more in keeping with their stage in the life cycle, Hispanic households move, an event that promotes spatial assimilation with Anglos.

The level and pattern of Hispanic segregation at any point depend on the balance between succession and assimilation, and this in turn depends on the history of economic expansion and immigration. During the 1960s the United States experienced rapid economic growth, upward mobility was widespread, and Hispanic immigration had not yet reached the mass levels of the 1970s. Spatial assimilation therefore predominated over residential succession, producing a moderate pattern of segregation from Anglos, one characterized by a paucity of established enclave areas, few succession areas, and many areas of recent entry.[19]

Puerto Ricans in New York represented an important exception to this generalization. They displayed an unusually high degree of segregation from Anglos and a prevalence of residential succession instead of spatial assimilation. Moreover, while the degree of segregation for most Hispanics was largely explained by their socioeconomic status and nativity, a crucial factor in accounting for the Puerto Rican pattern was race. Being of African heritage, Puerto Ricans were more prone to locate near black neighborhoods than other Hispanic groups, resulting in their spatial isolation from Anglos. Once racial heritage was controlled, Puerto Ricans conformed to the patterns observed for other Hispanic groups.[20]

During the 1970s the conditions affecting segregation changed dramatically. Hispanic immigration accelerated and the American economy went into recession. These changes imply less spatial assimilation and more residential succession, a possibility that is examined in Table 5.13, which presents patterns of residential change in neighborhoods of

[19]See Douglas S. Massey, "Residential Segregation of Spanish Americans in U.S. Urbanized Areas," *Demography* 16 (1979a):533–63; Douglas S. Massey, "Effects of Socioeconomic Factors on the Residential Segregation of Blacks and Spanish Americans," *American Sociological Review* 45 (1979b):1015–22; Douglas S. Massey, "Hispanic Residential Segregation: A Comparison of Mexicans, Cubans, and Puerto Ricans," *Sociology and Social Research* 65 (1981a):311–22; Douglas S. Massey, "Social Class and Ethnic Segregation: A Reconsideration of Methods and Conclusions," *American Sociological Review* 46 (1981b):641–50; and Massey and Mullan, "Processes of Assimilation."

[20]See Douglas S. Massey and Brooks Bitterman, "Explaining the Paradox of Puerto Rican Segregation," *Social Forces* 64 (1985):306–31.

TABLE 5.13

Classification of Hispanic Tracts by Type of Residential Change: 60 SMSAs by Census Region

Type of Change	Hispanic Tracts					Mixed Tracts				
	Northeast	North Central	South	West	Total	Northeast	North Central	South	West	Total
Established	4.7%	2.4%	15.7%	6.4%	7.6%	28.7%	9.5%	14.7%	18.6%	20.3%
Hispanic	4.7	2.4	15.7	6.4	7.6	5.3	3.0	3.5	4.0	4.2
Other	0.0	0.0	0.0	0.0	0.0	23.4	6.5	11.2	14.6	16.1
Succession	32.9	36.9	30.7	35.5	34.2	51.3	47.2	34.0	46.5	45.8
Late	13.3	18.7	15.0	10.4	13.0	34.7	25.2	17.1	23.8	26.0
Middle	10.0	9.1	8.2	9.2	9.1	11.5	15.4	10.6	16.0	13.7
Early	9.5	9.1	7.6	15.8	12.1	5.0	6.6	6.3	6.7	6.1
Invasion	48.0	50.3	31.5	17.8	30.0	8.4	22.6	19.3	4.1	9.5
Anglo Gain	7.9	9.1	21.8	10.1	12.0	1.8	8.8	14.3	3.3	5.2
Anglo Loss	40.2	41.2	9.7	7.7	18.0	6.7	13.8	5.0	0.8	4.2
Other	14.4	10.4	22.1	40.3	28.2	11.5	20.7	32.0	30.8	24.5
Growth	3.3	3.2	15.0	18.5	13.2	5.9	15.1	28.1	24.0	18.7
Displacement	2.2	0.5	1.2	5.6	3.5	0.6	0.3	1.5	2.0	1.4
Decline	8.9	6.7	5.9	16.2	11.6	5.0	5.3	2.4	4.8	4.5
Number of Tracts	548	374	648	1,509	3,079	1,232	305	743	1,845	4,125
Number of SMSAs	12	12	20	16	60	12	12	20	16	60

SOURCES: U.S. Bureau of the Census, *Census of Population and Housing: 1980*, Summary Tape File A; *Census of Population: 1970*, Fourth Count Summary Tapes, File A.

TABLE 5.14

Classification of Hispanic Tracts by Type of Residential Change,
1970–1980: 10 Hispanic SMSAs

Type of Change	Hispanic Tracts			
	Los Angeles	New York	Miami	Chicago
Established	10.3%	7.6%	11.0%	3.3%
Hispanic	10.3	7.6	11.0	3.3
Other	0.0	0.0	0.0	0.0
Succession	52.4	30.6	56.9	38.6
Late	19.8	9.7	39.5	22.7
Middle	12.4	9.4	10.1	10.1
Early	20.2	11.5	7.3	5.8
Invasion	14.9	47.6	11.9	49.1
Gain	4.7	5.5	9.2	7.2
Loss	10.1	42.1	2.8	41.9
Other	22.5	14.2	20.2	9.0
Growth	5.8	0.9	18.4	3.2
Displacement	2.5	2.1	0.0	0.4
Decline	14.2	11.2	1.8	5.4
Number of Tracts	485	330	109	277

SOURCES: U.S. Bureau of the Census, *Census of Population and Housing: 1980,* Summary Tape File A; *Census of Population: 1970,* Fourth Count Summary Tapes, File A.

Hispanic settlement in 60 metropolitan areas, including the 50 largest SMSAs in the United States, plus 10 other SMSAs with large concentrations of Hispanics.

Census tracts in each area were classified using a scheme developed by Massey and Mullan.[21] Census tracts are small, homogeneous areal units of between 2,500 and 8,000 people. The classification scheme divided them into two basic groups: "Hispanic tracts" contained at least 250 Hispanics in 1980 but fewer than 250 blacks and 250 Asians, while "mixed tracts" contained 250 or more Hispanics plus at least 250 of one of the other two groups. These two groups of tracts were then classified separately in the following order: established areas were 60 percent minority at both dates, invasion tracts had fewer than 250 minority members in 1970 but more than this number in 1980, succession tracts gained minority residents but lost Anglo residents over the decade, growth tracts gained members of both groups, displacement tracts gained Anglos but lost minorities, and declining tracts lost both groups. In addition, succession tracts were classified according to their stage in

[21]Massey and Mullan, "Processes of Assimilation."

TABLE 5.14 *(continued)*

Type of Change	Mixed Tracts			
	Los Angeles	New York	Miami	Chicago
Established	33.8%	30.2%	24.3%	7.5%
Hispanic	7.3	7.0	7.1	3.7
Other	26.5	23.2	17.2	3.8
Succession	48.2	56.0	45.7	49.1
Late	33.6	34.4	31.4	27.6
Middle	10.5	15.6	11.4	15.0
Early	4.1	6.0	2.9	6.5
Invasion	7.6	1.9	5.7	21.5
Gain	1.3	0.9	4.3	7.0
Loss	6.3	1.0	1.4	14.5
Other	10.4	11.9	24.3	22.0
Growth	4.8	9.2	21.4	17.3
Displacement	0.7	0.5	1.4	0.0
Decline	4.9	2.1	1.4	4.7
Number of Tracts	838	748	70	214

the succession process: early (under 20 percent minority), middle (20 to 40 percent minority), or late (more than 40 percent minority).

According to Table 5.13, the vast majority of neighborhoods inhabited by Hispanics in 1980 were either invasion or succession areas, and most of the former were losing Anglo residents. The 1970s were apparently a time when Hispanic neighborhoods were moving toward greater minority dominance, although few had yet become established enclave areas. In the SMSAs under study only 8 percent of Hispanic tracts and 4 percent of mixed tracts were established Hispanic areas, but 34 percent of the former and 46 percent of the latter were in the process of succession, and among the remaining tracts, very few were gaining Anglos. In all, only 29 percent of Hispanic tracts and 25 percent of mixed tracts gained Anglo residents during the 1970s.

Table 5.14 considers patterns of residential change within the four largest Hispanic communities in the United States: Los Angeles, New York, Miami, and Chicago. Earlier work has shown that during the 1960s Hispanic neighborhoods in these metropolitan areas were dominated by invasion areas, many of which were still gaining Anglo residents.[22] In Los Angeles, for example, invasion tracts outnumbered

[22]Massey and Mullan, "Processes of Assimilation"; and Massey and Bitterman, "Explaining the Paradox."

succession tracts by two to one in 1970, and more than half of the invasion tracts gained Anglo residents between 1960 and 1970. However, during the 1970s this pattern was decisively reversed. Nearly all of the Los Angeles neighborhoods invaded during the 1960s went on to lose Anglo residents in the subsequent decade, and most new invasion areas saw the number of Anglos decline.

A similar pattern of neighborhood transition typified the other three metropolitan areas. In New York the vast majority of tracts with Hispanics were either succession tracts moving toward minority dominance or were invasion areas that had already begun to lose Anglos. Similarly, most tracts in Miami were headed for eventual incorporation into the Hispanic enclave or were part of the enclave itself; and in Chicago a majority of tracts were either succession areas or invasion areas losing Anglos.

In short, during the 1970s Hispanics in all regions of the country, and especially those in the largest metropolitan areas, were heading toward greater spatial concentration and isolation within predominantly Hispanic enclaves. Table 5.15 measures the impact of these neighborhood changes on the level of Hispanic segregation by calculating the Hispanic-Anglo index of residential dissimilarity in 1970 and 1980. The index was computed over census tracts to give the proportion of Hispanics who would have to change tracts to produce an even residential distribution at each date. In 1980 Hispanics were identified using the 100 percent Spanish origin item, and in 1970 by the 15 percent Spanish American definition. Spanish Americans include all persons who spoke Spanish in 1970 or who were raised in a Spanish-speaking household, plus, in the southwestern states, persons of Spanish surname who were not of Spanish language.[23]

On the surface, aggregate level trends do not seem consistent with the data on neighborhood transition. For the 60 SMSAs as a whole there was very little change in the level of Hispanic segregation over the 1970s. The Hispanic-Anglo dissimilarity index was about .44 at both dates, representing a moderate level of segregation. (In general, dissimi-

[23]In 1970 the Spanish origin question was only a 5 percent sample item, and therefore too unreliable at the tract level. Moreover, substantial numbers of poorly educated blacks and whites in the South and North Central regions identified themselves as "Central or South Americans," producing large overcounts of Hispanics in those states. A preliminary examination of segregation indices and succession patterns using both the "Spanish American" and "Spanish Origin" definitions indicated that the latter substantially underestimated Hispanic segregation in 1970 by undercounting Hispanics in tracts where they were few in number (which is very likely with a 5 percent sample) and by misidentifying many Anglos and blacks as Hispanics living in Anglo neighborhoods. The most accurate estimates of Hispanic segregation in 1970 are therefore provided by the "Spanish American" definition, which was the identifier used earlier by Massey, "Residential Segregation."

TABLE 5.15

Dissimilarity Between Hispanics and Anglos in 60 SMSAs by Region and the 10 Largest Hispanic SMSAs (population in thousands)

Region or SMSA	Hispanic Population			Hispanic-Anglo Dissimilarity		
	1970	1980	Difference	1970	1980	Difference
All SMSAs (60)	7,204	10,324	3,120	.444	.437	-.007
Northeast (12)	1,814	2,229	415	.503	.540	.037
North Central (12)	555	865	310	.469	.439	-.030
South (20)	1,676	2,648	972	.426	.388	-.038
West (16)	3,158	4,583	1,425	.399	.415	.016
Los Angeles	1,288	2,065	777	.468	.570	.102
New York	1,335	1,494	159	.648	.656	.008
Miami	299	578	279	.503	.510	.007
Chicago	327	580	253	.582	.633	.051
San Antonio	385	481	96	.599	.571	-.028
Houston	213	423	210	.452	.463	.011
San Francisco	363	352	-11	.345	.401	.056
El Paso	204	297	93	.506	.514	.008
Riverside	189	290	101	.371	.363	-.008
Anaheim	160	286	126	.319	.416	.097

SOURCES: U.S. Bureau of the Census, *Census of Population and Housing: 1980*, Summary Tape File A; *Census of Population: 1970*, Fourth Count Summary Tapes, File A.

larity indices below .30 are considered low, those between .30 and .60 are moderate, and those above .60 are high.)[24] Hispanic segregation tended to be highest in the Northeast and North Central states and lowest in the South and the West. Over the decade, segregation increased in the Northeast and the West and declined in the North Central states and the South. The Northeast showed the greatest increase, about 4 points, moving from .50 to .54, while the South displayed the largest decline, also about 4 points, from .43 to .39. Thus, in the United States as a whole, and by region, Hispanic-Anglo segregation varied narrowly between about .40 and .54 over the 1970s.

However, this aggregate level stability masks some very pronounced shifts in several of the largest Hispanic metropolitan areas. For example, consistent with the information in Table 5.15, Los Angeles experienced a very sharp increase in the level of Hispanic-Anglo dissimilarity over the decade, moving from a moderate level of .47 in 1970 to a relatively high level of .57 in 1980. This increase is not surprising given the very large increase in the number of Hispanics over the decade. Of the increase of 777,000 persons, 78 percent were new immigrants, and since immigrants do not settle randomly, but in areas where Hispanics have already entered, these arrivals contributed directly to the ongoing process of succession and, hence, segregation.

By 1980 the level of Hispanic-Anglo dissimilarity in Los Angeles was beginning to approach that in New York, traditionally the most segregated Hispanic city in the United States.[25] Since New York's Hispanic population grew rather slowly over the decade and experienced a deteriorating economic position, there was little pressure for either segregation or desegregation. Invasion balanced succession, and the overall level of dissimilarity remained constant at about .65.

The next two largest Hispanic communities, Miami and Chicago, also experienced rapid population growth between 1970 and 1980, but displayed very different trends in dissimilarity from Anglos. In Miami the increase of 279,000 Hispanics (93 percent) left the index unaffected at about .50, but in Chicago a smaller proportionate change (253,000, or 71 percent) was accompanied by a significant increase in the level of dissimilarity, from .58 to .63.[26] This contrast is curious since invasion was the most prevalent kind of residential change in Chicago, while succession was more common in Miami. Apparently the relative num-

[24]These guidelines were first suggested by Nathan Kantrowitz, *Ethnic and Racial Segregation in the New York Metropolis* (New York: Praeger, 1973).
[25]See Massey, "Residential Segregation."
[26]These percentage increases in the sizes of the Hispanic populations do not agree exactly with those presented earlier in this chapter because they are based on different definitions of the populations in 1970 (see footnote 28).

ber of Hispanics moving to Chicago's succession areas exceeded the relative number entering new neighborhoods, while in Miami the relative concentration of Hispanics increased more or less equally in all areas.

Among the remaining six SMSAs in Table 5.15 the degree of segregation was inversely related to the size of the Hispanic community, in 1980 ranging from .57 in San Antonio, the fifth largest community, to .42 in Anaheim, the tenth largest. Older, well-established Hispanic areas like El Paso, San Antonio, and Riverside showed little change in dissimilarity over the decade, while newer, rapidly growing areas like Houston and Anaheim tended to increase. San Francisco's Hispanic population was the only one to register an absolute decline, and its segregation increased from .35 to .40.

Thus, data on Hispanic-Anglo dissimilarity suggest a moderate level of Hispanic segregation overall, but with considerable variability between metropolitan areas. During the 1970s the four largest Hispanic communities seemed to be converging toward a common high level of residential segregation, with Los Angeles, New York, and Chicago beginning to approach the very high levels typical of blacks in American cities, while smaller communities like Riverside and Anaheim displayed relatively low levels of segregation more characteristic of European ethnic groups.

Another way of looking at segregation is to compute the probabilities of intragroup and intergroup residential contact—that is, the likelihood of sharing a tract with a member of one's own group versus a member of another.[27] For Hispanics increasing segregation would be indicated by a falling probability of Anglo contact and a rising probability of contact with Hispanics or other minorities. These probabilities are presented in Table 5.16, and since they are strongly influenced by the relative number of Hispanics, the table also gives the Hispanic proportion for each metropolitan area.

Considering regional and national patterns, the proportion of Hispanics in the 60 SMSAs increased by about 2 percent, and this increase was accompanied by a corresponding decline in the probability of contact with Anglos and a rise in the probability of contact with other Hispanics. Overall, the likelihood of residential contact with Anglos decreased by 7 points while the probability of Hispanic contact increased by 3 points. The strongest decline in Anglo contact and the largest rise

[27]These probabilities represent the *P** family of indices recently popularized by Lieberson and his colleagues: Stanley Lieberson, "An Asymmetrical Approach to Segregation," in Ceri Peach, Vaughn Robinson, and Susan Smith, eds., *Ethnic Segregation in Cities* (London: Croom Helm, 1981); and Stanley Lieberson and Donna K. Carter, "Temporal Changes and Urban Differences in Residential Segregation: A Reconsideration," *American Journal of Sociology* 88 (1982):296–310.

TABLE 5.16

Probabilities of Residential Contact Between Hispanics and Anglos by Region and for 10 Largest Hispanic SMSAs

Region or SMSA	Hispanic Proportion			Probability of Hispanic-Anglo Contact			Probability of Hispanic-Hispanic Contact		
	1970	1980	Difference	1970	1980	Difference	1970	1980	Difference
All SMSAS (60)	.073	.095	.022	.708	.641	−.067	.172	.201	.029
Northeast (12)	.060	.077	.017	.730	.620	−.110	.124	.194	.070
North Central (12)	.022	.034	.012	.802	.745	−.057	.075	.095	.020
South (20)	.079	.098	.020	.673	.621	−.052	.191	.201	.010
West (16)	.140	.169	.029	.664	.606	−.058	.261	.287	.026
Los Angeles	.184	.276	.093	.522	.346	−.176	.377	.501	.124
New York	.135	.164	.029	.389	.331	−.058	.360	.399	.038
Miami	.237	.357	.121	.488	.340	−.147	.465	.580	.116
Chicago	.047	.082	.035	.648	.448	−.150	.250	.378	.128
San Antonio	.446	.449	.003	.283	.284	.001	.669	.660	−.009
Houston	.107	.146	.039	.582	.515	−.068	.268	.327	.058
San Francisco	.117	.108	−.009	.670	.581	−.089	.191	.193	.002
El Paso	.568	.619	.051	.265	.229	−.037	.702	.729	.027
Riverside	.166	.186	.020	.634	.548	−.036	.299	.314	.015
Anaheim	.113	.148	.035	.772	.609	−.163	.194	.310	.116

SOURCES: U.S. Bureau of the Census, *Census of Population and Housing: 1980, Summary Tape File A; Census of Population: 1970, Fourth Count Summary Tapes, File A.*

in Hispanic contact were in the Northeast, but all regions experienced the same basic pattern.

The pattern of a declining probability of Anglo contact and a rising probability of Hispanic contact was fairly universal among the SMSAs under study. The only exception was in San Antonio, where there was little change in either coefficient. Extremely sharp declines in the probability of residential contact with Anglos (10 points or more) were registered in Los Angeles, Miami, Chicago, and Anaheim, while slightly less extreme, but still quite large, declines were observed in New York and Houston. As one would expect, the probability of Anglo contact varied inversely with the proportion of Hispanics, ranging from .23 in El Paso (62 percent Hispanic) to .61 in Anaheim (15 percent Hispanic). Conversely, the probability of Hispanic contact varied indirectly with the Hispanic proportion, from .73 in El Paso to .31 in Anaheim. In general the SMSAs that experienced the greatest increase in the relative number of Hispanics also evinced the sharpest increase in Hispanic spatial isolation.

In many ways these contact probabilities give a clearer picture of the actual segregation experienced by Hispanics than the indices of dissimilarity. They measure the degree of exposure to Anglos experienced by the average Hispanic, and not some abstract ideal of "evenness." Indeed, even though the degree of residential unevenness remained fairly constant in Miami, Houston, El Paso, and Riverside, all these areas showed significant declines in the probability of Anglo contact, ranging from 4 to 15 points. The 1970s therefore appear to be a time of increasing spatial isolation for Hispanics, especially in the largest communities, and particularly in ones that experienced heavy immigration over the decade.

It is not possible to measure trends in segregation for different Hispanic groups over the 1970s, since comparable definitions of Mexicans, Cubans, and Puerto Ricans are not available at the tract level for both 1970 and 1980.[28] Therefore, Table 5.17 presents dissimilarity indices and contact probabilities measuring segregation for 1980 by itself. Mexicans, Cubans, and Puerto Ricans congregate in very different cities, so it does not make much sense to compare national and regional averages, although they are presented for comparative purposes. Since most of the SMSAs in the table contain few Cubans and Puerto Ricans, interpretation will focus on urban areas that serve as primary cities for the three main Hispanic groups: Puerto Ricans in New York, Mexicans in Los Angeles, and Cubans in Miami.

[28]In 1970 Mexicans, Cubans, and Puerto Ricans were identified at the tract level only on the basis of birth or parentage, leaving out all members of these groups above the second generation, and thus inflating their segregation indices considerably.

TABLE 5.17

Dissimilarities and Contact Probabilities Between Selected Hispanic Groups and Anglos in 60 SMSAs by Region and 10 Largest Hispanic SMSAs: 1980

| Region or SMSA | Hispanic-Anglo Dissimilarity | | | Probability of Contact Between Hispanic Group and | | | | | | | | |
| | Mexicans | Puerto Ricans | Cubans | Anglos | | | Itself | | | Other Hispanics | | |
				Mexicans	Puerto Ricans	Cubans	Mexicans	Puerto Ricans	Cubans	Mexicans	Puerto Ricans	Cubans
All SMSAs (60)	.512	.597	.680	.632	.675	.746	.133	.048	.023	.059	.121	.118
Northeast (12)	.623	.695	.709	.690	.562	.705	.009	.161	.042	.113	.070	.120
North Central (12)	.509	.716	.780	.719	.729	.835	.075	.045	.006	.030	.067	.043
South (20)	.483	.525	.610	.577	.706	.739	.155	.010	.035	.039	.123	.106
West (16)	.568	.518	.669	.589	.686	.722	.249	.008	.006	.064	.201	.188
Los Angeles	.611	.538	.596	.320	.445	.489	.458	.011	.027	.075	.363	.349
New York	.660	.723	.597	.433	.278	.510	.014	.324	.031	.257	.107	.256
Miami	.562	.441	.588	.467	.393	.311	.057	.055	.504	.268	.362	.132
Chicago	.640	.805	.671	.486	.450	.690	.311	.232	.022	.089	.211	.175
San Antonio	.589	.517	.582	.272	.548	.606	.635	.010	.003	.041	.349	.325
Houston	.504	.455	.509	.493	.666	.757	.324	.004	.007	.028	.153	.122
San Francisco	.476	.541	.642	.557	.560	.622	.135	.018	.006	.077	.181	.161
El Paso	.527	.360	.550	.222	.426	.469	.709	.017	.002	.039	.452	.483
Riverside	.391	.407	.596	.584	.699	.752	.300	.006	.005	.039	.207	.182
Anaheim	.479	.457	.516	.576	.746	.724	.305	.007	.007	.044	.173	.200

SOURCES: U.S. Bureau of the Census, Census of Population and Housing: 1980, Summary Tape File A; Census of Population: 1970, Fourth Count Summary Tapes, File A.

174

The New York SMSA represents the largest single community of Puerto Ricans in the United States, containing roughly 44 percent of the entire population. No matter which indicator of segregation one considers, the segregation of Puerto Ricans from Anglos in this metropolitan area is extremely high. The index of Puerto Rican–Anglo dissimilarity, .72, is among the highest observed for any Hispanic group in any area (indeed, the only higher coefficient is for Puerto Ricans in Chicago), and the probability of residential contact with Anglos is extremely low, about .28. Coefficients this low are usually only achieved when a group constitutes a majority, or near majority, of the urban population, as for Hispanics in San Antonio or El Paso; but Puerto Ricans constitute only about 10 percent of New York's population. At the same time, the probabilities of intragroup and inter-Hispanic contact are quite high for Puerto Ricans, .32 and .11, respectively, as is the probability of contact with blacks, .26 (not shown). In other words, Puerto Ricans in New York are a highly segregated, spatially isolated group who are much more likely to live near other minority members than Anglos.

Los Angeles is, of course, the largest and most important center of Mexican culture and population in the United States. Its Mexican origin population of 1.6 million represented 22 percent of the SMSA's population, and placed it behind only Mexico City, Guadalajara, and Monterrey as a Mexican city. In spite of its large size and the recent influx of immigrants, Mexican-Anglo dissimilarity, while relatively high, was 11 points below that of New York's Puerto Ricans, about .61. Similarly, although the percentage of Mexicans in Los Angeles was more than twice the share of Puerto Ricans in New York, the probability of Anglo contact was greater. Indications of Mexicans' lower segregation are also found in the lower probabilities of contact with other Hispanics (.08) and blacks (.09). On the other hand, the probability of intragroup contact was considerably higher than for Puerto Ricans, .46 compared with .32, reflecting the larger relative size of the Mexican community in Los Angeles.

Finally, Miami is the undisputed capital of the Cuban American community, containing 407,000 Cubans who represent over half of all those living in the United States and 25 percent of the SMSA's population. Of the three Hispanic groups, Miami's Cubans generally display the lowest level of dissimilarity (.59), which might suggest a low level of segregation. However, they also exhibit the highest probability of intragroup contact (.50), and a relatively low likelihood of Anglo contact (.31), although the latter is still higher than the level observed for Puerto Ricans in New York. They also have a fairly high probability of contact with other Hispanic groups (.13).

The unusual combination of a low level of dissimilarity and a high probability of intragroup contact probably reflects the unique history of Cubans in the United States. In 1960 there were virtually no Cuban neighborhoods in Miami. During the 1960s hundreds of thousands of Cuban émigrés entered the city. Since residential enclaves do not form overnight, these arrivals necessarily entered a wide variety of census tracts in the metropolitan area. With continuing immigration from Cuban and strong inmigration from the rest of the United States over the 1970s, these tracts formed the nucleus for an emerging enclave, and increased their Cuban proportions over the decade. However, the relative number of Cubans increased equally in each enclave tract, and this growth was balanced by the concomitant entry of Cubans into new Anglo areas. Thus, the unevenness of Cubans' residential distribution did not change markedly, even though the probability of intragroup contact did.

Comparing the cases of the three different groups in their primary cities, few general conclusions emerge. Both the Mexicans in Los Angeles and the Cubans in Miami are characterized by relatively high levels of residential dissimilarity from Anglos and are apparently organized into cohesive spatial communities typified by high probabilities of intragroup contact. However, in spite of the relatively large size and internal coherence of the two communities, the probability of contact with Anglos is significant, about 33 percent, while the probability of contact with blacks is small. In contrast, the relatively smaller Puerto Rican population displays a higher degree of spatial isolation from Anglos, a lower degree of internal coherence, and a higher probability of contact with other minority groups, especially blacks. This pattern replicates the essentials of the 1970 pattern and suggests a pattern of voluntary segregation for Mexicans and Cubans, reflecting a balance of succession and assimilation, but one of involuntary isolation for Puerto Ricans.

While such a conclusion follows from the three-way comparison we have made, the fact remains that the intergroup comparison is confounded with intercity differences in the pattern of segregation. The ecological structures of the three SMSAs obviously differ, which could account for some of the differences observed. The only SMSA with sufficient numbers of Hispanics from all three groups to conduct a reasonably sound intracity comparative analysis is Chicago, which houses 369,000 Mexicans, 127,000 Puerto Ricans, and 18,000 Cubans, who constitute 5.1, 1.8, and 0.3 percent of the SMSA's population, respectively. A comparison of segregation patterns for these three groups in Chicago only heightens the contrast and reinforces our earlier conclusions. Puerto Rican–Anglo dissimilarity (.81) is 13 points higher than that for Cubans and 16 points higher than that for Mexicans. Puerto Ricans also have the lowest probability of Anglo contact (.45 compared with .49 for

Mexicans and .69 for Cubans), and a relatively low likelihood of intra-group contact (.23 compared with .31 for Mexicans). Probabilities of contact with other minority groups are also the highest of the three, being .21 with Other Hispanics and .10 with blacks. Thus, data from the 1980 census reconfirm the unique position of Puerto Ricans in American society.

Summary and Conclusions

This review of data from the 1980 census has provided an assessment of the spatial position of Hispanics in the United States. In general Hispanics are a highly metropolitanized people, tending to live in metropolitan areas to a greater degree than do non-Hispanic whites. Although some indication of decreasing regional concentration of Hispanics is evident during the 1970s (at least among Mexicans), the decade also was a time of spatial consolidation for Hispanics within American cities, especially the largest ones. With strong immigration and a stagnant economy, spatial isolation within cities generally increased, especially in the cases of Cubans in Miami and Mexicans in Los Angeles. Puerto Ricans remained highly residentially segregated from Anglos throughout the decade, and their position as the most spatially isolated ethnic group remained unchanged. The consequences of high and growing Hispanic residential segregation are uncertain, but probably depend on the extent to which it is voluntary or involuntary. In this regard, Puerto Ricans are clearly at greatest risk of being denied equal access to spatially determined resources like education, health, security, and employment.

6

MARRIAGE, FAMILY, AND
HOUSEHOLD

P ATTERNS of marriage, family, and household behavior have changed substantially in the United States in recent years.[1] In fact, a considerable debate has arisen about whether or not the institutions of marriage and the family are in irrevocable decline. Increases in divorce rates, declines in first-marriage rates for women, and increases in the median age at first marriage[2] have led some observers to conclude that marriage and the family are losing their social importance. For example, Thomas Espenshade writes: "In recent years there have been considerable shifts in the decisions made by American adults regarding family formation and dissolution, and these shifts are consistent with the view that marriage is weakening as a social institution."[3] Other scholars, however, emphasize the resiliency of marriage and the family. Charles Westoff notes that despite the loss over several centuries of many of the family's productive, religious, and educational functions,

---

[1]Some of the material in this chapter originally appeared in W. P. Frisbie, F. D. Bean, and D. L. Poston, *Household and Family Demography of Hispanics, Blacks and Anglos*, Final Report, Center for Population Research, National Institute of Child Health and Human Development, Bethesda, Maryland, 1985.

[2]National Center for Health Statistics, "Advance Report of Final Marriage Statistics, 1982," *Monthly Vital Statistics Report*, vol. 34, no. 3, supplement (Hyattsville, MD: Public Health Service, 1985).

[3]Thomas J. Espenshade, "Marriage Trends in America: Estimates, Implications, and Underlying Causes," *Population and Development Review* 11 (1985):193–245.

the institution continues to thrive because it has retained responsibility for reproduction and socialization.[4] This view is echoed by Kingsley Davis, who observes that marriage is "the main institutional relationship through which societies license and encourage childbearing and child care."[5]

These issues attract particular interest in the case of Hispanics for whom family and kin relationships have been argued to assume greater importance than is the case among non-Hispanic whites. Because Hispanic groups are composed of relatively recent immigrants from less developed countries, they might be expected to adhere more closely to traditional patterns of marriage, family, and household behavior.[6] They might also be expected to subscribe more fully to familistic values, which have been defined as values that "give overriding importance to the family and the needs of the collective as opposed to individual and personal needs."[7] Whether or not these views accord with the available demographic evidence is a question we will address in this chapter. Its answer takes on added importance in light of the suggestion that familistic orientations may impede the socioeconomic achievement of racial/ethnic minority groups.[8] Hence, the extent to which Hispanic groups exhibit demographic behaviors consistent with familistic orientations not only is interesting in its own right, but also may have implications for the future prospects of these groups for further advances in socioeconomic achievement.

This chapter is thus concerned with demographic aspects of marriage, families, and households among the various Hispanic populations. In the next chapter, which focuses on fertility behavior, we examine in detail one of the most important factors affecting the size and composition of families and households. The present chapter explores three other aspects of marriage, family, and household behavior. The first of

[4]Charles F. Westoff, "Fertility Decline in the West: Causes and Prospects," *Population and Development Review* 9 (1983):99–104.

[5]Kingsley Davis, "Changes in Marriage Since World War II," paper presented at the conference on Contemporary Marriage: Comparative Perspectives on a Changing Institution, Center for Advanced Study in the Behavioral Sciences, Stanford, California, 1982.

[6]See Douglas S. Massey, "Dimensions of the New Immigration to the United States and the Prospects for Assimilation," *Annual Review of Sociology* 7 (1981):57–85; C. Heller, "Class as an Explanation of Ethnic Differences in Upward Mobility—The Case of Mexican Americans," *International Migration Review* 2 (1967):31–38; and S. E. Keefe, "Acculturation and Extended Family Among Urban Mexican Americans," in Amado Padilla, ed., *Acculturation: Theory, Models and Some New Findings* (Boulder: Westview Press, 1979).

[7]Frank D. Bean, R. L. Curtis, and J. P. Marcum, "Familism and Marital Satisfaction Among Mexican Americans: The Effects of Family Size, Wife's Labor Force Participation, and Conjugal Power," *Journal of Marriage and the Family* 39 (1977):759–67.

[8]Leo Grebler, Joan W. Moore, and Ralph C. Guzman, *The Mexican American People: The Nation's Second Largest Minority* (Glencoe, IL: Free Press, 1970).

these concerns patterns of marriage and marital dissolution. Increases in marital instability in the United States over the past two decades not only have contributed to the idea that marriage and family are in decline, but also have had a major influence on changes in household structure.[9] To what extent are the patterns of marriage and marital instability characteristic of the broader population evident among the Spanish origin groups? The second concerns patterns of household structure, which have implications for assessing marriage and family patterns. How do the various Hispanic groups differ with respect to the size and composition of households, and how have these changed over time? The third concerns the implications of changes in family/household structure for trends in economic inequality between the Spanish origin groups and non-Hispanic whites. This is important because it highlights the ways in which interethnic inequalities depend on family and household behavior.

Background and Definitions

"The distinguishing feature of household and family demography" is its focus on households and families as analytical units.[10] The terms "household" and "family" refer to different, though related, concepts. Following definitions set forth by Burch and based on current census procedures, we may speak of persons sharing the same dwelling unit as constituting a household.[11] The term "family" in its broadest usage refers to persons related by blood, marriage, or adoption. Consistent with census usage, however, and in keeping with present purposes, a family is taken here to mean those persons related by blood, marriage, or adoption who co-reside.[12] Hence, the concepts of family and household are not synonymous, although the latter establishes definitional boundaries for the former.

Although we present some data on the characteristics of individuals in order to assess aspects of family formation and marital dissolution,

[9]See Paul H. Glick, "Marriage, Divorce and Living Arrangements," *Journal of Family Issues* 5 (1984):7–26; and James A. Sweet, "Indicators of Family and Household Structure of Racial and Ethnic Minorities in the United States," in Frank D. Bean and W. Parker Frisbie, eds., *The Demography of Racial and Ethnic Groups* (New York: Academic Press, 1978).

[10]Thomas K. Burch, "Household and Family Demography: A Bibliographic Essay," *Population Index* 45 (1979):173; Paul H. Glick, "Family Statistics," in Philip M. Hauser and Otis D. Duncan, eds., *The Study of Population: An Inventory and Appraisal* (Chicago: University of Chicago Press, 1959).

[11]Burch, "Household and Family Demography."

[12]Burch, "Household and Family Demography."

for the most part we focus on characteristics of the household in terms of attributes of the household head. While it is clear that important familial relationships exist outside the confines of a given residence, it is equally true that "living in the same house or apartment facilitates (and often necessitates) the sharing of resources such as time and money."[13] In addition, nonfamily members may be important in the socialization of family members, and "the household, while lacking a legal role, is a more basic economic unit than is the family."[14] Also, as a practical matter, focusing on attributes of the head of the household allows for computing convenience and maximizes comparability between our results and not only published census reports, but also the work of other investigators in the field.[15]

Family Structure and Process

Our first concern is to examine the current marital status distribution among the various Hispanic groups, partly for the purpose of assessing group differences in marriage behavior, but mainly for the purpose of providing an assessment of group differences in "family stability."[16] Farley and Hermalin define a stable family system as "one in which adults marry and live with their spouses, in their own households and in which children are born into and raised in such a household."[17] The increasing prevalence of marital instability—defined here as ever having experienced divorce or separation—in the population at large is well documented. The increase results from a substantial rise in divorce and separation rates in the 1960s followed by an even sharper increase in the 1970s and a flattening of the trend line at high levels of marital disruption in the early 1980s.[18] Census data on the current prevalence of marital disruption can be less than ideal as indicators of marital instability, however, when "prevalence measures confound differ-

[13]Suzanne M. Bianchi, *Household Composition and Racial Inequality* (New Brunswick, NJ: Rutgers University Press, 1981), p. 9; and see Frances E. Kobrin, "The Fall in Household Size and the Rise of the Primary Individual in the United States," *Demography* 13 (1976):127–38.

[14]Daniel O. Price, *A Cohort Analysis*, Final Report to the Department of Health and Human Resources, University of North Carolina, Greensboro, 1981.

[15]In adopting this strategy, we follow the practice of Sweet, "Indicators."

[16]See Paul H. Glick, "Marital Stability as a Social Indicator," *Social Biology* 16 (1969):158–66.

[17]Reynolds Farley and Albert I. Hermalin, "Family Stability: A Comparison of Trends Between Blacks and Whites," *American Sociological Review* 36 (1971):1–17.

[18]Arthur J. Norton and Paul Glick, "Marital Instability in America: Past, Present, and Future," in George Levinger and Oliver C. Moles, eds., *Divorce and Separation* (New York: Basic Books, 1979).

ences in marital disruption, remarriage rates, age at marriage and age structure differences in a single measure."[19] To a certain extent, however, these problems are alleviated when census data allow a distinction to be made between remarried widows and remarried divorced, as is the case here.[20]

The current marital status distributions within the various populations of Spanish origin persons aged 14 and over in 1980 are presented in Table 6.1. The classification is defined by combining information on the number of times married and marital status to yield eight categories: (1) never married; (2) spouse present, married once; (3) spouse present, married more than once with first marriage ended by death of spouse; (4) spouse present, married more than once with first marriage ended because of divorce; (5) divorced; (6) separated; (7) widowed; and (8) spouse absent for other reasons. Compared with non-Hispanic whites, higher percentages of both males and females in the Spanish origin groups are never married, reflecting the younger age structures within these subpopulations. The Spanish origin groups also reveal higher percentages of both males and females in the "married, spouse absent" category than non-Hispanic whites. All of the Spanish origin groups also exhibit higher percentages in the "separated" category, perhaps because of the very high percentages of Catholics among Hispanics and the strictures of the Catholic church against divorce.[21] In the cases of the "remarried, previously divorced" and "divorced" categories, appreciable differences do not emerge between the Spanish origin groups and the non-Hispanic whites. To a certain extent whether these percentages are higher or lower than those of the majority group depends on gender. For example, among females the Spanish origin groups exhibit percentages very close to or even higher than the percentage currently divorced among non-Hispanic whites, whereas the percentages remarried among those previously divorced tend to be lower. Among males, however, almost all of the percentages for these two categories are lower than those for non-Hispanic whites.

It is extremely difficult, however, to reach conclusions about differences in the propensity toward various forms of marriage behavior from these figures because they are affected by differences in age structure

[19]Sweet, "Indicators," p. 225.

[20]See W. Parker Frisbie and W. Opitz, "Race/Ethnic and Gender Differentials in Marital Instability: 1980," *Texas Population Research Center Papers*, no. 7.007 (Austin: University of Texas, 1985); and W. Parker Frisbie, Frank D. Bean, and Isaac W. Eberstein, "Patterns of Marital Instability Among Mexican Americans, Blacks, and Anglos," in Frank D. Bean and W. Parker Frisbie, eds., *The Demography of Racial and Ethnic Groups* (New York: Academic Press, 1978).

[21]See Andrew M. Greeley, *The American Catholic: A Social Portrait* (New York: Basic Books, 1977).

TABLE 6.1

Marital Status by Sex and Spanish Origin Group, Persons Aged 14 and Over: 1980

Ethnic Group	Never Married	Married Once	Remarried, Previously Widowed	Remarried, Previously Divorced	Divorced	Separated	Widowed	Spouse Absent
MALE								
Non-Hispanic White	25.7%	53.0%	1.7%	9.2%	5.3%	1.3%	2.6%	1.2%
Mexican	32.3	48.5	0.9	5.6	4.3	2.1	1.6	4.7
Puerto Rican	36.5	42.3	0.7	6.2	5.3	4.5	1.4	3.3
Cuban	26.4	51.4	1.1	8.6	5.2	2.2	1.9	3.3
Central/South American	28.9	53.3	0.5	4.6	3.6	2.5	0.8	5.6
Other Hispanic	34.5	43.7	1.2	7.4	6.2	2.1	2.1	2.9
FEMALE								
Non-Hispanic White	19.2	48.7	1.9	7.6	6.9	1.7	13.0	1.0
Mexican	24.5	50.1	1.0	5.0	6.5	3.8	6.5	2.4
Puerto Rican	28.9	37.2	0.7	4.6	9.2	11.1	5.8	2.5
Cuban	21.1	48.1	0.9	4.9	8.9	2.9	10.4	2.8
Central/South American	21.4	52.7	0.7	4.0	6.2	4.9	6.3	4.1
Other Hispanic	26.6	42.5	1.1	6.3	9.0	3.4	9.0	2.1

SOURCE: 1980 Public Use Microdata Sample file.

between the Spanish origin groups and non-Hispanic whites. A clearer picture emerges when the data are organized so that they are less dependent on age composition. For example, Table 6.2 shows the percentages of 25-year-olds in the populations that have ever married (and by implication the percentages that have never married by that age). If the suggestion of many observers that family relationships are of particular importance within Hispanic groups is correct, then we might expect to find that higher percentages of both males and females among the Hispanic groups than among non-Hispanic whites have married by age 25. In 1980 this is true, however, only among Mexicans, whose percentages exceed those of non-Hispanic whites by 6 or 7 points. For both males and females all of the other groups in 1980 are either virtually identical with non-Hispanic whites (within 1 percent) or below them in their percentages ever-marrying by age 25. Interestingly, females in all of the Spanish origin groups in 1960 and in 1970 were less likely than non-Hispanic white females to marry by age 25, with the exception of Cubans in 1960.

Data on median age at first marriage, presented in Table 6.3, show a somewhat different picture.[22] In general, the Spanish origin groups exhibit slightly lower median ages at first marriage than do non-Hispanic whites. Also, their median ages have not increased as much as non-Hispanic whites have since 1960. When these findings are viewed in conjunction with those on the percentages marrying by age 25, they suggest a pattern of slightly earlier but less universalistic marriage among

TABLE 6.2

*Percentage of Ever-Married 25-Year-Olds
by Sex and Spanish Origin Group: 1960–1980*

	Male			Female		
Ethnic Group	1960	1970	1980	1960	1970	1980
Non-Hispanic White	71.4%	74.0%	59.1%	86.8%	85.6%	73.7%
Mexican	65.6	75.2	66.0	84.9	82.8	79.6
Puerto Rican	67.7	75.2	58.6	79.8	82.4	67.4
Cuban	77.8	75.9	60.0	88.9	74.4	72.2
Central/South American	38.9	65.9	59.9	71.4	79.6	72.8
Other Hispanic	50.0	75.3	60.1	66.7	83.1	74.4

SOURCES: 1960 and 1970 Public Use Sample files; Public Use Microdata Sample file.

[22]These figures are calculated based on approaches discussed in Henry S. Shryock and Jacob S. Siegel, and Associates, *The Methods and Materials of Demography,* 3rd ed. (Washington, DC: U.S. Government Printing Office, 1975), pp. 292–93.

TABLE 6.3

Median Age at First Marriage
by Sex and Type of Spanish Origin: 1960–1980

	Male			Female		
Ethnic Group	1960	1970	1980	1960	1970	1980
Non-Hispanic White	22.4	22.5	24.0	20.1	20.8	22.0
Mexican	22.4	22.1	22.8	19.5	20.7	20.9
Puerto Rican	21.4	22.1	23.2	19.1	20.0	21.4
Cuban	21.3	22.6	23.9	19.7	23.7	22.1
Central/South American	24.1	22.3	24.4	21.2	19.2	21.4
Other Hispanic	24.2	21.1	24.1	19.5	20.2	21.8

SOURCES: 1960 and 1970 Public Use Sample files; 1980 Public Use Microdata Sample file.

all of the groups except Cubans and Mexicans. Among Cubans, the pattern is virtually identical to that of non-Hispanic whites by 1980, while among Mexicans both earlier and more universalistic marriage seems to be characteristic.

These results thus seem to provide mixed support for the idea that Hispanic groups are more familistic than non-Hispanics. That Hispanics might be more familistic appears to have received some support, however, from recent studies of marital instability among Mexican Americans in five southwestern states (Arizona, California, Colorado, New Mexico, and Texas).[23] These investigations have found lower rates of instability among Mexican Americans compared with non-Hispanic whites and blacks living in this region. In order to examine this issue here, we combine three categories from Table 6.4 (the remarried, previously divorced; the divorced; and the separated) into a single category indicating prior experience with marital instability. We then compute the percentages of the populations falling into this category among the ever-married. The results, which are standardized for age and are presented for the entire country instead of only the southwestern states, do not lend a great deal of support to the idea that Mexican Americans and the other Hispanic groups are less likely than non-Hispanic whites to be characterized by unstable family situations. Although Mexican Americans exhibit slightly less instability than non-Hispanic whites in 1980 and Central/South Americans show substantially less instability, both of these groups reveal higher instability in 1960 and 1970 than non-

[23]See W.P. Frisbie, W. Opitz, and W. Kelly, "Marital Instability Trends among Mexican Americans as Compared to Blacks and Anglos," *Social Science Quarterly* 66 (1985):585–601.

TABLE 6.4

Age-Standardized Percentages
Experiencing Marital Instability Among Females Aged 15–64
by Type of Spanish Origin: 1960–1980

Ethnic Group	1960	1970	1980
Non-Hispanic White	15.8%	15.5%	23.3%
Mexican	18.7	17.4	21.2
Puerto Rican	22.0	26.2	36.2
Cuban	18.1	17.9	23.2
Central/South American	16.7	17.9	15.5
Other Hispanic	17.4	20.8	29.1

SOURCES: 1960 and 1970 Public Use Sample files; 1980 Public Use Microdata Sample A file.

Hispanic whites. The substantial differences observed in other research based on 1980 data for the southwestern states alone (for example, 31.6 percent unstable among ever-married non-Hispanic females versus 22.7 percent among ever-married Mexican origin females)[24] seem likely to derive from regional differences in age at marriage and religion among non-Hispanic whites.[25] Judging from the national comparisons presented here, one would conclude that the differences are minimal, or even that marital instability may be higher among many Hispanic groups.

Of greater significance, perhaps, is the fact that the Hispanic groups have followed the same trend of increasing instability characteristic of non-Hispanic whites since 1960. Among Puerto Ricans and Other Hispanics the increases have been substantial, resulting by 1980 in levels of instability substantially higher among females than those of the remaining Spanish origin groups. In summary, the national data examined here on levels of instability, together with the trends observed toward increasing instability among the Hispanic groups, do not provide a very strong basis for concluding that cultural orientations among Hispanics increase the likelihood of marital stability. If anything, instability is little different or even greater than that observed among non-Hispanic whites.

[24]Frisbie and Opitz, "Race/Ethnic and Gender Differentials."
[25]For age at marriage differences, see James A. Weed, "Age at Marriage as a Factor in State Divorce Rate Differentials," *Demography* 11(1974):361–75. For religion differences, see Greeley, *The American Catholic.*

Differences in Household Structure

In this section we present a number of indicators of household structure for the Spanish origin groups and for non-Hispanic whites in the United States in 1980. These indicators tap aspects of the size and composition of the household. Both of these are relevant to assessing differences among subpopulations in the extent to which their household structures reflect familistic emphases. The selection of indicators derives in part from the work of Sweet,[26] who has studied patterns of family/household structure based on 1970 census data from the standpoint of their implications for variation among racial and ethnic groups in measured economic welfare and inequality; phenomena that as we shall see depend on family/household structure. As noted above, the units of analysis are households, and the indicators are developed with respect to the attributes of the head of household.

One of the best documented trends regarding the structure of the American family is the secular decline in average size of household. Not surprisingly then, each of the Spanish origin groups except Central/South Americans is characterized by smaller households in 1980 than in 1960 (Table 6.5). The trend for Mexicans and Puerto Ricans is one of monotonic decline, with most of the reduction occurring between 1970 and 1980. A deviation from this pattern occurs among Cubans, Central/South Americans, and Other Hispanics, who show increases in average household size between 1960 and 1970, but overall decreases (at least among Cubans and Other Hispanics) between 1960 and 1980. The reason is probably that Cubans and Central/South Americans are relatively

TABLE 6.5

Mean Household Size and Mean Number of Adults per Household: 1960–1980

Ethnic Group	Mean Household Size			Mean Number of Adults per Household		
	1960	1970	1980	1960	1970	1980
Non-Hispanic White	3.2	3.0	2.7	2.1	2.0	1.9
Mexican	4.4	4.1	3.8	2.2	2.2	2.2
Puerto Rican	4.0	3.7	3.3	2.2	2.0	1.9
Cuban	3.2	3.4	3.0	2.2	2.3	2.2
Central/South American	3.3	3.4	3.4	2.1	2.1	2.2
Other Hispanic	3.2	3.7	3.0	2.2	2.1	2.0

SOURCES: 1960 and 1970 Public Use Sample files; 1980 Public Use Microdata Sample file.

[26]Sweet, "Indicators."

recent immigrants; many of them arrived during the late 1960s and 1970s, thus increasing average household size in 1970 when many households were in the early stages of the settlement process and the likelihood of sharing living quarters was probably greatest.

Despite the similarity in the direction of the trend lines for almost all of the groups, it is clear that Mexican Americans, Puerto Ricans, and Central/South Americans are characterized by larger households than are the other groups. Average household size among Mexican Americans declined from 4.4 persons in 1960 to 3.8 persons in 1980, but this figure is still above the 1960 mean for non-Hispanic whites by over half-a-person per household. Among Puerto Ricans the decline was from 4.0 persons per household in 1960 to 3.3 persons in 1980, a figure that placed them about where the average size of household among non-Hispanic whites was in 1960. In summary, all of the groups except Central/South Americans experienced shrinking household size between 1960 and 1980, with the pattern of monotonic decline that characterizes non-Hispanic whites also evident among Mexican Americans and Puerto

TABLE 6.6

Change in Mean Household Size and Decomposition into Change in Mean Number of Adults and Mean Number of Children: 1960–1970 and 1970–1980

Ethnic Group	Change in Mean Household Size	Change in Mean Number of Adults	Change in Mean Number of Children
Non-Hispanic White			
1960–1970	−.20	−.07	−.13
1970–1980	−.37	−.07	−.30
Mexican			
1960–1970	−.16	−.03	−.13
1970–1980	−.49	−.02	−.47
Puerto Rican			
1960–1970	−.23	−.21	−.02
1970–1980	−.47	−.07	−.40
Cuban			
1960–1970	.25	.16	.09
1970–1980	−.49	−.11	−.38
Central/South American			
1960–1970	.04	−.03	.07
1970–1980	.01	.08	−.07
Other Hispanic			
1960–1970	.50	−.15	.65
1970–1980	−.66	−.07	−.59

SOURCES: 1960 and 1970 Public Use Sample files; 1980 Public Use Microdata Sample file.

Ricans and with the latter two groups along with Central/South Americans evincing the largest households.

Table 6.6 presents the trends in mean household size for 1960–1970 and 1970–1980 among the Spanish origin groups and non-Hispanic whites decomposed into changes in the mean number of adults and the mean number of children. The child component of household size ought to assume particular significance for high fertility groups.[27] Thus, it might be expected that changes in the mean number of children would play a predominant role in the overall change among Mexican Americans and Puerto Ricans whose fertility levels are considerably above those of the other groups. But as the results in Table 6.6 reveal, there is no regular pattern along the lines of high versus low fertility groups. There are, however, a number of other interesting regularities. First, in the past decade every Spanish origin group except Central/South Americans experienced a drop in average household size. Second, it is clear that the pace at which households have been declining in size accelerated during the 1970s. Every group recording a decline in mean household size in both decades recorded a larger decline in the 1970s than in the 1960s. Undoubtedly this is due to the fertility declines beginning during the 1960s and continuing into the 1970s. Third, among all the groups showing declines from 1970 to 1980, 80 to 90 percent of the decline was due to the change in the mean number of children. This is in contrast to the 1960–70 pattern among Puerto Rican and Cuban groups, for whom half or more of the change in the earlier time interval resulted from change in the number of adults.

The average household sizes for the groups examined here may be viewed as a composite function of two parts—the average size of households of specific types and the distribution of households among these types.[28] For the purposes of this chapter, we make a distinction between three types of households:

1. *Husband-wife households.* These are families in which a married, spouse-present person is the head.

2. *Other family households.* These are households in which at least one other relative of the head is present. (A substantial component of these households consists of female-headed families. For instance, the proportion of other family households that is female-headed ranges from 74.9 percent among Mexican Americans to 88.2 percent among Puerto Ricans.)

3. *Nonfamily households.* These are households in which no relative of the head is present (a large share of such households are one-person households)

[27]Judith Treas, "Postwar Trends in Family Size," *Demography* 18 (1981):321–24.
[28]See Sweet, "Indicators."

TABLE 6.7

Mean Household Size and Percentage Distribution by Family Type and Ethnic Group: 1960–1980

Ethnic Group	Total Households			Husband-Wife Families			Other Families			Nonfamilies		
	1960	1970	1980	1960	1970	1980	1960	1970	1980	1960	1970	1980
MEAN HOUSEHOLD SIZE												
Non-Hispanic White	3.2	3.0	2.7	3.7	3.6	3.3	2.9	3.0	2.8	1.4	1.1	1.2
Mexican	4.4	4.1	3.8	4.9	4.6	4.4	3.9	3.8	3.7	1.2	1.2	1.3
Puerto Rican	4.0	3.7	3.3	4.4	4.2	4.0	3.7	3.8	3.6	1.2	1.2	1.2
Cuban	3.2	3.4	3.3	3.7	3.8	3.5	3.0	3.2	3.0	1.1	1.2	1.2
Central/South American	3.3	3.4	3.4	3.9	3.9	4.0	3.2	3.3	3.4	1.3	1.2	1.3
Other Hispanic	3.2	3.7	3.0	3.5	4.1	3.7	3.7	4.0	3.3	1.2	1.3	1.2
PERCENTAGE DISTRIBUTION												
Non-Hispanic White	100.0%	100.0%	100.0%	76.4%	70.8%	63.0%	9.4%	9.5%	10.1%	14.3%	19.6%	26.9%
Mexican	100.0	100.0	100.0	75.9	70.7	66.1	14.0	16.4	17.9	10.1	12.9	16.0
Puerto Rican	100.0	100.0	100.0	71.8	62.2	48.7	17.8	24.5	31.5	10.5	13.3	19.8
Cuban	100.0	100.0	100.0	72.1	74.4	65.7	13.3	13.2	14.1	14.6	12.4	20.2
Central/South American	100.0	100.0	100.0	68.0	64.1	56.8	14.5	18.8	23.6	17.5	17.1	19.6
Other Hispanic	100.0	100.0	100.0	75.7	70.6	58.1	10.3	13.4	16.7	14.0	16.0	25.2

SOURCES: 1960 and 1970 Public Use Sample files; 1980 Public Use Microdata Sample file.

Table 6.7 presents the mean household size distributions for these family types, together with the percentage of households falling into each type for the Spanish origin populations and for non-Hispanic whites in 1960, 1970, and 1980. It is clear in all cases that husband-wife households are larger than the other household types. For example, among Mexican Americans husband-wife households average 4.4 persons in 1980 versus 3.7 persons in other family households and 1.3 persons in nonfamily households. From the figures presented it is also evident that most of the decline in average household size occurring between 1960 and 1980 derives from decreases in the average size of husband-wife families, with a very small amount of the decline resulting from decreases in the size of other family households. The size of nonfamily households remained virtually constant over the 20-year period. It is also evident from the figures in the bottom panel of Table 6.7 that for most of the groups the percentage of husband-wife households has decreased since 1960, whereas the percentage of other family and nonfamily households has risen. As noted above, most of the increase in the percentage of households falling into the other family category derives from an increase in female-headed households between 1960 and 1980. We will return below to the implications of this shift for changes in patterns of income inequality between the Spanish origin groups and non-Hispanic whites.

In general, then, family/household structure among the Hispanic groups appears to be subject to the same forces affecting the structures of non-Hispanic whites. These forces have over the 20-year period (1960 to 1980) decreased the percentage of husband-wife families, increased the percentage of other families (the vast majority of which are female-headed), and increased the percentage of nonfamilies. The major difference in trend between the Hispanic groups and non-Hispanic whites, however, is the relatively greater growth in other family households and the relatively lesser growth in nonfamily households among Hispanics. These might be argued to reflect greater familism among the Hispanic groups. However, most of the other family households consist of female-headed households with children. If familistic emphases are comparatively strong among Hispanics, they apparently are not strong enough to ward off the forces making for these increases in families without fathers.

Female-Headed Families and Children in Two-Parent Households

Indicators of considerable interest because of their significance for economic well-being and for the social resources that can be brought to bear on childrearing are female headship rates and the percentages of children of various ages living with two parents or in female-headed families. Table 6.8 presents statistics on these indicators, standardized for age differences between the groups. The lowest percentage of families with a female head occurs among non-Hispanic whites, with only 13.6 percent of households falling into this category. The percentages among the Spanish origin groups are considerably higher, ranging from a low of 16.0 percent among Cuban Americans to 36.5 percent among Puerto Ricans. The figure for Mexican Americans, 18.9 percent, is only slightly higher than the figure for Cuban Americans. Hence, we find in these figures, as in other data we have examined, that Puerto Ricans closely approximate the situation of blacks, whose percentage of households headed by a female—40.6 percent—is virtually identical to that of Puerto Ricans.[29] As noted by Sweet, the "proportion of children in two-parent households is an indicator of the prevalence of marital disruption (and remarriage) looked at from the perspective of children rather than from the perspective of adults or marriages."[30] This measure includes children living with "step-parents" as well as with both "natural" parents, as well as a smaller number of children living with adoptive parents. By far the lowest prevalence of children under age 18 living in two-parent households occurs among Puerto Ricans, with only slightly more

TABLE 6.8

Female Headship Rates and Percentage of Children in Two-Parent Families, Standardized for Age: 1980

| Ethnic Group | Percentage of Families with Female Head | Percentage of Children Under Age 18 Living in Two-Parent Households | Percentage of Female-Headed Families With Children | |
			Under Age 6	Under Age 18
Non-Hispanic White	13.6%	83.1%	3.6%	19.1%
Mexican	18.9	74.5	7.0	33.2
Puerto Rican	36.5	51.9	8.5	36.1
Cuban	16.0	78.1	4.5	22.2
Central/South American	28.5	70.0	8.4	28.4
Other Hispanic	20.5	72.7	5.4	25.8

SOURCE: 1980 Public Use Microdata Sample file.

[29]1980 Public Use Microdata Samples.
[30]Sweet, "Indicators."

than half (51.9 percent) of children under age 18 residing in such a situation. The other Spanish origin groups show anywhere from 70.0 to 78.1 percent of children under age 18 living in two-parent households, figures that are somewhat below the 83.1 percent exhibited by non-Hispanic whites.

Another interesting question concerns the extent to which child-rearing occurs in female-headed families. Among non-Hispanic whites only 3.6 percent of female-headed households contained own children under age 6, a figure that is approximated among the Spanish origin groups only by Cuban Americans. The prevalence of children under age 6 among female-headed households among the remaining Spanish origin groups is considerably higher, ranging from 5.4 percent among the Other Hispanics to 8.5 percent among Puerto Ricans. A similar picture emerges when the percentage of female-headed households with own children under age 18 is examined. Puerto Ricans again exhibit a higher percentage (36.1) than the other groups. Cuban Americans show a low figure of 22.2 percent, but one that nonetheless exceeds the figure of 19.1 percent among non-Hispanic whites by a significant amount.

Marital Status of Female Household Heads

A popular image of female-headed households is that they consist of a female head residing with children. In actuality, as the figures in Table 6.9 reveal, this is far from the case. Among non-Hispanic whites the modal category consists of widows, with 42.7 percent of female

TABLE 6.9

Percentage Distribution of Marital Status of Female Household Heads, Standardized for Age: 1980

| Ethnic Group | Married | | Widowed | Divorced | Separated | Never Married |
	Spouse Present	Spouse Absent				
Non-Hispanic White	8.3%	1.5%	42.7%	22.8%	5.2%	19.6%
Mexican	9.9	1.2	26.5	29.6	7.0	25.0
Puerto Rican	10.6	1.8	17.5	32.7	8.0	29.2
Cuban	9.5	1.6	37.4	27.8	6.0	17.7
Central/South American	10.9	1.9	20.1	34.6	8.0	24.4
Other Hispanic	9.5	1.7	30.4	27.8	6.5	23.9

SOURCE: 1980 Public Use Microdata Sample file.

household heads falling into this category. The Spanish origin groups, however, are considerably different from non-Hispanic whites in this respect, partly as a consequence of their younger age structures. The proportion falling into the widowed category ranges from only about 18 percent to slightly more than 37 percent. All of the groups exhibit about the same tendency for married, spouse-present households to report a female head, although all of the Hispanic groups exceed non-Hispanic whites in this regard, which one would not expect given the allegedly greater emphasis on male dominance among Hispanics. Also, the percentages falling into the never-married category are higher (except for Cuban Americans) than they are for non-Hispanic whites. Another major difference between the Spanish origin groups and non-Hispanic whites is that higher percentages of female-headed families fall into the divorced and separated categories, especially the latter. Female household heads among Cubans exhibit the lowest proportion divorced or separated (33.8 percent), whereas Puerto Ricans show the highest (40.7 percent). These figures contrast rather sharply with the figure of 28.0 percent for non-Hispanic whites. Whereas the data presented above revealed patterns of marital instability among the Spanish origin groups that are not appreciably different from those of non-Hispanic whites, the present figures suggest a somewhat harsher picture insofar as the marital status composition of female household heads is concerned. Higher percentages of female-headed families among the Spanish origin groups result from divorce or separation than is the case among non-Hispanic whites, a result that does not accord well with the familistic hypothesis.

Adult Composition of Households

Another indicator that has significance both for economic well-being and for the question of the extent to which the Hispanic populations might be more familistic in orientation than majority whites is the presence of adults in households of various types.[31] Table 6.10 presents statistics on the mean number of adults in households of the various family types, as well as on the percentage of households containing three or more adults. For each of the Spanish origin groups except Puerto Ricans living in other families, the mean number of adults by type of family exceeds the comparable figure for non-Hispanic whites. For example, non-Hispanic whites living in husband-wife families aver-

[31]See Ronald Angel and Marta Tienda, "Determinants of Extended Household Structure: Cultural Pattern or Economic Need?" *American Journal of Sociology* 87 (1982):1360–83; and Marta Tienda and Ronald Angel, "Headship and Household Composition Among Blacks, Hispanics, and Other Whites," *Social Forces* 61 (1982):508–31.

TABLE 6.10

*Mean Number of Adults per Household
and Percentage of Households with Three or More Adults,
Standardized for Age: 1980*

Ethnic Group	Mean Number of Adults[a]			Percentage of Households with Three or More Adults	
	Husband-Wife Family	Other Family	Nonfamily	All Households	Husband-Wife Family
Non-Hispanic White	2.3	1.9	1.1	15.2%	20.5%
Mexican	2.6	2.1	1.2	27.5	35.2
Puerto Rican	2.5	1.9	1.2	20.3	32.0
Cuban	2.5	2.1	1.2	25.5	33.6
Central/South American	2.6	2.2	1.2	27.9	38.1
Other Hispanic	2.4	2.0	1.2	19.7	27.4

SOURCE: 1980 Public Use Microdata Sample file.

[a] Persons aged 18 and over.

age 2.3 adults per household, whereas the Spanish origin groups average from 2.4 adults per household among Other Hispanics to 2.6 adults per household among Mexicans and Central/South Americans. A similar pattern of results obtains in the case of the other two family types. Similarly, whether the focus is on all households or on husband-wife family households, the percentages of households containing three or more adults are greater among the Spanish origin groups than they are among non-Hispanic whites. Among Mexican Americans, for example, 27.5 percent of all households contain three or more adults, whereas only 15.2 percent do among non-Hispanic whites. To the extent that such adults provide supplemental sources of income, it is interesting that Puerto Ricans and Other Hispanics are the least likely of the various Spanish origin groups to contain three or more adults in households of any type.[32] Whatever economic deficiencies might be incurred by the Puerto Rican population, they are less likely to be overcome through the presence of supplemental earners in the household.

More relevant to the question of the familistic emphasis within Hispanic populations is the percentage of husband-wife families containing any related adult. These are presented for the various Spanish

[32] For more information on Puerto Rican family/household composition, see Rosemary S. Cooney, "Demographic Components of Growth in White, Black and Puerto Rican Female-Headed Families: A Comparison of the Cutright and Ross/Sawhill Methodologies," *Social Science Research* 8(1979):144–58.

TABLE 6.11

Presence of Adult Relatives in Husband-Wife Families,
Standardized for Age: 1980

	Percentage of Husband-Wife Families with:		
Ethnic Group	Any Related Adult	Own Child Aged 18 or Over	Other Relative Aged 18 or Over
Non-Hispanic White	19.9%	17.2%	3.9%
Mexican	34.4	28.1	9.8
Puerto Rican	30.8	24.6	9.2
Cuban	32.5	22.2	14.9
Central/South American	35.8	25.8	14.1
Other Hispanic	26.6	21.8	7.1

SOURCE: 1980 Public Use Microdata Sample file.

origin groups in Table 6.11, together with the percentages of households containing an own child aged 18 or over as well as the percentages of husband-wife families containing any other relative aged 18 or over. It is evident from the table that the Spanish origin groups are considerably more likely than non-Hispanic whites to contain adult relatives, especially adult relatives other than own children. Mexican and Central/South Americans are the groups most likely to have other related adults living with husband-wife families, and Other Hispanics the least likely. In all cases, however, the percentages exceed those for non-Hispanic whites.

Never-Married Persons Aged 18–24 Living in Parental Households

The final indicator we examine concerns the percentage of never-married persons aged 18 to 24 who are living in parental households. Although statistics on young, unmarried adults are somewhat problematic because disadvantaged minority males in this age range are the most underenumerated group in censuses and because many men are omitted by virtue of being overseas in the armed forces,[33] the measure nonetheless provides a rough suggestion of the extent to which persons within this age range continue to rely on their families of orientation for support beyond the age at which they could establish independent households. Interestingly, the data in Table 6.12 indicate that among never-married persons aged 18 to 24, the model living arrangement is to

[33]See Sweet, "Indicators."

TABLE 6.12

Percentage of Never-Married Persons Aged 18–24
Who Are Living in Parental Households

Ethnic Group	Male	Female
Non-Hispanic White	61.0%	60.5%
Mexican	60.4	66.1
Puerto Rican	64.9	56.2
Cuban	79.2	81.9
Central/South American	53.0	56.7
Other Hispanic	64.5	61.4

SOURCE: 1980 Public Use Microdata Sample file.

continue to reside in the parental household. Except among Central/South Americans and Puerto Rican females, this propensity is greater among the Hispanic origin groups than it is among non-Hispanic whites. In three of the five groups females are somewhat more likely than males to be living in parental households, and Cuban Americans of both sexes are much more likely than the other groups to adopt this living arrangement.

Household Composition and Economic Inequality

One of the difficulties in reaching conclusions about the importance of familism among Hispanic groups is that family/household patterns are affected by economic factors. That is, certain family or household arrangements that might be thought to reflect greater familistic values may in reality reflect responses to economic conditions. One of the strategies that may be relied on by the disadvantaged members of minority groups in order to compensate for inferior economic positions is the incorporation of supplemental earners within the household.[34] As many observers have noted, studies of economic inequality between minority and majority groups will vary in their results depending on whether households or individuals are being examined.[35] During the

[34]J. Aschenbrenner, "Extended Families Among Black Americans," *Journal of Comparative Family Studies* 4 (1973):257–68; Carol Stack, *All our Kin* (New York: Harper & Row, 1974); Angel and Tienda, "Determinants."

[35]Cf. Frank D. Bean, H. L. Browning, and W. P. Frisbie, "The Sociodemographic Characteristics of Mexican Immigrant Status Groups: Implications for Studying Undocumented Mexican Migrants," *International Migration Review* 18 (1984):672–91; Suzanne M. Bianchi, "Racial Differences in Per Capita Income, 1960–76: The Importance of Household Size, Headship, and Labor Force Participation," *Demography* 17 (1980):129–43; Reynolds Farley, "Trends in Racial Inequalities: Have the Gains of the 1960s Disappeared in the 1970s?" *American Sociological Review* 36 (1977):1–17.

1960s and 1970s, for example, average per capita and mean household income increased considerably in real dollar terms among both non-Hispanic whites and the members of the various Spanish origin groups (Table 6.13). As is evident from the figures on the percentage changes in per capita and mean household income between 1960–1970 and 1970–1980, the majority of this increase concentrated in the decade of the 1960s. Table 6.13 also shows the income gap for each year between the Spanish origin groups and non-Hispanic whites. Although there are dif-

TABLE 6.13

Per Capita and Mean Household Income for All Households by Ethnic Group: 1960–1980 (in 1979 dollars)

Ethnic Group	1960	1970	1980	Percentage Change, 1960– 1970	Percentage Change, 1970– 1980
PER CAPITA INCOME					
Non-Hispanic White	$4,771	$6,538	$7,635	37.0%	16.8%
Mexican	2,540	3,599	4,216	41.7	17.1
Puerto Rican	2,596	3,698	3,828	42.4	3.5
Cuban	3,983	5,183	5,744	30.1	10.8
Central/South American	4,191	5,175	4,900	23.5	−5.3
Other Hispanic	4,350	4,748	5,911	9.1	24.5
$ Gap to Non-Hispanic White					
Mexican	2,231	2,939	3,419		
Puerto Rican	2,175	2,840	3,807		
Cuban	788	1,355	1,891		
Central/South American	580	1,363	2,735		
Other Hispanic	421	1,790	1,724		
MEAN HOUSEHOLD INCOME					
Non-Hispanic White	15,267	19,615	20,615	28.5	5.1
Mexican	11,172	14,757	16,021	32.1	8.6
Puerto Rican	10,386	13,680	12,633	31.7	−7.6
Cuban	12,750	17,626	18,957	38.2	7.6
Central/South American	13,828	17,594	16,659	27.2	−5.3
Other Hispanic	13,920	17,568	17,733	26.2	.9
$ Gap to Non-Hispanic White					
Mexican	4,095	4,858	4,594		
Puerto Rican	4,881	5,935	7,982		
Cuban	2,517	1,989	1,658		
Central/South American	1,439	2,021	3,956		
Other Hispanic	1,347	2,047	2,882		

SOURCES: 1960 and 1970 Public Use Sample files; 1980 Public Use Microdata Sample file.

ferences among the various Spanish origin groups that warrant comment, we postpone a discussion of these until a later chapter. For the moment, our focus is on the role of family/household composition in accounting for economic inequality.

One of the most interesting results in Table 6.13 is that a much different picture about income inequality emerges depending on whether attention is focused on per capita or on mean household income. For example, the ratio of mean household income of Mexican Americans to that of non-Hispanic whites in 1960 was .73. This increased to .75 in 1970 and to .78 by 1980. When we focus our attention on per capita income, however, we find that the ratio of Mexican to non-Hispanic white income was only .53 in 1960, increasing to .55 in 1970, and remaining at this value in 1980. In short, Mexican American households had in 1980 more than three-fourths of the income available to them that non-Hispanic households did, but the individuals in Mexican American households had only a bit more than half as much income available as did the individuals in non-Hispanic white households. Essentially similar trends, if not actual values of income ratios, characterize the other Spanish origin groups compared with non-Hispanic whites.

As we noted above, the Spanish origin households contain larger numbers of adults than the non-Hispanic white households and probably also more earners.[36] This undoubtedly serves to narrow the gap between Spanish origin and non-Hispanic white household income. At the same time, however, most Spanish origin households contain more children, thus reducing the levels of per capita income and widening the per capita gap with non-Hispanic whites. In regard to the relative importance of these factors, it is interesting that the rate of improvement in real dollar terms of average household income between 1960 and 1980 is generally greater than that of per capita income within the Spanish origin groups. For example, the ratio of Mexican American to non-Hispanic average household income increased by 6.8 percent between 1960 and 1980, whereas the ratio of Mexican American per capita to non-Hispanic white per capita income improved by 3.8 percent. In short, the rate of improvement in narrowing the average household income gap was not matched at the per capita level. And in some cases (that of Cubans, for example), the per capita ratio decreased even as the household ratio increased.

These data make it clear that figures such as those in Table 6.11, which might be interpreted as reflecting a greater familistic orientation

---

[36]Tienda and Angel found this to be the case among Mexican and Central/South American but not Puerto Rican husband-wife and female-headed families. Tienda and Angel, "Determinants."

among Hispanics, may in reality derive from economic conditions. Given the magnitude of the per capita income gap between non-Hispanic whites and the various Hispanic groups, the presence of other adult earners in the household (or even adult nonearners who can help with child care so the husband or wife can more easily seek employment) takes on added importance. Differences that might seem to be cultural in origin may actually owe to economic factors.

Another important aspect of minority/majority economic inequality is revealed in the fact that such income patterns depend considerably on family/household structure. Table 6.14 presents per capita and mean

TABLE 6.14

Per Capita and Mean Household Income by Family Type and Ethnic Group: 1960–1980 (in 1979 dollars)

| | Husband-Wife Families | | | | |
Ethnic Group	1960	1970	1980	Percentage Change, 1960–1970	Percentage Change, 1970–1980
PER CAPITA INCOME					
Non-Hispanic White	$4,642	$6,423	$7,656	38.4	19.2
Mexican	2,569	3,706	4,192	44.3	13.1
Puerto Rican	2,644	4,001	4,280	51.3	7.0
Cuban	4,008	5,236	6,494	30.6	24.0
Central/South American	4,047	5,356	5,134	32.3	−4.1
Other Hispanic	4,372	5,000	5,918	14.4	18.4
$ Gap to Non-Hispanic White					
Mexican	2,073	2,717	3,464		
Puerto Rican	1,998	2,422	3,376		
Cuban	634	1,187	1,162		
Central/South American	595	1,067	2,522		
Other Hispanic	270	1,423	1,738		
MEAN HOUSEHOLD INCOME					
Non-Hispanic White	17,174	23,124	24,883	34.6	7.6
Mexican	12,593	17,042	18,444	35.3	8.2
Puerto Rican	11,636	16,802	17,118	44.4	1.9
Cuban	14,825	19,897	22,729	34.2	14.2
Central/South American	15,785	20,892	20,536	32.4	−1.7
Other Hispanic	15,299	20,498	21,898	34.0	6.8
$ Gap to Non-Hispanic White					
Mexican	4,581	6,082	6,439		
Puerto Rican	5,538	6,322	7,765		
Cuban	2,349	3,227	2,154		
Central/South American	1,389	2,232	4,347		
Other Hispanic	1,875	2,626	2,985		

household figures by family type for all three time periods. Husband-wife, other family, and nonfamily households all improved their income positions between 1960 and 1980 whether measured in terms of per capita or mean household income. The greatest improvements were concentrated among the nonfamily households. Among other family households, almost all of which are female-headed, the improvement depended considerably on the Spanish origin group being examined. Mexican Americans, for example, enhanced their per capita and household earnings positions considerably over the 20-year period. However, Puerto Ricans scarcely improved their situation at all; in fact, when measured in per capita terms, the income available to Puerto Rican other family households actually declined between 1970 and 1980.

TABLE 6.14 *(continued)*

	Other Families				Nonfamilies				
1960	1970	1980	Percentage Change, 1960–1970	Percentage Change, 1970–1980	1960	1970	1980	Percentage Change, 1960–1970	Percentage Change, 1970–1980
$4,306	$5,023	$5,694	16.6	13.4	$4,917	$8,336	$10,287	69.5	23.4
1,999	2,709	3,270	35.5	20.7	4,310	6,580	7,986	52.7	21.4
2,170	2,273	2,232	4.7	−1.8	4,829	6,956	7,434	44.0	6.9
3,214	3,918	4,622	21.9	18.0	4,891	7,860	8,521	6.07	8.4
3,869	3,776	3,496	−2.4	−7.4	5,704	9,058	8,608	58.8	−5.0
3,169	2,994	3,940	−5.5	31.6	6,738	7,179	9,386	6.5	30.7
2,307	2,314	2,424			607	1,756	2,301		
2,136	2,750	3,462			88	1,380	2,853		
1,092	1,105	1,072			26	476	1,766		
437	1,247	2,198			−787	−722	1,679		
1,137	2,029	1,754			−1,821	1,157	901		
12,487	15,070	16,170	20.7	7.3	6,884	9,170	12,242	33.2	33.5
7,797	10,295	12,101	32.0	17.5	5,173	7,896	10,382	52.6	31.5
8,030	8,640	8,035	7.6	−7.0	5,793	8,347	8,921	44.1	6.9
9,642	12,537	13,886	30.0	10.6	5,379	9,432	10,225	75.3	8.4
12,383	12,464	11,887	.6	−4.2	7,415	10,870	11,190	46.6	2.9
11,723	11,974	13,003	2.1	8.6	8,085	9,332	11,263	15.4	20.7
4,690	4,775	4,069			1,711	1,274	1,860		
4,457	6,430	8,135			1,091	823	3,321		
2,845	2,533	2,304			1,505	−262	2,017		
104	2,606	4,283			−531	−1,700	1,052		
764	3,096	3,167			−1,201	−162	979		

Of considerable significance is the fact that the per capita income of other family households is substantially below that of either husband-wife family households or nonfamily households. Furthermore, the economic position of such households relative to the other two types of households deteriorated during the 1960s and 1970s. Given that the percentages of households falling into the other family category increased among the Spanish origin groups between 1960 and 1980, the overall economic positions of the groups might have improved even more during the 20-year period than they did had it not been for the fact that increasing proportions of households shifted into this lower per capita income type of family. Table 6.15 presents a decomposition for 1960 and 1980 of the income gap between non-Hispanic whites and the two Spanish origin groups—Mexicans and Puerto Ricans—that had the lowest per capita incomes in 1980, breaking out that part of the gap due to differences between the population's family type distributions for each of the time periods.[37] As is clear, a very small portion of the difference in the case of both Mexicans and Puerto Ricans in 1960 was due to differences between the family type distributions of these populations and that of non-Hispanic whites. By 1980, however, the size of this component, as measured in both relative and absolute terms, increased considerably. Whereas differences in family type distributions in 1960 accounted for roughly one-twentieth of the total income gaps, by 1980 they accounted for roughly one-sixth in the case of Puerto Ricans and about one-seventh

TABLE 6.15

Decomposition of Differentials in Average per Capita Income of Mexicans and Puerto Ricans from Non-Hispanic Whites into Income and Family Type Distribution Components: 1960–1980 (in 1979 dollars)

	Mexican		Puerto Rican	
	1960	1980	1960	1980
Total Difference	$2,231	$3,419	$2,175	$3,807
Due to Differences in Income Within Family Types	1,958	3,092	1,824	3,300
Due to Differences in Family Type Distributions	102	485	123	662
Due to Interaction	171	−158	228	−155

SOURCES: 1960 Public Use Sample file; 1980 Public Use Microdata Sample file.

[37]See E. Kitagawa, "Components of a Difference Between Two Rates," *Journal of the American Statistical Association* 50 (1955):1168–94.

in the case of Mexicans.[38] In short, between 1960 and 1980 the increasing prevalence of family types with low income contributed an increasing amount to the per capita income gap between Mexicans and Puerto Ricans, on the one hand, and non-Hispanic whites, on the other. That these family types were largely female-headed families does not imply greater familistic emphases among Hispanic groups.

Summary and Conclusions

This chapter has examined a number of aspects of family and household structure and process, focusing on a variety of indicators which have not only significance in their own right, but also relevance for questions dealing with the extent of familistic emphasis among the various Spanish origin groups and significance for the study of economic inequality measured at the household level. These indicators, including measures of marital instability, yielded a mixed picture with respect to the issue of whether Spanish origin groups are more familistic in orientation than non-Hispanic whites. The larger household sizes, the presence of greater numbers of adults in households, and the greater tendency for unmarried persons aged 18–24 to live in parental households are consistent with the idea that more emphasis may be placed on family relationships within these groups than is the case among non-Hispanic whites. However, the Spanish origin groups are no more likely to live in husband-wife families than are non-Hispanic whites, nor do they exhibit levels of marital instability that are appreciably below those of the majority group. Considering this, as well as the fact that in those instances where the indicators seem to support a familistic interpretation, the results might just as well owe to economic factors,[39] we cannot conclude that the overall weight of the evidence supports the idea that these groups embrace cultural orientations that are more familistic than those of non-Hispanic whites.

The data examined in this chapter once again point to the distinctive position of Puerto Ricans and Cubans vis-à-vis the other Spanish origin groups. Most noteworthy is the especially high rate of marital instability among Puerto Ricans, whose family situations often more closely approximate those of blacks than they do those of the other

[38]Strictly speaking, it is not appropriate to speak of the components constituting a fraction of a difference when some of the components vary in sign. However, in this instance the nonpositive component is so small (and attaches to the interaction difference anyway) that it causes little distortion to talk in such terms.

[39]For example, see Tienda and Angel, "Determinants."

Spanish origin groups. This is evident in a number of indicators examined, but perhaps nowhere more critically than in the analyses of components of per capita income difference between Puerto Ricans and non-Hispanic whites. Between 1960 and 1980 the portion of the income gap due to differences in family type distributions between the two populations (which involved to a considerable degree a substantial increase of female-headed households among Puerto Ricans) increased enormously, accounting by 1980 for almost one-sixth of the total income difference between the two groups. Clearly, public policies that are designed to ameliorate the economic situations of minority groups must give considerable attention to how they would affect patterns of family and household structure. Unless such policies provide the means to reduce the higher proportions of minority populations living in low-income family situations, many of whom involve households headed by females, their chances for success would seem to be diminished.

7

FERTILITY PATTERNS WITHIN THE SPANISH ORIGIN POPULATIONS

O NE OF THE most important characteristics of a population is the rapidity with which it reproduces itself over time.[1] Despite high levels of both legal and undocumented immigration to the United States since 1965, what demographers call "natural increase," or the excess of a population's births over deaths for a given period of time, has constituted a larger share of the growth of most of the Spanish origin groups from 1970 to 1980 than has immigration.[2] The study of factors affecting reproductive patterns within the Spanish origin populations is thus relevant to the issue of how long these groups will sustain the rather remarkable rates of growth they exhibited from 1970 to 1980.[3]

This chapter thus has as its general purpose the examination of the fertility of the five Spanish origin populations. In addition to the insight this may reveal about the potential for future population growth, the

[1] Ansley J. Coale, *The Growth and Structure of Human Populations: A Mathematical Investigation* (Princeton, NJ: Princeton University Press, 1972).

[2] For a discussion of this issue in the case of the Mexican origin population, see Harley L. Browning and Ruth Cullen, "The Complex Formation of the U.S. Mexican-Origin Population: 1970–1980," in R. de la Garza and H. L. Browning, eds., *Mexican Immigrants and the Mexican Americans: An Evolving Relationship* (Austin: Center for Mexican American Studies, University of Texas, 1985). Also see Cary Davis, Carl Haub, and Jo-Anne Willette, "U.S. Hispanics: Changing the Face of America," *Population Bulletin*, vol. 38, no. 3 (Washington, DC: Population Reference Bureau, 1983), pp. 7–15.

[3] Davis, Haub, and Willette, "U.S. Hispanics."

fertility differences between the Spanish origin groups and non-Spanish whites can provide an indication of the nature and extent of demographic integration between the majority and these minority populations in the United States. We also compare fertility differences by education and other variables within the Spanish origin groups with those of non-Spanish whites. Most generally, we have two aims. The first is simply to describe, sometimes using data from the 1960 and 1970 censuses as well as data from the 1980 census, the fertility levels of women in the Spanish origin groups and the degree to which the levels are dissimilar to those of non-Spanish white women. The second is to ascertain under what circumstances observed differences in fertility might be expected to disappear.

As we shall see, not only do some of the groups of Spanish origin women exhibit levels of fertility that differ from those of non-Hispanic white women, but some of these differences persist even when we examine the data in ways that make the groups of women we are comparing as similar as possible with respect to the various characteristics known to influence fertility. Hence, we confront the tasks of both explaining these differences and interpreting what they mean for our more general examination of the social and economic positions held by the Spanish origin groups in American society. After first describing the fertility differences, we introduce several explanations of why racial/ethnic minority and majority groups often exhibit different patterns of fertility behavior.

The Fertility of Spanish Origin Groups Compared with Other Racial/Ethnic Groups

The first two questions to be asked about the reproductive behavior of the Spanish origin populations are the following: (1) Do the various groups of Spanish origin women have more (or fewer) children than non-Hispanic white women?; (2) How different are they in this respect from women who belong to other racial/ethnic minority groups in the United States? Table 7.1 presents data that provide at least rough answers to these questions. It contains information on the number of children ever born per 1,000 women aged 15 to 44 for various racial/ethnic groups, including the Spanish origin groups for each of the three most recent census years. (Central/South Americans are not shown here because they are not distinguished from Other Hispanics in published data.) The figures enable only rough comparisons to be drawn because the groups and time periods may differ with respect to their age and sociodemo-

TABLE 7.1

Number of Children Ever Born per 1,000 Women Aged 15–44
by Race and Type of Spanish Origin: 1960–1980

	1960	1970	1980	Percentage Change, 1960–1970	Percentage Change, 1970–1980
TOTAL	1,746	1,621	1,302	−7.2%	−19.7%
Non-Hispanic					
White	1,712	1,589	1,232	−7.2	−22.5
Black	2,016	1,862	1,575	−7.6	−15.4
Indian[a]	2,405	2,116	1,701	−11.0	−19.6
Asian[b]	1,521	1,421	1,184	−6.6	−16.7
Other[c]	1,984	1,550	1,164	−21.9	−24.9
Spanish					
Mexican	2,290	2,114	1,715	−7.7	−18.9
Puerto Rican	1,855	1,938	1,662	4.5	−14.2
Cuban	—	1,310	1,069	—	−18.4
Other Hispanic	—	1,719	1,355	—	−21.2
Total	—	1,919	1,591	—	−17.1

SOURCES: U.S. Bureau of the Census, Census of Population: 1980, "General Social and Economic Characteristics," PC80-1C-1, table 166; Census of Population: 1970, "Women by Number of Children Ever Born," PC2(3A), tables 8 and 13; Census of Population: 1960, "Women by Number of Children Ever Born," PC2(3A), tables 8, 9, and 10 (Washington, DC: U.S. Government Printing Office, 1964, 1973, and 1983).

[a]1980: American Indian, Eskimo, and Aleuts; 1970 and 1960: American Indian.
[b]1980: Asian and Pacific Islander; 1970: Japanese, Chinese, Filipino, Hawaiian, and Korean; 1960: Japanese and Chinese.
[c]1980: those not included in other categories (for example, Eurasian, Cosmopolitan, Interracial); 1970: those not of other categories; 1960: Filipinos, Koreans, Hawaiians, Asian Indians, Eskimos, Aleuts, Malayans, and so on.

graphic and socioeconomic composition. Such differences can affect the magnitude of the fertility differences observed among the groups. Despite this limitation, the data in Table 7.1 are advantageous in one very important respect—the figures represent actual numbers of children born to actual numbers of women.

The data reveal that by 1980 Spanish origin women had indeed borne larger numbers of children than had non-Hispanic white women (1,591 per 1,000 Spanish origin women versus 1,232 per 1,000 non-Hispanic origin white women). This difference is considerable, representing a Spanish origin level of childbearing more than 29 percent higher than that of non-Hispanic white women. The differential is also greater than it was in 1970, when Spanish origin fertility was 21 percent higher than non-Hispanic fertility. More significantly, the different Spanish origin groups exhibit substantial diversity in fertility, with Cuban origin women showing a level substantially below that of non-Hispanic white women and Mexican origin women exhibiting the highest level of any of the Spanish groups. If nothing else, these figures provide still further documentation for the notion that it is enormously misleading to lump the separate Spanish origin groups together into a single "Hispanic" category.

Turning to our second question concerning how the fertility levels of the Spanish origin groups compare with those of other racial/ethnic groups in the United States, we find that the data in Table 7.1 provide considerable support for the idea that most of the Spanish origin groups are characterized by relatively high fertility. Most strikingly, women of Mexican origin show a higher rate of childbearing in 1980 than any of the other groups displayed, including Native Americans. Also, the fertility of Mexican origin and Puerto Rican origin women exceeds that of black women by nearly 9 and 6 percent, respectively, and it surpasses that of non-Hispanic white women by 39 and 35 percent, respectively. As we will see below, much of this difference cannot be accounted for by differences among these groups in such factors as age, age at marriage, and education.

The data in Table 7.1 also provide dramatic confirmation of the reduction in fertility occurring in the United States since the beginning of the 1960s, the approximate end of the "baby boom." As with other women, the groups of Spanish origin women participated in the decline, although not quite to the degree that non-Hispanic white women did. Moreover, because women of Mexican and Puerto Rican origin were starting the decline from a higher level of childbearing to begin with, and because their fertility has not gone down as much on a percentage basis as that of non-Hispanic white women, relative fertility differentials between these groups and non-Hispanic whites have actually increased from 1970 to 1980 (in the case of Mexican origin women, for example, fertility increased from 33 percent higher in 1970 to 39 percent higher in 1980).

In Table 7.2 we present data on the fertility decline within the Spanish origin groups broken down by age. Only Mexican and Puerto Rican origin women have data going back to 1960, but they reveal, as is also true of non-Hispanic white women, that much of the fertility decline has been concentrated among younger women. The substantially higher fertility of Mexican women, especially, is evident among women of all ages in every census year, as is the lower fertility of Cuban origin women. The other groups are generally intermediate to these two extremes.

TABLE 7.2

Number of Children Ever Born per 1,000 Women Aged 15–44
by Type of Spanish Origin and Age: 1960–1980

	15–24 Years			25–34 Years			35–44 Years		
	1960	1970	1980	1960	1970	1980	1960	1970	1980
Non-Hispanic White	515	347	262	2,190	2,100	1,383	2,419	2,891	2,523
Total Spanish	—	502	475	—	2,460	1,922	—	3,523	3,202
Mexican	694[a]	492	528	2,950[a]	2,760	2,105	3,834[a]	4,222	3,646
Puerto Rican	770	657	548	2,302	2,507	1,986	2,873	3,240	3,202
Cuban	—	238	192	—	1,622	1,189	—	1,932	2,033
Other Hispanic	—	476	337	—	2,168	1,567	—	3,041	2,640

SOURCES: U.S. Bureau of the Census, *Census of Population: 1980,* "General Social and Economic Characteristics," PC80-1C-1,, table 166; *Census of Population: 1970,* "Women by Number of Children Ever Born," PC2(3A), tables 8 and 13; *Census of Population: 1960,* "Women by Number of Children Ever Born," PC2(3A), tables 8, 9, and 10 (Washington, DC: U.S. Government Printing Office, 1963, 1973, and 1983).

[a]Spanish surname population in the five southwestern states.

As noted above, all of these comparisons do not make allowance for other differences that affect the levels of fertility observed. Nonetheless, they provide ample documentation of the higher fertility of all of the groups of Spanish origin women compared with non-Hispanic white women, except those of Cuban origin and those in the residual Other Hispanic category. Much of the rest of this chapter is devoted to examining these fertility differences after the influence of other variables is taken into account. For example, we will ask: Does the difference continue to exist when we treat Mexican origin women, who have substantially lower levels of education than non-Hispanic white women, as if they had the same levels of education? The answer to this particular question is that the difference persists, albeit at a substantially reduced level. We will thus be left with the task of trying to explain why some of the Spanish origin groups show higher levels of childbearing than non-Hispanic white women. Our answer will not only advance our understanding of fertility differences, but also have implications for the more general questions we pose about the social and economic positions of peoples of Spanish origin in American society.

Theories of Fertility Differences

Why do some racial/ethnic minority groups in the United States exhibit higher fertility rates than majority whites? In considering this question, together with its relevance for groups of Spanish origin women, it is important first to note that at least three of the Spanish ethnic groups whose fertility we are examining would probably also be considered minority groups by many social scientists who study their behavior.[4] That is to say, they are groups that to at least some extent meet the following criteria: (1) each of them constitutes only a small proportion of the country's population; (2) their members experience some sense of self-awareness as belonging to that particular group; (3) they have experienced some degree and kind of discrimination at the hands of the majority group; and (4) their members are at least to some extent discernible in their appearance as members of a given racial/ethnic group. In the cases of the Mexican, Puerto Rican, and Cuban origin groups, it is reasonable to say that they could also be considered minority groups, although it is likely that many of their members are indistinguishable in appearance from many non-Hispanic whites. In the cases of Central or South Americans and Other Hispanics (especially), it may not be appropriate to designate them as minority groups, if for no other reason than it is not evident that the persons so categorized would perceive themselves as being members of a given ethnic group. As we shall see, the question of a racial/ethnic group's status as a minority group is one that some observers think has relevance for the patterns of fertility behavior exhibited by the group's members.[5]

In trying to explain differences in fertility between racial/ethnic minority groups and a majority group, observers have emphasized different kinds of factors.[6] Basically, explanations can be categorized according to whether they give greater weight to subcultural, sociodemographic, social psychological, or economic factors as determinants of differential fertility. Corresponding to these are what have come to be called the (1) subcultural, (2) social characteristics, (3) minority group status, and (4) economic hypotheses of minority/majority fertility differences.[7]

---

[4]Frank D. Bean and John P. Marcum, "Differential Fertility and the Minority Group Status Hypothesis: An Assessment and Review," in Frank D. Bean and W. Parker Frisbie, eds., *The Demography of Racial and Ethnic Groups* (New York: Academic Press, 1978); and C. Wagley and M. Harris, *Minorities in the World* (New York: Columbia University, 1959).

[5]Lincoln H. Day, "Natality and Ethnocentrism: Some Relationships Suggested by an Analysis of Catholic-Protestant Differentials", *Population Studies* 22 (March 1968):27–50; and Robert E. Kennedy, Jr., "Minority Group Status and Fertility: The Irish," *American Sociological Review* 38 (1973):85–96.

[6]For recent reviews of the literature, see Bean and Marcum, "Differential Fertility"; and Frank D. Bean and Gray Swicegood, *Mexican American Fertility Patterns* (Austin: University of Texas Press, 1985).

[7]Bean and Swicegood, *Mexican American Fertility Patterns.*

The Subcultural Hypothesis

The subcultural approach focuses on the fact that many groups immigrating to the United States have come from countries with higher fertility.[8] In most instances, this higher fertility is viewed as a reflection of stronger tendencies in the countries of origin to adhere to values giving "overriding importance to the family and the needs of the collective as opposed to individual and personal needs."[9] Some observers of traditional Mexican culture, for example, suggest that the family is its single most important component, with women finding their greatest satisfaction in the bearing and raising of children, and men in activities outside the home.[10] Although traditional Mexican familism may have declined among Mexican Americans the longer the time spent in the United States,[11] the subcultural hypothesis about fertility differences assumes that such values continue to exert at least a certain measure of influence on fertility behavior, thus encouraging higher levels of childbearing among many immigrant ethnic groups.

The Social Characteristics Hypothesis

A second approach does not deny that elements of traditional culture within many racial/ethnic groups may have represented a potent pronatalist force in the past, but emphasizes instead that once processes of acculturation and assimilation have begun, what matters most in bringing about convergence of minority/majority fertility levels is the structure of socioeconomic rewards in the society and the degree to

---

[8]Douglas S. Massey, "Dimensions of the New Immigration to the United States and the Prospects for Assimilation," *Annual Review of Sociology* 7 (1981):57–85; and Kathleen Ford, "The Fertility of Immigrants to the United States," unpublished paper, 1982.

[9]Frank D. Bean, Russell L. Curtis, and John P. Marcum, "Familism and Marital Satisfaction among Mexican Americans: The Effects of Family Size, Wife's Labor Force Participation, and Conjugal Power," *Journal of Marriage and the Family* 39 (1977):759–76.

[10]For discussions of this issue, see David Alvirez, Frank D. Bean, and Dorie Williams, "Patterns of Changes and Continuity in the Mexican American Family," in Charles H. Mindel and R. W. Haberstein, eds., *Ethnic Families in America: Patterns and Variations,* 2nd ed. (New York: Elsevier North-Holland, 1981); Nathan Murillo, "The Mexican American Family," in N. W. Wagner and M. J. Haug, eds., *Chicanos* (St. Louis: Mosby, 1971); Alfredo Mirande, "The Chicano Family: A Reanalysis of Conflicting Views," *Journal of Marriage and the Family* 39 (1977):747–56.

[11]Leo Grebler, Joan W. Moore, and Ralph C. Guzman, *The Mexican-American People: The Nation's Second Largest Minority* (New York: Free Press, 1970); and B. E. Farris and Norval Glenn, "Fatalism and Familism among Anglos and Mexican Americans in San Antonio," *Sociology and Social Research* 60 (1976):393–402.

which these are available to the members of the racial/ethnic group.[12] Hence, exponents of the social characteristics hypothesis often refer to the importance of "structural assimilation" as a factor affecting minority/majority group fertility differences. In tests of these ideas, however, structural assimilation has often been assessed by comparing the socioeconomic characteristics (especially education) of *people*, not by examining the reward structures of institutions, organizations, or societies. This approach thus begs the question of whether the properties of positions, institutions, and organizations, which more nearly constitute elements of social structure, affect the extent to which members of minority groups attain certain socioeconomic characteristics, such as a college education. We will return to these kinds of issues below. Suffice it to note for now that in its "strongest" form the social characteristics hypothesis would predict that *all* of the fertility differences between minority and majority groups can be accounted for by differences between them in the distribution of other characteristics known to affect fertility. In a somewhat "weaker" form it suggests that this will be true only among members of minority groups of higher socioeconomic standing because assimilation and acculturation processes are presumed to occur more slowly among the more disadvantaged.[13]

The Minority Group Status Hypothesis

Another approach focuses on the importance of minority group membership per se. It does not deny that different cultural systems and distributions of social characteristics might play a role in accounting for minority/majority fertility differences, but suggests that membership in a minority group itself may have an independent effect.[14] Researchers have differed in the degree to which they have considered the numerical smallness of the minority, apart from the social disadvantages experienced by members of minority groups, to be an important factor in explaining fertility differences. Those who have thought it to be important have tended to hypothesize that the independent effect of minority group status is pronatalist—that it operates to increase the level of fertility of the minority group.[15] Unfortunately, in cases where differences in fertility norms and values appear to exist between the members of

---

[12]Bean and Marcum, "Differential Fertility."

[13]Nan E. Johnson, "Minority Group Status and the Fertility of Black Americans, 1970: A New Look," *American Journal of Sociology* 84 (1979):1386–400.

[14]Calvin Goldscheider and Peter R. Uhlenberg, "Minority Group Status and Fertility," *American Journal of Sociology* 74 (1969):361–72.

[15]Kennedy, "Minority Group Status."

the minority and majority group, it is virtually impossible to ascertain whether an observed fertility difference owes its existence to subcultural factors or to minority group status per se.

Other observers have emphasized that feelings of frustration and marginality accompany minority group status and that these have the potential to reduce fertility, especially among women of higher socioeconomic status.[16] In this instance, the hypothesis would predict that minority women of higher socioeconomic status will exhibit lower fertility than majority women of comparable socioeconomic standing. The reason is not only that more highly educated women have higher aspirations for upward mobility than less educated women, but also that minority women find their aspirations more difficult to realize owing to societal patterns of discrimination. To compensate, they lower their fertility in order to achieve and sustain socioeconomic goals. For example, speaking of black women in the United States, E. Franklin Frazier said: "Men and women who have struggled to achieve a high position in the Negro community are not inclined to have the standards which they attempt to maintain lowered by the burden of children."[17]

The Economic Hypothesis

In certain respects, as we shall see, the economic approach is similar to both the social characteristics hypothesis and the minority group status hypothesis, but in other respects it is different. The hypothesis emerges out of the "economics of the family," which conceptualizes fertility as the result of household decisions about the allocation of scarce resources (time and money) for the acquisition of desired commodities, of which children are but one type.[18] Group differences in fertility, such as minority/majority differences, would then be presumed to be the result of differences between groups in the operation of these factors. It is not our purpose here to present a detailed discussion of economic approaches to fertility; such treatments are available elsewhere.[19] We note, however, that a chief contribution of these approaches is to emphasize the importance of the value of a woman's time as a factor af-

[16]Goldscheider and Uhlenberg, "Minority Group Status."

[17]E. Franklin Frazier, *The Negro in the United States* (New York: Macmillan, 1957).

[18]Gary S. Becker, "An Economic Analysis of Fertility," in Universities—National Bureau, Committee of Economic Research, ed., *Demographic and Economic Change in Developed Countries* (Princeton, NJ: Princeton University Press, 1960); and T. Paul Schultz, *Economics of Population* (Reading, MA: Addison-Wesley, 1981).

[19]Boone Turchi, "Microeconomics Theories of Fertility: A Critique," *Social Forces* 20 (1975):30–39; and Warren Sanderson, "On the Two Schools of the Economics of Fertility," *Population and Development Review* 2 (1976):469–77.

fecting the number of children she and her husband decide to have. A central supposition is that the demands of working and child care are often in conflict, and thus to at least some extent are "substitutes" for one another.[20] Women whose time is most valuable, who possess the characteristics that enable (or could enable) them to command the highest wages in a market economy, will be least likely to have large families, other things being equal. Within this framework even the highly educated woman committed totally to staying home to care for children would be predicted to have fewer children than the poorly educated woman who also stays home. The reason is that the "opportunity cost" of childbearing for the former—the wages she could have made if she had chosen to work—are potentially greater than they are for the latter woman.[21]

As applied to minority/majority fertility behavior, this approach would predict that group differences will be greatest where the potential earnings differences are greatest.[22] Thus, if minority women of higher education are able to achieve similar levels of earnings compared with majority women of higher education, their fertility will be similar as well. In this regard the hypothesis generates a prediction comparable to that of the "weak" form of the social characteristics hypothesis. It is more parsimonious than the social characteristics approach, however, because a single factor—the market value or potential market value of women's time—is presumably capable of explaining both between- and within-group fertility differences. The social characteristics approach must invoke one notion (structural assimilation) to explain between-group differences, but others (the point at which segments of the population are moving through the "demographic transition" or the notion that there are subcultural differences within the population) to explain within-group differences.

The Theories Applied to the Spanish Origin Groups

What would these hypotheses predict about fertility differences and patterns involving comparisons of the Spanish origin groups with non-Hispanic whites in the United States? The *social characteristics* hy-

[20]Frank D. Bean, Gray Swicegood, and Allan King, "Role Incompatibility and the Relationship between Fertility and Labor Supply among Hispanic American Women," in George J. Borjas and Marta Tienda, eds., *Hispanics in the U.S. Economy* (New York: Academic Press, 1985).

[21]Jacob Mincer, "Market Prices, Opportunity Costs, and Income Effect," in C. Christ, ed., *Measurement in Economics* (Stanford: Stanford University Press, 1963).

[22]Bean and Swicegood, *Mexican American Fertility Patterns;* and Frank D. Bean and Jeffrey Burr, "Black/White Fertility Differences Revisited: An Examination of Alternative Hypotheses," unpublished paper, 1985.

pothesis would predict that fertility differences between, say, Puerto Rican women and non-Hispanic white women will disappear once we have adjusted for differences between the two groups in age composition, rural–urban residence, levels of education, age at marriage, marital status, and so on. The *subcultural* approach would lead us to expect that higher fertility will persist even between groups of minority/majority women of higher socioeconomic status after such differences are taken into account. In this event, of course, we could not be certain that we had taken every characteristic into account that might be relevant to explaining differential fertility. The *minority group status* approach would predict that minority women of lower socioeconomic status will exhibit fertility levels above those of majority women of comparable socioeconomic standing, but that minority women of higher status will show fertility levels below those of comparable status. Finally, to the extent that the gap in potential earnings between minority and majority women narrows as socioeconomic status increases, the *economic* hypothesis would predict higher minority fertility than majority fertility among women of lower socioeconomic status and then a diminishing fertility differential with rising socioeconomic standing.

In the rest of this chapter we will examine fertility differences between each of the Spanish origin groups and non-Hispanic whites in order to see which of these hypotheses comes closest to fitting the patterns we observe. Because the minority group status and economic hypotheses predict a declining pattern of fertility differences by socioeconomic status, we will also examine fertility differentials between each of the Spanish origin groups and non-Hispanic whites by levels of female education.

We also present data on fertility separately for first-generation (foreign-born or island-born in the case of Puerto Ricans) and second- or later-generation (native-born or mainland-born in the case of Puerto Ricans) women in each of the Spanish origin groups. The major reason for doing this is simply to see if women who are born in this country and whose families have thus been here for a longer period of time show a level of childbearing more similar to that of non-Hispanic white women.[23] The other reason is that second- or later-generation women may provide a better test of the alternative hypotheses set forth above. First-generation women are a mixture of those who have been in the United States for varying lengths of time, as well as a mixture of women

[23]Frank D. Bean and Gray Swicegood, "Generation, Language and Mexican American Fertility." Final Report, Center for Population Research, National Institute for Child Health and Human Development, Bethesda, Maryland, 1983; Frank D. Bean, R. Cullen, E. Stephen, and G. Swicegood, "Generational Differences in Fertility Among Mexican Americans: Implications for Assessing Immigration Effects," *Social Science Quarterly* 65 (1984):573–82.

who have had varying amounts of their fertility in their countries of origin and in the United States.[24] Because it is impossible to adjust for this difference using census data, the second- or later-generation women may constitute the preferable group for the assessment of the theoretical perspectives, at least when measures of lifetime fertility are being used.

Patterns of Fertility Differences

Table 7.3 presents information on two measures of fertility for the various groups of ever-married Spanish origin women and for ever-married non-Hispanic white women in 1980. This information is based on data for all of the Spanish origin women and 1 in 30 sample of non-Hispanic white woman contained in the Public Use Microdata Sample-A file. In other words, the computations are for a 5 percent sample of Spanish origin women (1 in every 20) and a 0.17 percent sample of non-Hispanic white women (1 in every 600). We present estimates of both the number of children ever born to the women and of the number of a woman's own children under age 3 in the household at the time of the census. These measures provide somewhat different information about childbearing patterns. The measure of recent fertility (the number under age 3) reflects any differences that were occurring very close to a particular time, the time at which the 1980 census was taken. The cumulative measure (the number of children ever born) reflects differences that accumulated over a greater number of years. Also, among foreign-born women, the experience of migration may disrupt childbearing processes in ways that reduce fertility below what it otherwise might be. Because recent fertility is less likely to be affected by migration (except among very recent immigrants), it may provide a better basis than cumulative fertility for assessing patterns of differences in the case of the foreign-born women.

The data in Table 7.3 reveal the expected increases in the number of children ever born with age among women in all of the Spanish origin groups. The patterns evident in Table 7.1 generally repeat themselves when we examine marital fertility within age groups. The somewhat higher fertility of women of Other Hispanic origin, however, is concentrated among the two older age groups of women. The average number of children ever born to the two younger age groups is virtually identical

[24]Frank D. Bean, Gray Swicegood, and Tom Linsley, "Patterns of Fertility Variation Among Mexican Immigrants to the United States," in *U.S. Immigration Policy and the National Interest*, Staff Report (Washington, DC: Select Commission on Immigration and Refugee Policy, 1981), Appendix D.

TABLE 7.3

Mean Numbers of Children Ever Born and Under Age 3
by Ethnicity and Age Groups,
Ever-Married Spanish Origin and Non-Hispanic White Women
Aged 15–44: 1980

Ethnicity and Age	Number	Mean Number of Children Ever Born	Mean Number of Children Under Age 3
Non-Hispanic White			
15–19 Years	711	.53	.41
20–24 Years	3,937	.84	.45
25–34 Years	12,526	1.59	.34
35–44 Years	10,007	2.60	.06
Mexican			
15–19 Years	3,986	.77	.61
20–24 Years	13,068	1.30	.65
25–34 Years	30,148	2.38	.42
35–44 Years	19,268	3.83	.13
Puerto Rican			
15–19 Years	824	.70	.56
20–24 Years	2,698	1.22	.65
25–34 Years	7,210	2.12	.35
35–44 Years	5,314	3.28	.10
Cuban			
15–19 Years	256	.17	.12
20–24 Years	746	.64	.32
25–34 Years	2,076	1.35	.32
35–44 Years	2,656	2.13	.05
Central/South American			
15–19 Years	226	.50	.34
20–24 Years	1,972	.69	.32
25–34 Years	5,090	1.88	.41
35–44 Years	4,866	2.65	.08
Other Hispanic			
15–19 Years	712	.63	.49
20–24 Years	2,088	.98	.58
25–34 Years	7,920	1.80	.36
35–44 Years	5,294	3.09	.10

to those for the younger cohorts of non-Hispanic whites. As would be expected, the highest levels of recent fertility (the number of children under age 3) occur in every case examined among women aged 20 to 24, with recent fertility declining at older ages. The only exception to this pattern occurs among Cuban women aged 25 to 34, whose average number of children under age 3 is almost as high as that of any of the other groups of women of the same age. What is so notable about this is that it represents a departure from the noticeably lower fertility of Cuban women observed in every other instance, reflecting a pattern of delayed childbearing in this population that does not seem to be characteristic of any of the other Spanish origin groups.

Average levels of cumulative and recent fertility by generational status are shown in Table 7.4. In most instances they indicate that Spanish origin women born in the contiguous United States have lower fertility than those who are foreign-born or Puerto Rican–born. The major exception occurs among women of Central or South American origin and among women of Other Hispanic origin, in which cases native-born women show slightly higher levels of both cumulative and recent fertility. Mainland-born Puerto Rican women also evince higher recent fertility than island-born women, a result which we will see is due to their younger age composition.

The first column of Table 7.5 expresses these patterns in terms of the extent to which the first-generation or second- or later-generation segments of the Spanish origin groups differ from the fertility levels of non-Hispanic whites. Thus, for example, Mexican origin women born in Mexico have on the average almost one more child ever born (0.91) than do non-Hispanic white women, whereas Cuban-born women exhibit fewer children ever born (−0.16). The remaining columns in this table

TABLE 7.4

Mean Numbers of Children Ever Born and Under Age 3
by Generational Status and Ethnicity,
Ever-Married Spanish Origin and Non-Hispanic White Women
Aged 15–44: 1980

	Number	Children Ever Born	Children Under Age 3
Non-Hispanic White	27,182	1.83	.25
Mexican			
First-Generation	24,908	2.74	.43
Second- or Later-Generation	41,542	2.34	.37
Puerto Rican			
First-Generation	11,748	2.53	.30
Second- or Later-Generation	4,298	1.59	.40
Cuban			
First-Generation	5,158	1.66	.19
Second- or Later-Generation	576	.67	.13
Central/South American			
First-Generation	11,544	1.96	.25
Second- or Later-Generation	610	2.16	.50
Other Hispanic			
First-Generation	3,736	2.07	.30
Second- or Later-Generation	12,276	2.07	.32

TABLE 7.5

Gross and Net Mean Fertility Deviations
for Spanish Origin from Non-Hispanic White Women
by Generational Status, Ever-Married Women Aged 15–44: 1980

	Gross	$\text{Net}_1{}^a$	$\text{Net}_2{}^b$	$\text{Net}_3{}^c$
CHILDREN EVER BORN				
Mexican				
First-Generation	.91	1.04	.41	.35
Second- or Later-Generation	.52	.76	.49	.46
Puerto Rican				
First-Generation	.71	.64	.22	.17
Second- or Later-Generation	−.23	.30	.16	.14
Cuban				
First-Generation	−.16	−.36	−.53	−.47
Second- or Later-Generation	−1.15	−.47	−.64	−.51
Central or South American				
First-Generation	.13	.10	−.12	−.12
Second- or Later-Generation	.30	.30	.26	.28
Other Hispanic				
First-Generation	.24	.19	$.04^d$	$.02^d$
Second- or Later-Generation	.24	.31	.19	.19
Constant	1.83	.16	.92	1.10
R^2	.04	.27	.33	.35
CHILDREN UNDER AGE 3				
Mexican				
First-Generation	.18	.16	.12	.09
Second- or Later-Generation	.11	.07	.06	.05
Puerto Rican				
First-Generation	.05	.06	.04	.04
Second- or Later-Generation	.15	.04	.03	.03
Cuban				
First-Generation	−.06	$−.01^d$	$−.02^d$	$−.01^d$
Second- or Later-Generation	−.12	−.25	−.26	−.19
Central or South American				
First-Generation	$−.003^d$	$.004^d$	$−.01^d$	$−.02^d$
Second- or Later-Generation	.16	.15	.15	.16
Other Hispanic				
First-Generation	.04	.06	.05	$.03^d$
Second- or Later-Generation	.06	.05	.05	.05
Constant	.25	.47	.51	.60
R^2	.02	.12	.12	.15

[a]Net of age.
[b]Net of age and education.
[c]Net of age, education, income, rural/urban residence, labor force participation, ever maritally disrupted, and region.
[d]Not significant at $p = .01$.

show what these differences would be if there were no differences between the particular Spanish origin group and non-Hispanic whites in certain other characteristics. For example, the second column shows what the fertility differences would be if the groups were identical with respect to the ages of the women being compared, and the third column shows what the fertility differences would be if differences in levels of education were removed. The fourth column shows the results that are obtained after adjusting for still more factors that might account for a portion of the fertility differences between Spanish origin groups and non-Hispanic whites.[25]

Several interesting findings emerge from the analyses presented in Table 7.5. First, it is clear that differences in age composition among the groups of ever-married Spanish origin women and between these groups and non-Hispanic white women account for some of the "gross" fertility patterns observed. This is not surprising since both of the fertility measures vary so strongly with age. In the case of children ever born, for example, Mexican origin women would exhibit a level of fertility compared with non-Hispanic white women that would be even higher than the one initially observed were it not for the fact that they are younger and thus, on average, have had less time within which to finish their childbearing. The same is true of mainland-born Puerto Ricans, whose cumulative fertility would be about two-thirds of a child instead of about one-third of a child per woman more than that of non-Hispanic whites if the two groups had the same age distribution. Reflecting possibly a cessation and reversal of net migration between Puerto Rico and the mainland during the 1970s, island-born Puerto Ricans, however, are on the average older than non-Hispanic whites, and thus do not show this pattern. The Cuban-born women, who constitute most of the women of Cuban origin, and who also are considerably older since many of them came to the United States as political refugees during the mid-1960s,[26] would show even fewer children ever born than non-Hispanic white women if the two groups were similar in age composition.

Because younger women have higher recent fertility than older women, whereas the reverse is true in the case of cumulative fertility, the results obtained after adjusting for age differences in the case of the number of children under age 3 are generally the opposite of those obtained for children ever born. For example, the younger groups would show levels of recent fertility that do not exceed those of non-Hispanic whites as much as they would if their age distributions were the same.

[25]These include family income, rural/urban residence, labor force participation, ever-maritally disrupted, and region.
[26]Massey, "Dimensions of the New Immigration"; Davis, Haub, and Willette, "U.S. Hispanics."

The largest reduction of this type occurs among second- or later-generation Puerto Rican women, whose level of recent fertility (0.40 children under age 3 per woman compared with 0.25 for non-Hispanic white women) would be reduced (by 75 percent) to only 0.04 children per woman if the two groups of women had the same ages.

The second interesting finding in Table 7.5 is that the generally higher fertility of the Spanish origin groups would be reduced considerably, but by no means be eliminated, if they had the same levels of education as non-Hispanic white women. This can be seen in the third column, which presents the fertility differences that would result from controlling *both* age and education differences. The most dramatic changes involve Mexican origin and Puerto Rican origin women, whose higher cumulative fertility would be reduced anywhere from about 25 to 70 percent if they had non-Hispanic levels of education. The importance of lower levels of female education is evident even among Cuban origin women who, because they exhibit lower levels of cumulative fertility to begin with than non-Hispanic white women, would have *even* fewer children if they had higher levels of education. In the case of recent fertility, much the same pattern appears, although the changes that would result from holding constant education are not as pronounced, in part perhaps because much of recent fertility occurs to younger women when it is less subject to socioeconomic influence.[27]

The third major finding that appears in Table 7.5 is that controlling differences between the groups of Spanish origin women and non-Hispanic white women in characteristics other than age and education does not change substantially the nature and magnitude of the fertility differences previously observed, especially as viewed in comparison to the magnitude of the changes that result from holding education constant. Hence, the rest of this chapter will focus its attention on the patterns of fertility differences by education between each of the Spanish origin groups and the group of non-Hispanic white women.

In addition to its empirical importance, female education, as a major indicator of socioeconomic status, has considerable relevance for the explanations of differential fertility introduced above.[28] At this point in

[27]Norman B. Ryder, "Fertility Trends," in John A. Ross, ed., *International Encyclopedia of Population* (New York: Free Press, 1982); and Michael Hout, "The Determinants of Marital Fertility in the United States, 1968–1970: Inferences from a Dynamic Model," *Demography* 15 (1978):139–60.

[28]Theories about the influence of socioeconomic status on fertility are often couched in terms that imply that family socioeconomic status is important. However, many women live in households and without husbands; to exclude them in order to obtain a measure of husband's socioeconomic status is unwarranted. Thus, we use wife's education as a measure, which has the further advantage of making our results comparable to most of the previous research in this area.

our analysis we can see that controlling a wide variety of sociodemographic characteristics does not eliminate the fertility differences observed, especially the higher fertility among women of Mexican origin compared with non-Hispanic white women. Hence, the social characteristics hypothesis does not appear to explain fully the fertility behavior of Spanish origin women. Although we cannot say yet which of the three remaining hypotheses does the best job of explaining fertility patterns within the groups of Spanish origin women, from our discussions above clearly a key factor in enabling us to reach a decision in this regard are the fertility differences that occur by levels of education.

Fertility Differences by Education

Tables 7.6 and 7.7 present, respectively, average numbers of children ever born and children under age 3 by generational status and education for each of the Spanish origin groups and for non-Hispanic whites. In the case of cumulative fertility, women of higher education generally reveal smaller numbers of children ever born. The major ex-

TABLE 7.6

Mean Numbers of Children Ever Born
by Education, Generational Status, and Ethnicity,
Ever-Married Spanish Origin and Non-Hispanic White Women
Aged 15–44: 1980

	Years of Schooling				
	0–8	9–11	12	13–15	16+
Non-Hispanic White	2.62	2.32	1.90	1.67	1.30
Mexican					
First-Generation	3.16	2.33	2.12	1.90	1.70
Second- or Later-Generation	3.56	2.64	2.03	1.69	1.21
Puerto Rican					
First-Generation	3.30	2.52	2.09	2.01	1.51
Second- or Later-Generation	2.51	1.73	1.64	1.07	1.70
Cuban					
First-Generation	2.14	1.46	1.62	1.44	1.62
Second- or Later-Generation	.41	.50	1.31	1.07	.34
Central/South American					
First-Generation	2.49	1.80	1.96	1.75	1.42
Second- or Later-Generation	1.77	3.57	2.44	1.94	1.40
Other Hispanic					
First-Generation	2.66	2.18	2.18	1.73	1.40
Second- or Later-Generation	3.55	2.56	2.17	1.31	1.43

TABLE 7.7

*Mean Numbers of Children Under Age 3
by Education, Generational Status, and Ethnicity,
Ever-Married Spanish Origin and Non-Hispanic White Women
Aged 15–44: 1980*

	Years of Schooling				
	0–8	9–11	12	13–15	16+
Non-Hispanic White	.21	.25	.25	.26	.27
Mexican					
First-Generation	.45	.48	.40	.32	.27
Second- or Later-Generation	.33	.43	.38	.31	.23
Puerto Rican					
First-Generation	.23	.33	.31	.35	.42
Second- or Later-Generation	.42	.47	.40	.38	.19
Cuban					
First-Generation	.07	.18	.21	.27	.22
Second- or Later-Generation	.06	.11	.25	.30	.02
Central/South American					
First-Generation	.29	.32	.22	.26	.18
Second- or Later-Generation	.23	.48	.71	.41	.25
Other Hispanic					
First-Generation	.34	.37	.26	.13	.42
Second- or Later-Generation	.19	.44	.27	.35	.33

ception to this generalization occurs among Cuban origin women who, as we will increasingly see, constitute a special case. Also, second- or later-generation Puerto Rican and Other Hispanic women with 16 or more years of schooling show an "increase" in their numbers of children ever born, thus deviating from the pattern of linear decrease observed among the Mexican origin women. In the case of recent fertility, as noted above, we would expect to observe less variation with education because much of it occurs to women aged 20 to 24 and consists of births of lower parity, which have often been observed to be less influenced by socioeconomic variables.[29] For the most part, this is indeed the case; the women of Mexican origin are the only group which exhibits generally declining recent fertility with rising education, although even Mexicans do not exhibit a perfect linear pattern. In all of the other groups examined much less of a clear-cut relationship appears between female education and recent fertility. Hence, except within the group of Mexican origin women, our knowledge of a woman's educational level provides little guide to understanding her recent fertility.

[29]Ryder, "Fertility Trends"; and Hout, "Determinants of Marital Fertility."

This is not true of lifetime fertility, however, which varies strongly with education. Further testimony to the importance of female education as a factor influencing the magnitude of fertility differences is revealed in Table 7.8, which shows educational distributions for the Spanish origin groups and non-Hispanic white women. In almost every instance the Spanish origin women exhibit lower levels of education than non-Hispanic white women. If lower education tends generally to make for higher fertility, and if the Spanish origin women are relatively more concentrated in the lower educational categories, it is not difficult to see why higher fertility persists within many of the groups. Given the lower levels of education of even the Cuban origin women, many of

TABLE 7.8

Number and Percentage Distributions by Education and Generational Status, Ever-Married Spanish Origin and Non-Hispanic White Women Aged 15–44: 1980

	Years of Schooling					
	0–8	9–11	12	13–15	16+	Total
Non-Hispanic White	3.1%	12.3%	45.9%	21.9%	16.7%	99.9%
(N)	(854)	(3,355)	(12,464)	(5,960)	(4,548)	(27,181)
Mexican						
First-Generation	59.0	14.9	15.3	8.0	2.7	99.9
(N)	(14,704)	(3,708)	(3,816)	(2,004)	(678)	(24,910)
Second- or Later-Generation	16.5	24.7	38.3	16.0	4.5	100.0
(N)	(6,856)	(10,268)	(15,912)	(6,652)	(1,856)	(41,544)
Puerto Rican						
First-Generation	29.2	29.0	27.6	9.8	4.5	100.1
(N)	(3,428)	(3,406)	(3,238)	(1,146)	(532)	(11,750)
Second- or Later-Generation	5.5	23.2	43.3	21.5	6.4	99.9
(N)	(236)	(1,000)	(1,864)	(926)	(274)	(4,300)
Cuban						
First-Generation	19.8	13.0	34.1	21.5	11.6	100.0
(N)	(1,024)	(670)	(1,758)	(1,110)	(598)	(5,160)
Second- or Later-Generation	20.8	24.2	16.6	15.9	22.5	100.0
(N)	(120)	(140)	(96)	(92)	(130)	(578)
Central/South American						
First-Generation	23.4	13.9	33.7	16.1	12.8	99.9
(N)	(2,708)	(1,606)	(3,896)	(1,862)	(1,472)	(11,544)
Second- or Later-Generation	4.2	6.9	34.3	45.4	9.2	100.1
(N)	(26)	(42)	(210)	(278)	(56)	(612)
Other Hispanic						
First-Generation	23.5	11.2	28.3	19.0	17.9	99.9
(N)	(880)	(420)	(1,058)	(712)	(668)	(3,738)
Second- or Later-Generation	5.6	17.0	48.1	22.3	7.0	100.0
(N)	(694)	(2,084)	(5,904)	(2,736)	(860)	(12,278)

whom were political refugees fleeing the Cuban revolution and came from middle- or higher-class backgrounds before immigrating to the United States, perhaps the more interesting question in their case is: Why is their fertility so low? We shall return to this question below.

For the moment, however, we return to the issue of whether Spanish origin women of higher socioeconomic status, indicated here by female education, exhibit less of a fertility gap compared with similarly educated non-Hispanic women than do those of lower education. Stated differently, if a fertility gap persists between some of the groups and non-Hispanic whites, is this mostly true of less well educated women? Results relevant to answering this question are presented in Table 7.9, which shows the average fertility differences between the Spanish origin groups and non-Hispanic whites by generational status and education after holding constant all of the same factors that were controlled in Table 7.5.

The pattern predicted by the minority group status and the economic hypotheses—namely, that of a diminishing fertility differential as education increases—does not appear with any degree of consistency, except among women of Mexican origin and, to a lesser extent, among women of Other Hispanic origin. In the case of Puerto Rican women, those with higher levels of education are not appreciably less likely than those with lower levels of education to exhibit a smaller fertility gap with non-Hispanic women. Cuban women show generally lower fertility at most education levels, except at the higher levels among foreign-born women. In short, even after holding other factors constant, Spanish origin women generally continue to exhibit somewhat higher levels of cumulative and recent childbearing than do non-Hispanic white women, with two important exceptions.

The first exception is Cuban origin women, most of whom are concentrated in the first generation and who tend to exhibit lower fertility than non-Hispanic white women. This may reflect the disruptive effects of immigration on fertility, which Bean et al. have shown operate fairly strongly among Mexican immigrants.[30] Consistent with this interpretation is the fact that almost all of the groups of immigrant women show lower levels of children ever born than do their later generational counterparts, except Puerto Rican women, all of whom are U.S. citizens. The effects on Cuban women, who are not only immigrants but also political refugees, may be especially severe. As also would be expected if immigration has a depressing effect on fertility, the tendency for first-generation women to evince lower levels of children ever born does not repeat itself nearly as strongly in the case of the number of children

---

[30]Bean et al., "Generational Differences."

TABLE 7.9

Net Mean Fertility Differences
Between Spanish Origin Groups and Non-Hispanic Whites
by Education and Generational Status, Ever-Married Women Aged 15–44: 1980

	Years of Schooling				
	0–8	9–11	12	13–15	16+
CHILDREN EVER BORN					
Mexican					
First-Generation	.82	.25	.44	.30	.35
Second- or Later-Generation	1.12	.59	.46	.30	.26
Puerto Rican					
First-Generation	.49	.16	.14	.38	.25
Second- or Later-Generation	.42	−.03	.14	−.24	.73
Cuban					
First-Generation	−.82	−.71	−.36	−.23	.11
Second- or Later-Generation	−1.23	−.42	−.11	−.15	−.32
Central/South American					
First-Generation	−.22	−.47	−.10	.11	.12
Second- or Later-Generation	−.06	.26	.34	.32	.68
Other Hispanic					
First-Generation	.15	.17	.18	−.02	−.12
Second- or Later-Generation	1.08	.36	.30	−.21	.08
CHILDREN UNDER AGE 3					
Mexican					
First-Generation	.14	.14	.06	.03	−.02
Second- or Later-Generation	.07	.10	.06	−.01	−.10
Puerto Rican					
First-Generation	.06	.08	.06	.07	.15
Second- or Later-Generation	.10	.09	.08	.03	−.15
Cuban					
First-Generation	−.05	−.10	.00	.02	.01
Second- or Later-Generation	−.19	−.28	−.06	−.03	−.38
Central/South American					
First-Generation	.04	.00	−.03	−.02	−.13
Second- or Later-Generation	.11	.10	.26	.10	−.04
Other Hispanic					
First-Generation	.06	.04	.00	−.15	.19
Second- or Later-Generation	−.05	.18	.04	.08	.07

under age 3. Because the latter measure reflects recent behavior, it is less likely to be diminished by the prior experience of immigration. While the first-generation Cuban women exhibit lower fertility than second- or later-generation women, the latter also reveal lower fertility, however, which suggests that something other than just the disruptive aspects of immigration experience may be involved.

The second important exception to the pattern of generally higher Spanish origin fertility occurs in the case of recent fertility among women with 16 or more years of schooling. In most of the instances examined the levels of recent fertility are lower than those of non-Hispanic white women who have the same educational background. And in the cases of second- or later-generational Mexican, Puerto Rican, and Cuban origin women, the difference is fairly substantial, averaging from one-tenth to nearly four-tenths of a child per woman. It is important to note that this pattern does not emerge in the case of cumulative fertility (except among Cubans), suggesting that different forces may be influencing the earlier and later stages of childbearing. For example, since these women show fewer children under age 3, holding age constant, but more children ever born, the difference in the latter for whatever age is being compared would have to have arisen at an earlier stage of the childbearing process.

The Case of Mexican Origin Women

Since women of Mexican origin constitute such a large proportion of ever-married Spanish origin women (77.8 percent of ever-married women aged 15–44), and since the degree to which their fertility would continue to exceed that of non-Hispanic whites, even if other differences were removed, is generally greater than that of the other Spanish origin groups, we devote further attention here to analyzing the circumstances under which similarities and dissimilarities in their fertility compared with that of non-Hispanic whites occur. We ask first whether differences in age at marriage modify the generational status by education pattern observed in Table 7.9. As indicated in Table 7.10, when age at marriage is held constant the basic pattern remains unchanged, with more well-educated Mexican origin women showing higher cumulative but lower recent fertility than well-educated non-Hispanic white women.

Another question concerns whether this basic pattern (as displayed in Tables 7.9 and 7.10) was also characteristic of the population of Mexican origin women in 1970, or whether some change has occurred since then. Results relevant to this issue are presented in the bottom panel of Table 7.11, where we can see that the fertility differences by educational category were much the same in 1970 as in 1980 among women with a high school education or less. Among women with at least some higher

TABLE 7.10

Net Mean Fertility Differences
Between Mexican Origin and Non-Hispanic White Women,
Controlling for Age at Marriage,
Ever-Married Mexican Origin Women Aged 15–44: 1980

	Years of Schooling				
	0–8	9–11	12	13–15	16+
CHILDREN EVER BORN					
First-Generation	1.07	.58	.65	.48	.32
Second- or Later-Generation	1.10	.68	.53	.33	.23
CHILDREN UNDER AGE 3					
First-Generation	.13	.11	.05	.02	−.02
Second- or Later-Generation	.07	.10	.06	−.01	−.10

education, however, a shift has taken place. Overlooking first-genera-tion women, whose cumulative fertility especially is affected by the dis-ruptive impact of immigration, we see that more highly educated Mex-ican origin and non-Hispanic white women in 1970 were virtually indistinguishable in their levels of cumulative and recent fertility. In 1980, however, more highly educated Mexican origin women exhibit greater average numbers of children ever born but fewer average chil-dren under age 3.

TABLE 7.11

Net Mean Fertility Differences
Between Mexican Origin and Non-Hispanic White Women,
Ever-Married Women Aged 15–44: 1970

	Years of Schooling				
	0–8	9–11	12	13–15	16+
CHILDREN EVER BORN					
First-Generation	.96	.04	.27	−.06	−.34
Second- or Later-Generation	1.17	.68	.31	.10	−.02
CHILDREN UNDER AGE 3					
First-Generation	.19	.14	.16	.06	−.05
Second- or Later-Generation	.12	.10	.05	.02	−.02

TABLE 7.12

Net Mean Fertility Deviations
Between Mexican Origin and Non-Hispanic White Women
by Generational Status and English Proficiency,
Ever-Married Women Aged 15-44: 1980

English Proficiency	Years of Schooling				
	0–8	9–11	12	13–15	16+
CHILDREN EVER BORN					
Foreign-Born Low Proficiency	.81	.14	.49	.34	.96
Foreign-Born High Proficiency	.88	.56	.38	.27	− .09
Native-Born Low Proficiency	1.29	.56	.44	.40	.62
Native-Born High Proficiency	.92	.61	.47	.29	.21
CHILDREN UNDER AGE 3					
Foreign-Born Low Proficiency	.15	.15	.10	− .03	.04
Foreign-Born High Proficiency	.12	.11	.02	.06	− .06
Native-Born Low Proficiency	.09	.08	.04	.07	− .10
Native-Born High Proficiency	.04	.12	.07	− .02	− .10

Finally, we ask if linguistic factors could play any role in the patterns of fertility differences observed. Perhaps those women of Mexican origin, especially those who are native-born, who not only are highly educated but who also speak English most proficiently will be the most similar to non-Hispanic white women in their fertility behavior.[31] As the results in Table 7.12 indicate, however, variation in English proficiency makes very little difference for the basic pattern we have already observed. The amount by which both cumulative and recent Mexican origin fertility exceeds non-Hispanic white fertility declines with rising education. However, cumulative fertility remains higher even among highly educated native-born Mexican women with high English proficiency, whereas again their recent fertility is lower.

Summary and Conclusions

It is clear from the discussion above that most of the Spanish origin groups in the United States have higher fertility than non-Hispanic whites, with women of Cuban origin constituting a notable exception.

[31]Gray Swicegood, "Language, Opportunity Costs and Mexican American Fertility," unpublished doctoral dissertation, University of Texas, 1983.

Among all of the groups except the Cubans, but especially among Mexican origin women, this higher fertility is attributable only in part to differences between the group and non-Hispanic white women in such factors as age composition, educational attainment, and labor force participation. The analyses reveal that all of the Spanish origin groups except Cubans would continue to show higher overall levels of both cumulative and current fertility even if these other differences were eliminated.

Despite this fact educational differences between the populations and non-Hispanic whites explain a large part of the fertility differences between them. This is most precisely seen in the data for the second- or later-generation women, whose fertility is not affected by the disruptive impact of immigration. When the fertility differences are examined for these women, anywhere from about one-third to two-thirds of the age-adjusted fertility differences are observed to owe to the lower levels of female education in these groups. The further narrowing of the fertility gaps between these groups and majority whites would seem to be very much contingent on improvements in the levels of female education among Spanish origin women.[32]

The importance of female education for understanding the forces lying behind the higher fertility of the groups of Spanish origin women can also be seen in their patterns of fertility differences by educational level. With the exception again of the Cuban and Other Hispanic women, we find among highly educated native-born women (those with 16 or more years of schooling) that their cumulative fertility (the number of children ever born) *exceeds* that of non-Hispanic whites, but their current fertility (the number under age 3) *falls below* that of majority whites. Since we have held age differences constant in both sets of analyses involving these variables, this suggests that the Spanish origin groups may have had higher fertility than non-Hispanic white women at earlier points in their reproductive cycles. In short, highly educated Spanish origin women may have higher fertility than similar non-Hispanic white women at early stages of the reproductive process, but lower fertility later, a time pattern of fertility more like that of blacks than Anglos.[33]

What do all of these findings imply for the various explanations of differential fertility set forth above? Interestingly, they provide a measure of support for all of them, but they also indicate that none of them individually is fully adequate to explain the results. Clearly the *social*

[32]Bean, Swicegood, and Linsley, "Patterns of Fertility Variation."
[33]Craig St. John and Harold G. Grasmick, "Decomposing the Black/White Fertility Differential," *Social Science Quarterly* 66 (1985):132–46.

characteristics approach is correct in its prediction that differences in characteristics will account for a large part, if not all, of the fertility differences. However, substantial fertility differences between the Spanish origin groups and non-Hispanic whites remain after holding education and a number of other factors constant. This finding causes us not to be able to discard hastily the subcultural hypothesis that particular constellations of pronatalist norms and values within these groups might support their higher fertility. We should first consider whether higher Spanish origin fertility can be attributed to the fact that almost all of the women in these groups are Catholic. Evidence relevant to answering this question is available only for Mexican women among the various groups of Spanish origin women, but it does not suggest that religious differences would fully explain the fertility patterns observed. Research has shown, for example, that institutional affiliation with the Catholic church and degree of religiosity do not exert much of an effect on wanted family size or contraceptive efficacy among Mexican Americans.[34] Other research, however, suggests that religiosity does have an impact, but only among native-born Mexican origin women.[35] In any event, for religiosity to explain the fertility differences, large proportions of women would have to be involved. This does not seem likely given other evidence indicating that Mexican Americans are less likely to attend Mass weekly or to attend parochial schools than other Catholics and that they are less likely to agree with the positions of the Church on birth control.[36]

If the forces making for generally higher Spanish fertility do not seem to have their origin in Catholic pronatalism, and given that highly educated second- or later-generation Mexican, Puerto Rican, and Central/South American origin women all exhibit significantly *lower* recent fertility than non-Hispanic white women, other mechanisms than those posited by the subcultural approach would appear to be operating. It is here that the minority group status and economic hypotheses are relevant. These hypotheses are pertinent to the prediction of fertility differences by education. While not offering the possibility of explaining overall fertility differences (because they are not concerned with accounting for differences in levels of educational attainment), they are relevant to understanding the circumstances associated with some women having lower fertility than others. The mechanisms emphasized by the hypotheses are actually different sides of the same coin in that both posit

[34]David Alvirez, "The Effects of Formal Church Affiliation and Religiosity on the Fertility Patterns of Mexican American Catholics," *Demography* 10 (1973):19–36.

[35]Georges Sabagh and David Lopez, "Religiosity and Fertility: The Case of the Chicanos," *Social Forces* 59 (1980):431–39.

[36]Grebler, Moore, and Guzman, *Mexican-American People*.

231

fertility declines with increasing education because of the higher costs of childbearing among more highly educated women. The minority group status approach, however, invokes an additional aspect of motivation in its suggestion that minority group women must overcompensate through reduced childbearing in order to obtain the same rewards as majority women. Interestingly, in the lower recent fertility of highly educated native-born Mexican, Puerto Rican, and Central/South American women we find results consistent with this hypothesis.

This finding casts doubt on the idea that the subcultural hypothesis provides a general explanation of higher Spanish origin fertility, because it implies that these women reduce their fertility as childbearing costs increase, perhaps even disproportionately so, as the minority group status approach would predict. Nonetheless, more highly educated women also exhibit higher levels of children ever born. How can we explain this apparent anomaly? Perhaps minority women from groups with norms and values supporting higher fertility are more likely to exceed the fertility of majority group women in the earlier stages of the reproductive process when they are engaged in what Ryder has termed "normative" childbearing.[37] After that, as they move into what Ryder calls the "discretionary" phase of childbearing, the kinds of mechanisms posited by the minority group status and economic approaches may come more into play, bringing about reduced subsequent childbearing, especially in the case of more highly educated women. The results we have obtained are consistent with this possibility. Whatever the combination of mechanisms involved, the findings of this chapter underscore the crucial importance of female education for the explanation of fertility differences. This suggests that understanding fertility differences requires knowing something about the determinants of education differences, a topic we address further in the next chapter.

[37]Ryder, "Fertility Trends."

8

THE EDUCATIONAL STANDING
OF HISPANICS:
SIGNS OF HOPE AND STRESS

THIS CHAPTER documents the past and present Hispanic experience in the United States school system and, for the school-age population in 1980, analyzes the impact of socioeconomic background and ethnic characteristics on educational outcomes. Our main goals are (1) to document differentials in educational attainment and enrollment levels among Hispanic adults, (2) to examine enrollment patterns and sociodemographic characteristics of the school-age population of Hispanic origin, and (3) to analyze the determinants of the high rates of grade delay and high school noncompletion of Hispanic youth.

We organize this chapter into three sections corresponding to these broad objectives. First we document differentials in adult educational attainment and school enrollment levels between 1960 and 1980. This discussion is geared to illustrate key dimensions of variation in adult educational achievement according to national origin, nativity, age, and years of schooling. We also examine selected social and demographic characteristics of the small but growing segment of the population with four years of post-secondary schooling and compare this group with the population having less than a high school diploma. This comparison starkly illustrates the socioeconomic significance of higher education.

After examining empirically the school enrollment patterns of Hispanic young adults and school-age individuals, we discuss the theoretical issues that underlie the educational attainment process and, ultimately, help in understanding educational outcomes. This discussion attempts to identify those uniquely Hispanic factors that may clarify the low achievements of these groups. Subsequently, we present our empirical analyses of the factors contributing to high rates of grade delay and school noncompletion among Hispanic youth in 1980. We close the chapter with a discussion of policy issues for the 1990s and beyond. In assessing the future educational prospects of the Hispanic population, the sobering facts about high rates of high school noncompletion, particularly among Mexican and Puerto Rican origin youth, must be weighed against evidence of modest gains in average years of completed schooling for the total population. We discuss these issues in this chapter, as well as several others which bear on the importance of education in shaping the future demographic, social, and economic position of the United States Hispanic population.

Adult Education Differentials: 1960–1980

Despite the low educational attainment of Hispanics compared with blacks and whites, the average years of schooling completed by Hispanic adults has risen during the past two decades, as shown in Table 8.1. Nevertheless, the Hispanic population lags significantly behind the non-Hispanic white population in terms of educational attainment. In 1980, when the median schooling level of the adult non-Hispanic white pop-

TABLE 8.1

Median Years of Schooling of the Adult Population Aged 25 and Over by Race, Hispanic Origin, and Nativity: 1960–1980

	1960			1970			1980		
	Native	Foreign	Total	Native	Foreign	Total	Native	Foreign	Total
Mexican	7.6	3.6	6.4	9.2	5.6	8.2	11.1	6.1	9.1
Puerto Rican	9.8	7.1[a]	7.5	11.5	7.9[a]	8.2	12.0	9.2[a]	10.0
Cuban	8.4	8.4	8.4	11.8	10.0	10.0	12.1	11.7	11.7
Central/South American	11.6	11.5	11.6	12.0	11.6	11.7	12.4	11.7	11.7
Other Hispanic	10.7	7.6	8.0	10.5	9.2	10.0	11.9	11.3	11.8
Black	8.0	8.0	8.0	10.0	12.0	10.0	12.0	12.0	12.0
Non-Hispanic White	11.0	8.0	11.0	12.0	9.0	12.0	12.0	12.0	12.0

SOURCES: 1960, 1970, and 1980 Public Use Microdata Sample files.

[a]Foreign refers to island-born.

ulation was 12 years, the median education of Mexicans and Puerto Ricans was 9 and 10 years, respectively. Cubans, Central/South Americans, and Other Hispanics were less educationally disadvantaged than Mexicans and Puerto Ricans, as their educational levels approached those of non-Hispanic whites and blacks in 1980.

Despite the persistence of intergroup differences in schooling, Hispanics were more educationally homogeneous in 1980 than in 1960. The range of median education levels among the five origin groups in 1960 was 5.2 years compared with 3.5 and 2.7 years in 1970 and 1980, respectively. Blacks and whites became more educationally similar to each other during the 1960s and 1970s, and during the latter decade the nativity differences by race disappeared. However, among Hispanics nativity differentials in adult median education levels persisted throughout the period, and for Mexicans these discrepancies actually *increased* over time. For all groups and at all three time periods, United States-born Hispanics had completed higher levels of formal schooling than their counterparts born abroad. As we show below (Table 8.3), college-educated Hispanics are considerably more likely to be native-born. No doubt, the greater native-foreign educational differential among Mexicans reflects the presence of about 1.1 million undocumented Mexicans in the 1980 census,[1] as well as the presence of low-education legal immigrants admitted under the family reunification provisions of the 1965 Amendments to the Immigration and Nationality Act.

The Mexican pattern of widening nativity differentials contrasts with that of Other Hispanics, among whom the median education gap decreased between 1960 and 1980, and of Cubans, whose nativity differences in schooling converged during the 1970s. Although the median schooling level of all Central/South Americans remained fairly stable during the past two decades, the nativity differential in median education increased slightly owing to the higher levels of school completion among native-born adults. However, because the native-born segment of this population is quite small (refer to Chapter 3), the compositional effect of the overall average education is negligible. Puerto Ricans exhibit yet a third pattern of birthplace differentiation in schooling in that the median education gap between those born on the island and the U.S. mainland increased during the 1960s and fell back to its 1960 level by 1980. This results from the interaction of rising education levels on

---

[1]Robert Warren and Jeffrey S. Passel, "Estimates of Illegal Aliens from Mexico Counted in the 1980 United States Census," unpublished manuscript, U.S. Bureau of the Census, Population Division, 1983; Frank D. Bean, Allan King, and Jeffrey Passel, "The Number of Illegal Migrants of Mexican Origin in the United States: Sex Ratio-Based Estimates for 1980," *Demography* 20 (1983):99–109.

FIGURE 8.1

*Median Education of the Hispanic Population Aged 25 and Over
by Type of Origin and Broad Age Groups: 1960–1980*

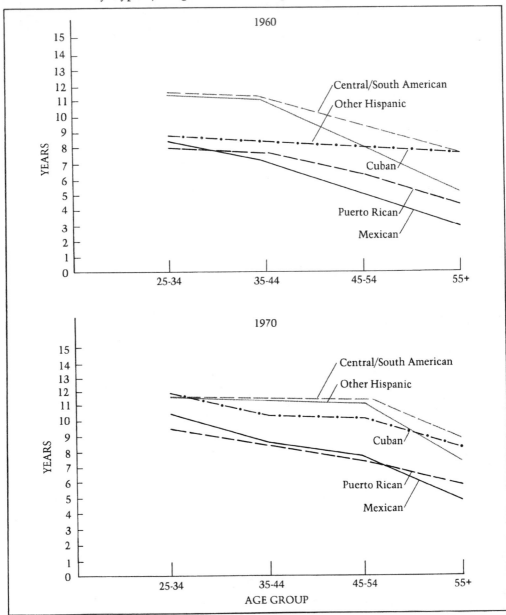

SOURCES: 1960, 1970, and 1980 Public Use Microdata Sample files.

FIGURE 8.1 *(continued)*

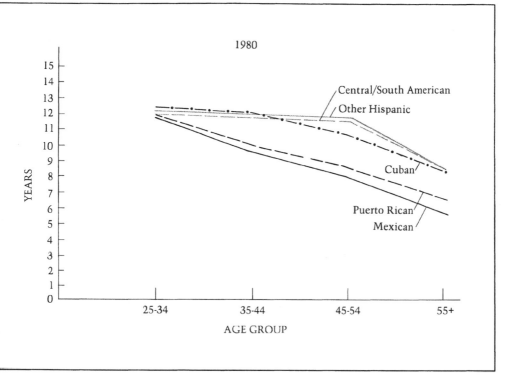

both the island and the mainland (albeit at different rates), coupled with changes over time in the selectivity of return and first-time migrants.[2]

Despite the complex pattern of educational differentials shown in Table 8.1, sex differentials (not reported) were relatively small throughout the period, and they were discernible mainly at older ages. By 1980 a median education gap of a full year was observed only among Cuban and Puerto Rican adults aged 55 and over who were born outside the United States. For example, the median education of foreign-born Cuban men aged 55 and over in 1980 was 10.4 years versus 8.7 years for their female counterparts. However, differentials of this magnitude were uncommon by 1980, especially compared with the gender differentials prevalent in 1960. For this reason we do not belabor these results in great detail.

The age-education profiles shown in Figure 8.1 support the interpre-

[2]Vilma Ortiz, "Changes in the Characteristics of Puerto Rican Migrants from 1955 to 1980," unpublished manuscript, Educational Testing Service, Princeton, New Jersey, 1985.

TABLE 8.2

*Percentage Distribution of Adults Aged 25 And Over
by Levels of School Completed, Race, Hispanic Origin, and Nativity:
1960–1980*

	Mexican			Puerto Rican[a]			Cuban		
	Native	Foreign	Total	Native	Foreign	Total	Native	Foreign	Total
1960									
High School	76.4%	89.6%	80.0%	59.6%	83.6%	81.8%	66.1%	68.0%	67.5%
12 Years	15.8	6.4	13.2	24.6	11.5	12.5	18.7	15.7	16.4
13–15 Years	4.8	2.2	4.1	8.8	3.2	3.6	6.4	8.0	7.6
16+ Years	3.0	1.8	2.7	7.0	1.6	2.0	8.8	8.2	8.4
1970									
High School	61.9	80.9	66.6	47.4	78.3	74.2	36.7	53.5	51.8
12 Years	24.7	11.8	21.5	31.5	15.9	17.9	33.4	23.2	24.3
13–15 Years	8.6	4.6	7.6	12.3	3.2	4.4	14.8	10.9	11.3
16+ Years	4.8	2.7	4.3	8.9	2.6	3.4	15.1	12.3	12.6
1980									
High School	50.6	77.4	60.6	30.1	63.6	57.7	31.0	43.9	43.0
12 Years	27.5	12.5	21.9	35.5	22.6	24.8	26.3	25.3	25.4
13–15 Years	14.7	6.8	11.8	21.5	8.9	11.1	19.9	13.6	14.1
16+ Years	7.2	3.2	5.7	12.8	4.9	6.3	22.8	17.2	17.5

SOURCES: 1960, 1970, and 1980 Public Use Microdata Sample files.

[a]Foreign refers to island-born.

tation of educational convergence among the national origin groups. Of course, age variation in median schooling levels is only one of many factors maintaining educational differentials among the Hispanic national origin groups. Younger cohorts exhibit a clear and pronounced educational advantage over their older counterparts, but the steepness of the curves differs by national origin. In 1960 the educational disadvantages of Mexicans and Puerto Ricans compared with Central/South Americans, Cubans, and Other Hispanics were already evident. Educational differentiation between Mexicans and Puerto Ricans was minimal among those aged 25 to 34, but beyond age 35 the disparity in median schooling levels increased, with the schooling advantage corresponding to Puerto Ricans.

Although the age-education profiles of all groups converged during the last two decades, especially among the three highest education groups (Central/South Americans, Cubans, and Other Hispanics), the age pattern of change was less uniform for Mexicans and Puerto Ricans.

TABLE 8.2 *(continued)*

Central/ South American			Other Hispanic			Black			Non-Hispanic White		
Native	Foreign	Total	Native	Foreign	Total	Native	Foreign	Total	Native	Foreign	Total
31.8%	47.5%	44.4%	47.9%	70.7%	67.8%	78.5%	64.8%	78.3%	52.3%	71.2%	54.0%
37.8	25.8	28.2	31.9	15.0	17.1	14.0	25.0	14.1	27.7	16.0	26.6
15.9	12.5	13.2	11.1	7.0	7.5	4.1	5.7	4.2	10.6	6.1	10.2
14.6	14.1	14.2	9.0	7.4	7.6	3.4	4.5	3.4	9.4	6.7	9.2
30.4	44.0	42.4	47.0	56.5	50.9	66.3	42.6	66.0	41.3	61.6	42.7
38.5	29.0	30.1	30.6	22.4	27.3	22.7	28.7	22.8	33.7	21.9	32.9
12.8	14.0	13.8	11.8	10.0	11.1	6.0	16.0	6.2	13.1	9.3	12.8
18.2	13.0	13.6	10.5	11.1	10.8	5.0	12.8	5.1	11.9	7.2	11.6
23.7	42.8	42.0	35.8	49.5	39.5	40.4	29.9	38.2	20.8	30.8	22.9
24.6	26.8	26.7	33.2	21.8	30.1	32.9	32.0	32.7	39.2	31.0	37.5
24.2	16.9	17.2	18.5	12.3	16.8	16.8	19.3	17.3	19.3	17.2	18.8
27.5	13.6	14.1	12.5	16.4	13.6	9.9	18.8	11.8	20.7	21.0	20.7

In 1970 the education differentials between Mexican and Puerto Rican adults occurred mainly at young and old ages, that is, among the 25-to-34 and over-55 age cohorts. Mexicans aged 25 to 54 had a slight educational advantage over Puerto Ricans, but those aged 55 and over were less well educated than their Puerto Rican age-mates. However, a short decade later Puerto Ricans enjoyed the educational advantage at all ages. This reflects the rapidly rising level of educational attainment in Puerto Rico, and of the migrant population in particular, coupled with a decline in the average attainment of the foreign-born Mexican origin population.[3]

Table 8.2 provides additional insight into the dimensions of educational differentiation among the Hispanic origin groups. Note that the

[3]We can only speculate how much the inclusion of a substantial number of undocumented Mexican immigrants contributed to the educational standing of Mexicans with respect to Puerto Ricans, but expect that these consequences are most pronounced among those individuals aged 25 to 34. Possibly—and this is only speculation on our part—the Puerto Rican and Mexican age-education profiles would be identical in the absence of the illegal immigration phenomenon.

proportion of adults aged 25 and over with less than a high school diploma declined steadily between 1960 and 1980, but Puerto Ricans and Mexicans lagged about 15 to 20 years behind Cubans and Other Hispanics in the proportion of high school graduates.[4] Thus, while all groups experienced gradual increases in the share of adults holding high school diplomas, in 1980 there remained pronounced national origin differences in the proportion of high school dropouts. Roughly three in five Mexicans and Puerto Ricans aged 25 and over had not completed high school in 1980 compared with two in five adults of other Hispanic nationalities.

The Hispanic experience when contrasted with that of blacks and non-Hispanic whites is instructive. Using the proportion of college graduates and high school dropouts as metrics, whites were educationally better off than all groups except Cubans and Central/South Americans in 1960 and 1970, but by 1980 the share of non-Hispanic white college graduates surpassed that of both Cubans and Central/South Americans. Blacks, while educationally disadvantaged throughout the period compared with all groups except Mexicans and Puerto Ricans, experienced considerably more educational upgrading than the latter. For example, in 1960 the share of adult high school dropouts was quite similar for Mexicans, Puerto Ricans, and blacks, but by 1980 Mexicans and Puerto Ricans were more disadvantaged educationally. Correspondingly, the share of black college graduates, while only marginally higher than that of Puerto Ricans and Mexicans in 1960, rose from 3.4 percent to 11.8 percent by 1980, or roughly double the shares of Mexican and Puerto Rican college graduates.

Figure 8.2 provides age detail about the pervasiveness of educational disadvantages among Hispanic adults as reflected by the proportion who had not completed high school in each period. In all three years, and for all age comparisons, Mexicans and Puerto Ricans stand apart from Cubans, Central/South Americans, and Other Hispanics in that they were least likely to have finished high school. Although the reduction over time in the proportion of high school noncompleters is encouraging, the dropout rates among the youngest age cohorts remained disturbingly high in 1980. That between 43 and 46 percent of all Puerto Rican and Mexican origin adults under age 35 had less than a high school education in 1980 does not bode well for their longer-term prospects in the labor market, particularly as the economy continues its shift toward ser-

[4]The share of persons not completing high school refers to all persons, not only those who entered high school. Restricting our analysis to those individuals who entered high school would exclude an important segment of the adult population—namely, those who dropped out at the middle school level. For Mexicans and Puerto Ricans this segment of the adult population is not trivial, as our discussion on dropouts shows.

vices and high-technology industries.[5] As we show in a subsequent section, this situation shows limited signs of improving among the school-age population. Thus, the proportion of high school dropouts among recently and currently enrolled Hispanics remains unacceptably high, despite the modest progress in reducing noncompletion rates over time.

On a more positive note it is encouraging that the decline in high school noncompletion rates increased the proportion of high school graduates, as well as the share of individuals with some post-secondary training. As indicated in Table 8.2, between 1960 and 1980 the proportion of high school graduates rose from 13 to 22 percent for Mexican origin adults, from 12 to 25 percent for Puerto Ricans, and from 16 to 25 percent for Cubans. That the percentage increases in the share of high school completers did not eliminate the educational disadvantages of Mexicans and Puerto Ricans with respect to Cubans, Central/South Americans, and Other Hispanics merely reflects the education discrepancies existing at the beginning of the period. In other words, all groups seem to have benefited by approximately similar amounts from the improvement in high school completion rates. Other Hispanics are an apparent exception, as their share of high school graduates rose by nearly 13 points to 30 percent by 1980. However, the noncomparability over time of this residual category overstates the amount of true change in high school completion rates. Thus, we believe that the gains in high school completion for this group were roughly similar to those observed for the other groups combined.

Gender differences in high school completion were smaller than the nativity differentials reported in Table 8.2. Hence we do not report them in detail. Essentially, these tabulations showed that the proportion of each group with a high school diploma was slightly greater for women, but men were more likely to hold college degrees or to have attended college. This generalization holds for all groups and at each point in time. As recently as 1980 gender differentiation in college completion was quite marked among Cubans, Central/South Americans, and Other Hispanics. For these three groups the proportion of men holding college degrees was 6 to 8 percent higher than their female national origin counterparts. Among Mexicans and Puerto Ricans roughly 6 percent of adult men aged 25 and over in 1980 held college degrees compared with 4 to 5 percent of the women.

---

[5]Joachim Singelmann and Marta Tienda, "The Process of Occupational Change in a Service Society: The Case of the United States, 1960–1980," in Bryan Roberts, Ruth Finnegan, and Duncan Gallie, eds., *New Approaches to Economic Life: Economic Restructuring, Unemployment and the Social Division of Labor* (Manchester, England: University of Manchester Press, 1985).

FIGURE 8.2

Proportion of the Hispanic Population Aged 25 and Over Not Completing High Schoo by Type of Origin and Broad Age Groups: 1960–1980

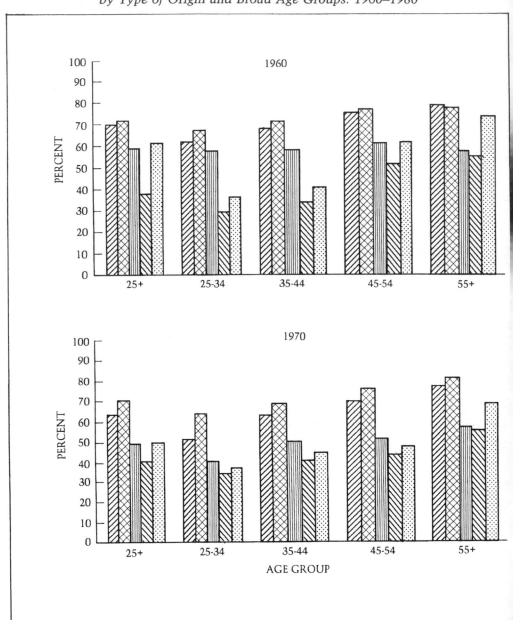

SOURCES: 1960, 1970, and 1980 Public Use Microdata Sample files.

FIGURE 8.2 *(continued)*

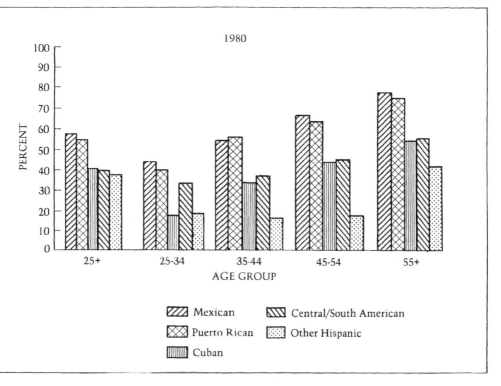

Gains in higher education were greatly facilitated by numerous privately and publicly funded fellowship and scholarship programs during the 1970s, yet the proportion of all Hispanic adults having completed 16 or more years of schooling in 1980 was discouragingly low compared with non-Hispanic whites and blacks. In 1980 roughly 6 percent of Mexican and Puerto Rican adults had completed four or more years of college compared with between 14 and 17 percent of the remaining Hispanic nationalities and roughly 12 and 21 percent of blacks and whites, respectively. Table 8.3 provides further information about the changing characteristics of Hispanics with post-secondary training versus those with less than high school diplomas.

The rising educational attainment of younger cohorts of Mexicans and Puerto Ricans manifests itself in the lowered average age of the college-educated population. In 1980 Mexicans and Puerto Ricans with completed baccalaureate degrees were 10 years younger, on average,

TABLE 8.3

Selected Characteristics of Adults Aged 25
Completing Less Than High School and Four or More Years of College
by Race and Hispanic Origin: 1970–1980

	Mexican		Puerto Rican		Cuban	
	Less Than High School Education	4 or More Years College	Less Than High School Education	4 or More Years College	Less Than High School Education	4 or More Years College
1970						
Mean Age	40.6	38.0	36.4	37.0	45.1	43.1
Percentage Married						
Men	81.5%	80.2%	78.0%	67.9%	84.6%	82.0%
Women	86.3	66.5	86.7	63.0	88.3	69.9
Percentage Native-Born	69.3	84.1	12.1	35.4	9.2	13.3
Median Earnings[a] (in thousands)						
Men	$5.0	$10.0	$5.0	$11.1	$5.0	$9.2
Women	$2.0	$5.8	$3.0	$10.6	$2.0	$4.8
Percentage Spanish Mother Tongue	94.9%	68.0%	98.6%	89.8%	99.0%	93.7%
1980						
Mean Age	39.8	34.9	39.6	35.0	52.1	45.0
Percentage Married						
Men	76.2%	67.2%	71.6%	61.0%	84.3%	74.2%
Women	85.3	59.2	77.5	57.0	90.7	62.5
Percentage Native-Born	51.5	76.7	17.6	38.0	6.0	8.7
Median Earnings[a] (in thousands)						
Men	$8.5	$15.5	$8.5	$13.0	$10.0	$14.5
Women	$4.6	$12.1	$5.0	$13.0	$6.0	$8.0
Percentage Speaking Spanish at Home	90.9%	73.1%	94.2%	80.1%	96.3%	90.0%

SOURCES: 1970 and 1980 Public Use Microdata Sample files.

[a]Applies only to those in the labor force. Earnings figures reflect actual dollars.
[b]Percentage speaking a language other than English at home.

than their education counterparts of Cuban origin, but there was less age differentiation with respect to similarly educated Central/South Americans and Other Hispanics. Blacks and non-Hispanic whites more clearly resembled Cubans in this respect. In large measure the youthfulness of the college-educated Mexican and Puerto Rican population reflects the impact of numerous programs explicitly designed to increase the number of Hispanics with advanced college degrees during the

TABLE 8.3 *(continued)*

Central/ South American		Other Hispanic		Black		Non-Hispanic White	
Less Than High School Education	4 or More Years College	Less Than High School Education	4 or More Years College	Less Than High School Education	4 or More Years College	Less Than High School Education	4 or More Years College
39.2	36.6	45.2	39.1	46.8	41.3	52.1	42.8
75.7%	78.1%	78.9%	78.7%	79.2%	83.1%	86.3%	86.6%
80.1	63.0	88.8	67.0	86.8	85.6	92.7	82.1
10.0	16.4	57.8	59.0	99.1	97.1	90.4	95.6
$6.0	$10.0	$5.0	$11.2	$4.0	$8.0	$6.5	$12.0
$2.6	$4.6	$1.8	$7.0	$1.6	$6.0	$2.9	$5.9
90.6%	73.7%	99.8%	77.1%	10.9%[b]	13.0%[b]	29.6[b]	21.9%[b]
39.4	37.8	46.9	38.4	41.8	36.7	44.1	39.0
72.8%	72.7%	77.3%	68.3%	69.7%	75.3%	82.2%	84.6%
82.3	61.4	87.7	60.1	79.3	72.2	90.5	76.8
2.9	8.0	68.2	66.1	84.9	72.9	73.6	80.9
$7.0	$19.5	$9.0	$16.4	$8.7	$16.0	$12.0	$22.6
5.0	$8.6	$4.7	$11.4	$5.0	$12.4	$5.9	$11.0
97.6%	86.9%	70.5%	35.3%	4.1%[b]	11.5%[b]	21.1%[b]	12.6%[b]

1970s,[6] but it also reflects the younger age structure of these populations compared with others (see Chapter 3). In the main Cubans and Central/South Americans tended not to qualify for many of these higher education programs because demonstrated economic need was a criterion for eligibility.

[6]The Ford Foundation doctoral fellowship program for Mexican Americans and Puerto Ricans was one of the best known and well funded of these programs. Parallel programs existed for blacks and Native Americans. Although the original program officially ended in 1981, the Ford Foundation and others continue to promote higher education programs for minority scholars under other auspices. Unlike the programs of the 1970s, whose focus was on predoctoral programs, those of the 1980s are geared more toward postdoctoral training and support.

Between 63 and 82 percent of all college-educated Hispanics were married in 1970, with Puerto Ricans at the lower end of this range and Cubans at the upper end. As a result of rising age at marriage, by 1980 the proportion married among those having completed four years of college was somewhat lower than had been true 10 years earlier, ranging from 57 percent for Puerto Ricans to 74 percent for Cubans. In both years college-educated women were less likely to be married than their race and national origin male counterparts.

In contrast to the modest age and marriage differentials between the population segments of each national origin group with less than 12 years of completed schooling versus those with college degrees, there exist pronounced differences in nativity composition, median earnings, and Spanish retention between these two education groups. In general, immigrants constituted smaller shares of the college-educated population than the segment with less than high school. These differences, however, varied according to national origin and time period. For example, in 1980, when 8.5 percent of Puerto Ricans aged 25 and over were mainland-born, 38 percent of those with four or more years of postsecondary schooling were mainland-born. For Cubans 9 percent of those aged 25 and over with four or more years of college training were native-born, twice the share of native-born among those aged 25 and over in 1980 (4.8 percent). That immigrants were less well represented among the college-educated than among the general population aged 25 and over can be traced largely to the less selective character of immigration since 1965 compared with earlier periods and the greater difficulties in the schools experienced by the foreign-born.[7] Thus, for all groups immigrants were more highly represented among the least educated. In considering the educational differences by nativity among the various national origin groups, we must keep in mind the relative youthfulness of the second generation of the Puerto Rican population, but especially the Cuban and Central/South American population, as documented in Chapter 3. As the second generation populations reach adulthood, their educational attainment will modify the overall profile reported in Table 8.3.

Two other noteworthy features about the college-educated Hispanic population are the variations in median earnings and language characteristics of the major national origin groups. With respect to earnings, those with college degrees earned roughly 1.5 to 2 times as much as their national origin and gender counterparts, but there was much greater variation among men than among women in both time periods.

[7]Candace Nelson, "Hispanic Educational Attainment: An Ethnic Issue?" Master's thesis, University of Wisconsin–Madison, 1984.

In 1970 the median earnings[8] for Hispanic men who completed four or more years of post-secondary schooling ranged from $9,200 (Cuban men) to $11,200 (Other Hispanic men), with Mexican and Central/South American men reporting median earnings of approximately $10,000 in 1970. As such, the 1970 median earnings of Hispanic men were intermediate to those of black and non-Hispanic men, whose respective medians were $8,000 and $12,000. That Cuban college-educated men did not exhibit the highest median earnings in 1970 can be explained partly by the recency of their arrival and the adjustment costs involved in recertifying foreign degrees. This situation, however, changed during the 1970s.

By 1980 not only had the median earnings of college-educated Hispanic men diverged, but the rank ordering of the groups also had changed. Whereas the lowest median earnings among the college-educated corresponded to Cubans in 1970, by 1980 Puerto Rican men reported the lowest median earnings. Central/South American and Other Hispanic men received the highest median earnings, at $19,500 and $16,400, respectively, but both earned less than non-Hispanic white men, whose 1980 median exceeded $22,000. Also, while black men reported the lowest median earnings in 1970, 10 years later their median topped that of Mexican, Puerto Rican, and even Cuban men.[9]

With the exception of Puerto Rican college-educated women, the median earnings of women exhibited less dispersion within education groups. In both time periods the highest median earnings corresponded to college-educated Puerto Rican women. The reasons for these differentials will be discussed in some detail in the following two chapters. For the present let it suffice that the median earnings are determined by the fluctuating availability of college-educated Hispanics (supply factors) and the changing job configurations in the diverse labor markets in which the various national origin groups are concentrated (demand factors). Since college-educated Puerto Rican women are relatively scarce, and they tend to receive their degrees after several years of job experience, they command higher wages than recent college graduates with no job experience.

[8]Earnings comparisons are based on current (actual) dollars because our comparisons emphasize within-year nationality differences.
[9]That the median earnings for Cuban college-educated men were below those of most groups, including black and Mexican men, results from the different levels of skewness of the earnings distributions of college-educated men, depending on race or national origin. Were we to report means, the rank ordering of the groups would conform to the results reported in chapter 10. Also responsible for these differences is the educational composition of these groups: There are relatively fewer college-educated men of Mexican and Puerto Rican origin than of Cuban and Central/South American origin, and consequently their earnings may be due to disproportionately higher supply shortages.

It is interesting that all groups exhibit a high level of Spanish retention in the home, but these are uniformly lower for those with college degrees. Because the language variables in the 1970 and 1980 censuses are not comparable, we cannot document changes in the rates of Spanish retention among the college-educated or high school dropouts. Rates of Spanish retention among the college-educated Hispanic population are impressive by any standards, particularly among groups like Mexicans, whose generational depth and diversity would lead one to predict low rates of Spanish use in the home, and Puerto Ricans, who are exposed to English throughout their schooling careers. Apparently, college education does not ensure a rapid and total loss of mother tongue for Hispanics, but the recency and as yet limited number of college-educated Hispanics make this interpretation tentative and somewhat premature.

In summary, while their educational standing has improved steadily over the past two decades, the adult Hispanic population, and adults of Mexican and Puerto Rican origin in particular, continues to lag far behind the non-Hispanic white population in terms of median school completed, the proportion of adults with high school diplomas, and the proportion with post-secondary school training. Besides national origin, nativity persists as a major axis of educational differentiation, but this situation may vary according to changes in the selectivity of migrants and the experience of the second generation of Puerto Ricans, Cubans, and Central/South Americans in the schools. While less salient, gender differentiation in adult educational outcomes persists. Women's achievements remain below those of men, and the completed schooling levels of the foreign-born remain below those of their native-born counterparts. Prospects for improving the educational condition of Hispanics greatly depend on the educational outcomes of those currently enrolled, particularly the youth and young adults. The following section provides some perspective on these possibilities.

School Enrollment Patterns and Differentials

Prospects for improving the educational condition of the Hispanic population depend directly on the current enrollment status of school-age children and young adults. Data from the decennial censuses are very telling on this matter, for they point to signs of hope and signs of stress. On a positive note a comparison of age-specific enrollment and completion rates by education levels shows a promising improvement in school attendance rates for all national origin and age groups.[10] On a less optimistic note 1980 census data suggest that the proportion of individuals lacking high school diplomas may decline very slowly because of age-grade delays which often result in leaving school before receiving the diploma. Table 8.4 provides some information about 1980 Hispanic enrollment patterns according to school levels.

School enrollment statuses reported in Table 8.4 were determined on the basis of the highest grade attended for each age and national origin group.[11] Because the cells in each of the age by education frames sum to 100 percent, we can trace both group differences in age-grade delay and age-specific dropout rates by school levels and the age progression of school completion within levels. For example, among Mexicans who had at least attended high school, the share of completers increases from 28 percent among those aged 17 to 19 to 41 percent among those aged 20 to 24 and declines to roughly 37 percent thereafter, reflecting the elevated high school dropout rates of earlier cohorts. High dropout rates in the past are further illustrated by the proportion among those aged 20 and over who failed to complete elementary school or high school.

Failure to complete elementary school is rare for Cubans, Central/South Americans, and Other Hispanics; and while high school noncompletion is more frequent, it was less pervasive than among Mexicans and Puerto Ricans. However, the proportion of Mexicans and Puerto Ricans aged 14 to 34 who had not completed elementary school in 1980 was disturbingly high, reaching 7 to 9 percent among those aged 30 to 34, and 5 to 7 percent among those aged 25 to 29.

Age-specific enrollment rates show the pervasiveness of age-grade delay among the Hispanic population. Because of the close association between age-grade delay and eventual noncompletion, these rates provide some idea about the likelihood that high dropout rates will persist in the future. For example, Mexicans and Puerto Ricans aged 14 to 16 were 4 to 5 percent more likely to be enrolled in elementary school than their Cuban, Central/South American, and Other Hispanic age-mates. That the psychological and social stigma of age-grade delay often results

---

[10]These tabulations are available from the authors but were omitted in the interest of brevity.

[11]We considered computing Table 8.4 separately for the native- and foreign-born because the processes of dropping out might be quite different in both places, with quite different policy implications. Because this would have greatly increased the number of cells with less than 20 observations, we opted not to do so. However, our multivariate analyses allow us to comment on the significance of nativity for high school noncompletion.

TABLE 8.4

School Enrollment Status of the Hispanic Population Aged 14–34
by National Origin, Education Level, and Age Group: 1980

Age and Enrollment Status	Mexican			Puerto Rican			Cuban		
	Elementary or Less	High School	College	Elementary or Less	High School	College	Elementary or Less	High School	College
14–16 Years									
Currently Enrolled	24.2	66.6	—[a]	25.5	66.9	—[a]	19.2	77.2	—[a]
Not Enrolled									
Completed	2.8	2.3	—	1.6	2.0	—	0.7	1.4	—
Not Completed	1.8	2.3	—	1.3	2.7	—	0.4	1.1	—
17–19 Years									
Current Enrolled	1.2	42.3	11.9	1.1	39.0	12.4	0.7	42.5	28.2
Not Enrolled									
Completed	10.0	27.8	1.0	3.4	25.7	0.7	1.2	18.3	1.4
Not Completed	3.7	1.3	0.9	2.5	14.7	0.6	0.5	6.2	0.8
20–24 Years									
Currently Enrolled	0.2	1.5	12.7	0.3	2.1	14.5	0.1	1.8	38.3
Not Enrolled									
Completed	15.5	41.4	8.7	5.9	44.1	10.0	2.6	36.0	5.1
Not Completed	5.5	11.0	3.5	3.5	15.1	4.6	1.0	7.0	8.2
25–29 Years									
Currently Enrolled	0.2	0.9	7.0	0.2	1.1	8.5	0.1	1.0	14.1
Not Enrolled									
Completed	19.7	37.3	14.4	9.3	41.8	16.4	4.1	33.8	31.7
Not Completed	7.3	8.7	4.5	4.7	12.5	5.4	1.5	4.8	8.9
30–34 Years									
Currently Enrolled	0.3	0.6	5.4	0.5	1.0	5.3	0.1	0.5	8.4
Not Enrolled									
Completed	22.8	34.5	14.9	15.0	43.6	13.1	8.1	35.3	33.1
Not Completed	9.2	7.5	4.8	7.4	9.8	4.3	2.3	3.8	8.3

SOURCE: 1980 Public Use Microdata Sample file.

NOTE: Persons who have never attended school are included in the cells "Not Completed Elementary or Less."

[a]Not reported; fewer than 20 cases.

in dropping out altogether is most dramatically illustrated by Puerto Ricans, whose share of high school dropouts reached 15 percent in 1980 among those aged 17 to 19 and 20 to 24. This is in addition to the 2 to 3 percent who did not complete elementary school. Mexicans appear to drop out of high school somewhat later than Puerto Ricans, thus a higher proportion eventually complete secondary programs. Yet, the 11 percent of Mexicans aged 20 to 34 in 1980 who had not completed high school remains disappointingly high.

Evidence of age-grade delay, while less dramatic for the remaining national origin groups, is nonetheless present. That between 2 to 3 percent of all Cubans and Central/South Americans aged 20 to 24 were

TABLE 8.4 *(continued)*

Central/ South American			Other Hispanic			Black			Non-Hispanic White		
Elementary or Less	High School	College	Elementary or Less	High School	College	Elementary or Less	High School	College	Elementary or Less	High School	College
19.2	60.6	—[a]	20.4	74.2	—[a]	18.1	78.4	0.1	23.3	72.2	0.1
1.0	1.3	—	0.9	1.9	—	0.5	1.1	—[a]	0.6	1.7	—[a]
0.6	17.3	—	0.6	2.1	—	0.5	1.3	—	0.7	1.4	—
1.1	44.3	22.7	0.6	38.2	20.1	1.0	46.4	20.9	—	42.1	19.6
4.4	18.0	1.1	2.2	26.5	1.0	0.6	20.3	0.6	0.7	26.7	1.4
1.5	6.0	0.9	1.4	8.8	1.1	1.4	8.6	0.2	0.5	8.4	0.7
0.3	2.8	28.4	0.1	1.2	21.7	—	2.2	18.4	0.1	0.7	21.9
11.1	31.9	11.6	4.3	43.1	13.7	1.1	47.5	13.9	1.3	43.7	19.4
3.4	5.8	4.6	2.1	8.3	5.5	2.0	10.1	4.9	1.2	5.9	5.8
0.3	1.1	13.6	0.2	0.6	11.3	—	1.3	13.7	—	0.1	9.2
14.8	34.4	19.5	6.1	40.0	25.0	3.4	43.9	20.1	3.4	43.3	31.8
4.7	5.3	6.2	3.0	6.8	7.0	2.5	9.1	6.1	0.9	4.7	6.6
0.3	1.0	9.7	0.1	0.6	7.4	0.2	1.2	9.5	—	—	7.5
16.8	36.1	22.1	7.8	39.3	28.5	4.5	45.3	25.4	2.7	34.2	43.0
5.4	4.2	4.5	3.6	5.8	6.8	0.9	7.4	5.5	0.6	4.5	7.5

enrolled in high schools (a clear indicator of grade delay) is less trouble-some than statistics showing that 6 to 7 percent of their age-mates dropped out altogether before completing a secondary curriculum. This is in addition to the 6 percent of those aged 17 to 19 who failed to complete secondary school. Again, these age-specific dropout rates are not as dramatic as those characterizing Mexicans and Puerto Ricans, but, when cumulated over the age categories, translate into low average schooling levels for all groups, as shown in the previous section of this chapter.

Our examination of gender and nativity differentials in enrollment patterns showed these to be relatively unimportant at young ages, that is, prior to age 14, but thereafter the higher toll of age-grade delay and noncompletion was greater for young men and the foreign-born. Gender and nativity appear to operate differently according to age and schooling levels. For example, auxiliary tabulations showed that Hispanic women aged 17 to 19 were more likely than their male age-mates to be enrolled in college; however, at older ages (20–24 and 25–29), the higher college enrollment rates corresponded to young men. Partly this reflects the differential effect of marriage on men's and women's conditional decisions about higher education, but these differences may be narrowing over time.

Age differences in enrollment and completion rates also depend heavily on family background and current living arrangements, as well as marital status of young adults. Table 8.5 provides insight into the importance of living arrangements in shaping decisions to remain in school or leave. For example, while virtually all youth under the legal age to quit school were enrolled in 1980, enrollment rates were between 3 and 5 percent higher among those who were living with their parents.[12] Among those enrolled in school and living with their parents, the majority (60 to 80 percent) were of mandatory school age. Obversely, most youth not enrolled in school are over age 18 and considerably more

TABLE 8.5

School Enrollment Status of Hispanic Youth Aged 5–25
by National Origin, Living Arrangements, and Age Group: 1980
(percentage enrolled in school)

Living Arrangements and Age Group	Mexican	Puerto Rican	Cuban	Central/South American	Other Hispanic
Living with Parents					
5–15 Years	95.0%	96.1%	97.4%	95.9%	96.5%
16–18 Years	78.0	76.5	86.8	84.1	81.5
19–25 Years	27.0	29.1	48.6	40.4	32.2
Living with Relatives					
5–15 Years	90.7	91.4	94.4	93.7	92.6
16–18 Years	40.6	62.2	66.1	71.9	55.0
19–25 Years	11.1	16.7	35.7	32.2	17.2
Living Independently					
5–15 Years[a]	—	—	—	—	—
16–18 Years	28.5	31.7	52.4	67.0	55.2
19–25 Years	10.3	14.2	26.3	27.0	21.8

SOURCE: 1980 Public Use Microdata Sample A (5%) file.

[a]Results are misleading owing to small sample sizes and skew within the age category.

[12]This includes individuals with one or both natural parents, but we excluded a handful of cases which were likely cases of adoption where the child's national origin was different from that of either parent. Since the number of affected cases was very small (4 to 5 percent), these deletions did not affect our tabulations or inferences in any appreciable manner. See Appendix C for further discussion of this issue.

likely to be living independently or with other relatives. We note with interest, however, that Cubans and Central/South Americans tend to stay in school longer and to live at home longer. Apparently, Cuban and other Latin American parents are more successful in holding their youth in school once they reach the age when they can legally drop out. A large part of the explanation for this phenomenon resides in their generally higher economic status.

The toll on educational achievement of not living with parents is best illustrated by the significantly lowered proportions of school-age young adults who were not enrolled in school. For example, whereas between 77 and 87 percent of all 16-to-18-year-olds living with their parents were enrolled in school, only between 41 and 72 percent of their age-mates residing with other relatives were enrolled in school in 1980. Compared with those living independently, Hispanic youth who resided with relatives in 1980 exhibited high enrollment levels. Although census data do not provide information about the reasons for not living with parents, it is conceivable that a large share of those living with relatives choose to do so in order to cut costs while attending college. This is more likely to be the case among Cubans and Central/South Americans, whose enrollment rates are 2 to 3 times higher than their age-mates (19 to 25) of other national origins.

In sum, for all national origin groups and at all ages the probability that Hispanic youth were enrolled in school was highest among those living with parents and lowest among those living independently. The differential school enrollment rate associated with living arrangements was most pronounced for the 16-to-18-year-olds, ranging from 57 to 68 percent lower among those living independently compared with those living with parents, and from 13 to 28 percent lower among those living with relatives compared with those residing with their parents. A similar pattern describes for the 19-to-25-year-olds, except that the proportions enrolled were lower for each age category and, consequently, the differentials between those living with parents and with relatives were smaller.

In discussing the differential enrollment rates associated with the three types of living arrangements reported in Table 8.5, we must acknowledge the real possibility that poor performance in school determines whether Hispanic youth live independently or with their parents. This is particularly relevant in situations where early marriage may contribute to age-grade delay and render high school completion difficult, if not virtually impossible. We examine this question in some detail in the analysis of the correlates and determinants of high school non-completion.

Table 8.6 highlights selected characteristics of the sample according to school status and living arrangements. As the most recent arrivals to this country, Cubans and Central/South Americans have the highest percentage foreign-born. For all five Hispanic groups, however, immigrants were less likely to be enrolled in school than their native-born counterparts. Partly this reflects the inverse relationship between foreign birth and probability of staying in school, but it largely captures differences in age composition. The nonenrolled population exhibited a slightly greater tendency to speak Spanish in the home, yet in Table 8.6 one observes great variation in the maintenance of Spanish at home among the national origin groups. Neither is the maintenance of Spanish strictly correlated with foreign birth and immigration. Spanish-speaking homes are only slightly less prevalent among Puerto Ricans compared with Cubans and Central/South Americans, even though the percentage of island-born Puerto Ricans is half that of Cubans.

That employment prospects challenge the holding power of school curricula is suggested by the higher participation rates among individuals not enrolled in school. Although labor market entry is limited by age requirements, the data in Table 8.6 show labor force participation of Hispanic youth to vary systematically by living arrangements, school status, and national origin. In general Cuban youth participated in the labor force at a higher rate than all other groups, irrespective of enrollment status, but the magnitude of the differentials depends on living arrangements. Rates of nonenrolled youth were higher than those of the student population, and the rates of young adults who lived independently were higher than those of youth living with their parents. Puerto Rican youth had the lowest percentages of labor force participants in 1980 and Cubans the highest, attesting that the patterns of labor force participation for Hispanic adults become established early in the socioeconomic life cycle.

This strictly descriptive overview of school enrollment patterns among Hispanic youth and young adults provides baseline information about the factors leading to low educational achievement among adults. While there are reasons to worry about the 1980 enrollment patterns of Hispanic youth, on balance there has been an improvement over time in the probability of completing a school level among those who enter it. However, as we have emphasized throughout, evidence of grade delay and high rates of high school (or elementary school) noncompletion are troublesome and warrant further investigation of their underlying causes. Because a clear understanding of the process that generates these unacceptably high rates of noncompletion and delay is an adjunct to informed policy, our attention now shifts to a closer examination of the correlates of school grade delay and noncompletion rates. First, we pre-

TABLE 8.6
Selected Characteristics of Hispanic Youth Aged 5–25 by National Origin, School Enrollment Status, and Living Arrangements: 1980

Living Arrangements	Mexican		Puerto Rican[a]		Cuban		Central/South American		Other Hispanic	
	Enrolled	Not Enrolled	Enrolled	Not Enrolled	Enrolled	Not Enrolled	Enrolled	Not Enrolled	Enrolled	Not Enrolled
Living with Parents										
Percentage Married	1.8%	14.3%	1.8%	11.1%	1.9%	15.8%	2.2%	16.2%	1.4%	11.0%
Percentage Foreign-Born	15.9	22.1	23.0	31.8	47.0	80.5	57.8	83.7	8.0	11.2
Percentage Speak Spanish at Home	67.6	74.1	81.0	85.3	89.0	92.6	87.9	94.7	40.3	43.5
Percentage in Labor Force[b]	39.4	73.7	25.6	59.1	49.9	79.3	37.5	74.2	43.6	74.7
Living with Other Relatives										
Percentage Married	11.8	34.1	9.2	28.6	12.4	41.4	9.2	30.8	9.4	32.9
Percentage Foreign-Born	29.9	57.2	33.3	54.3	54.1	80.9	83.4	96.3	17.9	31.0
Percentage Speak Spanish at Home	71.9	86.9	88.0	89.2	89.3	91.6	96.1	96.3	54.2	63.0
Percentage in Labor Force[b]	43.4	76.0	34.0	61.1	55.6	67.0	42.1	72.3	43.4	71.1
Living Independently										
Percentage Married	36.4	72.9	33.4	62.6	38.2	77.6	30.1	66.2	24.9	66.0
Percentage Foreign-Born	20.5	35.4	42.3	47.0	68.6	80.0	82.1	92.1	18.0	17.9
Percentage Speak Spanish at Home	66.2	75.6	77.1	87.7	80.1	86.5	88.0	93.9	40.6	48.3
Percentage in Labor Force[b]	56.3	72.6	43.2	46.7	57.0	81.2	38.2	67.7	56.0	75.8

SOURCE: 1980 Public Use Microdata Sample A (5%) file.

[a]Foreign-born refers to island-born.
[b]Refers to individuals aged 16–25.

255

sent a theoretical framework about the process of educational attainment, modifying the general framework to include those factors that are especially pertinent to Hispanics.

Hispanic Youth and Educational Underachievement: Issues and Evidence

Historically, the public school system implicitly or explicitly has assumed the challenges of equitably integrating foreign language students, minorities, and recent immigrants into American society. More recently, this mission has included the difficult goal of protecting cultural differences while ensuring that educational achievements will not be sacrificed. Nowhere is this philosophy better illustrated than in the often thwarted attempts to develop bilingual/bicultural and English as a Second Language (ESL) instructional programs in primary, middle, and secondary schools. Although these efforts to promote cultural pluralism have met with limited success, some evidence indicates that bilingual programs can improve the educational performance of children whose native language is not English. In the words of Fligstein and Fernandez:[13]

> Bilingual education programs and their evaluation techniques differ radically from situation to situation. That they are effective in some situations and not in others says more about the specific program than about the general idea of providing aid to students who are making a transition from one language to another. The important point is that effective programs *do* make a difference in the English and math proficiency of students, while poorly conceived and executed programs do not. [Emphasis added.]

Despite the broad and diffuse mission of the schools, the challenge of promoting equality of opportunity while preserving cultural pluralism has been continuously renewed and reformulated as the racial and ethnic composition of the school-age population and the political climate changed. For no other group has the mission of the schools taken on such degrees of complexity as with the Hispanic population in the United States. That Hispanic ethnicity poses a special challenge to the American educational system is reinforced by achievement statistics showing poor performance and critically high dropout rates. The loom-

---

[13]Neil Fligstein and Roberto M. Fernandez, "Hispanics and Education," in Pastora San Juan Cafferty and William C. McCready, eds., *Hispanics in the United States: A New Social Agenda* (New Brunswick: Transition Books, 1985), p. 125.

ing research question is: In what form must the schools incorporate variables of ethnicity, language, and immigration history into their curricula and programs to satisfy both the mandate of providing equal educational opportunity and that of improving Hispanics' school performance? To answer this question we must first establish whether these factors significantly influence educational outcomes.

The Educational Dilemma

We view the persistingly low educational attainment of Hispanic youth in U.S. schools as problematic, especially during a period when the educational attainments of the total population are improving. Test scores of Hispanic youth in reading, vocabulary, and mathematics remain consistently lower than those of non-Hispanic whites, and these differentials exist for all groups. In most cases they are only slightly higher than blacks' scores.[14] The far-reaching importance of test scores is that from the early stages of the formal educational process they are used to place students in curriculum tracks, shape teachers' attitudes toward students, determine the type of counseling they receive, and either open or close doors to higher education.

A more critical indication of low achievement is the high incidence of school delay. As a result of poor performance many Hispanic students are held back one grade or more and consequently find themselves older than the modal age for their grade. Hispanic rates of school delay are significantly higher than those of non-Hispanic whites and blacks.[15] Delay generally reflects poor grades and low achievement scores, but may also indicate discriminatory policies against minority students. Practically, experiences of delay imply spending more time and energy to complete school which, because of discouragement and the competing labor market alternative, the affected students are often unable or unwilling to do. The key significance of high delay rates lies in the fact that delay precedes dropping out of school altogether.

Statistics on dropout rates most pointedly illustrate the dimensions of the crisis in Hispanic education. For example, ASPIRA's[16] latest re-

[14]François Nielsen and Roberto Fernandez, "Achievement of Hispanic Students in American High Schools: Background Characteristics and Achievement," unpublished report, National Opinion Research Center, 1981; Annegret Harneschfeger and David E. Wiley, "Hispanic Americans: High School Learning and What Then?" *Policy Studies in Education* (Evanston, IL: Northwestern University, 1981).

[15]Nielsen and Fernandez, "Achievement of Hispanic Students"; Nelson, "Hispanic Educational Attainment."

[16]ASPIRA, "Racial and Ethnic High School Dropout Rates in New York City: A Summary Report, 1983" (New York: ASPIRA of New York, 1983).

257

port on racial and ethnic students in New York City estimated the Hispanic dropout rate at 80 percent, slightly higher than the black rate of 72 percent and considerably above the non-Hispanic white rate of 50 percent. Obviously, these high dropout rates reflect on the particular situation of the New York City school system and its special problems, but this fact does not detract from their significance.

The New York City problem is repeated in other large urban areas as well. In a recent testimony to the National Commission on Secondary Schooling for Hispanics, Charles Kyle reported "that more than one-half of all Hispanic youth who enter Chicago public high schools do not graduate or receive a high school diploma."[17] His research was modeled after a 1971 study which found that 71 percent of Puerto Rican youth in Chicago left school before completion.[18] Also, the increase in dropout rates in New York City and Chicago illustrate a nationwide trend for Hispanics for whom the rate of noncompletion rose from 30 to 40 percent between 1972 and 1976. During the same period the dropout rate for blacks remained constant, and non-Hispanic whites experienced a decline.[19]

The dimensions and consequences of the Hispanic education crisis take us beyond the confines of school corridors. Their educational experience raises the specter of the intersecting issues of social class, ethnicity, and minority status that get played out in the broader social arena. Yet the studies that examine these issues often refer to the schools as the spawning ground for societal patterns. On this basis, the scope of our remaining analyses is confined to the educational outcomes and the transitions of delay and noncompletion. An examination of the factors influencing educational attainment will invariably bring related socioeconomic issues into sharper focus.

Determinants of Educational Achievement

These well-researched factors influencing educational attainment can be grouped into four general categories: family background, ethnic/cultural, school, and community level variables. Family background refers to traditional indicators of socioeconomic position and is most commonly measured by father's education, mother's education, family in-

---

[17]Charles Kyle, "Testimony to National Commission on Secondary Schooling for Hispanics" (ASPIRA of Illinois, 1984), p. 17.

[18]Isidro Lucas, *Puerto Rican Dropouts in Chicago: Numbers and Motivations*, ERIC ED-035-235 (Washington, DC: Council on Urban Education, 1971).

[19]Kyle, "Testimony."

come, and the occupational status of the father.[20] There is substantial agreement that individuals' social background is the most significant factor determining their educational outcomes.[21] In addition, there is a strong correlation between class position and individual attributes such as IQ scores, motivation, and performance. Along with a family's ability to supplement free public education via extra educational materials (toys, games, books, computers, and so on) and experiences (special courses, trips, summer camp, and so on) are the equally important considerations of the value parents place on education and the psychoemotional support they provide. This economic, emotional, and psychological support gets translated into goals, attitudes, and motivation which are further reinforced within the school.[22]

Ethnicity and culture are of special significance to Hispanics as the fastest-growing minority group in the country, and as speakers of the second most prevalent language. In addition to language, this set of factors includes immigration status and history, as well as cultural orientations that shape behavior, perceptions, learning styles, and interpersonal relations. Of these factors, language is perhaps the most crucial, as Hispanic adults show a high degree of Spanish maintenance even among the native-born.[23] Also there is evidence that non–English-speaking students drop out of school at rates three to four times higher than native English speakers.[24] However, the impact of language on education is complicated by the need to consider the degree of proficiency in both Spanish and English and to assess the context and frequency of their respective use.

The broadest and certainly most difficult variable to address under the rubric of ethnicity is culture. This term is broadly used to explain the poor performance of Hispanics in schools as well as their low visibility in other social institutions. Stereotypically, Hispanics are noncompetitive, not future-oriented, and family-centered, all of which lead to poor performance in school. While the reality of cultural differences cannot be denied, a more perceptive interpretation of their impact would focus on the cultural conflict Hispanics experience as they are forced to become bicultural with respect to learning processes, commu-

[20]Neil Fligstein and Roberto M. Fernandez, "Hispanics' Educational Attainment: Descriptive Analysis and Model of the Process," National Opinion Research Center, 1984.

[21]Christopher Jencks, *Inequality: A Reassessment of the Effect of Family and Schooling in America* (New York: Harper & Row, 1972); Samuel Bowles and Herbert Gintis, *Schooling in Capitalist America: Educational Reform and the Contradictions of Economic Life* (New York: Basic Books, 1976); Robert Mare, "Social Background and School Continuation Decisions," *Journal of the American Statistical Association* 75 (1980):295–305.

[22]Fligstein and Fernandez, "Hispanics' Educational Attainment."

[23]Nelson, "Hispanic Educational Attainment."

[24]Kyle, "Testimony."

nication styles, and human relations in general. Schools rarely accommodate this duality. Rather, as agents of socialization and, specifically, Americanization, they have explicitly been the site of cultural homogenization and dilution of ethnic identity. Cultural denigration, when it occurs and is internalized by Hispanic students, translates into low self-esteem and further contributes to low achievement.

Both language and cultural differences are more pronounced among the foreign-born. This is certainly true for students who are recent immigrants. But the impact of foreign birth is attenuated across generations. While native-born youth whose parents are foreign may experience a stronger ethnic socialization process than their third-generation peers, the fact that their parents were immigrants may actually have a positive impact on their school performance. Those immigrants who bypass the schools for entry into the labor market often transmit their aspirations for a better life to their children, emphasizing the importance of education because of the barriers they often are ill equipped to overcome.

School level factors include those determined by the economic status of the community and its ability to financially support quality education as well as factors related to particular school systems as institutions. The first category embraces teacher-pupil ratios, quality of teachers (under the assumption that higher salaries attract better teachers), and school facilities. The latter consists of the degree of institutionalized discrimination, the racial and ethnic composition of the schools, the presence of Hispanic teachers and administrators, tracking policies, curriculum offerings, and social dynamics within the school (that is, race relations within the student body, level of violence, the prevalence of drug use, and so on). The atmosphere in the schools is particularly important for the quality of the day-to-day experience, as demonstrated by Kyle's respondents who reported fear of gangs as one of two major reasons for dropping out of school.

Despite the importance of school and community environment for the education process as students experience it, our empirical analyses will concentrate on the impact that the first two sets of factors discussed above—the family socioeconomic status and cultural characteristics—have on Hispanic educational outcomes. This decision is determined exclusively by the limitations of the census data, which do not include information on school characteristics or scholastic achievement. Moreover, these first two axes represent the major determinants of educational achievement among the host of possibilities, and together play a significant role in shaping the school and community characteristics as well as the range of opportunities facing individual children.[25]

[25]Fligstein and Fernandez, "Hispanics' Educational Attainment."

Summarily stated, middle- and upper-middle-class families tend to have the educational foundations, resources, and values conducive to positive school performance. The opposite is true for poor families. That Hispanics as a group consistently do worse in school than non-Hispanic whites and often worse than blacks raises questions about whether and how ethnicity structures educational outcomes. Our analyses question whether a strong ethnic identity maintained by students and their families lowers their chances for success in school above and beyond their social background. We address this issue in the analyses that follow.

School Delay

Age-grade delay is critical in the discussion of Hispanic educational attainment because students who have been held back a year have a greater propensity to drop out of school altogether due to the difficulties of being an older student among younger classmates, the embarrassment of being held back, the separation from one's peer group, and the attractions and/or necessity of entering the job market.[26] Because delay rates vary across states and metropolitan areas, several researchers[27] have suggested that the incidence of grade repetition among Hispanics may be the result of discriminatory school system policy rather than a generalized inability of Hispanics to function well in the mainstream owing to language or other socioeconomic handicaps.[28]

While lack of access to school level data prevents us from evaluating this premise, we can examine both traditional socioeconomic and cultural predictors of delay. Table 8.7 shows differential rates of school delay according to individual student characteristics and household level variables.[29] Delay is a measure of age-graded school achievement which could be determined only for individuals enrolled in school at the time of the census. This variable was computed by subtracting respondents' current grade plus six (for the first six years not in school) from their age. Values above zero indicate the number of years delayed. The sample in this analysis is, by necessity, limited to those students living at home and enrolled in school up to and including the 12th grade.[30]

[26]Unfortunately, it is not possible to evaluate the impact that school delay has on the probability of dropping out because the census does not allow us to know if a dropout was delayed before dropping out.

[27]See, for example, T. P. Carter and R. D. Segura, *Mexican Americans in School: A Decade of Change* (New York: College Entrance Examination Board, 1979); ASPIRA.

[28]Nielsen and Fernandez, "Achievement of Hispanic Students."

[29]The complexities of preparing the files for analyses of delay and dropout rates are detailed in Appendix C.

[30]It is not possible with the census data to know the year or age of a student at the point of leaving school. Therefore, we cannot analyze delay for those not currently enrolled.

TABLE 8.7

Rates of Grade Delay Among Enrolled Hispanic Youth by National Origin, Nativity, and Selected Student and Household Correlates of Educational Achievement: 1980

	Mexican		Puerto Rican	
	Native	Foreign	Native	Foreign[a]
AVERAGE DELAY RATE	9.8	19.8	10.9	21.2
STUDENT CHARACTERISTICS				
Sex				
Male	11.4	21.2	13.0	24.9
Female	8.1	18.3	8.8	16.6
Level in School				
Elementary (1–6)	8.5	19.1	9.2	17.8
Junior High (7–8)	13.1	20.0	13.9	28.7
High School (9-12)	13.8	23.5	15.9	23.8
English Ability				
Speaks Only English	7.2	10.6	7.5	13.8
Speaks Very Well	10.6	16.6	11.4	19.7
Speaks Well	12.7	21.5	13.1	21.3
Speaks Poorly	10.1	22.8	10.0	22.9
Speaks Not at All	15.7	27.0	24.1	24.6
PARENTAL AND HOUSEHOLD CHARACTERISTICS				
Household Type				
Both Parents	9.2	19.4	8.6	18.6
Single Parent	12.5	21.9	8.9	22.4
Nativity of Parents				
Both Parents Present				
Both Foreign	8.4	19.0	10.0	20.0
One Foreign	9.3	23.4	5.5	8.3
Both Native	9.0	15.0	4.7	20.0
One Parent Only				
Native	12.5	20.8	8.5	6.0
Foreign	12.4	21.6	15.4	22.6
Household Language Environment				
Spanish Monolingual	17.0	24.2	20.0	26.0
Spanish Dominant	12.0	20.5	13.3	22.6
Bilingual	8.8	13.1	7.6	11.2
English Dominant	7.7	10.7	8.7	11.8
English Monolingual	8.0	—	7.1	—
Below Poverty				
Both Parents Present	13.0	22.0	10.0	20.0
Single Parent	12.4	21.7	15.4	23.5

SOURCE: 1980 Public Use Microdata Sample A (5%) file.

[a]Foreign refers to island-born.
[b]Fewer than 20 cases.

TABLE 8.7 (continued)

Cuban		Central/ South American		Other Hispanic	
Native	Foreign	Native	Foreign	Native	Foreign
5.7	17.9	6.5	22.1	7.2	20.9
6.9	20.7	7.4	26.4	8.6	21.6
4.3	15.1	5.5	17.8	5.8	20.0
5.2	16.1	6.5	15.6	6.0	18.4
8.3	23.2	8.6	22.3	9.6	25.3
7.2	16.4	9.4	29.2	9.6	24.1
5.8	17.7	5.2	19.0	6.9	11.2
5.6	15.8	5.4	14.7	7.1	20.0
5.4	25.1	11.0	28.5	9.7	24.2
5.1	24.6	7.9	30.0	7.1	25.9
16.7	18.2	—[b]	27.8	16.7	—[b]
4.9	17.3	5.6	20.6	6.1	20.8
9.4	21.4	9.4	24.2	10.1	21.9
4.8	17.0	5.2	18.7	4.6	16.8
4.3	25.0	5.3	22.6	6.1	35.4
5.0	—	6.7	—[b]	5.8	—[b]
12.5	—	3.8	—[b]	10.4	—[b]
8.9	21.8	8.9	23.6	6.1	21.1
12.9	20.0	—[b]	25.3	10.0	—[b]
7.1	19.7	7.3	23.7	9.5	27.0
4.1	11.5	5.4	14.2	5.5	22.2
5.8	16.3	3.9	30.3	6.7	16.5
5.3	9.1	5.1	—[b]	5.9	14.8
6.5	20.6	9.0	17.5	9.6	24.3
9.9	23.0	—[b]	—[b]	15.4	—[b]

Therefore, our figures represent rates of delay among those enrolled in school as of 1980. Also, our descriptive tabulations do not exhaust the full set of variables used in the multivariate analyses in the interest of parsimony (see Appendix C).

Foreign-born Hispanic students were at least twice as likely to be delayed as their native-born national counterparts, but Table 8.7 shows that delay rates vary considerably by national origin. For both native- and foreign-born, young men show a higher incidence of delay than young women. As might be expected, the highest rates of delay are found among foreign-born students who speak little or no English. That the most proficient foreign-born students were more likely to be delayed in school suggests the importance of curriculum differences and the disruptive effects of migration per se in determining a student's grade level. Unfortunately, census data do not permit a precise calibration of the timing of immigration with respect to the schooling career, but it is a matter worthy of further exploration.[31]

Substantial differences in rates of delay also emerge for all groups according to household characteristics. Auxiliary tabulations reveal that delay rates for families below poverty and those receiving welfare were generally higher than the average rates for the total population. There is also some evidence of double disadvantages in that foreign-born youth from poor homes were more likely to be delayed in school than native-born youth from poor homes, but the strong effect of poverty on delay is clearly evident by comparing average delay rates of the native-born with those of poor native-born youth. Finally, from the descriptive tabulations it is difficult to say whether the often higher proportions delayed among single-parent families are related to the prevalence of poverty or to the absence of one parent.

Lower delay rates of youth residing in Spanish dominant homes compared with those in Spanish monolingual ones, and again between the former and bilingual homes, emphasize the importance of English for school performance. However, the bilingual household is composed of more English-speaking persons than the Spanish dominant home, and this may reflect higher educational attainment of parents and other siblings, as well as their employment in higher-status jobs that require En-

---

[31]For example, and contrary to expectations, additional tabulations revealed that the most recent immigrants did not have higher rates of delay than earlier arrivals who presumably had more time to adjust to the culture and educational system. One possible explanation is that insufficient time elapsed for delay to appear, especially since the majority of those delayed are held back during the transitional years of junior high. Recent immigrants who are young children in lower elementary grades generally learn languages more easily and make cultural transitions with less frustration. Without information about the availability of bilingual programs in the schools attended by recent arrivals, it is impossible to disentangle the reasons some students succeed while others fail.

glish. That is, given the strong relationship of language use to social background characteristics, the drop in delay rates for individuals from Spanish dominant homes compared with those from bilingual homes may also reflect the correlation between English proficiency and socioeconomic status of the parents. The delay rates for Cubans and Central/ South Americans from bilingual homes are interesting because these fall below the rates for students from homes where English is dominant and provide potential evidence to support claims that bilingualism actually has a positive effect on educational attainment or occupational status during the early career.[32]

Although suggestive, the observed differentials in delay rates in most instances overstate the unique importance of each variable considered because of intercorrelation among the independent variables. Estimating the net effects of ethnic and socioeconomic characteristics on rates of school delay requires a multivariate analysis, which we have computed using logistic regression.[33] The analyses reported in Table 8.8 regress a dichotomous variable—delayed versus not delayed—on a set of independent variables known to influence educational outcomes and a set of cultural indicators that conceivably influence schooling outcomes. The independent variables are dummies created from the categories of the various ethnic and socioeconomic indicators summarized in Appendix C. Exceptions are parental education and household income, which are both continuous. The effects reported represent the increase or decrease in the actual probability of being delayed that is associated with each variable or category. In the case of continuous variables this probability is associated with a one-unit increase; for dummy variables it reflects the impact of membership in the relevant category.[34]

Our analysis of delay has been executed on those youth residing with their parents and enrolled in school up to and including the 12th grade. This selection process eliminates those who are no longer in school but experienced delay when they were enrolled and those who dropped out before completing high school, as well as those who live with relatives or independently. The dropouts who may have been de-

---

[32]Roberto Fernandez and François Nielsen, "Bilingualism and Hispanic Scholastic Achievement: Some Baseline Results," unpublished manuscript, University of North Carolina, 1983; Marta Tienda, "Sex, Ethnicity, and Chicano Status Attainment," *International Migration Review* 16 (1982):435–72.

[33]This technique was employed in place of Ordinary Least Squares Regression because OLS produces biased parameter estimates and violates the heteroskedasticity assumption if the dependent variable is a dichotomy. Logistic analysis corrects this problem and assumes the proper functional form.

[34]The effects are first order partial derivatives, evaluated at the sample mean, P', using the formula: $b_i P' (1 - P')$ where b_i is the respective logit coefficient and P' the sample mean proportion delayed.

TABLE 8.8

Adjusted Effects of Individual and Household Characteristics
on the Probability of School Grade Delay
Among Enrolled Hispanic Youth Aged 5–25

	Mexican	Puerto Rican[a]	Cuban	Central/ South American	Other Hispanic
STUDENT CHARACTERISTICS					
Male	.038*	.064*	.054*	.059*	.031*
Foreign-Born	.082*	.053*	.086*	.124*	.082*
Level Enrolled in School					
Junior High	.018	.059*	.037*	.068*	.042*
High School	.030*	.065*	.003	.113*	.043*
English Ability					
Good English	.016	.006	−.053	.099*	.010
Poor English	.066*	.006	−.043	.105*	.012
No English	.040	.061	−.022	.094*	.072*
HOUSEHOLD CHARACTERISTICS					
Parents' Education	−.018*	−.011*	−.011*	−.006*	−.008*
Household Income	−.001*	.000	.000	−.000	−.000*
Household Language Environment					
Spanish Monolingual	−.013	.028	−.032	−.020	−.041
Spanish Dominant	.000	−.007	−.002	−.009	.000
Bilingual	−.010	−.050	−.037	−.006	−.015
English Dominant	−.024	−.001	−.044	−.037	−.016
Nativity/Headship of Parents					
Both Parents Foreign	−.075*	.067	.064	−.031	−.016
Single Parent Foreign	−.084*	.071	.078	.011	.019
Parents Mixed	−.032	.025	.049	−.085	−.049*
Single Parent Native	.012	.049	.164*	−.062*	.085*
Proportion of Sample Delayed	.133	.143	.110	.155	.084

SOURCE: 1980 Public Use Microdata Sample A (5%) file.

[a]Foreign refers to island-born.

*Significant at $p \leq .05$.

layed prior to leaving school constitute an important component of the delay story, but the absence of confidential information about individuals' educational history in the census makes it impossible to know whether those not enrolled in school at the time of census ever experienced delay and, if so, how much. This group includes disproportionate numbers of those living independently or with relatives for whom information about parental socioeconomic status was unavailable. Our sample does permit an analysis of the effects of individual and household socioeconomic and demographic characteristics on the probability of experiencing delay for those who are still enrolled in school.

Table 8.8 presents the adjusted effects of individual and household characteristics on the event of being held back one or more grades in school. As in the descriptive tabulations, delay probabilities vary according to national origin, but beyond that now-common theme the results contain some interesting twists that differentiate the groups. Briefly, immigrants and males are more likely to be delayed in school, but the effects of foreign birth are most pronounced for Central/South Americans. That the positive effects on delay of foreign birth are weakest among Puerto Ricans concurs with the ambivalence surrounding their immigrant status.

One clear message is that for all groups but Mexicans school delay begins at the junior high level; these processes continue through high school for all but Cubans. Puerto Rican students enrolled in high school were 7 percent more likely to be delayed than their counterparts enrolled in elementary school in 1980, while Mexican high school students experienced a 3 percent increase in the probability of grade retention beyond junior high school. The effect of high school enrollment on the probability of being delayed was negligible for Cubans. Since Cubans experience grade retention in junior high, the lack of significance of high school enrollment on this outcome may indicate that they eventually overcome the circumstances leading to delay.[35] This is not the case among Central/South Americans and Other Hispanics, whose chances of being held back a grade increase over the educational career. By 1980, when they were high school seniors—and assuming they are still enrolled in school—11.3 and 4.3 percent of Central/South American and Other Hispanic origin youth, respectively, had been retained one year or more in a grade.

For Mexican, Puerto Rican, and Central/South American youth English ability was important to school performance when considered separately from family background characteristics, but this was not the case for Cuban youth (these tabulations are not reported). While the inclusion of household variables did not change the effects of gender and nativity of the student on the probability of delay, the impact of language gave way to the strong effect exerted by parental education. This suggests that ethnicity is secondary, but not unrelated, to social background. However, the very strong positive effects of English ability on the age-grade delays

---

[35]An alternative explanation is that delayed Cubans drop out before entering high school, so that the negligible effect for these groups may be an artifact of our having to restrict the sample to enrolled students.

experienced by Central/South Americans point to the need for transitional language programs to facilitate the adjustment of new arrivals.[36]

On balance, these results point to quite diverse educational experiences among Hispanic students. While foreign-born Cubans face greater chances of being delayed, they seem to overcome them in the later stages of their educational career and are not adversely affected by their high levels of Spanish maintenance. Apparently, Spanish maintenance has not blocked their development of English proficiency. Conversely, poor language ability increases the chances of Mexicans, Central/South Americans, and Other Hispanics being held back one or more grades independently of their foreign birth.

Among the constellation of household variables hypothesized to influence the probability of grade retention, parental socioeconomic background measured by education exerted uniformly significant effects for all groups.[37] Exploratory analyses showed household language effects to be mediated through the strong negative impact of parents' education on children's delay rates. Cubans and Puerto Ricans were 1.1 percent less likely and Central/South Americans and Other Hispanics .6 to .8 percent less likely to be delayed in school for every year increase in their parents' education. Delay probabilities for Mexicans dropped almost 2 percent for each year increment in parental schooling. The importance of parental education cannot be overstated. Although the available data cannot completely confirm it, this variable should be viewed as a proxy

[36]The language results for Cubans and Puerto Ricans, however, differ in important ways. None of the language categories attained statistical significance, which indicates either that language has not been a barrier to Cubans' educational outcomes or that Cubans have little variance in English ability. The fact that foreign-born Cubans show a much higher probability of being delayed than Puerto Ricans suggests that Cubans may have experienced delay at their time of entry to this country, at which point their lack of English warranted such action. Thus, the impact of language in the Cuban case is mediated through their foreign birth, a situation not replicated by the more recent Central/South American arrivals. However, we stress the tentative nature of this suggested explanation for the strong impact of foreign birth on Cuban delay. To understand fully this effect would require including an "age at entry into the United States" variable in the equation predicting delay. This is difficult to estimate because response categories on the "year of immigration" variable cover five-year periods.

[37]The parental ethnicity item that measures the degree of ethnic identity in the household unfortunately cannot be used in these analyses due to extreme linear dependency with the headship/nativity variable. Because sample selection criteria result in all single parents having a Spanish origin that matches that of their child, complications arose in separating out headship, nativity, and ethnic identity. There was little variation, with single parents tending to be both homogeneous in ethnic identity (Spanish origin) and foreign. Combining single mothers and fathers into one single-parent category did not correct the problem of entering "empty" cell dummy variables into equations. Forced to choose between nativity and ethnic origin, we chose the former on the assumption that nativity would exert greater effects on educational outcomes than self-reported Spanish origin. This decision was based on numerous exploratory analyses which showed this to be the case.

for a host of socioeconomic indicators that could not be included in the model, such as labor force participation, occupational status, and class background.

The finding that household language environment is unrelated to school delay has important implications for the discussion of ethnicity, assimilation, and education. Contrary to popular belief, these results show that home bilingualism did not hinder students' school performance and challenge conclusions that "cultural disadvantages" fostered at home lie at the root of Hispanic students' educational problems. Although our data do not demonstrate a negative effect of home bilingualism on school delay, other studies have shown that if a child has solid English skills, a home bilingual environment can actually be an asset.[38] Our results are consistent with this interpretation to the extent that when language does contribute to delay, it is the individual English ability of the student rather than the home language that matters.

The other interesting, though less striking, result deserving comment is the effect on delay probabilities associated with having foreign-born parents. Only for Mexicans and Other Hispanics is this factor statistically significant, after controlling for the child's birthplace, although for Puerto Ricans this variable borders on the margin of significance. The negative probability means, of course, that Mexican and Other Hispanic students with foreign-born parents were, respectively, 8 and 5 percent *less* likely to be delayed a grade. Although not significant, the opposite holds for Puerto Rican students; those whose parents were born on the island were *more* likely to be delayed. Yet a third pattern arose, with Central/South Americans versus Cubans and Other Hispanic youth with native-born single parents, for whom this circumstance produced opposite effects on probabilities of grade delay. Similar effects in either direction do not appear for Mexicans and Puerto Ricans residing with a single, native-born parent. These results force us to recognize that native and foreign birth has different meanings for the differing Hispanic groups.

Even though we treat island-born Puerto Ricans as if they were "foreign," their immigration to the mainland cannot be equated with the Mexican movement across the border. This constitutes a significant point of difference between otherwise similar social classes. Mexicans experience greater risk with the decision to immigrate. Foreign-born parents who struggle with marginal jobs in the minority labor market pass their aspirations for success on to their children. The negative impact on delay rates exerted by Mexican immigrant parents might be ex-

[38]David Lopez, "The Social Consequences of Chicano Home/School Bilingualism," *Social Problems* 24 (1976):234–46; Tienda, "Sex, Ethnicity."

plained as a compensatory effect to overcome the strong handicaps with which they enter this country.

In contrast, Puerto Ricans are born as citizens of the United States and have the freedom of movement between the mainland and the island. Conceivably, a move to the mainland has different meaning than a move across international boundaries. Island-born Puerto Ricans are residents of an underdeveloped commonwealth, yet citizens of the wealthiest nation in the world. They are separate, unequal, and not in control of their resources. Their extreme marginality on both the island and mainland reduces the significance of the foreign-native distinction. Coupled with different motivational factors surrounding the decision to move to the mainland, it also helps to explain why foreign-born Puerto Rican parents increase a student's chances of being delayed.

The foregoing analysis has demonstrated the differential importance of cultural and social factors in determining grade delay probabilities among Hispanics. We also found that language effects on delay rates get mediated through parents' education, which lends strong support to the hypothesis that social class is a more important predictor of educational outcomes than is cultural background. Below we show that similar factors influence the probability of dropping out of high school.

School Dropouts

Completing high school is the most important transition in the formal schooling process, as a high school diploma is now a minimum credential for job entry, even at the lowest levels. Since school delay often leads to dropping out, the next logical step in our analysis of Hispanic youth entails comparisons of school dropouts across national origin groups. For the descriptive analysis all those who did not complete high school are included in our sample. However, in the multivariate analysis we were unable to examine differentials according to parental characteristics as was done for delay rates because this information is not available for over half the dropouts, many of whom live independently or with other relatives. Dropout rates presented in Table 8.9 are calculated on the entire population of those aged 18 to 25 in our sample of Hispanics, irrespective of living arrangements.

Differentials in average dropout rates clearly distinguish the foreign- from the native-born and Mexicans and Puerto Ricans from the other three origin groups. The highest rates of noncompletion correspond to foreign-born Mexicans and Puerto Ricans. Mexican origin youth born abroad were twice as likely as their native-born counterparts to drop out of school—60 and 30 percent, respectively. Puerto Rican noncompletion rates in 1980 are equally striking, 32 and 47 percent for those born on the U.S. mainland and the island of Puerto Rico, respectively. Cuban high school dropout rates fell below those of the foreign-born Central/South Americans and Other Hispanics, but the native-born among the latter two groups were more likely to have finished high school than Cuban youth born in the United States. Since over 70 percent of Other Hispanic youth were native-born, the low dropout rate represents a significant educational advantage of this group vis-à-vis others, but especially Mexicans and Puerto Ricans.

As expected, individuals with poor English skills dropped out at higher rates than proficient English speakers. For Cubans and Central/South Americans, however, these results were reversed; curiously, the English monolinguals of these origins left school at rates 6 to 7 percent higher than did those who spoke both languages. This most likely reflects sampling variability. For example, the overwhelming majority (73 percent) of foreign-born Cubans reported speaking English very well, but only a handful (2.5 percent) were English monolinguals or spoke English at home (3.2 percent).

The incidence of dropping out was notably lower among youth residing with parents than among those living on their own or with other relatives. Also, in every instance, married youth experienced higher dropout rates, although the differentials varied widely by nativity and national origin. Interestingly, the dropout rates of those living with relatives were in most instances higher than those of individuals living independently. Among native-born Mexicans and Other Hispanics in particular, youth living with relatives were considerably more likely to have dropped out of school. Finally, and as expected, there is a negative relationship between household income and the probability of dropping out of school. With rising household income, the dropout rates decreased in a roughly monotonic way. However, in most cases only the Hispanic youth from the poorest homes dropped out at rates exceeding the average.

Briefly, our descriptive results indicate that foreign birth, poor English skills, early marriage, living independently or with relatives, and poverty are associated with higher rates of high school noncompletion. The extremely high dropout rates for Mexicans and Puerto Ricans command our attention and concern; the sharp differentials between the dropout rates of these two groups and those of Cubans and Central/South Americans prompt us to raise again the question about the role of ethnicity and immigrant status in structuring educational outcomes. Explanations about the increased probability of immigrants dropping out of school are attenuated by the experience of Cubans and Central/South Americans. They have the highest percentages of foreign-born and

TABLE 8.9

School Noncompletion Rates Among Hispanic Origin Youth Aged 18–25
by National Origin, Nativity, and Selected Student and Household Correlates
of Educational Achievement: 1980

	Mexican		Puerto Rican	
	Native	Foreign	Native	Foreign[a]
AVERAGE DROPOUT RATE	30.4	59.4	31.9	47.2
STUDENT CHARACTERISTICS				
Sex				
Male	29.9	59.5	32.7	46.9
Female	30.9	59.2	31.2	47.8
Marital Status				
Ever Married	39.8	67.6	39.5	48.9
Single	23.1	50.7	27.9	45.6
English Ability				
Speaks Only English	25.5	41.1	25.1	25.8
Speaks Very Well	27.8	33.5	31.8	40.0
Speaks Well	42.5	47.4	38.0	48.5
Speaks Poorly	47.8	74.5	42.4	62.0
Speaks Not at All	62.5	83.2	—[b]	68.8
HOUSEHOLD CHARACTERISTICS				
Living Arrangements				
Living with Parents	23.7	40.4	28.0	39.4
Living with Relatives	41.3	68.1	34.3	54.4
Living Independently	35.0	65.2	34.9	49.1
Household Income				
Less than $10,000	44.1	65.7	42.5	56.5
$10,000–$20,000	30.3	62.2	28.7	43.7
$20,000–$30,000	23.0	55.9	23.4	38.5
$30,000–$50,000	22.7	45.1	17.4	34.9
More Than $50,000	15.7	44.7	23.3	—[b]

SOURCE: 1980 Public Use Microdata (5%) file.

[a]Foreign refers to island-born.
[b]Fewer than 20 cases.

the highest rates of Spanish maintenance in the home. Yet these ethnic traits have not deterred them from achieving schooling at levels close to those of whites and far surpassing those of Mexican and Puerto Rican youth. Apparently, their material and social resources, as manifested by income, parental education, and motivation, outweigh the impact of

TABLE 8.9 *(continued)*

Cuban		Central/ South American		Other Hispanic	
Native	Foreign	Native	Foreign	Native	Foreign
11.4	16.1	4.5	18.3	7.3	24.5
12.2	18.9	3.7	17.5	6.9	24.4
10.5	13.2	5.3	19.2	7.7	24.6
18.7	24.2	9.1	24.9	10.8	32.6
8.9	11.8	3.0	14.1	5.5	18.8
14.3	17.4	1.5	10.0	5.0	6.0
9.9	11.5	3.2	3.6	8.1	12.1
6.8	25.2	12.5	14.8	18.2	25.4
—[b]	38.3	—[b]	36.8	17.0	46.9
—[b]	50.5	—[b]	53.2	—[b]	69.8
10.5	13.4	4.0	11.2	5.8	17.8
19.6	16.2	—[b]	25.3	9.1	40.6
11.5	20.0	4.4	21.2	8.4	24.4
17.4	28.4	8.3	20.7	11.0	22.3
18.3	17.2	5.1	21.3	8.8	32.3
9.1	14.7	0.0	13.6	3.7	24.0
6.2	10.3	3.0	13.7	4.7	14.5
1.4	6.8	—[b]	5.2	1.3	—[b]

those cultural traits they have in common with Puerto Ricans and Mexicans.

Our multivariate analysis of dropping out of school was conducted for the population aged 18 and over. This age-selection criterion was chosen in order to analyze the event of dropping out with individuals who have had a chance to complete school. Thus, this sample consists mainly of school completers and dropouts, but also includes 18-year-olds who were about to finish their senior year at the time of the census and a handful of older delayed students who were still enrolled in high school. The analysis was further restricted to the subset of individuals residing with parents at the time of the interview; thus, we excluded the subset of individuals living independently or with relatives.[39] We estimated the same model used in the analysis of delay except to include respondents' marital status as an additional independent variable. This was justified by the more restrictive age criteria used to predict leaving school.

Results reported in Table 8.10 show that gender and nativity and marital status play a role in the story of school completion, but differentially so for the national origin groups. Young men were more likely to drop out than young women. Also foreign-born youth dropped out at a higher rate than native-born youth, although this effect was statistically significant only for Cubans and Other Hispanics. The event of marriage was statistically significant in all cases and exerted a strong positive effect on the probability of being a dropout, but we cannot infer its causality since we do not have information about the timing of the marriage with respect to leaving school, nor whether a pregnancy prompted the decision to leave school. Nonetheless, it is noteworthy that married Mexican and Puerto Rican youth were, respectively, 22 and 27 percent more likely to have dropped out of school than their non-married counterparts. Apparently, the exigencies of married life make it hard to stay in school and harder yet to return after having quit.

For all Hispanic groups except Cubans the self-reported English ability variables significantly influenced the failure to complete school. At lower levels of English proficiency the likelihood of dropping out of school increased. The effects were particularly strong for Central/South Americans. Among them, students who reported speaking English poorly were 33 percent more likely to leave school than those who reported speaking only English, while Spanish monolinguals (no English) were 42 percent more likely to have dropped out, holding constant other factors. As in the analysis of delay, the effects of language for Cuban dropouts followed a pattern similar to the other groups, but the net impact was much weaker and not statistically significant once other factors correlated with dropout status were taken into account.

A second interesting result is the stronger effect that being male has for Puerto Ricans compared with the other four Hispanic groups. Several factors contribute to a possible explanation. First, Puerto Ricans are the most marginal, socially and economically, of all Hispanic groups. Many

---

[39]In the subsample of individuals living with relatives or independently, only the effects of individual variables on the event of dropping out could be tested because parental information was not available.

TABLE 8.10

Adjusted Effects of Individual and Household Characteristics
on the Probability of School Noncompletion
Among Hispanic Youth Aged 18 and Over Living with Parents

	Mexican	Puerto Rican[a]	Cuban	Central/South American	Other Hispanic
INDIVIDUAL CHARACTERISTICS					
Male	.061*	.156*	.102*	.016	.009
Foreign-Born	.053	.056	.056*	.049	.047*
English Ability					
Good English	−.043	−.076	−.026	.175*	.071*
Poor English	.132*	.005	.040	.332*	.117*
No English	.291*	−.340*	.097	.422*	.248*
Ever Married	.218*	.269*	.150*	.088*	.060*
HOUSEHOLD CHARACTERISTICS					
Parents' Education	−.021*	−.026*	−.014*	−.018*	−.005*
Household Income	−.003*	−.002	−.002*	−.000	−.000*
Household Language Environment					
Spanish Monolingual	.092	.670*	.128	.044	.046
Spanish Dominant	−.018	.287	.077	.020	.105*
Bilingual	.036	.267	.077	.009	.061*
English Dominant	−.020	.173	.162	−.056	.042*
Persons Nativity/Headship					
Both Parents Foreign	−.044	−.040	−.085	.046	−.022*
Mixed/Foreign-Native	−.010	.045	.028	.035	.016
Single Parent Foreign	.041	.060	−.043	.088	−.024
Single Parent Native	.064	.290*	.060	.049	−.028
Proportion of Sample					
Dropped Out of School	.272	.316	.129	.168	.101

SOURCE: 1980 Public Use Microdata Sample A (5%) file.

Foreign-born refers to island-born.

Significant at $p \leq .05$.

youth are raised on the streets of urban slums where there is little encouragement to stay in school. However, the more concrete components of our hypothesized explanation reside in the high percentage of Puerto Rican households headed by single women and in widespread poverty. These circumstances lead us to believe that young men drop out of school to contribute to household income. Finally, the magnitude of this effect is also partly due to the selection of those aged 18 to 25.

As in the case of delay, the house language environment in most cases was not a statistically significant determinant of the propensity of Hispanic youth to drop out of school. The notable exceptions are Other

Hispanics and Spanish monolingual Puerto Ricans, and the effects are in the expected direction.[40] That is, Other Hispanics living in households where Spanish was spoken were more likely to leave school before completing, and this probability varied monotonically with the extent of Spanish use.

Our results suggest that ethnic traits contribute to school noncompletion only in conjunction with disadvantaged economic status, as manifested by parents' education and household income. For Cubans foreign birth was the only "ethnic" characteristic which affected the probability of dropping out, but apparently English ability was not a problem for them. For other groups one or more of the ethnic characteristics significantly influenced the probability of having dropped out of high school. That marriage exerts such a strong positive effect on the probability of dropping out of school is disturbing, given the cultural tradition of marrying young. At least this constitutes an area open to intervention, especially if the marriage effect is a disguised effect of teenage pregnancy. Such is not the case with foreign birth and a class structure that finds Mexicans and Puerto Ricans among the most marginal groups in this society.

The effects of household income on the probability of failing to complete school were also significant for most groups. Every $10,000 increment is associated with a 2 to 3 percent drop in the likelihood of Mexican, Puerto Rican, and Central/South American youth dropping out of school and a slightly lower decline for Cubans and Other Hispanics. Income and parental education were among the few significant variables in the multivariate model, thus lending support to the importance of socioeconomic status over ethnicity in predicting educational outcomes. Interestingly, income was not a significant predictor of school delay, which often precedes dropping out. That it emerged here as significant emphasizes the importance of the need for economic resources in ultimately pushing youth out of school.

Summary and Conclusions

Given the high levels of Spanish maintenance among Hispanics, and the obvious difficulties non-English speakers must face in school, the results of this multivariate analysis are somewhat surprising. While

[40]The effects of language on the probability of dropping out for Puerto Ricans is problematic. Although those who reported no English are on the margin of significance, the negative coefficient (suggesting that Spanish monolinguals are less likely to drop out) leads us to suspect high collinearity with the household language environment variable which was created using the English ability item.

foreign birth apparently does increase one's chances of being delayed in school and/or dropping out, the effects of language—both that spoken in the home and individual English ability—are overshadowed by those of family background as measured by household income and parents' education. Also, socioeconomic status is more powerful than headship as evidenced by the fact that in few cases did the circumstances of having single parents, either native or foreign, significantly influence the educational outcomes measured. That ethnicity plays second fiddle to class was foreshadowed by the Cuban experience. In addition, our brief foray into the history of the Hispanic groups in Chapter 1 shows clearly that the form in which ethnicity emerges is strongly related to class position.

These results raise several questions with respect to policy initiatives in the educational arena. Specifically, do they cast significant doubt about the real need for culturally specific policies? Even more critically, is there any way in which educational policy can change the class configuration of this society that finds Puerto Ricans and Mexicans in the position of disadvantaged ethnic minorities? Musing over these questions is the luxury we grant ourselves in the concluding section of this chapter.

Inherent in the findings reported in this chapter is a theme that we elaborated at the outset and have emphasized throughout the monograph: that the diversity among Hispanics is grounded in their different points of origin, immigration history, and class background. This diversity should undermine attempts to develop a single educational policy to serve all Hispanics. Yet, this is precisely what has emerged in the areas of bilingual education, staff training, and desegregation. While we cannot delve into the specifics of this policy history, we do want to comment on its future implications.

Since formal schooling is the key to subsequent employment opportunities and long-term life chances, justice, as defined by equal access to education, is served only when schools develop a culturally sensitive educational environment. Formerly, equal educational opportunity meant supplying minority students with equal facilities, textbooks, and teachers. This conception of the mandate implied the neutrality of culture which was challenged by ethnic groups and subsequently struck down in the courts. In the debate over bilingual education, its advocates reject transitional language training in favor of bicultural maintenance programs that incorporate the students' heritage and language into the school day on a permanent basis. Language skills, reading skills, and positive self-image are among the outcomes that presumably will improve when students have the advantage of a culturally sensitive educational environment.

In suggesting that ethnicity is less important than socioeconomic background in structuring individual educational outcomes, our findings could be used to critique bicultural educational programs as merely symbolic. Additional support is generated by the absence of conclusive evidence as to whether bilingual programs actually help to keep Hispanic students in school. Since cultural and structural assimilation have been the main avenues to overcome class barriers to upward mobility, an obvious school policy implication is to encourage mainstreaming. This would mean support for only those language programs that teach English to native Spanish-speaking students, as opposed to those that encourage both the maintenance of Spanish and the incorporation of Hispanic cultural heritage into the regular curriculum. By showing that the language of the home has little impact on educational outcomes, our results offer no evidence of the need to institutionalize Spanish in the schools beyond its limited use in transitional English training. And certainly desegregation efforts that disperse Hispanic students from minority schools could only benefit the mainstreaming goal and enhance student progress toward assimilation. Yet, a narrow interpretation of mainstreaming seems too harsh in that the assumption of an equally accessible educational system can be challenged. The pervasive educational underachievement of Mexicans and Puerto Ricans challenges this interpretation and suggests that access depends on both class and national origin.

This idea finds support in our results showing that when social and economic resources associated with middle- and upper-class status are accessible, ethnic traits do not hamper a student's educational attainment. For the Mexican and Puerto Rican minorities who are both ethnic and disadvantaged, however, these resources are not available. Compared with the children of non-Hispanic whites, these Hispanic youth have fewer opportunities because their parents are less likely to be in the labor force, have lower levels of education, and are more likely to have limited English skills. Mexican and Puerto Rican youth also have the highest rates of school delay and noncompletion—outcomes most strongly predicted by parental socioeconomic status. In that these outcomes translate into very limited life chances, they in turn contribute to the reproduction and transmission of disadvantage through generations.

Our empirical findings based on analyses of age-grade delay and high school noncompletion stress the importance of class background in determining educational attainment. Yet we were unable to test the effects of factors strongly related to minority status, including experiences of discrimination (experienced by Hispanics on the basis of color, accent in English, cultural differences, and so on), low self-concept, and motivation. Culturally supportive programs can address these issues not only for ethnic minority students, but for whites as well. They can help Hispanic students develop or maintain a sense of pride in themselves which ultimately may expose them to a wider range of life choices. In addition, only those schools with the personnel capable of communicating effectively in Spanish with parents can make progress in integrating the community into the educational process. This is clearly important for shaping children's motivation and subsequent academic performance.

Even without the economic resources to back up their efforts, determined parents can instill strong motivation in their children to work hard in school, as was suggested by our results of the impact of Mexican immigrant parents on school delay. But it may also prove to be important in bringing parents together and mobilizing them as a group to effect change. Finally, legitimatization of culturally specific policies recognizes the potential of Hispanics as a national resource whose future performance depends on present investments.

9

HISPANICS IN THE U.S. LABOR FORCE

F ROM THE vast number of studies documenting the labor market position of Hispanic origin workers,[1] three broad generalizations
emerge. First, the social and demographic heterogeneity of the population (see Chapter 3) is mirrored in varied employment and earnings
profiles according to national origin. Second, Puerto Ricans are the most
socially and economically disadvantaged of the Hispanic origin groups,
with poverty, labor force participation and unemployment rates, and average earnings comparable to those of Native Americans and southern
blacks.[2] Cubans and Central/South Americans fare much better in these
respects, and in some instances even better than native whites, although

[1]See reviews in George J. Borjas and Marta Tienda, eds., *Hispanics in the U.S. Economy* (Orlando, FL: Academic Press, 1985); A. J. Jaffe, Ruth M. Cullen, and Thomas D.
Boswell, *The Changing Demography of Spanish Americans* (New York: Academic Press,
1980); Marta Tienda, ed., *Hispanic Origin Workers in the U.S. Labor Market: Comparative Analyses of Employment Outcomes*, final report to the U.S. Department of Labor,
Employment and Training Administration (Springfield, VA: National Technical Information Service, 1981).

[2]Marta Tienda, "The Puerto Rican Worker: Current Labor Market Status and Future
Prospects," in *Puerto Ricans in the Mid-Eighties: An American Challenge* (Washington,
DC: National Puerto Rican Coalition, 1984); Marta Tienda and Leif Jensen, "Poverty and
Minorities: A Quarter Century Profile of Color and Socioeconomic Disadvantage," paper
presented at a conference on Poverty and Social Policy: The Minority Experience, Ailie,
UA, November 1986. This conference was co-sponsored by the Ford Foundation, Rocke-
feller Foundation, and the Institute for Research on Poverty, University of Wisconsin–
Madison.

recent immigrants are generally less successful in the United States labor market. Third, most of the differentials in labor market outcomes between Hispanic and non-Hispanic white workers reflect differing stocks of human capital, especially education and job experience, but labor market conditions and discrimination also contribute to the disadvantaged economic status of Hispanics as a group, and to Puerto Ricans in particular.[3]

Despite general consensus on these broad generalizations, there exists considerably more disagreement about the relative importance of individual and societal factors in determining labor market outcomes for several reasons. First, the frequent omission of market conditions in analyses of employment and earnings ignores an important component of variation in labor market experiences. These omissions result in overstating the importance of individual characteristics as factors which explain success and failure in the world of work. Second, variance in findings and conclusions about the labor market experiences of Hispanic workers reflects differing methods and models used to estimate the existence and extent of discrimination. Finally, although many students of racial and ethnic stratification have acknowledged the existence of premarket discrimination in determining the labor market standing of minority workers, data limitations preclude analysts from directly evaluating its impact on employment outcomes. For example, differences in educational achievement and job training themselves may result from premarket discrimination; thus, the total effect of discrimination on the socioeconomic well-being of Hispanics may have been understated.[4]

The ability of Hispanics to translate their human capital into social status (occupational position) and economic rewards (earnings) depends on national origin, a circumstance which raises many questions about the ascriptive versus meritocratic assignment of labor market positions. For Hispanics these questions revolve around the significance of two ascribed traits—ancestry and birthplace—versus achieved statuses (notably education and English proficiency) in stratifying the population. Much research has investigated these questions in recent years,[5] but little in the way of definitive conclusions has been forthcoming.

---

[3]Borjas and Tienda, *Hispanics in the U.S. Economy.*

[4]The counterargument, of course, is that the measured wage gap not attributable to measured characteristics included in a wage function results from omitted and crudely measured variables such as language, innate ability, job-specific skills, and other characteristics known to influence wages and labor supply.

[5]See reviews in Borjas and Tienda, *Hispanics in the U.S. Economy;* Tienda, *Hispanic Origin Workers;* National Commission on Employment Policy, "Hispanics and Jobs: Barriers to Progress," Report no. 14 (Washington, DC: National Commission on Employment Policy, September 1982); and Morris J. Newman, "A Profile of Hispanics in the U.S. Work Force," *Monthly Labor Review* 101 (1978):3–14.

Our purpose in this chapter and Chapter 10 on earnings and economic well-being is not to resolve the theoretical and empirical debates concerning the role of premarket versus labor market discrimination in stratifying the Hispanic work force. Rather, our objectives are more modest: (1) to document the relative socioeconomic standing of Hispanics, and changes in their labor market position between 1960 and 1980, and (2) to examine how *ascribed* characteristics (national origin, nativity, and gender), *achieved* characteristics (education, English proficiency, and job experience), and *labor market conditions* (unemployment rates, wage rates, and labor market ethnic composition) influence the performance of Mexicans, Puerto Ricans, Cubans, Central/South Americans, and Other Hispanics in the work force. Specifically, this chapter is concerned with labor force participation and positioning in the industrial and occupational structure, while the following chapter analyzes economic well-being based on earnings as well as personal and family income.

Our data analysis first examines differentials in participation rates by national origin, nativity, and gender between 1960 and 1980. For the most recent period we conduct a multivariate analysis to estimate the net influence of individual and labor market factors on the decision to participate in the labor market. We conclude the section on labor force participation by considering unemployment rates and documenting differentials between men and women by national origin and birthplace. Temporal comparisons establish whether the labor market position of each group has deteriorated, improved, or remained unchanged over time. Subsequently we examine the occupational and industrial positioning of Hispanic origin workers during the 1960–1980 period.

The socioeconomic significance of labor market standing cannot be understated: It determines both the relative economic well-being of the Hispanic national origin groups and their different class positions. Therefore, we conclude this chapter with a general discussion of the implications of contemporary employment trends for future patterns of social stratification, social mobility, and changes in economic well-being, a topic pursued in greater depth in Chapter 10.

Correlates and Determinants of Labor Market Activity

Most studies of ethnic variation in labor market position acknowledge the importance of ascribed characteristics, such as birthplace, national origin, and race in determining the employment opportunities of nonwhite people. While much research and writing on the question of labor market inequality has documented the significance of "race,"[6] until recently few scholars had examined in a parallel or as comprehensive manner the significance of ethnicity.[7] The importance of national origin and nativity in stratifying the Hispanic work force is now well documented, yet most studies fail to indicate in theoretical terms why national origin, as a proxy for ethnicity, should influence the labor market location of Hispanic workers once other factors which are correlated with labor market behavior have been taken into account.

Empirical research conducted within the human capital and status attainment traditions of the disciplines of economics and sociology, respectively, usually attribute varied labor market outcomes to differences in individual investments in education, on-the-job training, work experience, and other labor market skills, including English proficiency. These investments represent an array of achieved characteristics over which individuals presumably have some choice. These theoretical approaches to labor market experiences predict that Hispanics with lower stocks of human capital will be less successful than their counterparts with higher stocks of human capital. Success is measured in terms of labor force participation and unemployment rates, as well as occupational status and earnings.

Thus, the most common *explanation* for the well-documented labor market success of native white groups is that they have greater access to quality education and job training programs; that they are more proficient in English—a critical labor market skill for high-paying jobs; and

[6]Reynolds Farley, "Trends in Racial Inequalities: Have the Gains of the 1960s Disappeared in the 1970s?" *American Sociological Review* 42 (1977):189–208; O. D. Duncan, D. L. Featherman, and B. Duncan, *Socioeconomic Background and Achievement* (New York: Seminar Press, 1972); Bradley Schiller, *The Economics of Poverty and Discrimination* (Englewood Cliffs, NJ: Prentice-Hall, 1985).

[7]For exceptions, see Barry R. Chiswick, "An Analysis of Earnings Among Mexican Origin Men," *Proceedings of the American Statistical Association*, Business and Statistics Section (Washington, DC: American Statistical Association, 1977); Barry R. Chiswick, "The Effect of Americanization on the Earnings of Foreign-Born Men," *Journal of Political Economy* 86 (1978):897–921; George J. Borjas, "The Earnings of Male Hispanic Immigrants in the United States," *Industrial and Labor Relations Review* 35 (1982):343–53; George J. Borjas, "Assimilation, Changes in Cohort Quality, and the Earnings of Immigrants," *Journal of Labor Economics* 3 (1985):463–89; Cordelia W. Reimers, "Labor Market Discrimination Against Hispanic and Black Men," *Review of Economics and Statistics* 65 (1983):570–79; Cordelia W. Reimers, "A Comparative Analysis of the Wages of Hispanics, Blacks, and Non-Hispanic Whites," in George J. Borjas and Marta Tienda, eds., *Hispanics in the U.S. Economy* (Orlando, FL: Academic Press, 1985); Alejandro Portes and Robert L. Bach, "Immigrant Earnings: Cuban and Mexican Immigrants in the United States," *International Migration Review* 14 (1980):315–41; Kenneth Wilson and Alejandro Portes, "Immigrant Enclaves: An Analysis of the Labor Market Experiences of Cubans in Miami," *American Journal of Sociology* 86 (1980):295–19; Marta Tienda, "Socioeconomic and Labor Force Characteristics of U.S. Immigrants: Issues and Approaches," in Mary Kritz, ed., *U.S. Immigrant and Refugee Policy: Global and Domestic Issues* (Lexington, MA: Heath, 1983); and Marta Tienda, ed., *Hispanic Origin Workers*.

that they exercise greater political leverage to protect their advantaged economic and social status.[8] This set of circumstances, coupled with more favorable returns to education and job-specific experience, accounts for most, but certainly not all, of the differences in labor market outcomes (that is, participation rates, unemployment rates, and earnings) between Hispanics and non-Hispanic whites.

Within the human capital theoretical framework, foreign birth and time spent in the United States have been treated as investments because they represent differences in the level of knowledge and skills necessary to function in the U.S. labor market.[9] Presumably, with the passing of time and greater opportunities to gain experience and acquire skills necessary to operate efficiently, the initial handicaps associated with foreign birth diminish, and immigrants become indistinguishable from their native-born counterparts. Proponents of this approach argue that such findings constitute evidence of assimilation.

For most researchers working within the human capital approach, national origin is relevant in showing how group differences in achieved characteristics predict various labor market outcomes. Despite the dominant tendency to test for the existence of discrimination using residual techniques,[10] this line of reasoning begs the question as to why such differences, particularly educational underachievement and limited job skills, occur in the first place. Also, most empirical studies about wage gaps between Hispanics and non-Hispanic whites fail to explain *why* achieved or ascribed characteristics should be rewarded differently, except to suggest that models may have been misspecified or that discrimination may be partly responsible.

Consequently, the human capital and assimilation approaches to labor market differentiation of Hispanics have been subjected to extensive criticism not because their basic theoretical formulations are incorrect,[11] but because they underplay the importance of structural factors in shaping labor market outcomes. Also, they often dismiss the importance

---

[8]Marta Tienda and Ding-Tzann Lii, "Minority Concentration and Earnings Inequality: Blacks, Hispanics and Asians Compared," *American Journal of Sociology*, 93 (1987): 141–65.

[9]Barry R. Chiswick, "The Economic Progress of Immigrants: Some Apparently Universal Patterns," in W. Fellner, ed., *Contemporary Economic Problems* (Washington, DC: American Enterprise Institute, 1979); Borjas, "Earnings of Male Hispanic Immigrants"; and Tienda, "Socioeconomic and Labor Force Characteristics."

[10]R. Oaxaca, "Male-Female Wage Differentials in Urban Labor Markets, *International Economic Review* 14 (1973):693–709; S. Polachek, "Potential Biases in Measuring Male-Female Discrimination," *Journal of Human Resources* 10 (1975):205–29; Reimers, "Comparative Analysis."

[11]But see Borjas, "Assimilation," for a critique of previous assimilation research based on cross-sectional analyses of census data.

of ascribed characteristics in determining who has access to training and investment opportunities and frequently ignore how job assignments are influenced by ethnic affiliation. Critics of the human capital approach have argued that persisting differences in labor market outcomes among Hispanic national origin groups result from factors generally not included in formal models of labor supply and earnings, such as varying ethnic and racial make-up of labor markets, differences in labor market conditions (for example, unemployment rates and production structures), and intermarket variation in job and income opportunities.[12]

While not denying the importance of educational achievement and job experience in determining labor market success, an ethnic stratification perspective[13] recognizes that ascribed characteristics, such as race and national origin, significantly influence not only the allocation of social rewards, but also the ability of dominant groups to protect their interests.[14] This perspective suggests several reasons why Hispanics should be more disadvantaged in the labor market than non-Hispanic whites, and why Puerto Ricans and Mexicans are more disadvantaged than Cubans and Other Hispanics.

First, Hispanics have been subjected to greater discrimination in obtaining high levels of quality education through their segregation in low-income neighborhoods and their treatment as second-class citizens in areas of high Hispanic concentration. Consequently, this has limited their access to the more desirable jobs. Chapter 8 documented in detail the dimensions of educational disadvantages experienced by Hispanics, while Chapter 1 chronicled how different modes of incorporation shaped the class structures according to national origin. The idea that discrimination is partly responsible for these unequal outcomes centers on the ability of non-Hispanic workers to protect their economic and political interests through exclusion and residential segregation. Within the labor market employers may discriminate against Hispanic origin workers

---

[12]Additional critiques of human capital and assimilation perspectives based on ethnicity and gender are found in C. Arce, "A Reconsideration of Chicano Culture and Identity," *Daedalus* 110 (1981):171–91; and D. J. Treiman and H. I. Hartman, eds., *Women, Work, and Wages: Equal Pay for Jobs of Equal Value* (Washington, DC: National Academy Press, 1981); Alejandro Portes, "Illegal Immigration and the International System: Lessons from Recent Legal Mexican Immigrants to the United States," *Social Problems* 26 (1979):425–38.

[13]T. A. Sullivan, "Racial Ethnic Differences in Labor Force Participation: An Ethnic Stratification Perspective," in Frank D. Bean and W. Parker Frisbie, eds., *The Demography of Racial and Ethnic Groups* (New York: Academic Press, 1978); C. Hirschman, "Theories and Models of Ethnic Inequality," in C. Marett, ed., *Research in Race and Ethnic Relations*, vol. 2 (Greenwich, CT: JAI Press, 1980).

[14]Marta Tienda and Patricia Guhleman, "The Occupational Position of Employed Hispanic Women," in George J. Borjas and Marta Tienda, eds., *Hispanics in the U.S. Economy* (Orlando, FL: Academic Press, 1985); D. J. Noel, "A Theory of the Origin of Ethnic Stratification," *Social Problems* 16 (1968):157–72.

based on accented or imperfect English and/or Mestizo[15] racial characteristics, as well as Spanish surnames and other visible ethnic traits.

Second, Hispanic labor market outcomes could differ by national origin because work opportunities vary extensively across labor markets. From this perspective the poor labor market standing of Puerto Ricans would be explained partly by their geographic concentration in the Northeast, where employment opportunities in the garment and textile industries have declined sharply.[16] By itself this fact would be insignificant were it not for the disproportionate involvement of Puerto Ricans (especially women) in these enterprises. As we argue later in this chapter and the following one, the contraction of these industries contributed greatly to the deteriorated labor market position of Puerto Ricans. Similarly, the declining employment opportunities in many large, industrialized cities in the North Central states (for example, Michigan, Ohio, Indiana, and Illinois) during the 1970s may be pertinent for explaining rising unemployment rates for Mexican origin men because of their historical presence in these labor markets. Cubans and Other Hispanics, whose numbers in the midwestern states are relatively small, apparently have not been adversely affected by industrial restructuring.

Finally, the labor market position of the Hispanic national origin groups may reflect institutionalized practices of recruiting workers based on their ethnicity. The outcome of this process may be both favorable and unfavorable to the groups involved. For example, the Cuban enclave in Miami confers to this group relative economic advantages by shielding them from the competitive influences of the secondary labor market,[17] while the recruitment of immigrants to work as agricultural laborers and/or domestic servants tends to perpetuate the disadvantaged economic standing of Mexican origin workers residing in southern Texas and California or Puerto Ricans who live in the Northeast.

The role of national origin in stratifying the Hispanic labor force also must be interpreted in the context of differential control over social resources exercised by each group and labor market concentration patterns. As we showed in the previous chapter, Mexicans and Puerto Ri-

---

[15]Mestizo refers to a racial blend resulting from the miscegenation of Spaniards and other Europeans with the native peoples of Central and South America. Typical characteristics are brown skin, high cheekbones, dark, straight hair, and short physical stature, but there exists wide variation in skin pigmentation as well as in facial and physical features, depending on the native tribes involved and the extensiveness of interracial offspring.

[16]Tienda, "The Puerto Rican Worker"; Saskia Sassen-Koob, "Changing Composition and Labor Market Location of Hispanic Immigrants in New York City, 1960–1980," in George J. Borjas and Marta Tienda, eds., Hispanics in the U.S. Economy (Orlando, FL: Academic Press, 1985).

[17]Wilson and Portes, "Immigrant Enclaves"; Alejandro Portes and Robert L. Bach, Latin Journey: Cuban and Mexican Immigrants in the United States (Berkeley: University of California Press, 1985).

cans have the lowest levels of education, the most critical labor market resource. Others[18] have argued that Mexicans and Puerto Ricans have limited access to economic and political resources, despite their growing visibility in these social arenas. Alternatively, Cubans residing in Miami have formed and maintained their own institutional and economic structure,[19] thereby enhancing their political leverage in both the social and economic spheres.

To summarize, patterned differences in the labor market experiences and economic well-being of the Hispanic national origin groups reflect the operation of many processes, including (1) uneven access to education and other forms of market-enhancing skills; (2) ascribed characteristics, especially gender, national origin, and nativity, which trigger prejudice and ultimately result in premarket and labor market discrimination; (3) labor market conditions, including unemployment rates, wage rates, and the range of employment opportunities defined by the occupational and industry structure; and (4) the racial and ethnic composition of labor markets which establishes the viability of ethnic enclaves as labor allocation mechanisms.

Thus, our theoretical discussion suggests two types of variables to consider in examining Hispanic labor force participation patterns: those which pertain to individuals and those which pertain to labor markets. Individual variables of interest include an array representing achieved statuses (such as education, English proficiency, and post-school job experience), and those representing ascribed statuses, particularly nationality, nativity, and gender. In the remainder of this chapter we examine variation in labor force participation according to these individual and market characteristics.

Trends and Differentials in Labor Force Participation: 1960–1980

Our data analysis begins with a comparison of 1980 labor force participation rates of Hispanic men and women disaggregated by national origin and, for illustrative purposes, those of blacks and whites (Figure

---

[18]Arce, "Reconsideration of Chicano Culture"; A. F. Bonilla and R. Campos, "A Wealth of Poor: Puerto Ricans in the New Economic Order," *Daedalus* 110 (1981): 133–76.

[19]T. Sullivan and S. Pedraza-Bailey, *Differential Success Among Cuban American and Mexican American Immigrants,* final report to the U.S. Department of Labor, Employment and Training Administration, Washington, DC, 1979; Sullivan, "Racial Ethnic Differences"; Wilson and Portes, "Immigrant Enclaves"; Portes and Bach, *Latin Journey.*

FIGURE 9.1

*Labor Force Participation Rates of Men and Women Aged 16–64
by Race and Hispanic National Origin: 1980*

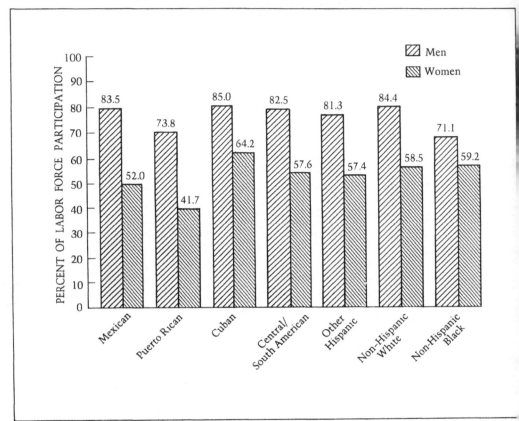

SOURCES: 1980 Public Use Microdata Sample A (5%) file; U.S. Bureau of Census, Census of Population: 1980, "Detailed Population Characteristics," U.S. Summary, Section A: U.S., PC 80-1-D1-A.

9.1).[20] Consistent with other reports,[21] among Hispanics Puerto Ricans exhibited the lowest rates of labor force participation in 1980, while the highest rates corresponded to Cuban men and women. The disadvantaged labor market position of Puerto Rican men can be appreciated by comparing them with blacks, the minority group historically subjected to the most extreme forms of discrimination. Roughly 3 percent differ-

[20]Both the black and white comparison groups are exclusive of Hispanics.
[21]Borjas and Tienda, *Hispanics in the U.S. Economy*; Newman, "Profile of Hispanics"; Jaffe et al., *Changing Demography of Spanish Americans*.

entiated the participation rates of black and Puerto Rican men, with the modest advantage corresponding to Puerto Ricans. However, black women enjoyed a 17 percent advantage over Puerto Rican women. Historical factors and the poor labor market standing of black men largely explain the high participation rates of black women.[22] The declining participation rates of Puerto Rican women have been associated with circular migration, the rising incidence of households headed by women, declining job opportunities in garment and textile firms, and the availability of means-tested transfer payments.[23]

Among men, in 1980 Cubans participated in the labor force 11 percent more than did Puerto Ricans, or at a rate comparable to non-Hispanic white men. The rates for the remaining national origin groups were between these extremes, ranging between 81 and 84 percent, but were more similar to those of Cubans. Dispersion in market activity rates was greater among women, ranging from 64 percent for Cubans to only 42 percent for Puerto Ricans. Other groups fell between these extremes, but nearly 7 points separated the Mexican women (52 percent) from Central/South American, Other Hispanic, and non-Hispanic white women.

These highly aggregated rates, while informative about gender and national origin differentiation in labor market activity, reveal little about the factors that produce them. As a first step in explaining the origins and sources of variation in Hispanic labor force participation rates, we disaggregated them by nativity and compared their evolution over time. Table 9.1 presents this detailed information.

Consistent with the national trends in labor force participation, we observe decreasing rates for men and increasing rates for women. The decrease in men's market activity occurred during the 1960s, falling from 86 to 82 percent, but remained constant throughout the 1970s. Participation rates of black men, lower at the start of the period, fell throughout the two-decade period, from 81 to 73 percent, while rates of white men converged over time with those of Hispanics.

In contrast to men, not only did women's economic activity rates increase during the past two decades, but the net change was much greater—rising 18 percent for Hispanic and non-Hispanic white women

[22]Shelley A. Smith and Marta Tienda, "The Doubly Disadvantaged: Women of Color in the U.S. Labor Force," in Ann Stromberg and Shirley Harkess, eds., *Working Women*, 2nd ed. (Palo Alto, CA: Mayfield, 1986).

[23]Marta Tienda and Ronald Angel, "Headship and Household Composition Among Blacks, Hispanics and Other Whites," *Social Forces* 61 (1982):508–31; Tienda, ed., *Hispanic Origin Workers*; Marta Tienda and Jennifer Glass, "Household Structure and Labor Force Participation of Black, Hispanic and White Mothers," *Demography* 22 (1985):381–94; Marta Tienda and Leif Jensen, "Immigration and Public Assistance: Dispelling the Myth of Dependency," *Social Science Research* 15 (1986):372–400.

TABLE 9.1

*Labor Force Participation Rates of Persons Aged 16–64
by Race, National Origin, Nativity, and Gender: 1960–1980*

Race and Hispanic National Origin	Men			Women		
	Native	Foreign	Total	Native	Foreign	Total
1960						
Total Hispanic	84.1%	87.5%	85.6%	33.1%	37.2%	34.8%
Mexican	84.1	90.4	85.7	32.1	29.3	31.5
Puerto Rican	76.6	85.6	84.7	47.7	39.5	40.3
Cuban	77.6	90.1	87.1	42.3	55.0	51.5
Central/South American	93.7	80.7	83.6	49.4	48.9	49.0
Other Hispanic	94.0	87.9	88.9	39.1	32.4	33.5
Black	80.6	90.2	80.6	47.2	57.8	47.2
Non-Hispanic White	88.3	90.8	88.5	39.4	41.0	39.5
1970						
Total Hispanic	80.4	84.0	81.9	41.1	41.2	41.2
Mexican	80.7	86.1	81.9	40.4	36.4	39.6
Puerto Rican	67.4	80.5	77.8	38.9	31.4	32.9
Cuban	81.0	86.7	86.0	46.2	53.8	52.8
Central/South American	76.8	84.5	83.2	48.6	52.7	52.1
Other Hispanic	84.3	83.1	83.9	44.5	47.0	45.4
Black	75.1	80.6	75.2	50.9	65.3	51.1
Non-Hispanic White	85.3	87.2	85.4	46.8	44.0	46.6
1980						
Total Hispanic	79.6	84.7	81.9	54.3	50.6	52.6
Mexican	81.2	87.7	83.5	54.2	47.5	52.0
Puerto Rican	67.2	77.0	73.8	47.6	39.0	41.7
Cuban	70.9	87.0	85.0	60.1	64.6	64.2
Central/South American	73.3	83.3	82.5	57.3	57.6	57.6
Other Hispanic	80.3	85.2	81.3	57.0	59.0	57.4
Black	72.6	76.4	73.3	59.5	67.8	61.1
Non-Hispanic White	84.5	85.2	84.6	58.7	54.8	57.9

SOURCES: 1960, 1970, and 1980 Public Use Microdata Sample files.

and 14 percent for black women between 1960 and 1980. The greatest change in the labor force participation rates for women was experienced during the 1970s, while for men this occurred in the 1960s. Women of Hispanic origin participated in the labor force at an average rate of 35 percent in 1960; their rate of labor market activity increased to 41 percent by 1970 and an additional 12 percent during the 1970s, reaching 53 percent by 1980.

The evolution of market activity rates also differed according to nativity and national origin. Throughout the period native-born Hispanic men participated in the labor force 3 to 5 percent less, on average, than did their foreign-born counterparts. Over time, the disparity in participation rates of black native-born and foreign-born men declined from 9.6 percent in 1960 to 3.8 percent in 1980, while the nativity differential for white men hovered around 1 to 2 percent throughout the period.

Nativity differentials for women evolved in a different manner. In 1960 the participation rates of foreign-born Hispanic women were 4 points higher than those of their native-born counterparts, but this gap virtually closed by 1970. In 1980 the nativity differentials in female labor force participation rates were opposite of what they had been 20 years earlier. Not only had the rates of all Hispanic women increased, but because those of native women rose faster, they surpassed the rates of immigrant Hispanic women. Thus, in 1980, 54 percent of U.S.-born women were in the labor force compared with 51 percent of immigrant women. Changes in labor force participation rates of white women paralleled those of Hispanic women, but the labor market activity pattern of black women differed in two respects. First, immigrants worked at higher rates than natives throughout the period, and, second, the black nativity differential increased from 11 to 14 percent during the 1960s, and then fell sharply to 8 percent during the 1970s.

Overall, the pattern of high labor force participation by Cuban and Central/South American women and low participation by Puerto Ricans and Mexicans persisted between 1960 and 1980. Moreover, the participation gap between Cubans and Puerto Ricans increased from 10 to 20 percent during the 1960s and remained unchanged during the 1970s. Similarly, and despite changes in the nativity-specific participation rates among the national origin groups, the 11 to 12 percent differential participation rate between Mexican and Cuban women persisted throughout the 1970s. Although these results suggest varying levels of market commitment among women of differing national origins, they also reflect differences in employability, as reflected by their varying stocks of human capital and market skills. We examine this question further following a brief discussion of nativity variation in men's labor market activity.

Closer examination of the differentials in Hispanic women's labor force activity shows that the rising participation rates among native-born Mexican women were largely responsible for the changed nativity differentials over the past 20 years. Because Mexican women are the largest of the five national groups, changes in their labor market behavior decisively influenced the average participation rates of the female Hispanic population. For example, market activity rates of native-born

Mexican women were consistently higher than those of their foreign-born counterparts. Over time, the participation differential between native-born and foreign-born Mexican women widened from roughly 3 percent in 1960 to 7 percent in 1980.

Participation rates among Cuban origin women were uniformly higher among the foreign-born compared with the native-born, but the extent of nativity differentiation decreased over time. Whereas foreign-born Cuban women's activity rates were 13 percent above their native-born counterparts in 1960, by 1980 this differential had closed to 4 percent. This change was due largely to the aging of the native-born female Cuban population, coupled with decreased participation among older foreign-born women, probably due to health reasons or retirement. That Cuban origin women in 1980 had the highest labor force participation rates of all native-born Hispanic women suggests an intergenerational transmission of norms about the acceptability of women's work.[24] Accordingly, we expect continued high levels of labor market involvement by Cuban origin women in the future.

Nativity-specific participation rates for Hispanic men evolved differently. First, there was relatively little differentiation in market activity among the national origin groups. Second, nativity differentials varied by national origin. In 1960 the foreign-born men of Mexican, Puerto Rican, and Cuban origin exhibited higher market activity rates than their native-born counterparts, whereas the opposite was true for Central/South American and Other Hispanic men.

By 1970 the deteriorating employment conditions in the New York–New Jersey SMSA fostered by the decline of employment in the textile and garment industry[25] had already taken their toll on the Puerto Rican population. While the labor force activity rate for all Hispanic men fell from 86 to 82 percent during the 1960s, that of Puerto Rican men declined from 85 to 78 percent. This decline resulted largely from the sharper drop in labor force participation among mainland-born Puerto Rican men. Although the market activity rate of mainland-born Puerto Rican men did not change much during the 1970s, that of island-born men fell throughout the period. Consequently, by 1980 the average participation rate of Puerto Rican men dropped to 74 percent.

The labor market experience of Mexican men contrasts sharply with that of Puerto Rican men in that the former actually *increased* their average market activity rates during the 1970s. This rise resulted from the increased economic activity of *both* native-born and foreign-

[24]Smith and Tienda, "Doubly Disadvantaged."
[25]Roger Waldinger, "Immigration and Industrial Change in the New York City Apparel Industry," in George J. Borjas and Marta Tienda, eds., *Hispanics in the U.S. Economy* (Orlando, FL: Academic Press, 1985).

born men. These increases in activity rates were relatively modest, but because of the size of the Mexican origin population relative to the total Hispanic population, they were sufficient to offset the lessened market activity of Puerto Rican men during the 1970s. Thus, the average participation rate for all Hispanic men was unchanged between 1970 and 1980.

In prior chapters we have shown that the Central/South American population exhibits considerable diversity along national origin lines. Unfortunately, this portrait of heterogeneity is concealed by tabulations which aggregate the nationalities into a single regional category. A disaggregation of participation rates according to national origin, as in Table 9.2, illustrates this point. For parsimony, we focus attention on 1980 rates.

TABLE 9.2

Labor Force Participation Rates
of Central/South Americans Aged 16–64
by Gender and Country of Origin: 1980

Country of Origin	Men	Women
CENTRAL AMERICAN AND THE CARIBBEAN	82.7%	58.0%
Dominican Republic	79.1	51.5
El Salvador	85.4	65.7
Guatemala	88.0	62.1
Nicaragua	82.9	58.0
Panama	81.8	62.0
Honduras	82.8	58.9
Costa Rica	85.8	55.0
Other Central American	78.3	56.6
SOUTH AMERICA	82.4	57.2
Colombia	84.8	59.0
Ecuador	82.9	58.5
Peru	88.3	60.1
Argentina	88.6	56.5
Chile	84.3	60.8
Venezuela	41.8	31.4
Bolivia	80.6	60.6
Uruguay	88.5	59.8
Paraguay	94.4	54.9
Other South American	83.3	54.6
Total	82.5	57.6

SOURCE: 1980 Public Use Microdata Sample file.

In contrast to the wide education differences documented in Chapter 8, average rates of labor force participation were quite similar between all Central Americans and all South Americans. However, there was appreciable diversity by nationality within these subgroupings. Gender differences in participation rates, of course, were quite pronounced, as is the case among the general population. Among Central Americans, Guatemalan and Costa Rican men exhibited the highest participation rates in 1980—88 and 86 percent, respectively—while among the South American nationalities, Paraguayan men's participation rate (94 percent) was notably higher than the regional average. At the opposite extreme was the labor participation rate for Venezuelan men (42 percent), which appears anomalous compared with rates of other national origin groups. That Venezuelan women also were half as likely to participate in the United States labor force as other Latin American women suggests that Venezuelan immigrants, at least those residing in the United States in 1980, are a peculiar group. We suspect that a large share of this group consists of individuals who are independently wealthy and not compelled to work.[26]

The average labor force participation rate of Central/South American origin women was roughly 25 percent below that of men. These gender differentials in participation rates also differed by country of origin. Among Central Americans the highest labor force participation rates were observed among Salvadoran, Guatemalan, and Panamanian women, while the lowest rates corresponded to Dominican women. These differentials are not simply explained by variation in educational attainment because Panamanian women were the most highly educated of the group (Chapter 8), while the other three nationalities exhibited the lowest educational levels among the Central American countries. Sex differences in participation rates for Central Americans range from a low of 10 percent for Venezuelans to a high of 40 percent for Paraguayan women. Thus, gender differences in participation rates were slightly greater among South American workers than Central American workers.

The observed differentials among the national origin groups, while informative about the evolving labor market attachment of Hispanics, reveal little about the relative importance of individual versus labor market characteristics in producing these differentials. We now turn our attention to this question and examine various correlates of labor force participation in 1980 among Hispanic men and women.

[26]Since these data were collected prior to the oil crisis, this explanation is plausible, but further verification must await comparisons based on subsequent censuses and possibly survey data.

Multivariate Analysis of Labor Force Participation

To further evaluate the relative importance of individual and market characteristics in determining the labor force response of Hispanics, we analyzed 1980 labor force participation rates using logistic regression.[27] Individual variables used to estimate the probability of entering the labor market include demographic characteristics that represent life cycle stages of individuals (age and marital status), human capital (English proficiency and education), and household constraints on labor market entry (for women the presence of children under age 6 and husband's income).[28]

We also included in our model two market level characteristics that influence individuals' participation decisions: the market unemployment rate and the average wage rate. These two indicators of labor market conditions should have opposite effects on the decision to enter the labor market. In places of high unemployment greater numbers of individuals should be discouraged from seeking work because they believe no jobs are available. Conversely, when higher average wage rates prevail in a labor market, greater numbers of individuals should be willing to enter the market because higher wages raise the cost of leisure (or home production) and result in a substitution of market work for leisure.

Tables 9.3 and 9.4 summarize the results of our logistic regression analyses for men and women, respectively. To facilitate interpretation of the multivariate results we report transformed coefficients that can be interpreted as the probability of participation in the labor force given membership in a category of a discrete variable.[29] For example, the −.041 (Table 9.3, col. 2) indicates that Mexican origin men with 8–11 years of schooling participated in the labor force 4 percent more, on average, than their (statistical) counterparts who completed primary school or less. We organize the presentation to highlight the pattern of relationships that are shared between the sexes and that either conform to or deviate from the predictions of the existing literature on this subject.

---

[27]A logistic regression was necessary because our dichotomous dependent variable is not normally distributed. Because logit coefficients are awkward to interpret, we transformed them by taking the first derivatives to render a more straightforward probabilistic interpretation.

[28]The justification for the latter is that the presence of young children deters women's entry into the labor market and also the well-established fact that women whose husbands' income is adequate to support the family tend not to participate in the labor force at rates comparable to those whose husbands' earnings are inadequate to support the family.

[29]Eric A. Hanushek and John E. Jackson, *Statistical Methods for Social Sciences* (New York: Academic Press, 1977).

TABLE 9.3

*Adjusted 1980 Labor Force Participation Differentials by National Origin:
Hispanic Men Aged 16–64*

	Mexican[a]		Puerto Rican[b]		Cuban[c]	
	Logit	1st Derivative	Logit	1st Derivative	Logit	1st Derivative
Education						
8–11 Years	−.308*	−.041	.318*	.064	.126	.016
12 Years	.704*	.094	1.235*	.248	.608*	.075
13–15 Years	.588*	.079	1.015*	.204	.684*	.085
16 + Years	.347	.046	1.114*	.224	.846*	.105
English Ability						
Fair	.006	.001	−.214*	−.043	.084	.010
Poor/None	.069	.009	−505*	−.102	−.237	−.029
Age						
25–54 Years	.604*	.081	.626*	.126	.870*	.108
55–64 Years	−.840*	−.112	−.613*	−.123	−.118	−.015
Marital Status						
Married, Spouse Absent	−1.097*	−.147	−.561*	−.113	−.709*	−.088
Single	−1.432*	−.192	−1.374*	−.276	−1.607*	−.199
Year of Immigration						
1975–1980	.511*	.068	—[g]	—	−.452*	−.056
1970–1974	.710*	.095	—	—	.459*	.057
1965–1969	.415	.056	—	—	.546*	.068
1960–1964	.107	.014	—	—	.653*	.081
1950–1959	.403	.054	—	—	.515*	.064
Before 1950	−.199	−.027	—	—	−.121	−.015
Island-Born[h]			−.258	−.052		
Unemployment Level						
Medium (6–8%)	−.191*	−.026	−.149	−.030	−.078	−.010
High (8 +)	−.119	−.016	.202	.041	−.076	−.009
Mean Wage Rate						
Medium (6.5–7.5)	.242*	.032	.235	.047	.560*	.069
High (7.5 +)	.331*	.044	.105	.021	.642*	.080

SOURCE: 1980 Public Use Microdata Sample file.

[a]Evaluated at p′ = .841.
[b]Evaluated at p′ = .721.
[c]Evaluated at p′ = .855.
[d]Evaluated at p′ = .825.
[e]Evaluated at p′ = .817.
[f]Evaluated at p′ = .849.
[g]Puerto Ricans are not considered to be immigrants; therefore year of immigration was not obtained.
[h]Native-born refers to mainland-born for Puerto Ricans.
*Significance level t ≥ 1.96.

TABLE 9.3 *(continued)*

Central South American/[d]		Other Hispanic[e]		Non-Hispanic White[f]	
Logit	1st Derivative	Logit	1st Derivative	Logit	1st Derivative
−.600*	−.087	.024	.004	.216	.028
−.089	−.013	1.023*	.153	1.154*	.148
−.424*	−.061	.711*	.107	.673*	.086
−.892*	−.129	1.258*	.189	1.103*	.141
−.131	−.019	−.309*	−.046	.101	.013
−.107	−.016	−.084	−.013	−.433	−.055
1.092*	.158	.665*	.100	.896*	.115
−.319*	−.046	−.975*	−.146	−1.032*	−.132
−.758*	−.110	−.877*	−.132	−1.305*	−.167
−1.344*	−.195	−1.612*	−.242	−1.716*	−.220
−.238	−.034	.083	.012	−1.078*	−.138
.246	.036	.578*	.087	−.414	−.053
.211	.030	.298	.045	.206	.026
.607*	.088	.105	.016	.277	.035
.675*	.098	.130	.020	.646*	.083
.179	.026	.102	.015	.186	.024
.063	.009	−.108	−.016	−.049	−.006
−.068	−.010	−.351*	.053	−.079	−.010
.337*	.049	.105	.016	.167	.021
.548*	.079	.172*	.026	.375*	.048

In accordance with expectations, increased levels of education generally were associated with higher probabilities of labor force participation. Central/South American men and women stand as a noteworthy exception, as the highest "adjusted"[30] participation rates correspond to the least-educated segments of the male working-age population. A similar result emerged for women, in that those with some secondary training or a high school diploma were less likely to work in 1980 than their counterparts with less than primary schooling. This scenario is consis-

[30]Our usage of the term "adjusted" indicates that the rates are net of the effects of other variables included in the model.

TABLE 9.4

Adjusted 1980 Labor Force Participation Differentials by National Origin:
Hispanic Women Aged 16–64

	Mexican[a]		Puerto Rican[b]		Cuban[c]	
	Logit	1st Derivative	Logit	1st Derivative	Logit	1st Derivative
Education						
8–11 Years	−.104	−.026	.237*	.057	.116	.027
12 Years	.690*	.172	.950*	.230	.591*	.135
13–15 Years	1.058*	.263	1.177*	.285	.946*	.217
16+ Years	1.343*	.334	1.594*	.386	.933*	.214
English Ability						
Fair	−.154*	−.038	−.236*	−.057	−.022	−.005
Poor/None	−.568*	−.141	−.809*	−.196	−.301*	−.069
Age						
25–54 Years	.273*	.068	.411*	.099	.448*	.103
55–64 Years	−.261*	−.065	.069	.017	−.145	−.033
Marital Status						
Married, Spouse Absent	.620*	.154	−.046	−.011	.229*	.052
Single	.381*	.095	−.156	−.038	−.151	−.034
Husband's Income						
$10,000–$25,000	−.113	−.028	.263*	.064	−.082	−.019
$25,000+	−.304*	−.076	.147	.036	−.569*	−.130
Children Under Age						
6 Present	−.099	−.025	−.514*	−.124	−.875*	−.200
Year of Immigration						
1975–1980	.148	.037	—[g]	—	−.464*	−.106
1970–1974	.074	.018	—	—	.353*	.081
1965–1969	.024	.006	—	—	.168	.038
1960–1964	.115	.029	—	—	.133	.030
1950–1959	−.100	−.025	—	—	−.065	−.015
Before 1950	−.261	−.065	—	—	−.499	−.114
Island-Born[h]			−.033	−.008		
Unemployment Level						
Medium (6–8%)	−.035	−.009	−.150	−.036	.053	.012
High (8+)	−.204*	−.051	−.275	−.067	.074	.017
Mean Wage Rate						
Medium (6.5–7.5)	.278*	.069	.037	.009	.340*	.078
High (7.5+)	.356*	.089	−.155	−.038	.133	.030

SOURCE: 1980 Public Use Microdata Sample file.

[a]Evaluated at $p' = .524$.
[b]Evaluated at $p' = .411$.
[c]Evaluated at $p' = .644$.
[d]Evaluated at $p' = .573$.
[e]Evaluated at $p' = .578$.
[f]Evaluated at $p' = .592$.
[g]Puerto Ricans are not considered to be immigrants; therefore year of immigration was not obtained.
[h]Native-born refers to mainland-born for Puerto Ricans.
*Significance level $t \geq 1.96$.

TABLE 9.4 (continued)

Central South American/[d]		Other Hispanic[e]		Non-Hispanic White[f]	
Logit	1st Derivative	Logit	1st Derivative	Logit	1st Derivative
−.323*	−.079	−.064	−.016	.437*	.106
−.072	−.018	.837*	.204	1.053*	.254
.036	.009	1.054*	.257	1.232*	.298
379*	.093	1.530*	.373	1.611*	.389
.003	.001	−.288*	−.070	.643*	.155
−.146	−.036	−.131	−.032	.461	.111
.491*	.120	.231*	.056	.337*	.081
−.218	−.053	−.433*	−.106	−.616*	−.149
.489*	.120	.457*	.111*	.637*	.154
.501*	.123	.299*	.073	.442*	.107
−.126	−.031	−.022	−.005	−.074	−.018
−.480*	−.118	−.438*	−.107	−.499*	−.121
−.232*	.057	−.526*	−.128	−.676*	−.163
−.292*	−.072	.057	.014	.850*	−.205
.073	.018	.505*	.123	.060	.014
.023	.006	.403*	.098	.465	.112
.197	.048	.190	.046	−.280	−.068
.495*	.121	.217	.053	−.132	−.032
.577*	.141	.111	.027	−.017	−.004
.000	.000	−.037	−.009	−.131	−.032
−.256	−.063	−.191*	−.047	−.207*	−.050
.343*	.084	.034	.008	−.050	−.012
.497*	.122	.130	.032	.054	.013

tent with the premise that lesser-educated Central/South Americans largely are labor migrants whose primary, if not sole, reason for being in the United States is to work. Among women those with post-secondary schooling were more likely to work than their counterparts with less than primary school.

The lower labor force participation rates among college-educated Central/South American men compared with their least-educated compatriots are somewhat puzzling. Central/South American men with 13–15 years and 16 or more years of education were between 6 and 13 percent *less* likely to participate in the labor market in 1980 than their statistical counterparts with fewer than 8 years of completed schooling. Additional tabulations revealed an interaction between the year of arrival and education, suggesting that most recent college-educated immigrants experienced greater difficulties in adjusting to the demands of the U.S. labor market. Once this effect was taken into account, the negative additive effect of 13–15 years of schooling on labor force participation for these education categories of Hispanic men disappeared.

Although the relationship between education and labor force participation is approximately monotonic for women, a nonlinear relationship emerged for men. Central/South American women were the main exception, an outcome which may reflect the relatively recent arrival of a large share of this group (see Chapter 3) and the extensive heterogeneity in socioeconomic backgrounds according to country of origin.

That the effect of education on labor force participation is stronger for women reflects the fundamentally different stance of each sex with respect to working. Because there is more variation in labor force participation among women than among men, on statistical grounds alone we would expect key variables to exert a larger influence on the market activity of women. Substantively, labor force participation is normatively required for men, so labor market activity is nearly universal. Education, therefore, does not exert such a strong influence on men's decision to work. For women, however, labor force participation is still normatively optional, so it is lower and not at all universal. Education, therefore, exerts a stronger influence on women's decision to work since it determines the opportunity costs of not working and also alters women's normative perceptions of the value of work itself.

English ability, another human capital characteristic, also performs as expected. In general, individuals with lower levels of proficiency in English were less likely to be in the labor force than their counterparts whose English proficiency ranged from fair to very good, but the effects differ by gender and national origin. Among men significant language effects emerged only for Puerto Ricans and Other Hispanics. Puerto Ricans with poor to no proficiency in English were 10 percent less likely to work in 1980 than proficient English speakers. Both Puerto Rican and Other Hispanic men with fair English skills participated in the labor market at a rate 4 percent below their national origin counterparts who were proficient in English. Like the effects of education, proficiency in English appears to be more influential in determining whether Hispanic women enter the labor market than men. Whereas only three of the estimated coefficients for English proficiency were statistically significant for men, seven were significant for women, including one for non-Hispanic whites.

Gender differences in the effect of English proficiency on labor force participation result partly from the different occupational choices available to men and women and partly because labor force participation is normatively optional for women. In clerical and sales occupations that employ disproportionate numbers of women and require contact with the general public, English proficiency should play a greater role in determining whether women consider their language skills adequate to obtain a job and in their decision to work outside the home. However, for many unskilled male-dominated jobs, such as laborer occupations in construction, agriculture, and manufacturing industries, English proficiency is less critical for job performance. Consequently, it may constrain their job choices to a lesser extent.

In general, the demographic and life cycle variables behaved as expected. Highest rates of labor force participation corresponded to individuals aged 25 to 54, while individuals aged 55 to 64 were as likely or slightly less likely to participate in the labor market than their ethnic counterparts aged 16 to 24.[31] However, age differences in labor force participation rates were less systematic for women than for men. For example, prime-age male workers were significantly more likely (8 to 16 percent for Mexicans and Central/South Americans, respectively) to be in the labor force than their national origin counterparts aged 16 to 24. Although this pattern generally obtained for Hispanic women, the differentials were less pronounced.

Marital status variations in labor force participation not only were less systematic for women than men, but also differed in direction. In contrast to men, single women, or married women whose spouses were absent, were considerably more likely to be in the labor force than their married, spouse-present counterparts. Puerto Rican women are the primary exception to this generalization, as marital status did not differentiate their labor market behavior. Elsewhere[32] we attributed the dis-

---

[31]For men the effects of age and marital status differed according to birthplace. Age effects on labor force participation usually were more pronounced for the native-born than the foreign-born. Likewise for the effects of marital status. The effects of marital status on probability of labor force participation were more pronounced for individuals born in the United States. In part this reflects compositional differences in marital status between native- and foreign-born men. Also, the observed differentials in age effects on labor force participation can be interpreted as stemming partly from differential access to social insurance benefits, such as social security income and pensions which covary with nativity. To the extent that eligibility for work-related insurance benefits is governed by length of job experience, native-born workers have a definite advantage over their foreign-born counterparts, other things being equal.

[32]Tienda, "The Puerto Rican Worker"; Tienda and Angel, "Headship and Household Composition"; Tienda and Glass, "Household Structure and Labor Force Participation."

tinctive labor force behavior of Puerto Rican women vis-à-vis other Hispanic women, blacks, or whites to the higher participation of Puerto Rican women in the public assistance programs. However, the causal linkages between the labor supply decision and the welfare participation decision have not been disentangled; hence such inferences are suggestive rather than conclusive. This is all the more so because most treatments of the subject have ignored the critical role of circular migration in jointly influencing marital disruption and subsequent decisions to enter the labor market or seek means-tested transfer income. That Puerto Ricans have the highest level of poverty and the highest rate of participation in welfare programs does suggest complex linkages among these variables.

Evidence that women's labor supply decisions are constrained by family and income factors resides in the strong negative effects of the presence of young children on the labor force participation rates of Hispanic origin women, except those of Mexican origin. Also, with the exception of Puerto Ricans, women whose husbands earned $25,000 or more in 1979 were 8 percent (Mexican origin) to 13 percent (Cuban origin) less likely to work than their (statistical) counterparts whose spouses earned less than $10,000 in 1979. The Puerto Rican anomaly can be traced to the sharply declining rates of labor force participation among men during the 1960s and 1970s, coupled with the sharp rise in the prevalence of female-headed households.

Labor market conditions generally influenced the labor force participation decisions of Hispanics in the manner hypothesized, but the effects of unemployment rates were largely insignificant. Residence in high wage areas increased the probability that Hispanics were in the labor force in 1980, but not uniformly among the national origin and gender groups. Uneven effects of labor market conditions on participation rates are consistent with pronounced differences in regional concentration.

Summary

The multivariate analysis helped in sorting the relative importance of individual and market characteristics in predicting labor market success. Differences in human capital—namely, education and English ability—partly explain the low labor force participation rates of Puerto Ricans, but not the higher average activity rates of Mexican men.

Most of our findings are consistent with the expectations set forth in the introductory sections of this chapter. However, several questions deserving further research attention emerged from the discussion. For example, it is not totally clear why the effects of English ability differ by gender. Our interpretations are more speculative than conclusive, and hence require further analyses with more fine-grained employment data than are available in the 1980 census. Results showing that education exerts a strong influence on labor force participation indicate the direction that policy might take in trying to alter labor force participation for some national origin groups, but they say little about why the effects differ by national origin. This issue should not be taken lightly, for it indicates directly the long-term prospects for improving the labor market standing of the Hispanic population overall, and the extent and nature of inequality according to national origin.

Unemployment Trends and Differentials: 1960–1980

Labor force participation rates include individuals who are actively employed (or with a job but not at work) and those who are looking for work, that is, the unemployed. Thus, participation rates reported in Table 9.1 and Figure 9.1 conceal an important aspect of labor market disadvantage in that they represent very different levels of joblessness according to national origin, nativity, and gender, as Figure 9.2 and Table 9.5 show. The now-familiar theme of Puerto Rican disadvantage is pointedly illustrated in Figure 9.2. Besides their extremely low rates of labor force participation (Figure 9.1 and Table 9.1), Puerto Ricans also experienced the highest unemployment rates of all Hispanics in 1980, with jobless rates similar to those of black men and women. Mexican unemployment rates, while lower than those of Puerto Ricans, also were above those of the other groups. In contrast, Cubans exhibited not only the highest labor force participation rates of all Hispanics in 1980, but also the lowest unemployment rates. In fact, the 1980 Cuban unemployment rates were most similar to those of non-Hispanic whites. Unemployment rates for Central/South American and Other Hispanic men and women fall between the extremes of Puerto Ricans and Cubans.

Among all groups except Other Hispanics and non-Hispanic whites, women's unemployment rates were 1 to 2 percent higher than those of their male counterparts. Although the gender differences in 1980 unemployment rates observed for non-Hispanic whites and Other Hispanics were quite small, the female advantage is not an artifact of sampling variability. Sigurd Nilsen[33] found similar gender differentials in unem-

[33]Sigurd Nilsen, "Recessionary Impacts of the Unemployment of Men and Women," *Monthly Labor Review* 107(1984):21–5.

FIGURE 9.2

Unemployment Rates of Men and Women Aged 16–64,
by Race and Hispanic National Origin: 1980

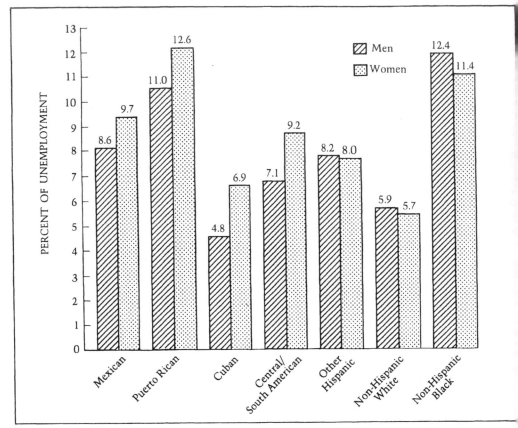

SOURCES: Public Use Microdata Sample A (5%) file; U.S. Bureau of Census, *Census of Population: 1980,* "Detailed Population Characteristics," U.S. Summary, Section A: U.S., PC 80-1-D1-A.

ployment, which he attributed to changes in the industrial composition of employment, coupled with the rise of new jobs highly conducive to female employment. That these industrial restructuring processes have not reversed the gender differentials in unemployment rates for minority workers might be due to the persisting differences in the occupational distributions of blacks and Hispanics compared with those of whites, an aspect of employment we consider in the final section of this chapter.

Table 9.5, which represents unemployment rates by national origin, gender, nativity, and age, shows that the unemployment differentials among Hispanics, like those of labor force participation, have existed for at least two decades. Age is an important dimension of variation in unemployment because of the well-documented problems associated with unemployment among youth, as well as among older workers who, when displaced by new technology, experience serious difficulties in re-entering the labor market.

High unemployment rates of Puerto Ricans already were evident in 1960. Temporal comparisons in unemployment rates reveal a worsening of the labor market position of Puerto Rican men and women, despite a slight interim improvement during the 1960s. In contrast, the unemployment rate for Cuban women in 1960 was similar to that of Mexicans and Puerto Ricans. Their disproportionately high rates of joblessness likely reflect their recent arrival following the overthrow of the Batista government in 1959. Many of these women probably experienced adjustment problems in securing employment shortly after their arrival, but these problems diminished as their familiarity with the United States labor market increased. The relatively low unemployment rates of Central/South American women in 1960 reflect the educational selectivity of earlier cohorts relative to those who arrived during the 1970s (see Chapters 3 and 8).

During the 1960s unemployment rates dropped for almost all groups, but not uniformly. Cuban origin men experienced the most precipitous decline in joblessness, with unemployment falling from 7 to 3 percent between 1960 and 1970. For Cuban women the unemployment rate fell by a less substantial, but nonetheless noteworthy, amount— from 10 to 8 percent. The differential rates of decline in unemployment by national origin altered somewhat the ranking of the groups with respect to levels of joblessness, such that Cuban men and women exhibited the lowest unemployment as early as 1970. Puerto Rican women experienced the highest unemployment rates of all the Hispanic origin and gender groups in 1970. Unemployment rates for Mexican and Puerto Rican men were roughly 1 percent higher than those for Central/South Americans and Other Hispanics.

The 1970s, a period of slow economic growth, were associated with a general rise in unemployment rates. For some Hispanic groups this meant an increase in joblessness above those levels observed in 1960. This generalization varied on gender, however. Only for Puerto Rican and Central/South American women were 1980 unemployment rates higher than those observed in 1960. Thus, despite the general increase in unemployment during the 1970s, the 1980 joblessness rate of Mexican, Cuban, and Other Hispanic women was below their respective

TABLE 9.5

Unemployment Rates by Hispanic National Origin, Race, Gender, Nativity, and Age: 1960–1980

	Mexican			Puerto Rican			Cuban		
	Native	Foreign	Total	Native	Foreign	Total	Native	Foreign	Total
1960									
Men									
16–24 Years	13.6	6.9	12.5	13.6	11.4	11.6	—[a]	11.1	10.4
25–54 Years	6.5	5.6	6.2	5.9	7.8	7.6	3.3	7.7	6.8
55–64 Years	9.5	8.4	8.9	—[a]	10.9	10.7	—[a]	8.0	9.1
Total	8.3	6.2	7.8	8.3	8.8	8.8	4.9	8.1	7.4
Women									
16–24 Years	11.3	8.8	11.0	8.2	15.7	14.4	—[a]	6.7	9.5
25–54 Years	8.7	11.9	9.4	11.1	9.3	9.4	6.4	10.6	9.7
55–64 Years	4.6	15.7	9.9	—[a]	10.0	12.9	—[a]	—[a]	—[a]
Total	9.4	11.8	9.9	10.6	11.0	10.9	10.6	9.9	10.1
1970									
Men									
16–24 Years	11.9	8.7	11.4	11.4	8.9	9.6	6.7	4.0	4.6
25–54 Years	4.3	4.7	4.4	5.7	4.8	5.0	1.6	2.3	2.2
55–64 Years	4.2	7.6	5.5	—[a]	5.0	4.6	—[a]	3.3	3.6
Total	6.3	5.8	6.2	7.7	5.7	6.0	3.2	2.6	2.7
Women									
16–24 Years	12.6	6.8	11.7	12.6	10.6	11.3	4.6	6.5	6.1
25–54 Years	6.6	8.9	7.0	3.6	8.5	7.7	6.6	8.5	8.3
55–64 Years	3.8	10.8	6.2	—[a]	13.0	11.5	—[a]	8.3	7.1
Total	8.4	8.6	8.4	8.2	9.4	9.2	5.0	8.2	7.8
1980									
Men									
16–24 Years	13.8	11.2	12.9	18.5	17.4	18.0	11.2	7.3	8.1
25–54 Years	6.3	7.7	6.8	8.8	8.9	8.9	5.5	3.9	4.0
55–64 Years	5.4	7.6	6.2	5.6	6.2	6.1	5.3	3.8	3.9
Total	8.5	8.6	8.6	13.5	9.9	11.0	7.9	4.4	4.8
Women									
16–24 Years	11.7	14.3	12.4	16.0	20.2	17.5	6.7	7.4	7.3
25–54 Years	6.8	12.1	8.5	8.7	11.2	10.6	5.7	6.8	6.7
55–64 Years	7.0	11.1	8.2	5.2	11.2	10.6	1.8	7.1	6.9
Total	8.5	12.6	9.7	12.6	12.6	12.6	6.0	7.0	6.9

SOURCES: 1960, 1970, and 1980 Public Use Microdata Sample files.

[a]Fewer than 20 cases.

TABLE 9.5 *(continued)*

Central/ South American			Other Hispanic			Black			Non-Hispanic White		
Native	Foreign	Total	Native	Foreign	Total	Native	Foreign	Total	Native	Foreign	Total
17.9	10.4	13.2	—[a]	—[a]	10.3	13.4	20.0	13.5	9.2	6.8	9.2
5.5	4.8	4.9	3.8	5.7	5.2	7.8	5.8	7.8	3.5	3.3	3.5
—[a]	4.6	4.2	—[a]	5.0	5.0	8.2	6.2	8.2	4.6	6.7	4.9
8.1	5.4	6.1	5.6	5.4	5.4	8.8	7.1	8.8	4.5	4.7	4.5
14.8	6.8	9.3	—[a]	—[a]	10.0	14.5	23.1	14.6	6.8	4.4	6.7
5.9	6.8	6.6	—[a]	7.9	9.9	7.9	3.0	7.8	4.5	5.2	4.5
—[a]	9.5	8.0	—[a]	7.1	7.1	5.5	12.0	5.6	3.6	4.7	3.7
8.5	7.0	7.3	16.0	7.7	9.3	8.7	7.7	8.7	4.8	5.0	4.8
12.7	7.4	8.7	11.8	5.4	10.1	14.0	4.4	13.9	7.1	11.6	7.2
7.5	3.6	4.1	3.6	2.7	3.3	4.9	2.9	4.9	2.5	2.7	2.5
—[a]	5.7	4.9	9.2	2.9	6.1	5.0	0.0	5.0	2.6	1.0	2.5
8.6	4.3	5.0	5.8	3.2	5.0	6.8	2.8	6.7	3.4	3.1	3.4
12.5	9.0	9.8	12.4	9.8	11.6	14.4	2.9	14.3	7.8	0.0	7.6
4.0	5.5	5.4	5.4	6.0	5.6	6.2	6.9	6.2	4.0	4.0	4.0
—[a]	3.3	4.6	0.0	16.7	5.9	4.6	5.0	4.6	3.7	3.4	3.6
8.0	6.0	6.3	6.9	7.7	7.2	7.8	5.9	7.8	5.0	3.3	4.9
9.5	12.2	11.9	14.4	9.8	13.8	23.4	17.0	22.3	11.2	8.6	11.0
5.4	6.0	6.0	6.2	6.4	6.3	9.7	8.0	9.3	4.4	3.8	4.3
.0	4.9	4.7	4.6	8.3	5.4	5.9	5.5	5.8	4.5	4.2	4.4
6.8	7.1	7.1	8.4	7.2	8.2	12.5	9.2	11.8	5.9	4.4	5.6
8.4	11.4	11.0	11.8	11.1	11.7	22.6	14.5	21.2	8.5	10.3	8.7
6.2	8.8	8.7	6.1	7.4	6.4	8.5	6.7	8.1	4.2	5.8	4.6
3.7	9.1	8.9	6.2	7.3	6.4	4.6	5.7	4.8	3.5	5.6	4.1
7.1	9.4	9.2	8.0	8.1	8.0	11.6	8.1	10.8	5.3	6.3	5.4

1960 average unemployment rate. For men this was not the case. The 1980 unemployment rates of all Hispanic men except Cubans exceeded the 1960 rates. Cuban men, the exception to this generalization, experienced a 5 percent joblessness rate in 1980 compared with their 7.4 rate in 1960. Not only does this suggest a swift socioeconomic assimilation process for this group, but also less deleterious effects of the business cycles.

That nativity differentiates Hispanic unemployment rates is evident in the sharp age differentials among the foreign- and native-born. The extensive diversity in nativity differentials over time and among gender and national origin groups defies any simple generalization about the importance of nativity. Focusing on 1980 for purposes of illustration, we note that the differentials in unemployment rates for Mexican origin men were trivial, whereas those for women favored the native-born. Among Puerto Ricans an opposite pattern obtained in that differentials in unemployment rates between native- and foreign-born women were nonexistent, while native-born men experienced the highest joblessness rates.

One final comment about Table 9.5 concerns the relationship between age and unemployment. It is clear that the youngest age group— 16 to 24—experienced the highest unemployment rates irrespective of national origin. In part this stems from their lower levels of labor market experience. Among the recent arrivals this outcome also reflects their limited familiarity with the U.S. labor market.

To summarize, in the two decades beginning in 1960 Puerto Ricans and Cubans emerge as showing generally more extreme and contrasting labor force experiences. Puerto Ricans experienced declining rates of labor force participation and rising rates of unemployment. The Cuban experience was one of increasing labor force participation rates and declining unemployment rates. In fact, for 1980 Cuban men and women were quite similar to white men and women in these respects. Further evidence about the advantaged labor market position of Cubans vis-à-vis others follows in the next section.

The Nature of Work:
Occupational and Industrial Location, 1960–1980

To complete the picture of the positioning of Hispanics in the labor market, we turn our attention to the industrial and occupational structures that define the range of job opportunities at any given time. The importance of this aspect of market activity resides in the centrality of work, and in particular occupational location, in determining social standing and economic well-being. Sociologists concerned with intergenerational and intragenerational occupational mobility have long recognized how industrial regimes constrain or amplify prospects for social mobility. In fact, a vast body of research in social stratification has shown that changes in the occupational structure were responsible for virtually all intergenerational mobility among U.S. workers.[34]

The most important source of change in the employment structure over the past half-century has been the industrial transformation of production involving the growth of service industries and the decline of the extraction industries. Concomitantly, the prevalence of blue collar jobs diminished, while the relative share of white collar jobs increased. Singelmann and Browning[35] demonstrated that industry shifts were largely responsible for the expansion of higher-status occupations up to 1970, particularly professional and managerial occupations, while Singelmann and Tienda[36] showed that the changing intra-industry occupational composition was the dominant force permitting continued upgrading of the occupational structure after 1975.

Our concern with industrial placement acknowledges that the shift in production from goods to services modifies not only the nature of available jobs, but also their attendant social and economic rewards. Accordingly, we first examine how the evolution of the industry employment structure has differentially modified the industrial placement of the Hispanic work force during the past two decades. Subsequently we consider the socioeconomic significance of these shifts by examining changes in the occupational distribution of the Hispanic work force and dispersions in earnings among broad occupational categories.

On the matter of occupational placement there exists a vast literature in sociology which discusses the status content of occupations[37] and changes in the positioning of various racial and ethnic groups in the hierarchy of occupations.[38] The list of studies which use scalar[39] and

[34]Robert Hauser, P.J. Dickenson, H.P. Travis, and J.N. Koffel, "Structural Changes in Occupational Mobility Among Men in the United States," *American Sociological Review* 40 (October 1975):585–98; David Featherman and R. Hauser, *Opportunity and Change* (New York: Academic Press, 1978).

[35]Joachim Singelmann and Harley Browning, "Industrial Transformation and Occupational Change in the U.S., 1960–70," *Social Forces* 59(1980):247–64.

[36]Singelmann and Tienda, "The Process of Occupational Changes"; Singelmann and Browning, "Industrial Transformation."

[37]O. Duncan, "A Socioeconomic Index for All Occupations," pp. 109–38 in A. Reiss, Jr., ed., *Occupations and Social Status* (New York: Free Press, 1961); P. Blau and O. Duncan, *The American Occupational Structure* (New York: Wiley, 1967); Duncan, Featherman, and Duncan, *Socioeconomic Background and Achievement*.

[38]Robert Hauser and David Featherman, *The Process of Stratification* (New York: Academic Press, 1977); Featherman and Hauser, *Opportunity and Change*; Tienda and Guhleman, "Occupational Position of Employed Hispanic Women"; C. Matthew Snipp and Marta Tienda, "Chicano Career Mobility," *Studies in Social Stratification and Mobility* 4 (1985):177–94.

[39]Duncan's Socioeconomic Index is the most commonly used scalar measure, although NORC prestige scales also have been widely used.

discrete measures of occupational standing is quite extensive, although writings comparing blacks and whites are far more voluminous than those involving Hispanic workers.[40] Scalar indexes of social standing are particularly useful for portraying the process of stratification within the framework of the socioeconomic life cycle.[41] However, census data are generally inappropriate for modeling the process of socioeconomic achievement because information on parental background is not available for most respondents except young workers who still reside with their parents. (See Chapter 8.)

In keeping with our general goal of describing the positioning of Hispanics in the U.S. labor market, we use broad occupational categories to compare the national origin groups rather than procedures based on scalar measures of socioeconomic status. That a status hierarchy underlies the occupational scheme which consists of upper and lower white and blue collar occupations[42] permits us to make approximate inferences about the social ranking of the national origin groups. Given the relatively limited amount of information about the occupational placement of Hispanic origin workers, we believe that categorical measures of occupational standing provide useful information about the stratification regime confronting Hispanic workers between 1960 and 1980.

Our discussion of the changing employment structure of the Hispanic work force begins with a presentation of industry participation and then proceeds to occupational placement. By organizing the presentation in this way we hope to convey the importance of industrial restructuring in shaping the occupational configuration over time.

Industry Distribution of the Hispanic Work Force

Tables 9.6 and 9.8 present the industry distributions of the Hispanic male and female work force, respectively, for 1960 to 1980. The six-sector industry scheme is based on a more detailed 37-industry classification which provides greater compositional detail about each of the sectors. This scheme, originally developed by Browning and Singel-

---

[40]See C. Matthew Snipp and Marta Tienda, "Chicano Career Mobility," *Studies in Social Stratification and Mobility* 4 (1985):177–94; and Borjas and Tienda, *Hispanics in the U.S. Economy*, chap. 1, for a discussion of these issues.

[41]Duncan, Featherman, and Duncan, *Socioeconomic Background and Achievement.*

[42]Snipp and Tienda, "Chicano Career Mobility"; Tienda and Guhleman, "Occupational Position of Employed Hispanic Women"; Featherman and Hauser, *Opportunity and Change.*

mann,[43] is summarized in Table 9.7. Although the Census Bureau did modify the industry classification schemes between 1960 and 1980, these changes were relatively modest and do not affect our intertemporal comparisons in any appreciable way.[44]

Men. The decline of agricultural employment as the economy shifted from goods to service production had its most pronounced effect on the employment of Mexican origin men, of whom 23 percent were occupied in extractive industries (virtually all in agriculture) in 1960.[45] Over the next decade the share of the Mexican men engaged in extractive pursuits dropped 10 points. However, the movement of Mexican origin men out of agriculture slowed during the 1970s, an outcome which can be traced to the persistence of Mexican immigrants in this industry. As recently as 1980, 17 percent of all foreign-born Mexican men worked in extractive industries—almost exclusively in agriculture. This represents roughly three times the share observed among other Hispanics born abroad. The continuing salience of farm jobs for people of Mexican origin, and immigrants in particular, reflects the distinctive role of Mexican labor in the development of capitalist agriculture in the United States as a whole, but the Southwest in particular (see Chapter 1). Only 20 years earlier, over one-third of Mexican immigrants worked in the extractive sector.

For no other group did agricultural employment acquire such importance as for Mexicans in the distant or recent past. Between 1960 and 1980 the share of Puerto Rican men working in extractive industries never reached 5 percent, and for Cuban and Central/South American men the respective share never exceeded 6 percent. Other Hispanic men stand as an exception, as just under one immigrant worker in five was engaged in extractive activities in 1960, but this share declined to 9.5 percent in 1970 and 6.3 percent in 1980.[46] Among non-Hispanic whites native-born workers were at least twice as likely to hold extractive jobs

---

[43]Harley L. Browning, and Joachim Singelmann, "The Emergence of a Service Society: Demographic and Sociological Aspects of the Sectoral Transformation of the Labor Force in the U.S.A." Final Report, Manpower Administration, U.S. Department of Labor, 1975.

[44]For further discussion of this point, see Marta Tienda and Joachim Singelmann, "The Process of Occupational Change in a Service Society: The Case of the United States, 1960–1980," in Bryan Roberts, Ruth Finnegan, and Duncan Gallie, eds., *New Approaches to Economic Life: Economic Restructuring Unemployment and the Social Division of Labor* (Manchester, England: University of Manchester Press, 1985).

[45]Percentages for the total population are not reported in Tables 9.6 and 9.7 even though part of the discussion refers to group averages pooled across nativity.

[46]Given that this group is the least comparable over time, and especially prior to 1970, their disproportionate agricultural participation should be interpreted with caution. More than likely this subgroup includes many Hispanics and third-generation Chicanos, but our data preclude a further verification of this suspicion.

TABLE 9.6
Sectoral Allocation of Men Aged 16–64 by Nativity: 1960–1980

	Mexican		Puerto Rican		Cuban	
	Native	Foreign	Native	Foreign	Native	Foreign
1960						
Extractive	17.9%	36.0%	1.6%	4.3%	1.1%	0.7%
Transformative	38.4	31.3	42.6	54.4	47.1	45.7
Distributive Services	21.8	17.4	22.4	14.7	20.5	19.3
Producer Services	2.4	1.9	5.4	3.7	4.3	5.0
Social Services	10.6	3.8	16.5	6.1	14.0	9.2
Personal Services	9.1	9.6	11.7	16.7	12.9	20.1
Total[a]	100.2	100.0	100.2	99.9	99.9	100.0
1960 Dissimilarity Index,[b] Native-Foreign	23.0		28.4		31.0	
1970						
Extractive	11.6	19.3	1.5	2.3	5.7	1.6
Transformative	38.3	43.0	29.0	46.2	30.6	41.7
Distributive Services	22.7	18.2	25.9	19.3	22.0	23.9
Producer Services	3.7	2.5	10.4	7.2	7.0	7.5
Social Services	14.6	6.1	18.8	10.9	25.3	9.3
Personal Services	8.9	10.9	14.6	14.2	9.3	15.8
Total[a]	99.8	100.0	100.2	100.1	99.9	99.8
1970 Dissimilarity Index,[b] Native-Foreign	19.0		26.4		34.8	
1980						
Extractive	9.1	17.0	1.8	2.9	2.6	1.8
Transformative	38.9	46.5	30.4	43.3	26.9	34.2
Distributive Services	22.0	14.5	25.1	18.7	28.3	28.1
Producer Services	4.9	3.1	11.5	8.5	10.7	11.5
Social Services	15.6	5.3	19.4	15.4	18.1	12.5
Personal Services	9.6	13.4	11.8	11.2	13.5	11.9
Total[a]	100.1	99.8	100.0	100.0	100.1	100.0
1980 Dissimilarity Index,[b] Native-Foreign	24.2		17.8		17.6	
Time Trend Comparisons Dissimilarity Index,[b] 1960–1970	11.4	21.8	20.9	15.2	35.4	20.2
Dissimilarity Index,[b] 1970–1980	8.3	8.4	11.6	11.6	22.3	15.7

SOURCES: 1960, 1970, and 1980 Public Use Microdata Sample files.

[a]Numbers may not sum to 100 percent because of rounding error.
[b]Compares industry distributions of native-born and foreign-born.

TABLE 9.6 (continued)

Central/South American		Other Hispanic		Black		Non-Hispanic White	
Native	Foreign	Native	Foreign	Native	Foreign	Native	Foreign
0.8%	2.4%	7.5%	17.2%	14.0	19.2%	10.4%	4.0%
40.5	35.6	43.9	32.9	39.6	29.7	42.9	48.9
23.4	20.4	17.2	17.4	19.2	14.3	23.2	20.7
9.4	8.3	6.5	3.4	2.8	8.2	5.7	5.9
18.0	19.0	16.2	10.6	12.4	13.2	11.3	8.6
7.8	14.2	8.6	18.4	12.1	15.4	6.4	11.9
99.9	99.9	99.9	99.9	100.1	100.0	99.9	100.0
27.8		36.2		23.3		17.0	
4.6	0.9	8.1	9.5	6.9	3.7	7.0	3.4
40.3	38.5	38.3	32.3	44.9	30.0	41.8	43.7
21.9	22.0	23.0	19.5	19.3	22.6	23.2	20.8
7.5	9.7	6.2	6.4	3.8	10.3	6.7	8.8
16.4	15.3	16.6	17.1	15.6	24.3	14.4	11.4
9.3	13.4	7.9	15.3	9.6	9.0	6.9	11.8
100.0	99.8	100.1	100.1	100.1	99.9	100.0	99.9
18.8		18.0		25.2		15.6	
2.0	1.2	6.3	6.3	3.6	1.6	6.3	2.6
28.1	39.6	33.8	39.8	41.4	33.4	39.5	40.8
23.1	20.5	22.8	18.6	19.3	19.4	22.9	19.4
11.7	10.6	7.7	7.3	6.1	12.6	8.2	10.0
19.5	11.9	18.2	14.3	20.7	22.8	15.0	15.3
15.4	16.1	11.2	13.6	9.0	10.1	8.1	12.0
99.8	99.9	100.0	99.9	100.1	99.9	100.0	100.1
20.9		17.4		17.2		12.0	
23.1	17.6	23.4	22.4	12.9	34.0	8.9	10.6
21.0	10.8	14.0	13.6	13.8	17.4	6.6	11.2

TABLE 9.7
Allocation Scheme for Sectors and Industries

EXTRACTIVE
 1 Agriculture, fishing, and forestry
 2 Mining

TRANSFORMATIVE
 3 Construction
 4 Food
 5 Textile
 6 Metal
 7 Machinery
 8 Chemical
 9 Miscellaneous manufacturing
10 Utilities

DISTRIBUTIVE SERVICES
11 Transportation and storage
12 Communication
13 Wholesale trade
14 Retail trade (except eating and drinking places)

PRODUCER SERVICES
15 Banking, credit, and other financial services
16 Insurance
17 Real estate
18 Engineering and architectural services
19 Accounting and bookkeeping
20 Miscellaneous business services
21 Legal Services

SOCIAL SERVICES
22 Medical and health services
23 Hospitals
24 Education
25 Welfare and religious services
26 Nonprofit organizations
27 Postal services
28 Government
29 Miscellaneous professional and social services

PERSONAL SERVICES
30 Domestic services
31 Hotels and lodging places
32 Eating and drinking places
33 Repair services
34 Laundry and dry cleaning
35 Barber and beauty shops
36 Entertainment and recreational services
37 Miscellaneous personal services

SOURCE: Harley S. Browning and Joachim Singelmann, "The Transformation of the U.S. Labor Force: The Interaction of Industry and Occupation," *Politics and Society* 8 (1978):481–509, table 1.

as their foreign-born counterparts throughout the period, but the share of whites engaged in extractive industries never exceeded 10.4 percent and fell to 6.3 percent by 1980.

Diversity describes the experience of Hispanic workers in the transformative or manufacturing sector during the past two decades. Some national origin groups increased, while others decreased, their participation in manufacturing industries. The representation of Mexicans and Central/South Americans in manufacturing industries increased by 7 and 3 percent, respectively, during the 1960–1980 period. By contrast, the relative shares of Puerto Rican and Cuban men engaged in manufacturing declined by 14 and 13 percent, respectively. Other Hispanic men maintained a steady share in transformative industries throughout the period, hovering around 35 percent.[47]

These aggregate patterns among national origin groups conceal further variation by nativity. For example, the increasing share of Mexican origin workers engaged in the transformative sector during the 1960s and 1970s was due almost exclusively to the increased participation of immigrants in manufacturing industries, as the share of manufacturing employment for native-born Mexican workers remained fairly steady throughout the period. Similarly, the increased Central/South American presence in the transformative sector can be traced to growing numbers of immigrants working in textile and miscellaneous manufacturing enterprises, as the native-born segment of this group was less likely to hold manufacturing jobs in 1980 than 1970 or 1960. Because of the substantial increase in volume of immigration from Central America during the 1970s, the changed industrial (and occupational) configuration of this group largely reflects the fact that this population was qualitatively different at the beginning and end of the period (see Chapter 3).

The sharp 10 percent drop in the share of Puerto Ricans engaged in manufacturing industries during the 1960s involved disproportionate numbers of mainland-born workers, whereas island-born men experienced greater declines in their share of transformative employment during the 1970s. However, the net shift of Puerto Ricans out of manufacturing was smaller during the latter period. Native-born Cubans left manufacturing industries at a faster rate than their foreign-born counterparts during the 1960s, but the 1970s witnessed a rapid shift of Cuban immigrants out of the goods-processing sector.

As service employment engaged an increasing share of the total U.S. work force, rising from 56.4 to 65.7 percent between 1960 and 1980,[48] we should expect the experience of Hispanic workers to follow suit. Our results reproduce this trend: All groups except Central/South Americans

---

[47]This is a pooled average across nativity groups.
[48]Singelmann and Tienda, "Process of Occupational Change."

TABLE 9.8
Sectoral Allocation of Women Aged 16–64 by Nativity: 1960–1980

	Mexican		Puerto Rican		Cuban	
	Native	Foreign	Native	Foreign	Native	Foreign
1960						
Extractive	7.7%	11.6%	0.6%	0.5%	0.0%	0.5%
Transformative	22.1	29.9	38.5	74.2	30.6	57.2
Distributive Services	23.9	17.1	20.5	7.1	21.3	16.0
Producer Services	5.6	3.0	14.1	3.0	16.0	4.0
Social Services	14.2	7.9	12.9	7.9	18.6	8.2
Personal Services	26.6	30.4	13.5	7.3	13.4	14.1
Total[a]	100.1	99.9	100.1	100.0	99.9	100.0
1960 Dissimilarity Index,[b] Native-Foreign	23.3		42.6		45.5	
1970						
Extractive	5.3	11.0	0.4	0.6	4.4	0.8
Transformative	20.8	32.6	18.3	55.6	16.7	47.2
Distributive Services	20.7	17.5	26.5	11.9	21.1	16.6
Producer Services	7.0	4.3	15.3	7.5	10.7	8.8
Social Services	24.9	13.1	27.9	16.5	33.2	15.4
Personal Services	21.2	21.4	11.6	8.0	13.8	11.3
Total[a]	99.9	99.9	100.0	100.1	99.9	100.1
1970 Dissimilarity Index,[b] Native-Foreign	25.0		38.7		42.9	
1980						
Extractive	4.0	10.0	0.8	0.7	1.1	0.6
Transformative	20.6	39.5	18.5	40.9	13.3	34.7
Distributive Services	19.3	12.7	20.9	13.0	29.1	19.8
Producer Services	9.2	5.6	16.4	8.9	15.2	14.8
Social Services	31.0	15.4	32.0	27.9	27.5	20.6
Personal Services	15.7	16.7	11.2	8.8	13.9	9.5
Total[a]	99.8	99.9	99.8	100.2	100.1	100.0
1980 Dissimilarity Index,[b] Native-Foreign	30.2		24.1		26.5	
Time Trend Comparisons Dissimilarity Index,[b] 1960–1970	17.4	17.6	32.1	23.1	34.7	20.1
Dissimilarity Index,[b] 1970–1980	12.0	13.4	16.0	18.8	26.6	17.6

SOURCES: 1960, 1970, and 1980 Public Use Microdata Sample files.

[a]Numbers may not sum to 100 percent because of rounding error.
[b]Compares industry distributions of native-born and foreign-born.

TABLE 9.8 *(continued)*

Central/South American		Other Hispanic		Black		Non-Hispanic White	
Native	Foreign	Native	Foreign	Native	Foreign	Native	Foreign
0.8%	0.4%	0.0%	3.6%	10.1%	0.0%	2.1%	1.2%
26.4	35.4	34.8	38.5	10.6	24.0	25.6	34.8
22.4	17.2	21.7	22.5	7.0	11.6	24.9	20.1
12.8	10.0	6.6	6.6	1.9	5.8	9.6	8.3
28.0	18.6	17.3	16.6	19.2	29.8	23.3	16.0
9.6	18.5	19.7	12.4	51.1	28.9	14.6	19.6
100.0	100.1	100.1	100.2	99.9	100.1	100.1	100.0
38.4		30.4		41.2		18.8	
0.5	0.5	3.2	1.9	3.2	0.0	1.5	1.4
18.1	35.5	21.7	27.2	17.7	14.7	21.9	26.4
22.2	15.1	18.4	15.1	12.2	15.6	22.8	22.9
12.6	13.1	9.7	10.6	4.5	10.7	10.4	11.4
34.9	20.6	29.8	27.5	30.4	36.2	29.1	22.3
11.7	15.3	17.1	17.6	32.0	22.8	14.2	15.6
100.0	100.1	99.9	99.9	100.0	100.0	99.9	100.0
31.5		16.5		25.5		12.0	
1.0	0.7	2.0	2.0	1.4	0.2	1.8	0.9
15.7	37.6	16.1	31.8	18.9	14.3	18.2	22.8
23.4	14.0	20.5	14.4	12.8	11.8	20.4	21.0
14.6	11.6	12.5	9.8	8.8	14.3	12.9	14.1
30.7	18.5	32.1	26.5	41.5	43.9	32.7	27.6
14.4	17.5	16.8	15.3	16.5	15.5	14.0	13.6
99.8	99.9	100.0	99.8	99.9	100.0	100.0	100.0
30.0		23.4		22.4		10.0	
27.6	16.8	30.0	23.9	30.4	26.7	9.8	19.6
19.1	10.4	14.1	11.2	22.3	20.4	10.2	12.6

increased their participation in service industries between 1960 and 1980, with the service employment gains ranging from a low of 5.5 percent among all Mexicans to a high of 15.6 percent among all Puerto Ricans. Cubans and Other Hispanics (pooled by nativity) increased their participation in service industries by 11.7 and 9.0 percent, respectively.

Not only did the level of service employment differ among the national origin and nativity groups, but so also did the interdecade pattern of sectoral changes among service sectors. For example, rising levels of service employment for Mexican and Other Hispanic men were possible largely because of their decreased participation in agricultural industries, while declining manufacturing employment was primarily responsible for the increased service employment of Puerto Rican and Cuban men. In 1980 the distributive services sector, which includes transportation, communication, and wholesale and retail trade, was the modal service employment sector for Hispanic men.

Although employment in personal services dropped between 1960 and 1980 for the country as a whole, most Hispanic groups did not conform to this pattern. For example, the share of Mexican men engaged in personal service industries *increased* over time owing largely to the growing presence of foreign-born workers engaged in personal services. A similar pattern obtained for Central/South American and Other Hispanic men, although the gains in personal service employment for the latter were more modest than those of Mexicans.

That nativity differentials in the industrial employment structures of Hispanic workers have persisted throughout the period does not preclude the possibility of increased similarity in their industry and sector distributions over time. To assess this question we computed for each time period indexes of dissimilarity (ID) between native- and foreign-born workers of each ethnicity. These computations were based on the 37-industry classification shown in Table 9.7. The ID indicates the percentage of workers who would have to change industry categories for the two distributions compared to be identical. While it does not tell where such changes must be made to achieve distributional parity, it is a convenient measure for summarizing trends.

Briefly, these calculations show that the nativity differentials in industry employment structures narrowed for all groups except Mexicans. For Puerto Ricans the index of dissimilarity based on the industrial distributions of mainland-born and island-born men dropped from 28 percent in 1960 to 18 percent in 1980, with most of the decline occurring during the 1970s. The Cuban ID value increased during the 1960s (from 31 to 35 percent), but thereafter fell 50 percent to just under 18 percent. The industrial employment structures of native and immigrant Central/South American and Other Hispanic men also converged during the period. That the ID value for Mexicans fell from 23 to 19 percent during the 1960s and then rose to 24 percent during the 1970s may partly reflect the increased presence of undocumented immigrants in the 1980 census and the persisting job segregation among Chicanos, Mexicanos, and Indocumentados.[49]

To summarize, the male Hispanic work force has participated in the industrial transformation of the U.S. employment structure, although the nature of their participation differs according to national origin and nativity. All groups but one increased their participation in the service sectors, but employment changes in the transformative sector varied from sharp declines (Cubans and Puerto Ricans) to moderate increases (Mexicans and Central/South Americans). Comparisons of industry structures over time showed that the process of industrial transformation proceeded somewhat faster during the 1960s than the 1970s. For example, ID values comparing the 1970 and 1980 industrial distributions ranged from 7 percent for Mexicans to 13 percent for Cubans, indicating a slower pace of industrial change overall, but particularly for Mexicans, whose movement into services has been slowed by their persistence in agricultural industries and a slow entry into the transformative sector. This occurred at a time when the other four Hispanic origin groups were moving rapidly into service employment.

Women. Although the share of all Hispanic women engaged in extractive jobs was considerably below that of all Hispanic men throughout the 1960s and 1970s, women of Mexican origin, like their male counterparts, were more highly represented in this sector. The fact that Mexican immigrant women continue to enter agricultural jobs at a rate faster than the growth of the total labor force,[50] despite shrinking extractive employment opportunities nationally, largely accounts for the disproportionate representation of Mexican origin women in extractive employment. The relative share of Mexican immigrant women occupied in extractive industries fell less than 2 percent over the 20-year period, while the respective decline in agricultural employment for native Mexican women was approximately 4 percent. For other groups employment in extractive industries was negligible between 1960 and 1980, with the exception of Other Hispanic women. This industrial configuration is consistent with the highly urban character of these groups.

[49]Bean, Browning, and Frisbie, "Sociodemographic characteristics of Mexican Immigrant Status Groups"; Harley L. Browning and Nestor Rodriguez, "The Migration of Mexican Indocumentados as a Settlement Process: Implications for Work," in George Borjas and Marta Tienda, eds., *Hispanics in the U.S. Economy* (Orlando, FL: Academic Press, 1985).
[50]Marta Tienda, Leif I. Jensen, and Robert L. Bach, "Immigration, Gender and the Process of Occupational Change," *International Migration Review* 18 (1984):1021–44.

Employment changes involving manufacturing and service industries varied in magnitude from modest to substantial, depending on time
period and national origin. For example, Mexican and Central/South
American origin women slightly increased their relative shares in manufacturing industries between 1960 and 1980, while the remaining
groups registered declines in manufacturing employment, ranging from
18 percent for Cubans and Other Hispanics to a whopping 38 percent
for Puerto Ricans. For this group the most precipitous fall occurred during the 1960s, when Puerto Rican manufacturing employment dropped
from 70 to 48 percent, but the 15 percent decline in manufacturing employment that occurred during the 1970s is equally impressive. The
movement of Cuban women out of manufacturing concerns resulted
from continuous declines throughout the period.

Decreasing opportunities in manufacturing are translated to expanded employment options in service industries for all women except
those of Mexican and Central/South American origin. These are the two
groups whose sociodemographic composition was most influenced by
immigration during the 1970s. The relative increases in service employment for Puerto Rican, Cuban, and Other Hispanic women were comparable in magnitude to the declines in manufacturing employment experienced by each group. This general pattern conforms with classic
statements about the sectoral transformation of employment which involves steady declines of agricultural and manufacturing employment
and the expansion of service employment.[51]

Within service industries the experience of Hispanic women varied
extensively along national origin lines. For example, three of the five
groups (Puerto Ricans, Cubans, and Other Hispanics) increased their
representation in distribution services, a change mainly involving retail
trade and communication industries, but Central/South American and
Mexican origin women decreased their shares in distribution industries
between 1960 and 1980. The lower participation of immigrants from
Central and South America in retail trade jobs accounts for their lower
representation in distributive industries in 1980, but there were no discernible nativity differentials in the share of Mexican origin women
who entered the distribution service sector during this period.

Producer services—which include banking, insurance, real estate,
engineering, and accounting services—absorbed larger shares of Hispanic women of all nationalities over time. Expanded employment opportunities for women in this sector resulted from the heavy reliance of

---

[51]See discussion in Browning and Singelmann, "Emergence of a Service Society."

producer service firms on clerical occupations which, because of sex-typing norms, absorb women in disproportionate numbers.[52]

During the past two decades Hispanic women made the greatest employment gains in the social service sector, which includes education and health industries. This trend reflects the rapid growth of these industries in the economy as a whole. Central and South American women were the only group whose representation in social service employment decreased between 1960 and 1980, but this decline was a phenomenon of the 1970s rather than the 1960s. This outcome partly reflects the changing country of origin and socioeconomic composition of Central/South American immigrants toward lower education levels and the possibility that many undocumented immigrants destined for unskilled jobs in personal services and manufacturing industries were included in the 1980 census. That is, the higher educational and certification requirements in the education and medical industries probably were inaccessible to many foreign-born Central/South American women seeking employment in social services industries.

Finally, the Hispanic female employment experience in personal services was mixed, involving small relative increases for Puerto Ricans, Central/South Americans, and Other Hispanics and more substantial decreases for Mexicans and Cubans. Nationally, personal service employment decreased by approximately 1 to 2 percent between 1960 and 1980; thus, the modest increases in personal service employment registered by some Hispanic women ran counter to the trend in the national economy as a whole.[53] Although the Mexican and Cuban experience conforms to the national trend, the dramatic decline in personal service employment by Mexican origin women is striking. This change was not confined to either decade, or to the native- or foreign-born segments of the population.

Aggregate changes in the sectoral allocation of Hispanic women workers conceal differential patterns of change according to nativity. Intersectoral shifts produced greater similarity between industry structures of native- and foreign-born women of like ethnicity. Mexican women, like their male counterparts, stand as the only exception to this generalization. The ID values comparing the industry distributions of native and immigrant women of Mexican descent rose slightly during the 1960s and even more during the 1970s, indicating growing dispari-

[52]Marta Tienda and Vilma Ortiz, "Hispanicity and the 1980 Census," *Social Science Quarterly* 67 (1986):3–20; Marta Tienda and Shelley A. Smith, "The Structural Transformation of Employment in Wisconsin, 1960–1980," Research Bulletin no. R3377, College of Agriculture and Life Sciences, University of Wisconsin–Madison, 1986.

[53]Singelmann and Tienda, "Process of Occupational Change."

ties over time. In large measure the growing nativity differentials in the industrial allocation of Mexican women resulted from the opposed tendencies of native and immigrant women to enter manufacturing jobs. That is, while the relative share of native-born Mexican women engaged in manufacturing enterprises fell between 1960 and 1980, the share of Mexican immigrant women working in transformation industries increased by 10 percent. Finally, ID values comparing the pace of the industrial transformation of the female Hispanic work force reveal that sectoral employment shifts were more rapid during the 1960s than the 1970s, as observed for men (and the total U.S. work force).

Summary. Although we have discussed the changing industrial employment patterns of Hispanic workers separately for men and women, we do not wish to leave the impression that the gender differences in industrial allocation patterns evident at the beginning of the period have remained unaltered through 1980. Both men and women of Hispanic origin increased their representation in service industries, while decreasing their presence in extractive and transformative industries, a pattern which mirrors the national trend in industrial restructuring. However, we have identified noteworthy departures from the general direction of change for men and women of different national origins and nativity statuses. Also, and consistent with national trends, the industrial employment structures of Hispanic men and women of like national origin have converged, indicating less gender differentiation in industrial employment structures. For example, in 1960, 45 percent of all Mexican origin workers would have had to change industries for the industry distributions of men and women to be identical, but by 1970 this proportion dropped to 35 percent. For Cuban workers the interdecade changes in their industrial distribution resulted in even greater gender similarity in industry distributions over time: ID values for this group dropped from 41 to 28 percent between 1960 and 1980.

In conclusion, there persisted in 1980 substantial differences in the industrial employment structures of Hispanic workers according to nativity and gender. For men nativity differentiation in industrial allocation was less than for women at all three time periods. But as recently as 1980 native and immigrant women differed in their industrial allocation patterns as much as men did from women.

Occupation Distribution of the Hispanic Work Force

Figures 9.3–9.7 and Tables 9.9 and 9.10 summarize changes in the occupational distributions of Hispanic men and women between 1960 and 1980 according to national origin and nativity. To highlight the key

FIGURE 9.3

Occupational Distribution for Mexicans Aged 16–64 by Year and Gender: 1960–1980

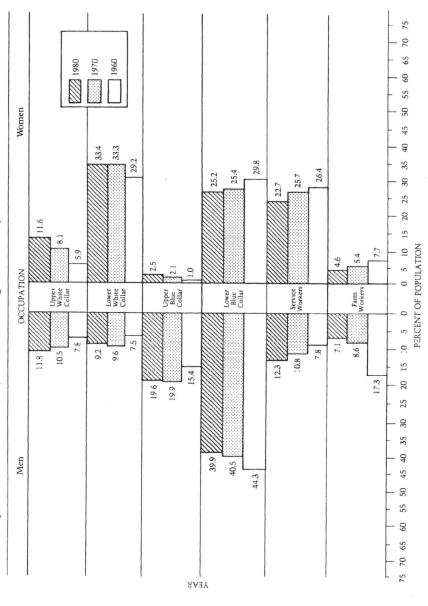

SOURCES: 1960, 1970, and 1980 Public Use Microdata Sample files.
NOTE: Upper white collar-professionals, semiprofessionals, and managers; lower white collar-clerical, sales; upper blue collar-crafts; lower blue collar-farmers, operatives, and laborers.

FIGURE 9.4

Occupational Distribution for Puerto Ricans Aged 16–64 by Year and Gender: 1960–1980

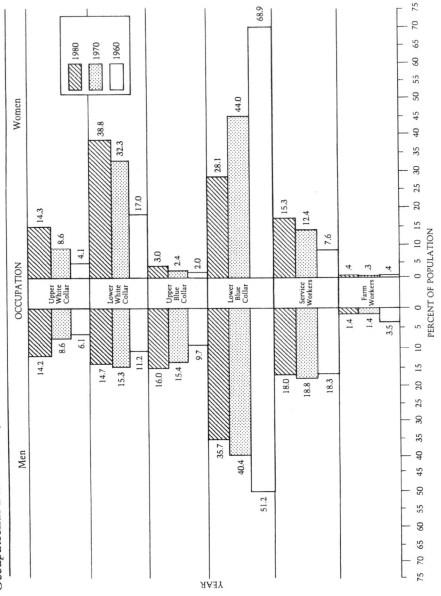

SOURCES: 1960, 1970, and 1980 Public Use Microdata Sample files.
NOTE: See Figure 9.3 for occupational codes.

FIGURE 9.5

Occupational Distribution for Cubans Aged 16–64 by Year and Gender: 1960–1980

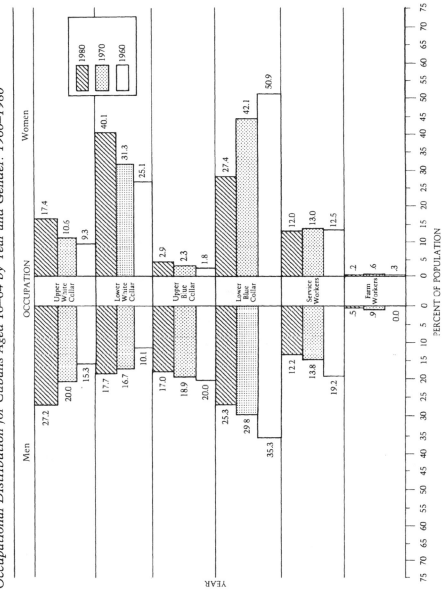

SOURCES: 1960, 1970, and 1980 Public Use Microdata Sample files.
NOTE: See Figure 9.3 for occupational codes.

FIGURE 9.6

Occupational Distribution for Central/South Americans Aged 16–64 by Year and Gender: 1960–1980

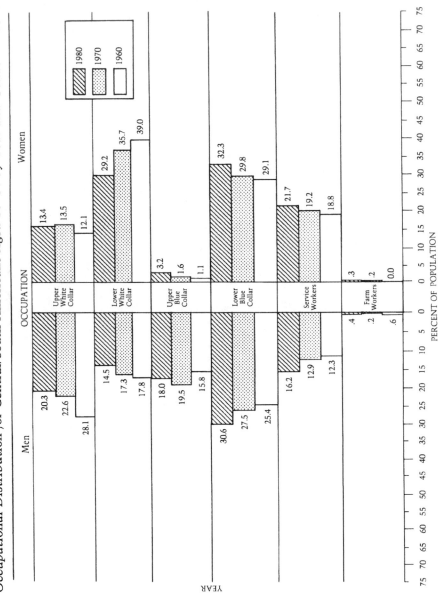

SOURCES: 1960, 1970, and 1980 Public Use Microdata Sample files.
NOTE: See Figure 9.3 for occupational codes.

FIGURE 9.7

Occupational Distribution for Other Hispanics Aged 16–64 by Year and Gender: 1960–1980

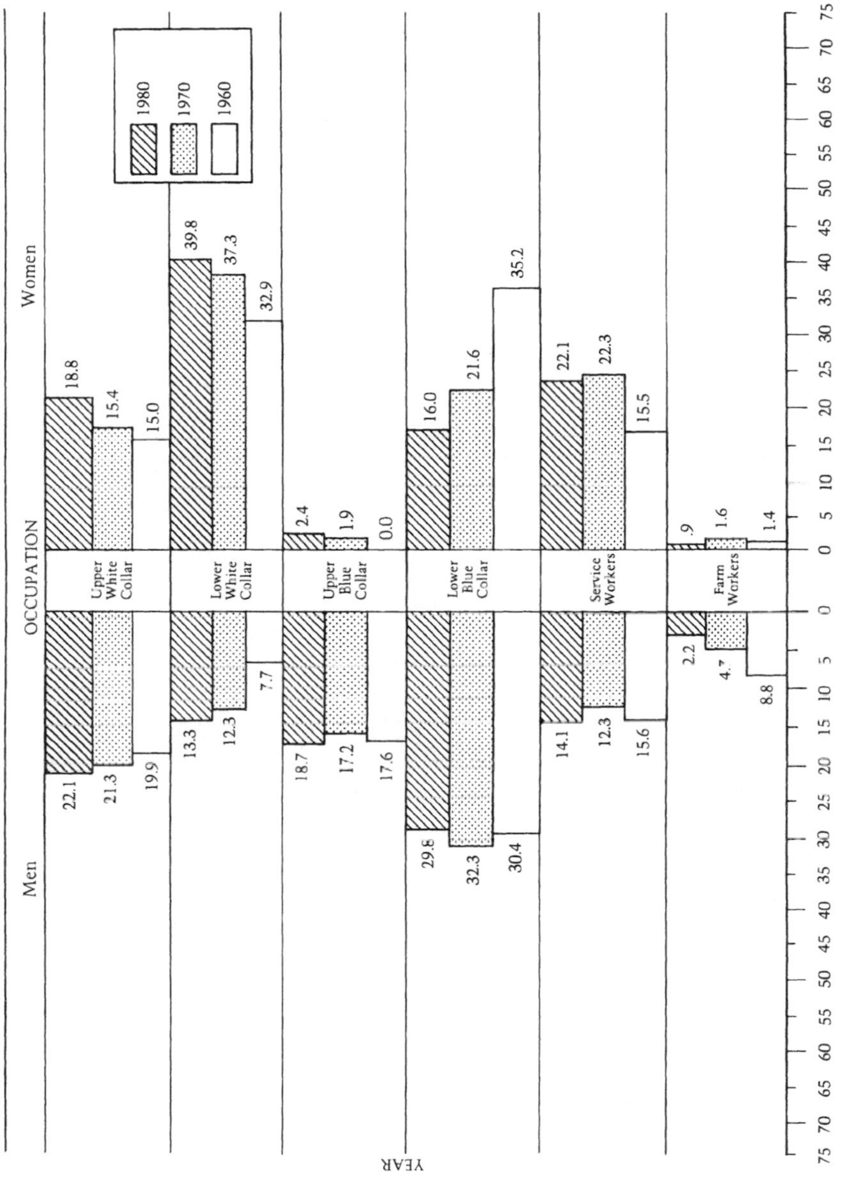

SOURCES: 1960, 1970, and 1980 Public Use Microdata Sample files.
NOTE: See Figure 9.3 for occupational codes.

TABLE 9.9
Occupational Distribution of Men Aged 16–64 by Nativity: 1960–1980

	Mexican		Puerto Rican		Cuban	
	Native	Foreign	Native	Foreign	Native	Foreign
1960						
Professional	3.3%	2.1%	5.9%	1.6%	9.9%	6.1%
Semiprofessional	1.3	0.4	2.7	0.9	3.3	0.3
Farmers	1.9	1.7	0.0	0.2	0.0	0.0
Managers	4.1	2.8	3.2	3.0	11.0	6.1
Clericals	5.2	2.4	12.4	6.9	6.6	6.5
Sales	3.4	2.1	7.0	3.5	3.3	3.7
Crafts	16.4	12.6	14.5	9.3	24.2	18.7
Operatives	26.8	19.0	30.1	43.8	18.7	31.3
Service Workers	8.0	7.5	15.6	18.6	15.4	20.4
Laborers	17.6	18.0	7.5	8.6	7.7	6.8
Farm Laborers	12.1	31.4	1.1	3.8	0.0	0.0
Total[a]	100.1	100.0	100.0	100.2	100.1	99.9
1960 Dissimilarity Index, Native-Foreign	19.8		20.6		18.1	
1970						
Professional	5.1	3.4	8.9	3.0	12.7	9.8
Semiprofessional	1.7	0.6	2.3	0.9	2.3	2.6
Farmers	0.7	0.6	0.2	0.1	0.0	0.1
Managers	4.9	2.9	6.4	2.8	14.1	6.2
Clericals	6.7	3.5	17.0	9.7	11.7	10.0
Sales	3.9	2.6	5.7	3.8	6.6	6.5
Crafts	20.2	18.8	15.2	15.4	19.7	18.8
Operatives	26.2	28.2	17.7	35.6	13.1	25.3
Service Workers	11.0	9.9	14.5	19.8	9.4	14.5
Laborers	13.0	14.3	11.5	7.2	7.0	5.7
Farm Laborers	6.7	15.2	0.5	1.6	3.3	0.5
Total[a]	100.1	100.0	99.9	99.9	99.9	100.0
1970 Dissimilarity Index, Native-Foreign	11.8		24.5		17.6	
1980						
Professional	5.7	2.5	8.1	4.8	11.8	11.2
Semiprofessional	2.1	0.8	2.6	1.7	3.4	2.7
Farmers	0.5	0.5	0.1	0.1	0.1	0.2
Managers	6.9	3.6	6.3	6.4	9.0	13.7
Clericals	7.9	3.7	15.8	9.6	13.0	10.3
Sales	3.7	1.7	5.0	2.4	8.1	7.0
Crafts	20.7	17.7	14.5	16.6	13.8	17.4
Operatives	24.0	30.0	19.7	30.6	14.1	18.5
Service Workers	11.8	13.0	18.0	18.1	15.5	11.8
Laborers	12.6	14.3	9.1	8.0	10.5	6.7
Farm Laborers	4.1	12.2	0.8	61.7	0.6	0.4
Total[a]	100.0	100.0	100.0	100.0	99.9	99.9
1980 Dissimilarity Index, Native-Foreign	17.0		14.1		12.8	
Time Trend Comparisons Dissimilarity Index, 1960–1970	11.8	21.0	15.8	12.0	17.7	13.1
Dissimilarity Index, 1970–1980	5.6	6.0	6.0	8.2	14.6	11.0

SOURCES: 1960, 1970, and 1980 Public Use Microdata Sample files.

TABLE 9.9 *(continued)*

Central/South American		Other Hispanic		Black		Non-Hispanic White	
Native	Foreign	Native	Foreign	Native	Foreign	Native	Foreign
16.7%	17.8%	10.0%	8.6%	2.5%	3.4%	9.3%	8.1%
2.4	2.9	4.4	1.1	0.4	1.7	2.0	1.8
0.8	0.2	3.3	5.5	3.7	0.6	5.3	1.7
8.7	7.5	8.9	9.6	1.6	2.8	11.2	12.8
12.7	12.9	7.8	3.7	5.4	8.5	7.9	7.0
9.5	3.6	2.2	3.5	1.3	1.7	7.6	5.2
20.6	14.4	28.9	15.4	10.2	12.4	21.3	26.1
16.7	21.7	16.7	13.6	26.8	17.5	21.1	21.6
6.3	14.1	3.3	18.0	16.6	20.9	5.0	8.8
5.6	4.1	11.1	11.2	23.2	12.4	6.7	6.0
0.0	0.7	3.3	9.9	8.2	18.1	2.6	0.9
100.0	99.9	99.9	99.9	99.9	100.0	100.0	100.0
15.3		25.5		23.2		10.6	
12.4	13.4	10.2	11.0	4.1	11.9	12.0	14.8
2.5	3.7	2.5	2.6	1.2	2.0	2.5	2.2
0.8	0.2	1.1	1.3	0.8	0.0	2.8	1.1
8.3	5.5	8.3	8.4	2.7	1.6	11.5	10.2
13.3	11.1	7.4	7.8	7.3	14.8	7.6	7.2
9.5	5.2	5.4	3.5	2.1	4.1	7.2	7.3
19.1	19.6	18.5	14.2	15.1	19.3	21.1	22.9
17.4	22.9	22.9	18.9	29.3	17.2	19.0	16.6
9.5	13.5	9.9	17.5	16.5	20.9	7.4	12.3
6.2	4.9	9.8	8.5	17.1	6.2	7.2	5.1
0.8	0.1	4.0	6.2	3.8	2.0	1.8	0.4
99.8	100.1	100.0	99.9	100.0	100.0	100.1	100.1
12.0		11.0		26.7		9.6	
15.0	8.8	9.2	10.5	5.3	10.7	12.1	17.0
4.5	2.5	2.8	2.7	2.0	3.8	2.7	3.2
0.3	0.1	0.9	0.6	0.4	0.1	2.1	0.5
10.0	8.3	10.3	7.8	5.4	6.0	13.6	16.5
11.9	10.1	8.8	7.4	9.6	13.2	6.9	5.5
7.4	4.1	5.1	3.5	2.3	3.2	7.0	5.2
14.7	18.2	19.1	17.2	15.1	16.5	20.7	22.1
12.9	25.8	18.0	21.3	27.5	22.1	17.4	14.6
14.7	16.3	13.8	15.3	16.8	17.0	8.6	9.8
8.3	5.3	10.2	10.0	13.9	6.7	7.5	5.1
0.4	0.4	1.7	3.7	1.6	0.7	1.3	0.4
100.1	99.9	99.9	100.0	99.9	100.0	100.0	99.9
18.1		8.0		13.8		10.9	
6.1	9.5	16.8	13.4	13.6	24.4	6.4	12.8
13.4	9.3	8.6	7.0	7.6	11.7	4.0	9.6

gender and ethnic differentials in occupational placement, we begin with a graphic display of broad occupational groupings for each national origin group and summarize changes and differentials in the occupational location of Hispanic workers using the index of dissimilarity (ID). Because ID tells whether and by how much two distributions differ, but not where changes must occur to achieve parity, we examine the more detailed occupational distributions in Tables 9.9 and 9.10 and locate the major sources of divergence among nationality, nativity, and gender groups.

The most general message portrayed in Figures 9.3–9.7 is that the Hispanic labor force experienced variable amounts of occupational upgrading over the last two decades, as evidenced by the increased representation in white collar occupations of all gender and origin groups except Central/South American men. However, the amount and pace of occupational upgrading differed markedly by gender and national origin. Mexicans and Puerto Ricans are similar in that the 1980 share of workers holding upper white collar occupations was virtually identical for men and women. However, the share of workers holding upper white collar jobs in 1980 was slightly larger for Puerto Ricans than Mexicans, 14 and 12 percent, respectively. This pattern emerged during the 1970s since in 1960 Mexicans were slightly better represented than Puerto Ricans in upper white collar jobs. Although this picture seems partly to contradict that of the previous two sections wherein Puerto Ricans emerged as the most disadvantaged of the Hispanic origin groups, the higher representation of Puerto Ricans in white collar occupations in 1980 reflects the more urban character of this group relative to Mexicans and the selective character of the sample of Puerto Rican workers with jobs. Because this occupational profile is based on a subset of employed workers, and we have already established that Puerto Ricans experienced not only the sharpest declines in labor force participation between 1960 and 1980, but also the highest unemployment rates, it appears that Puerto Ricans who actually secure jobs do quite well.

The Puerto Rican and Mexican scenario of limited gender differentiation in upper white collar occupations was not applicable to the remaining groups, especially Cubans and Central/South Americans. In 1980 the share of Cuban men and women holding upper white collar jobs differed by 10 percent, while among Central/South Americans the comparable gender differential was roughly 7 percent. Hispanic women of all the national origin groups were overrepresented in lower white collar jobs relative to men owing to the highly sex-typed character of clerical and sales occupations.[54]

[54]Tienda and Ortiz, "Hispanicity and the 1980 Census"; Tienda and Guhleman, "Occupational Position of Employed Hispanic Women"; Smith and Tienda, "Doubly Disadvantaged."

The main story from Figures 9.3–9.7 is that the interdecade pattern of occupational change differed by national origin and gender.[55] For example, Mexicans, whose mode of entry into the U.S. labor market was dominated by a presence in agriculture, experienced the greatest declines in farm occupations. Yet as recently as 1980 the Mexican presence in farm occupations, mainly laborer rather than operator jobs, far exceeded that of the other Hispanic groups. This is consistent with the results in Tables 9.6 and 9.7, which document the higher participation of Mexican immigrants in agricultural industries[56] and the more rural residential character of this group (Chapter 3). The decreased participation of Mexicans in farming pursuits was offset by a greater presence in white collar jobs and, to a lesser extent, in upper blue collar jobs. Also, the share of Mexicans holding lower blue collar jobs dropped by roughly 4 percent during the period. Gender differences in service employment resulted in declining shares of Mexican women involved in service occupations, owing largely to a decreased demand for domestic services, and a slight increase in the share of men holding service jobs.

In contrast to Mexicans, declining farm employment had little bearing on changes in the occupational structure of the remaining Hispanic groups.[57] Among Puerto Ricans the most striking intertemporal occupational changes involved the sharply declining shares of lower blue collar workers, ranging from 41 percent among women to 15 percent among men. This drop in blue collar jobs translated to an increased representation of men in upper blue and white collar occupations; concurrently, women increased their relative participation in white collar occupations. We reiterate that the impressive occupational upgrading experienced by Puerto Ricans must be interpreted as a highly selective process whereby those most likely to succeed have remained in the labor force, while those with limited prospects for occupational mobility have dropped out altogether, as suggested by the declining rates of labor force participation and increased rates of unemployment over time.

The Cuban labor market success story emerges clearly in the interdecade pattern of occupational changes. Not only were greater shares of Cuban men holding upper white collar jobs in 1980 compared with the other national origin and gender groups, but the increased representation of Cubans in the highest-status jobs between 1960 and 1980 also was impressive. By 1980, 45 percent of all employed Cuban men and 57 percent of all employed Cuban women worked in white collar jobs compared with 25 and 34 percent, respectively, in 1960. This impressive

---

[55]The next few paragraphs summarize the intertemporal change portrayed by Figures 9.3–9.7.

[56]Tienda, *Hispanic Origin Workers*.

[57]The only exception is Other Hispanics, but owing to the tenuous intertemporal comparability of this group, we do not elaborate on these differences.

occupational mobility was made possible by substantial decreases in the share of Cuban men holding blue collar and service jobs and Cuban women holding lower blue collar jobs over this period. Because immigrants often experience some downward occupational mobility immediately following their move to a new environment, some of the interdecade upward mobility observed among Cubans reflects a recovery of the status positions originally held in Cuba.[58] For a highly skilled labor force this is often possible only after recertifying professional titles and degrees, hence the time lag in the professionalization of the Cuban labor force.

Although Central and South Americans are often grouped with Cubans in terms of a relatively high-status positioning in the United States labor force, they differ from the latter in two important respects. Not only were the relative shares of Central/South American men and women holding white collar jobs in 1980 lower compared with Cubans, but Central and South Americans are the only group to decrease their representation in white collar compared with blue collar jobs over the period. Decreased white collar participation by Central and South Americans was accompanied by an increased presence in lower blue collar and service jobs. The changing country of origin composition of the Central and South American population during the 1970s (Chapter 3) largely explains the shifting interdecade occupational configuration toward a greater representation in blue collar as compared with white collar jobs.

Other Hispanics were similar to Mexicans, Puerto Ricans, and Cubans in their interdecade pattern of occupational change, except that the amounts of change differ. However, since this group is the most problematic with respect to interdecade comparability, we focus on the contemporary occupational profile. Based on the relative share of white collar workers, Other Hispanics were more similar to Cubans than to Mexicans and Puerto Ricans. Nearly 35 percent of all men and 59 percent of all women of Other Hispanic origin held white collar jobs in 1980. It appears that the high participation of Other Hispanic origin women in white collar occupations in 1980 was facilitated by dramatically reduced numbers engaged in lower blue collar jobs, but this cannot be established with certainty because of the comparability problems discussed in Chapter 2.

Tables 9.9 and 9.10 disaggregate the occupational distributions of Hispanic workers according to nativity, thus illustrating the importance of birthplace in stratifying the work force. Again, the index of dissimilarity provides a useful metric for identifying different patterns of change for native- and foreign-born workers.

---

[58]Portes and Bach, Latin Journey.

Among men only Cubans and Other Hispanics experienced a gradual convergence between the occupational structures of native and immigrant workers. The ID comparing the occupational structures of native- and foreign-born Cuban men dropped from 18 to 13 percent between 1960 and 1980, while for Other Hispanic men the respective ID value fell from 25 to 8 percent during the 20-year period. The movement of native Other Hispanic workers out of crafts and service jobs largely explains the narrowed differences in the occupational structures of native- and foreign-born workers, while for Cubans the exit of immigrants from operative jobs and native workers from crafts jobs accounts for the interdecade occupational convergence.

Among the remaining three groups changes in nativity differentials were mixed. That is, the occupational structures of native and immigrant men of Mexican and Central/South American origin converged during the 1960s, but diverged during the 1970s. That nativity differentials in occupational placement increased rather than decreased for these two groups points to the changing composition of recent immigrants, including larger shares of undocumented workers.[59]

Puerto Ricans illustrate yet a third pattern of temporal change in occupational differentiation according to nativity. Specifically, the occupational disparities between workers born in Puerto Rico and the U.S. mainland increased slightly during the 1960s, but declined sharply thereafter, from 24 to 14 percent. These striking fluctuations reflect not only the changing rates of labor force participation and unemployment of Puerto Ricans during the last two decades, but also the altered sociodemographic composition of labor migrants, as well as the massive shifts in the industrial structure of the Northeast.[60]

Nativity differentials in the occupational allocation of Hispanic origin women did not parallel those of their male counterparts of like ethnicity. For example, Mexican origin women were the only group for whom occupational disparities between native and foreign workers increased throughout the period. These increased occupational disparities involved clerical, operative, and farm laborer jobs. By contrast, nativity differentials in the occupational placement of Puerto Rican women declined continuously. Despite these opposed patterns of change, the nativity differentials in the occupational placement of Puerto Rican women were roughly similar in 1980 in that 26 to 28 percent of these workers would have to change occupations to achieve parity between native- and foreign-born women. Smaller disparities in the shares of mainland and island women engaged in clerical and operative jobs were

[59]See Chapter 4. Also see George J. Borjas, "Assimilation, Changes in Cohort Quality, and the Earnings of Immigrants," *Journal of Labor Economics* 3 (1985):463–89.
[60]Sassen-Koob, "Changing Composition and Labor Market Location."

TABLE 9.10
Occupational Distribution of Women Aged 16–64 by Nativity: 1960–1980

	Mexican		Puerto Rican		Cuban	
	Native	Foreign	Native	Foreign	Native	Foreign
1960						
Professional	3.9%	2.1%	4.5%	2.1%	5.4%	7.3%
Semiprofessional	0.7	0.4	1.3	0.6	0.0	1.0
Farmers	0.1	0.1	0.0	0.0	0.0	0.0
Managers	1.4	2.4	1.3	1.0	2.7	1.5
Clericals	22.1	9.5	40.1	9.9	35.1	15.6
Sales	9.9	7.0	11.5	2.8	8.1	2.9
Crafts	1.1	0.9	0.0	2.3	1.4	2.0
Operatives	27.0	36.2	28.0	72.9	33.8	55.6
Service Workers	25.7	29.3	11.5	7.1	13.5	12.2
Laborers	1.2	1.1	1.3	1.0	0.0	1.5
Farm Laborers	6.9	11.1	0.6	0.4	0.0	0.5
Total[b]	100.0	100.1	100.1	100.1	100.0	100.1
1960 Dissimilarity Index, Native-Foreign	18.0		47.2		27.2	
1970						
Professional	5.9	3.7	10.0	4.9	14.3	6.7
Semiprofessional	0.8	0.3	2.6	1.2	1.0	1.8
Farmers	0.1	0.1	0.0	0.0	0.0	0.0
Managers	2.0	1.7	0.9	1.1	2.5	1.0
Clericals	29.3	16.3	47.8	21.7	42.4	22.4
Sales	7.0	3.8	8.7	3.9	8.4	5.7
Crafts	2.0	2.4	1.3	2.6	1.5	2.5
Operatives	20.9	37.0	12.4	51.7	9.9	45.7
Service Workers	26.2	23.5	16.0	11.5	16.3	12.5
Laborers	1.4	1.7	0.4	0.9	0.5	1.6
Farm Laborers	4.4	9.6	0.0	0.4	3.4	0.1
Total[b]	100.0	100.1	100.1	99.9	100.2	100.0
1970 Dissimilarity Index, Native-Foreign	22.0		41.8		38.8	
1980						
Professional	8.0	3.5	10.1	8.2	12.2	9.8
Semiprofessional	1.9	0.9	2.5	2.4	2.9	2.4
Farmers	0.1	0.1	0.0	0.0	0.2	0.0
Managers	3.8	2.0	3.5	2.9	5.8	4.9
Clericals	33.7	15.7	46.4	26.9	45.4	32.9
Sales	5.5	3.2	6.9	3.6	9.3	5.6
Crafts	2.3	2.8	2.2	3.4	1.1	3.1
Operatives	16.6	37.2	10.8	35.2	7.3	28.0
Service Workers	22.9	22.2	15.8	15.0	14.5	11.7
Laborers	2.1	3.4	1.4	2.0	1.1	1.4
Farm Laborers	2.9	8.8	0.4	0.4	0.3	0.2
Total[b]	99.8	99.8	100.0	100.0	100.1	100.0
1980 Dissimilarity Index, Native-Foreign	28.3		26.2		23.0	
Time Trend Comparisons Dissimilarity Index, 1960–1970	11.5	11.3	20.3	21.2	24.2	11.4
Dissimilarity Index, 1970–1980	10.5	3.4	5.0	16.8	10.0	18.8

SOURCES: 1960, 1970, and 1980 Public Use Microdata Sample files.
[a]There were no observations in this category.
[b]Numbers may not sum to 100 percent because of rounding error.

TABLE 9.10 *(continued)*

Central/South American		Other Hispanic		Black		Non-Hispanic White	
Native	Foreign	Native	Foreign	Native	Foreign	Native	Foreign
15.7%	7.5%	6.5%	12.0%	5.5%	5.0%	10.9%	6.9%
0.8	0.7	2.2	0.6	0.4	2.5	1.4	1.4
0.8	0.0	0.0	1.2	1.0	0.0	0.3	0.4
0.8	2.2	2.2	3.6	0.9	0.0	3.4	4.6
48.8	26.9	37.0	19.8	7.4	20.2	37.8	24.0
9.9	6.3	10.9	9.0	1.6	4.2	11.0	8.7
1.7	1.0	—ᵃ	—ᵃ	0.6	1.7	1.1	1.7
9.9	33.7	23.9	36.5	14.4	24.4	16.6	30.1
11.6	20.9	17.4	15.9	58.1	42.0	15.7	21.1
0.0	0.7	0.0	0.6	1.2	0.0	0.5	0.6
—ᵃ	—ᵃ	0.0	1.8	9.0	0.0	1.3	0.6
100.0	99.9	100.0	100.0	100.1%	100.0	100.0	100.1
35.2		23.1		28.6		20.8	
12.9	8.9	10.5	11.8	8.1	9.6	13.4	12.1
4.0	2.1	1.6	1.9	1.1	1.8	1.6	1.2
0.5	0.0	0.3	0.6	0.2	0.0	0.2	0.0
4.0	1.4	3.5	1.2	1.3	1.3	3.3	3.4
43.8	29.1	31.5	28.1	19.8	29.4	37.2	30.5
9.0	3.9	8.5	4.0	2.9	2.6	8.6	9.8
2.0	1.6	2.1	1.3	1.6	1.3	1.7	2.0
9.5	32.2	17.9	25.1	17.3	13.6	14.1	20.4
13.9	20.0	21.2	24.5	43.8	38.6	18.4	19.3
0.5	0.5	0.9	0.7	1.7	1.8	1.0	0.9
0.0	0.2	2.0	0.7	2.2	0.0	0.7	0.3
100.1	99.9	100.0	99.9	100.0	100.0	100.2	99.9
29.1		53.9		11.9		9.0	
13.9	7.6	11.1	10.8	11.7	14.1	15.4	13.8
3.2	1.7	2.4	3.0	2.6	3.9	2.6	3.4
0.0	0.0	0.1	0.2	0.1	0.0	0.3	0.1
6.2	3.4	5.7	3.4	3.0	2.2	6.4	7.0
39.0	23.5	35.7	23.6	28.4	28.9	35.0	31.1
9.6	4.4	7.2	4.7	3.2	3.0	7.9	8.1
2.1	3.3	2.3	2.6	1.9	1.7	1.9	2.6
9.7	32.3	10.5	27.2	16.1	10.8	10.5	15.5
14.0	22.3	22.4	21.2	30.1	34.2	17.9	17.3
1.7	1.3	1.7	1.7	2.3	1.1	1.6	1.0
0.6	0.3	0.7	1.5	0.7	0.1	0.5	0.2
100.0	100.1	99.8	99.9	100.1	100.0	100.0	100.1
32.0		18.4		8.4		7.2	
9.4	5.8	14.4	20.6	21.8	16.9	6.4	13.5
6.0	7.4	9.2	10.2	16.6	8.4	7.1	8.8

largely responsible for the observed convergence in Puerto Rican occupational structures.

For Cuban and Other Hispanic origin women, rather substantial increases in occupational differentiation between native and immigrant workers during the 1960s were offset by a stronger tendency toward occupational convergence during the 1970s. The nonmonotonic occupational differentiation by nativity experienced by these two origin groups is somewhat surprising and derives from different sources. Socioeconomic assimilation is an important part of the explanation for Cubans, but for Other Hispanics we again must suggest that the noncomparability of this group over time may be partly responsible.[61]

Finally, the extensive occupational diversity of the Hispanic work force also manifests itself in differential rates and levels of gender differentiation in occupational roles. Although the 1960s and 1970s witnessed a convergence in the occupational structures of Hispanic men and women of similar national origin, rather substantial gender differences persisted into the 1980s. Between 26 percent (Central/South American) and 37 percent (Mexican) of Hispanic workers would have had to change jobs in 1980 to achieve gender equality in the occupational hierarchy. This suggests that sex is a more rigid dimension of labor market stratification than is nativity. It is not obvious why gender-based occupational differentiation varies so extensively by national origin, but surely this reflects the pronounced differences in opportunities faced by a regionally concentrated work force, as well as the diverse labor histories that shaped them.

Summary and Conclusions

On balance, our discussion of the labor market status of Hispanics reveals signs of progress for some groups and more limited advancement for others. In other words, results presented in this chapter underscore the now familiar theme of convergence and divergence according to national origin, gender, and nativity. The increased rates of female labor force participation demonstrate greater similarity with the rates of non-Hispanic whites, but the deteriorating labor market position of Puerto Rican workers—men and women alike—diverges from the experience.

In the main, changes in the occupational structure of Hispanic origin workers suggest continuous upgrading of occupational roles, al-

---

[61]See Singelmann and Tienda, "Process of Occupational Change," for substantial discussion on this point.

though at different rates for Hispanic workers who differ by gender, national origin, and nativity. How much change in the labor market position of the Hispanic work force can be expected during the 1980s depends on several factors, many of which are unknown because of their political and technological character. We do not yet know how the pace of technological change will continue to alter the job configuration and, consequently, the demand for native and immigrant workers, or men and women. Future nativity differentials in Hispanic occupational placement surely will depend on who gains admission (and in what legal status) as well as the availability of jobs for workers of varying skill levels. What is clear, however, is that Hispanics must first enter the labor market and obtain secure and better-paying jobs to improve their socioeconomic position.

If the slowed pace of occupational change during the 1970s compared with the 1960s is a signal of what the near-term future portends, it is conceivable that the Hispanic work force will continue to be over-represented in the lower-skill occupations relative to non-Hispanic whites. This scenario, which is quite plausible in light of the poor educational achievement of Hispanic workers discussed in the previous chapter, should be tempered by clear evidence of sustained occupational upgrading of Hispanic workers, despite the growing presence of low-skill, foreign-born workers.

The trend toward increased female labor force participation is likely to modify the economic well-being of the Hispanic population. Among married women labor force participation usually means a second paycheck to supplement the earnings of the primary worker. While directly increasing the family's resources, the employment of married women also can enhance the relative economic well-being of the family through its fertility-inhibiting effects. These potential benefits of increased market activity of Hispanic women, however, may be less salient for married women who enter the market after bearing and raising their children. Although we do not address these issues in this chapter, they are considered in the following chapter on economic well-being.

10

EARNINGS
AND ECONOMIC
WELL-BEING

THIS CHAPTER documents the relative economic well-being of the Hispanic population in terms of money income, poverty status, and earnings. We are interested in both period differentials and interperiod changes in the relative positioning of Mexicans, Puerto Ricans, Cubans, Central/South Americans, and Other Hispanics. Our analyses of family and personal income document the major dimensions of income differentiation among the national origin groups and trace changes in income according to market (wages and salaries) and nonmarket sources (transfer payments, social insurance, and other income).

While seemingly straightforward, the concept of economic well-being is complicated because its meaning hinges on several factors. That is, the socioeconomic significance of a fixed level of money income depends on absolute dollars, on the number of individuals who generate it and consume it, and on the relative prices of goods and services.[1] To account for these factors the first part of this chapter examines income adequacy and relative economic well-being using families as units of observation. We document variation in family income levels and poverty rates according to a set of sociodemographic correlates related to economic well-being.

---

[1]The latter are conventionally indexed by changes in the Consumer Price Index, which we use to deflate money income into a common metric.

The second part of the chapter, which focuses on individuals, examines the evolution of personal income of Hispanic men and women. Poverty rates are disaggregated according to nativity, gender, education, and age—factors which not only differentiate the Hispanic origin groups from one another, but also help to understand why Hispanic poverty changed in the manner it did between 1970 and 1980. This section concludes with a detailed analysis of earnings, by far the largest component of personal income, and involves both descriptive and multivariate analysis of variation in earnings.

Family Income and Economic Well-Being
Definitions

For the purpose of analyzing changes and differentials in family income, we have used the census definition of family to include a head and all members related by blood, marriage, or adoption.[2] This definition was relatively consistent between 1960 and 1980. If one or both family heads were of Mexican, Puerto Rican, Cuban, Central/South American, or Other Hispanic origin, we classified the family as Hispanic.

Current money income refers to the sum of money wages and salaries; net income from self-employment; social security income; and cash transfers from other government programs, property income (that is, interest, dividends, and net rental income), and other forms of cash income, including private pensions and alimony. The current money income concept as measured in census data excludes capital gains, imputed rents, and in-kind benefits whether provided by government sources (income transfers) or by private sources (health insurance and other fringes), but includes taxes paid by individuals. Thus, while seemingly comprehensive and inclusive, current money income does not account precisely for all components which affect a family's level of consumption and well-being. Moreover, the measurement of income, while reasonably comparable over time, must be adjusted to account for inflation and minor deviations in reporting procedures.

---

[2]The U.S. Census Bureau distinguishes between families and households, noting that families require relationship by blood, marriage, or adoption among all persons sharing a residence, while households do not. As such, households can and do include roomers/boarders and their spouses, as well as resident employees. Because the unrelated members are unlikely to pool their resources with the primary family, we have confined our analyses to family income rather than household income. However, auxiliary analyses showed relatively little difference between family and household income because Hispanic extended living arrangements largely involve related individuals.

Although the Census Bureau used roughly similar definitions of income between 1960 and 1980, except that the amount of detail on income sources increased over time, one change in reporting procedure did affect our presentation of results. Family incomes were truncated at $50,000 in 1970 and $75,000 in 1980. This truncation significantly affects comparisons of mean incomes, but not median incomes. Therefore, we restricted our temporal comparisons of family incomes to medians. Furthermore, we expressed incomes in constant dollars to adjust for rising prices over time, but in several tables we included nominal (actual) incomes to provide a perspective on the current income gaps among the national origin groups.

In portraying the Hispanic experience with poverty we use the official poverty measure, tabulating the proportions of families with incomes at or below the official poverty line. This approach differs from the relative approach to poverty which emphasizes the positioning of a given family's resources compared with those of other families. In contrast to the absolute definition, the relative definition of poverty draws attention to the degree of inequality at the lower end of the income distribution, a dimension of economic well-being we explore to only a limited extent in Table 10.1. Because the relative poverty threshold changes at about the same rate as average income, relative poverty conventionally is expressed in terms of the shape of the income distribution, and the poor are defined as those whose income is less than half of the median income.

Family Income Differentials: 1970–1980

Table 10.1 displays median family incomes for the Hispanic national origin groups, blacks, and whites for 1970 and 1980. To enable comparisons over time, these are expressed in both actual and constant dollars based on income received in the year preceding the census. Also presented are the income distributions in constant dollars for each year. Nominal median family incomes rose for all groups during the 1970–1980 decade, but not uniformly according to national origin and race. In current dollars median family incomes of Mexicans, Cubans, and Other Hispanics rose by approximately 130 to 135 percent during the 1970s, while the family incomes of Puerto Ricans and Central/South Americans rose slightly less, or approximately 91 and 87 percent, respectively. For blacks the corresponding increase in median family income was 114 percent, and for whites 109 percent. Rather than representing real gains in the relative economic well-being, the doubling of family incomes resulted largely, although not exclusively, from the double digit inflationary spiral that ensued after the 1973 oil embargo.

TABLE 10.1

Income Distribution and Median Income of Families by Hispanic National Origin and Race: 1970–1980

	Mexican	Puerto Rican	Cuban	Central/South American	Other Hispanic	Black	Non-Hispanic White
1970							
1970 Median Income							
Actual $	$6,150	$5,850	$8,150	$7,950	$7,350	$6,350	$10,150
Constant $[a]	5,601	5,328	7,423	7,240	6,694	5,783	9,244
Income Shares[b]							
$1–$4,999	39.7%	45.2%	26.2%	28.4%	32.2%	43.3%	20.1%
$5,000–$9,999	40.5	39.2	41.6	40.4	37.3	35.8	34.7
$10,000–$19,999	18.5	14.2	28.3	28.4	27.0	19.0	36.2
$20,000–$29,999	1.1	0.9	3.1	2.1	3.1	1.5	5.8
$30,000+	0.2	0.1	0.7	0.8	0.4	0.4	3.1
Total	100.0	99.9	99.9	100.1	100.0	100.0	99.9
1980							
1980 Median Income							
Actual $	$14,510	$11,168	$18,650	$14,840	$17,120	$13,558	$21,235
Constant $[a]	6,674	5,137	8,579	6,826	7,875	6,236	9,768
Income Shares[b]							
$1–$4,999	35.0%	48.3%	24.3%	35.3%	27.9%	39.8%	19.3%
$5,000–$9,999	38.0	32.8	35.1	36.9	35.9	33.5	31.9
$10,000–$19,999	24.0	17.1	34.0	23.3	28.7	23.0	38.0
$20,000–$29,999	2.3	1.5	4.4	2.8	5.2	3.1	7.4
$30,000+	0.7	0.4	2.3	1.6	2.2	0.6	3.3
Total	100.0	100.1	100.1	99.9	99.9	100.0	99.9

SOURCES: 1970 and 1980 Public Use Microdata Sample files.

[a]1969 = $1.098; 1979 = $2.174.
[b]Based on 1969 and 1979 income figures, expressed in constant 1967 dollars.

A comparison of changes in family income expressed in constant dollars indicates whether and how much the relative economic standing of Hispanic, black, and white families changed between 1970 and 1980. Median family incomes of blacks and whites increased 8 and 6 percent, respectively, in real terms during the 1970s. While Mexicans, Cubans, and Other Hispanics enjoyed a 16 to 19 percent real increase in median family income, Puerto Ricans' and Central/South Americans' income *declined* 4 to 6 percent in real terms. The share of Puerto Rican and Central/South American families with incomes under $5,000 in constant terms actually increased, rising 3 percent for the former and 7 percent for the latter. The improvements in the relative economic standing of Mexican and Cuban families can be traced to the increased shares of middle-income families, those with real incomes between $10,000 and $20,000.

FIGURE 10.1

Median Family Income by Hispanic National Origin: 1968–1980
(constant dollars)

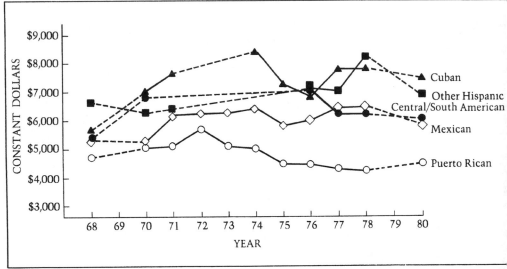

SOURCES: 1970 and 1980 Public Use Microdata Sample files; "Persons of Spanish Origin in the United States: March 1977," *Current Population Survey*, series P-20, no. 329, p. 11. table J; "Persons of Spanish Origin in the United States: March 1978," *Current Population Survey*, series P-20, no. 339, p. 13, table P; "Persons of Spanish Origin in the United States: March 1979," *Current Population Survey*, series P-20, no. 354, p. 14, table 26; "Persons of Spanish Origin in the United States: November 1969," *Current Population Survey*, series P-20, no. 213, p. 34, table 9.

Figure 10.1 provides further detail about the intercensal time trend in Hispanic median family incomes based on yearly estimates from the Current Population Surveys (CPS). For comparability over time and with the cross-section data in Table 10.1 we have converted the CPS income data into constant dollars. Although there is greater sampling variability in the annual CPS data, the time trends are consistent with the census data for 1970 and 1980. Thus, we have reason to believe that the intradecade variation is fairly accurate. In 1970 the highest median family income corresponded to Cubans, followed sequentially by Central/South Americans and Other Hispanics. Mexicans and Puerto Ricans ranked fourth and fifth in median family income in both years, despite the fact that real family income of Mexicans rose during the 1970s, while that of Puerto Ricans fell.

Figure 10.1 shows that the deterioration in Puerto Rican family income occurred gradually, except for the steep drop associated with the economic recession during the early 1970s. That median family incomes of Mexicans and Cubans also fell in real terms between 1973 and 1976 further attests to the negative cyclical effects on Hispanic economic well-being, but unlike Puerto Ricans, Mexican and Cuban origin families participated in the post-1976 recovery. Although the real family incomes of Central/South Americans fell by 6 percent during the 1970s, in 1980 this group apparently had not yet encountered the extreme economic hardships experienced by Puerto Ricans. Partly this is because Central/South Americans enjoyed a relatively high socioeconomic status at the start of the period owing to the highly selective character of immigration from South America during the 1960s.[3] However, the deteriorating family income of Central/South Americans did affect their economic ranking relative to Other Hispanics in 1980.

Our introductory chapter attempted to lay the historical and theoretical framework for interpreting persisting socioeconomic differentials along national origin lines. After examining recent differentials in economic well-being, we wish to reemphasize the profound significance of modes of incorporation and integration in fostering and maintaining socioeconomic inequities among the Hispanic national origin groups. Along some dimensions the data we present show greater, rather than lesser, income differentiation among Hispanics in 1980 than in 1970.

In general, evidence of greater income differentiation among Hispanics is consistent with information presented in Chapter 9, which showed a deterioration in the labor market standing of Puerto Rican and

[3]Alejandro Portes, "Determinants of the Brain Drain," *International Migration Review* 10 (1976):498–508.

Central/South American men and women between 1970 and 1980. On the one hand, the increased Mexican median family income signals an improvement in the relative economic standing of this group whose historical roots are deep and complex. However, this improvement was modest and apparently insufficient to alter the relative positioning of Mexicans vis-à-vis Cubans and Central/South Americans, whose history in the United States is much shorter.

Black median family incomes exceeded those of Mexican and Puerto Rican families in 1970, but fell behind Mexicans in 1980. By contrast, the median family income gap between blacks and Puerto Ricans widened substantially during the 1970s, reaching approximately $2,400 in nominal terms and $1,100 in constant terms. In both periods white families enjoyed the highest median incomes, but in real terms the median family income gap between whites and Hispanics narrowed during the 1970s for Mexicans, Cubans, and Other Hispanics, while it widened in real terms from $3,916 in 1970 to $4,631 in 1980 for Puerto Ricans, and from $2,004 to $2,942 for Central/South Americans.

Part of this tendency toward greater rather than lesser differentiation in family incomes can be traced to changes in the demographic composition of the national origin groups, a topic we discussed extensively in previous chapters. Family income differentials according to nativity and age of head, as well as headship type and family size, shown in Table 10.2 illustrate the implications of changing sociodemographic composition for changes in the economic well-being of the national origin groups and in comparison to blacks and whites. Two types of generalizations can be drawn from Table 10.2. The first concerns the pattern of differentials according to selected demographic characteristics among (and within) the national groups at each point in time, while the second concerns the ways these relationships changed over time.[4]

With respect to the former, the incomes of families with foreign-born heads were lower than those with native-born heads in both years. Blacks stood as the sole exception to this pattern in both years, owing to the positive selectivity of black immigrants,[5] and Cubans were an exception in 1970. Also, and partly due to differences in the prevalence of multiple earners among family units, families headed by a couple

---

[4]Our discussion focuses on the change in constant dollars, but we present the absolute dollars for purposes of comparison with other cross-sectional information sources.

[5]Robert L. Bach and Marta Tienda, "Contemporary Immigration and Refugee Movements and Employment Adjustment Policies," in Vernon M. Briggs, Jr., and Marta Tienda, eds., *Immigration: Issues and Policies* (Salt Lake City: Olympus Press, 1984).

received higher incomes than families headed by a single person in both years.[6]

In constant dollars family income differentials between units headed by couples and single persons were greater in 1980 than in 1970; that the income differentials by headship were not uniform by race and Hispanic origin points to greater income differentiation over time. In constant terms the 1970 family income differential between families headed by a couple and those headed by a single person ranged from a low of $637 for Other Hispanics to $3,734 for Central/South Americans, with Mexicans, Puerto Ricans, and Cubans exhibiting a $3,000 median income differential. For blacks and whites the comparable difference was $3,200 and $2,800, respectively. By 1980 the real income differential between families headed by a couple and those headed by a single person had increased for all groups, ranging from a low of $3,222 for Mexicans to a high of $4,577 for Central/South Americans. Headship differentials in 1980 median family income were on the order of $4,200 for both blacks and whites. This provides further evidence of greater rather than less diversity in this indicator of Hispanics' economic well-being.

Family income differentials according to age of the head were similar in both periods in that the highest incomes corresponded to units whose head was of prime working age. In general, income variation according to family size was directly and approximately monotonically related to family size at both time points, with the exception of Other Hispanics in 1970. On balance our tabulations suggest a pattern of multiple source income packaging which may involve several earners per family. Supplementary analyses revealed that in 1980 over 50 percent of Mexican, Cuban, and Other Hispanic families contained two or more earners compared with 35 percent of Puerto Rican families; comparable figures for three-earner families were 15 percent for the former groups and 7 percent for Puerto Ricans.

A comparison of changes in family income according to selected demographic characteristics of heads and family units during the 1970–1980 intercensal period provides further insight into the forces respon-

[6]Virtually all of the families headed by single persons were headed by women, as shown by the following tabulation:

	Mexican	Puerto Rican	Cuban	Central/South American	Other Hispanic
1970	71.2%	86.4%	72.5%	82.3%	75.2%
1980	74.9	88.0	76.1	82.4	78.4

TABLE 10.2

Differentials in Median Family Income According to Selected Head
and Family Characteristics, Hispanic National Origin, and Race: 1970–1980
(actual and constant dollars)

	Mexican		Puerto Rican		Cuban	
	Actual	Constant[a]	Actual	Constant[a]	Actual	Constant[a]
1970						
Overall Median	$6,150	$5,601	$5,850	$5,328	$ 8,150	$7,423
Nativity						
Foreign	5,450	4,964	5,650	$5,146	8,150	7,423
Native	7,050	6,421	7,250	6,603	8,150	7,423
Type of Headship						
Couples	7,250	6,603	7,050	6,421	9,150	8,333
Single Head[b]	4,250	3,871	3,750	3,415	5,650	5,146
Family Size						
1–2	3,650	3,324	4,550	4.144	5,850	5,328
3–5	6,950	6,330	6,050	5,510	9,050	8,242
6+	7,600	6,922	7,050	6,421	12,050	10,974
Age of Head						
24 Years and Under	4,650	4,235	5,250	4,781	7,750	7,058
25–59 Years	7,250	6,603	6,050	5,510	8,550	7,787
60 Years and Over	3,350	3,051	3,050	2,778	5,050	4,599
1980						
Overall Median	$14,510	$6,674	$11,168	$5,137	$18,650	$8,579
Nativity						
Foreign	13,005	$5,982	10,692	4,918	18,470	8,496
Native	16,010	7,364	11,375	5,232	17,005	7,822
Type of Headship						
Couples	15,905	7,316	14,710	6,766	20,015	9,206
Single Head[b]	8,900	4,094	5,525	2,541	12,600	5,796
Family Size						
1–2	11,522	5,300	10,098	4,645	13,312	6,123
3–5	15,005	6,902	11,025	5,071	20,428	9,396
6+	16,705	7,684	13,020	5,989	27,312	12,563
Age of Head						
24 Years and Under	10,790	4,963	5,735	2,638	13,825	6,359
25–59 Years	15,610	7,180	12,005	5,522	20,820	9,577
60 Years and Over	10,920	5,023	8,278	3,808	12,495	5,747

SOURCES: 1970 and 1980 Public Use Microdata Sample files.

[a]1967 = $1.00; 1969 = $1.098; 1979 = $2.174.
[b]Includes both men and women.

TABLE 10.2 *(continued)*

Central/South American		Other Hispanic		Black		Non-Hispanic White	
Actual	Constant[a]	Actual	Constant[a]	Actual	Constant[a]	Actual	Constant[a]
$7,950	$7,240	$7,350	$6,694	$6,350	$5,783	$10,150	$9,244
7,650	6,967	6,950	6,330	8,050	7,332	9,700	8,834
8,150	7,423	7,550	6,876	6,150	5,601	10,350	9,426
9,150	8,333	8,850	8,060	7,550	6,876	10,550	9,608
5,050	4,599	5,150	7,423	4,050	3,689	7,450	6,785
6,150	5,601	4,550	4,144	5,050	4,599	7,950	7,240
8,500	7,741	9,050	8,242	6,750	6,148	11,150	10,155
9,650	8,789	8,600	7,832	7,050	6,421	12,150	11,066
6,250	5,692	5,250	4,781	4,950	4,508	7,050	6,421
8,850	8,060	9,050	8,242	7,150	6,512	11,450	10,428
4,650	4,235	3,950	3,597	4,150	3,780	6,950	6,330
14,840	$6,826	$17,120	$7,875	$13,558	$6,236	$21,235	$9,768
14,400	6,624	17,150	7,889	15,640	7,194	19,935	9,170
18,060	8,307	17,005	7,822	12,908	5,937	21,810	10,032
17,790	8,183	18,820	8,657	17,762	8,170	22,490	10,345
7,840	3,606	10,780	4,959	8,678	3,992	13,355	6,143
12,008	5,523	14,010	6,444	10,600	4,876	17,005	7,822
15,005	6,902	18,010	8,284	14,708	6,765	23,418	10,772
19,010	8,744	21,210	9,756	16,575	7,624	27,315	12,564
9,110	4,190	10,010	4,604	7,355	3,383	12,790	5,883
15,312	7,043	18,208	8,375	15,010	6,904	23,948	11,016
13,612	6,261	13,695	6,299	10,035	4,616	15,315	7,045

sible for divergence and convergence in the relative economic standing of Hispanic, black, and white families. For example, among Mexican and Other Hispanic families the average 19 and 18 percent increase in median family income reflected slightly faster growth among the foreign-born, and for Cubans the growth in median family income during the 1970s was three times faster among the foreign-born than the native-born. This result is consistent with the Cuban story of economic prosperity narrated in Chapter 1. At first blush these results may appear to be inaccurate. That is, since immigrants usually earn less than their native counterparts of like national origin,[7] their faster income growth during the 1970s appears to be inconsistent. However, several factors may account for this outcome, including the higher labor supply of immigrant men,[8] as well as differences in income packaging among families with native- and foreign-born heads.

Net declines in real median incomes of Central/South American and Puerto Rican families must be interpreted in light of the changing character of recent immigration and migration between the island and the U.S. mainland. That the median incomes of Central/South American families with a foreign-born head declined by 5 percent, while those with a native-born head increased by 12 percent, is consistent with recent evidence showing that recent immigrants are less skilled than earlier waves.[9] A more conventional interpretation of the lowered economic standing of Central/South Americans is that recent cohorts (1970–1980 arrivals) are less selective than earlier cohorts (1950–1969 arrivals), partly because of the politically motivated character of the recent influx.[10]

Puerto Ricans, on the other hand, present a picture quite different from the other Hispanic national origin groups. Not only did both the mainland and island family incomes decline in real terms—21 and 4 percent, respectively—but the deterioration in real family income was almost five times greater among the families whose head was born on

---

[7]George J. Borjas and Marta Tienda, eds., *Hispanics in the U.S. Economy* (Orlando, FL: Academic Press, 1985); Marta Tienda, "Market Characteristics and Hispanic Earnings: A Comparison of Natives and Immigrants," *Social Problems* 31 (1983):59–72; Barry Chiswick, "The Economic Progress of Immigrants: Some Apparently Universal Patterns," in William Fellner, ed., *Contemporary Economic Problems* (Washington, DC: American Enterprise Institute, 1979); George J. Borjas, "The Earnings of Male Hispanic Immigrants in the United States," *Industrial and Labor Relations Review* 35 (1982):343–53.

[8]George J. Borjas, "The Labor Supply of Male Hispanic Immigrants in the United States," *International Migration Review* 17 (1983):653–71.

[9]George J. Borjas, "Assimilation, Changes in Cohort Quality, and the Earnings of Immigrants," *Journal of Labor Economics* 3 (1985):463–89.

[10]Esther Wicab Bach-y-Rita, "An Ethnographic and Psycho-social Study of Latin American Undocumented Women Immigrants in the San Francisco Bay Area," unpublished doctoral dissertation, Berkeley, California, Wright Institute, 1985.

the U.S. mainland than among families whose head was born in Puerto Rico. These findings challenge arguments about the role of assimilation as a vehicle to improve the income and employment possibilities of Puerto Ricans. Alternative interpretations should consider the importance of labor market conditions and employment discrimination in producing these results. That Puerto Ricans are likely to be mixtures of black and white races may be more significant in determining their labor market position than birthplace, but our finding that black median family incomes improved during the 1970s indicates that the reasons underlying the deterioration of Puerto Rican family incomes is far more complex.

Uneven rates of change in median incomes according to type of headship, family size, and age of the head were also telling about the dimensions of convergence and divergence in Hispanic family incomes. Differences by type of headship were especially revealing about the underlying factors contributing to the worsened economic status of Puerto Ricans and Central/South Americans. In real terms median family income of Puerto Rican families headed by a couple increased 5 percent, while the median income of families headed by a single person dropped 26 percent. That the share of Puerto Rican families headed by a single woman increased substantially during the past decade[11] makes the consequences of this income differential even more profound for the relative economic well-being of Puerto Ricans as a group. For Central/South Americans real incomes of families headed by both a couple and a single head decreased during the 1970s, but 10-fold more for the latter (2 and 22 percent declines, respectively).

Changes in the relative economic standing of the Hispanic population also can be understood in terms of intertemporal variation in the composition of family income. Table 10.3, which decomposes mean family income into four broad sources, allows us to address the question of whether the sources of family income have changed over time, and, if so, whether they help in understanding the net increases (or decreases) in median family incomes.[12]

One clear message is that wages and salaries (including self-employment income) were the major income source for Hispanic, black,

---

[11]Marta Tienda and Jennifer Glass, "Extended Household Composition and Female Labor Force Participation," in Jacques Boulet, Ann Marie DeBritto, and Aisha Ray, eds., *Understanding the Economic Crisis: The Impact of Poverty and Unemployment on Children and Families,* proceedings of a National Conference by the Bush Program in Child Development and Social Policy (Ann Arbor: University of Michigan, 1985).

[12]We use mean income for this analysis in order to show the relative shares of each income source, but because of the skewed income distributions, we also present the median incomes for each group in constant dollars.

TABLE 10.3

Components of Mean Family Income by Hispanic National Origin and Race:
1970–1980

	Mexican		Puerto Rican		Cuban	
	Constant Dollars	Percentage	Constant Dollars	Percentage	Constant Dollars	Percentage
1970						
Wages and Salary	$6,406	92.9%	$5,342	87.8%	$8,320	95.5%
Social Insurance	173	2.5	101	1.7	97	1.1
Public Assistance	149	2.2	523	8.6	154	1.8
Other Income	170	2.5	120	2.0	143	1.6
Mean, Constant $	6,898	100.1	6,086	100.1	8,714	100.0
Median, Constant $	6,239		5,510		7,650	
Mean, Actual $	7,590		6,701		9,584	
1980						
Wages and Salary	$6,872	89.4%	$5,021	82.5%	$8,817	89.8%
Social Insurance	210	2.7	157	2.6	301	3.1
Public Assistance	182	2.4	548	9.0	201	2.0
Other Income	419	5.4	361	5.9	503	5.1
Mean, Constant $	7,683	99.9	6,087	100.0	9,822	100.0
Median, Constant $	6,674		4,834		8,494	
Mean, Actual $	16,659		13,148		21,160	

SOURCES: 1970 and 1980 Public Use Microdata Sample files.
[a]1967 = $1.00; 1969 = $1.098; 1979 = $2.174.

and white families in both time periods. In 1970 wage, salary, and self-employment income constituted from 96 percent (Cubans) to 88 percent (Puerto Ricans) of average family income for all groups. By 1980 wage and salary income as a share of total family income actually decreased for all groups, from 91 percent (Central/South Americans) to 83 percent (Puerto Ricans). The public assistance component of total family income in both years was highest for Puerto Ricans, constituting nearly 9 percent of total family income. For all other groups, with the exception of blacks, public assistance income accounted for less than 3 percent of total family income in both years. During the 1970s reliance on public assistance increased modestly for all groups, with the largest changes occurring among Central South American and black families. The public assistance component in 1970 was highest for Puerto Ricans, with 8.6 percent, followed by blacks, with 3.5 percent. In 1980 Puerto Ricans

TABLE 10.3 *(continued)*

Central/ South American		Other Hispanic		Black		Non-Hispanic White	
Constant Dollars	Percentage	Constant Dollars	Percentage	Constant Dollars	Percentage	Constant Dollars	Percentage
$8,064	93.9%	$7,461	89.6%	$5,790	90.0%	$9,367	89.6%
152	1.8	236	2.8	239	3.7	307	2.9
98	1.1	130	1.6	227	3.5	37	0.4
275	3.2	498	6.0	175	2.7	743	7.1
8,589	100.0	8,325	100.0	6,431	99.9	10,454	100.0
7,787		7,332		5,510		9,153	
9,445		9,128		7,079		11,469	
$7,270	90.8%	$7,921	86.4%	$6,029	84.9%	$9,239	84.1%
133	1.7	309	3.4	344	4.8	493	4.5
214	2.7	171	1.9	304	4.3	69	0.6
391	4.9	766	8.4	426	6.0	1,182	10.8
8,008	100.1	9,167	100.1	7,103	100.0	10,983	100.0
6,695		7,702		5,752		9,962	
17,271		19,710		15,420		23,705	

and blacks still made up the larger share of public assistance with 9.0 and 4.3 percent, respectively.

The average share of mean family income derived from social insurance increased modestly during the 1970s for most groups, partly owing to changes in the age composition of the population. As a population ages, a higher proportion of individuals become eligible for social security pensions, survivors' benefits, and disability payments. Thus, the average share of family income derived from social insurance should continue to rise, but very gradually because these demographic changes unfold slowly. Also, the relative importance of social insurance as an income source depends on how well individuals fare in the labor market, and their eligibility for employer-provided pension benefits.

Receipt of public assistance income depends on the absolute income thresholds relative to minimum need levels represented by the array of poverty income cutoffs. Select demographic characteristics also are used to determine eligibility for programs aimed at special segments of the population (for example, single mothers with dependent children). In light of information presented in Table 10.1, we should expect public assistance income as an average share of total family income to increase for Puerto Ricans and Central/South Americans, the two groups whose real incomes declined during the 1970s, and to decrease for the remaining groups, who experienced real improvements in family income during the 1970s.[13] Our data also show increases in social insurance and other income as shares of Puerto Rican family income, but this could result from a greater reliance on unemployment benefits, child support payments, and allotment checks from servicemen. Unfortunately, census data do not allow us to examine this question further.

All told, the story of changes in Hispanic family income is one of increased heterogeneity rather than homogeneity. This is evident in opposed intertemporal changes in median real incomes according to national origin, with Mexicans, Cubans, and Other Hispanics showing improvements in relative economic standing, while Puerto Ricans and Central/South Americans experienced real declines in economic well-being relative to 1970. Within groups, increased income differentiation manifests itself as both narrowed and widened differentials according to some sociodemographic characteristics of families and family heads, in the packaging of family incomes, and in the pervasiveness of extreme economic deprivation. It is to the latter concern that our attention now turns. The following section examines in greater depth the most disadvantaged segment of the Hispanic population—those with below poverty incomes.

Poverty and Program Participation

Among the most revealing of social indicators reflecting the relative economic well-being of a population is the share of families and individuals in poverty. The official guidelines for establishing poverty status are based on a set of income cutoffs adjusted for household size, the age of the head, and the number of children under age 18.[14] Sex of the head and farm-nonfarm residence also were used through 1980 to determine poverty status, but since that time have been discontinued. The official

---

[13]Other Hispanics also are somewhat deviant in that, despite modest real increases in median family income, these families increased their reliance on public assistance income.

[14]Sheldon Danziger and Peter Gottschalk, "The Measurement of Poverty: Implications for Antipoverty Policy," *American Behavioral Scientist* 26 (1983):739–56. In 1982 the poverty line for a family of four was $9,862.

poverty income cutoffs provide an absolute measure of poverty intended to denote minimally decent levels of consumption in dollar terms, and these cutoffs are adjusted annually to account for changes in relative prices. Therefore, absolute poverty rates are comparable over time since they represent constant purchasing power each year.

Over the years the absolute poverty concept has been sharply criticized and its adequacy for representing the nature and extent of economic well-being in the United States disputed on several grounds. These include its unrealistically low minimum income threshold, its use of an emergency food plan as the foundation for determining minimum needs, and its reliance on untested normative assumptions about how poor families allocate their money resources among competing basic needs.[15] Controversies over the official poverty thresholds and minimum income concept notwithstanding, the adoption of an official measure of poverty and its use as a social indicator has symbolized the country's commitment to raising the living standard of the poorest citizens.[16] From an absolute perspective poverty will be eliminated once families achieve a minimum income threshold and, unlike the elimination of relative poverty, can be accomplished without altering the shape of the income distribution.

In this section we use the official absolute poverty cutoffs to analyze changes in the proportion of Hispanic families that are poor. Based on evidence presented in the prior section and in Chapter 9, we expected a mixed pattern of change in the percentage of Hispanic families with incomes at or below poverty. Figure 10.2, which shows the 1970 and 1980 percentages of Hispanic families with poverty level incomes or below, further contributes to a picture of increasing heterogeneity in the relative economic well-being of the Hispanic population.

Consistent with the analysis of changes in family income, the Hispanic experience with poverty shows signs of convergence and divergence. As expected, the proportion of families in poverty decreased for the three groups whose real family incomes rose during the 1970s—Mexicans, Cubans, and Other Hispanics. Poverty rates of Puerto Ricans and Central/South Americans increased during the 1970s, an outcome which mirrors their lowered real incomes. In both periods the lowest rates of poverty corresponded to white and Cuban families and the highest rates to black and Puerto Rican families. Puerto Rican and black families had virtually identical poverty rates in 1970—approximately 28

---

[15]Specifically, the Social Security Administration assumed that the poor spend approximately one-third of their income on food. Since the emergency minimum food plan value was determined, the first official poverty guideline was established by multiplying the food plan value by three.

[16]Danziger and Gottschalk, "Measurement of Poverty."

FIGURE 10.2

Percentage of Families in Poverty by National Origin and Race: 1970–1980

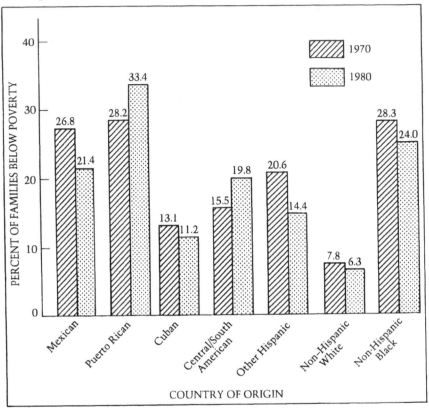

SOURCES: 1970 and 1980 Public Use Microdata Sample files.

percent. By 1980, however, the rate of poverty among Puerto Rican families was 9.4 percent higher than the rate among black families. Also, the relative positioning of Other Hispanics and Central/South Americans with respect to poverty rates changed slightly from 1970 to 1980. Poverty rates of Central/South American families increased by 4.3 percent, while those of Other Hispanics decreased by 6.2 percent.

Although the proportion of Mexican families in poverty fell by 5 percent during the 1970s, approximately one Mexican origin family in five had an income below the official poverty line. However, Mexican families were substantially less likely to be poor in 1980 than Puerto Rican families. Whereas in 1970 the poverty gap between Mexicans and Puerto Ricans was less than 2 percent, by 1980 this gap had *in-*

creased to 12 percent. Mexicans and Puerto Ricans were most disadvantaged of the Hispanic origin groups in 1980, but if current trends continue through 1990 it is possible that Central/South Americans will join Puerto Ricans among the most disadvantaged segments of the Hispanic population, with Mexicans assuming a middle posture between them and Cubans and Other Hispanics.

Table 10.4 provides additional insight into the correlates of poverty and their changes over time. That immigrants confront greater difficulties in earning a livelihood in the United States finds support in our results, which generally show higher rates of poverty among families whose head was born abroad. In 1970 Central/South Americans and Other Hispanics were an exception to this pattern, but in 1980 only the Other Hispanics exhibited higher rates of poverty among the native-born than the foreign-born.

Nativity differentials in poverty converged slightly for all national origin groups during the 1970s, despite the lack of uniformity in the direction of group-specific poverty rates. For example, nativity differentials in poverty rates for Mexicans dropped from 5.6 percent in 1970 to 4.8 percent in 1980. Despite the increases in Puerto Rican poverty during the 1970s, nativity differentials converged slightly from 8 to 6 percent. Only for Central/South Americans did nativity differentials in poverty increase during the 1970s, reflecting the changed socioeconomic composition of the recent immigrants from Central and South America. Finally, the convergence of nativity differentials in poverty were most pronounced for Cubans, for whom differences in the risk of being poor virtually disappeared during the 1970s.

Other noteworthy differentials in Hispanic poverty rates correspond to type of headship. Not surprisingly, families headed by a couple were considerably less likely to be poor in both years than families headed by a single person of either sex. Auxiliary tabulations showed that households headed by a single woman were more likely to be poor than those headed by a single man, a result which has been amply documented elsewhere.[17] However, the familiar theme of extensive differentiation according to national origin persists with respect to the differences in the rate of poverty among headship types. For example, in 1970 Mexican and black families headed by a single person were over twice as likely to be poor as those headed by a married couple. Central/South American, Cuban, and Other Hispanic and non-Hispanic white families

[17]See reviews in Marta Tienda and Jennifer Glass, "Household Structure and Labor Force Participation of Black, Hispanic and White Mothers," *Demography* 22 (1985):381–94; and Marta Tienda and Ronald Angel, "Headship and Household Composition Among Blacks, Hispanics and Other Whites," *Social Forces* 61 (1982):508–31.

TABLE 10.4

Differential Poverty Rates for Families
by Hispanic National Origin and Race: 1970–1980

	Mexican	Puerto Rican	Cuban	Central/South American	Other Hispanic	Black	Non-Hispanic White
1970							
Overall Rate	26.8%	28.2%	13.1%	15.5%	20.6%	28.3%	7.8%
Nativity							
Foreign	30.0	29.2	13.5	13.3	18.0	15.2	9.0
Native	24.4	21.1	3.6	17.4	21.5	29.5	7.3
Type of Headship							
Couple	21.5	18.1	9.4	9.9	11.5	19.6	6.3
Single Head[a]	41.6	51.7	26.4	29.1	37.0	47.3	18.9
Household Size							
1–2	32.3	26.2	16.9	17.6	27.8	25.3	9.7
3–5	20.3	25.3	11.1	12.0	11.8	24.5	6.0
6+	32.2	40.5	13.4	22.8	28.0	39.6	10.1
Age of Head							
24 Years and Under	29.5	27.1	7.7	17.5	24.1	37.4	13.3
25–59 Years	23.2	27.5	11.4	12.6	15.7	25.4	5.5
60 Years and Over	39.2	35.6	25.9	31.6	31.5	36.1	12.4
1980							
Overall Rate	21.4	33.4	11.2	19.8	14.4	24.0	6.3
Nativity							
Foreign	24.0	34.6	11.2	20.0	13.5	18.3	7.1
Native	19.2	28.4	10.2	15.4	15.0	25.7	6.0
Type of Headship							
Couple	17.1	17.2	8.7	11.0	11.0	13.0	4.6
Single Head[a]	38.3	59.9	21.5	38.6	26.6	40.1	17.7
Household Size							
1–2	19.0	27.2	16.4	18.1	12.8	20.8	6.7
3–5	19.1	34.4	8.7	20.6	13.8	23.4	5.7
6+	30.3	40.6	7.5	19.9	21.2	33.0	8.9
Age of Head							
24 Years and Under	27.6	50.7	16.4	29.9	32.0	45.3	17.0
25–59 Years	20.5	31.1	8.7	19.0	13.5	22.2	5.7
60 Years and Over	20.9	27.2	18.3	17.7	11.1	22.9	5.9

SOURCES: 1970 and 1980 Public Use Microdata Sample files.

[a]Includes both men and women.

headed by a single person were three times more likely to be poor as their counterparts headed by a married couple. Puerto Ricans stand apart from the other groups in that the absolute differences in poverty rates according to type of family headship were much greater—34 percent versus 17 to 28 percent for the other groups. Specifically, 18 percent of Puerto Rican families headed by a couple in 1970 were poor compared with 52 percent of families headed by a single person. In other words, Puerto Rican families headed by a single person were almost three times (2.8 times) more likely to be poor than families headed by a married couple. By 1980 this differential according to type of headship increased to 3.5 times.

Although couples were less likely to be poor than were single persons throughout the 1970s, for Mexicans, Puerto Ricans, and Central/South Americans the disparity in poverty rates between couples and single persons increased slightly, especially for the latter two groups. A 43 percent difference separated the probability of being poor for Puerto Rican families headed by a single person and those headed by a couple in 1980, up from 34 percent in 1970. Among Central/South Americans, 39 percent of the families headed by a single person were poor in 1980 compared with 29 percent in 1970. Although the poverty rate for Central/South American couples increased slightly between 1970 and 1980, because of the sharp increase in poverty among families with a single head, this group experienced an increased differentiation in poverty rates according to headship. Cubans and Other Hispanics presented an opposite pattern of interdecade change in that the amount of differentiation in poverty rates according to type of headship actually decreased by 4 percent for Cubans and by roughly 10 percent for Other Hispanics. For whites and blacks the headship differential in family poverty remained constant during the 1970s, although the overall poverty rate declined for both groups.

Age and household size differentiation in poverty rates decreased slightly during the 1970s, but in general the interdecade pattern of change was consistent with the existing literature about correlates of poverty. For example, families headed by an elderly adult were more likely to be in poverty compared with those headed by an adult of prime working age, but the race and national origin groups exhibited greater heterogeneity with respect to the probability that a head under age 24 would be in poverty. In part this has to do with the differences in the patterns of marriage and labor market experiences of the race and national origin groups, a phenomenon we documented extensively in Chapter 9. With the exception of Mexicans, the poverty rates among families with a young head increased during the 1970s, and the sharpest increase corresponded to Puerto Ricans. In 1970, 27 percent of Puerto Rican families with a young head were poor, but this figure nearly doubled by 1980.

There was no clear evidence of monotonicity in the likelihood of being poor according to the size of households. In 1970 we found a nonlinear pattern of variation according to household size among all groups except Puerto Ricans. Although there was greater evidence of monotonicity in the relationship between poverty rates and household size in 1980, the Cuban example defies this generalization; for them the relationship between household size and poverty rates was roughly inverse, while among Central and South Americans there was very little differentiation in poverty rates according to household size.

In its concern to eliminate poverty, as portrayed by the absolute measure, the government has designed several income maintenance programs to offset the income deficit of the poor. However, not all poor people who are eligible for means-tested transfer payments receive them. The 1980 census contains a question about the receipt of public assistance income, which shows cash payments under various assistance programs, including aid to families with dependent children, old age assistance, general assistance, aid to the blind, and aid to the permanently and totally disabled. Unfortunately, we are unable to separate Supplementary Security Income[18] from transfer programs generally referred to as "welfare." Although a less precise measure of receipt of welfare benefits, the proportion of families who received public assistance income largely represents the receipt of income-conditioned transfer payments, especially AFDC and other "welfare" benefits usually made available to only the very needy. Table 10.5 reports differences in the share of families who received public assistance income in 1970 and 1980 according to selected characteristics and serves as a rough measure of welfare dependence.

Given that Puerto Ricans experience the highest poverty rates of all Hispanic groups, it is unsurprising that they were more likely than other groups to have received transfer income. In fact, 21 percent of all Puerto Rican families received public assistance payments in 1970, and a slightly larger share, 24 percent, in 1980. Larger shares of Central and South American, non-Hispanic white, and black families received public assistance income in 1980 than in 1970, although the rate of poverty decreased for the latter two. Central/South American families increased their participation in transfer income programs from just under 6 percent in 1970 to 10 percent in 1980. Mexicans, Cubans, and Other Hispanics decreased their reliance on transfer income during the 1970s, but only slightly (by less than 1 percent). By and large, the picture is one of little change in welfare dependence for groups whose real family incomes did not deteriorate during the 1970s.

One of the most sensitive issues considered in recent years with respect to immigration has to do with the nativity differentiation in receipt of public assistance payments. Recently several authors have ad-

---

[18]Supplemental Security Income includes old age assistance, aid to the blind, and aid to the disabled; it does not include Social Security income.

TABLE 10.5

Differentials in Receipt of Public Assistance Income by Families
According to Hispanic National Origin and Race: 1970–1980

	Mexican	Puerto Rican	Cuban	Central/South American	Other Hispanic	Black	Non-Hispanic White
1970							
Overall Rate	9.5%	21.0%	7.4%	5.7%	7.8%	11.5%	2.0%
Nativity							
Foreign	11.2	21.7	7.6	4.4	5.6	4.2	1.8
Native	8.2	16.1	3.6	6.7	8.6	12.2	2.0
Type of Headship							
Couple	5.5	9.2	4.3	2.3	3.0	4.1	1.3
Single Head[a]	22.2	48.1	19.7	18.9	24.0	27.6	7.1
Age of Head							
24 Years and Under	6.6	19.1	0.0	7.1	9.9	17.4	3.0
25–59 Years	6.6	19.9	4.1	4.4	5.6	10.1	1.7
60 Years and Over	21.5	33.3	29.8	12.2	12.6	14.6	2.5
Median Payment							
Couple	$800	$1,500	$700	$950	$500	$800	$750
Single Head[a]	1,200	2,400	900	1,400	1,600	1,400	1,300
1980							
Overall Rate	8.7%	24.4%	7.1%	10.2%	7.4%	14.1%	3.2%
Nativity							
Foreign	7.4	25.0	7.4	10.3	5.6	6.3	3.2
Native	9.8	21.9	1.7	7.7	8.4	16.4	3.2
Type of Headship							
Couple	4.5	6.7	4.1	2.9	3.0	4.0	1.7
Single Head[a]	25.1	53.5	20.1	25.9	22.7	28.9	13.8
Age of Head							
24 Years and Under	7.2	33.8	8.2	12.2	16.8	26.6	7.8
25–59 Years	7.2	22.7	4.2	9.1	5.9	12.5	2.5
60 Years and Over	19.6	26.3	17.0	21.9	10.0	15.9	4.3
Median Payment							
Couple	$1,610	$3,005	$1,875	$1,375	$2,075	$1,920	$2,205
Single Head[a]	2,465	3,785	2,355	3,555	2,525	2,405	2,835

SOURCES: 1970 and 1980 Public Use Microdata Sample files.

Includes both men and women.

dressed this question.[19] Consistent with prior results, our tabulations show that in 1970 families with a foreign-born head of Mexican, Puerto Rican, and Cuban origin were slightly more likely than their native counterparts (on the order of 3 to 6 percent) to receive public assistance

[19]Francine D. Blau, "The Use of Transfer Payments by Immigrants," *Industrial and Labor Relations Review* 37 (1984):222–39; Julian Simon, "Immigrants, Taxes and Welfare in the United States," *Population and Development Review* 10 (1984):55–69; Marta Tienda and Leif Jensen, "Immigration and Public Assistance: Dispelling the Myth of Dependency," *Social Science Research* 15 (1986):372–400.

income. Because of their positive selection, Central/South American, Other Hispanic, black, and white families with a foreign head relied less on public assistance income than families with an immigrant head.

By 1980 nativity differences in public assistance participation decreased slightly for Mexicans and Puerto Ricans, although the latter increased their participation in programs overall: 25 percent of Puerto Rican families with an island-born head received public assistance income in 1980 compared with 22 percent of families with a mainland-born head. The most impressive increase in social program participation was experienced by Central/South American immigrants. In 1970 less than 5 percent of Central/South American families with a foreign-born head received public assistance payments compared with over 10 percent by 1980. However, there was relatively little change—1 percent—in the propensity of Central/South American origin families with a native-born head to receive public assistance income during the 1970s. The increased public assistance participation of black and white families resulted from increased shares of both native and immigrant families who received transfer income in 1980.

Given the eligibility rules governing participation in means-tested income programs, of which welfare income constitutes the greatest share, larger shares of families headed by a single person and by an elderly adult (over age 65) received public assistance income than families headed by a couple and by a working-age adult. In 1970 the proportion of families headed by a couple who received public assistance income was less than 6 percent for all groups except Puerto Ricans (who had 9 percent), while the share of single-head families receiving public assistance income ranged from 7 percent for white non-Hispanics to 48 percent for Puerto Ricans. By 1980 the headship-specific rates of participation in transfer income programs were higher, but the race and ethnic differentiation was similar. Specifically, the share of single-head families receiving public assistance income varied from a low of 14 percent for non-Hispanic whites to a high of 53 percent for Puerto Ricans. Roughly one Hispanic family in four headed by a single person of Mexican, Central/South American, or Other Hispanic origin received public assistance income in 1980. The 1980 rate for black families with a single head was slightly higher, or 29 percent.

The final comment on Table 10.5 concerns the median payments to families who are eligible for and actually receive public assistance income. That is, of those families who received any public assistance income in 1970, the payments were considerably larger for the families headed by a single person than those headed by a couple, indicating that the former had a greater income shortfall, on average. However, the difference in median payment received by couples and single heads varied extensively over time and according to national origin. Specifically, the payment differential received by single heads versus couples in 1970 ranged from $200 among Cubans to a high of $1,100 among Other Hispanics. Blacks and whites fell between these extremes, with a $550 to $600 median payment differential. For 1980 the differential payment received by families headed by a couple or a single head was generally under $1,000 for all groups, except for Central/South Americans. For this group alone the average payment for families headed by a single person was $2,200 above that for those headed by a couple. The reason for this large headship differential in transfer income payments received by families from Central and South America is unclear, but it may be related to the changing character of migration from Central America toward a greater representation of low-income refugees. From census data we cannot ascertain how many of the recent arrivals from Central and South America migrated as intact families and how many were in the process of reconstituting their families at the time of the 1980 census, but this is a question worthy of additional exploration.

To summarize, our examination of trends and differentials in Hispanic family income shows signs of increasing heterogeneity among and within groups. That real median family incomes of Mexicans, Cubans, and Other Hispanics increased (although at varying rates) while those of Puerto Ricans and Central/South Americans decreased in real terms provides the most striking testimony of greater socioeconomic disparities. Equally striking are the interdecade changes in poverty rates and participation in means-tested income programs. Furthermore, the correlates of poverty present a complex picture, showing signs of convergence along some sociodemographic dimensions and signs of divergence in poverty rates along others. As with the story on interdecade changes in family income, the general conclusion is one of greater differentiation in poverty rates according to national origin groups. This part of the story, which is based on analysis of family income, has its analogue in personal income, to which we now turn.

Personal Income and Earnings Differentials

Focusing on individuals rather than families as analytic units draws attention to the pronounced gender differences in personal income, above and beyond those associated with Hispanic national origin. As Figure 10.3 shows, with few exceptions mean personal incomes of men

FIGURE 10.3

*Mean Personal Income of Men and Women Aged 16 and Over
by Hispanic National Origin and Race: 1960–1980*

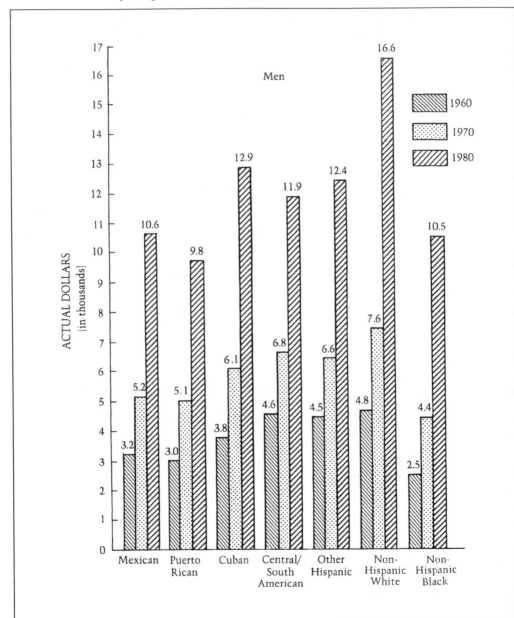

SOURCES: 1960, 1970, and 1980 Public Use Microdata Sample files.

FIGURE 10.3 *(continued)*

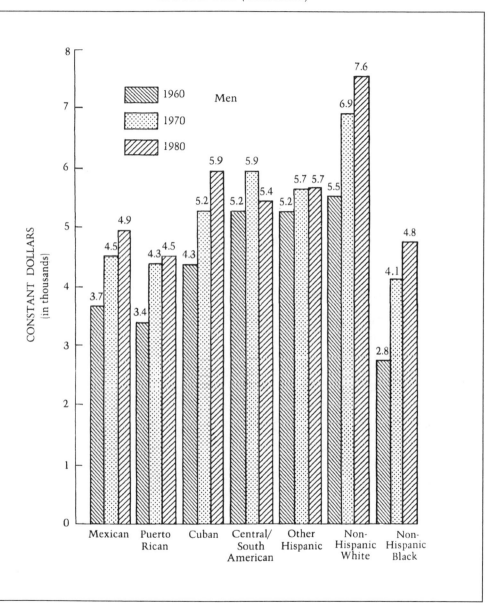

FIGURE 10.3 *(continued)*

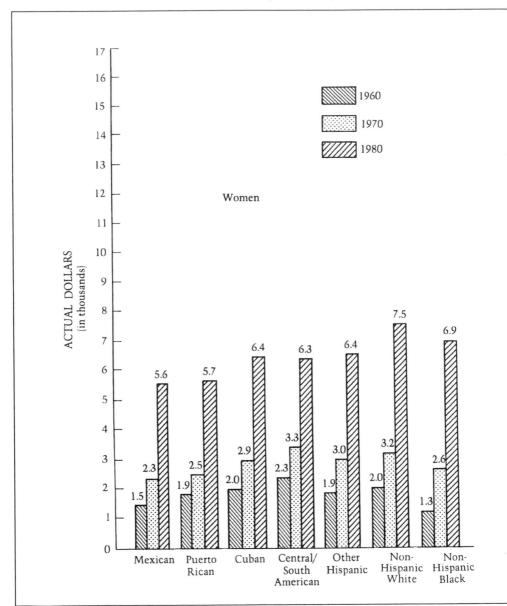

FIGURE 10.3 *(continued)*

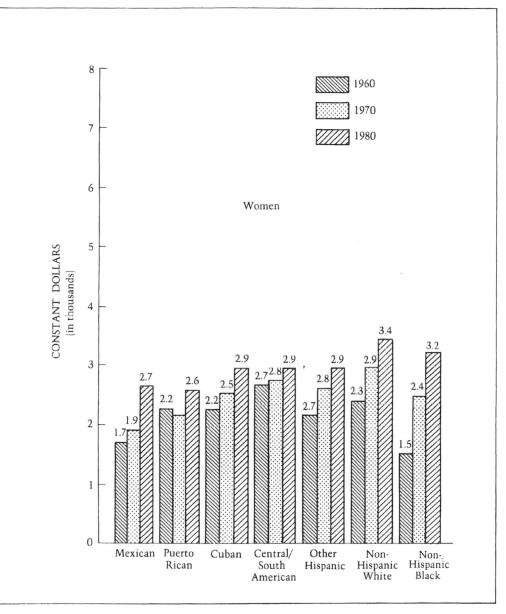

were approximately twice as large as those of their female counterparts in 1960, 1970, and 1980.[20] That all instances of female/male personal income ratios in excess of 50 percent involve Hispanics and blacks (see footnote 20) reflects on the particularly low incomes of minority men rather than economic advantages of the women. For all three years the extent of income differentiation according to race and Hispanic national origin consistently was greater among men than women.

Although the pattern of personal income differentiation according to national origin is generally consistent with that reported on family income, several noteworthy departures deserve mention. First, only Central/South American men experienced a real decline in personal income during the 1970s. The story based on family income included Puerto Ricans as well. Second, between 1960 and 1980 non-Hispanic white ($2,045), black ($1,899), and Cuban ($1,600) men received the largest absolute gains in real personal income, all net changes exceeding $1,500. For all other groups the 20-year increase in real average personal income was less than $1,500, and in two instances, specifically for Central/South Americans and Other Hispanics, it was less than $500. A disaggregation of the components of personal income between 1960 and 1980 provides some insights into the reasons for the different rates of income growth and aids in understanding why the pattern of change in personal income departs in some ways from that based on family income.

Table 10.6 displays the components of mean personal income for Hispanic, black, and non-Hispanic white men and women for all three census periods. Because of the aggregated nature of the income data in 1960 we could separate personal income only into two broad categories—wage and salary income (including self-employment income) and other income. In 1970 and 1980 we were able to disaggregate other income into social insurance, public assistance, and other income.[21]

Personal income increased for all groups and in both decades, but the rise in nominal terms was much greater during the 1970s than the 1960s owing to the higher rate of inflation during the latter period.

[20]The specific female/male earnings ratios for the 1960–1980 period were as follows:

	Mexican	Puerto Rican	Cuban	Central/South American	Other Hispanic	White	Black
1960	46.3%	64.5%	52.4%	51.5%	41.8%	52.9%	43.3%
1970	44.2	49.3	48.4	48.6	45.7	58.8	41.6
1980	56.0	58.7	50.0	53.5	51.6	66.0	45.1

[21]This residual could be broken down into two components—interest, dividend, or rental income, and a residual from all other sources—but we opted to pool these two categories since neither was sufficiently large to warrant further disaggregation.

However, in both periods the overall rates and component-specific rates at which personal income grew varied greatly according to race, national origin, and gender. Consequently, the interdecade changes in personal income translated into increasing income differentiation along race, national origin, and gender lines.

For Hispanic men the growth in real personal income during the 1960s ranged from a low of 9 to 12 percent for Other Hispanics and Central/South Americans to a high of 27 percent for Puerto Ricans. Personal incomes of black and non-Hispanic white men grew by 40 and 28 percent in real terms during this period. Among Hispanic and non-Hispanic white women the growth in real personal income was somewhat lower, ranging from 6 percent for Central/South Americans to 16 to 19 percent for Mexicans and Other Hispanics, respectively. Personal incomes of non-Hispanic white women rose 22 percent between 1960 and 1970 and those of black women rose 56 percent—more than those of Hispanic women, but slightly less than those of their male counterparts. However, Puerto Rican women experienced a net decline of 3 percent in real personal income between 1960 and 1970.

The 1970s further differentiated the change in personal income according to gender. That is, between 1970 and 1980 the rate of increase in men's real personal income slowed, while that of most Hispanic women accelerated. During the more recent period black and Cuban men experienced the largest increase in real personal income, 17 and 13 percent, respectively, compared with 8 and 3 percent, respectively, for Mexican and Puerto Rican men. Personal incomes of non-Hispanic white men rose 7 percent in real terms during the 1970s, while those of Other Hispanic men remained constant, and Central/South American origin men experienced a net decline of 7 percent in real personal income. For them, an 11 percent decline in wage and salary income was responsible for the loss in real personal income, but this was partly offset by relative gains in other income components.

Mexican origin and black women experienced the highest growth of real personal income during the 1970s, 37 and 32 percent, respectively, followed by Puerto Rican women (23 percent). Personal incomes of Cuban and non-Hispanic white women rose 16 percent in real terms during the 1970s, while the income of Central/South American women remained virtually constant.

Owing largely to the labor market hardships associated with the economic recessions of the 1970s, wage and salary income as a share of total personal income declined for several groups. Puerto Ricans and Other Hispanics were particularly affected by the labor market ills of the 1970s. The relative decline was particularly pronounced for Puerto Rican men, whose wage and salary income as a share of total personal

TABLE 10.6

Components of Mean Personal Income of Men and Women Aged 16 and Over by Hispanic National Origin and Race: 1960–1980 (in constant dollars[a])

Nativity by Income Type	Mexican Mean Dollars	Mexican Percentage	Puerto Rican Mean Dollars	Puerto Rican Percentage	Cuban Mean Dollars	Cuban Percentage
MEN						
All Persons, 1960						
Wages and Salary	$3,498	94.3%	$3,245	93.8%	$4,200	95.9%
Other Income	211	5.7	213	6.2	179	4.1
Total Income, Constant $	3,709	100.0	3,458	100.0	4,379	100.0
Total Income, Actual $	3,238		3,019		3,823	
All Persons, 1970						
Wages and Salary	$4,358	93.3	$4,272	97.4	$5,096	96.2
Social Insurance	8	0.1	6	0.0	5	0.0
Public Assistance	4	0.0	11	0.2	4	0.0
Other Income	156	3.4	98	2.2	191	3.6
Total Income, Constant $	4,526	99.8	4,387	99.8	5,296	99.8
Total Income, Actual $	5,264		5,103		6,160	
All Persons, 1980						
Wages and Salary	$4.550	92.7	$4,026	89.1	$5,483	91.8
Social Insurance	101	2.1	107	2.4	145	2.4
Public Assistance	43	.9	118	2.6	71	1.2
Other Income	213	4.3	265	5.9	272	4.6
Total Income, Constant $	4,907	100.0	4,516	100.0	5,971	100.0
Total Income, Actual $	10,688		9,819		12,982	
WOMEN						
All Persons, 1960						
Wages and Salary	$1,378	80.2	$1,920	86.0	$1,984	86.5
Other Income	339	19.7	312	14.0	309	13.5
Total Income, Constant $	1,717	99.9	$2,232	100.0	2,293	100.0
Total Income, Actual $	1,499		$1,948		$2,002	
All Persons, 1970						
Wages and Salary	$1,868	93.4	$1,997	92.3	$2,459	96.0
Social Insurance	10	0.5	9	0.4	7	0.3
Public Assistance	15	0.7	52	2.4	11	0.4
Other Income	106	5.3	105	4.8	85	3.3
Total Income, Constant $	1,999	99.9	2,163	99.9	2,562	100.0
Total Income, Actual $	2,324		2,516		2,980	
All Persons, 1980						
Wages and Salary	$2,207	80.3	$1,882	70.9	$2,539	85.1
Social Insurance	127	4.6	105	4.0	153	5.1
Public Assistance	274	10.0	485	18.3	152	5.1
Other Income	139	5.1	181	6.8	141	4.7
Total Income, Constant $	2,747	100.0	2,653	100.0	2,985	100.0
Total Income, Actual $	5,675		5,770		6,489	

SOURCES: 1960, 1970, and 1980 Public Use Microdata Sample files.

[a]1967 = $1.00; 1959 = .873; 1969 = $1.098; 1979 = $2.174.

TABLE 10.6 (continued)

| | Central/South American | | Other Hispanic | | Black | | Non-Hispanic White |
Mean Dollars	Percentage	Mean Dollars	Percentage	Mean Dollars	Percentage	Mean Dollars	Percentage
$4,876	92.3%	$4,625	88.1%	$2,695	91.9%	$5,147	91.6%
408	7.7	622	11.8	236	8.1	472	8.4
5,284	99.9	5,247	99.9	2,931	100.0	5,619	100.0
4,613		4,581		2,560		4,904	
$5,742	97.0	$5,357	93.6	$3,827	93.0	$6,526	91.0
6	0.0	12	0.2	128	3.1	168	2.3
2	0.0	3	0.0	51	1.2	15	0.2
173	2.9	352	6.2	111	2.7	466	6.5
5,923	99.9	5,724	100.0	4,117	100.0	7,175	100.0
6,888		6,658		4,522		7,878	
$5,099	92.8	$5,103	89.1	$4,458	92.3	$7,045	91.9
53	1.0	176	3.1	71	1.5	75	1.0
37	.7	43	.7	51	1.0	16	0.2
308	5.6	402	7.0	250	5.2	528	6.9
5,497	100.1	5,724	99.9	4,830	100.0	7,664	100.0
1,951		12,446		10,501		16,660	
$2,262	83.1	$1,784	81.3	$1,259	81.2	$1,931	79.3
460	16.9	409	18.6	291	18.8	505	20.7
2,722	100.0	2,193	99.9	1,550	100.0	2,436	100.0
2,377		1,914		1,353		2,127	
$2,697	93.7	$2,354	88.9	$2,007	82.9	$2,376	79.6
7	0.2	13	0.5	133	5.5	206	6.9
9	0.3	12	0.4	199	8.2	42	1.4
165	5.7	239	9.1	81	3.3	361	12.1
2,878	99.9	2,618	99.9	2,420	99.9	2,985	100.0
3,347		3,045		2,659		3,276	
$2,546	86.5	$2,375	80.3	$2,747	86.2	$2,982	86.2
74	2.5	187	6.3	78	2.4	86	2.5
164	5.6	115	3.9	198	6.2	46	1.3
158	5.4	280	9.5	163	5.1	346	10.0
2,942	100.0	2,957	100.0	3,186	99.9	3,460	100.0
6,396		6,429		6,926		7,522	

income fell from 97 percent in 1970 to 89 percent by 1980. The drop in the relative share of wage and salary income was approximately 4 percent for Cuban and Central/South American men, but the net change was imperceptible for Mexican, black, and non-Hispanic white men. Apparently greater reliance on public assistance income by Puerto Rican men prevented their personal income situation from worsening in real terms during the 1970s.

Among women the increase in real personal income experienced during the 1970s by all groups except blacks and non-Hispanic whites can be traced to the increasing shares of social insurance, public assistance, and other income. Without exception, wage and salary income as a share of total personal income for Hispanic women declined sharply, especially for Puerto Ricans. Central/South American women experienced the smallest increase in real personal income, only 2 percent between 1970 and 1980, one which compares favorably with the 7 percent decrease experienced by their male counterparts. By contrast, the rising personal incomes of black and non-Hispanic white women—32 and 16 percent, respectively—during the 1970s can be traced almost exclusively to greater shares of wage and salary income and lesser reliance on income transfers.

Overall, the picture of relative economic well-being based on personal income is one of stability and change. Signs of stability include the dominance of wages and salary in the personal income package of all groups, although work income has declined as a share of the total for virtually all Hispanic groups. On the other hand, the ranking of Hispanic men and women with respect to average personal income levels changed owing to differential rates of growth in personal income according to national origin and gender. Most pronounced were the declines in personal income experienced by Central/South Americans and Puerto Ricans, which have resulted in the relative impoverization of these two subgroups, as the following section shows.

Poverty Rates of Hispanic Persons

Consistent with evidence about families in poverty, Puerto Ricans emerge as the most disadvantaged of the Hispanic origin groups based on the share of persons with below poverty incomes. Table 10.7 shows that between 1970 and 1980 the poverty rate increased for Puerto Ricans and Central/South Americans, while the share of Mexican, Cuban, and Other Hispanic persons in poverty fell. So extreme was the economic disadvantage of Puerto Ricans in 1980 that the income of approximately one person in three of Puerto Rican ancestry was below the official pov-

TABLE 10.7

*Differential Poverty Rates of Persons
by Hispanic National Origin and Race: 1970–1980*

	Mexican	Puerto Rican	Cuban	Central/South American	Other Hispanic	Black	Non-Hispanic White
1970							
Overall Rate	27.5%	31.6%	13.5%	16.0%	21.3%	34.6%[a]	10.8%[a]
Nativity							
Foreign	28.8	30.7	13.5	17.0	21.7	18.6[a]	14.6[a]
Native	27.2	32.8	13.4	13.8	21.1	34.9	10.6
Age							
Under 18 Years	31.9	39.0	14.8	18.4	25.8	42.2[a]	10.9[a]
18–24 Years	27.3	28.1	17.9	22.9	30.9	29.3	11.7
25–59 Years	20.5	23.4	10.4	11.5	13.2	24.4	6.8
60 Years and Over	34.8	29.0	19.1	18.8	24.2	45.0	21.6
Sex							
Men	27.1	31.0	12.4	15.5	22.3	29.3[b]	8.2[b]
Women	27.9	32.2	14.4	16.4	20.3	35.0	10.7
1980							
Overall Rate	22.9	35.6	12.7	20.3	17.2	29.9[c]	9.4[c]
Nativity							
Foreign	26.5	35.4	12.9	20.0	17.2	*	*
Native	21.6	35.8	11.9	21.7	17.2	*	*
Age							
Under 18 Years	28.2	46.1	13.9	25.0	21.4	38.6[d]	11.6[d]
18–24 Years	20.7	31.8	10.8	25.3	16.2	31.1	11.7
25–59 Years	17.6	26.9	9.5	16.3	12.8	21.4	6.6
60 Years and Over	24.4	26.6	21.6	19.7	19.4	32.9	11.5
Sex							
Men	21.1	31.2	11.5	18.4	15.3	26.8[c]	8.2[c]
Women	24.7	39.6	13.8	21.9	19.0	32.5	10.6

SOURCES: 1970 and 1980 Public Use Microdata Sample files.

U.S. Bureau of the Census, *Census of Population: 1970,* "Low-Income Population," Subject Reports: Final Report PC(2)-9A.

"24 Million Americans—Poverty in the U.S.: 1969," *Current Population Reports,* series P-60, no. 76, table 4.

U.S. Bureau of the Census, *Census of Population: 1980,* "Detailed Population Characteristics," PC80-1-D1-, pt. 1, U.S. Summary, table 304.

U.S. Bureau of the Census, "Characteristics of the Population Below the Poverty Level: *Current Population Reports,* series P-60, no. 130, table 11.

Not applicable.

erty level in both years, with some evidence of increasing poverty rates during the period. Despite the lowered poverty rates for Mexicans, Cubans, and Other Hispanics during the 1970s, the incidence of poverty among these groups remained above that observed among native whites. Nearly one person in every four of Mexican origin was poor in 1980, down slightly from the rate in 1970. Cubans' poverty rate, which is relatively low compared with that of other Hispanic origin groups, changed little during the 1970s. The poverty rate of black persons fell almost 5 percent between 1970 and 1980, while that for whites dropped less than 2 percent.

Differentials in individual poverty rates according to nativity, age, and gender were less pronounced than those observed among families. That gender differences in poverty rates widened during the 1970s reveals the feminization of Hispanic poverty. Whereas the gender gap in the risk of being poor was less than 1 percent for Mexicans in 1970, this difference increased by 3.6 percent by 1980. Among Puerto Ricans women were approximately 1 percent more likely to be poor in 1970 than their male counterparts, but in 1980 the gender gap in poverty had grown to 8.4 percent. Similar gender differences emerged for the remaining Hispanic groups and blacks. These differences partly reflect the rise in the prevalence of female-headed households during the 1970s, as well as the disadvantaged positioning of minority women in the U.S. labor market.[22]

Age differentiation in poverty rates was not uniform among national origin and race groups. The broadest generalization we can make about age differentials in poverty rates is that the lowest rates correspond to individuals of prime working age, suggesting a close association between labor market position and the probability of being poor. Among the young and elderly, however, the risk of poverty varied considerably both along race and national lines. Poverty rates were strikingly high among Puerto Rican youth under age 18—39 percent in 1970 and 46 percent in 1980. These compare with rates of 42 and 39 percent of their black age-mates in 1970 and 1980, respectively. The high rates of poverty among Puerto Rican youth reflect their extremely poor labor market position, which is similar to that experienced by black youth.[23] Among Mexicans and Cubans it was the elderly, those aged 60 and

---

[22]This statement is documented extensively in Chapter 9. See also Shelley A. Smith and Marta Tienda, "The Doubly Disadvantaged: Women of Color in the U.S. Labor Force," in Ann Stromberg and Shirely Harkess, eds., Working Women, 2nd ed. (Palo Alto, CA: Mayfield, 1986).

[23]Robert D. Mare and Christopher Winship, "The Paradox of Lessening Racial Inequality and Joblessness among Black Youth: Enrollment, Enlistment and Employment, 1964–1981," American Sociological Review 49 (1984):39–55.

above, who experienced the highest poverty rates in 1970, but this circumstance changed for Mexicans by 1980. Why Central/South Americans and Other Hispanics aged 18 to 24 experienced higher poverty rates in 1970 than their younger or older nationality counterparts is unclear, but it may be related to transitory income effects associated with investment in schooling, as well as the pronounced effects of recent immigration on the age and socioeconomic composition of this group.

On balance, the information in Table 10.7 reaffirms our story about the extremely disadvantaged economic position of the Puerto Rican population and the lowered economic status of Central/South Americans during the 1970–1980 decade. Cubans fared best of all the groups, both in terms of their average personal income levels and in terms of their consistently lower rates of poverty throughout the 1970s. In large measure the growing affluence of the Cuban population derives from their general success in the U.S. labor market compared with Mexicans and Puerto Ricans, but increasingly compared with Central/South American workers. We explore this issue in the remaining part of this chapter through a more detailed analysis of earnings, which constituted the largest share of personal income for all groups.

Earnings

Despite continuing increases in women's labor force participation since 1945, as a group women have had more restricted access to the wide array of job opportunities in the United States labor market relative to men. That women have continued to be heavily concentrated in a small range of gender-typed jobs has direct implications for the persistence of gender differences in earnings.[24] Moreover, as shown in Chapter 9, because race and national origin influence occupational placement, differentials in the types of jobs held by men and women translate into uneven economic rewards according to Hispanic national origin.

"Fifty-nine cents for a dollar" became the familiar phrase when discussions of gender inequities in the labor market called attention to the seeming immutability of the male-female earnings disparity. That this ratio represents the differential in earnings between white men and

[24]Marta Tienda and Vilma Ortiz, "Hispanicity and the 1980 Census," *Social Science Quarterly* 67 (1986):3–20; Jennifer Glass, Marta Tienda, and Shelley A. Smith, "The Impact of Industry Growth and Intra-Industry Occupational Recomposition on Gender Wage Inequality," Working Paper no. 86-17, Center for Demography and Ecology, University of Wisconsin–Madison, 1986; Paul England and Steven D. McLaughlin, "Sex Segregation of Jobs and Male-Female Income Differentials," in Rodolfo Alvarez et al., eds., *Discrimination in Organization* (San Francisco: Jossey-Bass, 1979).

white women was less publicized. In the past the gender gap in earnings among people of color, including Hispanics, has been substantially lower than 59.[25] However, as the tabulations in Table 10.8 show, there is considerable variation in the female-male earnings ratio according to race and Hispanic national origin.

The data in Table 10.8 are restricted to the subset of individuals who worked on a full-time, year-round basis in order to make the comparisons of men and women more equal.[26] Consistent with the national picture,[27] men earned more than their female race or nationality counterparts in both years, but the size of the gender gap in earnings varied among groups and over time. In 1970 the female-male earnings ratio ranged from a low of 50 percent for Other Hispanics to a high of 66 percent for Puerto Ricans. By 1980 the female-male earnings disparity had narrowed for some groups and widened for others. For example, in 1980 Mexican origin women earned 56 percent as much as their male counterparts, up from 45 percent in 1970. For black and white workers the female-male earnings ratios were 66 and 45 percent, respectively, up from 52 and 43 percent in 1960 (see footnote 20). By contrast, the gender gap in earnings widened for Puerto Rican and Cuban origin women between 1960 and 1980, but the divergence between men's and women's earnings occurred during the 1960s. During the 1970s the wage gap between Puerto Rican and Cuban men and women began to converge.

An examination of the interdecade changes and differentials in median earnings between men and women provides some perspective on the forces responsible for the convergence of the Hispanic gender gaps in earnings. In current dollars the median earnings of all groups increased substantially during the 1970s, and, with the exception of Cubans, median earnings rose at a much faster rate for women than men. In constant or real terms, however, interdecade changes translated into net earnings declines for several of the gender and national origin groups. Among Mexicans and Puerto Ricans, for instance, the convergence of the gender gap in median earnings resulted from a 3 to 4 percent decrease in men's real median earnings versus a real increase in women's median earnings of 21 and 3 percent, respectively.

[25]See also Shelley A. Smith and Marta Tienda, "The Doubly Disadvantaged: Women of Color in the U.S. Labor Force," in Ann Stromberg and Shirley Harkess, eds., Working Women, 2nd ed. (Palo Alto, CA: Mayfield, 1986).
[26]This is important to avoid confounding gender differences in earnings with those arising because of male-female differences in the labor supply, and specifically the greater propensity of women to work part time.
[27]Janice Shack-Marquez, "Earnings Differences Between Men and Women: An Introductory Note," Monthly Labor Review 107 (1984):15–16; Janet Norwood, "The Female-Male Earnings Gap: A Review of Employment and Earnings Issues," Bureau of Labor Statistics Report 673 (1982):2.

Uniform rates of growth (4 percent) in the median earnings of Cuban men and women who worked on a full-time, year-round basis explain the slow convergence of gender differences for this group. Although the female-male earnings ratio for Central/South Americans and Other Hispanic workers narrowed slightly, this convergence resulted from the faster rate of decrease in men's versus women's real median earnings. That is, the real median earnings of these two groups fell during the 1970s, but the decline was steeper for men, ranging, respectively, from 7 to 16 percent for Other Hispanic and Central/South American men and 1 and 9 percent for women.

Additional dimensions of diversity in Hispanic median earnings reside in the differentials among the nativity and education groups. That immigrant workers received higher median annual earnings relative to their native-born counterparts in 10 out of 14 possible comparisons in 1980 and 8 out of 14 comparisons in 1970 was somewhat surprising in light of extensive empirical research showing average earnings penalties associated with foreign birth.[28] In these gross comparisons, however, we have not adjusted for the influence of various factors which are systematically correlated with foreign birth and earnings. Net differences based on our multivariate analysis are consistent with prior studies in showing a negative effect on earnings of foreign birth.

Gender differences in median annual earnings within the nativity groups also provide some useful information about the sources of disparity in median earnings between Hispanic men and women. In 1970 there was greater earnings parity between men and women among the foreign-born than among the native-born of every national origin group except non-Hispanic whites. For example, among Cubans, women earned only 39 percent as much as their male counterparts if they were native-born compared with 59 percent among those born abroad. Large gender disparities in earnings ratios also emerged among Other Hispanics and Central/South Americans depending on their birthplace. Among the native-born median earnings of Other Hispanics and Central/South American women were roughly 44 percent of that received by their male counterparts, while among immigrants women earned approximately 56 percent of what their male counterparts received in 1970.

In spite of a narrowing of the average gender gap in earnings during the 1970s, nontrivial earnings gaps persisted according to nativity and

[28]Marta Tienda, "Nationality and Income Attainment of Native and Immigrant Hispanic Men in the United States," *Sociological Quarterly* 24 (1983b):253–72; Cordelia W. Reimers, "A Comparative Analysis of the Wages of Hispanics, Blacks, and Non-Hispanic Whites," in George J. Borjas and Marta Tienda, eds., *Hispanics in the U.S. Economy* (Orlando, FL: Academic Press, 1985); Barry R. Chiswick, "The Effect of Americanization on the Earnings of Foreign-Born Men," *Journal of Political Economy* 86 (1978):897–921.

TABLE 10.8

Median Earnings Differentials of Individual Workers Aged 16–64
by Hispanic National Origin, Race, and Gender: 1970–1980[a]
(full-time, year-round workers)

	Mexican		Puerto Rican		Cuban	
	Men	Women	Men	Women	Men	Women
1970						
1970, All Persons						
Actual $	$5,050	$2,250	$5,050	$3,350	$5,550	$3,150
Constant $[b]	4,599	2,049	4,599	3,051	5,055	2,869
Nativity						
Foreign	4,417	1,867	4,599	3,051	4,872	2,869
Native	4,599	1,867	4,599	2,641	5,191	2,049
Education						
Less than 12 Years	4,053	1,412	4,599	2,778	4,599	2,687
12 Years	5,055	2,596	4,690	3,233	5,100	3,005
13–15 Years	5,510	2,778	4,918	2,778	5,328	2,960
16 Years or More	8,242	4,781	7,923	4,599	7,514	4,235
1980						
1980, All Persons						
Actual $	9,615	5,385	9,672	6,808	11,410	6,505
Constant $[b]	4,423	2,477	4,449	3,132	5,248	2,992
Nativity						
Foreign	3,682	2,302	4,602	3,222	5,062	2,868
Native	4,602	2,302	3,590	2,302	3,705	2,302
Education						
Less than 12 Years	3,682	1,842	4,069	2,440	4,167	2,633
12 Years	4,602	2,633	4,142	3,208	5,062	2,854
13–15 Years	5,430	2,762	4,441	3,222	4,489	2,875
16 Years or More	6,902	4,029	6,442	4,271	7,592	4,671

SOURCES: 1970 and 1980 Public Use Microdata Sample files.

[a]Based on 1969 and 1979 income figures, expressed in constant 1967 dollars.
[b]1969 = $1.098; 1979 = $2.174.

national origin in 1980. Gender differences in median earnings were much lower among the foreign-born than the native-born for all groups except Cubans and Puerto Ricans and non-Hispanic whites in 1980. Nativity differences in the relative male-female earnings disparity among Central/South Americans widened during the 1970s, as the median earnings of the foreign-born converged faster (rising from 55 to 61 percent) than those of the native-born (which rose from 44 to 46 percent). On balance, the general tendency in median earnings differentials was

TABLE 10.8 *(continued)*

Central/ South American		Other Hispanic		Black		Non-Hispanic White	
Men	Women	Men	Women	Men	Women	Men	Women
$6,050	$3,350	$6,050	$3,050	$6,000	4,000	$8,600	$5,000
5,510	3,051	5,510	2,778	5,464	3,643	7,832	4,554
5,510	3,051	4,918	2,778	5,920	4,189	8,834	4,554
5,328	2,322	5,510	2,413	5,464	3,643	7,741	4,554
4,599	2,778	4,599	1,867	4,554	2,732	6,557	3,643
5,510	3,506	5,965	3,097	5,738	4,098	7,468	4,554
5,510	2,778	5,510	2,778	6,375	4,554	8,379	5,282
8,698	4,098	9,153	4,599	8,197	6,557	11,840	7,104
10,005	6,005	11,170	6,005	12,005	9,805	18,005	10,005
4,602	2,762	5,138	2,762	5,522	4,510	8,282	4,602
4,547	2,762	4,846	2,762	5,522	4,602	9,151	4,752
4,506	2,072	5,062	2,509	5,522	4,377	7,953	4,602
3,682	2,486	3,760	1,842	4,694	3,590	6,442	3,912
4,602	2,762	4,602	2,762	5,522	4,372	7,399	4,418
4,602	2,955	5,513	2,762	6,023	4,759	8,282	4,959
6,902	3,811	7,822	4,512	8,052	5,982	10,582	6,235

one toward convergence between men and women, although there are some signs of pulling apart among nativity and national origin groups.

Education differentials in median earnings show a much clearer pattern in that the relationship between education and median earnings was roughly monotonic for both men and women in both years. However, there are some signs of nonlinearity involving the completion of 12 years of graded schooling and a baccalaureate degree. This suggests the importance of education in the determination of Hispanic earnings.[29]

[29]Marta Tienda and Lisa J. Neidert, "Language, Education, and the Socioeconomic Achievement of Hispanic Origin Men," *Social Science Quarterly* 65 (1984):519–36.

Within levels of schooling there was extensive variation in median earnings according to national origin and race. Among men who had completed 16 or more years of graded school in 1970, median earnings ranged from $11,800 for non-Hispanic whites to $7,500 for Cubans. That college-educated Cuban men received the lowest median earnings in 1970 is somewhat surprising in light of their image as a relatively successful ethnic group in the U.S. labor market. However, an accurate interpretation of this result must acknowledge that, because of their relatively short United States residence as of 1970, many professional Cuban men may not have completed the process of certifying their credentials (as required for teachers, lawyers, doctors, and so on, who were educated abroad). Their success in adapting to the U.S. labor market manifests itself in the comparisons of median earnings among college-educated men in 1980, when median earnings rose from last to fourth rank, superseded only by non-Hispanic white, black, and Other Hispanic origin men with college degrees.

Among college-educated men Puerto Ricans received the lowest median earnings. The median earnings of Central/South American and Mexican men converged, partly because of the changing composition of the recent immigrants from Central and South America toward individuals with less education (see Chapter 8). Women of Central/South American origin, however, fared worse than their male counterparts. However, as Table 10.9 shows, the average gap in earnings for this subgroup conceals extensive variation by country of origin.

The 1979 median earnings of South American origin men exceeded those of Central American origin men by roughly $3,200. Since Central Americans constituted a larger share of the Central/South American origin population in 1980 compared with previous decades, the decline in the economic position of the Central/South American population during the 1970s results from the compositional change toward lower earning groups. Furthermore, both Central and South Americans exhibited considerable diversity in median earnings. For example, among men the lowest earnings corresponded to Dominicans and Salvadorans, whose 1980 median among those employed full time stood just under $10,000. At the other extreme, the median earnings for Nicaraguan and Costa Rican men ranged between $14,000 and $15,000. South American men exhibited even greater variation in 1980 median earnings compared with those of Central American origin; their median earnings ranged from a high of $27,000 (Paraguayans) to a low of $12,000 (Ecuadorans). Most nationalities, however, earned close to the subregion median of $14,000.

Women of Central and South American origin exhibited less diversity in median earnings than men. Among women from Central America and the Caribbean, Panamanians received the highest median earn-

TABLE 10.9

*Median Earnings for Full-Time, Year-Round
Central and South American Workers Aged 16–64
by Gender and Country of Origin: 1980*

	Men	Women
CENTRAL AMERICA AND THE CARIBBEAN	$10,805	$7,850
Dominican Republic	9,880	7,005
El Salvador	9,885	7,005
Guatemala	11,005	7,345
Nicaragua	14,935	8,845
Panama	13,605	10,005
Honduras	12,005	8,305
Costa Rica	14,505	8,845
Other Central American	14,755	9,835
SOUTH AMERICA	$14,005	$9,005
Colombia	13,005	8,905
Ecuador	12,005	8,005
Peru	14,045	9,885
Argentina	16,755	10,005
Chile	15,445	10,005
Venezuela	16,315	9,885
Bolivia	16,650	10,005
Uruguay	14,885	9,105
Paraguay	26,915	6,255
Other South American	12,005	9,885
Total	12,005	8,205

SOURCE: 1980 Public Use Microdata Sample file.

ings in 1980, approximately $10,000. The remaining groups were within $1,000 below or above the median for the 1980 subregion average of $7,850. A similar pattern of dispersion in earnings characterized South American origin women, with most nationalities earning about $1,000 above or below the median for the subgroup. Paraguayan women, whose 1979 median earnings were approximately $3,000 *below* the subregion average of $9,000, were the sole exception. This result was somewhat surprising because the median earnings of Panamanian men were well above those of other South American nationalities, but it may be an artifact of the small sample size (N = 51) once restrictions for full-time, year-round workers were implemented.

Earning disparities between men and women according to national origin are easily summarized using a male/female earnings ratio. This

TABLE 10.10

Earnings Determination of Hispanic Men by National Origin: 1980
(standard error in parentheses)

	Mexican	Puerto Rican	Cuban	Central/South American	Other Hispanic
HUMAN CAPITAL					
Education	.045***	.056***	.043***	.054***	.060***
	(.002)	(.003)	(.002)	(.002)	(.003)
Experience	.037***	.037***	.034***	.033***	.043***
	(.002)	(.002)	(.002)	(.002)	(.002)
(Experience)^2	−.001***	−.001***	−.001***	−.001***	−.001***
	(.000)	(.000)	(.000)	(.000)	(.000)
English Ability[a]					
Good	.178***	.129**	.083*	.171***	.113*
	(.031)	(.048)	(.035)	(.036)	(.057)
Fair	.058	.080	−.039	.025	.113
	(.031)	(.050)	(.033)	(.035)	(.061)
YEAR OF IMMIGRATION[b]					
Before 1950	−.006		.044	.147*	.027
	(.046)		(.064)	(.068)	(.056)
1950–1959	.026		.054	.018	−.045
	(.035)		(.039)	(.048)	(.047)
1960–1964	−.023		.070*	−.014	.016
	(.037)		(.034)	(.042)	(.048)
1965–1969	−.003		−.055	−.060	−.097*
	(.032)		(.035)	(.040)	(.038)
1970–1974	−.081**		−.030	−.127**	−.058
	(.027)		(.038)	(.040)	(.035)
1975–1980	−.173***		−.334***	−.208***	−.221***
	(.029)		(.057)	(.040)	(.038)
Island-Born[c]		−.085***			
		(.019)			

SOURCE: 1980 Public Use Microdata Sample file.

*p ≤ .05
**p ≤ .01
***p ≤ .001
[a]Reference category is no English ability.
[b]Reference category is native-born.
[c]Reference category is mainland-born.

comparison revealed that gender differences in earnings were less pronounced among the Central American and Caribbean origin workers than those from South American, with male/female earnings ratios of 73 and 64 percent, respectively, in 1980. That there was greater gender parity in median earnings among Central Americans reflects the lower earnings of men rather than the higher earnings of women. The sex ratio

TABLE 10.10 *(continued)*

	Mexican	Puerto Rican	Cuban	Central/South American	Other Hispanic
DEMOGRAPHIC AND LIFE CYCLE					
Married[d]	.193***	.161***	.203***	.167***	.242***
	(.018)	(.017)	(.022)	(.021)	(.019)
Healthy[e]	.210***	.139***	.190***	.136*	.185***
	(.037)	(.036)	(.049)	(.056)	(.034)
Child Present[f]	−.008	−.026	.086**	.015	.003
	(.020)	(.022)	(.032)	(.024)	(.025)
LABOR SUPPLY					
Worked Full-Time	.350***	.384***	.347***	.319***	.402***
	(.027)	(.027)	(.032)	(.034)	(.029)
Weeks Worked, 1979	.033***	.035***	.036***	.034***	.314***
	(.001)	(.001)	(.001)	(.001)	(.007)
MARKET CONDITIONS					
Sector of Employment[g]					
Private	−.032	−.154***	−.110***	−.168***	−.032
	(.032)	(.040)	(.025)	(.032)	(.028)
Public	−.100**	−.203***	−.160***	−.269***	−.116***
	(.036)	(.042)	(.036)	(.042)	(.032)
Hispanic Concentration[h]					
Medium (3–9%)	−.041	.035	−.058	.013	−.014
	(.031)	(.023)	(.036)	(.035)	(.023)
High (10% +)	−.068*	−.083***	−.155***	−.092**	−.070***
	(.027)	(.021)	(.032)	(.031)	(.020)
Average Area Wage Rate	.103***	.066***	.055***	.013	.093***
	(.008)	(.010)	(.014)	(.013)	(.008)
Constant	5.308	5.474	5.841	6.177	5.360
R^2	.428	.405	.415	.455	.447

[d]Reference category is not married.
[e]Reference category is not healthy.
[f]Reference category is no child under age 6 present.
[g]Reference category is self-employed.
[h]Reference category is low concentration (<3%).

in earnings varied from a low of 59 percent for Nicaraguan women, showing them to be the most disadvantaged vis-à-vis their male counterparts, to a high of 74 percent for Panamanian women and 71 percent for Dominican and Salvadoran women. Among the South American nationalities Peruvians, Colombians, and Ecuadorans exhibited the highest gender parity in earnings in 1980, while the lowest parity corresponded to Paraguayan women (23 percent). For Argentinian, Venezuelan, Bolivian, and Uruguayan women[30] the gender ratio in earnings stood at roughly 60 percent.

To summarize, nativity differentials in the median earnings of full-time, year-round workers present a complex and diverse picture. Although results in Table 10.8 show that the better educated generally earned more than those less well-educated, the variation in median earnings within education levels suggests that several additional factors not considered in the bivariate tabulations are influential in producing the observed differentials in median earnings. To analyze these factors, we turn to a multivariate analysis of earnings determination for Hispanic origin workers.

Earnings Determination: A Multivariate Analysis

Labor economists and sociologists depict individual earnings as a function of a few widely agreed upon investment and background variables which we classify into four categories: (1) human capital, (2) demographic and life cycle factors, (3) labor supply, and (4) market conditions.[31] The specific variables we use in our multivariate analysis are summarized in Table 10.12. In the appendix to this chapter we also provide a brief theoretical rationale for our empirical specification.

For the empirical estimation we restricted the sample to civilian men and women aged 16 to 64 who were in the labor force in 1979 and who had nonzero earnings. Individuals enrolled in school at the time of the survey were excluded in the interest of eliminating voluntary part-time workers. Earnings, our dependent variable, was transformed into its logarithmic form because of the skewed distribution of earnings, so the coefficients can be interpreted roughly as percentage changes (or returns to investments). Our semilogarithmic earnings functions were estimated using ordinary least squares regression separately for men and women because of the well-documented differences in the structure of their earnings functions. We discuss the results accordingly.

Men. Table 10.10 reports the results of the regression analysis pre-

---

[30]The peculiar gender ratio in earnings partly reflects sampling variation due to the small sample sizes on which these calculations are based.

[31]Not all labor market analysts include all four categories of variables in their earnings functions, nor do economists and sociologists treat labor supply factors in the same manner. Although the recognition of the importance of market conditions in determining earnings has increased in recent years, many empirical studies have been slow to include them. Largely this reflects data problems, and in particular the difficulty of building multilevel files for analysis of individual labor market outcomes.

dicting men's 1979 (logged) annual earnings. As predicted by human capital theory, the educational experience variables positively influence earnings, but the rate of return to schooling varied according to national origin. While Mexicans and Cubans received a 4.6 percent return for each year of graded schooling, Puerto Ricans and Central/South Americans received a 5.6 percent return and Other Hispanics a 6 percent return for schooling. There was less differentiation in the relative returns to experience among the Hispanic nationalities, but the payoff to experience[32] was slightly higher for men of Other Hispanic origin. This also is evident in the steeper age-earnings profile for this group shown in Figure 10.4. Cubans, who received the highest average earnings in 1980, had the flattest age-earnings profile, but up to age 30 their average earnings exceeded those of all other groups; thereafter, they were surpassed only by those of Other Hispanics.

Arguments that earnings differentials for Hispanic workers stem partly from differences in English proficiency finds support in our results for men (but to a much lesser extent for women), yet the impact on earnings of language ability varied considerably according to nationality. Hispanic men with good English proficiency earned anywhere from 8 to 18 percent more than their national origin counterparts who were unable to speak English.

That recent immigrants (1975–1980 arrivals) earned between 17 and 33 percent less than their national origin counterparts who were native-born is consistent with other literature[33] showing that immigrants often earn less than otherwise similar U.S.-born workers, particularly immediately following their arrival in the United States. Some evidence suggests that nativity discrepancies in earnings narrow with increasing time spent in the U.S. labor market,[34] presumably because the foreign-born have greater opportunities to acclimate themselves to the U.S. labor market by adapting their skills and training to different opportunities. Among economists there is some debate as to how much and under which circumstances the earnings convergence between native and im-

---

[32]Since we do not have precise information on work experience, we use a conventional proxy which is a direct transformation of age [age − schooling − 6]. Essentially our experience effects are age effects, which is why we use them to compute age-earnings profiles.

[33]Reimers, "Comparative Analysis"; Chiswick, "Effect of Americanization"; "Economic Progress of Immigrants."

[34]Douglas S. Massey, "The Settlement Process Among Mexican Immigrants to the United States: New Methods and Findings," in *Migration Statistics, A Story of Neglect*, Final Report of the Panel on Immigration Statistics, Research Committee on National Statistics of the National Research Council (Washington, DC: National Academy of Sciences, 1985), Appendix C.

TABLE 10.11

Earnings Determination of Hispanic Women
by National Origin: 1980 (standard error in parentheses)

	Mexican	Puerto Rican	Cuban	Central/South American	Other Hispanic
HUMAN CAPITAL					
Education	.036***	.046***	.024***	.036***	.058***
	(.004)	(.003)	(.003)	(.003)	(.003)
Experience	.018***	.016***	.010***	.015***	.018***
	(.002)	(.002)	(.002)	(.002)	(.002)
(Experience)^2	−.000***	−.000***	−.000***	−.000***	−.000***
	(.000)	(.000)	(.000)	(.000)	(.000)
English Ability[a]					
Good	.001	−.053	.061	.125***	.072
	(.043)	(.054)	(.033)	(.032)	(.068)
Fair	−.048	−.122*	−.030	−.000	.060
	(.043)	(.057)	(.031)	(.031)	(.073)
YEAR OF IMMIGRATION[b]					
Before 1950	.018		−.108	−.136*	.042
	(.064)		(.070)	(.068)	(.068)
1950–1959	.050		−.078	−.045	.009
	(.050)		(.043)	(.051)	(.060)
1960–1964	−.012		.008	−.020	.042
	(.051)		(.036)	(.047)	(.053)
1965–1969	.068		−.075*	−.101*	.030
	(.044)		(.036)	(.044)	(.045)
1970–1974	−.038		−.108*	−.164***	−.104**
	(.040)		(.039)	(.044)	(.040)
1975–1980	−.079		−.184**	−.227***	.007
	(.043)		(.069)	(.045)	(.044)
Island-Born[c]		−.065**			
		(.022)			

migrant workers occurs,[35] and sociologists question whether and how much earnings convergence should be used to argue that immigrant adaptation and assimilation is taking place.[36]

Other life cycle and demographic variables that influence earnings perform as expected in that married men earned more than single men,

[35] See Borjas, "Assimilation." His cohort comparisons suggest that Chiswick's earlier work greatly overestimated the earnings convergence between native- and foreign-born workers.

[36] Alejandro Portes and Robert L. Bach, "Theoretical Overview," in Latin Journey: Cuban and Mexican Immigrants in the United States (Los Angeles: University of California Press, 1985).

TABLE 10.11 *(continued)*

	Mexican	Puerto Rican	Cuban	Central/South American	Other Hispanic
DEMOGRAPHIC AND LIFE CYCLE					
Married[d]	.035	.025	.002	.038*	−.007
	(.020)	(.018)	(.019)	(.019)	(.019)
Healthy[e]	.117*	.148**	.014	.101	.060
	(.056)	(.051)	(.058)	(.057)	(.050)
Child Present[f]	.035	−.015	.030	−.025	.062*
	(.028)	(.029)	(.035)	(.028)	(.031)
LABOR SUPPLY					
Worked Full-Time	.538***	.418***	.415***	.423***	.633***
	(.024)	(.024)	(.025)	(.025)	(.023)
Weeks Worked, 1979	.038***	.040***	.036***	.034***	.343***
	(.001)	(.001)	(.001)	(.001)	(.007)
MARKET CONDITIONS					
Sector of Employment[g]					
Private	−.033	.122	.005	.101	.030
	(.062)	(.074)	(.041)	(.054)	(.050)
Public	.067	.218**	.210***	.150*	.096
	(.065)	(.076)	(.048)	(.060)	(.052)
Hispanic Concentration[h]					
Medium (3–9%)	−.049	.057	−.077*	.032	.010
	(.042)	(.030)	(.040)	(.039)	(.027)
High (10% +)	−.071*	.046	−.059	.025	.042
	(.036)	(.028)	(.035)	(.035)	(.023)
Average Area Wage Rate	.116***	.051***	.124***	.048**	.094***
	(.010)	(.014)	(.015)	(.015)	(.010)
Constant	5.085	5.290	5.561	5.732	5.016
R^2	.516	.505	.444	.463	.501

SOURCE: 1980 Public Use Microdata Sample file.

*p ≤ .05
**p ≤ .01
***p ≤ .001
[a]Reference category is no English ability.
[b]Reference category is native-born.
[c]Reference category is mainland-born.
[d]Reference category is not married.
[e]Reference category is not healthy.
[f]Reference category is no child under age 6 present.
[g]Reference category is self-employed.
[h]Reference category is low concentration (<3%).

while the absence of work-limiting health conditions rendered Hispanic men's earnings between 14 and 21 percent higher than those of their nationality counterparts who reported one or more work-limiting health conditions. The variance in returns to good health among national ori-

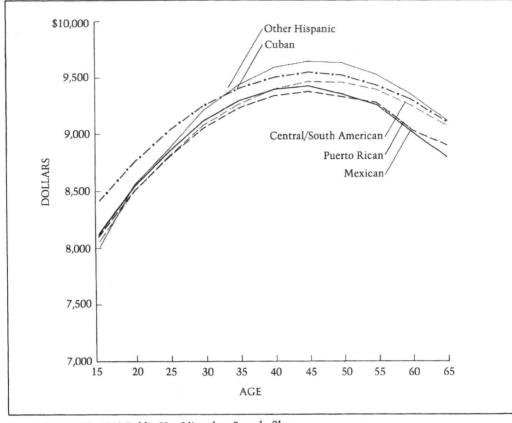

FIGURE 10.4

Age Earnings Profiles for Hispanic Men: 1980

SOURCE: 1980 Public Use Microdata Sample files.

gin groups may partly reflect class and cultural differences in perceptions of limiting health conditions.[37]

Labor supply effects on earnings, while not particularly interesting,
do conform with the predictions of economic theory. On average, 1979
annual earnings of full-time Hispanic workers were between 32 and 40
percent higher than those of part-time workers. Also, for each additional
week worked in 1979, Hispanic men's earnings increased by approximately 3 to 3.5 percent.

[37]Ronald J. Angel, "Disability for Hispanic Males," *Social Science Quarterly*, 65
(1984):426–43. Angel claims that individuals may normalize their health status by altering
their perceptions of states of diminished health and disability. To the extent this occurs,
disabled individuals will underreport health limitations. Moreover, if Hispanic men were
differentially inclined to underreport the presence of work-limiting disabilities (and Angel
shows that this is the case), the observed earnings differences associated with good health
status partly will reflect these reporting errors. Unfortunately there is no way to adjust for
such response errors in census data.

TABLE 10.12

Description of Variables Used in Earnings Regression Analyses

Variable	Description
DEPENDENT VARIABLE	
Log Earnings	Total 1979 labor income from wages and salaries and self-employment
INDEPENDENT VARIABLES	
I. Human Capital	
Education	Years of completed schooling
Experience	Age − Years of school completed − 6
(Experience)^2	Quadratic term
English Ability	Series of dummy variables coded 1 if reported English ability was good or fair; reference category is poor or no English ability
Interstate Mover	Dummy variable coded 1 if individual moved between states or countries during 1975–1980 time period; reference category is nonmovers
II. Demographic and Life Cycle	
Nativity	Dummy variable coded 1 if individual was born in the continental U.S.; reference category is born abroad, including Puerto Rico
Marital Status	Dummy variable coded 1 if individual was married; reference category is unmarried including divorced, widowed and separated
Health Status	Dummy variable coded 1 if individuals did not have any work limiting health conditions; reference category is individuals with work-limiting health conditions
Child Under Age 6	Dummy variable coded 1 if individual has a child under 6; reference category is individuals with no children under age 6
III. Labor Supply	
Worked Full-Time	Dummy
Weeks Worked, 1979	Number of weeks worked in 1979
IV. Market Conditions	
Sector of Employment	Series of dummy variables coded 1 if individual was employed in the private or public sector; reference category is self-employed
Hispanic Concentration	Proportion Hispanic in labor market, High = ≥ 10; Medium = ≥ 3 < 10; Low is the reference category <3
Average Wage Rate	Average wage rate in labor market

Of greater substantive and theoretical interest are the earnings effects of market conditions and employment sectors. The economic attractiveness of self-employment is revealed by findings showing lower returns to employment in the public or private sector for all national origin groups. The negative effects of public sector employment were especially pronounced among Puerto Ricans, Cubans, and Central/South Americans, but all Hispanic men employed in the public sector, which includes federal, state, and local levels, earned significantly less than their national origin counterparts who were self-employed. Average earnings differences associated with public sector employment versus self-employment ranged from 10 percent for Mexicans to 26 percent for Central/South Americans. Similarly, employment in the private sector in 1980 was associated with lower earnings compared with self-employment, on the order of 12 to 18 percent for Cubans, Puerto Ricans, and Central/South Americans, but Mexican and Other Hispanic men earned about the same in the private sector as in self-employment.

That labor market conditions influence earnings above and beyond individual productivity characteristics is evident in the statistically significant effects on earnings of the average market wage rate and Hispanic concentration measures. Employment in high wage areas rendered Hispanic men's income bonuses ranging from 6 to 7 percent for Cubans and Puerto Ricans to 9 to 10 percent for Other Hispanics and Mexicans, for each dollar increase in the average area wage rate. No such influence emerged among Central/South Americans, probably because this group is the most geographically dispersed and because the more diverse socioeconomic composition of this group has neutralized the uneven wage effects across labor markets.

Finally, and in accordance with our expectations, we observed that work and residence in areas where the percentage Hispanic was equal to or in excess of 10 percent of the total working-age population, Hispanic workers received lower earnings relative to otherwise similar men who worked in areas of lesser Hispanic concentration. However, the differential earnings losses associated with work in markets of high Hispanic concentration vary from 7 percent for Mexicans and Other Hispanics to 16 percent for Cubans. Discrimination and economic competition for higher-status, better-paying jobs produce these effects.[38] However,

---

[38]Marta Tienda and Ding-Tzann Lii, "Minority Concentration and Earnings Inequality: A Revised Formulation," Discussion Paper no. 791–85, Institute for Research on Poverty, University of Wisconsin-Madison, 1985. Although Tienda and Lii's analyses, which were confined to pooled comparisons among Asian, Hispanic, black, and white men, do not address the possibility of uneven influences among the Hispanic nationalities, our results suggest this possibility and invite further empirical scrutiny into this question because it appears that the meaning of "Hispanicity" as an ethnic construct can best be understood with reference to race and ethnic relations in specific labor markets.

FIGURE 10.5

Age Earnings Profiles for Hispanic Women: 1980

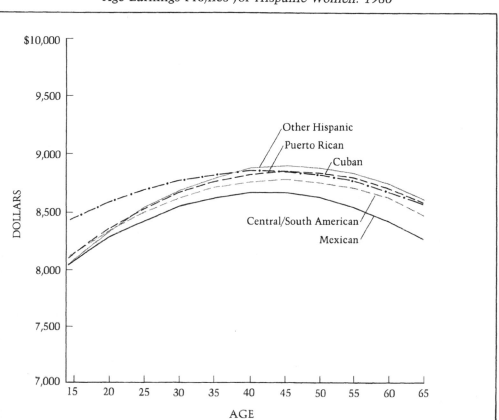

SOURCE: 1980 Public Use Microdata Sample files.

crowding, competition, and discrimination interpretations of minority concentration effects on patterns of earnings dispersion must probe deeper into the economic organization of power and privilege within labor markets and consider how ethnicity stratifies workers among various occupational roles and earnings strata.

Women. In light of our foregoing detailed discussion of the earnings determination of Hispanic men, and in striving for a more parsimonious interpretation of results, we provide an abridged presentation of the key findings for women. This discussion focuses on those aspects of earnings determination which distinguish women's experiences from those of men. An obvious starting point is the much flatter and lower age-earnings profiles of women (Figure 10.5) compared with the steeper and higher profiles of men (Figure 10.4). Women's age-earnings profiles reflect their lower economic returns to post-school job experience compared with men: whereas Hispanic men's returns to experience were approximately 3.5 to 4 percent, those received by Hispanic women never exceeded 2 percent, and were as low as 1 percent for Cuban women. Also, lower positioning of the female age-earnings profiles relative to those of men mirrors the 1980 gender gap in earnings (discussed in connection with Table 10.8), which arises partly because of the uneven occupational allocation of men and women and partly because of wage discrimination.[39]

As observed for Hispanic men, the economic returns to education among employed Hispanic women varied considerably according to national origin. Whereas Cuban women received a 2.4 percent return for each additional year of schooling, the earnings of Other Hispanic women increased 5.8 percent on an average annual basis for each additional year of school. Returns to education among Mexicans and Central/South Americans were roughly 3.6 percent, while those among Puerto Ricans, the most educationally disadvantaged group, were 4.6 percent. Possibly the higher schooling returns for Puerto Ricans reflect the relative shortage of educated women, which translates into a higher relative wage for those who are better schooled.[40] Also, the presence of greater numbers of undocumented immigrants among the Mexicans and Central/South Americans may account for their lower returns to education.

Another way the earnings determination of Hispanic women differs from that of men is in the comparatively lower importance of linguistic skills. Good proficiency in English improved the earnings of Central/South American origin women relative to their counterparts who spoke no English, but with one other exception (Puerto Rican women, with fair English proficiency) English proficiency did not affect earnings. For the remaining groups proficiency in English neither enhanced nor diminished earnings, net of other variables. Although these results may seem counterintuitive, on further reflection they are quite reasonable. Considering that many jobs which Hispanic women (and men) accept do not require proficiency in English (for example, garment and textile industries, electronics factories, hotel service work, and agricultural

---

[39]Marta Tienda, Vilma Ortiz, and Shelley Smith, "Industrial Restructuring and Earnings: A Comparison of Men and Women," *American Sociological Review* 52, 1987; England and McLaughlin, "Sex Segregation of Jobs."

[40]Lisa J. Neidert and Marta Tienda, "Converting Education into Earnings: The Patterns among Hispanic Origin Men," *Social Science Research* 13 (1984):303–32; Marta Tienda and Patricia Guhleman, "The Occupational Position of Employed Hispanic Women," in George Borjas and Marta Tienda, eds., *Hispanics in the U.S. Economy* (Orlando, FL: Academic Press, 1985); Marta Tienda, "The Puerto Rican Worker: Current Labor Market Status and Future Prospects," in *Puerto Ricans in the Mid-Eighties: An American Challenge* (Washington, DC: National Puerto Rican Coalition, 1984).

work), it is conceivable that women with low education and limited English skills are systematically selected into these jobs. This may help explain the anomaly for Puerto Rican women with "fair" skills. Thus, for women more than men, English ability may serve as a screening or signaling device for prospective employers. It is also conceivable that the earnings effect of English proficiency is mediated largely by women's educational attainment, more so than is the case for men, who generally face a less restricted array of job opportunities. That Central/South American women received an earnings bonus for good ability in English probably signals positive selectivity, giving this group access to a broader spectrum of higher-paying jobs for possessing the requisite English speaking and comprehension skills.

Compared with men fewer of the demographic and life cyle factors emerged as significant factors influencing women's earnings. These results are consistent with findings of other studies showing considerably less wage differentiation among women than men.[41] In contrast to men marital status did not significantly influence the earnings of Hispanic women, except those of Central/South American origin, and the positive effect of health status was significant only for Mexican and Puerto Rican women. Also, the labor supply variables behaved as predicted and were similar to those observed for men except that the influence of full-time work status on earnings was considerably larger for women than men. This is because part-time work is more common among women and thus constitutes a much greater component of earnings variation for females.

The patterning of nativity effects does warrant further discussion not only because of the departures from the results for men, but also because of the differences by national origin among the women. Puerto Ricans exhibit the most consistent results in that both men and women born were penalized (8.5 to 6.5 percent, respectively) for island birth. Although recent Mexican immigrant men earned less than their native-born counterparts, there was no nativity differentiation in earnings of Mexican origin women. Cuban women who entered the United States after 1964 earned significantly less than their native-born (statistical) equivalents, suggesting that the labor market adjustment process may be longer for them than their male counterparts, but this was not the case for Central/South Americans. For them the pattern of nativity effects was roughly similar for men and women. All told, the picture of nativity effects on Hispanic earnings is highly complex, varying as it does according to gender and national origin.

The influence on earnings of market factors differed notably by gender. For example, public sector employment rendered most Hispanic

---

[41]Reimers, "Comparative Analysis."

women substantial and significant earnings bonuses compared with their counterparts who were self-employed in 1979. For Hispanic men public sector employment was an economic liability relative to self-employment. These positive earnings returns received by Puerto Rican, Cuban, and Central/South American women ranged from 15 to 22 percent, but excluded Mexican and Other Hispanic women. One explanation for the gender differences in earnings associated with public sector employment is that for women these jobs often provide clearly defined job ladders and job security, as well as good fringe benefits. These advantages are less often guaranteed to women employed in the private sector. Also, and in contrast to men, women's earnings were relatively impervious to the share of Hispanic workers in the labor market; but with the exception of Puerto Ricans, female earnings were more sensitive to variations in the market wage rate than those of Hispanic men. Specifically, variation in market wage rates increased women's average annual earnings by 5 percent (Puerto Ricans and Central/South Americans) to 12 percent (Mexicans) for each dollar increase in the average market wage rate.

On balance, there are many similarities between Hispanic men and women in the factors which influence their earnings, and consequently their relative economic well-being, but there are also some puzzling differences. For example, it is unclear why education, experience, and English proficiency should be rewarded differently according to gender and national origin, but there are strong possibilities that discrimination may be involved. This tentative conclusion begs the question about the mechanisms which sustain these differences over time, but this line of questioning transcends those suited for census data. An additional point of contrast between men and women centers on the importance of public service employment as an avenue for closing the gender gap in earnings. That Hispanic women employed in government industries earned more than those employed in the private sector suggests a future potential to close the gender gap in earnings among Hispanics through policies designed to broaden employment opportunities for minority women. However, in light of the efforts of the current administration to shrink the size of the public sector, it is unlikely that public sector employment will serve as a vehicle for raising the earnings of Hispanic workers in the future.

Conclusions

In reflecting on the results in this chapter and the previous two which addressed educational and employment aspects of socioeconomic status, we are struck by the extent to which they underscore our organizing theme of diversity, one which seems to be increasing rather than decreasing over time. Although there is evidence of improvement in the relative economic well-being of the Hispanic population overall, our analyses of trends and differentials in income growth clearly show that national origin and gender remain important axes of socioeconomic differentiation for people of Hispanic origin. In many ways their salience has increased over time; for despite many indications of convergence in the economic well-being among the Hispanic groups, there was as much evidence of divergences among other subgroups. These were documented in the summaries for each section and will not be repeated.

A clear case in point is provided by the Central/South American population whose relative socioeconomic standing has been modified extensively because of the substantially changed character of immigrants who entered since 1970. Partly the lowered socioeconomic position of Central/South Americans may reflect the greater prevalence of undocumented migrants during the most recent period. Although this is also true of Mexicans, the intertemporal socioeconomic impacts may be less evident because of the low economic standing of Mexicans at the start of the period and because of the greater size of the native-born Mexican population which serves to attenuate these differences.

The experience of Puerto Ricans is problematic in many ways. Briefly, the economic disadvantages they have experienced over the past two decades defy easy explanation for several reasons. First, Puerto Ricans are not immigrants, and thus birthplace should not emerge as an important axis of socioeconomic differentiation for this group, yet it does. This fact challenges conventional models of immigrant assimilation and forces us to consider the role of discrimination as well as market conditions as two additional determinants of economic well-being which may account for the deterioration in relative economic well-being of this group. That Puerto Ricans are more racially heterogeneous than the other Hispanic origin groups lends support to a discrimination interpretation of their worsened economic position, but it is not one we considered in our analyses. Nor is it one which can be addressed convincingly with census data.

A promising line of research for exploring further the declining economic well-being of Puerto Ricans compared with the modest to moderate improvements experienced by Mexicans and Cubans during the 1960s and 1970s would involve relating internal migration flows to labor market outcomes. Recently Tienda and Lii[42] showed that Puerto Ricans who participated in dispersed migration flows—that is, streams away from high-density areas—benefit financially from such movement.

[42]Marta Tienda and Ding-Tzann Lii, "Migration, Market Insertion and Earnings Determination of Mexicans, Puerto Ricans, and Cubans," paper presented at the 1986 annual meeting of the American Sociological Association, 1986.

This finding suggests that Puerto Ricans are responsive to market opportunities outside the areas of their traditional concentration. Moreover, to the extent that the pattern of dispersed concentration continues into the 1990s (see Chapter 4), it is conceivable that the economic well-being of the Puerto Rican population that moves away from the Northeast will improve considerably. However, this optimism about the potential for migration flows to improve the economic well-being of Puerto Ricans must be tempered with evidence that recent migrants from the island tend to concentrate in the New York and New Jersey SMSA, where the industrial restructuring away from jobs traditionally occupied by Puerto Ricans does not bode well for their employment prospects. As we noted in Chapter 9, disproportionately high rates of joblessness have become a defining feature of the Puerto Rican employment experience. The prospects of obtaining higher earnings are meaningless for those who cannot find work in the first place.

Nevertheless, in the interest of preventing any further deterioration in the relative economic standing of Puerto Ricans through the 1980s, the evidence presented here should be used as a baseline for more in-depth analyses designed to establish causal relationships among the determinants of economic well-being. This, after all, is the most basic input into policy formulation. Our results also bring into focus the need to monitor the socioeconomic diversification of the Central/South American origin population, which is tied to the process of international migration and the internal conflicts in Central America. Our evidence points to a deterioration in the relative socioeconomic standing of this group, but the fluidity of this situation makes it difficult to draw firm conclusions. Results from the 1990 census should be revealing, however.

Appendix:
Theoretical Specification of Earnings Functions

The importance of education and work experience in determining earnings has been discussed extensively elsewhere[43] and needs no fur-

---

[43]Borjas and Tienda, Hispanics in the U.S. Economy; Marta Tienda, ed., Hispanic Origin Workers in the U.S. Labor Market: Comparative Analysis of Employment Outcomes, final report to the U.S. Department of Labor, Employment and Training Administration, with the collaboration of Ronald Angel, George Borjas, Rosemary S. Cooney, Patricia Guhleman, John A. Garcia, and Lise Neidert (Springfield, VA: National Technical Information Service, 1981); Mark Blaug, "The Empirical Status of Human Capital Theory: A Slightly Jaundiced Survey," Journal of Economic Literature 14 (1976):827–55; R. Roy Marshall, M. Carter, and A. G. King, Labor Economics: Wages, Employment and Trade Unionism (Homewood, IL: Richard D. Irwin, 1976); William Sewell and Robert M. Hauser, Education, Occupation and Earnings: Achievement in the Early Career (New York: Academic Press, 1975).

ther elaboration. An additional investment variable we include in our model—English proficiency—deserves some justification even though it has been used in prior analyses of Hispanic earnings.[44] Proficiency in English should improve Hispanic earnings because language is an economic skill which enhances productivity in jobs requiring communication skills and because linguistic skills serve as an indicator of the transferability of skills.[45] Also, linguistic skills may determine labor market outcomes by affecting information about job alternatives. Finally, if accented speech serves as a signal, language can differentiate earnings by encouraging employer discrimination for such behavior.[46] English proficiency is a relevant investment variable for native-born as well as foreign-born Hispanics, because, for reasons noted in Chapter 1, many persons of the second and third generation have limited English speaking and comprehension skills. For these reasons we expected better proficiency in English to be associated with higher earnings.

Among the demographic and life cycle factors associated with earnings, we include nativity, marital and health status, and the presence of a child under age 6. Foreign birth should negatively influence Hispanic earnings because it represents cultural and social differences in preparedness for the United States labor market, as well as differences in the transferability of specific employment skills. Following the pioneering work of Chiswick,[47] several scholars have used length of United States residence as a general proxy for the complex processes by which immigrant workers integrate themselves into the United States labor market by acquiring specific skills and adapting old ones. In support of this claim labor market analysts have shown that the longer immigrants spend in the United States, the better they perform in the labor market. Because the use of cross-sectional measures of length of United States residence to portray labor market assimilation and integration processes has been criticized,[48] we confine our analyses to a simple additive specification of nativity in our earnings model.

The remaining demographic and life cycle factors and labor supply variables which influence earnings have been discussed extensively in various theoretical and empirical studies and need no further discus-

---

[44]Geoffrey Carliner, "Returns to Education for Blacks, Anglos, and Five Spanish Groups," *Journal of Human Resources* 2 (1976):172–83; Gilles Grenier, "An Analysis of the Effects of Language Characteristics on the Wages of Hispanic-American Males," revised version of a paper presented at the meeting of the Société Canadienne de Science Economique, Sherbrooke, Quebec, May 13–14, 1981; Marta Tienda, "Sex, Ethnicity and Chicano Status Attainment," *International Migration Review* 16 (1982):435–72.

[45]Chiswick, "Economic Progress of Immigrants"; Tienda and Neidert, "Language, Education, and the Socioeconomic Achievement of Hispanic Origin Men."

[46]Grenier, "Analysis of the Effects of Language Characteristics."

[47]Chiswick, "Effect of Americanization,"; "Economic Progress of Immigrants."

[48]Borjas, "Assimilation."

sion.[49] However, our inclusion of market and job characteristics in the earnings functions warrants some additional explanation. Reimers[50] has documented systematic wage differences according to sector of employment, but economists generally exclude the self-employed as a labor group. Because of the importance of self-employment for Cubans, and the differential prevalence of self-employment among Hispanics according to nativity,[51] we have added this variable to our earnings functions. Specifically, our functions include a trichotomous variable designating whether respondents were employed in the private or public sector, versus self-employed, to monitor systematic differences in earnings associated with class of worker.

Finally, we included indicators of labor market characteristics to portray the influence of structural forces on individual earnings. Two variables of demonstrated importance for Hispanic earnings are the Hispanic concentration and the average wage rate in a designated labor market.[52] Previous findings that residential concentration of minority groups fosters income inequities among geographic units is significant for the Hispanic population given its high regional concentration according to national origin. Another justification for including an indicator of Hispanic concentration is that worker outcomes are shaped by the extent of job competition with other minority and majority groups. The average wage rate taps market variation in wages which ultimately constrain income frontiers.

---

[49]See various studies in Borjas and Tienda, *Hispanics in the U.S. Economy.*
[50]Reimers, "Comparative Analysis."
[51]George J. Borjas, "The Self-Employment of Immigrants," unpublished manuscript, Department of Economics, University of California at Santa Barbara, 1985.
[52]Tienda, "Market Characteristics"; Tienda and Lii, "Minority Concentration."

11

EPILOGUE

OUR major purpose in writing this book has been to study in as much detail as possible the social, demographic, and economic situations of the various groups of Hispanic origin living in the United States. In the course of pursuing this objective we have examined the growth and structure of the subpopulations, including the ways in which these have been affected by changing patterns of immigration. We have also scrutinized the geographic distribution and residential patterns of the groups, as well as their family/household characteristics, fertility behavior, educational attainment, patterns of labor force participation, and income and earnings characteristics. In order to achieve these goals we have drawn primarily on data from the three most recent decennial censuses (1960, 1970, and 1980), focusing especially on data from the 1980 census. As this epilogue was being written—nearly three-fourths of the way through the 1980s—the 1980 census remained the single most comprehensive source of statistical information about these subpopulations. Many surveys carried out subsequent to the 1980 census, despite their seemingly large sample sizes in certain instances, simply do not provide sufficiently large numbers of cases to enable reliable examination of the sociodemographic characteristics of many of the Hispanic national origin groups. Hence, any more recent study of these subpopulations beyond what has been possible with 1980 census data will have to await the publication and release of information from the 1990 census.

It is not possible to summarize succinctly the results of this study. In fact, because we have included extensive individual chapter summaries and statements of conclusions, we think it serves little purpose to repeat such material here. What we do wish to reiterate at this point is one overarching and important conclusion that we feel emerges from our endeavors, as well as some general thoughts about factors that might be affecting the sociodemographic differences we have observed among the groups.

The conclusion worth emphasizing is one that repeats a theme that has been sounded over and over again during the course of the book: the theme of diversity and heterogeneity. Because of the magnitude of some of the differences that we have found among the groups, it is clear that it is impossible to speak of a single, unified "Hispanic population" in any strict sense of the term. It is only through some rather vague, historical connection to the use of the Spanish language that it is even appropriate at all to speak of an "Hispanic population." In virtually every other respect the groups and subpopulations that we have examined appear to be different from one another. They vary not only in their immigration histories—in where they came from, in when they arrived, and in how favorably they were received when they got here—but also in their reasons for coming and in the social class backgrounds they brought with them. Hence, it is not surprising that we have found considerable differences among the groups in almost all of the sociodemographic and economic characteristics that we have examined. Thus, if we were able to make no other point, we would emphasize that the Hispanic population of the United States consists of very diverse and heterogeneous national origin groups. At a minimum, those who seek to study "Hispanics" must disaggregate this population by national origin, and preferably also by nativity and gender. To treat Hispanics as a single population risks overlooking differences that are so great that such an approach becomes virtually meaningless.

Beyond the documentation of sociodemographic and economic differences among the various Hispanic subpopulations, the outlines of a rudimentary pattern of differences can be discerned among the groups, at least with respect to sociodemographic and economic characteristics. Cubans and Other Hispanics tend to exhibit the least socioeconomic differences compared with non-Hispanic whites, ranking above Mexicans, who in turn rank above Puerto Ricans. Central/South Americans show a less clear pattern of results because of the recency of their arrival during the 1970s. Some light may be shed on these patterns by considering the factors introduced in Chapter 1 concerning the immigration histories, ethnic consciousness, and class backgrounds of the various groups. A useful example can perhaps be constructed from the results about the fertility behavior of the various groups.

All of the Spanish origin groups except Cubans revealed higher levels of children ever born than non-Hispanic whites, even after adjusting for differences between the groups and non-Hispanic whites in age, education, and other compositional factors. This is consistent with the fact that most of the members of these groups are more recent arrivals in the United States and come from countries with higher levels of fertility than is the case for non-Hispanic whites. It is also congruent with the fact that most of these groups continue to suffer a disadvantaged, minority position in the United States, thus limiting the access of their members to the kinds of socioeconomic opportunities that increase the opportunity cost of childbearing. We also found evidence, however, that several of the groups showed levels of recent fertility that were little different from those of non-Hispanic whites, and in some instances even below those of non-Hispanic whites, especially in the cases of women with higher levels of education. This suggests that while these groups may begin their fertility at levels higher than those of whites, they may not terminate childbearing that way.

Interestingly, the most pronounced tendency in this regard occurs among Cuban women, whose recent fertility behavior falls substantially below that of non-Hispanic white women. In seeking to explain this pattern, we think the notion of *ethnic resilience* invoked by Portes and Bach in their study of Mexican and Cuban immigrants might offer a basis for interpreting this pattern, as well as perhaps some of the other differences that we have observed among the groups.[1] Their hypothesis suggests that a heightened sense of ethnic solidarity often occurs among minority immigrant groups who have achieved considerable socioeconomic assimilation but whose pathway to total acceptance and equality remains blocked to a certain extent. This emergent sense of ethnic solidarity serves as a resource to be drawn upon for further, renewed efforts toward socioeconomic achievement. More highly educated Cuban women (who may be the most disposed to reduce their childbearing in order to achieve socioeconomic goals) may thus find such ethnic solidarity an additional source of motivation to draw upon in their efforts to achieve better jobs and higher earnings. Among Mexicans and (especially) Puerto Ricans, whose lower socioeconomic standing upon arrival in this country and whose less favorable reception in the United States has made achievement more difficult, such tendencies may be less pronounced. In the case of Central/South Americans, it is difficult to even speak of such inclinations because this population is composed so substantially of recent immigrants. And highly educated Other Hispanics, many of whom have been in the United States for several generations

[1]Alejandro Portes and Robert L. Bach, *Latin Journey: Cuban and Mexican Immigrants in the United States* (Los Angeles: University of California Press, 1985).

and many of whom trace their ancestry to European origins, exhibit fertility behavior that is often little different from that of more highly educated non-Hispanic whites.

In general, then, we find that Cubans and Other Hispanics have achieved the greatest degree of socioeconomic success in the United States and that their demographic behavior is most likely to reflect this fact. Other Hispanics, however, are so diverse in origin, have been in the country so long, and are so likely to have come from European origins that it is difficult to generalize further about their experiences compared with the rest of the population. But in the case of Cubans, their residential concentration in an ethnic enclave in Florida, their considerable but not total socioeconomic assimilation, and their relative recency of arrival may increase the likelihood that processes of ethnic resilience operate in an especially forceful way among the members of this group. If ethnic resilience is the product of both success *and* continued discrimination, then Cuban Americans may be the group most likely to experience such processes.

At the other end of the spectrum, Puerto Ricans exhibit the least socioeconomic success of all of the groups, as well as many of the sorts of demographic behavior that are often associated with economic disadvantage. In the case of persons of Puerto Rican origin, racial discrimination cannot be eliminated as a factor contributing to their extremely impoverished position in the United States. The social and economic resources that Cubans brought with them and that have facilitated their socioeconomic success have largely been absent among Puerto Ricans, thus diminishing the development of comparable ethnic resilience in the case of the members of this group. Central/South Americans and (especially) Mexicans seem to fall in between these two extremes. They have experienced neither the success of Cubans nor the deprivation of Puerto Ricans. The improvement of their socioeconomic positions, as well as their further demographic integration vis-à-vis the rest of the population, is likely to depend both on the extent to which their resource position can be enhanced and on the degree to which majority non-Hispanic whites can continue to eliminate barriers to total integration into the culture and institutions of American society. Both of these will continue to be challenges as not only Puerto Ricans but also the other Spanish origin groups move into the 1990s.

APPENDIX A
SELECTION CRITERIA
USED TO IDENTIFY HISPANICS
1960, 1970, AND 1980

B ECAUSE the criteria used to identify Hispanics have not been uniform over time, we attempted to maximize intertemporal comparability by using several indicators available in the microdata samples to delineate the ethnic boundaries for the total Hispanic population and its constituent subgroups. Although interdecade comparability is necessarily imprecise due to the substantial changes in the availability and coverage of various indicators of Hispanic ethnicity, our strategy entailed selecting a broadly inclusive universe of Hispanics and delineating the constituent subgroups in the most consistent fashion possible.

The purpose of this appendix is to outline the criteria used to define the Hispanic population using the 1960, 1970, and 1980 censuses, and to document the major discrepancies among the three data sources which challenge intertemporal comparability of the results we present in Chapters 3 through 11. As the 1980 census is the benchmark for this monograph, we begin our discussion with the most recent period and then proceed to the two earlier censuses.

The 1980 U.S. Public Use Microdata Sample

The 1980 Public Use Microdata Sample (PUMS)[1] consists of three independent, stratified subsamples of the full census sample (19.4 percent of all households) that received long-form questionnaires. These three samples differ in their identification of geographic areas and their sample sizes. We use the A sample, a 5 percent national sample which contains over one-fourth of all households that received the census long-form questionnaire (11 million persons and over 4 million housing units). Our preference for the A over the B and C samples was governed by our interest in conducting detailed analyses of as many national origin groups as was feasible—a task which required a large sample.

Because our analysis of consistency among various Hispanic identifiers, including self-reported Spanish origin, ancestry, Spanish home language, birthplace, and a Spanish write-in entry for race, indicated that the Spanish origin item was the best identifier of the population, we use this as the major criterion for identifying Hispanics. However, we excluded all Mexican Americans who indicated that they were black and who resided outside the Southwest because evidence indicates that these individuals are likely to have misinterpreted the intent of the Spanish origin question.[2] We further differentiated the "Other Spanish/Hispanic" category into two groups: Central and South Americans and Other Hispanics. To accomplish this differentiation, we used birthplace data for the foreign-born and ancestry data for the native-born.

In comparison with the 1970 and 1960 data, the 1980 data are unique in that three new Hispanic identifiers are available, including a 100 percent self-identification item, an ancestry item, and a measure of Spanish language usage in the home. Although the 1980 census constitutes the most recent national source of information about Hispanics with sample sizes sufficient for detailed analyses among national origin groups, one disadvantage of this data source is the loss of information about parentage which would have allowed a disaggregation of the native-born population into second and third or higher "generations." The omission is compensated for, however, by the availability of the Spanish origin item which has the effect of more third- or higher-generation Hispanics being included than is the case when parentage and mother tongue items must be used.

---

[1]For complete details about the 1980 sample, see U.S. Bureau of the Census, *Census of Population and Housing: 1980*, Public Use Microdata Samples, Technical Documentation (Washington, DC: U.S. Government Printing Office, 1983).

[2]See U.S. Bureau of the Census, "Persons of Spanish Origin by State: 1980," PC80-S1-7 (Washington, DC: U.S. Government Printing Office, 1982).

The 1970 U.S. Public Use Sample

The 1970 Public Use Sample (PUS)[3] consists of six files based on 1 percent samples of households. The Census Bureau prepared one sample each based on the 5 and 15 percent questionnaires for each of three areal units—states, county groupings, and neighborhoods. In our analyses we use both the state and county grouping files based on the 15 percent questionnaire.

Unlike the 1980 census the 1970 (and 1960) data contain information from a question on birthplace of parents. Thus, the 1970 (and 1960) data permit "three-generational" breakdowns of Mexican Americans, Puerto Ricans, and other Hispanics (excluding the Central and South Americans, whose native-born groups were insufficiently large to warrant disaggregation in 1970).

Although the 5 percent questionnaire of the 1970 census contained a Spanish origin item, the parentage and mother tongue items were available only on the 15 percent questionnaire. Birthplace data, however, were obtained in both the 5 and 15 percent questionnaires. Thus, we are able to utilize both the birthplace and parentage information in identifying the largely foreign-born Cuban and Central/South American populations. Our decision to use the 15 percent sample came at the expense of being able to use detailed data on year of arrival to the United States.

Our delineation of Hispanic ethnic boundaries with the 1970 (and 1960) census involved recode statements for 14 subgroups representing a combination of national origin, parentage, and birthplace combinations. We present these at the end of this appendix, following a brief description of the 1960 census sample data.

The 1960 U.S. Public Use Sample

The 1960 Public Use Sample (PUS)[4] is a 1 percent sample of households which is parallel in structure and content to the 1970 PUS. The file contains all individual and household items obtained in the 25 percent sample questionnaire. As this was the first year in which the Census Bureau released census data in a machine readable format for public

---

[3]For complete details about the 1970 sample file, see U.S. Bureau of the Census, *1970 Census Users' Guide* (Washington, DC: U.S. Government Printing Office, 1970).

[4]See U.S. Bureau of the Census, *A Public Use Sample of Basic Records from the 1960 Census: Description and Technical Documentation* (Washington, DC: U.S. Government Printing Office, 1971).

use, it is less versatile in its geographic detail and its content than the 1970 census. To delineate ethnic boundaries for the Hispanic population in historical perspective, we manipulated the data on parentage, birthplace, Spanish surname, and mother tongue and derived categories roughly comparable to those of 1970.

Operational Criteria for Identifying Hispanics: 1960–1970

Because the Spanish origin item was asked only on the 5 percent census questionnaire in 1970, and not at all in the 1960 census, we identified the Hispanic population, and its constituent subgroups, using several identifiers that were available in both years: birthplace, parentage, surname, and state of residence. We opted for an inclusive universe by selecting all individuals who were themselves born or whose parents were born in Central or South America, Spain, Mexico, Cuba, Puerto Rico, or Spanish-speaking Caribbean nations, or who had a Spanish surname (if they resided in the Southwest), or who reported a Spanish mother tongue. From this universe we defined 14 mutually exclusive groupings which exhausted all of our sample observations. These are as follows:

1. *Mexican foreign-born:* if respondent born in Mexico.

2. *Mexican native of foreign parentage:* if respondent U.S.-born and either parent born in Mexico.

3. *Mexican native of native parentage:* if respondent U.S.-born and both parents U.S.-born, and state of residence in 1970 (or 1960) was Arizona, California, Colorado, New Mexico, or Texas.

4. *Puerto Rican, island-born:* if respondent born in Puerto Rico.[5]

5. *Puerto Rican, native of Puerto Rican parentage:* if respondent born on U.S. mainland and either parent born in Puerto Rico.

6. *Puerto Rican, native of native parentage:* if respondent born on U.S. mainland, and both parents U.S.-born, and state of residence in 1970 (or 1960) was New Jersey, New York, or Pennsylvania.

7. *Cuban foreign-born:* if respondent born in Cuba.

---

[5] As residents of a commonwealth of the United States, Puerto Ricans are legal U.S. citizens and cannot be classified technically as foreign-born. However, as many studies have demonstrated, the island-mainland distinction operates essentially as a foreign-native distinction for other Hispanic origin groups. See Marta Tienda, "The Puerto Rican Worker: Current Labor Market Status and Future Prospects," in *Puerto Ricans in the Mid-Eighties: An American Challenge* (Washington, DC: National Puerto Rican Coalition, 1984).

8. *Cuban native of foreign parentage:* if respondent U.S.-born and either parent born in Cuba.

9. *Cuban native of native parentage:* If respondent U.S.-born and both parents U.S.-born, and state of residence in 1970 (or 1960) was Florida.

10. *Central or South American foreign-born:* if respondent born in one of the following countries: Guatemala, Honduras, Nicaragua, El Salvador, Costa Rica, Panama, Dominican Republic, Venezuela, Ecuador, Peru, Bolivia, Paraguay, Uruguay, Chile, Argentina, Colombia, other Central/South American country not specified.

11. *Central or South American native of foreign parentage:* if respondent U.S.-born and either parent born in one of the countries listed in 10.

12. *Other Hispanic foreign-born:* if respondent born abroad, but not in Mexico, Puerto Rico, Cuba, or the countries listed in 10.

13. *Other Hispanic native of foreign parentage:* if respondent U.S.-born, and parents born abroad, but not in Mexico, Puerto Rico, Cuba, or the countries listed in 10.

14. *Other native of native parentage:* if respondent U.S.-born, and parents U.S.-born, and state of residence in 1970 (or 1960) is other than New Jersey, New York, Pennsylvania, Florida, Arizona, California, Colorado, New Mexico, or Texas.

The three categories designated as "Other Hispanics" are a residual group from those that preceded. One might surmise that these groups were composed largely of European Spanish respondents. However, they also include descendants of mixed Hispanic or Hispanic/non-Hispanic couples, and those who selected nonspecific labels (for example, Latino, Hispano) to identify themselves.

Appendix Table A.1 presents the percentage distribution of the national origin groups for the 1960 and 1970 censuses using our classification scheme based on the birthplace, parentage, residence, language, and surname identifiers. All five items served as selection criteria, but only the first three were used for classification purposes. We present the 1980 distribution based on the 100 percent Spanish origin item as a basis for evaluating the plausibility of the 1960 and 1970 distributions. By and large, the 1960 and 1970 distributions appear to be quite reasonable, despite the absence of a consistent Spanish origin identifier over all three periods. That the 1970 and 1980 distributions are quite similar— in fact much more so than the 1970 distribution based on the Spanish origin item available in the 5 percent questionnaire—lends credibility to

APPENDIX TABLE A.1

Percentage Distribution of Hispanic Subgroups: 1960–1980

National Origin, Nativity, and Parentage	1960	1970	1980
Mexican	71.3%	59.1%	59.8%
Foreign-Born	11.2	9.7	15.5
Native of Foreign Parentage	22.3	16.4	44.3
Native of Native Parentage[a]	37.8	33.1	—
Puerto Rican	17.5	16.2	13.8
Island-Born	12.0	8.9	6.8
Mainland Born of Puerto Rican Heritage	5.5	6.3	⎫ 7.0
Mainland Born of Mainland Parentage[b]	—	1.0	⎭
Cuban	2.3	6.7	5.5
Foreign-Born	1.5	5.0	4.3
Native of Foreign Parentage	.9	1.2	1.2
Native of Native Parentage[c]	—	.5	—
Central and South American	4.3	6.7	7.2
Foreign-Born[d]	2.7	4.5	5.8
Native of Foreign Parentage[e]	1.7	2.1	⎫ 1.4
Native of Native Parentage	—	—	⎭
Other Hispanic	4.6	11.4	13.7
Foreign-Born	2.4	3.7	2.3
Native of Foreign Parentage	2.3	3.7	⎫ 11.4
Native of Native Parentage[f]	—	4.0	⎭

SOURCES: 1960, 1970, and 1980 Public Use Microdata Sample files.

[a]Also resided in five Southwest states in 1960 or 1970.
[b]Also resided in New York, New Jersey, and Pennsylvania in 1960 or 1970.
[c]Also resided in Florida in 1960 or 1970.
[d]Excludes Brazil, Mexico, Cuba, Puerto Rico, and all non-Spanish-speaking countries in Latin America and the Caribbean.
[e]Same foreign-birth restrictions apply.
[f]Essentially includes persons of Spanish language who resided outside the Southwest.
[g]Blanks indicate groups that could not be separately identified.

the structure of our logic in classifying Hispanics according to major national origin categories.

The seemingly greater differences between the 1960 and 1970 distributions according to national origin reflect real changes in the national origin composition of the population. For example, by 1960 the impact of the Cuban refugee migration had not yet peaked, and the migration flow from Central and South America had not gained the momentum characteristic of the 1970s. With fewer absolute and relative shares of Cubans and Central/South Americans in the United States, it is not unreasonable to expect higher relative shares of Puerto Ricans and Mexicans. However, some of the observed differences among the three distributions reflect problems of noncomparability and warrant further discussion, as they will hamper our inferences about change over time to varying degrees.

For instance, the rather substantial increase in the relative size of the Other Hispanic population between 1960 and 1970 stems largely from the increasing difficulty of identifying third and higher generations of Mexican origin people with the birthplace and parentage items. Since the Chicano population is the most generationally diverse, it is highly likely that the 1960–1970 difference in the proportion classified as Other Hispanic resulted from greater coverage of the Mexican origin population residing outside of the Southwest with the broader language concept adopted in 1970. Thus, in subsequent interpretations one must understand that in 1970 the other Hispanic group probably includes a disproportionate number of individuals who with 1960 criteria would have been classified as Mexican or mixed-Mexican origin.

Of the remaining problems with our classification scheme, the one deserving additional comment is the use of residence to classify the native of native parentage groups. Because our residence categories had to be mutually exclusive, we were unable to differentiate between Cubans and Puerto Ricans residing in the Northeast. Thus, we have probably underestimated the number of Cuban natives of native parentage residing in the Northeast, but given the timing of the Cuban exodus to the United States, this classification error is probably very small. Most of the Cubans residing in the Northeast in 1970 were either foreign-born or native of foreign parentage, and thus easily identifiable with the per- centage item. Similar problems affect our classification of the native of native parentage among the remaining groups, but for Puerto Ricans the classification error also is likely to be small (although larger than that for Cubans) also because as of 1970 only about 10 percent of the popu- lation was "third generation," and over 75 percent resided in the three states we used to differentiate this Hispanic group from others.[6]

On balance, and despite certain noncomparabilities in the bases used to delineate the Hispanic population and its major national origin segments in successive censuses, we believe that our classification scheme is defensible and provides an acceptable basis for drawing infer- ences about changes in the characteristics of the populations between 1960 and 1980.

---

[6]U.S. Bureau of the Census, "Persons of Spanish Origin," table 8.

APPENDIX TABLE B.1

Total Hispanic Distribution by State: 1960–1980

State	1960	1970	1980
Alabama	.1%	.1%	.2%
Alaska	.0	.0	.1
Arizona	4.4	3.3	3.1
Arkansas	.0	.1	.1
California	30.9	30.7	31.2
Colorado	3.2	2.9	2.4
Connecticut	.4	.7	.9
Delaware	.0	.1	.1
District of Columbia	.1	.1	.1
Florida	1.7	4.5	5.9
Georgia	.1	.2	.3
Hawaii	.1	.2	.5
Idaho	.1	.2	.2
Illinois	2.2	3.4	4.4
Indiana	.5	.6	.6
Iowa	.1	.1	.2
Kansas	.3	.3	.4
Kentucky	.1	.1	.2
Louisiana	.4	.6	.6
Maine	.0	.0	.0
Maryland	.2	.4	.4
Massachusetts	.2	.7	1.0
Michigan	.6	1.1	1.1
Minnesota	.1	.2	.2
Mississippi	.0	.0	.1

APPENDIX TABLE B.1 *(continued)*

State	1960	1970	1980
Missouri	.2	.3	.3
Montana	.0	.1	.1
Nebraska	.1	.1	.2
Nevada	.1	.2	.4
New Hampshire	.0	.0	.0
New Jersey	1.6	3.3	3.4
New Mexico	5.4	4.3	3.3
New York	15.3	14.7	11.5
North Carolina	.1	.2	.3
North Dakota	.0	.0	.0
Ohio	.5	.8	.8
Oklahoma	.1	.3	.4
Oregon	.1	.3	.4
Pennsylvania	.6	1.0	1.0
Rhode Island	.0	.1	.1
South Carolina	.0	.1	.2
South Dakota	.0	.0	.0
Tennessee	.0	.1	.2
Texas	28.8	21.6	20.6
Utah	.2	.4	.4
Vermont	.0	.0	.0
Virginia	.2	.4	.5
Washington	.4	.5	.8
West Virginia	.0	.0	.1
Wisconsin	.3	.4	.4
Wyoming	.0	.2	.2
Total	99.8	100.0	99.9

SOURCES: 1960, 1970, and 1980 Public Use Microdata Sample files.

APPENDIX TABLE B.2
Residential Redistribution[a] of the Hispanic Population Aged 5 and Over by National Origin: 1960–1980

	Mexican			Puerto Rican		
	1960	1970	1980	1960	1970	1980
Same House	44.9%	50.1%	46.8%	26.0%	40.8%	40.0%
Interstate	45.2	40.5	40.4	52.5	42.3	42.1
Different State	5.6	5.3	5.3	4.6	5.9	7.3
Abroad	4.4	4.0	7.5	17.0	10.9	10.6
Total	100.1	99.9	100.0	100.1	99.9	100.0
(N)	(30,643)	(45,487)	(186,702)	(7,504)	(11,633)	(44,831)

	Cuban			Central/ South American			Other Hispanic		
	1960	1970	1980	1960	1970	1980	1960	1970	1980
Same House	30.1%	23.1%	43.6%	27.5%	30.1%	29.9%	44.8%	41.6%	48.1%
Interstate	32.5	32.0	40.9	34.7	35.7	37.5	36.7	34.7	38.0
Different State	7.1	10.5	9.8	8.8	9.0	7.5	5.7	14.6	8.6
Abroad	30.3	34.4	5.6	29.1	25.2	25.0	12.8	9.0	5.4
Total	100.0	100.0	99.9	100.1	100.0	99.9	100.0	99.9	100.1
(N)	(1,008)	(5,330)	(19,897)	(1,922)	(5,055)	(25,414)	(1,253)	(8,128)	(45,165)

SOURCES: 1960, 1970, and 1980 Public Use Microdata Sample files.

[a]Based on question about residence five years prior to the census.

APPENDIX C
DATA AND FILE CONSTRUCTION

To conduct the analysis of school delay and noncompletion, a file of Hispanic children aged 5 to 25 was constructed from the 5 percent Public Use Microdata Sample (PUMS) of the 1980 census. From the 5 percent PUMS 1 percent of Puerto Ricans and Mexicans and all of the Cubans, Central/South Americans, and Other Hispanics were drawn. As children were the unit of analysis, to the personal records of those children who were still living with their parents at the time of the census we appended selected parental characteristics which are pertinent for studying schooling processes. This construction yielded three basic groups—those living with their parents, those living with relatives, and those living independently. The first group consists largely of children under age 18, the majority of whom are enrolled in school. Those living with other relatives constitute the smallest group and are more evenly divided between students and those not enrolled. The last group is largely older and out of school. Because information on family background is not available for either the youth living with relatives or on their own, these groups did not enter into the discussion of school delay.

The census includes several items for identifying ethnic and, in particular, Spanish heritage, as discussed in Chapter 2. A broad definition of Hispanic can be derived from any combination of positive responses on language, ancestry, Spanish origin, Spanish surname, and birthplace items. However, we used narrow selection criteria for defining this sample: Only those youth who identified themselves or whose parents identified them (in the case of young children) as Hispanic on the Spanish origin question were included. As noted in Chapter 2, our conclusions would not have changed in any appreciable manner had we opted for a more inclusive definition. In addition, from the population living at home only those children who had one or both parents with a matching self-identification were included in the final sample. This restriction resulted in the loss of a small proportion (4 to 5 percent) of the cases owing to the lack of matching Hispanic identity between parents and children.

Definition of Variables

The independent variables are organized into two groups: the individual characteristics of the child and the characteristics of their households. The latter group of variables generally combine responses of both parents if both are present. Because household characteristics are available only for youth who live with their parents, youth living independently or with relatives can be compared with the former only on the basis of their individual characteristics. Consequently, in the multivariate analysis the latter groups had to be analyzed separately. The individual and household variables introduced in the empirical analysis are identified and their operational definitions summarized in Table C.1. Most are self-explanatory, but because of complexities inherent in the living arrangements of children, the household variables require further explanation.

The inclusion of parental and household characteristics is critical given our focus on ethnicity, which is contextually determined at the household level. In order to capture the effects of household ethnic characteristics, several variables were created which combine responses of both parents and, where applicable, of the child as well. The most complex of these constructed variables is the "Household Language Environment" which combines responses of the parents and child on the two language items contained on the census—Language Spoken in the Home and English Ability. The created variable classifies households into five categories: Spanish monolingual, Spanish dominant, bilingual, English dominant, and English monolingual. To be classified as Spanish monolingual, all respondents (two parents and one child or one parent and one child) reported Spanish as the language spoken in the home and all reported little or no English ability. In addition, at least one must have reported *no* English ability. It is assumed that the presence of one family

APPENDIX TABLE C.1
Operational and Conceptual Definition of Dependent
and Independent Variables for Analysis of Delay and Dropping Out

Variable	Definition
DEPENDENT VARIABLES	
Dropout	Any person who did not complete the 12th grade. Includes all those who completed any grade up to and including 11th grade plus those who attended 12th grade but did not complete it.
Delay	Any person still enrolled in school whose age is one year or more above the modal age for the grade in which respondent is enrolled (delay = age − grade −6).
INDEPENDENT VARIABLES	
Individual Level	
Age	Respondent's age expressed in years, but limited in this sample to those aged 5–25.
Sex	Sex of the respondent.
Nativity	Whether the respondent was born in the United States or abroad, including Puerto Rico.
English Ability	Respondent's report of proficiency in English. There are five values: Speaks Only English, Speaks Very Well, Speaks Well, Speaks Not Well, Speaks Not at All. In most instances, the categories "Speaks Very Well" and "Speaks Well" have been collapsed into one.
Level in School	Those enrolled in school are grouped into three levels—elementary, junior high, and high school.
Living Arrangements	Whether the child lives with parents, with other relatives, or independently. In the latter two cases, parental information is not available.
Household Level	
Headship	Whether one or two parents are present in the household.
Nativity of Parents	Combines the birthplace of mother and father to create five categories: both parents foreign, both parents native, one native/one foreign, single parent native, single parent foreign.

APPENDIX TABLE C.1 *(continued)*

Variable	Definition
Immigration of Parents	Year of immigration of mother and father, within a five-year period, from 1950 to 1980. The categories are: 1975–1980, 1970–1974, 1965–1969, 1960–1964, 1950–1959, before 1950. Their responses cannot be pooled given that in some cases the parents did not come together.
Household Language Environment	Combines responses of child and each parent on "Language Spoken in the Home" and "English Ability." Consists of five categories: Spanish monolingual, Spanish dominant, bilingual, English dominant, English monolingual.
Parent Education	Where two parents are present this variable is the mean of their combined education measured by highest grade completed. If only one parent is present, that parent's highest grade completed is used.
Poverty	This variable is dichotomized into two categories denoting poverty status as poor/nonpoor. The cutpoint was established at 150 percent of the official poverty line used by the census based on 1969 income levels.
Public Assistance	On the census this variable indicates the dollar amount either parent receives in public assistance. Here it is dichotomized to recipients and nonrecipients. If either parent or both parents are recipients, so is the household.

member who speaks no English will force the others to speak Spanish exclusively, especially given that no one speaks much English.

A Spanish dominant household is one in which the child and at least one of the parents reported Spanish as the language spoken at home. A household is defined as bilingual if (1) all respondents reported speaking Spanish at home and reported strong English ability; (2) the child speaks English at home and both parents speak Spanish; or, in the case of a single-parent family, (3) the child speaks Spanish while the parent speaks English in the home.

English dominant households are those in which (1) the child reported speaking English in the home and at least one parent reported the same; (2) the child reported Spanish but both parents reported speaking English in the home; (3) in the case of single-parent families, the child speaks English and the parent speaks Spanish; or (4) all three respondents speak English in the home but are *not* English monolinguals. Finally, an English monolingual home is one in which all respondents identify themselves as English monolingual speakers.

The other created household variable listed in Table C.1 that requires some additional explanation is the ethnicity variable, which has been derived from parental responses on the Spanish Origin item on the census. By combining the responses of both parents we sorted households according to the degree of homogeneity in the self-identified ethnic origin. For youths living with their parents, at least one parent must have a matching response on this item. When both parents' responses match the child's, the household is considered homogeneous. If one parent matches the child and the other is Hispanic, but not of the same origin as the child and the other parent (for example, if the child and mother identify as Mexican and the father is Puerto Rican), then the couple is labeled as Mixed Hispanic. The third possibility consists of those cases in which one parent is Hispanic (and by selection, of the same origin as the child) and the other parent is not Hispanic. By default, all single-parent families will be homogeneous—that is, the parent and child report the same Spanish origin.

All of the economic measures combine responses from the mother and father and most were dichotomized (that is, below poverty or not, receiving public assistance or not). The exception is household income which, for convenience of presentation, has been recoded into five categories. In the multivariate analyses, this variable is entered as a continuous variable, divided by 1,000.

The dependent variables used to measure educational attainment are school delay and school completion versus dropping out. Both are created via a combination of the school enrollment, highest grade attended, and highest grade finished items on the census. Delay is a measure of age-graded school achievement which could be determined only for those enrolled in school at the time of the census. This variable was calculated by subtracting respondents' current grade + 6 (for the first six years not in school) from their age. This results in a distribution of values ranging from -4 to 10. Any value above zero indicates the number of years delayed. However, the majority of cases are delayed one to three years with only a few outliers in the upper end of the distribution. The values -1 and 0 account for all those not delayed while negative values below -1 represent those few students who are younger than the modal age for their grade. Because most delayed students are behind only one year, the construct is analyzed as a binary variable denoting whether students are delayed or not delayed.

The second measure of attainment is school completion versus dropping out, and when evaluated against specific education thresholds (that is, primary, middle, high school) portrays successive transitions in the educational process. For purposes of the tabular and multivariate analyses, individuals are assigned a score of 1 if they completed any grade up to and including 11th grade, or attended but did not complete the 12th grade.

Bibliography

Acuña, Rudolfo *Occupied America: The Chicano Struggle Toward Liberation.* San Francisco: Canfield Press, 1971.

Alba, Richard D., and Katherine Trent "Population Loss and Change in the North: An Exploratory Analysis of New York's Migration to the Sunbelt." Unpublished paper, Center for Social and Demographic Analysis, State University of New York at Albany, 1985.

Almaguer, Tomas "Historical Notes on Chicano Oppression: The Dialectics of Race and Class Domination in North America." *Aztlan* 5 (1974):1.

Alvarez, Rodolfo "The Psycho-Historical and Socioeconomic Development of the Chicano Community in the United States." *Social Science Quarterly* 53 (1973):4.

Alvirez, David "The Effects of Formal Church Affiliation and Religiosity on the Fertility Patterns of Mexican American Catholics." *Demography* 10 (1973):19–36.

———**; Frank D. Bean; and Dorie Williams** "Patterns of Change and Continuity in the Mexican American Family." In Charles H. Mindel and R. W. Haberstein, eds. *Ethnic Families in America: Patterns and Variations,* 2nd ed. New York: Elsevier North-Holland, 1981.

Anderson, G. M. *Networks of Contact: The Portuguese and Toronto.* Waterloo, Ontario: Wilfrid Laurier University Press, 1974.

Angel, Ronald J. "Disability for Hispanic Males." *Social Science Quarterly* 65 (1984):426–43.

———**, and Marta Tienda** "Determinants of Extended Household Structure: Cultural Pattern or Economic Need?" *American Journal of Sociology* 87 (May 1982):1360–83.

Arce, Carlos H. "A Reconsideration of Chicano Culture and Identity." *Daedalus* 110 (1981):177–91.

Aschenbrenner, J. "Extended Families Among Black Americans." *Journal of Comparative Family Studies* 4 (1973):257–68.

ASPIRA "Racial and Ethnic High School Dropout Rates in New York City: A Summary Report, 1983." New York: ASPIRA of New York, 1983.

Bach, Robert L. "The New Cuban Immigrants: Their Background and Prospects." *Monthly Labor Review* 103 (1980):30–46.

———**; Jennifer B. Bach; and Timothy Triplett** "The Flotilla 'Entrants': Latest and Most Controversial." *Cuban Studies* 11 (1981):29–49.

Bach, Robert L., and Marta Tienda "Contemporary Immigration and Refugee Movements and Employment Adjustment Policies." In Vernon M. Briggs, Jr., and Marta Tienda, eds. *Immigration: Issues and Policies.* Salt Lake City: Olympus Press, 1984.

419

Bach-y-Rita, Esther Wicab "An Ethnographic and Psycho-social Study of Latin American Undocumented Women Immigrants in the San Francisco Bay Area." Unpublished doctoral dissertation, Berkeley, CA: Wright Institute, 1985.

Barrera, Mario *Race and Class in the Southwest.* Notre Dame, IN: University of Notre Dame Press, 1979.

Bean, Frank D.; H. L. Browning; and W. P. Frisbie "The Sociodemographic Characteristics of Mexican Immigrant Status Groups: Implications for Studying Undocumented Migrants." *International Migration Review* 18 (1984): 672–91.

Bean, Frank D., and Jeffrey Burr "Black/White Fertility Differences Revisited: An Examination of Alternative Hypotheses." Unpublished paper, 1985.

Bean, Frank D.; Ruth M. Cullen; Elizabeth H. Stephen; and Gray Swicegood "Generational Differences in Fertility among Mexican Americans: Implications for Assessing Immigration Effects." *Social Science Quarterly* 65 (June 1984):573–82.

Bean, Frank D.; R. L. Curtis; and J. P. Marcum "Familism and Marital Satisfaction Among Mexican Americans: The Effects of Family Size, Wife's Labor Force Participation, and Conjugal Power." *Journal of Marriage and the Family* 39 (1977):759–76.

Bean, Frank D.; Allan G. King; and Jeffrey S. Passel "The Number of Illegal Migrants of Mexican Origin in the United States: Sex Ratio Based Estimates for 1980." *Demography* 20 (1983):99–109.

———"Estimates of the Size of the Illegal Migrant Population of Mexican Origin in the United States: An Assessment, Review and Proposal." In Harley L. Browning and Rodolfo O. de la Garza, eds. *Mexican Immigrants and Mexican Americans: An Evolving Relation.* Austin: Center for Mexican American Studies, University of Texas, 1986.

Bean, Frank D.; B. L. Lowell; and L. Taylor "Undocumented Mexican Immigrants and the Earnings of Other Workers in the United States." *Demography* 25 (1988): forthcoming.

Bean, Frank D., and John P. Marcum "Differential Fertility and the Minority Group Status Hypothesis: An Assessment and Review." In Frank D. Bean and W. Parker Frisbie, eds. *The Demography of Racial and Ethnic Groups.* New York: Academic Press, 1978.

Bean, Frank D.; E. Stephen; and W. Opitz "The Mexican Origin Population in the United States: A Demographic Overview." In R. de la Garza, F. Bean, C. Bonjean, R. Romo, and R. Alvarez, eds. *The Mexican American Experience: An Interdisciplinary Anthology.* Austin: University of Texas Press, 1985.

Bean, Frank D., and Teresa Sullivan "Immigration and the Consequences: Confronting the Problem." *Society* 22 (May-June 1985):67–73.

Bean, Frank D., and Gray Swicegood "Generation, Female Education and Fertility Among Mexican Americans." *Social Science Quarterly* 63 (March 1982):131–44.

——— "Generation, Language and Mexican American Fertility." Final Report, Center for Population Research, National Institute for Child Health and Human Development, Bethesda, Maryland, 1983.

——— *Mexican American Fertility Patterns.* Austin: University of Texas Press, 1985.

———; **and Allan King** "Role Incompatibility and the Relationship between Fertility and Labor Supply among Hispanic American Women." In George J. Borjas and Marta Tienda, eds. *Hispanics in the U.S. Economy.* New York: Academic Press, 1985.

Bean, Frank D.; Gray Swicegood; and Tom Linsley "Patterns of Fertility Variation Among Mexican Immigrants to the United States." In *U.S. Immigration Policy and the National Interest.* Staff Report. Washington, DC: Select Commission on Immigration and Refugee Policy, 1981, Appendix D.

Becker, Gary S. "An Economic Analysis of Fertility." In Universities—National Bureau, Committee of Economic Research, ed. *Demographic and Economic Change in Developed Countries.* Princeton: Princeton University Press, 1960.

Berry, Brian J., and Lester P. Silverman, eds. *Population Redistribution and Public Policy.* Washington, DC: National Academy of Sciences, 1980.

Bianchi, Suzanne M. "Racial Differences in Per Capita Income, 1960–76: The Importance of Household Size, Headship, and Labor Force Participation." *Demography* 17 (1980):129–43.

—— *Household Composition and Racial Inequality.* New Brunswick, NJ: Rutgers University Press, 1981.

Biggar, Jeanne "The Sunning of America: Migration to the Sunbelt." *Population Bulletin,* vol. 34, no. 1. Washington, DC: Population Reference Bureau, 1979.

Blau, Francine D. "The Use of Transfer Payments by Immigrants." *Industrial and Labor Relations Review* 37 (1984):222–39.

Blau, P., and O. Duncan *The American Occupational Structure.* New York: Wiley, 1967.

Blaug, Mark "The Empirical Status of Human Capital Theory: A Slightly Jaundiced Survey." *Journal of Economic Literature* 14 (1976):827–55.

Blauner, R. *Racial Oppression in America.* New York: Harper & Row, 1977.

Bonacich, Edna "Class Approaches to Ethnicity and Race." *Insurgent Sociologist* 10 (1980):9–23.

Bonilla, A. F., and R. Campos "A Wealth of Poor: Puerto Ricans in the New Economic Order." *Daedalus* 110 (1981):133–76.

Bonilla, Frank "Por que seguiremos siendo puertorriqueños." In Alberto Lopez and James Petras, eds. *Puerto Rico and Puerto Ricans.* Cambridge, MA: Schenkman, 1974.

Borjas, George J. "The Earnings of Male Hispanic Immigrants in the United States." *Industrial and Labor Relations Review* 35 (1982):343–53.

—— "The Labor Supply of Male Hispanic Immigrants in the United States." *International Migration Review* 17 (1983):653–71.

—— "The Substitutability of Black, Hispanic and White Labor." *Economic Inquiry* 21 (1983):93–106.

—— "The Impact of Immigrants on the Earnings of the Native-Born." In V. M. Briggs, Jr., and M. Tienda, eds. *Immigration: Issues and Policies.* Salt Lake City: Olympus, 1984.

—— "Assimilation, Changes in Cohort Quality, and the Earnings of Immigrants." *Journal of Labor Economics* 3 (1985):463–89.

—— "The Self-Employment of Immigrants." Unpublished manuscript, Department of Economics, University of California at Santa Barbara, 1985.

——, and Marta Tienda, eds. *Hispanics in the U.S. Economy.* Orlando, FL: Academic Press, 1985.

—— "The Economic Impact of Immigration." *Science* (February 6, 1987).

Bowles, Samuel, and Herbert Gintis *Schooling in Capitalist America: Educational Reform and the Contradictions of Economic Life.* New York: Basic Books, 1976.

Brown, David L., and Calvin Beale "Diversity in Post-1970 Population Trends." In Amos Hawley and Sara Mills Mazie, eds. *Nonmetropolitan America in Transition*. Chapel Hill: University of North Carolina Press, 1981.

Browning, Harley L., and Ruth Cullen "The Complex Formation of the U.S. Mexican-Origin Population: 1970–1980." In R. de la Garza and H. L. Browning, eds. *Mexican Immigrants and the Mexican Americans: An Evolving Relation*. Austin: Center for Mexican American Studies, University of Texas, 1985.

Browning, Harley L., and Nestor Rodriguez "The Migration of Mexican Indocumentados as a Settlement Process: Implications for Work." In George J. Borjas and Marta Tienda, eds. *Hispanics in the U.S. Economy*. Orlando, FL: Academic Press, 1985.

Browning, Harley L., and Joachim Singelmann "The Emergence of a Service Society: Demographic and Sociological Aspects of the Sectoral Transformation of the Labor Force in the U.S.A." Final Report, Manpower Administration, U.S. Department of Labor, 1975.

Bryan, S. "Mexican Immigrants in the Labor Market." In W. Moquin and C. Van Doren, eds. *A Documentary History of the Mexican Americans*. New York: Bantam, 1971.

Burawoy, Michael "The Functions and Reproduction of Migrant Labor: Comparative Material from Southern Africa and the U.S." *American Journal of Sociology* 81 (1976):1050–87.

Burch, Thomas K. "Household and Family Demography: A Bibliographic Essay." *Population Index* 45 (1979):173.

Bustamante, J. A., and G. Martinez "La Emigracion a la Frontera Norte del Pais y a los Estados Unidos." In M. M. Kritz, ed. *Migraciones Internacionales en las Americas*. Caracas: CEPAM, 1980.

Cafferty, Pastora San Juan; Barry R. Chiswick; Andrew M. Greeley; and Teresa A. Sullivan *The Dilemma of American Immigration*. New Brunswick, NJ: Transaction Books, 1985.

Cardoso, L. *Mexican Emigration to the United States: 1897–1931*. Tucson: University of Arizona Press, 1980.

Carliner, Geoffrey "Returns to Education for Blacks, Anglos, and Five Spanish Groups." *Journal of Human Resources* 2 (1976):172–83.

Carter, T. P., and R. D. Segura *Mexican Americans in School: A Decade of Change*. New York: College Entrance Examination Board, 1979.

Casal, Lourdes, and Andres Hernandez "Cubans in the U.S.: A Survey of the Literature." *Cuban Studies* 5 (1975):25–51.

Centro de Estudios Puertorriqueños "The History Task Force." In *Labor Migration Under Capitalism*. New York: Monthly Review Press, 1979.

Chiswick, Barry R. "An Analysis of Earnings Among Mexican Origin Men." *Proceedings of the American Statistical Association*, Business and Statistics Section. Washington, DC: American Statistical Association, 1977.

_____ "The Effect of Americanization on the Earnings of Foreign-Born Men." *Journal of Political Economy* 86 (1978):897–921.

_____ "The Economic Progress of Immigrants: Some Apparently Universal Patterns." In William Fellner, ed. *Contemporary Economic Problems*. Washington, DC: American Enterprise Institute, 1979.

Coale, Ansley J. *The Growth and Structure of Human Populations: A Mathematical Investigation*. Princeton, NJ: Princeton University Press, 1972.

Cooney, Rosemary S. "Demographic Components of Growth in White, Black and Puerto Rican Female-Headed Families: A Comparison of the Cutright and Ross/Sawhill Methodologies." *Social Science Research* 8 (1979):144–58.

Danziger, Sheldon, and Peter Gottschalk "The Measurement of Poverty: Implications for Antipoverty Policy." *American Behavioral Scientist* 26 (1983):739–56.

Davis, Cary; Carl Haub; and JoAnne Willette "U.S. Hispanics: Changing the Face of America." *Population Bulletin*, vol. 38, no. 3. Washington, DC: Population Reference Bureau, 1983.

Davis, Kingsley "Changes in Marriage Since World War II." Paper presented at the conference on Contemporary Marriage: Comparative Perspectives on a Changing Institution, Center for Advanced Study in the Behavioral Sciences, Stanford, California, 1982.

Day, Lincoln H. "Natality and Ethnocentrism: Some Relationships Suggested by an Analysis of Catholic-Protestant Differentials." *Population Studies* 22 (March 1968):27–50.

Dinerman, I. R. "Patterns of Adaption among Households of U.S.-bound Migrants from Michoacan, Mexico." *International Migration Review* 12 (1978):485–501.

Duncan, O. D. "A Socioeconomic Index for All Occupations." In A. Reiss, Jr., ed. *Occupations and Social Status*. New York: Free Press, 1961.

———; D. L. Featherman; and B. Duncan *Socioeconomic Background and Achievement*. New York: Seminar Press, 1972.

England, Paul, and Steven D. McLaughlin "Sex Segregation of Jobs and Male-Female Income Differentials." In Rodolfo Alvarez et al., eds. *Discrimination in Organization*. San Francisco: Jossey-Bass, 1979.

Espenshade, Thomas J. "Marriage Trends in America: Estimates, Implications, and Underlying Causes." *Population and Development Review* 11 (1985):193–245.

Estrada, Leo F.; Jose Hernandez; and David Alvirez "Using Census Data to Study the Spanish Heritage Population of the United States." In *Cuantos Somos: A Demographic Study of the Mexican-American Population*. Austin: Center for Mexican American Studies, University of Texas, 1977.

Farley, Reynolds "Trends in Racial Inequalities: Have the Gains of the 1960s Disappeared in the 1970s?" *American Sociological Review* 42 (1977):189–208.

———, and Albert I. Hermalin "Family Stability: A Comparison of Trends Between Blacks and Whites." *American Sociological Review* 36 (1971):1–17.

Farris, B. E., and Norval Glenn "Fatalism and Familism among Anglos and Mexican Americans in San Antonio." *Sociology and Social Research* 60 (1976):393–402.

Featherman, David, and Robert Hauser *Opportunity and Change*. New York: Academic Press, 1978.

Ferdandez, E., and Nampeo R. McKinney "Identification of the Hispanic Population: A Review of Census Bureau Practices." Paper presented at the annual meeting of the American Statistical Association, Houston, Texas, August 1980.

Fernandez, Roberto, and François Nielsen "Bilingualism and Hispanic Scholastic Achievement: Some Baseline Results." Unpublished paper, University of North Carolina, 1983.

Fitzpatrick, Joseph P., and Douglas M. Gurak *Hispanic Intermarriage in New York City*. Hispanic Research Center Monograph. New York: Fordham University, 1979.

Fligstein, Neil, and Roberto M. Fernandez "Hispanics' Educational Attainment: Descriptive Analysis and Model of the Process." National Opinion Research Center, 1984.

—— "Hispanics and Education." In Pastora San Juan Cafferty and William C. McCready, eds. *Hispanics in the United States: A New Social Agenda*. New Brunswick, NJ: Transition Books, 1985.

Frazier, E. Franklin *The Negro in the United States*. New York: Macmillan, 1957.

Frey, William H. "Population Movement and City-Suburb Redistribution: An Analytic Framework." *Demography* 15 (1978):571–88.

Frisbie, W. Parker; Frank D. Bean; and Isaac W. Eberstein "Patterns of Marital Instability Among Mexican Americans, Blacks, and Anglos." In Frank D. Bean and W. Parker Frisbie, eds. *The Demography of Racial and Ethnic Groups*. New York: Academic Press, 1978.

Frisbie, W. Parker; Frank D. Bean; and Dudley L. Poston "Household and Family Demography of Hispanics, Blacks and Anglos." Final Report, Center for Population Research, National Institute of Child Health and Human Development, Bethesda, Maryland, 1985.

Frisbie, W. Parker, and W. Opitz "Race/Ethnic and Gender Differentials in Marital Instability: 1980." *Texas Population Research Center Papers*, no. 7.007. Austin: University of Texas, 1985.

——; and W. Kelly "Marital Instability Trends among Mexican Americans as Compared to Blacks and Anglos." *Social Science Quarterly* 66 (1985):585–601.

Gans, Herbert J. "Symbolic Ethnicity: The Future of Ethnic Groups and Cultures in America." *Ethnic and Racial Studies* 2 (1979):1–19.

Gardner, Bruce *Bilingual Schooling and the Survival of Spanish in the United States*. Rowley, MA: Newbury House, 1977.

Gardner, Robert W.; Peter C. Smith; and Herbert R. Barringer "The Demography of Asian Americans: Growth, Change and Heterogeneity." Paper presented at the annual meeting of the Population Association of America, Boston, March 1985.

Geertz, C. *Old Societies and New States*. New York: Free Press, 1963.

Glass, Jennifer; Marta Tienda; and Shelley A. Smith "The Impact of Industry Growth and Intra-Industry Occupational Recomposition on Gender Wage Inequality." Working Paper no. 86-17, Center for Demography and Ecology, University of Wisconsin–Madison, 1986.

Glenn, Norval "Suburbanization in the United States since World War II." In L. H. Massoti and J. K. Hadden, eds. *The Urbanization of the Suburbs*. Beverly Hills, CA: Sage, 1973.

Glick, Paul H. "Family Statistics." In Philip M. Hauser and Otis D. Duncan, eds. *The Study of Population: An Inventory and Appraisal*. Chicago: University of Chicago Press, 1959.

—— "Marital Stability as a Social Indicator." *Social Biology* 16 (1969):158–66.

—— "Marriage, Divorce and Living Arrangements." *Journal of Family Issues* 5 (1984):7–26.

Goldscheider, Calvin, and Peter R. Uhlenberg "Minority Group Status and Fertility." *American Journal of Sociology* 74 (1969):361–72.

Gomez-Quinones, J. "The First Steps and Chicano Labor, Conflict and Organizing, 1900–20." In M. P. Servin, ed. *An Awakening Minority: The Mexican-Americans*. New York: Free Press, 1974.

Gordon, Milton *Assimilation in American Life: The Role of Race, Religion and National Origins*. New York: Oxford University Press, 1964.

Grasmuck, Sherri, and Patricia Pessar "Undocumented Dominican Migration to the United States." Research Project Center for International Studies, Duke University, 1982.

Grebler, Leo; Joan W. Moore; and Ralph C. Guzman *The Mexican American People: The Nation's Second Largest Minority.* Glencoe, IL: Free Press, 1970.

Greeley, Andrew M. *The American Catholic: A Social Portrait.* New York: Basic Books, 1977.

Greenwood, Michael J. "Regional Economic Aspects of Immigrant Location Patterns in the United States." In Mary M. Kritz, ed. *U.S. Immigration and Refugee Policy: Global and Domestic Issues.* Lexington, MA: Lexington Books, 1983.

Grenier, Gilles "An Analysis of the Effects of Language Characteristics on the Wages of Hispanic-American Males." Revised version of a paper presented at the meetings of the Société Canadienne de Science Economique, Sherbrooke, Quebec, May 13–14, 1981.

Grossman, Jean B. "The Substitutability of Natives and Immigrants in Production." *Review of Economics and Statistics* 54 (1982):596–603.

Hanushek, Eric A., and John E. Jackson *Statistical Methods for Social Sciences.* New York: Academic Press, 1977.

Harneschfeger, Annegret, and David E. Wiley "Hispanic Americans: High School Learning and What Then?" *Policy Studies in Education.* Evanston, IL: Northwestern University, 1981.

Hauser, Robert; P. J. Dickenson; H. P. Travis; and J. N. Koffel "Structural Changes in Occupational Mobility Among Men in the United States." *American Sociological Review* 40 (October 1975):585–98.

Hauser, Robert, and David Featherman *The Process of Stratification.* New York: Academic Press, 1977.

Heer, David M., and Jeffrey S. Passel "Comparison of Two Different Methods for Computing the Number of Undocumented Mexican Adults in the Los Angeles SMSA." Paper presented at the annual meeting of the Population Association of America, Boston, April 1985.

Heller, C. "Class as an Explanation of Ethnic Differences in Upward Mobility— The Case of Mexican Americans." *International Migration Review* 2 (1967):31–38.

Hernandez, Jose; Leo Estrada; and David Alvirez "Census Data and the Problem of Conceptually Defining the Mexican American Population." *Social Science Quarterly* 53 (1973):671–87.

Higham, John *Strangers in the Land: Patterns of American Nativism, 1860–1925*, 2nd ed. New York: Atheneum, 1971.

Hirschman, Charles "Theories and Models of Ethnic Inequality." In C. Marett, ed. *Research in Race and Ethnic Relations*, vol. 2. Greenwich, CT: JAI Press, 1980.

———— "America's Melting Pot Reconsidered." *Annual Review of Sociology* 9 (1982):397–423.

Hispanic Policy Development Project *The Hispanic Almanac.* Lebanon, PA: Sowers, 1984.

Hout, Michael "The Determinants of Marital Fertility in the United States, 1968–1970: Inferences from a Dynamic Model." *Demography* 15 (1978):139–60.

Hutchinson, E. P. *Immigrants and Their Children, 1850–1950.* New York: Wiley, 1956.

Jaffe, A. J.; Ruth M. Cullen; and Thomas D. Boswell *The Changing Demography* *of Spanish Americans.* New York: Academic Press, 1980.

Jencks, Christopher *Inequality: A Reassessment of the Effect of Family and Schooling in America.* New York: Harper & Row, 1972.

Johnson, Nan E. "Minority Group Status and the Fertility of Black Americans, 1970: A New Look." *American Journal of Sociology* 84 (1979):1386–400.

Jones, K., and A. D. Smith *The Economic Impact of Commonwealth Immigration.* Cambridge: Cambridge University Press, 1970.

Jordan, Terry G. "The 1887 Census of Texas' Hispanic Population." *Aztlan* 12 (1982):271–77.

Kantrowitz, Nathan *Ethnic and Racial Segregation in the New York Metropolis.* New York: Praeger, 1973.

Kasarda, John D. "Hispanics and City Change." *American Demographics* 6 (1984):25–30.

Keefe, S. E. "Acculturation and Extended Family Among Urban Mexican Americans." In A. M. Padilla, ed. *Acculturation: Theory, Models and Some New Findings.* Boulder: Westview Press, 1979.

Keely, Charles B. Affidavit submitted for Plaintiffs in *Cumo et al.* v. *Baldridge et al.,* United States District Court, Southern District of New York, 80 Div. 4550 (JES), 1984.

_____ "Illegal Migration." *Scientific American* 246 (1982):41–47.

_____ *U.S. Immigration: A Policy Analysis.* New York: Population Council, 1979.

Kennedy, Robert E., Jr. "Minority Group Status and Fertility: The Irish." *American Sociological Review* 38 (1973):85–96.

King, Allan G.; B. L. Lowell; and Frank D. Bean "The Effects of Hispanic Immigrants on the Earnings of Native Hispanic Americans." *Social Science Quarterly* 67 (1986):672–89.

Kitagawa, E. "Components of a Difference Between Two Rates." *Journal of the American Statistical Association* 50 (1955):1168–94.

Kobrin, Frances E. "The Fall in Household Size and the Rise of the Primary Individual in the United States." *Demography* 13 (1976):127–38.

Kritz, Mary M., and Douglas T. Gurak "Kinship Networks and the Settlement Process: Dominican and Colombian Immigrants in New York City." Paper presented at the annual meeting of the Population Association of America, Minneapolis, May 1984.

Kyle, Charles "Testimony to National Commission on Secondary Schooling for Hispanics." ASPIRA of Illinois, 1984.

Lieberson, Stanley "A Societal Theory of Race and Ethnic Relations." *American Sociological Review* 26 (1961):902–10.

_____ *A Piece of the Pie: Black and White Immigrants Since 1980.* Berkeley: University of California Press, 1980.

_____ "An Asymmetrical Approach to Segregation." In Ceri Peach, Vaughn Robinson, and Susan Smith, eds. *Ethnic Segregation in Cities.* London: Croom Helm, 1981.

_____ , **and Donna K. Carter** "Temporal Changes and Urban Differences in Residential Segregation: A Reconsideration." *American Journal of Sociology* 88 (1982):296–310.

_____ "A Model for Inferring the Voluntary and Involuntary Causes of Residential Segregation." *Demography* 19 (1982):511–26.

Loomis, Charles P. "A Backward Glance at Self-Identification of Blacks and Chicanos." *Rural Sociology* 39 (1974):96.

Lopez, Alberto "The Puerto Rican Diaspora." In Alberto Lopez and James Petras, eds. *Puerto Rico and Puerto Ricans.* Cambridge, MA: Schenkman, 1974.

Lopez, David "The Social Consequences of Chicano Home/School Bilingualism." *Social Problems* 24 (1976):234–46.

Lowry, Ira S. "The Science and Politics of Ethnic Enumeration." Rand Paper Series no. P-6435. Santa Monica, CA: Rand Corporation, 1980.

Lucas, Isidro *Puerto Rican Dropouts in Chicago: Numbers and Motivations.* Washington, DC: Council on Urban Education, 1971.

Mare, Robert D. "Social Background and School Continuation Decisions." *Journal of the American Statistical Association* 75 (1980):295–305.

———, **and Christopher Winship** "The Paradox of Lessening Racial Inequality and Joblessness among Black Youth: Enrollment, Enlistment and Employment, 1964–1981." *American Sociological Review* 49 (February 1984):39–55.

Marshall, R. Roy; M. Carter; and A. G. King *Labor Economics: Wages, Employment and Trade Unionism.* Homewood, IL: Irwin, 1976.

Massey, Douglas S. *Residential Segregation of Spanish Americans in United States Urbanized Areas.* Unpublished doctoral dissertation, Department of Sociology, Princeton University, 1978.

——— "Effects of Socioeconomic Factors on the Residential Segregation of Blacks and Spanish Americans." *American Sociological Review* 45 (1979a): 1015–22.

——— "On the Measurement of Segregation as a Random Variable." *American Sociological Review* 43 (1979b):587–90.

——— "Residential Segregation of Spanish Americans in the United States Urbanized Areas." *Demography* 16 (1979c):553–64.

——— "Dimensions of the New Immigration to the United States and the Prospects for Assimilation." *Annual Review of Sociology* 7 (1981a):57–85.

——— "Hispanic Residential Segregation: A Comparison of Mexicans, Cubans, and Puerto Ricans." *Sociology and Social Research* 65 (1981b):311–22.

——— "Social Class and Ethnic Segregation: A Reconsideration of Methods and Conclusions." *American Sociological Review* 46 (1981c):641–50.

——— *The Demographic and Economic Position of Hispanics in the United States: The Decade of the 1970s.* Washington, DC: National Commission for Employment Policy, 1983.

——— "Ethnic Residential Segregation: A Theoretical Synthesis and Empirical Review." *Sociology and Social Research* 69 (1985a):315–50.

——— "The Settlement Process Among Mexican Migrants to the United States: New Methods and Findings." In Daniel Levine, Kenneth Hill, and Robert Warren, eds. *Immigrant Statistics: A Story of Neglect.* Washington, DC: National Academy Press, 1985b.

——— "Do Undocumented Migrants Earn Lower Wages?" Unpublished paper, 1986.

———; **R. Alarion; J. Durand; and H. Gonzalez** *Return to Atzlan.* Berkeley: University of California Press, 1987.

Massey, Douglas S., and Brooks Bitterman "Explaining the Paradox of Puerto Rican Segregation." *Social Forces* 64 (1985):306–31.

Massey, Douglas S., and Nancy A. Denton "Spatial Assimilation as a Socioeconomic Outcome." *American Sociological Review* 50 (1985):94–105.

Massey, Douglas S., and Brendan P. Mullan "Processes of Hispanic and Black Spatial Assimilation." *American Journal of Sociology* 89 (1984):836–73.

Mincer, Jacob "Market Prices, Opportunity Costs, and Income Effect." In

C. Christ, ed. *Measurement in Economics*. Stanford, CA: Stanford University Press, 1963.

Mintz, Sidney "Puerto Rico: An Essay on the Definition of National Culture." In Francesco Cordasco and Eugene Bucchioni, eds. *The Puerto Rican Experience*. Totowa, NJ: Rowan and Littlefield, 1973.

Mirande, Alfredo "The Chicano Family: A Reanalysis of Conflicting Views." *Journal of Marriage and the Family* 39 (1977):747–56.

Moore, Joan "Colonialism: The Case of the Mexican Americans." *Social Problems* 17 (1970): 463–72.

Muller, T., and T. Espenshade *The Fourth Wave*. Washington, DC: Urban Institute Press, 1985.

Murguia, Edward *Assimilation, Colonialism and the Mexican American People*. Mexican American Monograph Series no. 1. Austin: University of Texas Center for Mexican American Studies, 1975.

Murillo, Nathan "The Mexican American Family." In N. W. Wagner and M. J. Haug, eds. *Chicanos*. St. Louis: Mosby, 1971.

National Center for Health Statistics "Advance Report of Final Marriage Statistics, 1982." *Monthly Vital Statistics Report*, vol. 34, no. 3, supplement. Hyattsville, MD: U.S. Public Health Service, 1985.

National Commission on Employment Policy "Hispanics and Jobs: Barriers to Progress." Report no. 14. Washington, DC: National Commission on Employment Policy, 1982.

National Puerto Rican Coalition *Puerto Ricans in the Mid '80s: An American Challenge*. Washington, DC: National Puerto Rican Coalition, 1985.

Nelson, Candace "Hispanic Educational Attainment: An Ethnic Issue?" Master's thesis, University of Wisconsin–Madison, 1984.

————, **and Marta Tienda** "The Structuring of Hispanic Ethnicity: Historical and Contemporary Perspectives." *Ethnic and Racial Studies* 8 (1985):49–74.

Newman, Morris J. "A Profile of Hispanics in the U.S. Work Force." *Monthly Labor Review* 101 (1978):3–14.

Nielsen, François, and Roberto Fernandez "Achievement of Hispanic Students in American High Schools: Background Characteristics and Achievement." Unpublished report, National Opinion Research Center, 1981.

Nilsen, Sigurd "Recessionary Impacts of the Unemployment of Men and Women." *Monthly Labor Review* 107 (1984):21–25.

Noel, D. J. "A Theory of the Origin of Ethnic Stratification." *Social Problems* 16 (1968):157–72.

Norton, Arthur J., and Paul Glick "Marital Instability in America: Past, Present, and Future." In George Levinger and Oliver C. Moles, eds. *Divorce and Separation*. New York: Basic Books, 1979.

Norwood, Janet "The Female-Male Earnings Gap: A Review of Employment and Earnings Issues." *Bureau of Labor Statistics Report* 673 (1982):2.

Oaxaca, R. "Male-Female Wage Differentials in Urban Labor Markets." *International Economic Review* 14 (1973):693–709.

Olzak, Susan "Contemporary Ethnic Mobilization." *Annual Review of Sociology* 9 (1980):355–74.

Ortiz, Vilma "Changes in the Characteristics of Puerto Rican Migrants from 1955 to 1980." Unpublished manuscript, Educational Testing Service, Princeton, New Jersey, 1985.

Padilla, Amado, ed. *Acculturation: Theory, Models and Some New Findings*. Boulder: Westview Press, 1979.

Passel, Jeffrey S. "Undocumented Immigrants: How Many?" Paper presented at the annual meeting of the American Statistical Association, Social Statistics Section, Las Vegas, August 1985.

————; J. S. Siegel; and J. G. Robinson "Coverage of the National Population by Age, Sex, and Race in the 1980 Census: Preliminary Estimates by Demographic Analysis." *Current Population Reports*, P-23, no. 115. Washington, DC: U.S. Government Printing Office, 1982.

Passel, Jeffrey S., and Karen A. Woodrow "Geographic Distribution of Undocumented Immigrants: Estimates of Undocumented Aliens Counted in the 1980 Census by State." *International Migration Review* 18 (1984):642–71.

———— "Growth of the Undocumented Alien Population in the United States, 1979–1983, as Measured by the Current Population Survey and the Decennial Census." Paper presented at the annual meeting of the Population Association of America, Boston, April 1985.

———— "Undocumented Immigration." *Annals* 487 (September 1986): 181–200.

Passel, Jeffrey S., and David L. Word "Constructing the List of Spanish Surnames for the 1980 Census: An Application of Bayes' Theorem." Paper presented at the annual meeting of the Population Association of America, Denver, April 1980.

Piore, M. J. *Birds of Passage: Migrant Labor and Industrial Societies.* New York: Cambridge University Press, 1979.

Polachek, S. "Potential Biases in Measuring Male-Female Discrimination." *Journal of Human Resources* 10 (1975):205–29.

Portes, Alejandro "Dilemmas of a Golden Exile: Integration of Refugee Families in Milwaukee." *American Sociological Review* 34 (1969):505–19.

———— "Determinants of the Brain Drain." *International Migration Review* 10 (1976):498–508.

———— "Illegal Immigration and the International System: Lessons from Recent Legal Mexican Immigrants to the United States." *Social Problems* 26 (1979):425–38.

————, and Robert L. Bach "Immigrant Earnings: Cuban and Mexican Immigrants in the United States." *International Migration Review* 14 (1980):315–41.

———— *Latin Journey: Cuban and Mexican Immigrants in the United States.* Berkeley: University of California Press, 1985.

Portes, A.; J. M. Clark; and R. L. Bach "The New Wave: A Statistical Profile of Recent Cuban Exiles to the United States." *Cuban Studies* 7 (1977):1–32.

Poston, Dudley, and W. Parker Frisbie "Ecological Models of Migration." *Texas Population Research Center Papers*, no. 6.004. Austin: University of Texas, 1984.

Price, Daniel O. *A Cohort Analysis.* Final Report to the Department of Health and Human Resources. University of North Carolina at Greensboro, 1981.

Reimers, Cordelia W. "Labor Market Discrimination Against Hispanic and Black Men." *Review of Economics and Statistics* 65 (1983):570–79.

———— "A Comparative Analysis of the Wages of Hispanics, Blacks, and Non-Hispanic Whites." In George J. Borjas and Marta Tienda, eds. *Hispanics in the U.S. Economy.* Orlando, FL: Academic Press, 1985.

Reimers, David M. "Post–World War II Immigration to the United States: America's Latest Newcomers." *Annals* 454 (1981):1–12.

Rodriguez, Clara "Economic Factors Affecting Puerto Ricans in New York." In *Labor Migration Under Capitalism.* New York: Monthly Review Press, 1979.

Rogg, Eleanor *The Assimilation of Cuban Exiles: The Role of Community and Class.* New York: Aberdeen Press, 1974.

————, and Rosemary Cooney *Adaptation and Adjustment of Cubans: West*

New York, N.J. Hispanic Research Center Monograph. New York: Fordham University, 1980.

Ross, Heather, and Isabel V. Sawhill *Time of Transition: The Growth of Families Headed by Women.* Washington, DC: Urban Institute, 1975.

Ryder, Norman B. "Fertility Trends." In John A. Ross, ed. *International Encyclopedia of Population.* New York: Free Press, 1982.

Sabagh, Georges, and David Lopez "Religiosity and Fertility: The Case of the Chicanos." *Social Forces* 59 (1980):431–39.

Samora, Julian *Los Mojados: The Wetback Story.* Notre Dame, Indiana: University of Notre Dame Press, 1971.

Sanderson, Warren "On the Two Schools of the Economics of Fertility." *Population and Development Review* 2 (1976):469–77.

Saragoza, Alex "The Conceptualization of the History of the Chicano Family." In A. Valdez, A. Camarillo, and T. Almaguer, eds. *The State of Chicano Research in Family, Labor and Migration: Proceedings of the Symposium on Work, Family and Migration.* Palo Alto: Stanford Center for Chicano Research, 1983.

Sassen-Koob, Saskia "Changing Composition and Labor Market Location of Hispanic Immigrants in New York City, 1960–1980." In George J. Borjas and Marta Tienda, eds. *Hispanics in the U.S. Economy.* Orlando, FL: Academic Press, 1985.

Schiller, Bradley *The Economics of Poverty and Discrimination.* Englewood Cliffs, NJ: Prentice-Hall, 1985.

Schultz, T. Paul *Economics of Population.* Reading, MA: Addison-Wesley, 1981.

Sewell, William, and Robert M. Hauser *Education, Occupation and Earnings: Achievement in the Early Career.* New York: Academic Press, 1975.

Shack-Marquez, Janice "Earnings Differences Between Men and Women: An Introductory Note." *Monthly Labor Review* 107 (June 1984):15–16.

Shryock, Henry S., and Jacob S. Siegel, and Associates *The Methods and Materials of Demography,* 3rd ed. Washington, DC: U.S. Government Printing Office, 1975.

Siegel, Jacob S., and Jeffrey S. Passel "Coverage of the Hispanic Population of the United States in the 1970 Census: A Methodological Analysis." *Current Population Reports,* special studies, series P-23, no. 82. Washington, DC: U.S. Government Printing Office, 1979.

Simon, Julian "Immigrants, Taxes and Welfare in the United States." *Population and Development Review* 10 (1984):55–69.

———, **and S. Moore** "The Effect of Immigration Upon Unemployment: An Across-City Estimation." Unpublished paper, 1984.

Singelmann, Joachim, and Harley L. Browning "Industrial Transformation and Occupational Change in the U.S., 1960–70." *Social Forces* 59 (1980):247–64.

Singelmann, Joachim, and Marta Tienda "The Process of Occupational Change in a Service Society: The Case of the United States, 1960–1980." In Bryan Roberts, Ruth Finnegan, and Duncan Gallie, eds. *New Approaches to Economic Life: Economic Restructuring, Unemployment and the Social Division of Labor.* Manchester, England: University of Manchester Press, 1985.

Smith, Shelley A., and Marta Tienda "The Doubly Disadvantaged: Women of Color in the U.S. Labor Force." In Ann Stromberg and Shirley Harkess, eds. *Working Women,* 2nd ed. Palo Alto, CA: Mayfield, 1986.

Snipp, C. Matthew, and Marta Tienda "Chicano Career Mobility." *Studies in Social Stratification and Mobility* 4 (1985):177–94.

St. John, Craig, and Harold G. Grasmick "Decomposing the Black/White Fertility Differential." *Social Science Quarterly* 66 (1985):132–46.

Stack, Carol *All Our Kin.* New York: Harper & Row, 1974.

Sullivan, T. A. "Racial Ethnic Differences in Labor Force Participation: An Ethnic Stratification Perspective." In Frank D. Bean and W. Parker Frisbie, eds. *The Demography of Racial and Ethnic Groups.* New York: Academic Press, 1978.

———, **and S. Pedraza-Bailey** *Differential Success Among Cuban American and Mexican American Immigrants.* Final Report to the U.S. Department of Labor, Employment and Training Administration, Washington, DC, 1979.

Sweet, James A. "Indicators of Family and Household Structure of Racial and Ethnic Minorities in the United States." In Frank D. Bean and W. Parker Frisbie, eds. *The Demography of Racial and Ethnic Groups.* New York: Academic Press, 1978.

Swicegood, Gray "Language, Opportunity Costs and Mexican American Fertility." Unpublished doctoral dissertation, University of Texas, 1983.

Tienda, Marta "Familism and Structural Assimilation of Mexican Immigrants in the United States." *International Migration Review* 14 (1980):383–408.

——— "The Mexican American Population." In Amos Hawley and Sara Mills Mazie, eds. *Nonmetropolitan America in Transition.* Chapel Hill: University of North Carolina Press, 1981.

——— "Sex, Ethnicity and Chicano Status Attainment." *International Migration Review* 16 (1982):435–72.

——— "Market Characteristics and Hispanic Earnings: A Comparison of Natives and Immigrants." *Social Problems* 31 (1983a):59–72.

——— "Nationality and Income Attainment of Native and Immigrant Hispanic Men in the United States." *Sociological Quarterly* 24 (1983b):253–72.

——— "Residential Distribution and Internal Migration Patterns of Chicanos: A Critical Assessment." In Armando Valdez, Albert Camarillo, and Tomas Almaguer, eds. *The State of Chicano Research on Family, Labor and Migration: Proceedings of the Symposium on Work, Family and Migration.* Palo Alto: Stanford Center for Chicano Research, 1983c.

——— "Socioeconomic and Labor Force Characteristics of U.S. Immigrants: Issues and Approaches." In Mary Kritz, ed. *U.S. Immigrant and Refugee Policy: Global and Domestic Issues.* Lexington, MA: Heath, 1983d.

——— "The Puerto Rican Worker: Current Labor Market Status and Future Prospects." In *Puerto Ricans in the Mid '80s: An American Challenge.* Washington, DC: National Puerto Rican Coalition, 1984.

———, **ed.** *Hispanic Origin Workers in the U.S. Labor Market: Comparative Analyses of Employment Outcomes.* Final report to the U.S. Department of Labor, Employment and Training Administration. Springfield, VA: National Technical Information Service, 1981.

———, **and Ronald Angel** "Headship and Household Composition Among Blacks, Hispanics, and Other Whites." *Social Forces* 61 (1982):508–31.

Tienda, Marta, and Elizabeth Evanson *Statistical Policy and Data Needs for Hispanic Studies.* Final Report to the Ford Foundation. Madison: Institute for Research on Poverty, University of Wisconsin, 1983.

Tienda, Marta, and Jennifer Glass "Extended Household Composition and Female Labor Force Participation." In Jacques Boulet, Ann Marie DeBritto, and Aisha Ray, eds. *Understanding the Economic Crisis: The Impact of Poverty and Unemployment on Children and Families.* Proceedings of a National

Conference by the Bush Program in Child Development and Social Policy. Ann Arbor: University of Michigan, 1985a.

_____ "Household Structure and Labor Force Participation of Black, Hispanic and White Mothers." *Demography* 22 (1985b):381–94.

Tienda, Marta, and Patricia Guhleman "The Occupational Position of Employed Hispanic Women." In George J. Borjas and Marta Tienda, eds. *Hispanics in the U.S. Economy.* Orlando, FL: Academic Press, 1985.

Tienda, Marta, and Leif Jensen "Immigration and Public Assistance: Dispelling the Myth of Dependency." *Social Science Research* 15 (1986):372–400.

_____; and Robert L. Bach "Immigration, Gender and the Process of Occupational Change." *International Migration Review* 18 (1984):1021–44.

Tienda, Marta, and Ding Tzann Lii "Minority Concentration and Earnings Inequality: A Revised Formulation." Discussion Paper no. 791–85, Institute for Research on Poverty, University of Wisconsin–Madison, 1985.

_____ "Migration, Market Insertion and Earnings Determination of Mexicans, Puerto Ricans, and Cubans." Paper presented at the 1986 annual meeting of the American Sociological Association, 1986.

_____ "Minority Concentration and Earnings Inequality: Blacks, Hispanics and Asians Compared." *American Journal of Sociology* 52(1987).

Tienda, Marta, and Vilma Ortiz "Hispanicity and the 1980 Census." *Social Science Quarterly* 67 (1986):3–20.

_____; and Shelley A. Smith "Industrial Restructuring and Earnings: A Comparison of Men and Women." *American Sociological Review* (forthcoming).

Tienda, Marta, and Shelley A. Smith "The Structural Transformation of Employment in Wisconsin, 1960–1980." Research Bulletin no. R3377, College of Agriculture and Life Sciences, University of Wisconsin–Madison, 1986.

Treas, Judith "Postwar Trends in Family Size." *Demography* 18 (1981):321–24.

Treiman, D. J., and H. I. Hartman, eds. *Women, Work, and Wages: Equal Pay for Jobs of Equal Value.* Washington, DC: National Academy Press, 1981.

Turchi, Boone "Microeconomics Theories of Fertility: A Critique." *Social Forces* 20 (1975):30–39.

U.S. Bureau of the Census *Historical Statistics of the United States: Colonial Times to 1957.* Washington, DC: U.S. Government Printing Office, 1960.

_____ *1970 Census Users' Guide.* Washington, DC: U.S. Government Printing Office, 1970.

_____ "Persons of Spanish Origin in the United States: November, 1969." *Current Population Reports,* series P-20, no. 213. Washington, DC: U.S. Government Printing Office, 1971a.

_____ *A Public Use Sample of Basic Records from the 1960 Census: Description and Technical Documentation.* Washington, DC: U.S. Government Printing Office, 1971b.

_____ "Population Profile of the United States: 1980." *Current Population Reports,* series P-20, no. 363. Washington, DC: U.S. Government Printing Office, 1981.

_____ *Statistical Abstract of the United States: 1982–83.* Washington, DC: U.S. Government Printing Office, 1982.

_____ "Persons of Spanish Origin by State: 1980." Supplementary Report, PC80-S1-7. Washington, DC: U.S. Government Printing Office, 1982.

_____ *Census of Population and Housing: 1980.* Public Use Microdata Samples, Technical Documentation. Washington, DC: U.S. Government Printing Office, 1983.

——— *The Condition of Hispanics in America Today.* Washington, DC: U.S. Government Printing Office, 1984.

——— *Statistical Abstract of the United States:* Washington, DC: U.S. Government Printing Office, 1986.

U.S. Commission on Civil Rights *Puerto Ricans in the United States: An Uncertain Future.* Washington, DC: U.S. Government Printing Office, 1976.

U.S. Department of Justice *Statistical Yearbook of the Immigration and Naturalization Service: 1980.* Washington, DC: U.S. Government Printing Office, 1981.

——— *Statistical Yearbook of the Immigration and Naturalization Service: 1983.* Washington, DC: U.S. Government Printing Office, 1983.

Vincent, Joan "The Structuring of Ethnicity." *Human Organization* 33 (1974):375–79.

Wagley, C., and M. Harris *Minorities in the World.* New York: Columbia University, 1959.

Waldinger, Roger "Immigration and Industrial Change in the New York City Apparel Industry." In George J. Borjas and Marta Tienda, eds. *Hispanics in the U.S. Economy.* Orlando, FL: Academic Press, 1985.

Warren, Robert, and Jeffrey S. Passel "A Count of the Uncountable: Estimates of Undocumented Aliens Counted in the 1980 United States Census." *Demography* (forthcoming).

Weed, James A. "Age at Marriage as a Factor in State Divorce Rate Differentials." *Demography* 11 (August 1974):361–75.

Westoff, Charles F. "Fertility Decline in the West: Causes and Prospects." *Population and Development Review* 9 (1983):99–104.

Willette, JoAnne; Robert Haupt; Carl Haub; Leon Bouvier; and Cary Davis "The Demographic and Socioeconomic Characteristics of the Hispanic Population in the United States: 1950–80." Report prepared by Development Associates and the Population Reference Bureau for the U.S. Department of Health and Human Services. Washington, DC: Development Associates, 1982.

Wilson, Kenneth, and Alejandro Portes "Immigrant Enclaves: An Analysis of the Labor Market Experiences of Cubans in Miami." *American Journal of Sociology* 86 (1980):295–319.

Yancey, William; Eugene Erikson; and Richard Juliani "Emergent Ethnicity: A Review and Reformulation." *American Sociological Review* 41 (1976):391–403.

Yinger, Milton "Ethnicity." *Annual Review of Sociology* 11 (1985):151–80.

Zelinsky, Wilbur *Immigration Settlement Patterns: The Cultural Geography of the U.S.* Englewood Cliffs, NJ: Prentice-Hall, 1973.

Name Index

Boldface numbers refer to figures and tables.

A

Acuña, Rudolfo, 19n, 107n
Alarion, R., 123n
Alba, Richard D., 162n
Almaguer, Tomas, 17n, 18n, 21n, 33n, 86n
Alvarez, Rodolfo, 17n, 18n, 20n, 373n
Alvirez, David, 39n, 40n, 211n, 231n
Anderson, G. M., 123n
Angel, Ronald, 91n, 194n, 197n, 199n, 203n, 289n, 301n, 355n, 386n, 394n
Arce, Carlos H., 22n, 285n, 287n
Aschenbrenner, J., 197n

B

Bach, Jennifer B., 28n
Bach, Robert L., 28n, 29n, 31n, 32n, 33n, 72n, 122n, 123n, 140n, 283n, 286n, 287n, 319n, 332n, 384n, 399, 399n
Bach-y-Rita, Esther Wicab, 348n
Barrera, Mario, 20n, 22, 22n, 33–34
Barringer, Herbert R., 59n
Beale, Calvin, 145n
Bean, Frank D., 17n, 52n, 55n, 104n, 116n, 117n, 118n, **119**, 119n, 120n, 124n, 126n, 127n, 133n, 134, 134n, 178n, 179n, 180n, 182n, 197n, 210n, 211n, 212n, 214n, 215n, 216n, 225n, 230n, 235n, 285n, 319n
Becker, Gary S., 213n
Berry, Brian J., 141n, 152n
Bianchi, Suzanne M., 181n, 197n
Biggar, Jeanne, 141n, 152n
Bitterman, Brooks, 26n, 164n, 167n
Blau, Francine D., 359n
Blaug, Mark, 394n
Blauner, R., 107n
Bonacich, Edna, 9n

Bonilla, A. F., 287n
Bonilla, Frank, 27, 27n
Bonjean, C., 17n
Borjas, George J., 92n, 101n, 129n, 133n, 214n, 280n, 281n, 283n, 284n, 285n, 286n, 288n, 292n, 310n, 319n, 333n, 348n, 375n, 384n, 390n, 394n, 395n, 396n
Boswell, Thomas D., 19n, 280n
Boulet, Jacques, 349n
Bouvier, Leon, 62n
Bowles, Samuel, 259n
Briggs, V. M., Jr., 133n
Brown, David L., 145n
Browning, Harley L., 52n, 55n, 119n, 126n, 129n, 134n, 197n, 205n, 309, 309n, 310–311, 311n, 314n, 319n, 320n
Bryan, S., 107n
Bucchioni, Eugene, 23n
Burawoy, Michael, 21n
Burch, Thomas K., 180, 180n
Burr, Jeffrey, 214
Bustamente, J. A., 123n

C

Cafferty, Pastora San Juan, 12n, 256n
Camarillo, Albert, 21n, 86n
Campos, R., 287n
Cardoso, L., 18, 18n
Carliner, Geoffrey, 395n
Carter, Donna K., 163n, 171n
Carter, M., 394n
Carter, T. P., 261n
Casal, Lourdes, 29n, 30n
Castro, Fidel, 28, 70
Chiswick, Barry R., 12n, 283n, 284n, 348n, 375n, 383n, 384n, 395, 395n

Clark, J. M., 29n
Coale, Ansley J., 205n
Cooney, Rosemary S., 31n, 91n, 94n, 195n, 395n
Cordasco, Francesco, 23n
Cullen, Ruth M., 19n, 127n, 205n, 215n, 280n
Curtis, Russell L., 179n, 211n

D

Danziger, Sheldon, 352, 353n
Davis, Cary, 39n, 48n, **50**, 58n, **59**, 62n, 72n, **105**, 105n, 205n, 220n,
Davis, Kingsley, 179, 179n
Day, Lincoln H., 210n
DeBritto, Ann Marie, 349n
de la Garza, Rodolfo O., 17n, 119n, 205n
Denton, Nancy A., 163n
Dickenson, P. J., 309n
Dinerman, I. R., 123n
Duncan, B., 283n, 309n, 310n
Duncan, Otis D., 180n, 283n, 309n, 310n
Durand, J., 123n

E

Eberstein, Isaac W., 182n
Eisenhower, Dwight D., 30
England, Paul, 373n
Erikson, Eugene, 9n, 11n
Espenshade, T., 133n, 134n, 178, 178n
Estrada, Leo F., 39n, 40n, 47n, 48n
Evanson, Elizabeth, 36n, 37n

F

Farley, Reynolds, 181, 181n, 197n, 283n
Farris, B. E., 211n
Featherman, D. L., 283n, 309n, 310n
Fellner, W., 284n, 348n
Fernandez, Edward, 47n
Fernandez, Roberto M., 256, 256n, 257n, 259n, 260n, 261n, 265n
Finnegan, Ruth, 13n, 241n, 311n
Fish, Hamilton, 118–119
Fitzpatrick, Joseph P., 27n
Fligstein, Neil, 256, 256n, 259n, 260n
Ford, Kathleen, 211n
Frey, William H., 148n
Frazier, E. Franklin, 213, 213n

Frisbie, W. Parker, 52n, 55n, 126n, 145n, 178n, 180n, 182n, 185n, 186n, 197n, 210n, 285n, 319n

G

Gallie, Duncan, 13n, 241n, 311n
Garcia, John A., 394n
Gardner, Bruce, 22n
Gardner, Robert W., 59n
Geertz, C., 8, 8n
Gintis, Herbert, 259n
Glass, Jennifer, 91n, 289n, 301n, 349n, 355n, 373n
Glenn, Norval, 148n, 211n
Glick, Paul H., 180n, 181n
Goldscheider, Calvin, 212n, 213n
Gomez-Quinones, J., 107n
Gonzalez, H., 123n
Gordon, Milton, 44n
Gottschalk, Peter, 352n, 353n
Grasmick, Harold G., 230n
Grasmuck, Sherri, 101n
Grebler, Leo, 145n, 179n, 211n, 231n
Greeley, Andrew M., 12n, 182n, 186n
Greenwood, Michael J., 122n
Grenier, Gilles, 395n
Grossman, Jean B., 133n
Guhleman, Patricia, 285n, 309n, 310n, 330n, 390n, 394n
Gurak, Douglas M., 27n, 101n
Guzman, Ralph C., 145n, 179n, 211n, 231n

H

Haberstein, R. W., 211n
Hadden, J. K., 148n
Hanushek, Eric A., 295n
Harkness, Shirley, 289n, 372n, 374n
Harneschfeger, Annegret, 257n
Harris, M., 210n
Hartman, H. I., 285n
Haub, Carl, 39n, **50**, 58n, **59**, 62n, 105n, 205n, 220n
Haug, M. J., 211n
Haupt, Robert, 62n
Hauser, Philip M., 180n
Hauser, Robert M., 309n, 310n, 394n
Hawley, Amos, 12n, 48n, 84n, 145n
Heer, David M., 120n

Heller, C., 179n
Hermalin, Albert I., 181, 181n
Hernandez, Andres, 29n, 30n
Hernandez, Jose, 39n, 40n, 44n, 47n, 48n
Higham, John, 116n
Hill, Kenneth, 140n
Hirschman, Charles, 10n, 285n
Hout, Michael, 221n, 223n
Hutchinson, E. P., 145n

J

Jackson, John E., 295n
Jaffe, A. J.,·19n, 23n, 24n, 28n, 280n, 288n
Jencks, Christopher, 259n
Jensen, Leif I., 280n, 289n, 319n, 359n
Johnson, Charles E., Jr., 51n
Johnson, Nan E., 212n
Jones, K., 133n
Jordan, Terry G., 107n
Juliani, Richard, 9n, 11n

K

Kantrowitz, Nathan, 170n
Kasarda, John D., 152n
Keefe, S. E., 179n
Keely, Charles B., 20n, 117n, 120, 120n
Kelly, W., 185n
Kennedy, John F., 30
Kennedy, Robert E., Jr., 210n, 212n
King, Allan G., **119**, 119n, 120n, 127n,
 133n, 214n, 235n, 394n
Kitagawa, E., 202n
Kobrin, Frances E., 181n
Koffel, J. N., 309n
Kritz, Mary M., 101n, 122n, 123n, 283n
Kyle, Charles, 258, 258n, 259n, 260n

L

Levine, Daniel, 140n
Levinger, George, 181n
Lieberson, Stanley, 11n, 13n, 163n, 171n
Lii, Ding-Tzann, 284n, 388n, 393, 393n,
 396n
Linsley, Tom, 216n, 230n
Loomis, Charles P., 22n
Lopez, Alberto, 26n, 27n
Lopez, David, 231n, 269n
Lowell, B. L., 133n, 134n

Lowry, Ira S., 38n
Lucas, Isidro, 258n

M

McCready, William C., 256n
McKinney, Nampeo R., 47n
McLaughlin, Steven D., 373n
Marcum, John P., 179n, 210n, 211n, 212n
Mare, Robert, 259n, 372n
Marett, C., 285n
Marshall, R. Roy, 394n
Martinez, G., 123n
Massey, Douglas S., 19n, 22n, 24n, 26n,
 28n, 30, 30n, 38n, 54n, 115n, 123, 123n,
 124n, 134, 134n, 137n, 140n, 142n,
 147n, 163n, 164n, 166, 166n, 167n,
 168n, 170n, 179n, 211n, 220n, 383n
Massoti, L. H., 148n
Mazie, Sara Mills, 12n, 48n, 84n, 145n
Mincer, Jacob, 214n
Mindel, Charles H., 211n
Mintz, Sidney, 23n
Mirande, Alfredo, 211n
Moles, Oliver C., 181n
Moore, Joan W., 22n, 145, 179n, 211n,
 231n
Moore, S., 133n
Moquin, W., 107n
Mullan, Brendan P, 163n, 164n, 167n
Muller, T., 133n, 134n
Murguia, Edward, 17n
Murillo, Nathan, 211n

N

Neidert, Lisa J., 377n, 390n, 394n, 395n
Nelson, Candace, 7n, 34n, 43n, 86n, 94n,
 246n, 257n, 259n
Newman, Morris J., 39n, 281n, 288n
Nielsen, François, 257n, 261n, 265n
Nilsen, Sigurd, 303–304, 303n
Noel, D. J., 285n
Norton, Arthur J., 181n
Norwood, Janet, 374n

O

Oaxaca, R., 284n
Olzak, Susan, 11n
Opitz, W., 17n, 182n, 185n, 186n

Ortiz, Vilma, 38n, 43n, 49n, 51n, 52n, 237n, 321n, 330n, 373n, 390n

P

Padilla, Amado, 179n
Passel, Jeffrey S., 46n, 49n, 52n, 58n, 62n, **64**, 64n, 65n, 76n, 118n, **119**, 119n, 120n, 124n, 125, 125n, 126, 126n, 127n, 235n
Peach, Ceri, 171n
Pedraza-Bailey, S., 287n
Pessar, Patricia, 101n
Petersen, William, 50n
Petras, James, 26n, 27n
Piore, M. J., 123n
Polachek, S., 284n
Portes, Alejandro, 29n, 30n, 31n, 32n, 33n, 122n, 123, 123n, 283n, 285n, 286n, 287n, 332n, 343n, 384n, 399, 399n
Poston, Dudley, 145n, 178n
Price, Daniel O., 181n

R

Ray, Aisha, 349n
Reimers, Cordelia W., 283n, 284n, 375n, 383n, 391n, 396, 396n
Reimers, David M., 116n
Reiss, A., 309n
Roberts, Bryan, 13n, 241n, 311n
Robinson, J. G., 120n
Robinson, Vaughn, 171n
Rodino, Peter, 118
Rodriguez, Clara, 25n
Rodriguez, Nestor, 129n, 134n, 319n
Rogg, Eleanor, 29n, 31n, 94n
Romo, R., 17n
Ross, Heather, 91n
Ross, John A., 221n
Ryder, Norman B., 221n, 223n, 232, 232n

S

Sabagh, Georges, 231n
St. John, Craig, 230n
Samora, Julian, 19n, 20n
Sanderson, Warren, 213n
Saragoza, Alex, 21n
Sassen-Koob, Saskia, 101n, 286n, 333n
Sawhill, Isabel V., 91n

Schiller, Bradley, 283n
Schultz, T. Paul, 213n
Schumer, Charles, 133n
Segura, R. D., 261n
Servin, M. P., 107n
Sewell, William, 394n
Shack-Marquez, Janice, 374n
Shryock, Henry S., 184n
Siegel, Jacob S., 49n, 62n, 76n, 120n, 184n
Silverman, Lester P., 141n, 152n
Simon, Julian, 133n, 359n
Singelmann, Joachim, 13n, 241n, 309, 309n, 310–311, 311n, 314n, 315n, 321n
Smith, A. D., 133n
Smith, Peter C., 59n
Smith, Shelley A., 289n, 292n, 321n, 330n, 372n, 373n, 374n, 390n
Smith, Susan, 171n
Snipp, C. Matthew, 309n, 310n
Stack, Carol, 197n
Stephen, Elizabeth H., 17n, 127n, 215n
Stromberg, Ann, 289n, 372n, 374n
Sullivan, Teresa A., 12n, 104n, 116n, 117n, 118n, 119n, 124n, 285n, 287n
Sweet, James A., 180n, 181n, 182n, 187, 187n, 189n, 192, 192n, 196n
Swicegood, Gray, 127n, 210n, 214n, 215n, 216n, 229n, 230n

T

Taeuber, Alma, 41–42, 42n
Taeuber, Karl, 42, 42n
Taylor, L., 134n
Tienda, Marta, 7n, 12n, 13n, 17n, 20n, 21n, 25n, 26n, 34n, 36n, 37n, 43n, 48n, 49n, 51n, 52n, 53n, 84n, 86n, 88n, 91n, 92n, 94n, 101n, 129n, 133n, 194n, 197n, 199n, 203n, 214n, 241n, 265n, 269n, 280n, 281n, 283n, 284n, 285n, 286n, 288n, 289n, 292n, 301n, 309, 309n, 310n, 311n, 315n, 319n, 321n, 330n, 331n, 348n, 349n, 355n, 359n, 372n, 373n, 374n, 375n, 377n, 388n, 390n, 393, 393n, 394n, 395n, 396n, 404n
Travis, H. P., 309n
Treas, Judith, 189n
Treiman, D. J., 285n
Trent, Katherine, 162n
Triplett, Timothy, 28n
Turchi, Boone, 213n

U

Uhlenberg, Peter R., 212n, 213n

V

Valdez, Armando, 21n, 86n
Van Doren, C., 107n
Vincent, Joan, 13–14

W

Wagley, C., 210n
Wagner, N. W., 211n
Waldinger, Roger, 101n, 292n
Warren, Robert, 58n, **64,** 64n, 65n, **119,**
    120n, 125, 125n, 126, 126n, 140n, 235n
Weed, James A., 186n
Westoff, Charles, 178, 179n

Y

Yancey, William, 9n, 11, 11n, 12, 14, 14n
Yinger, Milton, 7–8, 8n

Z

Zelinsky, Wilbur, 145n

Wiley, David E., 257n
Willette, JoAnne, 39n, **50,** 58n, **59,** 62n, 69,
    69n, 88n, **105,** 105n, 205n, 220n
Williams, Dorie, 211n
Wilson, Kenneth L., 30n, 31n, 32n, 283n,
    286n, 287n
Winship, Christopher, 372n
Woodrow, Karen A., 58n, 119n
Word, David L., 46n

Subject Index

Boldface numbers refer to figures and tables.

A

accounting, 320
acculturation, 92–94; see also
  assimilation; culture
accuracy of measurement, 4
achieved characteristics, 282, 284, 287
adults, in households, 194–197, **195, 196**
Afro-Americans, 43n
age: on arrival, 31; of Central/South
  Americans, 98, **99;** and earnings, 383,
  383n, **386, 389,** 390; and education, **236–
  237,** 237–239, 239n, 240–241, **242–243,**
  248–249, **250–251, 252;** and family
  income, 344, 345, 349; and fertility,
  208–209, **209,** 216–218, **217,** 220; -grade
  delay, 249–252, 261–270, 261n, **262–263,
  266,** 278; and labor force participation,
  295, 301, 301n; at marriage, 91, 184–
  185, **185, 228,** 246; of population, 63, **68,**
  89; and poverty, 339; -sex structure, 57,
  63, **65,** 66–67, **66, 67,** 69–71, **69, 71,** 73,
  74, 75, 76, 127, **128;** and unemployment,
  305, **306–307,** 308
agriculture, 18, 19, 20, 21, 22, 26, 286, 301,
  331; families in, and undercount, 48n;
  Mexicans and, 86, 88, 130; in Puerto
  Rico, 24; sector, 311–312, 318, 319
Aid to Families with Dependent Children
  (AFDC), 358
air travel: for Cuban refugees, 29; for
  Puerto Ricans, 24, 24n
Albuquerque, N. Mex., 152
alimony, 339
"Americanization," 10
Amerindians, 34
Anaheim, 171, 173
ancestry, 42 43, 43n, 51; and
  comparability, 55; multiple, 43n; see

also national origin groups
"Ancestry and Language in the United
  States" (U. S. Bureau of the Census), 51n
Argentinians, 97, 101, 111, 114–115, 382
Arizona, 17, 82, 83, 138, 185
ascribed characteristics, 282–283, 284–286,
  287
Asians, 8, 11, 59, 59n, 115, 116, 135, 166
ASPIRA, 257–258, 257n
assimilation (integration), 10, 21, 34, 44,
  93–94, 94n, 336; Cuban experience, 14,
  34, 308, 400; diversity of experiences
  among Hispanic groups, 13, 14, 94, 400;
  and education, 278; and labor market
  outcomes, 284–285, 284n, 285n; and
  language, 43–44, 45; Mexican
  experience, 14, 33–34, 125, 126n;
  parentage data and analysis of, 42n;
  Puerto Rican experience, 14, 33, 34;
  "structural," 212; see also acculturation

B

banking, 32, 320
barrios, 22, 33
bilingual education, 1, 256, 277–278
bilingualism, 265, 269; data on, 45, 45n,
  413–416
birthplace identifier, 39, 40–42, 42n, 44n,
  51, 54
blacks, 4, 13, 34, 176, 402; census tracts,
  166; earnings, 247, 247n; and education,
  235, 240, 243, 245n, 247, 257, 258, 261;
  family incomes, 340, 342, 344, 348, 349;
  fertility, 208, 213, 230; geographic
  distribution, 147; growth rate of, 59;
  Hispanic, 51–52, 164; labor force
  participation, 287–288, **289, 290, 291;**

marriage and family, 185, 192, 203; personal incomes, 366, 367, 370; and poverty, 353, 373; and public assistance, 358, 360; socioeconomic status, 280; undercount of, 58n, 120; unemployment, 303, 304; *see also* race
blue-collar workers, 21, 26, 30, 309, 331, 332
Bolivians, 97, 101, 111, 382
bracero program, 20, 127
business, repair and personal services, 131

C

California, 17, 78, 80, 82, 83, 88, 98, 100, 101, 138, 149, 185, 286; migration flows, **162**
capital: for ethnic enterprises, 32; gains income, 339
Caribbeans, 3, 378, 380; demographic and socioeconomic characteristics of, 95, **96**, 97, 98; immigration and population, 63
Catholic church, 182, 231
census: regions, 138n; tracts, **165,** 166–168, **166–167**
Central and South Americans, 3, 4, 56, 57, 62n; ages of, 89, 98, **99;** age-sex structure of, 73, **74**, 76; Central vs. South Americans, 95, 97; demographic and socioeconomic diversity within, 95–102, **96**; earnings, 247, 247n; earnings, female, 390, 391, 392; earnings, female vs. male, 375, 376, 378–380, **379**; earnings, male, 383, 388; economic and cultural integration of, 33; economic well-being, 338; education, 235, 238, 240, 241, 244, 245, 246, 247, 247n, 248, 249, 250–251, 253, 254, 265, 267, 268, 268n, 269, 412; enumeration and identification of, 36, 46, 49, 52, **53,** 402, 403, 405; family income, 339, 340, 342, 343, 344, 345, 348, 349, 350, 352, 361; fertility, 206, 210, 218, 232, 399; foreign-born, 89, 90, 109–115, **112, 113;** generations, 42; geographic distribution of, 80, 82, 83, 88, 98–102, **100**, 139, 141, 144; household structures, 187–188, 189, 195, 196, 197; immigration by, 72–73, 76, 106, 109–115, **113**, 115n, 124, 135; included in "Other Hispanics," 72, 72n;

incomes, 199n; industry distribution of employment, 311, 315, 318, 319, 320, 321; internal migrations by, **157;** labor force participation, 93, 280–281, 289, 291, 292, 293–294, **293,** 297–300, 301; linguistic practices of, 93, 94; marriage and family patterns, 185–186; metro-nonmetro residence patterns, 84–85, 88, 145; misreporting of others as, 168n; national origin, and age, **99;** national origin, and nativity, **96;** national origin, and residential distribution, **100;** naturalizations, 109; occupational distribution, **326,** 330, 332, 333, 336; overcount of, 72; as percent of Hispanic population, 2, **53, 60, 60,** 406; personal incomes, 366, 367, 370; population growth, 62, 72–73, 76; and poverty, 354, 355–356, 357, 358, 360, 361, 370, 373; and public assistance, 358, 360, 361; school dropout rates, 271–273, 276; school enrollment, 249, 250–251, 253, 254; socioeconomic status of, 92, 93, 94, 103, 393, 394, 398, 400; time of arrival, 110–114; unemployment, 303, 305
central cities, 26, 84, 147–149, **147,** 147n
Centro de Estudios Puertorriquenos, 24n
Chicago, Ill., 149, 167, 168, 170–171, 173, 175, 258; segregation patterns, 176–177
Chicanos, 17n; movement, 21–22; *see also* Mexicans
children, 55; cost of, and fertility, 213–214; data and file construction, 412–417; in female-headed households, 192–193, **192;** and labor force participation by women, 295, 295n; number of, **188,** 189; *see also* education; fertility
Chileans, 97, 101
circular migration, 24, 26–27, 26n, 68, 105, 289, 302
citizenship, of Puerto Ricans, 23, 26; *see also* naturalization
class: of Cubans, 31, 33; and diversity of Hispanics, 398; divisions view of ethnicity, 10; vs. ethnic divisions, 22; integration, of Mexicans, 33–34; *see also* socioeconomic status; *and specific classes*
classification problems: of Other Hispanics, 74–75; of Other South Americans, 97n

clerical occupations, 321, 330, 333
college education, 235, 240, 241–248, **244–245**; and earnings, 247; and gender, 251–252; and language, 248
Colombians, 97, 98, 101, 111–112, 115, 115n, 381
Colorado, 3, 17, 80, 82, 83, 86, 138, 185
communication industries, 320
Communist governments, 28, 29
community: leadership, among Puerto Ricans, 2; variables, and education, 258
comparability, 46, 58; and children of Spanish origin, 55; of mother tongue items, 44–45; of surname identifier, 46; and underenumeration, 55; see also time trend analyses
Conference on the Political Economy of National Statistics, 50n
conquest, 16, 17–18, 33
"Consistency of Reporting of Ethnic Origin" (Johnson), 51n
"Constructing the List of Spanish Surnames for the 1980 Census" (Passel and Word), 46n
construction industry, 130, 301
contact probabilities, **174**
contract labor system, 20
contract workers, 25
Costa Ricans, 112, 294, 378
coverage errors, 62, 62n, 63, 70, 72, 73, 76, 82
"Coverage of the Hispanic Population of the United States in the 1970 Census" (Siegel and Passel), 62n
Cubans, 3, 4, 7; ages of, 89; age-sex composition of, 70–71, **71**, 76; in central cities, 147, 149; earnings, 247, 247n, 396; earnings, female, 390, 391, 392; earnings, male, 383, 388; earnings, male vs. female, 374, 375, 376, 378; economic well-being, 338; education, 235, 237, 238, 240, 241, 244, 245, 246, 247, 247n, 248, 249, 250–251, 253, 254, 265, 267, 267n, 268, 268n, 269, 277, 412; enclave economy, 32–33, 286, 287; enumeration and identification of, 36, 40, 43, 43n, 404–405, 407; family income, 339, 340, 342, 343, 344–345, 348, 350, 352, 361; family size, 91; female-headed households, 192, 193; fertility, 208, 209, 210, 217–218, 220, 221, 223, 224–227,

229–230, 400; generations, 42; geographic concentration of, 80n, 82, 83, 88, 102, 141, 144; historical comparisons, 8; household structures, 187–188, 189, 197, 203; immigration of, 28–29, 70, 70n, 72, 76, 97, 105–106, 117, 124, 135; incomes, 199; index of dissimilarity, 175–176; industry distribution of employment, 311, 315, 318, 319, 320, 321, 322; influx of, 2; integration experience of, 14, 16, 27–33; internal migrations, 153, **156**, 161; labor force participation, 93, 280–281, 289, 290, 291, 292, 302; and labor market, 285, 286; linguistic practices of, 93, 94, 94n; marriage and family patterns, 184, 185, 194; metro-nonmetro residence patterns, 84–85, 88, 145, 152; as minority group, 210; nativity, 407; naturalizations, 109; number of refugees, 28; occupational distribution, **325**, 330, 331–332, 333, 336; as percent of Hispanic population, 2, 27, **53**, 60, **60, 61**, 406; personal incomes, 366, 367, 370; as political refugees, 115; population growth, **61**, 62, 70–72, 76; and poverty, 353, 355–356, 357, 358, 359, 361, 370, 372–373; and public assistance, 358, 359, 361; race mixture of, 34; Refugee Program, 30, 31; regional distribution of, 138; relocation assistance, 25; residential segregation, 173, 173n, 175–177; school dropout rates, 271–273, 274, 276; school enrollment, 249, 250–251, 253, 254; self-employment, 396; socioeconomic status of, 13, 14, 88, 92, 93, 94, 103, 393, 398, 399, 400; unemployment, 303, 305–308
culture or cultural: assimilation, 21, 34, 44, 93–94, 94n; deficiencies view of ethnicity, 10; diversity of Hispanics, 1; dual identity of Puerto Ricans, 27; and educational achievement, 256–257, 258, 259–260, 269, 277–279; and educational policy, 277–279; and fertility, 211–212; identity of Cubans, 30–31; and residential segregation, 163
Current Population Surveys, 39, 45n, 52, 72n, 73, 343; vs. Census enumerations, 52–54, **53**, 55

D

data: and file construction, 412–417; historical sources of, 14; strengths and limitations of, 36–55, 37n, 57

demographic characteristics, 56–57; and diversity, 89–91, **90**; and earnings, 382, 383–385, 391, 395–396; and family incomes, 344–349, **346–347**

"Demography of Asian Americans, The" (Gardner, Smith, and Barringer), 59n

desegregation, 277

developed countries, 122–123

Development Associates, 58n

disability payments, 351

discretionary childbearing, 232

discrimination, 1, 13, 14; and earnings, 388–389; and labor force participation, 281; and labor market outcomes, 283, 284–286; against Mexicans, 18, 21, 22, 26; against Puerto Ricans, 25, 26, 393, 400; and school grade delay, 261; and socioeconomic status, 393

distributive services sector, 318, 320

diversity, 2–4, 14, 33, 37, 56, 89–94, 398–400; among Central and South Americans, 95–102; and demographic and socioeconomic positions, 56–57, 89–94, 103, 398–400; and economic well-being, 392–394; and educational achievement, 277–278; and ethnicity, 14–16; see also generational diversity

divorce, 178, 181, 182, 194

Dominican Republic, 95, 95n

Dominicans, 95, 100–101, 111, 112, 294, 378, 381

downward mobility, 30, 31

E

earnings, 338, 339, 373–392, 397; and education, 246–247, 247n; functions, theoretical specification of, 394–396; husband's, 295, 295n; and labor market conditions, 281, 283; variables used in analyses of, **387**; see also family incomes; personal incomes

Eastern European immigration, 123

ecological foundations of residential segregation, 12, 163–164, 163n, 176

economic conditions: and fertility, 210, 213–214, 215, 225, 231–232; and immigration flows, 122–123; inequality, and household composition, 197–203, 204; and integration, 16, 28, 33, 34; international, 101; and international migration of labor, 123; and labor market position, 287; and residential segregation, 164, 170, 177; see also economic well-being

economic well-being, 1, 338–396; and diversity, 392–394; and ethnic vs. minority groups, 13–14; and family and household behavior, 179, 180, 187, 197–203; and labor force participation by married women, 337; and labor market conditions, 281, 282; see also economic conditions; socioeconomic status

Ecuadorans, 97, 98, 101, 111–112, 378, 381

education, 5, 163, 233–279, 397; and age, **236–237**; of Cuban refugees, 28, 31; data and file construction, 412–417; and discrimination, 284; diversity among national origin groups, 92; and earnings of males vs. females, 377–378, 383, 392; and earnings of women, 390; and fertility, 209, 212, 213, 214, 215, 221, 222–228, **222**, **223**, **224**, **226**, **228**, **229**, 230, 231–232, 399–400; and labor force participation, 295, 299–300, 303; and labor market position, 281, 283, 285, 286, 287, 302; levels of Puerto Ricans, 25; median years of schooling, **234**; of Mexicans, 129, **130–131**; policy questions, 277–279; and poverty, 339; of Puerto Ricans, 177; school enrollment patterns, 248–256; services, 321; underachievement issues, 256–276; see also college education; school

elderly, 357, 372–373

El Paso, Tex., 171, 173, 175

El Salvador, 95, 95n, 106, 114; see also Salvadorans

employment, 163; for Cubans, 29; of illegal immigrants, 118, 133–134; and labor market conditions, 281; of Mexicans, 129–131, **132**, 134; opportunities, 22, 91–92, 286, 289, 308; of Puerto Ricans, 25, 177, 289; see also labor force participation; labor market

enclave economy, 31, 32–33, 163, 286, 287

engineering, 320

English as a Second Language (ESL)
  programs, 256, 278
English language proficiency, 5, 30; of
  Cubans, 30, 31; data on, 413–416; and
  earnings, 383, 390–391, 392, 395; and
  educational achievement, 259, 264–265,
  267–268, 269, 271, 274, 275–277, 276n,
  278, 413–416; and fertility, 229, **229;**
  and labor force participation, 295, 300–
  301, 302, 303; and labor market
  experiences, 283, 286, 287; of Mexicans,
  129, **130–131;** and mother tongue
  concept, 45, 45n; by national origin
  groups, 93–94, **93,** 94n; and
  socioeconomic status, 281; and
  socioeconomic well-being, 93–94; see
  also language
entrepreneurial skills, 32
entry mode, 16, 33, 103; of Mexicans, 107–
  109
enumeration practices, 4, 36–55
equal opportunity, 277
ethnic: antagonism and hostility, 11;
  consciousness, 398; enclave economy,
  31, 32–33, 163, 286, 287; groups, and
  immigration, 115–116; groups, reporting
  by, 51n; vs. minority groups, 13–14;
  resilience concept, 399; stratification,
  and labor market outcomes, 285–286;
  see also ethnicity; ethnic solidarity
ethnicity: class factors and, 10; cultural
  aspects of, 10; dynamic process of, 10–
  11; and educational achievement, 258,
  259–260, 261, 268n, 271, 276, 277, 278;
  emergence of Hispanic, 14–16;
  identifiers of, 38, 39; interactive aspect
  of, 11; and labor market position, 282–
  287, 285n; and lower socioeconomic
  status, 33; meaning of, 4, 7–8;
  multidimensional construction of
  Hispanic, 38; social construction of, 8–
  14; sociological concept of, 39, 48;
  structuring of Hispanic, 7–35, **15;**
  symbolic, 15, 16, 103; see also ethnic;
  ethnic solidarity; Hispanics; specific
  ethnic and national-origin groups
ethnic solidarity, 34; and fertility, 399–
  400; and regional concentration, 82–83;
  and residential segregation, 83, 163; see
  also ethnic; ethnicity
European immigrants, 8, 11, 12–13, 14, 34,
  115–116, 145, 147

European origin, 43, 171
extractive industries, 309, 311–312, 319,
  322

F

family, 91, 178–204, 397; defined, 180–
  181, 339, 339n; economics of, and
  fertility, 213; and educational
  achievement, 258–259, 260–276, **262–
  263, 266, 272–273, 275,** 276–277, 278,
  279; extended, 91; headship, and public
  assistance, 360–361; and poverty, 352–
  361, **354, 356;** public assistance income,
  358–361, **359;** reunification criteria for
  immigration, 124; size, and income, 349;
  stability, 181; structure, 181–197, **190;**
  type, and income, 200–203, **200–201,
  202;** values, and fertility, 211; see also
  family income; household
family income, 220n, 338, 339–352, **341,
  342, 345, 346–347, 350–351,** 361;
  defined, 339–340; and educational
  achievement, 258–259; headship and,
  344, 345–349, **345n, 346–347;** see also
  earnings; personal income
farm laborers, 333; see also agriculture;
  extractive industries
father: education, 258; occupational status,
  259
female- or single-person-headed
  households, 191–194, **192, 193,** 199n;
  and children's educational achievement,
  275; incomes, 201, 204, 344, 345–349,
  345n, 346–347; and labor force
  participation, 289; Mexican, 189; and
  poverty, 355–357, 372; and public
  assistance, 360–361; Puerto Rican, 91,
  189; see also gender; women
fertility, 4, 9, 59–60, 62, 66, 134, 205–232,
  397; and age, **217;** of Cubans, 70, 91,
  217–218; diversity among Hispanics
  and, 398–400; and education, **222, 223,
  224, 226, 228, 229,** 399–400;
  generational status and ethnicity, **218,
  219;** of Mexicans, 91; by national origin
  and age, **209;** of Puerto Ricans, 91; by
  race and origin, **207;** of South
  Americans, 98; see also education, and
  fertility
Filipinos, 46

first generation, 41–42, 42n, 44n, 130, 215–216, 224–226; *see also* foreign-born; nativity

first marriage, 178, 184–185, **185**

Florida, 2, 28, 30, 78, 80n, 82, 83, 84, 88, 98, 100, 101–102, 137, 138, 144, 400; migration flows, **161**, 162

food retailing, 130–131

Ford Foundation, 245n

foreign-born: and fertility, 215–216; and geographic distribution, 140–141, **140**; and language, 94n; metropolitan residence patterns, 146–147, **146, 147**; number of, by national origin, 89–90, **96**, 97–98; parents, and educational achievement, 269–270; percentage of, and timing of arrival, 109–115; *see also* first generation; generational diversity; generations; immigrants; immigration; nativity

foreign stock identifier, 40–43, **41**, 43n, 46

Frostbelt, 26

future orientation, 31

G

garment industry, 25, 286, 289, 292

gender, 398; and age structure, 57, 63, **65, 66–67, 66, 67,** 69–71, **69, 71,** 73, **74, 75,** 76, 127, **128;** and earnings, 373–392, 374n, 382n; and education, 237, 241, 246–247, 251–252, 264, 274–275; and industrial sector employment, 322; and labor force participation, 288–294, 295–302, **288, 290, 293, 296–299,** 303; and labor market, 285n, 287; and occupational distribution, **323–329,** 330–332, 333–336, **334–335;** and personal income, 361–370, **363–365, 368–369;** and poverty, 339, 372; and unemployment, 303–308, **304, 306–307;** *see also* female- or single-person-headed households; men; women

generational diversity: of Cubans, 28; and fertility, 215–216, 218, **218, 219, 222, 223, 224, 226,** 230; of Mexicans, 21, 42; and Puerto Ricans, 27

generations, identification of, 41–42, 42n, 404–407, **406;** *see also* foreign-born; generational diversity; nativity; *specific generations*

geographic distribution, **77, 78–88, 78–79, 81,** 137–177, 397; measures of concentration, 141–144; by region and nativity, **140;** by state, **142–143, 144**

Great Britain, 133

Great Depression, 19, 107

Guatemala, 95n

Guatemalans, 95, 97, 98, 101, 111, 112, 114, 294

H

head of household, 181

health, 163, 321, 385–386, 386n

Hispanic Almanac (Hispanic Policy Development Project), 84, 84n

"hispanicity," 14–16

Hispanic Policy Development Project, 59n, 61n, 76n, 80n

Hispanics: age-sex structure of, **65;** availability of data on, 3, 4; census tracts, **165,** 166, **166–167;** critique of data on, 4; defining population, 4, 38–54, 412–413; demographic and socioeconomic profile of, 56–103; demographic characteristics of, 4, 89–91, **90;** distribution of, by state, **409–410;** diversity of, 2–4, 14–16, 33, 37, 56, 89–94, 95–102, 103, 277–278, 392–394, 398–400; earnings and economic well-being, 338–396; economic and cultural integration of, 33; education, 233–279; enumeration and identification of, 36–55, 38n, **41,** 52n; ethnicity, and residential concentration, 83–84; ethnic labels, changing, 9; vs. European immigrants, 34; family incomes, 220n, 338, 339–352, **341, 342, 345, 346–347, 350–351,** 361; fertility patterns within, 205–232, 398–400; geographic distribution, 77, 78–88, **78–79, 81,** 137–177; identifiers, 38–54, 168, 168n, 401–407; immigration, 104–136; immigration, and population growth, 62–76; immigration experiences, 33–35; impact of, in U.S., 1–3; incomes, and household composition, 198–203; internal migrations, 152–163; intrastate concentration of, 83–84; and labor force participation, 280–337; marriage, family, and household, 178–214; meaning of ethnicity, 4, 8–9; metro vs. nonmetro

Hispanics *(continued)*
concentration, 84–88, **85, 87;**
metropolitan concentrations, 145–152,
146, 148, 150, 151; non-white, 46;
number of, 36; overcount of, 168*n;*
percentage distribution of subgroups,
406–407, **406;** personal incomes, 361–
370, 366*n;* population growth, 52–53,
53, 57–62, **59, 60, 61,** 62–76, 62*n;*
poverty, 339, 352–361, 370–373, **371;**
and public assistance, 358–361, **359;**
racial classification of, 13, 34; residential
redistribution, **410–411;** residential
segregation of, 163–177, **165, 166–167,
169;** socioeconomic characteristics, 4–5,
12, 13–14, 16, 399–400; structuring of
ethnicity, 7–35, **15;** terms for, 37*n;*
timing of immigration, 12–13; undercounting of, 48, 48*n,* 52–54, 55, 58, 58*n,*
168*n;* visibility of, 1–2, 9; white, 46; *see
also specific national-origin groups*
Hispanos, 1, 3, 61, 74
historical comparisons, 8
Hondurans, 97, 98, 112
household: characteristics, and school
noncompletion, 270–276, **272–273, 275,**
277, 413–416, **414–415;** composition and
economic inequality, 197–203; defined,
180–181, 339; income, 198–203, **198,
200–201,** 271, **272–273,** 275, 276, 277,
339*n;* size, 91, 187–191, **187, 188, 190;**
size, and poverty, 357–358; structure,
180, 187–197; *see also* family; family
income
housing, 163; discrimination, 25
Houston, Tex., 171, 173
human capital, 218, 283, 284–285, 285*n,*
295, 302, 382, 383
husband: earnings, 295; -wife households,
189, 191, 194–196, **196,** 199*n,* 201, 202,
203

I

identifiers, 38–54, **41;** comparability, 55;
selection criteria, 401–407; subjective
vs. objective, 48, 54
illegal immigrants or undocumented
migrants, 52, 104, 117–121, 136; and
comparability, 55; connotation of term,
117–118; education of, 239*n;* future
"flood" of, 122; increase in, 115; and

industry sector employment, 319; labor
market impact of, 133–134; laws to
curb, 116; Mexicans, 20, 52–53, 64–66,
83*n,* 107, 117, 119–121, **119, 121,** 125–
127, 126*n;* number of, 118–121; and
population growth data, 58, 62, 63–66;
and undercounting, 48*n,* 58*n*
Illinois, 80, 81, 83, 84, 286; migration
flows, **162,** 163
immigrants: change in ethnic composition
of, 115–116; and earnings, 383–384;
geographic distribution of, vs. native
born, 144; labor force participation, 93,
281; and labor market, 395; vs.
migrants, 117; percent admitted by type
of admission, **124–125;** *see also* illegal
aliens; immigration; *and specific
national-origin groups*
immigration, 104–136; by Asians, 59*n,*
115; by Central and South Americans,
72–73, 76, 83, 85, 97–98, 100–102;
context and consequences of, 115–117;
continued, 34; by Cubans, 27, 70, 70*n,*
72, 76, 85; diverse experiences of, 7, 8,
397, 398; issue, 1; and education, 246,
254, 260, 264, 264*n;* and emergence of
ethnicity, 16, 34–35; ethnic composition
of, 115–116; and fertility, 216, 224, 225–
227; future, 122–124; historical and
contemporary features of, 105–109; and
industry distribution of employment,
320; and intercensal growth of
population, 57, 59–60, 62, 63–76; and
labor market, 133–134; laws, 104, 115,
116, 122; and meaning of ethnicity, 8–
10, 11–12; by Mexicans, 18–21, 26, 63–
67, **64,** 76, 83, **106,** 107–110, 125–131,
132; by national origin, **105;** nativity
composition and time of arrival, 109–
115; by Other Hispanics, 73–76;
political guidelines, 12; by Puerto
Ricans, 22–25, 26, 68–70, 85; rates, 4;
and residential segregation, 164, 173,
177; time of, 12–13; undocumented,
117–121; *see also* foreign-born; illegal
aliens; immigrants; nativity
Immigration and Nationality Act, 115
Immigration and Naturalization Service
(INS), 70, 70*n,* 73, 109, 111, 112–114,
115, 118
incomes, 338, 397; current money, 339;
defined, 339–340, 339*n;* and educational

attainment, 272; family, and economic well-being, 339–352; personal, and earnings differentials, 338, 339, 361–370, **362–365, 368;** *see* earnings; poverty
index of dissimilarity, 141–143, 142*n*, **144;** for industry and sector distributions, 318–319, 321–322; for occupational distributions, 330, 332–333; of residential dissimilarity, 168–175, **169, 174;** scalar, of occupational standing, 309–310, 309*n*
Indian (American) origin, 3
Indiana, 81, 286
individualism, 31
Indochina, 115
industrial: flight to Sunbelt, 26; structure, 12, 34, 286, 287, 304, 308, 309, 333
industry: distribution of Hispanics, 310–322, **312–313, 314, 316–317;** employment by, 130–131, **132**
inequality: cultural vs. class factors and, 10; economic, 180; economic, and household composition, 197–203; interethnic, and family behavior, 180; labor market, 281, 283; of Mexicans, 22
insurance, 320
integration experiences: of Cubans, 29–33, 34; diversity of, by Hispanics, 14–16, 33–35; of Mexicans, 18, 21–22, 33–34; of Puerto Ricans, 25–27, 33, 34
intermarriage, 27, 46
internal migration, 4, 137, 152–163, **154–161;** defined, 153*n*; and labor market outcomes, 393–394
invasion tracts, 167, 168, 170
Iowa, 81
isolation, 33, 34
Italians, 46, 122

J

Japanese, 32
job or work: experience, 281, 283, 284, 287, 383*n*; segregation, 319; skills, and discrimination, 284; training, 29, 281, 283, 285

K

kinship ties, and immigration, 20–21
Koreans, 32

L

labor: international migration of, 115, 122–123; patterns of Mexicans, 129–134, **132**
labor force participation, 220*n*, 397; and education, 254; and nativity, 93; of Puerto Ricans, 25; trends and differentials in, 287–303; and unemployment, 303; *see also* labor market
labor market, 5, 8, 12, 280–337, 343–344; activity, correlates and determinants of, 282–287; conditions, 281–282, 302, 382; conditions, and earnings of men, 382, 388–389, 388*n*; and Cuban immigration, 30–31, 94; deterioration of standing in, 343–344; and earnings, 378, 382, 391–392, 396; and education, 240–241, 247; ethnically split, vs. enclave economy, 31, 32; and family incomes, 349; impact of immigration on, 133–134, 395; and internal migrations, 393–394; and Mexican immigration, 18–19, 20, 26; and metro vs. nonmetro residence, 85; minority, 34; in New York City, 101; and personal incomes, 367–370; and poverty, 372; and Puerto Rican immigration, 24, 25, 26; secondary, 33; in Southwest after annexation, 18
labor supply, 382, 386, 391
language, 5, 9; and education, 246, 248, 259, 260, 261, 264, 268, 268*n*, 269, 274, 275–277, 276*n*, 413–416; and fertility, 229; as Hispanic identifier, 38, 43–45, 51; practices, among national origin groups, 93–94, **93,** 94*n*, 248; question, 45, 45*n*; *see also* English language proficiency; Spanish language
Latin American immigrants, 104–136; vs. Asian immigrants, 11; vs. European immigrants, 11; illegal aliens, 58*n*; immigration and growth of population, 63; linguistic practices, 5, 9; rising percentage of, 115–116; socioeconomic status, 14; *see also* immigrants; immigration
"Latino" term, 37*n*
legal immigration, 116–117; by Mexicans, 106–109, **106**
less-developed countries, 115
life cycle factors, 383
linguistic assimilation, 43*n*

living arrangements, 4; and education, 252–254, **252, 255,** 265–266, 413; and school dropouts, 270, 271, 274, 274*n*
logistic analysis, 265*n*, 295, 295*n*
Los Angeles-Long Beach, 149, 149*n*, 152, 167–168, 170, 173, 175, 176, 177
low-skilled jobs, 102, 337

M

managers, 30
manufacturing sector, 26, 130, 301, 315, 318, 320, 321
Mariel incident, 28, 70, 72
marital: disruption, 181–182, 220*n*, 302; instability, 180, 181–182, 185–186, **186,** 194, 203; status, 181, 182–186, **183, 184;** status, and labor force participation, 295, 301–302, 301*n*; status of female household heads, 193–194, **193;** see also marriage
marriage, 4, **90,** 91, 178–180, 181–186, **183, 184, 185, 186;** and earnings of men, 384–385; and education, 246, 271, 275; exogamous, 94; and labor force participation, 337; and poverty, 357; see also marital
married, spouse absent category, 182
married women, fertility of, 216–218, **217, 218, 219, 222, 223, 224, 226**
mass communication, 25
mass transit, 26
mean family incomes, 340, 349*n*, **350–351**
means-tested transfer payments, 289, 302, 358, 360, 361
measurement errors, 62
median family incomes, 340–349, **341, 342, 346–347**
men: earnings, 373–389, 392, **376–377, 379, 380–381;** earnings, vs. women, **366,** 373–374, 380–382, 392; education and earnings, 247; education, vs. female education and English proficiency, 129, **130–131;** employment, vs. female, 130–131, **132;** and industry distribution of employment, 311–319, **312–313;** labor force participation, 288–291, 292–302, **288, 290, 293, 296–297,** 301*n*; occupational distribution for, **328–329;** personal incomes and earnings of, 361–

370, **362–363,** 366*n*, **368–369;** and school noncompletion, 274–275; unemployment, 303, **304,** 305, **306–307,** 308; young, 196
Mestizo, 17*n*, 286, 286*n*
metropolitan areas (SMSAs): defined, 145*n*; vs. nonmetro residential concentration, 57, 84–88, **85, 87;** residential segregation in, 168–177, **169**
metropolitanization, 145–152, 177
Mexican-American War, 17, 40, 107, 109
Mexican Revolution of 1910, 18, 19
Mexicans (Chicanos), 1, 3, 4, 7; age-sex structure of, 66–67, **67,** 89, 127, **128;** ages of, 89, 127, **128;** in central cities, 149; characteristics of immigrant groups, 125–133, **128;** coverage errors, 72; vs. Cubans, 28; diversity of, 33; earnings, 247, 247*n*; earnings, female, 390, 391, 392; earnings, male, 383, 388; earnings, male vs. female, 374, 378; economic well-being, 338; education, 234, 235, 238–239, 240, 240*n*, 241, 243, 244, 245*n*, 247, 247*n*, 248, 249, 250, 251, 267, 268, 269–270, 277, 278, 279; emergence of ethnicity, 16, 17–22; entry by conquest, 16, 17–18, 23, 107–109, 135; enumeration and identification of, 36, 38, 39*n*, 40, 42, 43*n*, 46, 48, 48*n*, 49, 49*n*, 51–54, 55; family income, 339, 340, 342, 343, 344, 345, 348, 352, 361; family size, 91, 191; female-headed families, 192; fertility, 205*n*, 208, 209, 210, 211, 218, 220, 221, 222, 223, 225, 227–229, **228, 229,** 230, 231, 232, 399; forced emigration of, 19, 21; foreign-born, 89, 90, 109–110, 144; generational diversity of, 21, 42; geographic distribution of, 80–81, 82, 83, 83*n*, 88, 102, 138, 141, 143, 144; historical comparisons, 8; household structures, 187, 188, 189, 191, 195, 196, 199*n*; identification, 402, 403, 404, 407; illegal immigrants, 58*n*, 103, 105, 107, 117, 119–121, **119, 121,** 125, 126, 126*n*, 127; immigration by, 14, 16, 17–21, 33, 63–67, **64,** 76, 97, 103, 105, 123, 124, 135; incomes, 199, 199*n*, 201, 202–203, **202;** index of dissimilarity, 175, 318–319; industry distribution of, 311, 315, 318, 319, 320, 321–322; integration by, 21–22, 33–34; internal

migration by, 152, **155**, 161, 162–163, **162**; labor force participation, 93, 289, 292–293, 295, 301, 302; and labor market, 285, 286–287; legal immigration by, 106–109, **106**; linguistic practices, 9, 22, 93, 94, 94*n*, 248; marriage patterns, 184, 185–186; metro-nonmetro residence patterns, 86, 88, 145, 146, 148, 149; as minority group, 210; misclassification as, 63; native-born, 126, 144; naturalizations, 109; naturalized citizens, 126; noncitizens, 125; number of illegal immigrants, 118–121, **119, 121**; occupational distribution, **323**, 330, 331, 332, 333, 336; as percent of Hispanic population, 2, 17, **53**, 60, 61–62, **60, 61**, 406, 407; and personal incomes, 367, 370; population growth, 61–62, 63–67, **64**, 103; and poverty, 353, 354–355, 357, 358, 359–360, 361, 370, 372, 373; and public assistance, 358, 359, 360; vs. Puerto Ricans, 25–26; race of, 39*n*, 51–52; residential segregation, 173, 173*n*, 175, 176–177; rural-urban distribution of, 86, 87; rural vs. urban migrants, 123–124; school dropout rates, 270, 271, 272, 274, 276; school enrollment patterns, 249, 250, 251; socioeconomic status of, 13, 14, 20, 21, 25–26, 33, 88, 92–93, 94, 103, 393, 398, 400; socioeconomic status of, before immigration, 123; term to describe, 17*n*, 49, 49*n*; timing of immigration, 12; undercounting of, 48, 48*n*, 52–54, 55, 58, 80, 83; unemployment, 286, 303, 305, 308
"Mexican wages," 18
Mexico, 20, 63; illegal immigration from, 52–53
Miami, 2, 30, 31, 32, 83, 101, 138, 145, 149–152, 167, 168, 170, 171, 173, 175–176, 177, 286, 287
Michigan, 81, 286; migration flows, **162**, 163
Middle Atlantic states, 47
middle-class: Cubans, 29, 31; and education, 261, 278; increase in, 342; Mexicans, 33–34; role models, and Mexicans, 21
midwestern states, 81
"migrants" vs. immigrants, 117
migration patterns, 12

military service, 23, 25
mining, 18, 19
minority group status, 176; defined, 210; and education, 278–279; vs. ethnicity, 13–14; and fertility, 210, 212–213, 215, 225, 231–232; and integration experiences of Hispanics, 15–16; symbolic, vs. minority status, 103
minority labor markets, 34
mixed: census tracts, 166; Hispanic origin, 61, 73, 416; origins, 43, 60–61
mother's education, 258
mother tongue, 39, 44–45, 44*n*; *see also* Spanish language
multivariate analysis: of earnings determination, 382–392, 382*n*; of labor force participation, 295–302

N

Nassau-Suffolk, 149
National Center for Health Statistics, 178*n*
National Commission on Secondary Schooling for Hispanics, 258
national origin groups, 36; of Central and South Americans, 95–97, **96, 293**, 378–382, **379**; and Central/South American age structures, 98, **99**; and Central/South American earnings, **379**; and Central/South American immigration, 111–114, **112, 113**; and Central/South American nativity, **96, 112**; and Central/South American residence distribution, **100**; composition of Hispanic population by, 53, **53**, 56, 60–62, **60, 61**; demographic diversity among, 89–91, **90**, 397; distribution of, **406**; diversity among, 89, 398–400; and earnings, 372–394, **379, 380–381; 384–385, 386, 389**; and education, 234–256, **234, 236–237, 238–239, 242–243, 244–245, 250–251, 252, 255**; family incomes, 340–352, **341, 342, 345, 346–347, 350–351**; female/male earnings ratios, **366***n*; and fertility, 223–227, **222, 223, 224, 226**; geographic distribution of, by region, **139**; geographic distribution of, by state, **78–79, 81**; as Hispanic identifier, 38, 43*n*; household structures, 187–191, **187**; immigration by, **105**; and industry distribution of employment, 310–322,

national origin groups *(continued)*
312–313, 316–317; and interregional migration, 155–161; and labor force participation, 281, 282, 283, 287–289, 288, 290, 291–302, 293, 296–297, 298–299, 303; and labor market outcomes, 284, 285, 286–287; linguistic practices of, 93–94, 93, 94n, 248; marriage and family patterns, 184–186, 184, 185, 186, 190; median age by, 68; metro vs. nonmetro distribution by, 84–88, 85, 149–152; metropolitan areas by, 149–152, 150; nativity by, 110, 111, 404–407, 406; naturalizations by, 108, 109; and occupational distribution, 310, 322–336, 323–329, 334–335; and personal incomes, 361–370, 362–365, 368–369; population growth by, 61–62, 61, 63; and poverty, 353–361, 354, 356, 359, 370–373, 371; and public assistance, 358–361, 359; residential redistribution by, 410–411; residential segregation compared, 173–177, 174; and school noncompletion, 270–276, 272–273, 275; socioeconomic diversity among, 91–94, 92, 93, 94n, 103, 310, 399–400; and unemployment, 303–308, 304, 306–307; *see also* specific groups
National Origins Quota System, 115, 116
National Puerto Rican Coalition, 23n, 25n, 26n
Native Americans, 23, 208, 245n, 280
nativity, 89–90, 91, 110, 111, 398; and central city concentration, 147, 149; and earnings, 375–377, 382, 383–384, 384n, 391, 395; and education, 234, 235–237, 238–239, 246, 248, 249n, 251, 254, 260, 262–263, 264, 267, 268n, 269–270, 274, 277; and dropout rates, 270–272; and family income, 344–345, 348–349; and fertility, 218, 218, 219; and geographic distribution, 140–141, 140, 144; identification of, 404–407, 406; and industry distribution of employment, 312–313, 315, 316–317, 318–319, 320, 321–322; and labor force participation, 93, 284, 290, 291–292, 301n; and labor market outcomes, 287; and linguistic practices, 94n; and metropolitanization, 146; of Mexicans, 125–131; misreporting of, 126n; and occupational distributions,

328–329, 330, 333, 334–335, 336, 337; and poverty, 339, 355, 356; and public assistance, 360; and timing of arrival, 109–115; and unemployment, 303, 305, 306–307, 308; *see also* foreign born; specific generations
natural increase, 205
naturalizations, 108, 109
naturalized citizens, 126; misreporting of, 126, 126n
neighborhood transition, 163–168
never-married, 182, 194; in parental households, 196–197, 197, 203
Newark, N.J., 149
New Jersey, 47, 80, 81, 82
New Mexico, 3, 17, 82, 83, 84, 86, 138, 185
New York City, 27, 30, 83, 85, 145, 149, 149n, 167, 168, 170, 173, 175, 258
New York-New Jersey SMSA, 293, 394
New York State, 47, 78, 81–82, 83, 88, 98, 100, 101, 137, 161, 161, 162
New York Times, 122, 133
Nicaraguans, 101, 106, 378, 381
nonfamily households, 189, 191, 201, 202
non-Hispanic whites, 4, 34; earnings, 247; earnings, male vs. female, 373–374; education, 235, 240, 243, 247, 258, 278–279; employment, 92; family incomes, 340, 342, 348; fertility, 206–209, 216–218, 220–226, 230; household structure, 187, 188, 189, 192, 193, 195; incomes, 198, 199, 202, 202, 203; industry distribution of employment, 311–315; internal migration, 152, 153, 160; labor force participation, 287–288, 289, 291; labor market success of, 283–284, 285; marriage and family behavior, 179, 182, 184, 185–186, 191, 193–194, 196, 197; personal incomes, 366, 367, 370; and poverty, 353, 355–356; and public assistance, 358, 360; residential patterns, 84, 146, 177; settlement of Southwest by, 18; unemployment, 303; *see also* whites
nonmetropolitan residential concentration, 84–88, 85, 87, 87n
NORC prestige scales, 309n
normative childbearing, 232
North Central region, 139, 141, 168n; defined, 138n; labor market, 286;

migrations to and from, 153–158, 161, 162; residential segregation in, 170

Northeast, 2, 25, 26, 407; concentration of Hispanics in, 78, 80, 81–82, 88, 138, 141, 145; labor market, 286, 333; migrations to and from, 153, 158, 160, 161, 394; residential segregation in, 170, 173

"Nuyoricans," 27

O

occupation or occupational: choices, 301; concentration, and ethnic solidarity, 12; distribution, 322–337, **323, 324–329, 334–335;** of father, and educational achievement, 258–259; high-status, 13, 309; location, 308–310; mobility, 309; mobility of Cubans, 30, 31, 332; patterns, 16; segregation of Puerto Ricans, 27; status, 283

Ohio, 81, 286

oil crisis, 101–102, 114, 294n, 340

older workers, 305

on-the-job training, 283

Operation Bootstrap, 24

operatives, 333

opportunity cost, and fertility, 214

Ordinary Least Squares Regression (OLS), 265n

other family households, 189, 191, 194, 201, 202

"Other Hispanics," 62n; ages of, 89; age-sex composition of, **75,** 76, Central and South Americans included in, 72, 72n, 82; classification problems, 74; diversity of, 2–3; earnings, 247, 247n; earnings, female, 390; earnings, male, 383, 388; earnings, male vs. female, 374, 375, 378; economic and cultural integration of, 33; economic well-being, 338; education of, 240, 241, 244, 247, 247n, 249, 267, 268, 269, 412; enumeration and identification of, 36, **53,** 405; family income, 339, 340, 342, 343, 344, 345, 348, 352, 361; fertility, 209, 210, 216, 218, 223, 225, 230, 399–400; foreign-born, 89, 93, 109; geographic distribution of, 80, 82, 139, 141; household structures, 187, 195, 196; immigration by, 73, 74, 75–76, 106;

industry distribution of employment, 311, 311n, 315, 318, 319, 320, 321; internal migrations by, **157,** 158; labor force participation, 93, 289, 300; and labor market, 285, 286; metro-nonmetro residence patterns, 86–88; metropolitan area, 152; as minority group, 210; nativity, 305; occupational distribution, **327,** 332, 333, 336; as percent of Hispanic population, **53,** 60, **60, 61,** 72; personal incomes, 366, 367, population growth, 62, 73–76; and poverty, 353, 354, 355–356, 357, 358, 360, 361, 370, 372, 373; and public assistance, 352n, 358, 360, 361; school dropout rate, 271, 274, 275–276; school enrollment, 249; socioeconomic status of, 103, 398, 400; unemployment, 303, 305–308

"Other South American" category, 97n

P

P* family of indices, 171n

Panamanians, 95, 97, 294, 378–379, 381

Paraguayans, 97, 111, 294, 378, 379, 382

parentage identifier, 39, 40–43, 42n, 43n, 44n, 48, 54, 55, 404–405, **406**

parental: background, 310, 413–416, **414–415;** education, 268–269, 272, 276, 277

part-Hispanics, 60–61, 73

Pennsylvania, 47

pensions, 301n, 339

per capita income, 198–203, **198, 200–201, 202**

personal income, 338, 339, 361–370, **362–365, 368;** and poverty, 370–373, **371**

personal services, 318, 321

"Persons of Spanish Origin by State" (U. S. Bureau of the Census), 52n

Peruvians, 98, 101, 111–112, 381

Philadelphia, 149

political: leverage, and data, 37, 48; resources, and labor market position, 287; strength of Hispanics, 9

political refugees: from Central America, 112–114; ease of entry, 70n, 72, 115; vs. economic refugees, 28, 29, 106

"Politics and the Measurement of Ethnicity" (Petersen), 50n

population age-sex structure, 57, 63, 66–67, 127, **128;** of Central and South

population age-sex structure *(continued)*
Americans, 72–73, **74, 99;** Cuban, 70–72, **71;** Hispanic, **65;** Mexican, by nativity, **67:** of Other Hispanics, **75,** 76; Puerto Rican, 69–70, **69;** total U.S., **66**
population growth, 1; Central and South Americans, 72–73, 97–98; components of, 62–76, 102–103, 205; of Cubans, 70–72, 70n; of Hispanics, 56, 57–76, **59;** of Mexicans, 62, 63–67; by national origin, **61,** 63; of Other Hispanics, 73–76; projections, 76; of Puerto Ricans, 24, 68–70; rate, 59; *see also* fertility
Population Reference Bureau, 58, 58n
population shifts, 141
population size, 57–58; by national origin, 60–61, **60**
Portuguese, 46
post-industrial economy, 34
poverty: definitions, 340, 352–353, 352n, 353n; diversity among national origin groups, 92–93, 338; and educational achievement, 261, 264, 271; families in, 352–361, **354, 356;** among individuals, 339; persons in, 370–373, **371;** and public assistance income, 351; and Puerto Ricans, 25, 280, 302; rates, 338, 339
presidential elections, 23
primordial ties, 10
producer services, 320–321
professional and managerial occupations, 309
professionals, 28, 30; recertification, 29, 332
professional services, finance, and public administration, 131
property incomes, 339
public assistance, 302, 350–352, 352n, 358–361, **359**
public schools, 29
public sector employment, 388, 391–392, 396
Public Use Microdata Sample Tapes, 55, 78, 82; (PUMS) of 1980, 402, 412; (PUS) of 1970, 403; (PUS) of 1960, 403–404
Puerto Ricans, 3, 4, 7; age-sex composition of, 69–70, **69;** ages of, 89; in central cities, 147; circular migration, 105; citizenship, 23, 26; and comparability, 55; concentration of, in N.Y. City, 2; vs.

Cubans, 28, 29; earnings, 247, 247n; earnings, female, 390, 391, 392; earnings, male, 383, 388; earnings, male vs. female, 374, 376, 378; economic well-being, 338; education, 234, 235, 237, 238–239, 239n, 240, 240n, 241, 243–244, 245n, 246, 247, 248, 249–250, 251, 254, 258, 267, 268, 268n, 269, 270, 277, 278, 412; enumeration and identification of, 36, 38, 40, 43n, 47, 49n; ethnic structuring of, 22–27, 33; family income, 339, 340, 342, 343–344, 345, 348–349, 350–351, 352, 361; family size, 91; female-headed families, 192, 193, 194; fertility, 208, 210, 218, 220, 221, 223, 225, 227, 231, 232; generations, 42; geographic distribution of, 80, 81–82, 83, 88, 102, 138–139, 141, 143–144; historical comparisons, 8; household structures, 187, 188, 189, 194, 195, 195n, 197, 203–204; identification, 403, 404, 407; immigration (migration) by, 22–25, 29, 33, 68–70, 97, 105, 106, 135; incomes, 199n, 201, 202–203, **202,** 204; index of dissimilarity, 175–176; industry distribution of employment, 311, 315, 318, 319, 320, 321; integration experience of, 14, 16, 25–27, 33, 34; internal migrations, **156;** island born, 89, 404, 404n; labor force participation, 288–289, 291, 292–293, 300–302; and labor market outcomes, 280, 285, 286–287; linguistic practices, 9, 94, 248; marriage patterns, 91; metro-nonmetro residence patterns, 84–85, 88, 145, 149; vs. Mexicans, 25–26; as minority group, 210; net migration, 68–70; occupational distribution, **324,** 330, 331, 332, 333, 336; as percent of Hispanic population, 2, 22–23, **53,** 60, **60, 61,** 406, 407; personal incomes, 366, 367–370; population growth, **61,** 62, 68–70; position vs. other Hispanics, 25–26; and poverty, 353–355, 356–357, 358, 359–360, 361, 370–372, 373; and public assistance, 358, 359–360; and racial discrimination, 13, 34, 400; regional distribution of, 138; residential segregation, 164, 173, 173n, 175–177, 393–394; school dropout rates, 270–271, 272, 273, 274–275, 276, 276n; school

enrollment, 249–250, 251, 254;
socioeconomic status of, 13, 14, 25–26,
88, 92–93, 94, 103, 280, 393–394, 398,
400; and unemployment, 303, 305, 308
Puerto Rico: Commonwealth status, 23;
and Dominicans, 101; economy of, 24,
25; industrialization of, 24; population
size, 57; and race, 164
"push-pull" model, 122–123, 124

R

race: classification of Hispanics, 13, 34;
Cubans and, 34; and earnings, **376–377,**
378; and education, **234,** 235, 258; and
family incomes, 340, **341, 346–347, 350–
351;** and fertility, 207–210, **207;** of
Hispanics, 38; identification of, 50, 50*n*;
and labor force participation, **290;** and
labor market position, 282–283, 285,
286, 287; Mestizo, 286*n*; of Mexicans,
39*n*; and personal income, 367, **368–369;**
and poverty, **354,** 357, **371;** and public
assistance, 358, **359;** Puerto Ricans and,
27, 34, 164; Spanish write-in on, 50,
50*n*, 51; and unemployment, **304, 306–
307;** *see also* racial discrimination
racial discrimination, 13, 34–35; and
Mexicans, 18, 21; and Puerto Ricans,
400; *see also* discrimination
railroad industry, 18, 19
real estate, 320
"Recent Immigration and the Foreign
Born" (Taeuber and Taeuber), 42*n*
"Reconsideration of Chicano Culture and
Identity, A" (Arce), 285*n*
regions or regional: concentration of
Hispanics, 56, 57, 78–84, 88, 138–144,
139, 177; and internal migration, 153–
160, **154–161;** labor markets, 26;
measures of, 141–144; nativity and,
140–141; probabilities of residential
contacts in, **172,** 173; residence change
by, **165**
religion, 38
remarried, 182
resettlement assistance, 25, 29–30, 31
residential patterns, 16, 56, 57, 168, 397;
of Central and South Americans, 98–
102, **100;** and contact probabilities, **172,**
173–177, **174;** of Cubans, 30;

distribution, 77–88; and earnings, 388–
389, 396; and ethnic solidarity, 12, 82–
83; and labor market outcomes, 285;
metro vs. nonmetro distribution, 84–88,
85, 87; of Mexicans, 22; redistribution,
by national origin, **410–411;** and
residence change type, **165, 166–167;**
and residential segregation, 83, 137,
163–177, **165, 166–167, 169, 172, 174;**
and residential succession, 163–164,
163*n*; by state, **77,** 78–84, **78–79, 81,** 98–
102, **100**
retail trade, 320
return migration: of Mexicans, 19, 21; of
Puerto Ricans, 24, 25; *see also* circular
migration
Rhode Island, 161
Riverside, 171, 173
Roybal Resolution, 37*n*
rural settlement, 12, 86, 87–88, **87,** 87*n*,
220*n*; by Mexicans, 20, 145

S

sales occupations, 330
Salvadorans, 95, 97, 101, 111, 112, 114,
294, 378, 381
San Antonio, 171, 173, 175
scalar indexes of occupational standing,
309–310, 309*n*
scholars, 29
school: age-grade delay, 257, 276, 279,
412–417, **414–415;** data, 413–417, **414–
415;** enrollment patterns, 248–256, **250–
251, 252,** 255; noncompletion, 240–241,
240*n*, **242–243, 244–245,** 249–256, 249*n*,
258, 261*n*, 270–276, **272–273, 275,** 278;
variables, 258, 260, **414–415;** *see also*
education; college education
secondary labor market, 286
second-class citizens, 285
second-class workers, 31
second generation, 44*n*; and fertility, 215–
216; identification of, 41–42, 42*n*;
Puerto Ricans, 27
segregation in low-income neighborhoods,
285
self-employment, 339, 388, 392, 396
self-identification, 39, 42–43, 54, 402
separation, 181, 182

service sector, 26, 309, 315–318, 319, 320–321, 322
settlement patterns, 7, 8, 12, 18; see also residence patterns
Simpson-Rodino bill, 116
skilled workers, 101
small farmers, 21
small-scale, private enterprises, 32
social: characteristics hypothesis, 210, 211–212, 214–215, 222, 230–231; distance, 163; mobility, 18, 42n, 309; networks, and international migration flows, 123, 124; services, 321
social insurance, 338, 339, 351
social security, 301n, 338, 339, 351, 358n
Social Security Administration, 353n
Socioeconomic Index, 309n
socioeconomic status: of Cubans, 28, 29, 30, 33; and demographic profile of Hispanic population, 56–103; diversity of, among Hispanic groups, 13, 14, 56, 91–94, **92**, 103, 392–393, 398–400; diversity of, and integration experiences, 14–16; downward bias of, and undocumented aliens, 55; and economic well-being, 338; and education, 253, 258–259, 260, 261–270, 276–277, 278–279; and ethnicity, 10, 13–14, 16, 33; and family incomes, 343; and family values, 179; of female-headed households, 191–192; and fertility, 211–212, 213, 221, 221n, 223, 225, 398–400; and labor force participation, 280–281, 282; and metro-nonmetro residence patterns, 84, 88; of Mexicans, 20, 33–34, 88; and migration and settlement patterns, 12; and occupational structure, 308–310; parentage data, and analysis of assimilation, 42n; of Puerto Ricans, 25–27, 33, 280; and school noncompletion, 274–275, 276; and Spanish origin identifier, 51
South, 138, 141, 152, 168n, 170; defined, 138n; migrations flows, 153, 158, 160, 161, 162
Southeast Asians, 25, 59n
Southwest, 1, 17–20, 21, 26, 40, 46, 46n, 47, 53, 61, 78, 80–81, 82, 83, 88, 123, 137, 185, 186, 311, 407; annexation of, 17–18, 107; residential patterns of Hispanics in, 86–88, **87**, 149

Spain, immigrants from, 1, 3, 43n, 73, 86, 405; see also Hispanos
Spanish American identifier, 168, 168n
Spanish Heritage concept, 47
Spanish language: comparability of items, 44–45, 55; and education level, 248, 272, 275–277, 276n, 415–416; -English bilingualism, 5, 415; home use of, 93–94, **93**, 413–416; identifier, 43–45, 43n, 47, 48, 51, 54, 55; language shift away from, 22
Spanish origin: vs. ancestry, 43n; and comparability, 55; European, 43n, 405; identifier, 168, 168n, 416; self-identification question, 39, 43, 47–54, **50**, 50n, 51n, 54, 55; use of term, 37n
Spanish surname, 39, 45–46, 46n, 47, 48, 51, 53, 54, 55; population, residential configuration of, 86–88, **87**
spatial assimilation, 163, 164
spatial isolation, 173–177
Standard Metropolitan Statistical Areas (SMSAs), 145; defined, 145n; dissimilarity between Hispanics and Anglos in, **169, 174**; with large concentration of Hispanics, **148**, 149–152, **150, 151**, 167, **174**; migrations between, 161; probabilities of residential contact in, **172**; residence change in, 165, **166–167**
states; distribution of Hispanics in, **78–79**, 81, 141–144, **142–143, 409–410**; migrations between, 161–163, **161**, **162**
Statistical Policy (Tienda and Evanson), 37n
status attainment, 283
"Structuring of Hispanic Ethnicity, The" (Nelson and Tienda), 43n, 94n
subcultural hypothesis, 210, 211, 215, 231, 232
suburbanization: of Hispanics, 148–149; of industry, 26
succession tracts, 167–168, 170
Sunbelt, 26, 141, 152
Supplemental Security Income, 358, 358n
Survey of Income and Education (1976), 45n
survivors' benefits, 351
symbolic ethnicity, 15, 16, 103

T

taxes, 23
technicians, 30
test scores, 27
Texas, 17, 18, 26, 78, 80, 83, 84, 138, 149, 185, 286; migration flows, **162**, 163
textile industry, 25, 286, 289, 292, 315
third generation, 41–42, **42**, 48, 74, 402
Third World, 116
time spent in U.S., and labor force participation, 284
time trend analyses, 40–41, 43, 44–45, 46; of incomes, 343; limitations on, 55; and poverty rates, 353
timing of arrival, 109–115
transfer payments, 338, 339, 358
transformative sector, 315, 319, 322; *see also* manufacturing
Treaty of Guadalupe Hidalgo, 17, 107, 135

U

undercounting: of Hispanics, 58; of Mexicans, 48, 48n, 52, 120–121; Puerto Ricans and, 25; of undocumented aliens, 120–121, 121n
undocumented immigrants, *see* illegal aliens
unemployment, 1, 19, 91, 133, 280, 283, 286, 287, 295, 302; trends and differentials, 303–308, **304, 306–307**
unions, 21, 22
United States: age-sex structure of population, **66**; aid to Cuban exiles, 29–30; immigration policy, 19, 20; Puerto Rican citizenship, 23
U.S. Bureau of the Census, 28n, 51n, 57n, 59n, 73n, 80n, 107n, 112n, 114n, 141n, 153n; definition of families, 339, 339n, enumeration and identification procedures, 36–55, 43n; income definitions, 339–340; and industry classification, 311
U.S. Census: of 1850, 40, 41; of 1870, 40; of 1910, 44; of 1930, 39n; of 1940, 39n; of 1950, 41, **41**, 44; of 1960, 4, 37, 38n, 41, **41**, 44, 46, 58, 397; of 1970, 4, 37, 38n, 39, 41, **41**, 44, 45, 46, 47, 48–50, **50**, 51n, 55, 58, 187, 397; of 1970, coverage problems, 63, 64, 72, 72n, 76, 80; of

1990, 43n, 72; *see also* U.S. Census of Population and Housing of 1980
U.S. Census of Population and Housing of 1980, 3, 4, 46, 120, 397; Cubans in, 28; enumeration and identification procedures, 37–55, 38n, 39n, **41**, 45n, 46n, **50**, 58, 63–64, 401–402; number of illegal Mexican immigrants included in, 120–121; and undercount, **121**
U.S. Commission on Civil Rights, 26n
U.S. Congress, 23, 37, 37n, 122n
U.S. Department of Justice, 70n, 73n, **106, 107n, 113,** 114n, 115n, 116n
U.S. House of Representatives, 23
U.S. Senate, 23
unskilled workers, 26, 30, 124; *see also* blue-collar workers; low-wage jobs
upper classes, 29, 31, 32
upward mobility, 31
Uraguayans, 97, 111, 382
urban areas: defined, 145n; and education, 258; fragmented, 164
urbanized area, defined, 145n
urban population, defined, 145n
urban settlement patterns, 88, 145–152, 220n; of Cubans, 28; of Hispanics in Southwest, 86–88, **87,** 87n; of Mexicans, 20, 21, 22, 86, 145; of Puerto Ricans, 26

V

value systems: of Cubans, 30–31; dual, of Puerto Ricans, 27; and education, 259; and family, 179, 197, 211; and fertility, 231
Venezuelans, 97, 98, 101–102, 111, 114, 294, 380

W

wage(s), 21, 338, 350, 367–370; gap, and discrimination, 281, 281n, 284; impact of immigration on, 133–134; low, 21, 25, 32, 92; low, and recruitment of immigrant labor, 122–123; and migration flows, 124; rates, and labor force participation, 295; and residential concentration, 396
Washington, D.C., 100, 102
Washington State, **162**

welfare, 302, 358, 360; *see also* public
  assistance
West, 18, 138, 139, 141; defined, 138*n*;
  migrations to and from, 153, 158, 160,
  161; residential segregation in, 170
white collar jobs, 309, 330, 331, 332
whites: growth rate of, 59; Hispanic, 38,
  38*n*, 46*n*; Spanish surname population,
  residential configuration of, 86 88, **87;**
  undercount of, 58*n*; *see also* non-
  Hispanic whites
widows, 193–194
women or female: age-earnings profiles for,
  389, 390; earnings, **384–385,** 389–392;
  earnings and education, 247; earnings
  ratios vs. males, **366,** 373–392, **376–377,**
  392; education, 246, 247, 248, 251–252,
  300; education and English proficiency,
  129, **130–131;** education and fertility,
  209, 212, 213, 214, 215, 221, 222–228,
  222, 223, 224, 226, 228, 229, 230, 231–
  232, 399–400; employment, 130–131,
132; immigration, 129; industry
  distribution of employment, **316–317,**
  319–322; labor force participation, 288–
  302, **288, 290, 293, 298–299,** 337; and
  labor market, 285*n*; marital instability,
  185–186, **186;** occupational distribution,
  330–336, **334–335;** personal incomes and
  earnings of, **364–365,** 366–367, **368–369,**
  370; and poverty, 372; unemployment,
  303–308, **304, 306–307;** working vs.
  childcare, 214; *see also* fertility
Women, Work, and Wages (Treiman and
  Hartman), 285*n*
worker hostility, vs. Mexicans, 21

Y

young adults: families headed by, 357;
  mobile families, 48*n*; and poverty, 372;
  unemployment, 305, 308; unmarried,
  196–197, **197**